Visit the companion website for *Entrepreneurship and Small Business* at www.palgrave.com/business/burns for access to valuable learning material for all students of entrepreneurship, including:

▷ an interactive test to discover your entrepreneurial tendency
▷ pro forma business plans, plus samples
▷ video commentaries from the author
▷ exercises relevant to basic business skills
▷ revision questions

Entrepreneurship & Small Business
start-up, growth & maturity

Third Edition

| home | about this book | lecturers' zone | students' zone | order title |

About This Book

Reviews
About the author
Table of contents

Lecturers' Zone

Powerpoint slides
Teaching notes for cases
Teaching notes for specimen business plans
Answers to additional exercises on basic business skills
Selected case studies

Students' Zone

Video commentaries
Interactive chapter tests
General Enterprise Tendency (GET) test
SME Growth Audit
Downloadable versions of the cases
Pro-forma business plan
Four entrepreneurship exercises
Additional exercises
Checklist of regulations
Sources of information
Selected websites
Leadership Style Questionnaire
Corporate Entrepreneurship Audit Tool

Home

Students' Zone

- **Video commentaries** by the author
- **Interactive chapter tests**
- **General Enterprise Tendency (GET) test**
- **SME Growth Audit**
- **Downloadable versions of the cases** with questions, including additional cases not included in the book
- **Downloadable versions** of a pro forma business plan and the specimen plans for Sport Retail, Jean Young and Dewhurst Engineering
- **Four entrepreneurship exercises**
- **Additional exercises** on basic business skills such as accounting, financial management and marketing
- **Checklist of regulations** to be met in setting up a business in the UK
- **Sources of information, help and advice** in the UK
- **Selected websites offering further learning resources** and practical, up-to-date help and advice, with hyperlinks
- **Leadership Style Questionnaire** - a self assessment questionnaire that allows you to assess you own leadership style
- **Corporate Entrepreneurship Audit Tool**

'A highly engaging, contemporary text, Paul Burns' revised edition provides a practical approach to the study of entrepreneurship and small business. The case studies and questions are challenging and encourage students to reflect on their learning and understanding.'
Colette Henry, Norbrook Professor of Business & Enterprise, The Royal Veterinary College

'A well structured contemporary overview of key aspects of the entrepreneurial process.'
Sue Marlowe, Professor of Entrepreneurship, De Montfort University

'This text should be indispensable to any student of entrepreneurship. I strongly recommend it to anyone who wants to learn more about entrepreneurship or actually set up their own enterprise.'
Elizabeth Chell, Professor of Entrepreneurial Behaviour, Kingston University

'An excellent text for students to refer to time and time again. Very comprehensive.'
Julie Logan, Professor of Entrepreneurship, City University

'A highly readable, comprehensive text for all students of small business. It is adorned with rich examples and mini case studies, offering readers a solid learning experience related to the essentials of small business management.'
Jay Mitra, Head of Entrepreneurship and Innovation Group, University of Essex

'A refreshing approach to Entrepreneurship. This book is packed full of student friendly insights and cases. A must for any course on Entrepreneurship.'
Spinder Dhaliwal, Senior Lecturer in Entrepreneurship, University of Surrey

'The 3rd edition of Paul Burns' Entrepreneurship and Small Business was a joy to read. Its improved format and updated case studies make it ideal for teaching at undergraduate and postgraduate levels. It is also an excellent handbook for practitioners who want to launch their own enterprises.'
Mike Wells, Teaching Fellow, Entrepreneurship, City University

'This is one of the most thorough texts that I have seen on the topic of entrepreneurship. The book could easily be used on an entrepreneurship or small business management course.'
Matt Allen, Assistant Professor of Entrepreneurship and Innovation, Northeastern University

Entrepreneurship and small business

Start-up, growth and maturity

Third edition

PAUL BURNS

Professor of Entrepreneurship and Dean,
University of Bedford Business School, UK

palgrave
macmillan

First edition 2001
Reprinted 8 times
Second edition 2007
Reprinted 4 times
This edition 2011
Published by
PALGRAVE MACMILLAN

Palgrave Macmillan in the UK is an imprint of Macmillan Publishers Limited,
registered in England, company number 785998, of Houndmills, Basingstoke,
Hampshire RG21 6XS.

Palgrave Macmillan in the US is a division of St Martin's Press LLC,
175 Fifth Avenue, New York, NY 10010.

Palgrave Macmillan is the global academic imprint of the above companies
and has companies and representatives throughout the world.

Palgrave® and Macmillan® are registered trademarks in the United States,
the United Kingdom, Europe and other countries

ISBN 978-0-230-24780-2

This book is printed on paper suitable for recycling and made from fully
managed and sustained forest sources. Logging, pulping and manufacturing
processes are expected to conform to the environmental regulations of the
country of origin.

A catalogue record for this book is available from the British Library.

A catalog record for this book is available from the Library of Congress.

10   9   8   7   6   5   4   3   2   1
20   19   18   17   16   15   14   13   12   11

Printed and bound in China

Contents overview

Preface to the third edition   xix
How to use the book and website   xxi
Guided tour of the book and website   xxvi

Part 1   **Entrepreneurship**   1

    1   **Entrepreneurship in the twenty-first century**   3
    2   **Entrepreneurs and owner-managers**   31
    3   **Innovation and entrepreneurship**   63
    4   **Social and civic entrepreneurship**   83

Part 2   **Start-up**   107

    5   **Developing creativity and the business idea**   109
    6   **Evaluating the business idea**   141
    7   **Launching the business**   167
    8   **International entrepreneurship**   201
    9   **Running the business**   221
   10   **Financing the business**   257

Part 3   **Growth**   287

   11   **Planning for growth**   289
   12   **New products and services**   325
   13   **Growing the business**   343
   14   **Developing the business plan**   363
   15   **Exit: failure and success**   385

Part 4   **Maturity**   407

   16   **The family firm**   409
   17   **From entrepreneur to leader**   431
   18   **Corporate entrepreneurship**   469

To my parents, Jim and Jeanne,
who gave me life and taught me how to live it
And to my wife, Jean,
who gives me love and makes my life a joy

Contents

List of figures		xvi
List of tables		xviii
Preface to the third edition		xix
How to use the book and website		xxi
Guided tour of the book and website		xxvi

Part 1   Entrepreneurship   1

   1   Entrepreneurship in the twenty-first century   3

The stuff of dreams   5
The entrepreneurial revolution   8
The economics of entrepreneurship   9
Entrepreneurs and owner-managers   11
Small firms   16
The differences between small and large firms   18
Lifestyle and growth firms   19
The UK small firms sector   21
Global Entrepreneurship Monitor (GEM)   24
Summary   27

Case insights

Bill Gates and Microsoft   6
Michael Dell and the Dell Corporation   8
Richard Branson and Virgin   13
Shaa Wasmund and Brightstation Ventures   15
Marc Demarquette   17
Joseph Bamford and JCB   23

Cases with questions

Julie Spurgeon   20
Sara Murray – Serial entrepreneur   26

   2   Entrepreneurs and owner-managers   31

Start-up influences   33
Personal character traits   34
Character traits of owner-managers   36

Character traits of entrepreneurs   38
Antecedent influences   42
Ethnicity and immigration   44
Gender   46
Growth businesses   48
National culture   49
Situational factors   53
Summary   58

Case insights
Steve Hulme   33
Simon Woodroffe and YO! Sushi   39
Market traders   43
Kenyan Asians   45
Elizabeth Gooch and EG Solutions   47
Will King and King of Shaves   54

Cases with questions
Duncan Bannatyne, Dragon   55
Hilary Andrews and Mankind   57

3 Innovation and entrepreneurship   63
Innovation   65
Innovation and competitive advantage   65
Discontinuous innovation   69
Innovation and entrepreneurship   71
Creativity and entrepreneurship   74
Innovation and size   75
Innovation and location   77
Summary   80

Case insights
James Dyson   67
McDonald's   69
Who invented the world wide web (www)?   71
Trevor Baylis   72
Great Ormond Street Hospital for Children   73
Swarfega   73

Case with questions
Big companies and new ideas   79

4 Social and civic entrepreneurship   83
The rise of social entrepreneurship   85
Social enterprise and the social economy   87
Legal forms of social enterprise in the UK   88
The social entrepreneur   92
The growth and development of the social enterprise   94
The civic entrepreneur   96
The dangers of social entrepreneurship   99
Summary   102

Case insights

The Maggie Keswick Jencks Cancer Caring Centres Trust	91
Abs-Kids	91
Bright Ideas Trust	91
Seven Stories	91

Cases with questions

Big Issue	89
Ridgeway Primary School	98
Nin Castle, Phoebe Emerson and Goodone	100

Part 2 Start-up 107

5 Developing creativity and the business idea 109

Creativity	111
Barriers to creativity	113
The creative process	113
Techniques for generating new ideas	116
Recognising opportunity	121
The business idea	125
The internet	128
Safeguarding your ideas	129
Summary	137

Case insights

Martin Dix and Current Cost	115
Bruce Bratley and First Mile	116
Tom Mercer and mOma	123
Adrian Wood and GTI	125

Cases with questions

Alex Tew and the Million Dollar Homepage	118
eBay	131
Andrew Valentine and Streetcar	136

6 Evaluating the business idea 141

What you need to start a business	143
Personal attributes	143
Knowing your customers	145
Knowing your competitors	146
Marketing strategies	148
Resources	154
Capital	155
The importance of networks	157
Planning and evaluation	159
Summary	163

Case insights

Quad Electroacoustics	152
Morgan Motor Company	153
Alan Pound and Aculab	153
Richard Branson	155

Robbie Cowling and Jobserve   155
Big companies and strategic alliances   159

Cases with questions
David Sanger and Rollover   160
Mark Constantine and Lush   161

7 **Launching the business**   167
Marketing strategies   169
Pricing   172
Differentiation   177
Developing customer focus   178
Entrepreneurial marketing   180
Undertaking market research   182
Developing selling skills   185
Retailing on the internet   188
Legal forms of business   190
Summary   196

Case insights
Martin Penny and Good Hair Day   173
Jean Young   175
Radio Spirits   178
Mark Dorman and Black Vodka   184
Mark Goldsmith and Goldsmith's Fine Foods   186
Gary Frank and the Fabulous Bakin' Boys   189

Cases with questions
The Body Shop franchise   193
Stephen Waring and Green Thumb   194
Calypso Rose and Clippy   195

8 **International entrepreneurship**   201
Globalisation and international entrepreneurship   203
The international start-up   205
The stage model of internationalisation   207
The influence of networks and learning theory   209
Export strategies   210
The agency dilemma   213
Summary   216

Case insights
Michael Ross and Figleaves   208
John and Julie Gilbert and Hop Back   211
Julie Diem Le and Zoobug   213

Cases with questions
B&Q   204
Hightech Components   214

9 **Running the business**   221
Cash flow and Death Valley   223
The profit statement   224
The balance sheet   229

Planning and control   232
Financial drivers   233
Break-even   236
Decision-making   238
Summary   243
Case insights
Jean Young   225, 226, 228, 231
Chris Hutt and the Newt & Cucumber   234
David Speakman and Travel Counsellors   237
Flitwick Manor Hotel   237
Penforth Sofa Beds   239
Appendix 1: Forecasts and budgets – an example   246
Appendix 2: Accounting records – an example   252

10   Financing the business   257
Money   259
Bank finance   263
The bank's perspective   267
Banking relationships   269
Venture capital institutions and business angels   270
The equity investor's perspective   272
Stock market floatation   273
Is there a financing gap?   275
Gender, ethnicity and finance   278
Summary   281
Case insights
Martyn Dowes and Coffee Nation   264
Peter Kelly and Softcat   267
Andrew Barber, Robin Hall and FBS Engineering   271
Fred Turok and LA Fitness   274
Bob Holt and Mears Group   275
Elizabeth Gooch and EG Solutions   280
Cases with questions
Specsavers   272
NDT   276

Part 3   Growth   287

11   Planning for growth   289
Ingredients of success   291
A framework for developing strategy   292
Sustainability and corporate social responsibility   293
Vision and mission   297
Values and ethics   299
The SWOT analysis   300
Financial performance analysis   304
Value chains   308
SLEPT analysis   309

Strategy intent   310
Securing competitive advantage   311
Successful entrepreneurial strategies   313
Developing entrepreneurial strategies in the real world   314
Summary   320

Case insights
Jordans   294
Dale Vince and Ecotricity   295
Abel & Cole   296
J. J. Cash   303
Dell Computer Corporation   312

Cases with questions
Dmitry Kotenko and Nitol Solar   312
Lastminute.com   316
easyJet   318

12   New products and services   325
Product life cycles   327
Product portfolios   330
Portfolio strategies   332
Managing the product life cycle   335
Financial implications of the product portfolio   338
Implications for the entrepreneur   339
Summary   340

Case insights
Heinken   331

Cases with questions
Cadbury 1   333
Barbie and Mattel Corporation   336

13   Growing the business   343
Growth options   345
Market penetration   346
Product/service development   348
Market development   349
Diversification   350
Risk   352
Buying growth   355
Summary   360

Case insights
Wilson & Sons   347
Virgin   348
Tim Slade, Julian Leaver and Fat Face   350
Wing Yip   352

Cases with questions
Jim Ratcliffe and Ineos Group   357
George Brian Boedecker Jr. and Crocs   358
Cadbury 2   359

14 Developing the business plan 363

Why you need a business plan 365

The planning process 365

What a business plan looks like 369

Using the plan to obtain finance 371

The bankers' view 374

The investors' view 375

Presenting a case for finance 377

Pro forma business plan 378

Summary 382

Cases with questions

Chris Hutt and the Newt & Cucumber 372

15 Exit: failure and success 385

Stagnate and die 387

Failure 388

The ingredients of failure 390

Predicting failure 394

Dealing with failure as an individual or a sole trader 396

Dealing with failure as a company 397

Success – selling the business 400

Company valuation 403

Summary 404

Case insights

Nick Kenton, Rob Taub and Sportsbase 387

Nicholas Hall 390

Tech Board and Imperial Board Products 392

ZedZed.com 393

Alex Meisl and Taotalk, then Sponge 394

Peter Durose and the English Grocer 397

Kristian Segerstrale and Playfish 401

Vivid Imaginations 401

The Body Shop 402

Julian Harley, Ian West and Harley West Training 403

Anne and Simon Notley and Feather and Black 404

Cases with questions

Cobra Beer 399

Part 4 Maturity 407

16 The family firm 409

The advantages of family 411

Family business is big business 413

The conflict between family and business cultures 414

Succession 417

Points of conflict 419

The introvert firm 421

Resolving conflict: the family constitution 422

Succession planning 425
Summary 428

Case insights
Doreen Lofthouse and Fisherman's Friend 412
Adidas vs Puma 414
Values and beliefs 415
Ferrero Rocher 416
Noon Products 419
Littlewoods 420
Alex Ramsay 420
J&B Wild 421
Everards Brewery 423

Cases with questions
Timberland 416
Wates Group 424
Mars Inc. 427

17 From entrepreneur to leader 431
Growth and crises 433
Changing skills 435
Coping with crises 439
The role of leader 440
The evolving vision 442
Leadership style 444
Building the management team 448
The board of directors 450
Entrepreneurial structures 451
Traditional large firm structures 453
Structure, change and task complexity 454
Creating culture 456
Entrepreneurial leadership skills 459
Summary 465

Case insights
David Poole and DP&A 455
Gary Redman and Now Recruitment 460

Cases with questions
Michael Dell 461

18 Corporate entrepreneurship 469
Defining corporate entrepreneurship 471
Entrepreneurial architecture 474
Learning organisations 475
Building the architecture for entrepreneurial
    transformation 477
The role of culture 480
The role of structure 482
Management, structure and control 485
Intrapreneurship 489

Organising new venture ideas   491
Corporate venturing   492
Summary   498

Case insights
Julian Metcalf, Sinclair Beecham and Pret a Manger   472
Richard Branson's Virgin Group   484

Cases with questions
David Hall and HFL   487
Nokia   494
3M   496

Further reading and journals   505
Subject index   508
Author index   513
Quotes index   516

Companion resources

Visit www.palgrave.com/business/burns for an accompanying students' website and password-protected lecturers' website:

Students' website
▷ Video commentaries by the author
▷ Interactive chapter tests
▷ General Enterprise Tendency (GET) Test
▷ Corporate Entrepreneurship Audit Tool
▷ Leadership Style Test
▷ Small business audit checklists
▷ Five entrepreneurship assignments including a small business growth audit
▷ Downloadable versions of the cases with questions, including additional cases not included in the book
▷ Downloadable versions of a pro forma business plan and the specimen plans for Sport Retail, Jean Young and Dewhurst Engineering
▷ Additional exercises on basic business skills such as accounting, financial management and marketing
▷ Checklist of regulations to be met in setting up a business in the UK
▷ Sources of information, help and advice in the UK
▷ Selected websites offering further learning resources and practical, up-to-date help and advice, with hyperlinks

Lecturers' website
▷ Powerpoint slides for each chapter
▷ Notes on the entrepreneurship exercises
▷ Teaching notes for cases with questions
▷ Teaching notes for the specimen business plans
▷ Selected case studies from the European Case Clearing House, many with related DVDs. These are particularly valuable for postgraduate teaching.

List of figures

A	Wheel of learning	xxii
1.1	Entrepreneurs, managers and owner-managers	14
1.2	Policy options for encouraging survival and growth	22
1.3	The GEM approach to measuring entrepreneurial activity	25
2.1	Start-up influences	34
2.2	Character traits of owner-managers and entrepreneurs	36
2.3	Hofstede's dimensions of culture	51
2.4	Reasons for setting up in business	53
3.1	Product/service and processes development: a spectrum	68
3.2	Innovation and competitive advantage	69
3.3	Creativity, invention, opportunity and entrepreneurship	74
3.4	Invention and entrepreneurship	75
4.1	The three systems of the economy	88
4.2	Multidimensional social entrepreneurship construct	93
4.3	The virtuous circle of social capital	94
4.4	The life cycle of the social entrepreneur	95
4.5	The spectrum of entrepreneurship	97
5.1	Dimensions of creative (lateral) vs logical (vertical) thinking	112
5.2	The creative process	113
5.3	Sources of awareness and ideas	114
5.4	Generating a viable business idea	122
5.5	Why? Why? diagram	124
6.1	What you need to start a business	143
6.2	Porter's Five Forces	147
6.3	Generic marketing strategies	148
6.4	Economies of scale	149
6.5	Economies of scale in two industries	150
6.6	Economies of small scale	151
6.7	The credibility merry-go-round	154
6.8	Start-up capital	155
6.9	Generating a viable business idea	156
6.10	Innovation networks	158
7.1	Marketing mix: the five Ps	170
7.2	Generic marketing strategies	172
7.3	Cost, volume and revenue	174
7.4	The pricing range	176
7.5	The customer loyalty ladder	178
7.6	Entrepreneurial vs non-entrepreneurial planning pathway	181
7.7	The entrepreneurial marketing planning process	182
7.8	The selling potential matrix	185
8.1	Factors influencing the early internationalisation of international start-ups	206
8.2	International development	207
8.3	Entry and exit barriers, profitability and risk	212
9.1	The Death Valley curve	223
9.2	The flow of money	224
9.3	Cash flow forecast for Jean Young 2011/12	225
9.4	Cost–profit–volume chart	236
9.5	Profit–volume chart	236
9.6	Cash receipts book	253
9.7	Cash payments book	253
9.8	Accounting worksheet for ACE Computers	254
10.1	How to finance the entrepreneurial business	263

11.1	The ingredients of success	291
11.2	The strategic planning process	292
11.3	Values, vision, strategy and tactics	300
11.4	The business planning process	301
11.5	Financial ratio checklist	307
11.6	The value chain	308
11.7	Generic marketing strategies	311
11.8	The strategy formulation cycle	316
12.1	The product/service life cycle	328
12.2	The life cycle and competitive position	330
12.3	The Boston matrix	331
12.4	The Boston matrix – strategy implications	332
12.5	Boston matrix for hypothetical company	333
12.6	Product life cycle management	336
12.7	Cash flow implications of the Boston matrix	338
12.8	ABC analysis contribution chart	339
13.1	The product/market matrix	346
13.2	Growth and risk	354
14.1	The business planning process	368
15.1	The ingredients of business failure	390
16.1	Family vs business cultures	415
16.2	The family business life cycle	418
17.1	The Greiner growth model	434
17.2	Churchill and Lewis growth model	435
17.3	The growth process	439
17.4	Work effectiveness through change	439

17.5	Leadership style	444
17.6	Leader and task	445
17.7	Leader and group	446
17.8	The role of the board of directors	450
17.9	The Institute of Management model of board-level competencies	451
17.10	The entrepreneurial spider's web	451
17.11	People and interactions	452
17.12	The entrepreneurial spider's web grows	452
17.13	The hierarchical structure	453
17.14	The matrix structure	454
17.15	Structure, change and task complexity	455
17.16	Constructing culture	456
18.1	The wheel of learning and our mental models	476
18.2	Building entrepreneurial architecture	478
18.3	The cultural web hierarchy in an entrepreneurial organisation	481
18.4	Entrepreneurial culture summarised in Hofstede's dimensions	482
18.5	An organic structure	483
18.6	Organisational structure and management style	485
18.7	Organisational structure, management style and the concept of cycling	486
18.8	Freedom vs control	487
18.9	Dealing with new venture developments	

List of tables

1.1 The antecedence of modern entrepreneurship 14

1.2 Comparison of UK enterprises by size, 2007 21

3.1 Two approaches to problem-solving 68

7.1 Price cuts – percentage increase in sales volume required to generate the same level of profit after a price cut 176

7.2 Price increases – percentage decrease in sales volume required to generate the same level of profit after a price increase 176

7.3 Relationship vs transactional marketing 180

7.4 Advantages and disadvantages of field vs desk research 183

7.5 Advantages and disadvantages of different types of field research 184

7.6 Advantages and disadvantages of different forms of business 192

7.7 Advantages and disadvantages of being a franchisee or franchisor 192

9.1 Balance sheet, 31 December 2015 246

9.2 Preliminary sales budget 247

9.3 Production budget 247

9.4 Budgeted purchases, overheads and wage payments 248

9.5 Final sales budget 249

9.6 Budgeted income statement, 2016 249

9.7 Cash flow forecast 2016 250

9.8 VAT quarterly returns summary 250

9.9 Budgeted balance sheet, 31 December 2016 251

9.10 Analysis of accounts 252

10.1 Sources and uses of finance 259

10.2 Advantages and disadvantages of different forms of finance 262

10.3 Balance sheet structures – small and large companies 265

10.4 Asset security values 266

11.1 Tools of the SWOT analysis 303

12.1 New products: average time-to-take-off in Europe 329

16.1 The family constitution checklist 423

17.1 Churchill and Lewis's growth stage imperatives 436

17.2 Scott and Bruce growth model 437

17.3 Burns growth model 438

17.4 Entrepreneurial vs administrative cultures 458

17.5 Entrepreneurial leadership skills 461

18.1 Traditional vs entrepreneurial management 479

Preface to the third edition

The major challenge facing business schools today is how to encourage and develop the entrepreneurial skills of students. This book is designed to address this issue. It is written to motivate students to become more entrepreneurial at the same time as providing frameworks to nurture these precious skills in a systematic way. It covers all of the main theoretical aspects of entrepreneurship as well as being a 'how-to-do-it' text – synthesising good management practice for entrepreneurs involved in start-ups and growing firms. It is informed by research and based on my own experience of over thirty years' working with entrepreneurs, small firm advisors and bankers as a researcher and teacher, as well as running my own firm for five years.

Entrepreneurship and Small Business has been the market-leading textbook on entrepreneurship in the UK now for nearly a decade. The major strengths of the book have been retained in the third edition:

▷ The unique breadth of coverage which allows a holistic approach to the issues facing the entrepreneurial organisation.
▷ The way it synthesises theory with practice, reinforcing the theory with practical examples and quotes from entrepreneurs in the real world.
▷ The informal style that makes the book so accessible and easily understood by students.

All chapters have seen extensive updating and rewriting in the third edition. What is new in this edition is the integration of the expanding range of topics into a framework that looks firstly at entrepreneurship and then at the start-up, growth and maturity of the small and medium-sized enterprise (SME) and how this might develop into corporate entrepreneurship. This integration means that there is better cohesion and logical flow in the narrative. Social entrepreneurship and international entrepreneurship are now treated as mainstream issues. The early emphasis on creativity and innovation has been maintained but better focused on the development of start-up ideas. The section on networks has been expanded, as has the chapter on corporate entrepreneurship.

New topics in the third edition include sustainability and corporate social responsibility, issues of gender and ethnicity in entrepreneurship, social capital, intellectual property rights as well as an expanded coverage of social entrepreneurship and business failure. There are new cases and those retained from the previous edition have been updated. Websites are now included for cases so that students can update information through their own research.

Keeping up to date is a challenge in any text that sets out to be practical and current. This is achieved by the extensive signposting to websites that offer up-to-date information and practical help and advice. It is an unfortunate sign of the times that the web resource also contains a warning about plagiarism – particularly necessary since business plans of any sort can now be so easily downloaded.

I would like to thank all those academic colleagues who continue to recommend the book and those who have suggested improvements. I hope I have met your expectations with this third edition.

How to use the book and website

The book is written for a range of undergraduate and postgraduate courses with the aim of fostering entrepreneurial talent and developing entrepreneurial skills. It is supported by a website (www.palgrave.com/business/burns) which contains additional teaching resources, including video commentaries by the author.

Firstly, the book can be used as a specialist text on entrepreneurship for both undergraduate and postgraduate courses such as a MBA. Whilst entrepreneurship is recognised as a topic in its own right, for students who have previously studied business and management, an entrepreneurship course typically aims to integrate and apply most of the functional areas they have previously studied and give it a creative and practical focus. This helps them to see better the interconnections in the topics they have already studied and realise that the solutions to real business problems require the application of all the areas they have studied. For these students the case studies are particularly important whilst some of the chapters that cover the 'basics' of business (such as Chapters 7 and 9), can be skimmed over. The book covers all of the main theoretical aspects of entrepreneurship and is comprehensively referenced throughout for further reading.

Secondly, the book can be used as a comprehensive core text for an 'introduction to business' course, albeit with an entrepreneurial focus – aimed particularly at students that are studying subjects where self-employment is a real option. It covers core areas such as management, strategy, marketing, accounting and finance. However, rather than teach the subject in subject-based compartments, relevant chapters are designed to act as a holistic introduction to the topic of business studies in the practical context of a business start-up and growth. Again, students can better see the interconnections and realise that solutions to real business problems require the application of a wide range of business subjects. Relevance and practicality can also aid motivation. Additional exercises on basic business skills such as accounting, financial management and marketing are available on the website.

For all students the practical focus of what is needed to start up and grow your own business is both motivating and practical. But, whilst I do believe that you can enhance entrepreneurial skills through education, I also believe that you really learn these skills by 'doing' rather than by just reading a book. This is why the learning resources contained in the book and on the supporting website are important. They are an integral part of the 'learning'.

Learning styles and the learning resources

Daniel Kim (1993) suggests that effective learning can be considered to be a revolving wheel (Figure A). During half of the cycle you test and experiment with concepts and observe what happens through concrete experience – learning 'know-how'. In the second half of the cycle you reflect on the observations and form concepts or theories – learning 'know-why'. This is often called 'double-loop learning' – the best sort of learning which links knowing how with knowing why, linking theory with practice. So effective learning involves forming concepts, testing concepts, experience and reflection. Traditionally education has focused too much on the second half of the cycle – forming concepts or theories and reflection – and it is difficult to break away from this in a textbook which, inevitably, focuses on the concepts and theories. However, I have tried to do so by including a number of learning resources. Each learning resource is designed to influence a particular learning style. Taken together, they should complete the wheel of learning.

Cases with questions

Embedded in each chapter are cases with questions, designed to make students think about and apply the concepts being explained and discussed in that chapter. This is the testing stage of the wheel of learning. Additional cases are available on the supporting website. Case notes are available on the lecturers' website. Other recommended cases, which are typically longer and more complex are given in the Learning Resources section on the website.

Exercises and assignments

In the testing and experimenting phase of the cycle are exercises and assignments, which involve doing something, in the main further research. This research is often desk-based – including visits to websites – but some of the most popular assignments, in my experience, involve students going out to do things – such as interviewing entrepreneurs. This is very much the 'test concepts' part of the wheel of learning.

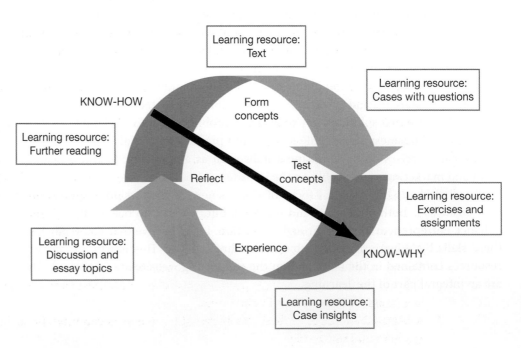

 **F.A** Wheel of learning

Source: Kim, D.H. (1993) 'The Link between Individual and Organizational Learning', *Sloan Management Review*, Fall.

Case insights and summaries

Spread throughout this book, there are case insights and quotes from entrepreneurs around the world. They are designed to illustrate and reinforce the theoretical points being made in the text with practical examples and opinions from the real world – there is nothing like an endorsement from an entrepreneur. The summary at the end of each chapter links cases to the main points being made in that chapter. This is the experience element of the wheel of learning, linked to the concepts and theories through the summaries and case questions.

Discussion and essay topics

Each chapter has topics for group discussion or essay writing. These can be used as a basis for tutorials. They are designed to make students think about the text material and develop their critical and reflective understanding of it and what it means in the real world. The summary and discussion topics help students discriminate between main and supporting points and provide mechanisms for self-teaching. The discussion and essay topics also form the reflective element of the wheel of learning, forcing students to think through the theories and concepts, often linking them to the real world.

Selected further reading and journals

Each chapter has full journal and book references. There are also selected further textbooks, organised by topic, and selected journals and their quality ranking on the website.

Website (www.palgrave.com/business/burns)

The students' website accompanying this book provides further resources:

▷ Video commentaries by the author.
▷ Interactive chapter tests – multiple choice tests to assess your understanding of each chapter.
▷ General Enterprise Tendency (GET) Test – an interactive version of the entrepreneurship test produced by Durham University Business School that allows you to assess whether you are entrepreneurial.
▷ Corporate Entrepreneurship Audit Tool – an interactive tool that matches the entrepreneurial orientation of an organisation against the commercial environment that it faces.
▷ Leadership Style Test – a self assessment test that allows you to assess your own leadership style.
▷ Small Business Audit Checklists – five checklists to help evaluate the preparedness for growth of a small firm.
▷ Entrepreneurship Assignments – five major assignments comprising entrepreneurial self-assessment, business idea generation, the development of a start-up business plan, a small business growth audit and an entrepreneurship audit. They use book and website resources and can be used for assessment purposes.
▷ Downloadable and printable versions of the cases with questions, including additional cases not included in the book.
▷ Downloadable and printable pro forma business plan.
▷ Downloadable and printable specimen plans for three businesses: Sport Retail, Jean Young and Dewhurst Engineering.
▷ Additional exercises on basic business skills such as accounting, financial management and marketing.

▷ Checklist of regulations to be met in setting up a business in the UK.
▷ Sources of information, help and advice in the UK.
▷ Selected websites offering further learning resources and practical, up-to-date help and advice, with hyperlinks.
▷ Any updates or revisions.

There is a password-protected lecturers' website which contains:

▷ Powerpoint slides for each chapter.
▷ Teaching notes for cases with questions.
▷ Teaching notes for the three specimen business plans.
▷ Selected case studies from the European Case Clearing House, many with related DVDs. These are particularly valuable for postgraduate teaching.
▷ Notes on the entrepreneurship assignments.

Learning outcomes

Each chapter has clear learning outcomes that identify the key concepts to be covered. These assume that students will undertake the essays and discussion topics as well as assignments and exercises, at the end of each chapter.

On completing the course based on this book a student should be able to:

1 Write a business plan for a start-up business.
2 Evaluate the entrepreneurial orientation of an organisation and its 'fit' with the commercial environment it faces.
3 Describe the problems and issues facing small and family firms and how they might be resolved.
4 Describe the nature of entrepreneurship in individuals – character traits and approaches to business and management – and evaluate their own entrepreneurial qualities.
5 Describe the process of creativity and innovation and explain how it might be encouraged in others and in themselves.
6 Explain what is required to become an entrepreneurial leader and manager and how entrepreneurship can be embedded in a larger organisation.
7 Develop strategies for an entrepreneurial organisation and explain which strategies are most likely to lead to successful start-up and growth, even in an international context.
8 Describe how the concept of entrepreneurship can be extended to non-commercial fields.

Key and cognitive skills for the course

Having completed a course in entrepreneurship using this book, with the seminar discussion topics, exercises and activities designed around it, a student should have developed a number of important skills:

▷ Information interpretation, critical analysis and evaluation skills.
▷ Data analysis and interpretation skills.
▷ Problem identification and solving skills.
▷ ICT skills, in particular the use of the internet.
▷ Independent and/or team-working skills.
▷ Writing and presentation skills.

Students should also have developed a range of applied business and management skills in a holistic way that can be applied to help a developing or existing organisation become more entrepreneurial.

In the final analysis, any course on entrepreneurship must challenge students to think entrepreneurially. It must make them aware of opportunities in the market place and generate a 'can-do' mentality. It must empower them and convince them that they can shape their own destinies. It must make them realise how important the entrepreneur is to the small firm and to society as a whole. It must make them realise how business problems do not come in neatly labelled boxes reflecting the way the subject is taught. But, most of all, it must be interesting and fun.

Acknowledgements

Every effort has been made to trace all the copyright holders, but if any have been inadvertently overlooked the publishers will be pleased to make the necessary arrangements at the first opportunity.

I would particularly like to thank Durham University Business School for permission to reproduce an electronic version of their GET Test on the website accompanying this book. Their work on entrepreneurship over the years has inspired all of us.

I would also like to thank my editor, Ann Edmondson, for her hard work, particularly on the last-minute revisions. Without her diligence this book would be littered with errors and omissions. Any that remain I claim as my own.

Guided tour of the book ...

Learning outcomes identify the key concepts to be covered

Quotes illustrate theoretical points with opinions from entrepreneurs

Case insights illustrate theoretical points with practical examples from the real world

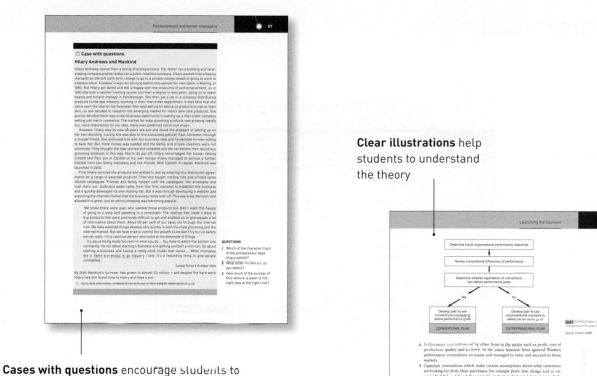

Cases with questions encourage students to apply theory to real-world situations

Clear illustrations help students to understand the theory

Summaries link the in-chapter case insights and quotes to the main points discussed in the chapter

Essays, discussion topics, exercises and assignments give opportunities for revision and reinforce the chapter contents

...and the website

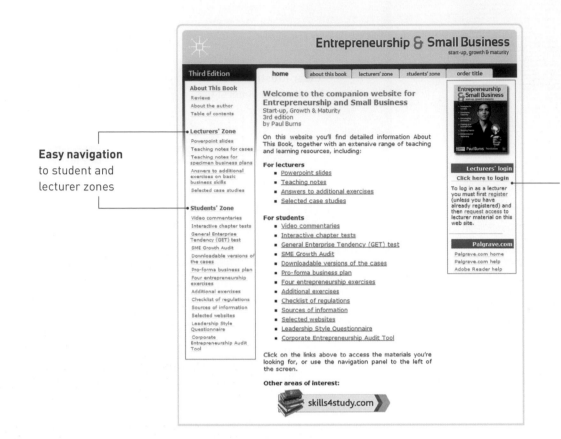

Easy navigation to student and lecturer zones

Password protected lecturer resources

Powerpoint slides to accompany every chapter

Detailed teaching notes for cases and specimen business plans

1 Entrepreneurship in the twenty-first century

2 Entrepreneurs and owner-managers

3 Innovation and entrepreneurship

4 Social and civic entrepreneurship

1 Entrepreneurship

1 Entrepreneurship in the twenty-first century

▷ **The stuff of dreams**
▷ **The entrepreneurial revolution**
▷ **The economics of entrepreneurship**
▷ **Entrepreneurs and owner-managers**
▷ **Small firms**
▷ **The differences between small and large firms**
▷ **Lifestyle and growth firms**
▷ **The UK small firms sector**
▷ **Global Entrepreneurship Monitor (GEM)**
▷ **Summary**

Case insights
▷ Bill Gates and Microsoft
▷ Michael Dell and the Dell Corporation
▷ Richard Branson and Virgin
▷ Shaa Wasmund and Brightstation Ventures
▷ Marc Demarquette
▷ Joseph Bamford and JCB

Cases with questions
▷ Julie Spurgeon
▷ Sara Murray – serial entrepreneur

Learning outcomes

By the end of this chapter you should be able to:

▷ Explain why small firms and entrepreneurs are so important to the economies of modern countries;

▷ Describe the influences that have contributed to their increasing importance;

▷ Explain the economic underpinning for entrepreneurship;

▷ Explain the meaning of the terms entrepreneur and owner-manager and how they are different;

▷ Explain the differing statistical definitions of small firms;

▷ Describe the relationship between small firms and entrepreneurship;

▷ Describe the characteristics of the UK small firms sector compared to other countries and the significant contribution it makes to the economy;

▷ Explain the consequences of differing policy options for stimulating SMEs;

▷ Explain what data is gathered by the annual GEM surveys.

♀ The stuff of dreams

Over the last thirty years the business world has fallen in love with the idea of entrepreneurship. Entrepreneurs have evolved to become super-heroes who valiantly and single-handedly battle to make the most of business opportunities, pulling together resources they do not own, finding willing suppliers and eager customers and, just sometimes, against all the odds, winning out to become millionaires. The entrepreneur has emerged as a new 'cultural hero' (Cannon, 1991; Carr and Beaver, 2002). This is the stuff of dreams. Entrepreneurs are held up as role models. They are said to embody ephemeral qualities that we ought to emulate – freedom of spirit, creativity, vision, zeal. Above all, they have the courage and self-belief to turn their dreams into reality. Is it any wonder that we envy them?

Entrepreneurs, like super-heroes, valiantly make the most of opportunities

Yet take time to get a perspective on this. As we entered the twentieth century, the focus was on big. Big was beautiful and size really mattered. Big was respectable, it was political-establishment. Big was the future. It offered economies of scale; mass production that brought well being, if not wealth, to the masses. It was how the Western democracies would keep the common man, not only in food, shelter and life's necessities, but also in his place. It even spawned its own professional elite – managers. Whilst running a business has been a fundamental activity throughout history, the recognition and study of it as a discipline and profession is a thoroughly modern, twentieth century phenomenon. Harvard Business School awarded its first Masters degree in the discipline in 1910. And all of this was based upon the best practices in large corporations. Business schools have reflected the wider establishment view; they have traditionally eschewed the arts of running a small business and largely ignored the skills of entrepreneurialism (Crainer and Dearlove, 1998).

But have small firms, like David, suddenly triumphed over the Goliath of large firms? In fact small firms, new firms and entrepreneurs never went away. And in the later part of the twentieth century reality began to dawn. In 1974 E.F. Schumacher, in his somewhat romantic book *Small is Beautiful*, asserted that giant organisations and increased specialisation resulted in economic inefficiency, environmental pollution and inhumane working conditions, and he proposed a system of intermediate technology based on smaller working units. Others began to doubt even the hard-nosed economic orthodoxy. In 1983 Jim Dewhurst wrote:

> In all the short history of modern business there is nothing so strange as this. On the one hand we have the traditional belief in the rightness and power of size. Rationalisation, standardisation and concentration are the watchwords. Economies of scale rule the industrial world. And in the UK we have gone further along this road of concentration than any other country in the world. Yet this predilection for economic orthodoxy has not brought us economic success.
>
> Dewhurst and Burns, 1983

The reality is that large firms were not so much the future of business but the natural consequence of businesses being set up by entrepreneurs and then growing. Unfortunately, like many things in life, they have a natural life expectancy and prolonging this is not always beneficial – to the firm or to society. According to Arie de Geus (1997) large organisations have proved amazingly inept at survival. He quoted a Dutch survey showing that the average corporate life expectancy in Japan and Europe was 12.5 years. 'The average life expectancy of a multinational corporation – the Fortune 500 or equivalent – is between 40 and 50 years.' The reality is that large companies die young, or at least their ownership changes fairly quickly.

Since the late twentieth century we have come to realise that new firms have done more to create wealth than firms at any time before them – ever! Ninety-five per cent of the wealth of the USA has been created since 1980. When Bill Gates founded Microsoft, IBM dominated the computer market with over 70 per cent of the market and more cash on its balance sheet than the sales of the rest of the industry. During the early 1990s IBM's share price plummeted and its workforce was slashed as it struggled to stay alive, while the new entrepreneurial companies, like Microsoft and Dell, prospered. By the start of the twenty-first century, one in every three households in the USA – 37 per cent or 35 million households – had at least one person who was involved in a primary role in a new or emerging business (*Economic News*, 1997).

Furthermore, people have begun to appreciate the sheer proportion of firms that can be described as small – by any definition, in any country. Small firms, virtually no matter how they are defined, make up at least 95 per cent of enterprises in the European Community. Their contribution to the economies of their countries also began to be appreciated around 1980. It was David Birch (1979) who, arguably, started this process with his seminal research which showed that 81.5 per cent of net new jobs in the USA, between 1969 and 1976, were created by small firms (under

📇 Case insight Bill Gates and Microsoft

We start with what is probably the outstanding business success story of a generation. Born in 1955 in Seattle, Bill Gates and his friend Paul Allen, 'begged, borrowed and bootlegged' time on his school's computer to undertake software commissions. The two went to Harvard University together, using the University's computer to start their own business. Bill's big break came when he approached Altair, a computer company in Albuquerque, New Mexico, trying to sell it a customised version of the programming language, BASIC, for its PC. The only problem was that, at the time, he and Paul Allen had not finished writing it. He had a vision of what it would look like and how it would operate, but no software. That was not finished until some weeks later and with it Microsoft came about. The package was later licensed to Apple, Commodore and IBM. IBM then commissioned Microsoft to develop its own operating system and that was how Microsoft Disk Operating System (MS DOS) was born. Founded in the late 1970s, by 1980 Microsoft was seen as a successful start-up with turnover of $8 million from just 38 employees. The company floated its shares on the US stock market in 1986; the ensuing rise of the company's stock price has made four billionaires and an estimated 12000 millionaires from Microsoft employees.

Microsoft's growth has been amazing. With a turnover of over $58 billion and 93000 employees, Microsoft is now the world's largest software company, producing a range of products and services that includes the Windows operating system and Microsoft Office software suite. And its ambitions are still anything but small. The company has expanded into markets such as video game consoles (Xbox), interactive television, internet access (MSN) and search engines (Bing). With its core markets maturing, it is targeting services for growth, looking to transform its software applications into web-based services.

In 2008 Bill Gates retired from day-to day-activities in the company a multimillionaire. He remains Chairman of the Board of Directors, and will continue to act as an advisor on key projects.

☐ Up-to-date information on Microsoft can be found on their website: www.microsoft.com

500 employees). The general pattern has been repeated since. Small, growing firms have outstripped large ones in terms of job generation, year after year. At times when larger companies retrenched, smaller firms continued to offer job opportunities. There are now about 10 million self-employed people in the USA and it has been estimated that small firms generate some 50 per cent of GDP, with over 50 per cent of exports coming from firms employing less than 20 people.

Small firms are just as important in Europe. In 2005 enterprises employing up to 249 employees made up 98.8 per cent of all firms in the EU – a total of 19.6 million enterprises (Eurostat, 2008). That compares to 84 per cent in the USA – although this data is not exactly comparable as it relates to 'establishments' rather than enterprises (OECD, 2008). These small firms in the EU generated 67.1 per cent of employment and 57.6 per cent of value added (Eurostat, op. cit.). By just about any measure the contribution small firms make to the economy of any country is considerable and their importance is now fully recognised.

But the focus is not just on small firms. It is also on high-growth firms. Despite being few in number, high-growth businesses are disproportionately important to national economies. Harrison and Taylor (1996) claim that in the USA it has been estimated that, whilst 15 000 medium sized businesses represent just 1 per cent of all businesses, they generate a quarter of all sales and they employ a fifth of all private sector labour. In the UK, Storey et al. (1987) asserted that 'out of every 100 small firms, the fastest growing four firms will create half the jobs in the group over a decade' – an assertion that has stood the test of time.

This book looks at a range of things that make up this whole romanticised, but blurred, vision of entrepreneurs and small business. It looks at entrepreneurs – how they start up businesses, grow them, and nurture them to maturity, many failing on the way. It links theory – how things ought to be done – with practice – how they are done in the real world – to find best practice through the minefield of starting and growing a business. It looks in depth at:

▷ *Entrepreneurs*. Who are they? Are all owner-managers entrepreneurial? What is their link with the process of innovation and economic growth, so loved by governments in most countries? Are they born rather than made and how are they shaped? Can they manage large firms or do they have to change as the business grows? Are they any different from managers or leaders in larger firms? Can they adapt to work in social enterprises with not-for-profit objectives? And, the important question for this millennium, can entrepreneurship be engendered in larger companies or other sorts of organisations?
▷ The *start-up*. How do you develop a business idea, one that is viable? How do you develop a plan that allows you to successfully launch the business – linking the marketing strategy that has the best chance of success with the resources you need to implement it? And where might those resources come from? Indeed once set up, what controls do you need to put in place to run the business?
▷ The *growth* of small firms. What growth strategies give the best chance of success? How do you find new customers or introduce new products or services? How do you develop a business plan that will get the backing of financiers? And what are the things that might go wrong and lead the business to failure, or how might you cash in on your success and sell the business?
▷ The *maturity* of these businesses. How do family firms pass from generation to generation – or not? How does the entrepreneur have to change with the business

as it grows if he wants to lead it effectively? Can we put in place the structures, systems and processes that ensure that the firm continues to be entrepreneurial as it grows? Can we understand the DNA of the entrepreneur sufficiently to transplant it into the very architecture of a large firm?

This book attempts to answer these questions. With over thirty years of research into entrepreneurship and small business there are now many answers. We do know what to do and what not to do, what works and what does not. This book will take a conceptual perspective to develop a theoretical framework for understanding the area and, based on this, move forward to show how many of these concepts may be operationalised and developed into practical help in successfully launching and growing a business – indeed any organisation. In other words it will link theory with practice to show that organisations can successfully start up, grow and stay entrepreneurial in their maturity.

🛄 Case insight Michael Dell and the Dell Computer Corporation

Michael Dell purchased his first computer – an Apple II – in 1980 and immediately took it apart to see how it was built. Only three years later he started a lucrative business selling upgraded PCs and add-on components out of his dormitory room at the University of Texas with capital of only $1000. Securing capital of $300 000 through his family, Michael registered the name Dell Computer Corporation in 1984 when he decided to leave college and start selling custom-built computers directly to end-users, ignoring the more normal channel of selling mass-produced computers through computer resellers. This not only eliminated the substantial middleman mark-up, but also the costly inventories required. In 1985, the company produced the first computer of its own design, the 'Turbo PC', which sold for $795.

> 'We built the company around a systematic process: give customers the high-quality computers they want at a competitive price as quickly as possible, backed by great service.'
>
> Dell, 1999

In the 1980s Dell pioneered the 'configure to order' approach to manufacturing, producing individual PCs configured to customers' specifications and, in so doing, minimising its inventories and its costs. In contrast, most manufacturers at that time delivered large orders to intermediaries on a quarterly basis. Dell currently sells PCs, servers, data storage devices, network switches, software, and computer peripherals. It also sells HDTVs, cameras, printers, MP3 players and other electronics built by other manufacturers. Dell grew during the 1980s and 1990s to become, for a time, the biggest marketer of PCs and servers. It is currently the second largest company in the industry after Hewlett-Packard and employs over 76 500 people worldwide.

In 2004 Michael Dell stepped aside as CEO of Dell while retaining his position as Chairman of the Board. Kevin Rollins became the new CEO but Michael Dell returned in 2007 to become CEO once more. Like Bill Gates, he also is a multimillionaire and has become a truly exceptional entrepreneurial leader.

☐ Up-to-date information on Dell can be found on their website: www.dell.com

💡 The entrepreneurial revolution

What we are seeing now is nothing short of an entrepreneurial revolution. The major factors causing this are change and the pace at which it is accelerating. Change itself has changed to become discontinuous, abrupt but all pervasive. And small, entrepreneurial firms are better able to cope. Their flexibility and speed of response to changing market circumstances is well documented. In a turbulent world, full of uncertainties, they seem better able to survive and prosper. This is the essence of their success – their ability to spot an opportunity arising out of change or even to create it and then focus resources on delivering what the market wants quickly. In essence they are expert in innovation. And that often means taking risks that larger businesses are unwilling or unable to take. This all boils down to one word – entrepreneurship. It is the entrepreneurial small firms that have been able to capitalise most on the turbulent world we face today – entrepreneurial firms led by founders like Bill Gates, Michael Dell and Richard Branson.

A number of other influences have accelerated this trend towards smaller firms. Firstly there has been the shift in most economies away from manufacturing towards the service sectors where small firms often flourish because of their ability to deliver a personalised, flexible, tailor-made service at a local level. The 'deconstruction' of larger firms into smaller, more responsive units concentrating on their core activities, often sub-contracting many of their other activities to smaller firms, has also contributed to the trend. Large firms and even the public sector became leaner and fitter in the 1980s in a bid to reduce fixed costs and reduce risks. Small firms have benefited, although they may be seen as dependent on large ones.

Technology has played its part. It has influenced the trend in three ways. Firstly, the new technologies that swept the late twentieth century – computers and the internet – were pioneered by new, rapidly growing firms. Secondly, these technologies actually facilitated the growth of self-employment and small business by easing communication, encouraging working from home and allowing smaller and smaller market segments to be serviced. Indeed information has become a product in its own right and one that can be generated anywhere around the world and transported at the touch of a button. Thirdly, many new technologies, for example in printing, have reduced fixed costs so that production can be profitable in smaller, more flexible units.

Social and market trends have also accelerated the growth of small firms. Firstly, customers increasingly expect firms to address their particular needs. Market niches are becoming slimmer and markets more competitive – better served by smaller firms. Secondly, people want to control their own destiny more. After periods of high unemployment, they may see self-employment as more attractive and more secure than employment. In the late twentieth century, redundancy pushed many people into self-employment at the same time as the new 'enterprise culture' gave it political and social respectability. The growth of 'new age' culture and 'alternative' lifestyles also encouraged the growth of a whole new range of self-employment opportunities.

> *The Entrepreneurial Revolution is here to stay, having set the genetic code of the US and global economy for the 21st century, and having sounded the death knell for Brontosaurus Capitalism of yesteryear. Entrepreneurs are the creators, the innovators, and the leaders who give back to society, as philanthropists, directors and trustees, and who, more than any others, change the way people live, work, learn, play, and lead. Entrepreneurs create new technologies, products, processes, and services that become the next wave of new industries. Entrepreneurs create value with high potential, high growth companies which are the job creation engines of the US economy.*
>
> ☐ Jeffrey Timmons, author, 1999

> *We now stand on the threshold of a new age -- the age of revolution. In our minds, we know the new age has already arrived: in our bellies, we're not sure we like it. For we know it is going to be an age of upheaval, of tumult, of fortunes made and unmade at head-snapping speed. For change has changed. No longer is it additive. No longer does it move in a straight line. In the twenty-first century, change is discontinuous, abrupt, seditious.*
>
> ☐ Gary Hamel, author, 2000

💡 The economics of entrepreneurship

The question arises as to whether there are any underlying theories to explain the growth in number and importance of small firms. Marxist theory predicts that capitalism will degenerate into economies dominated by a small number of large firms and society will polarise between those that own them and those that work in them. To a Marxist, the rise of small firms is just another, subtler way for this trend to manifest itself. Small firms are dependent upon larger firms for their custom and well being; they absorb risk and push down pay and conditions for workers as they are rarely unionised. However, the successful growth of so many small firms since the 1980s, the increasing fragmentation of industries and markets and the increasing popularity of self-employment by choice would seem to belie this theory.

People like Fritz Schumacher (1974) would have us believe that the growth of small firms is part of a social trend towards a more democratic and responsive society – 'small is beautiful'. To him the quality of life is more important than materialism. He is very much in favour of 'intermediate technology' – simpler, cheaper and easier to use – with production on a smaller scale and more locally based. However, the technologies that fuelled the growth of small firms at the end of the twentieth century were far from simple and, for many, quality of life improved alongside materialism. This leads us on to free-market economics. At one extreme the growth of small firms can be seen as the triumph of the free market and the success of the 'enterprise culture' promulgated by politicians like Ronald Reagan and Margaret Thatcher. Increasing numbers of small firms are the natural result of increased competition and a drive to prevent private and public monopoly. But what exactly does economic theory have to say about the creation of small firms?

Traditional industrial economists would explain the growth of new firms in terms of industry profitability, growth, barriers to entry and concentration. However, they are more concerned with 'entry' to an industry, rather than whether this is by a new or an existing firm. They assume an endless supply of potential new entrants. They would say that entry to an industry is high when expected profits and growth are high. It is deterred by high barriers to entry and high concentration, when collusion between existing firms can take place. However, much of this work does not specifically consider the role of new or smaller firms. Indeed, Acs and Audretsch (1989) show that entry by small, primarily new, firms is not the same as entry by large firms and that the birth of small firms is lower in highly concentrated industries and ones where innovation plays an important part.

By way of contrast, labour market economists have been more interested in what influences individuals to become potential entrants to an industry by becoming self-employed. Psychologists have also contributed greatly to this work, which has focused on the character or personality of the individual, the antecedent influences on them, such as age, sex, education, employment status, experience and ethnicity, as well as other societal influences. This work has proved far more successful and informative, and we examine it in detail in Chapter 2.

The link between entrepreneurship – the creation of new firms – and economic growth has until recently been far from clear, as far as economists are concerned. Traditional theories tended to suggest that entrepreneurship impeded rather than encouraged growth. Classical economics focused on optimising existing resources within a stable environment and treated any disruptions, such as entrepreneurial new firms creating whole new industries, as 'god sent' external forces. It was Joseph Schumpeter (1934), an Austrian economist, who created the link between entrepreneurship, innovation and growth. Schumpeter sought to explain economic development as a process caused by enterprise – or innovation – and carried out by entrepreneurs. We shall return to this in Chapter 3. This process of 'creative destruction', whereby new entrants displaced inefficient firms was formally restated by Aghion and Howitt (1992).

More recent theories of 'industrial evolution' have linked entrepreneurship and economic growth directly (Jovanovic, 1982; Lambson, 1991; Hopenhayn, 1992; Audretsch, 1995; Ericson and Pakes, 1995; Klepper, 1996). These theories focus on change as the central phenomenon and emphasise the role knowledge plays in charting a way through this. Innovation is seen as the key to entry, growth and survival for an enterprise and the way entire industries change over time. But the information they need in order to innovate is crucial – being inherently uncertain, asymmetric (one party may have more than another) and associated with high transaction costs. As a result there are differences in the expected value of new ideas, and people therefore have an incentive to leave secure employment to start up a new enterprise in order to capitalise on a commercial idea they believe in more than others. Once established, if economies of scale are important (see Chapter 6), the enterprise must grow, simply to survive. In this way the economic performance of nations is linked to how well the potential from innovation is tapped – start-ups encouraged and growth facilitated. And inherent in the process is churning – firms being displaced by newer, more innovative rivals.

These new evolutionary theories, supported by empirical evidence, therefore state that entrepreneurship encourages economic growth for three reasons:

1 It encourages competition by increasing the number of enterprises. Whilst this increases growth in itself, it is a cumulative phenomenon because competition is more conducive to knowledge externalities – new ideas – than is local monopoly. And so entrepreneurship encourages entrepreneurship – a factor to which we return in Chapter 2.

2 It is a mechanism for 'knowledge spillovers' – transmission of knowledge from its point of origin to other individuals or organisations. Knowledge spillover is an important mechanism underlying endogenous growth, and start-ups – entrepreneurs – are seen as being particularly adept at appropriating knowledge from other sources. In other words entrepreneurs spot opportunities and innovate – a factor to which we shall also return in Chapter 2.

3 It generates diversity and variety among enterprises in any location. Each enterprise is in some way different or unique and this influences economic growth.

☿ Entrepreneurs and owner-managers

Before we go much further we need to define some terms. There is no universally accepted definition of the term 'entrepreneur'. The *Oxford English Dictionary* defines an entrepreneur as 'a person who attempts to profit by risk and initiative'. This definition emphasises that entrepreneurs exercise a high degree of initiative and are willing to take a high degree of risk. But it covers a wide range of occupations, including that of paid assassin. No wonder there is an old adage that if you scratch an entrepreneur you will find a 'spiv' (somebody who makes a living from unlawful work). The difference is more than just one of legality. Therefore a question you might ask is, how do they do it?

> *We learned the importance of ignoring conventional wisdom and doing things our way ... It's fun to do things that people don't think are possible or likely. It's also exciting to achieve the unexpected.*
>
> ☐ Michael Dell, 1999

Back in the 1800s, Jean-Baptist Say, the French economist, said: 'entrepreneurs shift economic resources from an area of lower productivity into an area of higher productivity and greater yield' (1803). In other words entrepreneurs create value by exploiting some form of change, for example in technology, materials, prices or demographics. We call this process innovation and this is an essential tool for entrepreneurs. We shall examine it in greater detail in Chapter 3. Entrepreneurs, therefore, create new demand or find new ways of exploiting existing markets. They identify a commercial opportunity and then exploit it.

Central to all of this is change. Change causes disequilibrium in markets out of which come the commercial opportunities that entrepreneurs thrive upon. To them change creates opportunities that they can exploit. Sometimes they initiate the change themselves – they innovate in some way. At other times they exploit changes created by the external environment. Often, in doing so, they destroy the established order and complacency of existing social and economic systems. How entrepreneurs manage and deal with change is central to their character and essential if they are to be successful. Most 'ordinary people' find change threatening. Entrepreneurs welcome it because it creates opportunities that can be exploited and they often create it through innovation.

How entrepreneurs deal with change is a key part of their success

Another key feature of entrepreneurs is their willingness to accept risk and uncertainty. In part this is simply the consequence of their eagerness to exploit change. However, the scale of uncertainty they are willing to accept is altogether different from that of other managers. It reflects itself in the risks they take for the business and for themselves. And for some this can be so addictive that they become 'serial entrepreneurs', best suited to continuing to start up businesses and unwilling to face the tedium of day-to-day management.

It is no wonder that entrepreneurship has been described as 'a slippery concept ... not easy to work into a formal analysis because it is so closely associated with the temperament or personal qualities of individuals' (Penrose, 1959). We shall examine it in more detail in Chapter 2 where we attempt to differentiate entrepreneurs from others by their character traits. We shall also address the question of whether entrepreneurs are born or made.

Notice that in these definitions that there is no mention of small firms. Indeed, Richard Branson, a successful entrepreneur in his own right, is quoted as saying:

> I am often asked what it is to be an 'entrepreneur' and there is no simple answer. It is clear that successful entrepreneurs are vital for a healthy, vibrant and competitive economy. If you look around you, most of the largest companies have their foundations in one or two individuals who have the determination to turn a vision into reality.
>
> Anderson, 1995

The point is that entrepreneurs are defined by their actions, not by the size of organisation they happen to work within. Any manager can be entrepreneurial. The manager of a small firm may not be an entrepreneur – an important distinction that is often missed in the literature. Equally, entrepreneurs can exist within large firms, even ones

🗀 Case insight Richard Branson and Virgin

Richard Branson is probably the best known entrepreneur in Britain today and his name is closely associated with the many businesses that carry the Virgin brand name. He is outward-going and an excellent self-publicist. He has been called an 'adventurer', taking risks that few others would contemplate. This shows itself in his personal life, with his transatlantic power boating and round-the-world ballooning exploits, as well as in his business life where he has challenged established firms like British Airways and Coca-Cola. He is a multimillionaire with what has been described as a charismatic leadership style. The Virgin Group is characterised as being informal and information driven – one that is bottom-heavy rather than strangled by top-heavy management.

Now in his sixties, Richard Branson's business life started as an 18-year-old schoolboy when he launched Student magazine, selling advertising space from a phone booth. He started selling mail-order records but soon decided he needed a retail site. In 1972 he got his first store, above a shoe shop on London's Oxford Street, rent-free on the grounds that it could not be let and would generate more customers for the shoe shop. It was a great success and Richard earned enough money from it to buy a country estate, in which he installed a recording studio and started Virgin Records.

Since those early days the Virgin brand has found its way onto aircraft, trains, cola, vodka, mobile phones, cinemas, a radio station, financial services and most recently the internet. Virgin Atlantic Airways was launched in 1984. In 1986 Virgin was floated but later reprivatised because Richard did not like to be accountable for his actions to institutional shareholders. In 1992, to keep his airline company afloat, he sold the Virgin record label to EMI for $1 billion. In 1999 a 49 per cent stake in the airline was sold to Singapore Airlines. In the same year Virgin Mobile was launched. Today Virgin describes itself as a 'branded venture capital company', comprising over 360 separate businesses.

'Virgin is not a big company – it's a big brand made up of lots of small companies. Our priorities are the opposite of our large competitors ... For us our employees matter most. It just seems common sense that if you have a happy, well motivated workforce, you're much more likely to have happy customers. And in due course the resulting profits will make your shareholders happy. Convention dictates that big is beautiful, but every time one of our ventures gets too big we divide it up into smaller units ... Each time we do this, the people involved haven't had much more work to do, but necessarily they have a greater incentive to perform and a greater zest for their work.'

Branson, 1998

🗆 Up-to-date information on the Virgin Group can be found on their website: www.virgin.com

that they did not set up themselves. How large firms encourage and deal with this is an important issue to which we shall return in Chapter 18: 'Corporate entrepreneurship'.

The way our notion of entrepreneur has been crafted has a long history, dating back to Cantillon (1755). Table 1.1 summarises some of the major developments in the concept. It charts the academic history and maps the antecedence of modern entrepreneurship. Trying to combine these shifting concepts and definitions with elements of character, I would propose the following definition for this elusive term:

> Entrepreneurs use innovation to exploit or create change and opportunity for the purpose of making profit. They do this by shifting economic resources from an area of lower productivity into an area of higher productivity and greater yield, accepting a high degree of risk and uncertainty in doing so.

You do not have to own a firm to manage it. However, some managers do own the firms they manage and these make up the majority of managers of small firms. These are owner-managers. Sole traders are owner-managers. Limited companies, however, have share capital. The term owner-manager, therefore, needs further refinement. An obvious one would be that to qualify as an owner-manager requires ownership (or beneficial ownership) of over 50 per cent of the share capital, thereby giving control of the business.

Date	Author	Concept
1755	Cantillon	Introduced the concept of entrepreneur from 'entreprendre' (ability to take charge).
1803, 1817	Say	Emphasised the ability of the entrepreneur to 'marshal' resources in order to respond to unfulfilled opportunities.
1871	Menger	Noted the ability of entrepreneurs to distinguish between 'economic goods' – those with a market or exchange value – and all others.
1893	Ely and Hess	Attributed to entrepreneurs the ability to take integrated action in the enterprise as a whole, combining roles in capital, labour, enterprise and entrepreneur.
1911, 1928	Schumpeter	Envisioned that entrepreneurs proactively 'created' opportunity using 'innovative combinations' which often included 'creative destruction' of passive or lethargic economic markets.
1921	Knight	Suggested that entrepreneurs were concerned with the 'efficiency' in economic factors by continually reducing waste, increasing savings and thereby creating value, implicitly understanding the opportunity-risk-reward relationship.
1948, 1952, 1967	Hayek	Continued the Austrian tradition of analytical entrepreneurs giving them capabilities of discovery and action, recognising the existence of information asymmetry which they could exploit.
1973, 1979, 1997, 1999	Kirzner	Attributed to entrepreneurs a sense of 'alertness' to identify opportunities and exploit them accordingly.
1974	Drucker	Attributed to entrepreneurs the capacity to 'foresee' market trends and make a timely response.
1975, 1984, 1985	Shapero	Attributed a 'judgement' ability to entrepreneurs to identify 'credible opportunities' depending on two critical antecedents – perceptions of 'desirability' and 'feasibility' from both personal and social viewpoints.

Source: Adapted from Etemad (2004).

T 1.1 The antecedence of modern entrepreneurship

These definitions are, however, restrictive. For example, if a company is owned equally by two managers they would not be called owner-managers. Would this be any different if it were a partnership? Many people would call the managers in both situations 'owner-managers'. But where does this dilution begin and end? How many managers owning part of the business do you need before they cease being called owner-managers? Are all the employees of the John Lewis Partnership owner-managers? The real issue is not ownership, but control. Owner-managers significantly control the operations of their firm on a day-to-day basis. Notice, however, that this is a question of judgement and therefore this term, as with 'entrepreneur', is likely to be used very loosely.

Notice also that, using these definitions, owner-managers need not be entrepreneurs. Indeed, most owner-managers are not entrepreneurial. This book argues that entrepreneurs can be described in terms of their character and judged by their actions and one of the major factors differentiating them from owner-managers is the degree of innovation they practise.

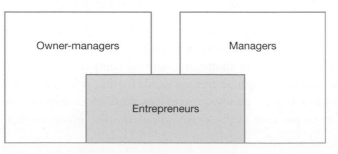

F1.1 Entrepreneurs, managers and owner-managers

Many managers of small firms do not own or control the firm they are employed by. The firm may be controlled by its larger, parent company. The manager is therefore not an owner-manager. Paradoxically, however, they might be entrepreneurs, depending on the way they act. Figure 1.1 shows these relationships. Whilst managers are different from owner-managers, both can be entrepreneurial. Similarly both managers and owner-managers may not be entrepreneurial. The entrepreneur is a unique individual with characteristics that are found in both owner-managers and managers.

🖻 Case insight Shaa Wasmund and Brightstation Ventures

Shaa Wasmund is a graduate of the London School of Economics. In her last year at the London School of Economics she won a writing competition which led to a chance to interview the boxer Chris Eubank for *Cosmopolitan*. Eubank was impressed with Shaa and the interview led to a job with him, promoting his fights. After Eubank retired in 1994 she set up her first business, a PR and marketing company, with James Dyson as her first client. In 1999, a chance meeting with pop star and businessman Sir Bob Geldof led her to join him in launching the travel company Deckchair.com.

A year later, Shaa raised £6 million to launch her own company Mykindaplace.com a combination of online teenage girls' magazine and an early social networking site. By working with large companies like BSkyB and Freeserve – who also provided funding – to drive traffic to the site, the business prospered. So much so that by 2006 it was worth £10–£15 million and she decided to sell half her share in the business to BSkyB.

In 2007, together with entrepreneur Dan Wagner, she launched Brightstation Ventures, an investment vehicle with $100 million of capital dedicated to investing in internally generated ideas and seeding young companies that use information technology in innovative ways.

In a podcast interview for *Leadership Week* in 2008, she reflected on her experience:

Business is like a relay race and I am very, very good at the first leg and I am very, very good at the last leg, and I'm really not the best person

to do the second and third legs. So you have to learn to pass that baton over to somebody else and more often than not that person will be somebody from a more corporate background than you, who has probably more experience at systems and procedures and who … and enjoys developing and growing the business but also managing the business, whereas an entrepreneur will typically really enjoy the first part – getting the business off the ground, getting the funds in and making the ideas happen, probably to the point of bringing a business to profitability … At that point I start to lose focus and so that's when you need to recognise what your strengths and your weaknesses are and then you come back in to sell the business. It's not that you disengage completely during the second and third legs, but you certainly pass the responsibility over to somebody who is more capable than you.

I believe in as flat a management structure as possible … in leading without title … I never put any emphasis on my title. I most certainly try to lead by example and I'm very much a big believer in making all of my mistakes public so that other people feel confident and comfortable to be able to air their own mistakes.

Management Today 18 July 2008,
www.managementtoday.co.uk

☐ Up-to-date information on Brightstation Ventures can be found on their website: www.brightstation.com

💡 Small firms

As with the other terms, there is no uniformly acceptable definition of a small firm. Back in 1971, the Bolton Report (Bolton, 1971), which is usually held to be a definitive report on the state of small business in Britain at the time, made heavy weather of providing a statistical definition. Recognising that one definition would not cover industries as divergent as manufacturing and service, it used eight definitions for various industry groups. These ranged from under 200 employees for manufacturing firms to over £50 000 turnover (in 1971) for retailing, and up to five vehicles or less for road transport. So many definitions clearly cause practical problems. What is more, definitions based on financial criteria suffer from inherent problems related to inflation and currency translation.

The European Commission coined the now widely used term 'small and medium enterprise' (SME) and in 1996 defined it as an organisation employing fewer than 250 people – a criterion that continues to be used for most statistical purposes. It defines these further categories:

	Number of employees
Micro	0–9
Small	10–49
Medium	50–249
Large	250 or more

The EU goes further to define the SME as having a turnover of less than €50 million and an annual balance sheet total of €43 million when it comes to establishing which SMEs might benefit from EU programmes, policies and competitiveness rules.

Being a small firm is not just about size, defined in simple statistical terms. Small firms also have important defining characteristics. The Bolton Committee described a small firm as satisfying three criteria, all of which defy practical statistical application:

1 *Market influence.* In economic terms, the small firm has a small share of the market. Therefore it is not large enough to influence the prices or national quantities of the good or service that it provides. Unfortunately, two fundamental problems arise with this, firstly with the definition of market and secondly with the ability of the small firm to influence price and the quantity sold in that market. Many of the most successful small firms operate in market niches so slim that they dominate that market segment, with no clear competition, and they can and do influence both price and quantity sold. In that respect Bolton's definition looks naïve and dated and was probably influenced by the economists' definition of perfect competition. It is certainly not one that most entrepreneurs would agree with.

2 *Independence.* The small firm is independent in the sense that it does not form part of a larger enterprise and that the owner-managers are free from outside control in taking their principal decisions. This means that only owner-managed firms are considered small firms. This is clearly unsatisfactory if you believe that there are certain specific characteristics about managing a small firm that mark it out as different from a large one.

3 *Personal influence.* The small firm is managed in a personalised way and not through the medium of a formalised management structure. This person is involved in all aspects of the management of the business and is involved in all major decision-making. Frequently there is little devolution or delegation of authority.

📁 Case insight Marc Demarquette

Half French and half Chinese, Marc Demarquette was born and lives in London. He was a management consultant until an accident caused him to reconsider his priorities. His interest in catering led him to the prestigious Maison Lenôtre in Paris to learn the art of making chocolate and then to the Alps to work with a master chocolatier. In 2006 he opened an up-market chocolate shop, Demarquette, in Fulham, in south west London, and a small production facility nearby with the help of a £40 000 bank loan. He employed a chocolatier to help him create his range of high quality chocolates.

Three years later the business was well established. The £40 000 was spent within the first six months but since then the business has been entirely funded out of cash flow. Marc now produces a range of chocolates for Fortnum & Mason, but about one-third of sales come through the website. He has talked to other stores around the world about producing bespoke ranges of chocolate for them but has not moved forward on any of these. He also thought about opening a second shop in 2008, but decided not to because of the economic down turn. Since then his

margins have been squeezed as chocolate prices rose by some 40 per cent in 2008 at a time when Marc felt unable to increase his prices. Marc still employs the chocolatier.

'After week one you can rip up your business plan because, although theories are wonderful, you have to respond to the real market. You need to have nerves of steel but it has been a fantastic experience. I'm loving it. I just wish I had a couple of extra hours in the day to enjoy my own life.'

Sunday Times, 24 May 2009

☐ Up-to-date information on Marc Demarquette can be found on his website: www.demarquette.com

Small firms start to make managerial appointments when they have some 10–20 employees and at this point they begin to take on the appearance of more formal structures (Atkinson and Meager, 1994). Nevertheless, this third point is the key to a definition of the real small firm – the one with potential, the one that economists cannot understand, the one that makes it so different from the large firm. Essentially the real small firm can be described as having 'two arms, two legs and a giant ego'. In other words it is an extension of a person – the owner-manager or entrepreneur and their character traits – into the firm. Their personality is imprinted on the way it operates. The risks they and their family face if the firm fails influences how business decisions are made.

○ The differences between small and large firms

Small firms are not just scaled down versions of large ones. They go about their business in a number of fundamentally different ways. The key to understanding how a particular small firm goes about management and why and how decisions are made is to understand the personality of the owner-manager. Their personality and their behavioural characteristics will strongly influence this. More than large firms, small firms are social entities that revolve around personal relationships. They approach risk and uncertainty in a particular way that sometimes seems far from rational, which may explain why they are so little understood by economists.

There are a number of other characteristics that are typical of small firms and underline their different approach to management and business. The first is that they are typically short of cash. They cannot raise capital in the same way that a large company can. This has major strategic implications. Firstly, it constrains the strategies that they can adopt. For example, they cannot afford to adopt expensive advertising and promotion campaigns, so instead managers develop close relationships with customers and prospective customers, investing their time rather than money. Secondly, it dictates that business decisions must have a quick pay-off and therefore decision-making is short-term. For a growing business it means that raising finance becomes a major strategic issue and relationships with financing institutions such as banks and venture capitalists can become a major resource issue.

The second characteristic is that small firms are likely to operate in a single market, or a small number of markets, probably offering a limited range of products or services. This means that their scope of operations is, or at least should be, limited. In that sense they face fewer strategic issues than larger firms and often business strategy is synonymous with marketing strategy. However, unlike large firms, they find it difficult to diversify their business risk, which is another reason why they find it hard to raise finance.

Related to this is the characteristic that most small firms are over-reliant on a small number of customers. This means that they are particularly vulnerable to losing any one customer and the effect on the firm of such a loss will be disproportionately large. This is yet another reason why they are riskier prospects than large firms and find difficulty raising finance.

The fourth characteristic is the effect of scale on the economics of the business and how that translates into financial evaluation and decision-making. Most business finance textbooks are written with large companies in mind; consequently, whilst the principles they espouse are sound, the examples they use and generalisations that result are not. For example, taking on an additional member of staff for a small firm is a major strategic decision involving relatively large sums of money that represent a step increase in their fixed costs. Consequently they are reluctant to do so unless absolutely necessary. Yet in most business finance textbooks wage costs are treated as a variable cost, a view that can only be justified when there is a large number of employees. As we shall see in Chapter 9, this error can lead to quite incorrect business decisions being made. It is little wonder that managers of small firms have little faith in professional advisors and accountants. Banks have for some time realised that traditional financial analysis says little about the health of the small firm and have started to broaden their approach.

These characteristics start to combine to distinguish small firms from large ones on a basis other than scale. Wynarczyk et al. (1993), strongly influenced by Casson (1982), argue that the much greater role played by uncertainty, innovation and firm evolution is the real defining characteristic of small firms. Small firms face more uncertain markets than large firms. They have a limited customer base and often cannot influence price. The owner-manager's own aspirations and motivations may also be uncertain. The effect of this high degree of uncertainty is to force decision-making to become short-term. Small firms also innovate in a particular way that makes them different from large firms (see Chapter 3). The final distinguishing characteristic is evolution – the recognition that the nature, style and functions of management change considerably as the small firm grows and evolves. Once more, we shall explore this in detail, in particular looking at the 'stage theories' of how firms grow (see Chapter 17).

Lifestyle and growth firms

Small firms and entrepreneurship have often been linked together in a very loose fashion. They are broadly overlapping sets. As Storey and Sykes (1996) explain:

> the small firm is less concerned with formal systems and its decision-making process will be more judgemental, involving fewer individuals, and can therefore be quicker. It can be much more responsive to changes in the market-place but, conversely, is much less able to influence such developments. Hence the small firm is likely to adjust more quickly than the large firm to situations of market disequilibrium and, in these senses, embodies the characteristics of the classic entrepreneur.

However, this is a question of scale and, just as it was necessary to distinguish between owner-managers and entrepreneurs, it might be useful to distinguish between two categories of small firms:

1 *Lifestyle firms.* These are businesses that are set up primarily to undertake an activity that the owner-manager enjoys or gets some comfort from whilst also providing an adequate income, for example craft-based businesses. They are not set up to grow and, therefore, once a level of activity that provides the adequate income is reached, management becomes routine and tactical. There is probably little thought about strategic management unless things start to go wrong, and the most likely thing to go wrong is that the market changes without the owner-manager realising it. These firms are rarely managed by entrepreneurs and, if they are, the entrepreneur will be extremely frustrated. Most owner-managed firms fall into this category. Many are sole traders (unincorporated businesses). However, a lifestyle business can change if the owner-manager's motivations change and they have the entrepreneurial qualities to see it through.

2 *Growth firms.* These are set up with the intention of growth, usually by entrepreneurs. Occasionally a lifestyle business can turn into a growth business unintentionally. However, if the manager does not have entrepreneurial characteristics they are unlikely to succeed in the long run. Rapid growth is risky and creates major problems that must be addressed within very short time frames. Effective strategic management is vital if the firm is to succeed, indeed possibly survive. Notwithstanding this, these firms will face numerous problems and crises as they grow, some of which are predictable, others that are not. This is the classic entrepreneurial firm so beloved by the financial press.

It is important to realise that the small firm sector is far from homogeneous. Consider issues of size and age of business, sector, location, growth and decline, economic and market conditions. What is more, the people that manage them are many and varied. You do not have to own a small firm to manage it and you certainly do not have to be an entrepreneur. Consider also issues of age, sex, ethnicity, social origins, family relationships and then you start to realise the scale of the complexity.

Generalisations about small firms and the people that manage them are therefore just that – vast generalisations that are supposed to cover what makes up some 95 per cent of firms in most countries. Small firms are not homogeneous but, notwithstanding this, let us try to paint a broad picture of their nature and role in the UK.

🗀 Case with questions Julie Spurgeon

In her mid-forties, Julie Spurgeon graduated with a first in ceramic design from London's Central Saint Martin's College of Art and Design in the summer of 2008. As part of her final project to design a range of tableware she had to seek critical appraisal from retailers and industry experts. One of the firms she contacted was up-market retailer Fortnum & Mason and they were sufficiently impressed to commission a range of bone china tableware, called Material Pleasures, that was launched in August 2009.

The trade mark Material Pleasures, which goes on the reverse of each piece, is registered (cost £200) and Julie joined Anti Copying in Design (ACID), which allowed her to log her design trail as proof against copying. Julie has had to pay for tooling and manufacturing costs herself. The moulds cost £5000 and the factory in Stoke on Trent required a minimum order of 250 pieces. The contract with Fortnum's involved exclusivity for six months. All this was funded with a £5000 loan from the Creative Seed Fund and a part-time job.

'In the future I'd like to continue creating specialist tableware, as well as handmade pieces. Material Pleasures stands for individual design, not big-batch production.'

Sunday Telegraph, 12 July 2009

QUESTIONS

1 In your opinion, is Julie's a lifestyle or a growth business?

2 How do you differentiate between the two?

💡 The UK small firms sector

During much of the twentieth century, the UK saw a decrease in the importance of small firms, measured in terms of their share of manufacturing employment and output. The proportion of the UK labour force classified as self-employed was at its lowest point in the 1960s. It was no wonder that the Bolton Committee (op. cit.), set up in the late 1960s to investigate the role of small firms in the economy, concluded that 'the small firm sector was in a state of long-term decline, both in size and its share of economic activity'. From the 1970s the situation has been reversed. Small firms have increased in importance, measured in terms of their number and their share of employment and turnover, and the number of small firms continues to rise, as does the number of people classified as self-employed. In 1979 there were only 2.4 million SMEs in the UK (see preceding definition). By 2007 this had grown to 4.7 million – an increase of almost 96 per cent in 28 years.

In the UK a range of SME statistics are produced and are available free on www. statistics.gov.uk. These are updated annually. The statistics for 2007 (Table 1.2) show that 99.9 per cent of firms were SMEs (all but 6000 out of 4.7 million) and they generated 59.2 per cent of employment (out of 22.7 million) and 51.5 per cent of turnover (out of £2.8 billion).

However, the detailed statistics also show that 73.9 per cent of all firms in the UK had no employees (3.5 million). These comprise sole proprietors, partnerships with only self-employed partners and companies with only an employee/director. These firms generated 16.6 per cent of UK employment for their proprietors (3.8 million) and 7.6 per cent of UK turnover (£222 billion).

These statistics reinforce the view that most UK small firms really are small, offering no more than self-employment. Most of these are probably lifestyle businesses. Few firms grow to any significant size. What is more, employment in small firms varies widely from sector to sector. Over 70 per cent of employment in both construction and agriculture is in SMEs. At the other extreme, less than 10 per cent of employment in financial intermediaries and mining is in SMEs. Small firms are not a homogeneous group.

In fact, small firms are increasing in number in most advanced countries, as is their share of employment. In 2005, 99.8 per cent of enterprises in the EU were SMEs which generated 67.1 per cent of employment and 57.6 per cent of value added (Eurostat, op. cit.). They employed on average 4.3 people, varying between 12 people in Slovakia and upwards of 7 in Estonia, Ireland Latvia and Germany, to less than 3 in the Czech Republic and Greece. SMEs are a vital part of all EU economies. They dominate many service sectors, particularly hotels, catering, retailing and wholesaling, and are important in construction. What is more, SMEs in the EU display many of the same characteristics as those in the UK. Most display modest growth rates and only about 50 per cent survive beyond their fifth year.

	Number (%)	Employment (%)	Turnover (%)
Micro	95.7	33.2	22.8
Small	3.6	14.3	14.6
Medium	0.6	11.7	14.1
Large	0.1	40.8	48.5

T1.2 Comparison of UK enterprises by size, 2007

An EU report (European Commission, 2008) comparing EU to US SMEs found that US SMEs were on average larger than EU firms with proportionately fewer micro firms generating less employment. It observed that entry, exit and survival rates were roughly comparable and that the main differences were:

▷ in the US new firms expand more rapidly than in the EU;
▷ in the US new firms display a higher dispersion of productivity;
▷ in the US the more productive firms have a stronger tendency to increase their market shares than in the EU.

The report concluded that the US market was probably therefore more competitive than the EU and had fewer barriers to growth.

The issue about encouraging survival and growth for SMEs pervades much of government policy. Some academics, like Storey and Greene (2010), remain unconvinced by the arguments for government intervention, except in cases of 'market failure'. For them governments cannot justify policy interventions related to provision of finance, advice and assistance for particular groups and the general creation of an 'enterprise culture'. They only remain convinced of intervention in support of technology business in terms of R&D support and the case for a publicly-funded loan guarantee scheme. Others support the view that there is little evidence of success in government interventions in supporting SMEs (Bill et al., 2009; Bridge et al., 2009; Davidsson, 2008). Not withstanding these reservations. Hölzl et al. (2006) provided a stylised typology for looking at the issue of government intervention, reproduced as Figure 1.2. The horizontal axis depicts the degree of successful exploitation of opportunities in terms of survival and growth, and the vertical axis represents the smoothed frequency distribution of firms. The strongly skewed shape of the curve reflects the large number of start-ups that may be thought about (latent or nascent entrepreneurship), with decreasing numbers of businesses that are actually set up only to fail, those that survive and those that go on to grow. Policy might simply encourage more start-ups, but this is likely to lead to more start-ups failing early. On the other hand, a policy of encouraging surviving firms to grow – even if it does not involve 'picking winners', which most policy advisors would be sceptic of the ability of government to do – may result in fewer start-ups because of reduced opportunities.

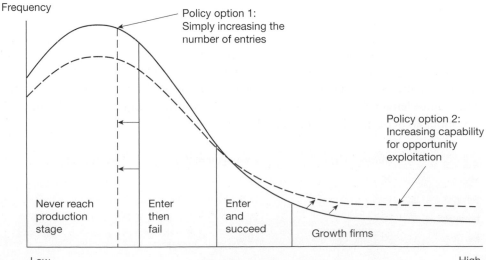

F1.2 Policy options for encouraging survival and growth

Source: Hölzl et al. (2006), quoted in European Commission (2008)

As with so many things, there is a balance to be achieved – that is of course, if you believe in government intervention at all. But whilst many academics feel these micro-economic policies might be ineffectual, even Storey and Greene (op. cit.) would agree that the broader macro-economic policies of taxation, regulation, competition and even immigration can have a powerful effect on SMEs, simply because they affect the economic environment in which they operate.

In the UK, there are also a range of VAT statistics that inform us about SMEs. These are available free from the Office of National Statistics in a series called 'Business Demography' (www.statistics.gov.uk). Information about VAT registrations and de-registrations is widely used as the best guide to patterns of change in the small-firm sector – levels of entrepreneurship and the health of the business population. They are also used in regional and local economic planning. The net change in business stocks is a particularly important figure that is often reported in national newspapers. The net change in stock tends to be highly related to the state of the economy. Small firms are particularly vulnerable to economic changes because of their frequently precarious financing situation. In times when the economy is in recession there tends to be a net decrease in the stock of businesses and vice versa. So, the 1980s saw a large increase in the stock of registered companies, whereas the stock decreased between 1991 and 1994. From 1995 net stocks have increased. 2008 saw a net increase of 2 per cent or 51 000 firms (270 000 registrations less 219 000 deregistrations) – down from 57 900 in 2007. These statistics are also broken down by sector and region. The highest

📖 Case insight Joseph Bamford and JCB

Stories of successful entrepreneurs always make good reading. And successful entrepreneurs have been with us for many, many years in Britain. Joseph Cyril Bamford gave his initials to the ubiquitous yellow hydraulic excavator and digger seen on just about every building site or road works – the JCB. In fact JCB became one of the few post-war British industrial success stories. By the time of Joseph Bamford's death in 2001 the company employed over 4500 people across three continents and had a turnover of £833 million. Over 70 per cent of JCB production is for overseas markets.

Joseph Bamford came from a prosperous Staffordshire engineering family which had been making agricultural equipment since mid-Victorian times. When he returned to civilian life after the Second World War he decided to start up on his own doing what he knew best. Starting his business with only an electric welder he bought for £2.50, he started producing tipping farm trailers from a garage in Uttoxeter, using materials from old air-raid shelters. These sold well, but in 1948 he decided to branch out into hydraulic equipment and, in 1953, went into partnership to produce a range of earth-moving machines before eventually coming up with the famous backhoe loader that combined the two functions of excavator

and shovel and became the visual embodiment of the initials JCB.

Joseph Bamford was a paternalistic employer, who provided a social club and a fishing lake next to his factory in Rochester. He ran a tight ship but rewarded effort. He also knew how to get PR. In 1964, when he famously paid his workers £250 000 in bonuses because the company's turnover had topped £8 million, he personally handed out the bonus to each employee, standing on the first farm tractor he had designed in 1947.

Joseph Bamford made JCB into one of the most successful privately owned companies in Britain. Eventually the company diversified from his central control into a group of several operating companies. He gave up his chairmanship of the group in 1975, handing it over to his eldest son, now Sir Anthony Bamford, and retired to Montreux, Switzerland where he enjoyed yacht designing and landscape gardening. Today the company is the third-biggest maker of construction equipment in the world, with about 12 per cent of the global market. It employs around 7000 people on 4 continents and sells its products in 150 countries through 1500 dealer depot locations. It remains a family business.

☐ Up-to-date information on JCB can be found on their website: www.jcb.com

birth rate in 2008 was in business administration and support services (16.2 per cent), followed by professional, scientific and technical (14.6 per cent). London had both the highest birth and death rates at 15.0 and 10.3 per cent, respectively. Northern Ireland had the lowest birth and death rates at 9.5 and 7.3 per cent, respectively. One interesting point is that areas with high registrations, like London, also tend to have high deregistrations – an effect called 'churning' – indicating that high economic growth may cause or be caused by more firms coming into existence (registering) but the increased competition means that more will cease (deregister).

These VAT statistics have also been used to show that the most dangerous time for a new business is its first three years of existence. Almost 50 per cent of businesses will cease trading within that period. This does not, of course, mean that the closures represent failure in terms of leaving creditors and unpaid debts. Most are simply wound down. Businesses that cease trading do so for a number of reasons. Some will close because the business ceases to be lucrative. Others because of the death or retirement of the proprietor, or changes in their personal motivations and aspirations. Some will simply close to move on to other, more lucrative opportunities. This 'churning effect' of small firms closing and opening is part of the dynamism of the sector as they respond to changing opportunities in the market place and is why the net change in the stock of businesses is more important than the individual number of failures.

Other studies have given an insight into the UK small firms sector. Small firms tend to have lower productivity than large firms, even in the same industry – a conclusion supported across Europe (Eurostat, 2009). Firms with fewer than 200 employees had 55 per cent of the productivity (measured in value added per employee) of firms with 1000 or more employees. In the computer and office machinery sectors SME productivity is only one-third that of larger firms'. These differences are largely because of lower capital backing. Research also indicates that SMEs have a disproportionately high number of 'bad jobs' (McGovern et al., 2004) and higher accident rates (Walters, 2001). The availability of flexible working practices to encourage family-friendly working appears arbitrary in SMEs (Dex and Smith, 2002) and there is low take-up of training initiatives such as NVQs (national vocational qualifications) and IIP (Investors in People) (Matlay, 2002). However it would be wrong to characterise SMEs as poor employers as there is enormous diversity of practice (Barrett and Rainnie, 2002; Ram and Edwards, 2003).

♀ Global Entrepreneurship Monitor (GEM)

GEM is a research programme which was started in 1999 in 10 countries. By 2008 it had been extended to 43 countries. It is a harmonised assessment of the level of national entrepreneurial activity in each of the countries. In the UK it is based upon an annual survey of 32 000 adults of working age. It asks a number of questions but a central one is whether or not they are starting up a business (nascent entrepreneurs – the stage at which individuals begin to commit resources, such as time or money, to starting a business), or already own or manage a business (new business owner-managers – those whose business are paying income, such as salaries or drawings). From this information a figure for total entrepreneurial activity (TEA) is calculated for each country as the proportion of nascent entrepreneurs and new business owner-managers. In 2008 the TEA index for the UK was 5.5 per cent, the

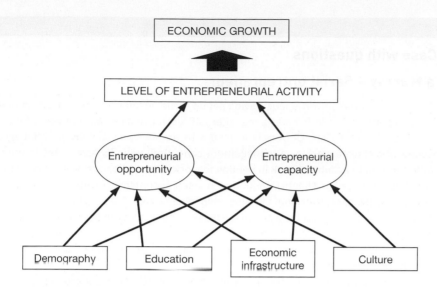

ECONOMIC GROWTH

LEVEL OF ENTREPRENEURIAL ACTIVITY

Entrepreneurial opportunity

Entrepreneurial capacity

Demography
Education
Economic infrastructure
Culture

F1.3 The GEM approach to measuring entrepreneurial activity

Source: Adapted from GEM (2001) Executive Report

same as in 2007' – in other words 5.5 per cent of the UK population were engaged in some form of entrepreneurial activity (GEM, 2009). As you might expect, the USA with a score of 10.8 per cent ranked higher. This continued a long-term pattern in the UK of lower TEA rates than the USA, Canada, Brazil, India and China, and higher TEA rates than other G7 nations and Russia. The UK TEA rate has closely tracked the G7 average since 2002. The report also showed that the UK had intermediate rates of established business ownership and business 'churn' in comparison to other G7 nations. The proportion of entrepreneurs reporting high growth expectations, new product/market combinations, and new technology applications was also intermediate. 'Necessity-driven' entrepreneurship in the UK was relatively low.

GEM 2008 came up with some interesting conclusions about gender and race to which we shall return in Chapter 2. It found that in most high-income countries, men are around twice as likely to be entrepreneurially active as women. The UK rate of TEA in males was 7.4 per cent compared to 3.6 per cent for women. It found that immigrants who identify with the white British ethnic group have higher rates of TEA than UK-born white British. UK-born and immigrant mixed ethnic individuals have similar TEA rates. Black and Asian immigrants have lower TEA rates than their UK-born peers.

Central to the GEM approach is the hypothesis of a causal relationship between entrepreneurial activity in the economy and the level of economic growth. The GEM model is shown in Figure 1.3. The demand side is represented by entrepreneurial opportunity and the supply side by entrepreneurial capacity. These are affected in different ways by demography, education, economic infrastructure and culture.

GEM is an enormous research endeavour generating quantitative data that can be used for both cross-sectional analysis and, probably most importantly, longitudinal analysis, allowing us to track individuals from entrepreneurial aspiration ('nascent entrepreneurship') to action. Obvious methodological problems exist. For example, GEM does not attempt to measure differences in culture. Also the use of a single questionnaire across all the countries is clearly problematic. Nevertheless data from GEM is increasingly being pored over by econometricians eager to find statistical relationships of any kind, no matter how unsupported by theory or other research. GEM reports can be downloaded free of charge from www.gemconsortium.org.

📖 Case with questions

Sara Murray – Serial entrepreneur

Sara Murray is a serial entrepreneur, having set up three businesses so far. Born in 1968 to professional parents (her father was a manager at Chloride and her mother was a teacher), Sara graduated from Oxford University in 1990 with an MA in physiology, psychology and philosophy. She started work as a management consultant with ZS Associates in the USA and in 1991 moved to Hambros Bank in London to work in asset finance. In 1993 she started her first business, called Ninah Consulting. It used technology to improve companies' marketing effectiveness, working for blue-chip clients like Coca-Cola and SmithKline Beecham. In 1999 she started her second business, inspop.com, an insurance comparison website. She expanded the site to more than 250 000 customers within 18 months and then sold it to Admiral Group who renamed it 'Confused.com'. In 2002 Sara sold Ninah to Publicis, the French media group.

Sara is married with one daughter and three step-children. She is a keen sportswoman – a runner, skier and yachtswoman who helmed an America's Cup boat across the Atlantic. She claims that her mother encouraged her to set up her own business, telling her she would be in 'control' and that it was 'better for having a family'.

The idea for Sara's latest business came when her daughter disappeared in a supermarket and she wondered whether there was a technological solution to this problem. She decided to find a satellite navigation tracking device that could be used in such situations and eventually found a company in California that had already spent $180 million on developing one. However it was not yet on sale and, anyway, would only work in US metropolitan areas. Having set up businesses before and with a range of contacts in finance through her brief City career, Sara decided to investigate the opportunity herself. A friend introduced her to two engineers.

> 'I decided to make one myself ... I knew the difficult thing would be building the hardware, because I had never done it before ... I was completely consumer-orientated. I said – this is what I would like it to do for my child. They were completely technology-orientated. There was a gap ... Most technology companies build technology and look at where they can sell it.'

The Times, 3 January 2009

Sara spent £200 000 of her own money on building a working prototype. Relying heavily on her network of finance contacts she then went on to obtain the first round of funding from business angels in 2005. The first Buddi device went on sale in 2007.

A Buddi is about the size of a wrist watch and is hung around the neck. It sells for a small fixed amount above the cost of manufacture plus a monthly charge for unlimited use. By logging on to the Buddi website it is possible to find someone's whereabouts on the relevant page of Google Maps. Their movements can even be tracked in real time. The device also contains a panic button, which alerts one of two constantly monitored call centres and has an audio feed to assess whether there is a real emergency. If there is an emergency, the centres contact a nominated guardian. It can be used for any vulnerable people, not just children, and operates anywhere in the world.

So far the venture has cost just over £1.3 million, funded by two rounds of calls on business angels and further injections of cash will be necessary. Turnover in 2008 was £3 million

☐   Up-to-date information on Buddi can be found on their website: www.buddi.co.uk

QUESTIONS

1   In what ways is Sara different from most women? How might these characteristics contribute to her drive and determination in setting up her own firms?

2   What challenges has Sara faced in setting up her businesses? How has she overcome them?

3   How much of what she has achieved has been down to luck?

▷ Summary

▷ In the late twentieth century the focus of business interest shifted from large to small firms. Their contribution to the economy became recognised, as did the shortcomings of large companies. Start-up entrepreneurs like **Bill Gates**, founder of **Microsoft**, **Michael Dell**, founder of **Dell Computer Corporation**, **Richard Branson,** founder of **Virgin** and **Joseph Bamford**, founder of **JCB**, demonstrated they could become world-class, outstanding successes very quickly, and at the same time they became 'the stuff of dreams' – at least in the financial press. Some entrepreneurs, like **Shaa Wasmund** and **Sara Murray**, become 'serial entrepreneurs, starting up and selling multiple businesses.

▷ Many politicians would claim that the growth of small firms is a manifestation of the success of free-market capitalism, although Marxist theory does seem to be able to accommodate it. But whilst industrial economists would have little to say to explain the phenomenon, labour economists and psychologists have been more successful. It was Schumpeter who first linked entrepreneurs with economic growth through innovation and 'creative destruction'. Theories of 'industrial evolution' link entrepreneurship and economic growth through the tendency of entrepreneurial companies to increase competition, make the most of knowledge spillovers and create increased diversity.

▷ Entrepreneurs use innovation to exploit or create change and opportunity for the purpose of making profit. They do this by shifting economic resources from an area of lower productivity into an area of higher productivity and greater yield, accepting a high degree of risk and uncertainty in doing so.

▷ Owner-managers own the business they manage. Sole traders are owner-managers. Managers of companies owning over 50 per cent of the share capital, and thereby controlling the business, are owner-managers. However, the term is also used loosely when a small group of managers own and control the business. Not all owner-managers are entrepreneurs.

▷ Small firms and entrepreneurship are broadly overlapping sets. However, the two concepts are not necessarily synonymous. We broadly characterise small firms as either lifestyle – set up to allow the owner-manager to pursue an activity they enjoy – or growth – set up to make money and grow. Some owners, like **Julie Spurgeon**, have lifestyle businesses by choice. Others, like **Marc Demarquette**, have businesses that might grow if opportunities present themselves.

▷ Entrepreneurs are defined primarily by their actions although, as we shall see in the next chapter, they can have certain identifiable personal characteristics. They are the particular type of owner-manager that the financial press love so much. They make 'the stuff of dreams' come true.

▷ A small or medium-sized enterprise (SME) is one with fewer than 250 employees. A micro business has up to 9 employees, a small business up to 49 employees and a medium-sized business up to 249 employees. A defining characteristic of the small firm is the influence of the owner-manager. It is managed in an informal, personalised way and the character and preoccupations of the manager are significant influences on decision-making.

▷ SMEs have a number of other significant characteristics, which include shortage of cash and difficulty in raising finance, limitations in product or service range and the markets they operate in, reliance on a small number of customers and the effects of their small scale on financial evaluation and decision-making. But the other defining characteristics of entrepreneurial SMEs are uncertainty, innovation and firm evolution.

▷ Until the 1960s the UK saw a decrease in the importance of small firms. Since the 1970s this has been reversed and SMEs are now an important part of the UK and EU economies, generating significant employment and wealth. However, most small firms in the UK do not grow to any size. The increasing number of small firms is a result of many trends – the move from manufacturing to the service sectors, the 'deconstruction' of many large firms and the trend towards sub-contracting, the influence of new technologies, and social and market changes.

⏻ **Further resources are available at www.palgrave.com/business/burns**

📄 Essays and discussion topics

1 Are small firms worthy of special treatment? If so, by whom and what form should it take?
2 List the pros and cons of running your own business.
3 Do you think you might have what it takes to be an entrepreneur? Return to this question after you have read the next chapter.
4 Do you dream of starting your own business? If so, why? If not, why not? What do you think will be the main challenges you would face?
5 Do you think the definition of an entrepreneur is adequate?
6 How does the management of a small firm differ from the management of a large one?
7 What are the characteristics of small firms that distinguish them from large firms and what are their implications? Do these mean that small firms really are sufficiently different to warrant special study?
8 Are small firms sufficiently homogeneous to justify special study? What further segmentation might you suggest and what are the special and different characteristics of these segments?
9 Is it good that so many businesses close in their first three years?
10 Why has the number of small firms been increasing in the UK since the late 1960s?
11 Does Marxism say anything to explain the increasing number of small firms?
12 How does entrepreneurship encourage economic growth?
13 How might entrepreneurship be encouraged?
14 Should governments encourage an increase in the number of start-ups or encourage opportunity exploitation? Are the two mutually exclusive?
15 How can you encourage opportunity exploitation?
16 Are lifestyle firms worth encouraging?
17 Should art students who want to be self-employed be taught entrepreneurship?
18 Should all students at university be taught entrepreneurship?
19 Is small really beautiful?
20 What are the real defining characteristics of a small firm?
21 What are nascent entrepreneurs? What does their number tell us that start-up statistics do not?
22 Do you see any similarities between the entrepreneurs profiled in this chapter?

↻ Exercises and assignments

1 Research the history and profile of an entrepreneur who set up their own business and grew it successfully.
2 Update the statistics on small firms in Britain and in the EU. Alternatively, obtain similar statistics on the performance of small firms in your country. What does this tell you about recent developments? Summarise your findings in a report.
3 Access the latest GEM report for your country and summarise its findings in a report.

📖 References

Acs, Z.J. and Audretsch, D.B. (1989) 'Births and Firm Size', *Southern Economic Journal*, 55.

Aghion, P. and Howitt, P. (1992) 'A Model for Growth through Creative Destruction', *Econometrica*, 60.

Anderson, J. (1995) *Local Heroes*, Glasgow: Scottish Enterprise.

Atkinson, J. and Meager, N. (1994) 'Running to Stand Still: The Small Business in the Labour Market', in J. Atkinson and D.J. Storey (eds), *Employment, The Small Firm and the Labour Market*, London: Routledge.

Audretsch, D.B. (1995) *Innovation and Industry Evolution*, Cambridge: MIT Press.

Barrett, R. and Rainnie, A. (2002) 'What's So Special About Small Firms? Developing an Integrated Approach to Analysing Small Firm Industrial Relations', *Work, Employment and Society*, 16(3).

Bill, F., Johannisson, B. and Olaison, L. (2009) 'The Incubus Paradox: Attempts at Foundational Rethinking of the "SME Support Genre"', *European Planning Studies*, 17(8).

Birch, D.L. (1979) 'The Job Creation Process', unpublished report, MIT Program on Neighbourhood and Regional Change, prepared for the Economic Development Administration, US Department of Commerce, Washington, DC.

Bolton, J.E. (1971) *Report of the Committee of Inquiry on Small Firms*, Cmnd. 4811, London: HMSO.

Branson, R. (1998) *Losing my Virginity*, London: Virgin.

Bridge, S., O'Neill, K. and Martin, F. (2009) *Understanding Enterprise, Entrepreneurship and Small Business*, Basingstoke: Palgrave Macmillan.

Cannon, T. (1991) *Enterprise: Creation, Development and Growth*, Oxford: Butterworth-Heinemann.

Cantillon, R. (1755) *Essai sur la Nature du Commerce en General*, London and Paris: R. Gyles (trans. H. Higgs (1931), London: Macmillan). See also www.newschool.edu/nssr/het/profiles/cantillon.htm.

Carr, P. and Beaver, G. (2002) 'The Enterprise Vulture: Understanding a Misunderstood Concept', *Strategic Change*, 11.

Casson, M. (1982) *The Entrepreneur: An Economic Theory*, Oxford: Martin Robertson.

Crainer, S. and Dearlove, D. (1998) *Gravy Training: Inside the Shadowy World of Business Schools*, Oxford: Capstone.

Davidsson, P. (2008), 'Some Conclusions about Entrepreneurship and its Support', Paper presented at the World Entrepreneurship forum, November, Evian, France.

de Geus, A. (1997) *The Living Company*, Boston, MA: Harvard Business Press.

Dell, M. (1999) *Direct from Dell: Strategies that Revolutionised an Industry*, New York: Harper Business.

Dewhurst, J. and Burns, P. (1983) *Small Business Finance and Control*, London: Macmillan – now Basingstoke: Palgrave Macmillan.

Dex, S. and Smith, C. (2002) *The Nature and Pattern of Family-Friendly Employment Policies in the UK*, Abingdon: Policy Press.

Drucker, P.F. (1974) *Management Tasks, Responsibilities, Practices*, New York: Harper & Row.

Economic News (1997) 'The Small Business Advocate', February 1997, Washington, DC, Office of Advocacy, SEA.

Ely, R.T. and Hess, R.H. (1893) *Outline of Economics*, New York: Macmillan.

Ericson, R. and Pakes, A. (1995) 'Markov-Perfect Industry Dynamics: A Framework for Empirical Work', *Review of Economic Studies*, 62.

Etemad, H. (2004) 'International Entrepreneurship as a Dynamic Adaptive System: Towards a Grounded Theory', *Journal of International Entrepreneurship*, 2.

European Commission (2008) *European Competitiveness Report 2008*, available free online at www.ec.europa.eu/enterprise.

Eurostat (2008) *Enterprises by Size Class – Overview of SMEs in the EU, Statistics in Focus, 31/2008*. Available on epp.eurostat.ec.europa.eu.

Eurostat (2009) *European Business Facts and Figures, 2009 Edition*, Luxembourg: Eurostat. Available on epp.eurostat.ec.europa.eu.

GEM (2001) *Executive Report*, Babson College, Boston, USA/London Business School.

GEM (2009) *Global Entrepreneurship Monitor 2008*, reports by individual GEM national teams available free online at www.gemconsortium.org.

Harrison, J. and Taylor, B. (1996) *Supergrowth Companies: Entrepreneurs in Action*, Oxford: Butterworth-Heinemann.

Hayek, F.A. (1948) 'The Use of Knowledge in Society', in *Studies in Philosophy, Politics and Economics*, Chicago: University of Chicago Press.

Hayek, F.A. (1952) *The Sensory Order*, Chicago: University of Chicago Press.

Hayek, F.A. (1967a) 'Competition as a Discovery Procedure', in Hayek, *New Studies in Philosophy, Politics, Economics and History of Ideas*, Chicago: Chicago University Press.

Hayek, F.A. (1967b) 'The Results of Human Action, but not Human Design', in Hayek, *New Studies in Philosophy, Politics, Economics and History of Ideas*, Chicago: Chicago University Press.

Hölzl, W., Huber, P., Kaniovski, S. and Peneder, M. (2006) 'Neugründung und Entwicklung von Unternehmen, Teilstudie 20', in K. Aiginger, G. Tichy and E. Walterskirchen (eds), *WIFO-Weißbuch: Mehr Beschäftigung durch Wachstum auf Basis von Innovation und Qualifikation*, Vienna: WIFO.

Hopenhayn, H.A. (1992) 'Entry, Exit and Firm Dynamics in Long Run Equilibrium', *Econometrica*, 60.

Jovanovic, B. (1982) 'Favorable Selection with Asymmetrical Information', *Quarterly Journal of Economics*, 97(3).

Kirzner, I.M. (1973) *Competition and Entrepreneurship*, Chicago: University of Chicago Press.

Kirzner, I.M. (1979) *Perception, Opportunity and Profit: Studies in the Theory of Entrepreneurship*, Chicago: University of Chicago Press.

Kirzner, I.M. (1997) 'Entrepreneurial Discovery and Competitive Market Processes: An Austrian Approach', *Journal of Economic Literature*, 35.

Kirzner, I.M. (1999) 'Creativity and/or Alertness: A Reconsideration of the Schumpeterian Entrepreneur', *Review of Austrian Economics*, 11.

Klepper, S. (1996) 'Entry, Exit, Growth and Innovation over the Product Life Cycle', *American Economic Review*, 86(3).

Knight, F. (1921) *Risk, Uncertainty and Profit*, Chicago: University of Chicago Press.

Lambson, V.E. (1991) 'Industry Evolution with Sunk Costs and Uncertain Market Conditions', *International Journal of Industrial Organisations*, 9.

Matlay, H. (2002) 'Training and HRD Strategies in Family and Non-Family Owned Small Business: A Comparative Approach', *Education and Training*, 44.

McGovern, P., Smeaton, D. and Hill, S. (2004), 'Bad Jobs in Britain: Non-standard Employment and Job Quality', *Work and Occupations*, 31.

Menger, C. (1871/1981) *Principles of Economics*, New York: New York University Press.

OECD (2008) *Measuring Entrepreneurship: A Digest of Indicators*, Paris: OECD. Available on www.oecd.org.

Penrose, E.T. (1959) *The Theory of the Growth of Firms*, Oxford: Basil Blackwell.

Ram, M. and Edwards, P. (2003) 'Praising Caesar Not Burying Him – What We Know About Employment in Small Firms', *Work, Employment and Society*, 17(4).

Say, J.B. (1803) *Trait d'Economie Politique ou Simple Exposition de la Manière dont se Forment, se Distribuent, et se Consomment les Riches*; revised (1819); translated (1830) by R. Prinsep, *A Treatise on Political Economy: On Familiar Conversations on the Manner in Which Wealth is Produced, Distributed and Consumed by Society*, Philadelphia: John Grigg and Elliot. See also Resources for Say at cepa.newschool.edu/het/profiles/say.htm.

Say, J.B. (1817) *Catechisme d'Economie Politique*, translated (1821) by John Richter, *Catechism of Political Economy*, London: Sherwood, Neely & Jones.

Schumacher, E.F. (1974) *Small is Beautiful*, London: Abacus.

Schumpeter J.A. (1928) 'The Instability of Capitalism', *Economic Journal*, 38.

Schumpeter J.A. (1934) *The Theory of Economic Development: An Inquiry into Profits, Capital, Credit and Interest and the Business Cycle* (trans. R. Opie), Cambridge, MA: Harvard University Press. (First published in 1911 as *Theorie der Wirtschaftlichen Entwicklung*, Munich and Leipzig: Dunker und Humblat).

Shapero, A. (1975) 'The Displaced, Uncomfortable Entrepreneur', *Psychology Today*, 8.

Shapero, A. (1984) 'The Entrepreneurial Event', in C. Kent (ed.) *Environment for Entrepreneurship*, Lexington, MA: DC Heath.

Shapero, A. (1985) 'Why Entrepreneurship?', *Journal of Small Business Management*, 23(4).

Storey, D. and Greene, F.J. (2010) *Small Business and Entrepreneurship*, Harlow: Pearson Education.

Storey, D. and Sykes, N. (1996) 'Uncertainty, Innovation and Management', in P. Burns and J. Dewhurst (eds), *Small Business and Entrepreneurship*, London: Macmillan – now Basingstoke: Palgrave Macmillan.

Storey, D., Keasey, K., Watson, R. and Wynarczyk, P. (1987) *The Performance of Small Firms, Profits, Jobs and Failure*, London: BCA.

Timmons, J.A. (1999) *New Venture Creation: Entrepreneurship for the 21st Century*, Boston: Irwin/McGraw-Hill.

Walters, D. (2001) *Health and Safety in Small Enterprise*, Oxford: PIE Peter Lang.

Wynarczyk, P., Watson, R., Storey, D.J., Short, H. and Keasey, K. (1993) *The Managerial Labour Market in Small and Medium Sized Enterprises*, London: Routledge.

2   Entrepreneurs and owner-managers

▷ **Start-up influences**
▷ **Personal character traits**
▷ **Character traits of owner-managers**
▷ **Character traits of entrepreneurs**
▷ **Antecedent influences**
▷ **Ethnicity and immigration**
▷ **Gender**
▷ **Growth businesses**
▷ **National culture**
▷ **Situational factors**
▷ **Summary**

Case insights
▷ Steve Hulme
▷ Simon Woodroffe and YO! Sushi
▷ Market traders
▷ Kenyan Asians
▷ Elizabeth Gooch and EG Solutions
▷ Will King and King of Shaves

Cases with questions
▷ Duncan Bannatyne, Dragon
▷ Hilary Andrews and Mankind

Learning outcomes

By the end of this chapter you should be able to:

▷ Explain the factors that influence the start-up decision;

▷ Describe the character traits of owner-managers;

▷ Describe the character traits of entrepreneurs;

▷ Explain the methodological problems associated with trying to measure character traits and the linkages with growth businesses;

▷ Describe the antecedent influences that are likely to influence owner-managers and entrepreneurs;

▷ Recognise the importance of national culture in influencing entrepreneurship;

▷ Explain what constitutes an entrepreneurial culture and how it might be measured;

▷ Recognise the importance of female and ethnic minority entrepreneurs;

▷ Explain the situational factors influencing start-ups and how blocks to start-up might be overcome.

💡 Start-up influences

Why does anybody want to take the risk of starting up their own business? It is hard work without guaranteed results. But millions do so every year around the world. The start-up is the bedrock of modern-day commercial wealth, the foundation of free-market economics upon which competition is based. So can economists shed light on the process?

Economists would tell us that new entrants into an industry can be expected when there is a rise in expected post-entry profitability for them. In other words, new entrants expect to make extra profits. Economists tell us that the rate of entry is related to the growth of that industry. They also tell us that entry is deterred by barriers such as high capital requirements, the existence of economies of scale, product differentiation, restricted access to necessary inputs and so on. What is more, the rate of entry is lower in industries with high degrees of concentration where it may be assumed that firms combine to deter entry. However, research also tells us that, whereas the rate of small firm start-up in these concentrated industries is lower, the rate of start-up for large firms is higher (Acs and Audretsch, 1989).

These seem useful, but perhaps obvious, statements about start-ups. But do they really explain what happens and why? Somehow economists fail to explain convincingly the rationale for, and the process of, start-up. They seem to assume that there is a continuous flow of entrants into an industry just waiting for the possibility of extra profits. But people are not like that. They need to earn money to live; they have families who depend on them. Leaving a secure job to start up a business, for example, needs more of a rationale than just 'extra profits'. Certainly the personal characteristics of owner-managers and entrepreneurs and their antecedents — their history and the environment they grow up in — are factors that economists are both unfamiliar and uncomfortable with. Economists are not really interested in individuals who are likely to set up their own firms, or their personal motivations for doing so. Economists are just interested in explaining how many might consider doing so and into which sectors they might be expected to go. What is more, economists are generally not altogether happy with the idea that the number of start-ups can be influenced by non-economic factors like personal situation, character traits and the antecedent influences on it like family and national culture; but most people believe they are.

Figure 2.1 shows all these start-up influences. The model proposes that owner-managers and entrepreneurs are in fact both born and made. We are all born with certain personal character traits. Research indicates that owner-managers have a certain identifiable set and entrepreneurs — who want to set up growth firms — have a somewhat different set. Entrepreneurs share the character traits of owner-managers but they have certain additional, almost magical, qualities that the average owner-manager does not possess. However, these character traits are also shaped by antecedent influences — your history and experience

> *Many people talk about business ideas but don't get on and do them. Starting up a business is like taking part in an amateur boxing match. You don't know how good either guy is – but unless you get in there and have a go, you never will.*
>
> ☐ Gary Redman, founder of Now Recruitment
> *Sunday Times* 8 August 2004

📂 Case insight Steve Hulme

Steve Hulme retired from teaching on health grounds in 1997. For two-and-a-half years he and his wife got by on his pension and her salary. However, he became restless and decided to become self-employed. He had previously written a textbook for teenagers about problem-solving and lateral thinking, and based on this experience, he wanted to run courses for the young unemployed to introduce them to the kind of 'joined up' thinking skills he believed industry wanted. Aged 52, he set up his training business with the help of the Prince's Initiative for Mature Enterprise (Prime). Prime was set up in 1999 to provide advice, support and loans for over-45s who are jobless.

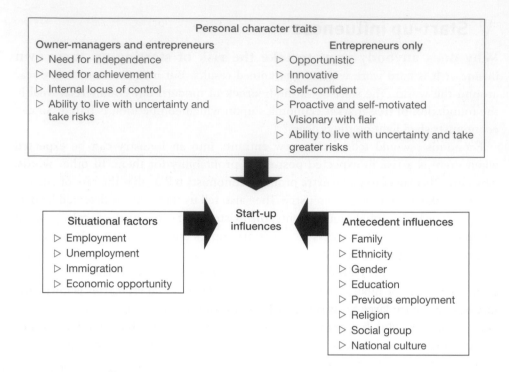

F2.1 Start-up influences

of life and the environment they grow up in. This includes their family, ethnic origins, gender, education, previous employment, religion and social group. The national culture of the country that they grow up in also seems to be an important influence. As we saw in Chapter 1, the GEM studies show that entrepreneurial activity varies significantly from country to country. Finally there are situational factors that influence the decision to start up your own business. As well as the positive economic influences – the opportunities that may attract, or 'pull', people into self-employment – there may also be the negative ones such as unemployment or immigration that 'push' them into it.

All these factors influence the decisions on whether to start up a business and whether to grow it. If all the factors are favourable the volume of start-ups should increase, as should the number of businesses that grow. Indeed, both antecedent influences and the dominant culture of the society will almost certainly influence the personal character traits of individuals as they develop over time and vice versa – over time entrepreneurial characters will start to shape society and influence those they come in contact with. These three factors are inter-related.

Therefore, if owner-managers are the heroes of this book, then entrepreneurs must be the super-heroes. Were it not for those who have a vested interest in identifying our super-heroes at an early stage in their business development, it is unlikely that economists, sociologists and psychologists would have paid this area so much attention. Because of this it remains an area of heated academic debate and constant development, not least over the question as to whether entrepreneurs are born rather than made.

💡 Personal character traits

The issue of linking the character traits of an individual to the success of a business – picking winners – needs to be approached with caution. Even if it is possible to identify the personal characteristics of owner-managers and entrepreneurs, it is not always possible to link them directly with a particular sort of business. So far we have considered three types of managers and implicitly linked them to three types of small firm:

Type of manager	Type of business
1 Owner-manager	Lifestyle firm.
	Often trade- or craft-based. Will not grow to any size.
2 Entrepreneur	Growth firm.
	Pursuit of growth and personal wealth important.
3 Manager	Manages a business belonging to someone else.
	Will build an organisation by putting in appropriate controls, similar to a large firm.
	May be entrepreneurial.

These were broad generalisations. The linkages are not that simple or direct all of the time. For example, an entrepreneur might manage a business belonging to someone else, at least for a time. Similarly, an owner-manager may find himself with a growth business, either by accident or design. Success or failure in business, as we shall see later, comes from a mix of many different things. The character traits of the manager are just one factor in the equation. What is more, it takes time for entrepreneurs to prove that the business they manage is in fact a growth business. So do you measure aspirations or reality?

A further difficulty is that much of the research often fails to distinguish between owner-managers and entrepreneurs, assuming anyone who starts their own business is an entrepreneur. However, research into the character traits of owner-managers of growth businesses, who should mainly be entrepreneurs, does allow us to come to some broad conclusions and to paint a picture of the different characters of owner-managers compared to entrepreneurs.

There are also a number of methodological problems associated with attempting to measure personality characteristics (Deakins, 1996):

▷ They are not stable and change over time.
▷ They require subjective judgements.
▷ Measures tend to ignore cultural and environmental influences.
▷ The role of education, learning, and training is often overlooked.
▷ Issues such as age, sex, race, social class and education can be ignored.

The last three issues we shall address in looking at the antecedent influences on entrepreneurship, but they go to the heart of the question of whether entrepreneurs are born or made. The area, therefore, is an academic minefield. Notwithstanding this, many researchers do believe that, collectively, owner-managers have certain typical character traits, although the mix and emphasis of these characteristics will inevitably be different for each individual. Whether a clearly definable set of entrepreneurial characteristics exists is more controversial. Furthermore, many so-called 'entrepreneurial' character traits are similar to those found in other successful people such as politicians or athletes (Chell et al, 1991). Perhaps, the argument goes, it just happens that the individual has chosen an entrepreneurial activity as a means of self-satisfaction. Certainly, even if you believe the character traits can be identified, they do not explain why the individual chose to apply them in an entrepreneurial context.

Notwithstanding these issues, most researchers believe that, collectively, owner-manager entrepreneurs have certain typical character traits, although, as for

F2.2 Character traits of owner-managers and entrepreneurs

Sources: Aldrich and Martinez, 2003; Andersson et al., 2004; Baty, 1990; Bell et al., 1992; Blanchflower and Meyer, 1991; Brockhaus and Horwitz, 1986; Brush, 1992; Buttner and More, 1997; Caird, 1990; Chell et al., 1991; Cuba et al., 1983; de Bono, 1985; Hirsch and Brush, 1987; Kanter, 1983; Kirzner, 1973, 1979, 1997, 1999; McClelland, 1961; Pinchot, 1985; Rosa et al., 1994; Schein et al., 1996; Schumpeter, 1996; Schwartz, 1997; Shapero, 1985; Shaver and Scott, 1992; Storey and Sykes, 1996.

Owner-managers
Need for independence
Need for achievement
Internal locus of control
Ability to live with uncertainty
and take measured risks

Entrepreneurs
Opportunistic
Innovative
Self-confident
Proactive and self-motivated
Visionary with flair
Willing to take greater risks and live
with even greater uncertainty

non-entrepreneurial owner-managers, the mix and emphasis of these characteristics will differ between individuals. The character traits of the owner-manager might be characterised as an instinct for survival – most owner-managed businesses never grow to any size – and those of the entrepreneur might be characterised as an instinct for growth. Figure 2.2 summarises these character traits, accumulated from numerous research studies. Those associated with owner-managers are also present in entrepreneurs, but those associated with entrepreneurs are not necessarily present in owner-managers – particularly if they run a lifestyle business.

Character traits of owner-managers

Need for independence

Owner-managers have a high need for independence. This is most often seen as 'the need to be your own boss' and is the trait that is most often cited, and supported, by researchers and advisors alike. However, independence means different things to different people, such as controlling your own destiny, doing things differently or being in a situation where you can fulfil your potential. It has often been said that once you have run your own firm you cannot work for anybody else.

Entrepreneurs don't like working for other people ... I was once made redundant by the Manchester Evening News. I had a wife who had given up a promising career for me, and a baby. I stood in Deansgate with £5 in my pocket and I swore I would never work for anyone else again.
□ Eddy Shah, founder of Messenger Group
The Times, 16 March 2002

Need for achievement

Owner-managers typically have a high need for achievement, a driving force that is even stronger for entrepreneurs. Achievement for individual owners means different things depending on what type of person they are; for example, the satisfaction of producing a beautiful work of art, employing their hundredth person, or making the magic one million pounds. Often money is just a badge of achievement to the successful entrepreneur. It is not an end in itself.

You have to enjoy what you do and have a passion for it, otherwise you're bound to fail. But of course the financial rewards are important and apart from anything else reflect how successful your company is.
□ Martyn Dawes, founder of Coffee Nation
Startups: www.startups.co.uk

Money doesn't motivate me. But it's not to say I don't drive a Bentley Continental T2.
□ Stephen Waring, founder of Green Thumb
Sunday Times 2 October 2005

As a child I never felt that I was noticed. I never felt that I achieved anything or that there was any expectation of me achieving anything. So proving myself is something that is important to me and so is establishing respect for what I have achieved.
□ Chey Garland, founder of Garlands Call Centres
Sunday Times 27 June 2004

Public recognition of achievement can be important to some owner-managers and entrepreneurs. And this can lead to certain negative behaviours or unwise decisions. For example, overspending on the trappings of corporate life – the office, the company car and so on (often called the corporate flagpole syndrome) – or the 'big 'project' that is very risky but the entrepreneur 'knows' they can do. These can lead to cash flow problems that put at risk the very existence of the business.

Internal locus of control

If you believe that you can exercise control over your environment and ultimately your destiny, you have an internal locus of control. If, however, you believe in fate, you have an external locus of control and you are less likely to take the risk of start-ing a business. Owner-managers typically have a strong internal locus of control, which is the same for many senior managers in large firms.

In extreme cases this trait can also lead to certain negative behaviours. In particular, it can show itself as a desire to maintain personal control over every aspect of the business. That can lead to a pre-occupation with detail, overwork and stress. It also leads to an inability or unwillingness to delegate as the business grows. Again, in extreme cases it might show itself as a mistrust of subordinates. Kets de Vries (1985) thinks that these behaviours lead to subordinates becoming 'infantilised'. They are expected to behave as incompetent idiots, and that is the way they act. They tend to do very little, make no decisions and circulate very little information. The better ones do not stay long.

Most of the pleasure is not the cash. It is the sense of achievement at having taken something from nothing to where it is now.

☐ Charles Muirhead, founder of Orchestream, acquired by MetaSolv in 2003 for £8 million
Sunday Times 19 September 1999

We don't feel like millionaires at all. Money doesn't come into it. It's not really why you do it, it really isn't.

☐ Brent Hoberman, co-founder of Lastminute.com
Sunday Times 19 September 1999

I want to take control of my life and achieve something.

☐ Jonathan Elvidge, founder of Gadget Shop
Sunday Times 17 March 2002

This need for control also shows itself in the unwillingness of many owner-managers to part with shares in their company. They just do not want to lose control, at any price.

Ability to live with uncertainty and take measured risks

Human beings, typically, do not like uncertainty and one of the biggest uncertainties of all is not having a regular pay cheque coming in. That is not to say owner-managers like it. Uncertainty about income can be a major cause of stress. The possibility of missing out on some piece of business that might affect their income is one reason why they are so loath to take holidays.

There are also other commercial aspects of uncertainty that owner-managers have to cope with. Often they cannot influence many aspects of the market in which they operate, for example, price. They must therefore react to changes in the market that others might bring about. If a local supermarket has a special price promotion on certain goods it may well affect sales of similar goods in a local corner shop. A business with a high level of borrowing must find a way of paying interest charges but has no direct influence over changes in interest rates. Many small firms also have a limited customer or product base and this can bring further uncertainty. If, for whatever reason, one large customer ceases buying it can have an enormous impact on a small firm.

Hand in hand with owner-managers' ability to live with uncertainty is their willingness to take measured risks. Most people are risk averse. They try to avoid risks and insure against them. Setting up your own

Owner managers must be willing to take measured risks

When I was made redundant self-employment was my only option and the work with the Business Link made it possible. The money was good, but I don't like the uncertainty – where the money for next month is coming from. It did not help to have three young boys to support. Eventually I went back into teaching.

☐ Jean Young, self-employed 1998–99

You have to be prepared to lose everything and remember that the biggest risk is not taking any risk at all.

☐ Jonathan Elvidge, founder of Gadget Shop
Sunday Times 17 March 2002

business is risky and owner-managers are willing to take more risks with their own resources than most people. They might also risk their reputation and personal standing if they fail. However, they do not like it and try always to minimise their exposure, hence their preference to risk other peoples' money and borrow, sometimes too heavily, from the bank. Another example of this is the way they often 'compartmentalise' various aspects of their business. For example, an owner-manager might open a second restaurant but set it up as a separate limited company just in case it fails and endangers the other. In this way they sometimes develop a portfolio of individually small businesses and their growth and success is measured not just in the performance of a single one but rather by the growth of the portfolio.

One important characteristic of owner-managers is their approach to dealing with uncertainty and risk is the short-term view they take on all business decisions. It really is a case of not being certain that the business will survive until tomorrow.

Taking a chance, a risk or a gamble is what unites entrepreneurs. Without risk there is no reward. You won't discover America if you never set sail.

☐ Jonathan Elvidge, founder of Gadget Shop
The Times 6 July 2002

Therefore decision-making is short-term and incremental. Strategies often evolve on a step-by-step basis. If one step works then the second is taken. At the same time owner-managers will keep as many options open as possible because they realise the outcome of their actions is very uncertain.

Prudent entrepreneurs also seek to keep their investment and fixed costs as low as possible, trying to minimise the risk they face. We discuss ways to do this later in the book. Owner-managers also see assets as a liability, limiting the flexibility that they need, which is just as well since finding the resources to start a business is usually a problem.

💡 Character traits of entrepreneurs

Entrepreneurs share the characteristics of owner-managers. However, they have certain additional traits. Nevertheless, owner-managers can be entrepreneurial in some of their actions and the boundaries between the two are not always clear. Consequently, many of these traits are present in owner-managers, but to a far lesser extent.

Opportunistic

I have always lived my life by thriving on opportunity and adventure. Some of the best ideas come out of the blue, and you have to keep an open mind to see their virtue.

☐ Richard Branson quoted by Anderson (1995)

By definition, entrepreneurs exploit change for profit. In other words, they seek out opportunities to make money. Often entrepreneurs see opportunities where others see problems. Whereas ordinary mortals dislike the uncertainty brought about by change, entrepreneurs love it because they see opportunity and they do not mind the uncertainty.

With many entrepreneurs the problem is getting them to focus on just one opportunity, or at least one opportunity at a time. They see opportunity everywhere and have problems following through on any one before becoming distracted by another. This is one reason why some entrepreneurs are not able to grow their business beyond a certain size. They get bored by the routines and controls; they see other market opportunities and yearn for the excitement of another start-up. They probably would be well advised to sell up and do just that. However, others recognise this element of their character and become serial entrepreneurs, moving to set up and sell on one business after another. You see this very often in the restaurant business where an entrepreneurial restaurateur launches a new restaurant and makes it successful, then sells it on so as to move onto another new venture. They make money by creating a business with capital value, not necessarily income, for themselves.

📁 Case insight Simon Woodroffe and YO! Sushi

Simon Woodroffe, founder of YO! Sushi, took a while to home in on his final business idea. His first idea was to drive a van on the hippy trail to India, charging passengers to accompany him, but he did not have enough money to buy a van and his father declined to invest. Soon after this he started producing belts. He put together £100, bought an old sewing machine, some buckles and snakeskin trimmings. The belts sold well. Later he intended to make indoor rock climbing popular – another idea he never got round to pursuing. Then a Japanese man over a sushi lunch suggested what he really needed to do was open a conveyor-belt sushi bar with girls dressed in black PVC mini skirts. The idea stuck. Two years later, in 1997, he opened his first YO! Sushi bar in London – but without the girls in mini skirts. Simon sold his majority shareholding to Primary Capital in 2003, who in turn sold it to Quilvest and the company's management team in 2008.

Innovative

The ability to spot opportunities and to innovate are the most important distinguishing features of entrepreneurs. Innovation is the prime tool entrepreneurs use to create or exploit opportunity. These characteristics set entrepreneurs apart from owner-managers. Entrepreneurs link innovation to the market place so as to exploit an opportunity and make their business grow. Although innovation is difficult to define and can take many forms, entrepreneurs are always, in some way, innovative. We shall explore this in more detail in the next chapter.

> *True innovation is rarely about creating something new. It's pretty hard to recreate the wheel or discover gravity; innovation is more often about seeing new opportunities for old designs.*
>
> ☐ Neil Kelly, owner and managing director of PAV
> *Sunday Times* 9 December 2001

Self-confident

Facing uncertainty, you have to be confident in your own judgement and ability to start up your own business. Many start-up training programmes recognise this and try to build confidence by developing a business plan that addresses the issue of future uncertainty. As well as a useful management tool, the plan can become a symbol of certainty for the owner-manager in an otherwise uncertain world and some even keep it with them at all times, using it almost like a bible, to reassure them of what the future will hold when the business is successful.

> *My mother gave me a massive self-belief. I will always try things – there is nothing to lose.*
>
> ☐ Richard Thompson, founder and chairman of EMS, quoted in Steiner (1999)

Entrepreneurs, therefore, need self-confidence aplenty to grow their business given the extreme uncertainty they face. If they do not believe in the future of the business, how can they expect others to do so? However, the self-confidence can be overdone and turn to an exaggerated opinion of their own competence, and even arrogance.

Some researchers believe entrepreneurs are actually 'delusional'. In an interesting piece of research, two American academics tested the decision-making process of 124 entrepreneurs (defined as people who started their own firm) and 95 managers of big companies in two ways (Busenitz and Barney, 1997). Firstly, they asked five factual questions, each of which had two possible answers. They asked respondents to rate their confidence in their answer (50 per cent, a guess; 100 per cent, perfect confidence). Entrepreneurs turned out to be much more confident about their answers than managers, especially those who gave wrong answers. Secondly, they were given a business decision. They were told they must replace a broken foreign-made machine and they had two alternatives. The first was an American-made machine, which a friend had recently bought and had not yet broken down, and the second a foreign-built machine, which was statistically less likely to break down than the other; 50 per cent of the entrepreneurs opted for the American machine but 90 per cent of the managers opted for the foreign one. The researchers concluded that the entrepreneurs were more prone to both delusion and opportunism than normal managers. So the question is raised, is entrepreneurial self-confidence so strong as to make them delusional, blinding them to the reality of a situation?

> *An entrepreneur is unfailingly enthusiastic, never pessimistic, usually brave, and certainly stubborn. Vision and timing are crucial. You have to be something of a workaholic, too. You have to be convinced that what you are doing is right. If not you have to recognise this and be able to change direction swiftly – sometimes leaving your staff breathless – and start off again with equal enthusiasm.*
>
> ☐ Chris Ingram founder of Tempus
> *Sunday Times* 17 March 2002

Proactive and self-motivated

Entrepreneurs tend to be proactive rather than reactive and more decisive than other people. They are proactive in the sense that they seek out opportunities, they do not just rely on luck. They act quickly and decisively to make the most of the opportunity before somebody else does.

Entrepreneurs have drive and determination. They are often seen as restless and easily bored. They can easily be diverted by the most recent market opportunity and often seem to do things at twice the pace of others, unwilling or unable to wait for them to complete tasks. Patience is certainly not a virtue many entrepreneurs possess. They seem to work 24 hours a day and their work becomes their life with little separating the two. It is little wonder that it places family relationships under strain. One important result of this characteristic is that entrepreneurs tend to learn by doing. They act first and then learn from the outcomes of the action. It is part of their incremental approach to decision-making, each small action and its outcomes contribute to the learning process.

> *Neither my grandfather nor my father would be surprised if they could see me now. My success didn't just happen As a young boy, I was always working. My parents and my brothers and sisters all had high energy.*
>
> ☐ Tom Farmer, founder of Kwik-Fit
> *Daily Mail* 11 May 1999

> *Enthusiasm is my strength. And good health, and energy and endeavour. I love what I do. It's just so interesting, it is new every day, exciting every day. I work 364 days a year. The only day I don't work is Christmas Day, because it's my wife's birthday.*
>
> ☐ Bob Worcester, founder of MORI
> *Financial Times* 7 April 2002

> *I have never had anything to do in my life that provides so many challenges – and there are so many things I still want to do.*
>
> ☐ Martha Lane Fox, co-founder of Lastminute.com
> *Sunday Times* 19 September 1999

Entrepreneurs' drive and determination comes from being highly self-motivated, amounting almost to an irresistible urge to succeed in their economic goals. This intrinsic motivation is, in turn, driven by their exceptionally strong inner need for achievement, far stronger than with the average owner-manager. Running your own business is a lonely affair, without anyone to motivate and encourage you. You work long hours, sometimes for little reward. You, therefore, need to be self-motivated, committed and determined to succeed.

I am motivated by my success not money. But success is partly measured by money.

☐ Wing Yip, founder of W. Wing Yip & Brothers
   Sunday Times 2 January 2000

This strong inner drive – what psychologists call type 'A' behaviour – is quite unique and can be seen as almost compulsive behaviour. This is not to say that entrepreneurs are not motivated by other things as well, such as money. But often money is just a badge of their success that allows them to measure their achievement. What drives them is their exceptionally high need to achieve. 'A' types tend to be goal-focused, wanting to get the job done quickly. However, they also tend to be highly reactive, focusing on the future and often not in control of the present.

Be incredibly focused on what you're trying to achieve. You can't do everything well, because you spread your attention, talents and money, thinly, but you can do things you focus on well, if you really focus properly.

☐ Martyn Dawes, founder of Coffee Nation
   Startups: www.startups.co.uk

Fun is at the core of the way I like to do business and has informed everything I've done from the outset. More than any other element, fun is the secret of Virgin's success.

☐ Richard Branson

An important part of this self-motivation comes from enjoyment – enjoyment in the challenges of being entrepreneurial. Entrepreneurs do what they do because they enjoy doing it, not because they are forced in any way. The entrepreneur will actually enjoy their work, often to the exclusion of things that are important in other people's lives – such as spouse and family. The long hours worked by entrepreneurs have often been known to break marriages. But ultimately the entrepreneur will always regard their business as 'fun', and this is one reason they can be so passionate about it. It provides an intrinsic motivation and, generally, people with an intrinsic motivation outperform those who undertake tasks because of extrinsic motivation – doing something because of an external influence or simply because they 'have to'.

Visionary with flair

In order to succeed, entrepreneurs need to have a clear vision of what they want to achieve. That is part of the fabric of their motivation. It also helps them to bring others with them, both employees and customers. The flair comes with the ability to be in the right place at the right time. Timing is everything. Innovation that is before its time can lead to business failure. Innovation that is late results in copy-cat products or services that are unlikely to be outstanding successes. A question constantly asked about successful entrepreneurs is whether their success was due to good luck or good

My strength and my weakness is that I am very focused. Some people would describe me as obsessive … The secret is to have vision and then build a plan and follow it. I think you have to do that, otherwise you just flounder about … You change your game plan on the way, as long as you are going somewhere with a purpose … I wouldn't say it was at the cost of everything else, but when I am at work, I work hard and do long hours – and when I am not at work my mind still tends to be there anyway.

☐ Mike Peters, founder of Universal Laboratories
   Sunday Times 11 July 2004

judgement? The honest answer in most cases is probably a bit of both. But, as we shall see, real entrepreneurs can help to make their own luck.

Willingness to take greater risks and live with even greater uncertainty

You have to have nerves of steel and be prepared to take risks. You have to be able to put it all on the line knowing you could lose everything.

☐ Anne Notley, co-founder of The Iron Bed Company
Sunday Times 28 January 2001

It is worth stressing that, whilst all owner-managers are willing to take risks and live with uncertainty, true entrepreneurs are willing to take far greater risks and live with far greater uncertainty. Often they are willing to put their own home on the line and risk all, so strong is their belief in their business idea.

What is more, growth businesses face rapid change. Even with careful management they are extremely risky. Growth businesses require large amounts of capital and entrepreneurs are, if necessary, willing to risk all they own for the prospect of success. Faced with such extreme uncertainty a high degree of self-confidence is essential.

♀ Antecedent influences

Whilst inherent character traits are important, there are other influences at work and there are other approaches to trying to explain the complicated process of entrepreneurship. Cognitive theory shifts the emphasis from the individual towards the situations that lead to entrepreneurial behaviour. Research has identified certain 'antecedent influences' – the entrepreneur's history and experience of life (Carter and Cachon, 1988). We are all born with certain character traits. However, we are also influenced by the social environment that we find ourselves in, for example, our family, ethnic group, education and so on. They influence our values, attitudes and even our behaviours. These are also antecedent influences.

In many ways the academic research in this area is even more confusing, and sometimes contradictory, than with personal character traits. There are a myriad of claimed influences that are difficult to prove or, indeed, disprove. There are simply too many variables to control. A further confusion is the one noted before; differentiating between owner-managers and entrepreneurs. Most of the research is about influences on start-ups. But start-ups comprise both owner-managers and entrepreneurs. However, there is a body of research on antecedent influences on managers of growth businesses which can apply, in the main, to entrepreneurs. The problem here is that some of the influences that seem to influence growth are not those that can be proved to influence start-ups. The only really safe conclusion is that, except for a handful of influences, the research is inconclusive.

One influence that comes through on many studies for both start-up and growth is educational attainment. Clearly there are problems with measuring educational attainment consistently over studies. However, particularly in the USA, research consistently shows a positive association between the probability of starting up in business and increasing educational attainment (Evans and Leighton, 1990). Similar research in other countries tends to support this result, albeit less strongly and not consistently. However, what is altogether stronger is the relationship between educational attainment and business growth. Storey (1994) reviewed seventeen multivariate studies of antecedent influences and found that educational attainment was a positive

🗁 Case insight Market traders

Notwithstanding the research, there are a number of millionaire entrepreneurs in the UK who started out as stall-holders in a market. They learnt their trade the hard way and they learnt the need for hard work. Indeed, the giant shop-chains of Marks & Spencer (M&S) and Morrison both started out as market stalls. Here are just seven entrepreneurs that featured in the *Sunday Times* Rich List in 2010.

Sir Ken Morrison, boss of the 375-store Morrison supermarket chain is estimated to be worth £1.4 billion. He started out by joining the family market stall in Bradford.

Lord Alan Sugar, these days better known for his appearances on *The Apprentice* TV show, set up Amstrad and Viglen. He began by boiling beetroot to sell from market stalls in London's East End.

Julian Dunkerton launched his clothing firm on a market stall in Cheltenham in 1984. His fashion business, Supergroup, owns the Superdry label favoured by many celebrities and he realised £200 million in a stock market float in 2010.

John Hargreaves founded the Matalan clothing chain which he sold to a private equity firm for £1.5 billion in 2009. A docker's son who left school at 14, he started out with a market stall in Liverpool selling M&S seconds.

David Whelan, founder of JJB Sport and owner of Wigan Athletic football club, started by selling toiletries from a market stall after being told by his mother to get a 'real job'.

Peter Simon, chairman of the Monsoon fashion chain started by selling knitted coats from a stall in London's Portobello Road.

Bill Adderley started selling curtains in Leicester market but went on to set up the Dunelm Mill homeware chain.

influence in eight. This led him to conclude that there was 'fairly consistent support for the view that educated entrepreneurs are more likely to establish faster-growing firms'. The GEM studies suggest that people with higher incomes and better education are more likely to be entrepreneurs.

This is not a widely acknowledged result and perhaps one that is more true of the USA than Britain. It is the stuff of folk lore that the entrepreneur comes from a poor, deprived background and has little formal education. In fact, some writers go further and claim that 'anecdotal evidence' suggests that too much education can discourage entrepreneurship (Bolton and Thompson, 2000). But times are changing and if you ask venture capitalists why they think certain firms will grow rather than others, they will tell you that they are looking for background and track record in the firm's management, and education counts. It is also particularly true of the new generation of entrepreneurs pursuing technology-based opportunities.

The rationale for the relationship might be two-fold. Firstly, educational attainment might provide the basis for better learning through life, enabling entrepreneurs to deal better with business problems and giving them a greater openness and more outward orientation. Secondly, it might give them higher earning expectations that can only be attained by growing the business. What is more, it might also give them greater confidence in dealing with customers and other business professionals.

Other influences on start-ups have been cited, many supported by univariate research (linking the characteristic on its own with start-ups), for example the influence of family. In a survey of 600 respondents, Stanworth et al. (1989) found that between 30 per cent and 47 per cent of individuals either considering, about to start, or in business had a parent who had been in business. However, Storey (1994) in his review of antecedent influences concluded that there is little support from multivariate studies (linking more than one characteristic) for the impact of family, family circumstances, cultural or ethnic influences on self-employment decisions. He could not prove the following factors had any influence on start-up propensity:

▷ Marital status;
▷ Dependants (children);
▷ Previous wage level;
▷ Length of experience;
▷ Age;
▷ Gender;

▷ Ethnicity;
▷ Social class;
▷ School type;
▷ Personality;
▷ Being a manager in a previous job.

One interesting perspective on entrepreneurship is provided by Kets de Vries (1997) who believes that entrepreneurs often come from unhappy family backgrounds. This makes them unwilling to accept authority or to work closely with others. He paints the picture of a social deviant or misfit who is both hostile to others and tormented in himself:

> A prominent pattern among entrepreneurs appears to be a sense of impulsivity, a persistent feeling of dissatisfaction, rejection and pointlessness, forces which contribute to an impairment and depreciation of his sense of self-esteem and affect cognitive processes. The entrepreneur is a man under great stress, continuously badgered by his past, a past which is experienced and re-experienced in fantasies, daydreams and dreams. These dreams and fantasies often have a threatening content due to the recurrence of feelings of anxiety and guilt which mainly revolve around hostile wishes against parental figures, or more generally, all individuals in a position of authority.

In reality there is little support for this extreme view.

A further strand of cognitive theory is worthy of note because it reinforces at least two elements of trait theory. Chen et al. (1998) set out the idea that successful entrepreneurs possess high levels of 'self-efficacy'. Self-efficacy is 'the strength of an individual's belief that he or she is capable of successfully performing the roles and tasks of an entrepreneur'. Clearly this is part of the self-confidence of entrepreneurs described in the last section, but it is also created by their internal locus of control and rooted firmly in their need for achievement and, therefore, it is more than just self-confidence. Chen et al. argue that it is self-efficacy that motivates entrepreneurs and gives them the dogged determination to persist in the face of adversity when others just give in. With this characteristic entrepreneurs become more objective and analytical and attribute failure to insufficient effort or poor knowledge. They argue that self-efficacy is affected by a person's previous experiences – success breeds success.

♀ Ethnicity and immigration

Despite Storey's conclusion, immigration is often cited as a positive influence on the propensity to start up a business. In fact, self-employment rates in the UK for ethnic minorities are not uniform. Those for Asians (Indian, Pakistani, Bangladeshi and so on) and Chinese are higher than those for white males, whilst those for black Africans and black Caribbeans are lower (Annual Population Survey, 2004). There are some 200 000 Asian-owned businesses in the UK, collectively punching above their weight in their contribution to the economy. Asians are recognised as the most likely ethnic minority group in the UK to become entrepreneurs. They are represented across all sectors of business. The case insight on Kenyan Asians gives some examples of these successes.

One reason for the high self-employment rate for Asians compared to black Africans and black Caribbeans appears to be family background and expectations. Traditionally Asian families have valued the independence of self-employment. This seems to be changing, with second generation Asians in the UK being encouraged to enter more traditional professions. However, one of the problems with looking for a pattern is that these ethnic groups are no longer homogenous and there is a complex set of family, community and societal influences at play. There is also some evidence of different financing patterns for ethnic businesses. This is addressed in Chapter 10.

It's an Asian way of working. We are all focused on what we are doing and we are working for succession. It's all in the family. We are not growing the business for an exit route. We all had one thing in common – we came to a country where we had to make it and our families supported us. My wife didn't mind me working 14 hours a day on the business and not being home to read the children bedtime stories. But we had, and still have, a good relationship. We have no regrets.'

☐ Bharat Shah, founder of Sigma Pharmaceuticals
Kenyan Jewels, www.alusainc.wordpress.com

💼 Case insight Kenyan Asians

It is an astonishing fact that six of the most successful wholesale companies supplying drugs and medicines to Britain's retail pharmacies and hospitals were founded by Kenyan Asians who are now in their fifties. All left poverty in Kenya to come to Britain in the late 1960s and early 1970s where they went to college to achieve pharmacy qualifications, generally supporting themselves with menial part-time jobs. Then they set up their own retail pharmacies before building their much bigger wholesale businesses. All are now multimillionaires.

Bharat Shah has built up the family firm of **Sigma Pharmaceuticals**. It sells some 100 generic medicines and also deals in parallel imports – whereby drugs are bought in a country where wholesale prices are much lower and repackaged for a country where the price is higher. Two of his brothers work in the business – Manish is an accountant and Kamal works in operations – and his son Halul runs retail pharmacies.

Bharat and **Ketan Mehta** founded **Necessity Supplies** in 1986. It also sells generic drugs and deals in parallel imports.

Vijay and **Bikhu Patel** have built up **Waymade Healthcare** into a business with 700 employees. They have ambitions to turn the company into a 'mini-Glaxo' and in 2003 launched Amdipham to develop medicines that are too small for the big pharmaceuticals.

Ravi Karia founded **Chemilines** in 1986. It claims to be one of Britain's fastest growing companies.

Naresh Shah founded **Jumbogate** with his wife Shweta in 1982. Whilst still involved in retailing the business is predominantly wholesale.

Navin Engineer came to London with only £75 in his pocket in 1969 at the age of 16 to live with his aunt. He worked in a Wimpy burger restaurant in Oxford Street in the evenings to support himself through sixth form and then the London School of Pharmacy. On graduation he took a job with Boots, the retail chemist. Eventually he opened his own pharmacy in Chertsey, Surrey, working long hours to make money to buy other pharmacies. By 1999 he had 14 such shops and, when the German group GEHE offered him £12 million for the retail chain, he decided to take it. He invested most of the proceeds in his much smaller wholesale business. He bought a range of small turnover branded pharmaceuticals from bigger companies, switched production to established factories in Eastern Europe and the Far East, and realised cost savings as profit. He then went into generic medicines – copies of branded drugs produced after the expiry of their patent. This involves checking patents and making certain the drug can be developed without infringing the patent. At the same time regulatory authorities have to be satisfied. His company, **Chemidex**, is now a wholesaler of both branded and generic medicines including treatments for gout, depression and an antibiotic for anthrax.

It has to be admitted that Storey's cold analytical approach to the immigrant issue does not stand the test of observation. As Harper (1985) observed:

> The Indians in East Africa, the Armenians in Egypt, the Lebanese in West Africa, the Kikuyu in Masailand, the Mahajans all over India except in their desert homeland of Rajasthan, the Tamils in Sri Lanka, the Palestinians in Arabia and the British almost everywhere except in Britain; all have shown that dislocation and hardship can lead to enterprise. The very experience of living in a difficult environment, and of planning, financing and executing a move and then surviving in a new and often hostile environment requires the qualities of self-restraint, abstinence, hard work and voluntary postponement of gratification which are normally far more severe than those demanded by the lifestyle of those who remain at home, or of the indigenous people of the place in which these refugees relocate.

Starting and running your own business is not easy and immigrants often have the motivation to work the long hours. Often with few options open to them, they have little to lose from failure and much to gain from success.

♀ Gender

In the UK, and in most of the rest of the world, women are less likely to start up a business than men. Self-employment rates in the UK for women are almost half those for men (7 per cent compared to 13 per cent (Annual Population Survey, 2004)). As Gordon Brown observed when he was Chancellor of the Exchequer: 'If the UK could achieve the same levels of female entrepreneurship as the US, Britain would gain three quarters of a million more businesses' (Advancing Enterprise Conference, 4 February 2005).

More recent data from the Global Entrepreneurship Monitor in 2008 (GEM, 2009) show that:

▷ In most high income countries, men are about twice as likely to be entrepreneurially active as women.
▷ In the UK female early-stage entrepreneurial activity was about 49 per cent that of men – a figure that has held for some years: 3.6 per cent compared to 7.4 per cent. This compares to about 70 per cent in the USA, up from 60 per cent in 2007.
▷ In the UK female entrepreneurs of established businesses were just 40 per cent that of males: 3.4 per cent of the population compared to 8.6 per cent. This compares to about 62 per cent in the USA.

What is more, a consistent research finding is that women-owned businesses are likely to perform less well than male-owned businesses, however measured – turnover, profit or job creation (Kalleberg and Leicht, 1991; Rosa et al. 1996; Cliff, 1998). There are also differences in business and industry choice. For example, whilst male-owned businesses are represented across all industries, female-owned businesses are concentrated in the retail and service sectors (Carter and Shaw, 2006). There are also differences in financing strategies and governance structures. We shall look at some of the reasons for this 'under-performance' of women-owned businesses in Chapter 10, since a major factor appears to be start-up capital, defined in its broadest sense.

Notwithstanding these issues, women-owned businesses are among the fastest growing entrepreneurial populations in the world and make significant contributions to innovation, employment and wealth creation in all economies. They can be a force to be reckoned with. The Center for Women's Business Research (2008) showed that there were over 1 million women-owned businesses in the USA, employing 13 million people and generating almost $2 trillion in sales annually.

🗎 Case insight Elizabeth Gooch and EG Solutions

Elizabeth Gooch was named as the seventh most successful female entrepreneur in the UK by *Management Today* in 2006. About 25 per cent of the top 100 entrepreneurs in the list are female. Elizabeth is founder and CEO of EG Solutions, a company selling operations management software that helps clients to generate improvements in operational performance. EG prides itself on implementing its programmes on a fixed cost, fixed timescale basis. It is the only company that guarantees return on investment and its sales receipts are based on the results delivered. Typically implementation will pay for itself within six months.

Elizabeth started work for HSBC aged 18 but left after only 12 months to work for a consultancy that helped large firms find better ways to use their staff. Eight years later she started her own business, EG Consulting, aged 26, financed by £1000 borrowed from family and friends and a credit card. EG Consulting initially offered consultancy and training on operations management to financial services companies. In its first year turnover reached £600 000. However, the complexity of collecting the information needed to advise on improving efficiency led Elizabeth to develop software to help in the task. In 1993 the software, called Operational Intelligence, was launched as a product in its own right. It allowed data to be collected in real time, enabling all departments of a company to monitor the production process. At that point the business had six employees, several contract workers and a turnover of £1 million.

It was not until Elizabeth met Rodney Baker-Bates, then CEO of Prudential Financial Services, that things changed dramatically. He believed she was not making enough of the business and said she should focus on the software rather than the consultancy work. The company changed its name to EG Solutions and he became Chairman, engaging the services of a strategic planning consultant to help them develop the business in a focused way. The strategy worked, increasing turnover by 28% a year until 2005. At this point turnover was £4.2 million and the business needed more capital to meet some ambitious growth

targets. Elizabeth decided to float the company on the Alternative Investment Market (AIM) rather than going for venture capital because she did not want to lose control.

> 'We had two options really – venture capital or floatation. I liked the float model where you had several institutional investors with a range of views and advice rather than a venture capital investor with a large stake in the business.'

The float was successful, but the problem with the stock market is that it expects the company to deliver good results year after year. Unfortunately in 2006 EG Solutions failed to make its sales targets by £700 000. Worse still, in 2007 it posted loses of £800 000. The analysts and shareholders were damning.

> 'I had really personal attacks from analysts and shareholders alike. They told me they had never seen anything so bad and that the business would never recover. I took it all very personally.'

Elizabeth's reaction was to cut costs by £1.2 million, returning the business to profit by 2008, admitting that she took her eye off the UK market as she looked overseas for business opportunities that would help her achieve her ambitious growth targets.

> 'Floatation gives a public face to your business and access to finance that is so often key to development. But there needs to be a lot more attention to strategy.
> Persevere and never see anything as failure. Look at what you can learn from something that does not go the way you want. It's all about attitude. I do not believe in failure. I have needed sheer determination – although my shareholders would probably describe it as stubbornness.'
>
> *Sunday Times* 23 November 2008

➡

By 2009 the company was back on track. Cutting costs ahead of the recession stood them in good stead, and the recession was actually helping the recovery because companies were looking to improve their efficiency. Elizabeth's objectives in 2009 involved growing the business and then exiting via a trade sale within the next two or three years.

Asked for the best advice she would give to prospective entrepreneurs, she gave six tips:

▷ 'When the going gets tough – pitch in and keep working. Nothing comes easy so you should expect it to get tough and to have to work hard.

▷ Cash is king – everybody says that, but fulfilling orders so you can raise invoices and collect the cash are the most important things you can do.

▷ Focus – have a clear strategy and don't get side tracked by activities that don't enable you to achieve this. Review your strategy constantly to ensure you are meeting market demands.

▷ Think big, act small. Reach for the stars and you will get there (or at least close). Aim low and you'll get there too. But always retain the fit, fast and flexible culture of a small business.

▷ Agility is a major strength that big businesses would die for.

▷ Starting your own business doesn't mean doing everything yourself, that's a recipe for staying small. Delegation is an important skill to learn.'

Launch Lab (www.launchlab.co.uk) 13 January 2009

☐ Visit the EG Solutions website: www.eguk.co.uk

💡 Growth businesses

Storey's review of the research (op. cit.) concludes that there are three further factors that are positively correlated with growth companies:

1 Growth companies are more likely to be set up by groups rather than individuals. This proves the venture capitalists' view that they invest in a management team not in a business, and explains why they are so willing to invest in management buy-outs and buy-ins. Managing growth needs a range of different skills with managers able to work as a team. Attracting a strong management team can be a problem for a start-up. How do you tempt successful managers to leave secure jobs and face the risks associated with a start-up? The answer is that you offer them a share in the business. In that way they share in the success of the business as well as the risks that it faces.

2 Middle-aged owners are more likely to be associated with growth companies. Middle age does have some advantages. It brings experience, credibility and financial resources. With the family possibly grown up, middle-aged entrepreneurs can devote more time and resources to the business.

However, as with all research these results must be treated with caution. Findings like these come from looking at what has happened in the past and if situations change, the past may not be a good indication of what might happen in the future. As we shall see in subsequent chapters, opportunities in the new technologies, most lately the internet, have often been grasped by very young entrepreneurs, many of whom have become millionaires as a consequence.

3 Owners with previous managerial experience are more likely to be associated with growth companies. This is likely to be the case because they bring with them both managerial and, probably, market experience. They also know their previous worth, which may create salary expectations that can only be satisfied by a growth business.

The factors that Storey could not prove influenced growth were:

▷ Gender (see previous section);
▷ Prior firm size experience;
▷ Prior sector experience;
▷ Training;

▷ Social marginality;
▷ Ethnicity (see previous section);
▷ Family history;
▷ Prior self-employment.

However, he also concluded that the picture was 'fuzzy' and that what the entrepreneur has done prior to establishing the business 'only has a modest influence on the success of the business'. One frequently debated factor is entrepreneurs' experience of prior business failure. Whether or not this is a positive experience is still to be adequately researched. Until then no conclusion can be drawn.

One curious conclusion is that the influence of training cannot be proved. If you believe that entrepreneurs are both born and made, then you must accept that they can be influenced. Just like an athlete or a musician, if they have the basic ingredients, then training should improve their performance. There are at least two major problems related to this variable. Firstly, there is the question of what constitutes training. Smaller firms are notoriously poor at undertaking formal training but that does not necessarily mean they do not undertake informal training. Secondly, those small firms that do seek out formal training are also likely to seek out other sources of help and so the influence of the formal training becomes more difficult to measure.

These studies of growth businesses allow us to draw an, albeit tentative, identikit picture of the antecedent influences on an entrepreneur which are most likely to result in them successfully growing their business. Founders of growth businesses are likely to be:

▷ Middle-aged (or very young?);
▷ White, Asian or Chinese male;
▷ Well educated;

▷ Leaving a managerial job;
▷ Willing to share ownership.

Remember, however, that these are generalisations. Whilst broadly supportable because of the samples on which they are based, they do not apply to every individual. Just like small firms, entrepreneurs are not homogeneous. The results are also based on ex-post research, that is, analysis based on the past. Circumstances change and the past is not always a good predictor of the future. What is more, if picking winners were really that easy there would be an awful lot of rich people around.

💡 National culture

The final element in the jigsaw puzzle is culture. In his seminal work on the subject, Hofstede (1980) defined culture as the 'collective programming of the mind which distinguishes one group of people from another'. It is a pattern of taken-for-granted assumptions. Different groups have different cultures and most people operate in groups that have different subcultures – family, ethnic groups, religious groups, companies and so on. However the over-riding culture of the nation in which we live is a significant over-arching influence. An entrepreneurial culture is one that fosters positive social attitudes towards entrepreneurship. Cultures can change over time, albeit slowly. So, most people would argue that Britain has developed a more entrepreneurial culture from the 1970s through to today. Similarly the subcultures within which we live will be more or less entrepreneurial and also may have changed over time.

It has been argued that there is no such thing as one identifiable entrepreneurial culture; what is needed is a favourable environment which combines social, political and educational attributes (Timmons, 1994). However, many would consider the culture in the USA to be the most entrepreneurial in the world. It is an achievement-orientated society that values individualism and material wealth. According to Welsch (1998):

> Entrepreneurship is ingrained in the fabric of North American culture. It is discussed at the family dinner table among intergenerational members, practised by pre-school children with their lemonade stands, and promoted every day through personal success human interest stories in the media. Furthermore, entrepreneurship is taught in school from kindergarten through to the twelfth grade, it has been integrated into college and university curricula, and is taught and promoted through various outreach and training programmes including government Small Business Development Centres in every state of the nation. Consequently, through one's life as an American citizen, entrepreneurship as a career option is espoused early and reinforced regularly.

Americans are said to have a 'frontier culture', always seeking something new. They are restless, constantly on the move. They have a strong preference for freedom of choice for the individual. The individual is always free to compete against established institutions. Rebellious, non-conformist youth is the accepted norm. If there is an 'American dream' it is that the humblest of individuals can become the greatest of people, usually measured in monetary terms. Achievement is prized and lauded throughout society. Individuals believe they control their destiny. Americans think big. Nothing is impossible. They prefer the new, or at least the improved. They worship innovation. Time is their most precious commodity. They are tolerant of those who make mistakes as long as they learn from them. Things need to get done quickly rather than always get done perfectly.

Measuring the dimensions of culture in a scientific way is extremely difficult. The most widely used dimensions are those developed by Hofstede (1981) who undertook an extensive cross-cultural study, using questionnaire data from some 80 000 IBM employees in 66 countries across seven occupations. From his research he established four dimensions (Figure 2.3):

1 *Individualism vs collectivism* This is the degree to which people prefer to act as individuals rather than groups. Individualistic societies are loosely knit social frameworks in which people primarily operate as individuals or in immediate families. Collectivist societies are composed of tight networks in which people operate as members of ingroups and outgroups, expecting to look after, and be looked after by, other members of their ingroup. In the individualist culture the task prevails over personal relationships. The atmosphere is competitive. In the collectivist culture the opposite is true. 'Anglo' countries (USA, Britain, Australia, Canada and New Zealand) are the highest scoring individualist cultures, together with the Netherlands. France and Germany just make it into the upper quartile of individualist cultures. South American countries are the most collectivist cultures, together with Pakistan.

Low (lower quartile countries)		High (upper quartile countries)
South America Pakistan	**INDIVIDUALISM**	**USA UK Australia** New Zealand Canada France
USA UK Germany Scandinavia	**POWER DISTANCE**	France Malaysia Philippines South America
USA UK Hong Kong Singapore	**UNCERTAINTY AVOIDANCE**	France Greece Portugal Uruguay Guatemala
North Europe	**MASCULINITY**	**USA UK Germany** Austria Italy Japan

F2.3 Hofstede's dimensions of culture

2 *Power distance* This is the degree of inequality among people that the community is willing to accept. Low power distance countries endorse egalitarianism, relations are open and informal, information flows are functional and unrestricted and organisations tend to have flat structures. They are more empowered cultures. High power distance cultures endorse hierarchies, relations are more formal, information flows are formalised and restricted and organisations tend to be rigid and hierarchical. Austria, Ireland, Israel, New Zealand and the four Scandinavian countries tend to be low power distance countries. The USA, Britain and Germany also make it into the lower quartile. High power distance countries are Malaysia, the Philippines and four South American countries, with France also making it into the upper quartile.

3 *Uncertainty avoidance* This is the degree to which people prefer to avoid ambiguity, resolve uncertainty and favour structured rather than unstructured situations. Low uncertainty avoidance cultures tolerate greater ambiguity, prefer flexibility, stress personal choice and decision-making, reward initiative, risk-taking and team-play and stress the development of analytical skills. High uncertainty avoidance cultures prefer rules and procedures, stress compliance, punish error and reward compliance, loyalty and attention to detail. The lowest uncertainty avoidance countries are Hong Kong, Ireland, Jamaica, Singapore and two Scandinavian countries. The USA and Britain are in the lowest quartile group. The highest uncertainty avoidance countries are Greece, Portugal, Guatemala and Uruguay, with France also in the highest quartile group. Germany is about halfway.

4 *Masculinity vs femininity* This defines quality of life issues. Masculine virtues are those of assertiveness, competition and success. Masculine cultures reward financial and material achievement with social prestige and status. Feminine virtues are those such as modesty, compromise and cooperation. In feminine cultures, issues such as quality of life, warmth in personal relationships, service and so on are important, and in some societies having a high standard of living is thought to be a matter of birth, luck or destiny (external locus of control). The most masculine countries are Japan, Austria, Venezuela, Italy and Switzerland. The USA, Britain and Germany all fall into the highest quartile. Four North European countries are the highest scoring feminine countries. France is about halfway.

Hofstede and Bond (1991) have added a fifth dimension – short/long-term orientation. A short-term orientation focuses on past and present and therefore values respect for the status quo, including, for example, an unqualified respect for tradition and for social and status obligations. A long-term orientation focuses on the future and therefore the values associated with this are more dynamic. For example, they include the adaptation of traditions to contemporary conditions and promote only qualified respect for social and status obligations.

Using Hofstede's dimensions, therefore, the USA, our role model for entrepreneurial culture, emerges as a highly individualistic, masculine culture, with low power distance and uncertainty avoidance. It is a culture that tolerates risk and ambiguity, has a preference for flexibility and it is an empowered culture that rewards personal initiative. It is a highly individualistic and egalitarian culture, one that is fiercely competitive and the home of the 'free-market economy'. Assertiveness and competition are central to the 'American dream'. If there is a key virtue in the USA it is achievement, and achievement receives its monetary reward. It is an informal culture. According to the Declaration of Independence, all men are created equal, but they also have the freedom to accumulate sufficient wealth to become very unequal. The USA is the original 'frontier culture'. It actually seems to like change and uncertainty and certainly rewards initiative and risk-taking.

The American Dream proposes that every individual can become successful

This, then, is the anatomy of an enterprise culture: one that encourages enterprise and entrepreneurship, one where the probability of an entrepreneur being made, rather than just born, is highest. This is the sort of culture that many other countries have been trying to promote and develop because it seems to encourage the characteristics that are needed for successful management. This culture, combined with the other antecedent influences, is said to be likely to develop the largest number of that most valuable resource – entrepreneurs.

However, notice one thing from Figure 2.3. Alongside the USA, at the extreme ends of these dimensions, is the UK and that country can hardly have been held to be the epitome of an enterprise culture at the time these studies were conducted. The explanation may lay in the timing of the study. In the 1970s, in both the UK and USA, political interest focused on enterprise as a means of rescuing their stagnant economies (O'Connor, 1973). It was argued that structural change was needed to achieve an 'enteprise culture' (Morris, 1991; Carr, 2000) and this would have to be accompanied by cultural change at the level of the individual, so much so that it would bring about a revolution that was moral, economic and enduring. And in the UK it was, arguably, the Thatcher government that brought about that change at the end of the 1970s.

It is also possible, however, that the dimensions measured by Hofstede are just not relevant to entrepreneurship. Perhaps there are other equally relevant, important but uncharted dimensions. After all, his work was based upon IBM employees and they can hardly be described as the most entrepreneurial in the world, particularly at the time when Microsoft was setting out in business. Whilst other countries try to emulate the enterprise culture of the USA, the jury is out on how precisely the dimensions of their enterprise culture are to be measured.

Notwithstanding this serious reservation about measurement, we know that deep cultures take time to change, if indeed they can be changed. There is little evidence, as yet, of different cultures around the world converging. What is more, we do not understand how best to go about changing national cultures, even if we believe it desirable. Rather than trying to change a nation's culture perhaps it would be best just to ensure that, at the very least, it does not inhibit entrepreneurship.

Culture is, however, something that can be influenced and shaped in an organisational context and we return to this important issue in Chapters 11, 17 and 18.

♀ Situational factors

Most people, at some time in their life, have an idea that could form the basis for establishing their own business. But few people choose to do so. What is needed is a trigger to spur them into action, to turn the idea into reality. These triggers can take the form of 'push' or 'pull' factors. Push factors are those that push you into self-employment – unemployment or forced redundancy, disagreement with your boss, being a 'misfit' and not feeling comfortable in an organisation for some reason, or simply having no alternative because, for example, you have a physical disability or illness. These are very strong motivations for self-employment, but not necessarily to grow your business. Pull factors – the need for independence, achievement and recognition, personal development and wealth – are positive reasons for setting up a business. Sometimes the factors combine and an entrepreneur emerges with a positive motivation, for example, to make a success of an innovative idea, having felt a 'misfit' in their old organisation.

We got the inspiration (for Lush) because we were broke. The previous business had gone bust. We had three mortgages, three children and no money. So – make a living!

□ Mark Constantine, founder of Lush
   RealBusiness interview 26 May 2009

All too often these triggers are blocked by other factors – the need for regular income, a family to support, no capital or a doubt about your own ability. These all boil down to two things – insufficient self-confidence and an inability to cope with high risk and uncertainty. Without these key ingredients the business will not get past the ideas stage. Figure 2.4 summarises these influences.

It is no coincidence that many people try to start up their own businesses either at an early age or in their late thirties and forties. At those ages, the blocks are fewer. This is particularly the case later in life when children will probably have grown up and left home and there might be some capital in savings that can be used in the start-up. At the same time the prospective entrepreneur will have gained experience and confidence and, very possibly, be seeking new challenges for self-development.

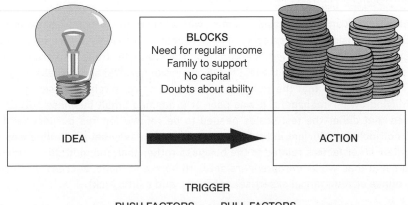

BLOCKS
Need for regular income
Family to support
No capital
Doubts about ability

IDEA → ACTION

TRIGGER

PUSH FACTORS	PULL FACTORS
Unemployment	Independence
Disagreement with management	Achievement/Recognition
Does not 'fit in' to company	Personal development
No other alternatives	Personal wealth

F2.4 Reasons for setting up in business

Storey's (1994) review of antecedent literature also came to some important conclusions regarding the influence of employment and unemployment. Reviewing three multivariate studies, he found two had statistically significant relationships between unemployment and the probability of starting up in business. However, when he came to look at growth, four out of eight studies showed a negative relationship and the other four showed no relationship at all. What is more, four out of seven studies found a positive relationship between positive motives for setting up the business (for example, market opportunity, making money) and subsequent growth. This led Storey to conclude that 'if the founder is unemployed prior to starting a business, that firm is unlikely to grow as rapidly as where the founder is employed'.

It would seem that unemployment gives people a strong push into self-employment. They possibly have limited options open to them. However, they may not have the skills needed to grow the business and may

---

🛆 Case insight Will King and King of Shaves

Will King has sensitive skin and had started mixing his own shaving oils. However, when he was made redundant in 1992 he decided to try to make this into a business. He mixed the oils in his kitchen and spent two weeks hand filling 9600 bottles with his girlfriend's help. He managed to sell the shaving oil to Harrods using the brand name King of Shaves. Today KMI, Will's toiletries and fragrance business, employs 50 people and has a turnover in excess of £42 million. His products are now sold in Harrods, Bentalls, Boots, Tesco and Sainsbury. What is more, his new Azor razor, has overtaken Wilkinson Sword in the UK market and is second only to Gillette.

☐ Up-to-date information on King of Shaves can be found on their website: www.shave.com

---

🛆 Measuring Entrepreneurial Personality

The **General Enterprise Tendency (GET)** test has been developed by staff at Durham University Business School over several years to measure a number of personal 'tendencies' commonly associated with the enterprising person. The test aims to measure 'tendency' rather than traits and was developed following research into a variety of dimensions used to measure entrepreneurship and enterprise. It was validated with a number of different groups of people and amended accordingly. It is a 54-question instrument that measures entrepreneurial personality traits in five dimensions:

▷ Need for achievement – 12 questions.
▷ Autonomy – 6 questions.
▷ Drive and determination – 12 questions.
▷ Risk-taking – 12 questions.
▷ Creativity and potential to innovate – 6 questions.

It is relatively quick and simple to administer – with either agree or disagree questions – and score. Each dimension receives a score of up to 12 points (Autonomy six points) and the final composite score measures inherent entrepreneurial character traits on a scale of 0–54.

Stormer et al. (1999) applied the test to 128 owners of new (75) and successful (53) small firms. They concluded that the test was acceptable for research purposes, particularly for identifying owner-managers. It was poor at predicting small business success. They concluded that either the test scales needed to be refined for this purpose or that the test did not include sufficient indicators of success such as situational influences on the individual or other factors related to the business rather than the individual setting it up. It would seem that, while entrepreneurs are both born and made, success requires more than an ounce of commercial expertise ... oh yes ... and a little luck!

An electronic version of the tool is available online at the website accompanying this book (www.palgrave.com/business/burns). Why not try it and see whether you are entrepreneurial?

have lower aspirations than those who leave employment to start their own business. It would seem that what is needed to make the firm grow is positive motivation – a real desire, an ambition, almost a need to achieve certain internally generated goals or pursue some market opportunity. Growth does not happen (often) by chance. The entrepreneur must want it.

Research in France also casts doubt on the long-term viability of start-ups generated by unemployed people (Abdesselam et al., 1999). They found that firms with the shortest life-spans were set up by the young (under 30) and unemployed. They also found that there was a high probability that the fledgling business people would be female and the business would be in the retail or wholesale sector. These results cast worrying doubt on the wisdom of any government policy to encourage the unemployed to start up their own business – one aspect of policy option 1, which was outlined on p. 22.

Motivations can be difficult to disentangle and, although growth businesses are more likely to be set up as a result of pull factors, often people face a combination of push and pull factors. What is more, size of business may not feature in their vision at start-up. Indeed motivations change over time. Many owner-managers may start out with no wish to grow their company to be a future Microsoft or Virgin. However, if a business shows potential for being successful, few owners will hinder growth until their personal resources are really stretched. At this point the owner reaches a watershed.

👜 Case with questions Duncan Bannatyne, Dragon

Duncan Bannatyne is probably the best known entrepreneur in the UK because of his appearances on the BBC TV series *Dragons' Den* rather than his achievements as a serial entrepreneur. His life has, however, been a colourful one. He was born in 1949 into a relatively poor family in the town of Clydebank, Scotland. The second of seven children, his father was a foundry-man at the local ship yard. When told that the family could not afford to buy him a bicycle Duncan tried to get a job delivering newspapers for the local newsagents, only to be set the challenge of finding 100 people who wanted a newspaper to be delivered. By knocking on doors he collected the names, got his newspaper round and eventually was able to buy his bicycle.

Duncan left school at 15 to serve in the Royal Navy. He served for five years before receiving a dishonourable discharge – after 9 months detention – for threatening to throw an officer off a jetty. He spent his twenties moving from job to job around the UK, including taxi driving and selling ice creams, ending up in Stockton-on-Tees. It was here, in his early 30s, that Duncan's entrepreneurial career started when, using his personal savings, he bought an ice cream van for £450. He built this business into a fleet of vans selling 'Duncan's Super Ices'. Even here he showed entrepreneurial flair. He was innovative – he started using a scoop that speeded up serving and made a shape like a smile in the ice cream, which the children loved. He was good at spotting opportunities – he bought one pitch in a local park for £2000 which gave him profits of £18 000 in one summer. He eventually sold the business for £28 000, but not before he had spotted another opportunity. In the 1980s the government started helping unemployed people by paying their rent. Duncan used his profits from the ice cream business to buy and convert houses into bedsits for rent. He rented to the unemployed, so the rents were guaranteed by the government.

Duncan used the proceeds from the sale of the ice cream business – and almost everything else he owned – to move into residential care homes with a business partner. He

➡

took out a bank loan, re-mortgaged his own home and started building up credit card debt. The building costs of the care home were to be financed by a 70 per cent mortgage, but this would only be released when building work was complete and the home was available for occupation. When building costs for the first home spiralled out of control and no more funds were available, he, his partner, friends and family decided to finish the work themselves. The total costs for the care home came to £360 000, and nearly bankrupted Duncan. But the bank then valued the finished home at £600 000, giving a mortgage of £420 000. This meant that Duncan could recover his costs, pay off his debts and still have equity to put into the next care home. Using a mix of retained profits and borrowings, and by offering shares in the company, he expanded the number of homes.

'When I opened my first nursing home, I had considered newsagents and bed and breakfast establishments but then Margaret Thatcher started to revolutionise care for the elderly ... I spotted an opportunity. I came to the conclusion that landlords who owned nursing homes could make a lot of money from the scheme. I took advantage and bought a plot of land with a bank loan and set up my first nursing home in Darlington as soon as I could. When that was full, I paid off all my debts, bought another plot and repeated the process until the portfolio included 45 homes.'

The company was called Quality Care Homes and it was eventually floated on the Stock Exchange. Duncan also went into children's nurseries with the Just Learning chain. In 1996 he sold Quality Care Homes for £26 million and Just Learning for £22 million. By now, however he had expanded into health clubs with the popular Bannatyne's chain.

'I remember while I was working in the nursing home industry, I injured my knee and used to travel 30 minutes to a local gym in the North East for exercise and physiotherapy. While working out my knee, I also tried to work out the gym's business plan. I knew the membership fees and the number of members and I calculated approximately how much the building cost because I sat and counted the number of tiles on the ceiling and equated them to square footage in my nursing homes. I did the necessary sums and worked out that, if I opened my own health club, I would make a 35%-40% return on capital. It was a no-brainer.'

Daily Telegraph 30 July 2009

By buying plots of land next to the health club sites Duncan expanded into the hotel business. He worked out that by sharing staffing, reception and other facilities he could save costs and offer hotel residents use of the health club facilities during their stay. So Bannatyne Hotels was born. Duncan has since acquired 26 health clubs from Hilton Hotels making it the largest independent chain of health clubs in the UK. He has also launched Bar Bannatyne and, in October 2008, opened Bannatyne Spa Hotel in Hastings.

Duncan's wealth is estimated by the *Sunday Times* 2009 Rich List at £320 million, which places him as the 167th richest person in the UK. He is also by far the wealthiest of the Dragons in the Den.

QUESTION

What entrepreneurial character traits can you spot in Duncan?

🛄 Case with questions Hilary Andrews and Mankind

Hilary Andrews comes from a family of entrepreneurs. Her father ran a building and land-scaping company and her sister ran a public relations company. Hilary wanted to be a beauty therapist so she left sixth form college to go to a private college ahead of going to work in a beauty salon. However it was not too long before she opened her own salon in Woking, in 1983. But Hilary got bored and felt unhappy with the insecurity of self-employment, so in 1990 she took a teacher training course and then a degree in education, going on to teach beauty and holistic therapy in Farnborough. She then got a job in a company distributing products to the spa industry, working in their mail order department. It was here that she came upon the idea for her business. Men kept asking for advice on products to use on their skin, so she decided to research the emerging market for men's skin care products. She quickly decided there was a real business opportunity in setting up a mail order company selling just men's cosmetics. The market for male grooming products was growing rapidly but, more importantly for her idea, many men preferred not to visit shops.

However, Hilary was by now 38 years old and she found the prospect of setting up on her own daunting. Luckily she was able to find a business partner, Paul Jamieson, through a mutual friend. She enthused him with her business idea and he decided he was willing to back her. But more money was needed and the banks and private investors were not convinced. They thought the idea untried and untested and did not believe men would buy grooming products in this way. Not to be put off, Hilary remortgaged her house, raising £10 000 and Paul put in £20 000 of his own money. Hilary managed to borrow a further £20 000 from two family members and two friends. With £50 000 of capital, Mankind was launched in 2000.

First Hilary secured the products she wished to sell by entering into distributor agreements for a range of selected products. Then she bought mailing lists and printed some 100 000 catalogues. Friends and family helped stuff the catalogues into envelopes and mail them out. Sufficient sales came from this first mailshot to establish the business and it quickly developed its own mailing list. But it was through developing a website and exploiting the internet market that the business really took off. This was a key decision that allowed it to grow, just as online shopping was becoming popular.

'We knew there were guys who wanted these products but didn't want the hassle of going to a shop and speaking to a consultant. The internet has made it easy to buy products that were previously difficult to get and enabled us to give people a lot of information about them. About 99 per cent of our sales are through the internet now. We have watched things develop very quickly in both the male grooming and the internet market. But we have tried to control the growth so we don't try to run before we can walk. I'm a cautious person who looks at the downside of things.

It's about being really focused on what you do ... You have to watch the bottom line constantly. Its not about starting a business and getting yourself a nice car; its about starting a business and having a really solid model that works ... What motivates me is being successful in an industry I love. It's a rewarding thing to give people confidence.'

Sunday Times 9 October 2005

By 2005 Mankind's turnover had grown to almost £3 million – and despite the hard work Hilary had still found time to marry and have a son.

☐ Up-to-date information on Mankind can be found on their website: www.mankind.co.uk

QUESTIONS

1 Which of the character traits of the entrepreneur does Hilary exhibit?

2 What other influences can you detect?

3 How much of the success of this venture is down to the right idea at the right time?

▷ Summary

▷ The decision to start your own business is influenced by your own character traits, antecedent influences and the situation you face at any point in time. You can assess your character traits using the GET test.

▷ Owner-managers and entrepreneurs have certain personal character traits that they are born with but that can be developed over time. These character traits are summarised in Figure 2.2. Entrepreneurs like **Simon Woodroffe, Richard Thompson, Duncan Bannatyne** and **Hilary Andrews** exhibit many of these traits.

However, the issue of linking the character traits of an individual to the success of a business – picking winners – needs to be approached with caution. Success or failure in business comes from a mix of many different things. The character traits of the manager are just one factor in the equation. What is more, there are a number of methodological problems associated with trying to measure personality traits:

▷ Traits are not stable and change over time.
▷ They require subjective judgements.
▷ Antecedent influences can be overlooked or ignored:
– cultural and environmental influences;
– education, learning and training;
– age, sex, race and social class.

▷ Women are generally less likely to start up a business than men and, even when they do, that business is likely to perform less well than male-owned businesses, however measured. There are, however, many exceptions to this, such as **Elizabeth Gooch**.

▷ By way of contrast, self-employment rates in the UK for ethnic minorities are not uniform and many ethnic minority-owned businesses exhibit above-average performance. Asian-owned businesses perform particularly well – as was the case with the **Kenyan Asians**.

▷ Education is an important antecedent influence on start-ups but more particularly entrepreneurial growth businesses. Whilst unemployment is a strong push into self-employment, entrepreneurial growth businesses are more likely to be set up for more positive motives. Growth companies are also more likely to be set up by groups than individuals, often sharing ownership to attract experienced managers. They are more likely to be set up by middle-aged owners with previous managerial experience who leave their job for the start-up.

▷ National culture – 'the software of the mind' – also influences the decision whether to set up one's own firm and whether to grow it. Culture can be measured in four dimensions: individualism vs collectivism; power distance; uncertainty avoidance; and masculinity vs femininity. The USA is probably the role model for an entrepreneurial culture. It emerges as a highly individualistic, masculine culture, with low power distance and low uncertainty avoidance. Whether or not you accept these dimensions of culture as saying anything about entrepreneurship, what is true is that entrepreneurship is ingrained into the fabric of culture in the USA, part of the 'American dream'.

▷ Situational factors also influence the start-up decision. Many people have business ideas but few have the confidence to start up their own business. The blocks to doing so include the need for regular income to support a family, the lack of capital and self-doubt. What is needed is a trigger. This can be a push factor such as unemployment – as in the case of **Will King** – or immigration – as was the case with the **Kenyan Asians**. It can also be a pull factor such as a desire to make money through an economic opportunity. As we saw with **Steve Hulme** and **Duncan Bannatyne**, it can be a combination of these factors. Generally businesses set up for positive motives or pull factors are most likely to grow.

Further resources are available at www.palgrave.com/business/burns

Essays and discussion topics

1 Are entrepreneurs born or made?
2 Do you think you have what it takes to be an owner-manager or entrepreneur?
3 Which character traits of owner-managers and entrepreneurs might have negative effects on a business?
4 What factors do you think affect the success or otherwise of a business venture?
5 Can you 'pick winners'?
6 How do entrepreneurs cope with risk and uncertainty?
7 What are the defining characteristics of an entrepreneur?
8 Are immigrants more entrepreneurial?
9 Why are women less entrepreneurial than men?
10 Can training help develop entrepreneurship?
11 Has your education, so far, encouraged you to be entrepreneurial? If so, how? If not, how could it be changed?
12 Does this course encourage entrepreneurship?
13 Is entrepreneurship really just for the middle-aged?
14 Are there advantages to setting up your own business when you are young?
15 What are the blocks you personally face in starting your own business? Against each block consider the changes that would be needed for it to be removed.
16 Why might so many dot.com entrepreneurs be young and well educated?
17 Is it really better to set up in business with other individuals?
18 Does previous business failure mean that you are more likely to succeed in the future?
19 Have attitudes to entrepreneurs changed in this country over the last twenty years?
20 Does this country have an enterprise culture?
21 How can enterprise culture be encouraged?
22 Why is the USA considered to be the most entrepreneurial culture in the world?
23 Which other countries would you consider to have an entrepreneurial culture?
24 Are there any other dimensions along which an enterprise culture could be measured?

Exercises and assignments

1 Write a mini case study on the motivations and other influences on an entrepreneur you know who set up their own business.

List the questions you would ask an owner-manager or entrepreneur in trying to assess their character traits.

Use the list of questions to conduct an interview with an owner-manager of a local small firm. Once you have done this get them to complete the GET test. Summarise the most important observation and insights you have gained from the interview. Make sure you justify your conclusions about their character with evidence from the interview and the GET test.

2 Find out all you can about a well known entrepreneur and write an essay or report describing their character. Give examples of their actions that lead you to make your conclusions.

3 Using the GET test and the questions developed in exercise 1 as a basis, evaluate your own entrepreneurial character. Write a report describing your character. Give examples of actions or behaviours that support these conclusions.

References

Abdesselam, R., Bonnet, J. and Le Pape, N. (1999) 'An Explanation of the Life Span of New Firms: An Empirical Analysis of French Data', *Entrepreneurship: Building for the Future*, Euro PME 2nd International Conference, Rennes.

Acs, Z. and Audretsch, D.B. (1989) 'Births and Firm Size', *Southern Economic Journal*, 55.

Aldrich, H.E. and Martinez, M. (2003) 'Entrepreneurship as a Social Construction: A Multi-Level Evolutionary Approach', in Z.J. Acs and D.B. Audretsch (eds),

Handbook of Entrepreneurship Research: A Multidisciplinary Survey and Introduction, Boston, MA: Kluwer Academic Publishers.

Anderson, J. (1995) Local Heroes, Scottish Enterprise, Glasgow.

Andersson, S., Gabrielsson, J. and Wictor, I. (2004) 'International Activities in Small Firms – Examining Factors Influencing the Internationalisation and Export Growth of Small Firms', *Canadian Journal of Administrative Science*, 21(1).

Annual Population Survey (2004) *Annual Population Survey, January–December, 2004*, London: Office for National Statistics.

Baty, G. (1990) *Entrepreneurship in the Nineties*, Englewood Cliffs, NJ: Prentice Hall.

Bell, J., Murray, M. and Madden, K. (1992) 'Developing Expertise: An Irish Perspective', *International Small Business Journal*, 10(2).

Blanchflower, D.G. and Meyer, B.D. (1991) 'Longitudinal Analysis of Young Entrepreneurs in Australia and the United States', National Bureau of Economic Research, Working Paper no. 3746, Cambridge, MA.

Bolton, B. and Thompson, J. (2000) *Entrepreneurs: Talent, Temperament, Technique*, Oxford: Butterworth-Heinemann.

Brockhaus, R. and Horwitz, P. (1986) 'The Psychology of the Entrepreneur', in D. Sexton and R. Smilor (eds), *The Art and Science of Entrepreneurship*, Cambridge, MA: Ballinger Publishing Co.

Brush, C.G. (1992) 'Research on Women Business Owners: Past Trends, A New Perspective and Future Directions', *Entrepreneurship: Theory and Practice*, 16(4).

Busenitz, L. and Barney, J. (1997) 'Differences between Entrepreneurs and Managers in Large Organisations: Biases and Heuristics in Strategic Decision Making', *Journal of Business Venturing*, 12.

Buttner, E. and More, D. (1997) 'Women's Organisational Exodus to Entrepreneurship: Self-Reported Motivations and Correlates with Success', *Journal of Small Business Management*, 35(1).

Caird, S. (1990) 'What Does it Mean to be Enterprising?', *British Journal of Management*, 1(3).

Carr, P. (2000) *The Age of Enterprise: The Emergence and Evolution of Entrepreneurial Management*, Dublin: Blackwell.

Carter, S. and Cachon, J. (1988) *The Sociology of Entrepreneurship*, Stirling: University of Stirling Press.

Carter, S. and Shaw, E. (2006) *Women's Business Ownership: Recent Research and Policy Developments*, Report to the Small Business Service, London: DTI.

Center for Women's Business Research (2008), *Key Facts*, Center for Women's Business Research, Washington, DC, www.nfwbo.org/facts/index.php.

Chell, E., Haworth, J. and Brearley, S. (1991) *The Entrepreneurial Personality*, London: Routledge.

Chen, P.C., Greene, P.G. and Crick, A. (1998) 'Does Entrepreneurial Self Efficacy Distinguish Entrepreneurs from Managers?', *Journal of Business Venturing*, 13.

Cliff, J. (1998), 'Does One Size Fit All? Exploring the Relationship Between Attitudes Towards Growth, Gender and Business Size', *Journal of Business Venturing*, 13(6).

Cuba, R., Decenzo, D. and Anish, A. (1983) 'Management Practises of Successful Female Business Owners', *American Journal of Small Business*, 8(2).

Deakins, D. (1996) *Entrepreneurs and Small Firms*, London: McGraw-Hill.

de Bono, E. (1985) *Six Thinking Hats*, Boston: Little Brown & Company.

Evans, D.S. and Leighton, L.S. (1990) 'Small Business Formation by Unemployed and Employed Workers', *Small Business Economics*, 2(4).

Harper, M. (1985) 'Hardship, Discipline and Entrepreneurship', Cranfield School of Management, Working Paper no. 85.1.

Hirsch, R.D. and Brush, C.G. (1987) 'Women Entrepreneurs: A Longitudinal Study', *Frontiers in Entrepreneurship Research*, Wellesley, MA: Babson College.

Hofstede, G. (1980) *Culture's Consequences: International Differences in Work-related Values*, Beverly Hills, CA: Sage.

Hofstede, G. (1981) *Cultures and Organisations: Software of the Mind*, London: HarperCollins.

Hofstede, G. and Bond, M.H. (1991) 'The Confucian Connection: From Cultural Roots to Economic Performance', Organisational Dynamics, Spring.

Kalleberg, A.L. and Leicht, K.T. (1991), 'Gender and Organisation Performance: Determinants of Small Business Survival and Success', *Academy of Management Journal*, 34(1).

Kanter, R.M. (1983) *The Change Masters*, New York: Simon & Schuster.

Kets de Vries, M.F.R. (1985) 'The Dark Side of Entrepreneurship', *Harvard Business Review*, November–December.

Kets de Vries, M.F.R. (1997) 'The Entrepreneurial Personality: A Person at the Crossroads', *Journal of Management Studies*, February.

Kirzner, I.M. (1973) *Competition and Entrepreneurship*, Chicago: University of Chicago.

Kirzner, I.M. (1979) *Perception, Opportunity and Profit: Studies in the Theory of Entrepreneurship*, Chicago: University of Chicago.

Kirzner, I.M. (1997) 'Entrepreneurial Discovery and Competitive Market Processes: An Austrian Approach', *Journal of Economic Literature*, 35.

Kirzner, I.M. (1999) 'Creativity and/or Alertness: A Reconsideration of Schumpeterian Entrepreneur', *Review of Austrian Economics*, 11.

McClelland, D. C. (1961) *The Achieving Society*, Princeton, NJ: Van Nostrand.

Morris, P. (1991) 'Freeing the Spirit of Enterprise: The Genesis and Development of the Concept of Enterprise Culture', in R. Keat and N. Abercrombie (eds), *Enterprise Culture*, London: Routledge.

O'Connor, J. (1973) *The Fiscal Crisis of the State*, New York: St. Martin's Press.

Pinchot, G. (1985) *Intrapreneuring*, New York: Harper & Row.

Rosa, P., Hamilton, S., Carter, S. and Burns, H. (1994) 'The Impact of Gender on Small Business Management: Preliminary Findings of a British Study', *International Small Business Journal*, 12(3).

Rosa, P., Carter, S. and Hamilton. D. (1996). 'Gender as a Determinant of Small Business Performance: Insights from a British Study', *Small Business Economics*, 8.

Schein, V., Mueller, R., Lituchy, T. and Liu, J. (1996) 'Thinking Manager – Think Male: A Global Phenomenon?', *Journal of Organisational Behaviour*, 17.

Schumpeter, J.A. (1983/1996) *The Theory of Economic Development*, New Brunswick, NJ: Transaction Publishers.

Schwartz, E.B. (1997) 'Entrepreneurship: A New Female Frontier', *Journal of Contemporary Business*, Winter.

Shapero, A. (1985) *Managing Professional People – Understanding Creative Performance*, New York: Free Press.

Shaver, K. and Scott, L. (1992) 'Person, Processes and Choice: The Psychology of New Venture Creation', *Entrepreneurship Theory and Practice*, 16(2).

Stanworth, J., Blythe, S., Granger, B. and Stanworth, C. (1989) 'Who Becomes an Entrepreneur?', *International Small Business Journal*, 8(1).

Steiner, R. (1999) *My First Break: How Entrepreneurs Get Started*, Sunday Times Books.

Storey, D.J. (1994) *Understanding the Small Business Sector*, London: International Thomson Business Press.

Storey, D. and Sykes, N. (1996) 'Uncertainty, Innovation and Management', in P. Burns and J. Dewhurst (eds), *Small Business and Entrepreneurship*, London: Macmillan – now Basingstoke: Palgrave Macmillan.

Stormer, R., Kilne, T. and Goldberg, S. (1999) 'Measuring Entrepreneurship with the General Enterprise Tendency (GET) Test: Criterion-Related Validity and Reliability', *Human Systems Management*, 18(1).

Timmons, J. (1994) *New Venture Creation*, Boston, MA: Irwin.

Welsch, H. (1998) 'America: North', in A. Morrison (ed.), *Entrepreneurship: An International Perspective*, Oxford: Butterworth Heinemann.

3 Innovation and entrepreneurship

▷ **Innovation**
▷ **Innovation and competitive advantage**
▷ **Discontinuous innovation**
▷ **Innovation and entrepreneurship**
▷ **Creativity and entrepreneurship**
▷ **Innovation and size**
▷ **Innovation and location**
▷ **Summary**

Case insights
▷ James Dyson
▷ McDonald's
▷ Who invented the world wide web (www)?
▷ Trevor Baylis
▷ Great Ormond Street Hospital for Children
▷ Swarfega

Cases with questions
▷ Big companies and new ideas

Thomas Edison was so poor at marketing his inventions that he was removed from every new business he founded

of a cheaper material in an existing product, or a better way of marketing an existing product or service, or even a better way of distributing or supporting an existing product or service. Entrepreneurial firms in particular are often innovative in their approach to marketing, finding more effective, often cheaper routes to market. Direct Line pioneered the sale of car insurance – a mature, long-established product – to the UK public in a way that was innovative at the time – directly, firstly by telephone then over the internet, cutting out insurance brokers. Interestingly it was copying a US firm that had done the same. It looked at the value chain (see Chapter 11) for insurance and concluded that the broker network added substantial cost but little or no value to the customer. Innovation, therefore, is about doing things differently in some way.

Mintzberg (1983) defined innovation as 'the means to break away from established patterns', in other words doing things really differently. So, simply introducing a new product or service that has customers willing to buy it is not necessarily innovation. For Mintzberg true innovation has to break the mould of how things are done. Put another way, there has to be a high degree of innovation – it is a question of scale. New cars are rarely truly innovative, despite what the marketing hype might say. However, the Mini was truly innovative because it changed the way cars were designed and changed the way people perceived vehicle size. But how high a degree of innovation does there have to be for it to cross the line to become invention?

Schumpeter (1996) described five types of innovation:

1 The introduction of a new or improved good or service.
2 The introduction of a new process.
3 The opening up of a new market.
4 The identification of new sources of supply of raw materials.
5 The creation of new types of industrial organisation.

In fact there are considerable problems with interpreting these criteria for innovation. For example, what constitutes a new product or service? When a sofa manufacturer produces a 'new' sofa, is that a new product? Economists would probably argue that it was not (because the cross elasticity of demand[1] is unlikely to be zero) – but the entrepreneur might disagree.

What if the sofa manufacturer starts manufacturing chairs? At what point does the firm start producing genuinely new products? As Porter (1998a) observed, 'much innovation is mundane and incremental, depending more on an accumulation of small insights than on a single major technological breakthrough'. If Schumpeter's description of innovation is inadequate it is because of the myriad forms it can take. What is more, the central role of the entrepreneurial firm in taking the innovation to the market needs to be explicitly acknowledged in any definition.

---

[1] Cross elasticity of demand measures the responsiveness of demand for a product to the change in price of other related products. When there is zero elasticity of demand there is no relationship between the products. Thus if elasticity is not zero, customers require some price inducement to try the 'new' product.

💼 Case insight James Dyson

James Dyson is the inventor of the revolutionary cyclone vacuum cleaner who challenged established large companies in the market and gained a significant market share. Having already invented the 'Ballbarrow', a light plastic wheelbarrow with a ball rather than a wheel, the idea for the cleaner came to Dyson in 1979 because he was finding that traditional cleaners could not clear all the dust he was creating as he converted an old house. Particles clogged the pores of the dust bags and reduced the suction. He had developed a small version of the large industrial cyclone machines which separate particles from air by using centrifugal force in order to collect paint particles from his plastic-spraying operation for the Ballbarrow. He believed the technology could be adapted for the home vacuum cleaner, generating greater suction and eliminating the need for bags.

Working from home, investing all his own money, borrowing on the security of his home and drawing just £10 000 a year to support himself, his wife and three children, he produced 5000 different prototypes. However, established manufacturers rejected his ideas and venture capitalists declined to invest. In 1991 he took the product to Japan and won the 1991 International Design Fair prize. He licensed the manufacture of the product in Japan where it became a status symbol selling at $2000 a time. On the back of this and twelve years after the idea first came to him, he was able to obtain finance from Lloyds Bank to manufacture the machine under his own name in the UK.

Early sales were through mail order, then followed a deal with John Lewis and later Comet and Currys. There are now many different sorts of Dyson cleaner and, at its peak in the 1990s, the company had captured 38 per cent of the UK market. But the Dual Cyclone was nearly never made due to patent and legal costs. Unlike a songwriter who owns his songs, an inventor must pay substantial fees to renew his patent each year. This nearly bankrupted Dyson in the development years.

Dyson's major competitor, Hoover, paid him the ultimate compliment of copying his design with their Vortex range. In 2000 he won his case against them for infringing his patents. With a turnover of £628 million, profits of £85 million and 2500 employees, his business was still growing in 2009. And he, his wife and three children still owned 100%. In 2010 he had an estimated wealth of £920 million according to the *Sunday Times* – although he been a billionaire three years earlier. In 2010 he stood down as Chairman of the company he founded. Dyson is one of that rare breed – inventor, innovator and entrepreneur.

☐ Up-to-date information on Dyson can be found on the company website: www.dyson.co.uk

Morris and Kuratko (2002) expand on Schumpeter's list and talk about the range or continuum of possibilities shown in Figure 3.1. These relate to either the introduction of new products/services or new processes. New processes can be administrative or service delivery systems, new production or financing methods, different marketing, sales, distribution or procurement approaches, new information or supply chain management systems. This is a frequent route to innovation for entrepreneurial firms. One point to note is that Morris and Kuratko's continuum of possibilities does not include innovations in marketing, a form of innovation that is used very effectively by many entrepreneurial firms. Whether a concept or activity may be described as innovative depends on whether it represents a 'departure from what is currently available' – that is, whatever makes it unique or different. This is what makes the concept or activity an innovation.

Kirton (1976) distinguishes between an innovator and an adaptor in terms of the approach each takes to problem-solving, rather than the outcome itself. One engages in divergent thinking aimed at innovation; the other engages in convergent thinking aimed at perfection. These are contrasted in Table 3.1.

What constitutes innovation is therefore contentious. But this fails to recognise that there is a second dimension to innovation, and that is how frequently it is practised. Arguably, a firm that practises frequent small-scale innovation is just as innovative as one that has the occasional large-scale innovation. And what is true is that the

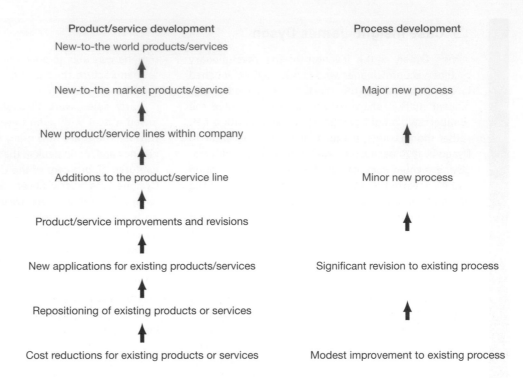

Product/service development	Process development
New-to-the world products/services	
↑	
New-to-the market products/service	Major new process
↑	
New product/service lines within company	↑
↑	
Additions to the product/service line	Minor new process
↑	
Product/service improvements and revisions	↑
↑	
New applications for existing products/services	Significant revision to existing process
↑	
Repositioning of existing products or services	↑
↑	
Cost reductions for existing products or services	Modest improvement to existing process

F3.1 Product/service and processes development: a spectrum

sum of many small, incremental innovations can have an enormous impact on competitive advantage (Bessant, 1999). Often these innovations are introduced during the later stages of the life cycle of a product or service so as to maintain or improve competitive advantage and extend its life. Indeed, there is evidence that the majority of commercially significant innovations are indeed incremental rather than radical (Audretsch, 1995). This leads to the idea that the impact of innovation on competitive advantage might be measured on two dimensions – frequency of innovation and scale or degree of innovation. This is shown in Figure 3.2. Frequent small innovations may compensate for the occasional 'big-bang' breakthrough. What is more, frequent small innovations may also be less risky.

But entrepreneurial innovation is even more than this. What is needed to make the innovation successful is for it to be linked to customer demand – existing or in the future – that is, a market opportunity. Whilst some entrepreneurs might achieve this

Adaptor	Innovator
Employs a disciplined, precise, methodical approach	Approaches task from unusual angles
Is concerned with solving, rather than finding, problems	Discovers problems and avenues of solution
Attempts to refine current practices	Questions basic assumptions related to current practices
Tends to be means-orientated	Has little regard for means; is more interested in ends
Is capable of extended detail work	Has little tolerance for routine work
Is sensitive to group cohesion and cooperation	Has little or no need for consensus; often is insensitive to others

Source: Kirton, M. (1976) 'Adaptors and Innovators: A Description and Measure', *Journal of Applied Psychology*, October.

T3.1 Two approaches to problem-solving

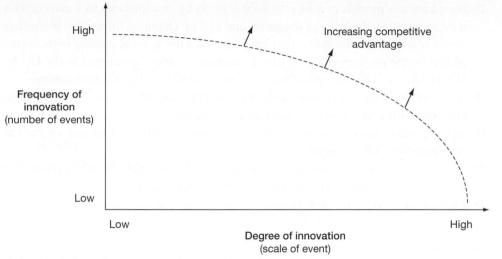

F3.2 Innovation and competitive advantage

link through luck, it is the link between innovation and opportunity in the market place that reduces the risk for the entrepreneurial firm and gives it the competitive advantage it seeks – and that market linkage needs to be developed and embedded in the processes of the firm. Even process innovation, which may involve no change in the product itself, must be linked to customer demand through cost/price, quality, lead times and so on if it is to be successful. Finding opportunities must become a systematic process for the entrepreneurial firm.

💡 Discontinuous innovation

Innovation is not always a continuous process. It can also be triggered by dramatic changes to the status quo (in technology, market, social and regulatory environments) that lead to 'discontinuous innovation' – step changes in products or processes. These are difficult to predict, even if a company is sensitive to the expressed needs of its customers. Famously, Henry Ford once said that if he had asked people what they wanted, they'd have said faster horses, rather than 'new-fangled' things called cars. Tidd et al. (2005) give some examples of these discontinuities:

▷ New technologies can emerge as step changes in product or process technologies (e.g. mobile phones or the internet) or as the result of a single breakthrough (e.g. LED as a white light source). These can occur in high-technology niches, evidenced by pioneering breakthroughs (Utterback and Acee, 2005), or in low-technology niches, evidenced by new configurations of existing technologies (Schmidt, 2004), blurring somewhat the distinction between incremental and radical innovation.

▷ New markets can emerge unpredictably – one example of disruption that led to the extinction of many large firms, as highlighted by Christensen (1997), is the dot.com bubble.

🗁 Case insight McDonald's

Like it or loath it, McDonald's, the ubiquitous hamburger chain, brought true innovation to the food industry. It developed a standardised, high quality hamburger sandwich, produced using entirely new cooking procedures and delivered with the speed of just-in-time preparation by meticulously trained people, in clean surroundings and at a bargain price. This was something entirely new for customers and it spawned a completely new market called 'the fast-food industry'. In doing this not only did McDonald's have first mover advantage, they also created the rules for a whole new industry. And if you write the rule book, inevitably you have an incredible competitive advantage. The question today is whether the product has finally come to the end of its life cycle?

▷ New business models may be established, often by new entrants to a market who dare to question the 'rules of the game' and end up changing them. This is another instance of market disruption that large firms are not good at dealing with, exemplified by the emergence of the direct insurance market, pioneered in the UK by Direct Line, and the success of internet businesses like eBay and Lastminute.

▷ New political rules can cause markets to change dramatically, such as the end of communism or the drive for lower carbon emissions.

▷ Market exhaustion for firms in mature industries may lead to exit or radical reorientation of the business.

▷ Sea change in market sentiment or behaviour – for example the move from CDs to music downloads, or the growing popularity of organic foods.

▷ Deregulation or shifts in regulatory regimes can lead to new markets or new market rules – for example the privatisation of much of the UK's public sector by Margaret Thatcher in the 1980s.

▷ Fracture along 'fault lines' can occur when minority opinions gather momentum and cause systems to 'flip' – for example, opinions over smoking or the environment.

▷ Unthinkable events that cannot be prepared for, like '9/11' and the consequences for business or the BP Gulf of Mexico oil spill in 2010.

▷ Shifts in the 'techno-economic paradigm' are systems-level changes involving the convergence of technological and market changes such as electricity replacing steam power or the emergence of social media as a new dimension to advertising and communication.

▷ Architectural innovations which rewrite the 'rules of the game' as to how things are done; for example, who might hold the knowledge to drive innovation.

Arguably the most significant recent discontinuous innovation has been the internet and the development of the World Wide Web. The impact of its arrival has been likened to that of the railways in the nineteenth century. The internet has created significant entrepreneurial business opportunities, particularly for start-ups, and made many entrepreneurs into millionaires along the way. It spawned the 'dot.com boom' and the 'dot.com bust'. It created the base for the development of social media. We shall look at the history of its commercial development and the business ideas it has spawned in Chapter 5. We shall also look at how it might be incorporated into mainstream business activities in Chapter 6.

Another powerful driver of innovation in the twenty first century is 'sustainability' – environmental responsibility, ethical business practices and other issues often wrapped up in the term 'corporate social responsibility' (CSR). We look at this in greater detail in Chapter 11. Innovation linked to sustainability often has major systems-level implications, demanding a holistic and integrated approach to innovation management, offering ideal entrepreneurial opportunities. The commitment of the retailer M&S to be completely carbon-neutral by 2012 requires the company to completely re-engineer many of its operations. Berkhout and Green (2003) argue for a systems approach to innovation, linking innovation with sustainable research, policy and management, and they conclude that 'greater awareness and interaction between research and management of innovation, environmental management, corporate social responsibility and innovation and environment will prove fruitful.'

Although the innovations coming from these discontinuities are far from incremental or part of a continuous process of improvement, they can still be managed

💼 Case insight Who invented the world wide web (www)?

The first electronic mail transfer took place in July 1970 in the laboratories of consultants Bolt, Baranek and Newman. Building on the work of Paul Baran of the RAND Corporation, it was the result of a contract placed by the US Advanced Research Projects Agency (ARPA) to build a distributive network that enabled researchers at one site to log onto and run programs at another. Roy Tomlinson, who wrote the program, initiated the use of the symbol '@' to separate the name of the sender from the mailbox ID. He chose it because it was the only symbol that was unlikely to form part of a name or an ID.

Computer networks were also being built elsewhere and ARPA brought researchers from Britain, France, Italy and Sweden to form an international Network Working Group to investigate how the various networks could be connected. In 1973 there was a breakthrough as researchers realised that instead of trying to create a common specification, all they had to do was use dedicated computers as gateways between each network, thus creating a 'network-of-networks'. In 1977 the concept was made a reality as a message was sent on a 94000-mile round trip from San Francisco to University College, London and back to the University of Southern California. An international network – or 'internet' – was created. The system continued to be used but only by scientists and specialists for many years.

In 1990 an Englishman, Tim Berners-Lee, working at CERN, the European Particles Physics Laboratories in Geneva, proposed a solution to the problem of capturing and coordinating the work of the scientists and then locating it in such a way that this accumulating knowledge was easily available. He devised a 'hypertext' system that would give access across the internet, allowing users to access the same information from different computer systems and add their own links to information. It also enabled links to be made to live data that kept changing. The system was called the world wide web. Shortly after this he devised a 'browser' that linked the resources on the internet in a uniform way. He also devised a protocol to specify the location of the information – the Unique Resource Locator (URL) – and one to specify how information exchanges between computers should be handled – the HyperText Transport Protocol (HTTP). Finally, he invented a uniform way to structure documents, proposing the use of HyperText Mark-up Language (HTML). In 1992 the browser was made publicly available to anyone with an internet connection to download.

In 1993 a University of Illinois team working at the National Center for Supercomputer Applications (NCSA) developed the CERN system, which used high powered workstations and the Unix operating system, to operate on PCs and Macintosh. In the same year one of the team, Marc Andreesen, posted a message on some specialist Usenet conferences. It read: 'By the power vested in me by nobody in particular, alpha/beta version 0.5 of NCSA's Motif-based networked information systems and World Wide Web browser, X Mosiac, is hereby released. Cheers, Marc.' The World Wide Web, as we know it, had been born.

With the help of Jim Clark, the wealthy founder of Silicon Graphics, Marc Andreesen and others in the team went on to set up Netscape. When the company went public it was valued at $3 billion, a valuation that in those days was huge.

within established frameworks. This involves dealing with rapidly changing and disparate information in a wide range of new technologies and in diverse, fragmented and often geographically widespread markets; charting a way through often uncertain political and unstable regulatory environments; facing competitors emerging from unexpected directions. So knowledge can be a powerful source of innovation. In these circumstances effective knowledge management – picking up and making sense of knowledge signals – is vital and knowledge networks, considered in Chapter 6, have an important part to play in this.

💡 Innovation and entrepreneurship

As we noted in Chapter 1, it is the work of Joseph Schumpeter that most strongly links entrepreneurship to innovation. He was the first person to challenge classical economics and the way it sought to optimise existing resources within a stable environment and treated disruptions as a 'god sent' external force. In his primary work, Schumpeter (1934) set out his overall theory of economic development – an endogenous process within capitalism of wrenching the economy out of its tendency towards one equilibrium position and towards a different one – a process of 'creative destruction'. This fundamental phenomenon entails the development of new combinations of the means of production, which Schumpeter labels 'enterprise' but we could equally call 'innovation', while the individuals carrying them out are called 'entrepreneurs'. These new combinations 'as a rule … must draw the necessary means of production from some old combinations'.

Schumpeter was arguing against traditional economic theory which presumed that the economy always tended towards equilibrium and that changes in that equilibrium could only occur through changes in the underlying conditions of the economy, such as population growth or changes in savings ratios, or external shocks, such as wars or natural disasters. The former were thought to change only slowly and the latter only occurred unpredictably. Schumpeter sought to explain the process of economic development as a process caused by enterprise – or innovation – and carried out by entrepreneurs.

For Schumpeter a normal healthy economy was one that was continually being 'disrupted' by technological innovation, producing the 50-year cycles of economic activity noticed earlier by the Russian economist, Nikolai Kondratieff. Using data on prices, wages and interest rates in France, Britain and the USA, Kondratieff first noticed these 'long waves' of economic activity in 1925.

⬚ Case insight   Trevor Baylis

In 1991 Trevor Baylis was watching a TV programme about the AIDS epidemic in Africa. It got him thinking about how information on AIDS prevention might be broadcast to people in a country where there was no electricity and batteries were prohibitively expensive. He quickly came up with a design for a clockwork radio. Despite being featured on radio and TV he could not convince people that it was a commercially viable product.

It was only when he teamed up with an entrepreneur, Christopher Staines, and a company called Liberty Life that the radio was produced and marketed. The entrepreneur was able to exploit the innovation in a way the inventor was not able to do. Production of his clockwork radio began in 1994. It can now be found across Africa. Without the entrepreneur the invention would not have reached the market place.

Unfortunately he was executed by Stalin some ten years later because he (accurately as it turned out) predicted that Russian farm collectivisation would lead to a decline in farm production. It was therefore left to Schumpeter to study these waves in depth.

Schumpeter said that each of these cycles was unique, driven by different clusters of industries. The upswing in a cycle started when new innovations came into general use:

▷ Water power, textiles and iron in the late eighteenth century.
▷ Steam, rail and steel in the mid nineteenthth century.
▷ Electricity, chemicals and the internal combustion engine in the early twentieth century.

These booms eventually petered out as the technologies matured and the market opportunities were fully exploited, only to start again as a new set of innovations changed the way things were done. For the last twenty years of the cycle the growth industries of the last technological wave might be doing exceptionally well. However they are, in fact, just repaying capital that is no longer needed for investment. This situation never lasts longer than twenty years and returns to investors then start to decline with the dwindling number of opportunities. Often this is precipitated by some form of crisis. After the twenty years of stagnation new technologies will emerge and the cycle will start again.

The other factor is that innovation – particularly technological innovation – also seems to generate growth that cannot be accounted for by changes in labour and capital. Although the return on investment may decline as more capital is introduced to an economy, any deceleration in growth is more than offset by the leverage effects of innovation. Because of this the rich Western countries have seen their return on investment increasing, whilst the poorer countries have not caught up.

By the time Schumpeter died in 1950 the next cycle of boom was starting, based upon oil, electronics, aviation and mass production. Another started in the 1980s based upon digital networks, software and new media. The internet and e-commerce triggered an even shorter boom in the late 1990s. One reason for this shortening cycle may be the more systematic approach entrepreneurs now have towards exploiting innovation.

But innovation does not happen as a random event. Central to the process are the entrepreneurs. It is they who introduce and then exploit the new innovations. For Schumpeter, 'the entrepreneur initiates change and generates new opportunities. Until imitators force prices and costs into conformity, the innovator is able to reap profits and disturb equilibrium'. By way of contrast, early classical economists such as Adam Smith saw the entrepreneurs as having a rather minor role in overall economic activity. Smith thought that they provided real capital, but did not play a leading or direct part in how the pattern of supply and demand was determined.

Aghion and Howitt (1992) have produced a formal restatement of Schumpeter's theories whereby new entrants replace existing inefficient firms. Other economists have emphasised the Schumpeterian assumption that innovation-based growth needs entrepreneurs and effective selection among entrepreneurs (Michelacci, 2003; Acemoglu et al., 2006). The theories of 'industrial evolution' mentioned in Chapter 1 focus on change as the central phenomenon and emphasise the role that knowledge plays in charting a way through the process. Acs et al. (2004, 2005) and Audretsch

🗁 Case insight
Great Ormond Street Hospital for Children

Ideas for innovations can come from unusual sources. The Great Ormond Street Hospital for Children took its inspiration from watching the McLaren and Ferrari Formula 1 racing teams take only six seconds to turn a car around at a pit stop. Doctors at the hospital were concerned by the time they took to move patients from the operating theatre to the intensive care unit where they recovered. Delays in emergency handover could cost lives, so they contacted Ferrari to see how the process might be improved. Ferrari explained that their pit-stop procedure was kept simple, with minimal movements all planned in advance. In fact it was so simple that it could be drawn on a single diagram. From that every member of the Ferrari team knew exactly what they had to do and when to do it in a coordinated fashion.

Ferrari then videoed the hospital's handovers. When the doctors watched it they were shocked at the lack of structure. Ferrari concluded that, with an ever-changing team and unpredictable demand, the hospital's handover teams needed a simple formula they could understand and work to – just like a pit-stop. And Ferrari helped the hospital to design it.

🗁 Case insight Swarfega

Not all innovations find a commercial application in the way they were originally envisaged. Swarfega is a green gel which is a dermatologically safe cleaner for the skin. It is widely used to remove grease and oil from hands in factories and households. In 2004 Audley Williamson sold the business he set up to manufacture his innovation for £135 million.

But the original product, developed in 1941, was not intended for degreasing hands at all. It was intended as a mild detergent to wash silk stockings. Unfortunately the invention of nylon and its application to nylon stockings rendered the product as obsolete as silk stockings. Watching workmen trying to clean their hands with a mixture of petrol, paraffin and sand which left them cracked and sore led Williamson to realise that there was a completely different commercial opportunity for his product.

(2007) have expanded on the notion that the important feature of entrepreneurs is their role as 'knowledge filters', facilitating 'knowledge spillovers' or 'knowledge transfers'.

Pulling together these strands, therefore, real innovation might be defined as a single 'mould-breaking' development in new products or services – or how they are produced (the materials used, the process employed or how the firm is organised to deliver them) or how or to whom they are marketed – that can be linked to a commercial opportunity and successfully exploited. However, in the real world frequent, incremental small-scale 'innovations' can create similar competitive advantage, with lower associated risk. And in the commercial world, both degree and frequency of innovation combine to produce competitive advantage.

Returning to Michael Porter's issue of national advantage, the agent which takes invention to the market place is indeed the entrepreneur or the entrepreneurial firm but what they are really seeking in doing this is innovation – difference – rather than invention, per se. It is innovation and entrepreneurship that are at the heart of success for the individual firm and of national advantage.

♀ Creativity and entrepreneurship

Bolton and Thompson (2000) stress the importance of creativity in the process of invention and innovation. They associate invention closely with creativity but also link it with entrepreneurship if an invention is to become a commercial opportunity to be exploited. 'Creativity is the starting point whether it is associated with invention or opportunity spotting. This creativity is turned to practical reality (a product, for example) through innovation. Entrepreneurship then sets that innovation in the context of an enterprise (the actual business), which is something of recognised value'. Like Porter, they perceive that creativity and invention need the entrepreneurial context, including the perception of opportunity, to become a business reality. These links between creativity, invention and innovation, opportunity perception and entrepreneurship are represented in Figure 3.3.

Another way of looking at the relationship between creativity and entrepreneurship and its real outcomes is shown in Figure 3.4. Only in quadrant A is there a winning combination of creativity and entrepreneurship. All other quadrants fail to

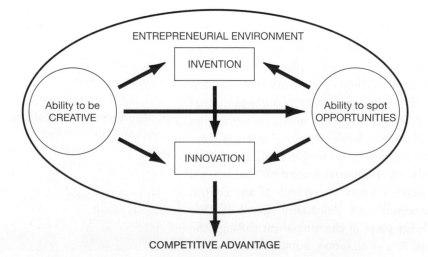

F3.3 Creativity, invention, opportunity and entrepreneurship

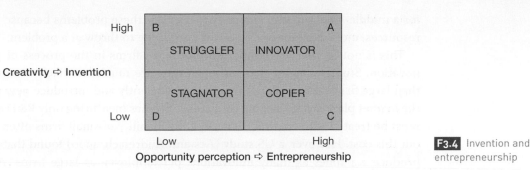

F3.4 Invention and entrepreneurship

achieve their full potential. In quadrant B there is a firm struggling with too many wasted ideas. It lacks an entrepreneurial orientation with the ability both to see the commercial application of the idea and to exploit it. In quadrant C there is a firm that lacks creativity but can at least copy and perhaps improve on the creative inventions coming from other firms if they have a commercial application. Firms in quadrant D, lack both creativity and entrepreneurship, are certain never to grow and indeed their very survival may be questioned.

Innovation and size

Just as entrepreneurs are not defined simply as owner-managers, entrepreneurial firms are not defined, necessarily, in terms of size. But there are linkages between size and innovation. Few small firms introduce really new products into their product range. Even fewer introduce really new products into the economy as a whole. This role is more likely to be undertaken by larger firms because of the resources they command. However, small firms can, and often do, introduce products or services that are clearly differentiated from those of the 'competition', to the point where one might question whether there is any direct competition. Indeed, this ability to differentiate clearly is a major element in their success. Is this innovation? Perhaps it is, but one would have to stretch Schumpeter's first or even his third criterion (opening up of a new market) to accommodate it.

Small firms are most likely to provide something marginally different from the competition in terms of the product or service, and thus find a gap in the market. They are also far more likely to innovate in terms of marketing and customer service (often low-cost options). They frequently find new routes to market first, for example 'direct' selling, via the phone, with call centres located in low-cost areas, or via the internet, offering similar advantages through the 'virtual' organisation. Small firms are often innovative in their approach to key account management and customer relationships. They find ways of networking with customers and suppliers so as to cut costs and lead times. Which of Schumpeter's categories do these fall into? They are all approaches an entrepreneurial firm of any size can adopt.

Many truly successful innovations, particularly product innovations but certainly the ones involving large amounts of capital, originate from large not small companies. There are few Dysons in this world who successfully struggle to bring a genuinely new product to the market themselves, against all the odds. There are just too many problems to sort out – not least of which is finding the finance. Moreover it is easier for a middle-sized or large company to sort out these problems because it has more resources, more experience ... more of everything to throw at a problem.

This is not to decry the importance of small firms in the process of product innovation. Studies suggest that, although they are much less likely to conduct R&D than large firms, they conduct them more efficiently and introduce new products to the market place faster than big companies. Studies measuring only R&D expenditure must be treated with caution because of the inability of small firms often to separate out this cost. However, a US study (Acs and Audretsch, 1990) found that small firms produce 2.4 times as many innovations per employee as large firms. A UK study covering a similar period (Pavitt et al., 1987) concluded that small firms are more likely to introduce fundamentally new innovations than large firms. In their review of innovation in small firms Deakins and Freel (2009) concluded that 'the innovative contributions of small firms vary across industry sectors and through the industry life cycle, at least with respect to technical innovations. In new industries, where technology is still evolving, small firms have a more significant role to play than in mature industries, where the innovation focus has switched to cost-reducing process innovation and minor product enhancements. However, in mature industries small firms may benefit from innovations in structure, supply or markets. In addition, small firms may enjoy comparative advantage in industries that serve smaller, fragmented markets where consumers value variety and where manufacturing flexibility carries a premium – irrespective of the age of the industry.

What seems clear is that innovative behaviour is not entirely related to firm size. It also relates to business activity, the industry, the nature of the innovation, and the type of company. Large firms outperform small firms where resources are important – because of capital intensity or because of scale of spending on R&D, advertising etc. or simply because of barriers to entry. Rothwell (1989) shows that, where no such prerequisite exists, the share of small firms in innovation is substantial. He concludes that 'innovative advantage is unequivocally associated with neither large nor small firms. The innovatory advantages of large firms are in the main associated with their relatively greater financial and technological resources, i.e. they are material advantages; small firm advantages are those of entrepreneurial dynamism, internal flexibility and responsiveness to changing circumstances, i.e. they are behavioural advantages'. It has also been pointed out that the advantages of large firms are generally the disadvantages of small firms, and vice versa, and therefore collaboration between the two sizes (inside or outside the same corporation) can create powerful synergistic relationships which benefit all parties (Vossen, 1998).

Innovation is important if a small firm wants to grow and be successful. In a study of fast-growing small firms matched against slow-growing firms, Storey et al. (1989) concluded that the owner-managers of the fast-growing firms were much more likely to emphasise their competitive advantage in areas such as innovation and product or service quality. By way of contrast, the owner-managers of the slow-growing firms emphasised price. Innovation, therefore, is not only the vehicle for faster growth but also a means of fending off competition and being able to charge a higher price.

In fact, Schumpeter said nothing about whether innovation could be best carried out by small or large firms. To him this was irrelevant. An entrepreneur could just as easily work in a large firm as in a small one. However, small firms do have the inherent flexibility needed to spot market opportunities and capitalise on them quickly if, that is, they are run by an entrepreneur. Small firms typically lack the bureaucratic, hierarchical structures of large firms.

◌ Innovation and location

There is evidence that innovation can be geographically concentrated in certain areas, particularly with respect to smaller firms, and this leads to 'clusters' of small firms that form mutually supportive networks. This is often referred to as 'innovative milieu' theory (Camagni, 1991; Keeble and Wilkinson, 1999). This theory is based on the assumption that knowledge is a crucial element in the process of innovation (Simmie, 2002) and, whereas large firms have their own R&D functions to help generate this, small firms have to rely on networking and a process of 'socialisation' that allows them to collect information and accumulate knowledge (Capello, 1999). Geographical proximity facilitates this process of knowledge transfer and hence these clusters of small firms can be observed (Porter, 1998b; Keeble and Wilkinson, op. cit.).

Within these clusters, where there is the development and sharing of a common base of knowledge, 'collective learning' is taking place. This allows the firms to coordinate their actions so as to solve the technological and organisational problems they face (Lorenz, 1996, quoted in Keeble and Wilkinson, op. cit.). 'Collective learning' can be either conscious – as in research collaborations – or unconscious. Unconscious learning occurs where the skills and knowledge are vested in a workforce that is shared between the small firms. These clusters therefore attract similar small firms because it is a low-cost way of gaining knowledge. This underlines the importance of networking, particularly in relation to knowledge transfer – something to which we shall return in Chapter 7. It will be interesting to see how far the development of the internet affects the formation of clusters based on geographic proximity in future years.

Cambridge, UK, is home to a number of high technology clusters

Cambridge in the UK is home to a number of high technology clusters and is an example of both types of learning. In computing, not only are there research collaborations between Cambridge University and the firms in the cluster, but there is also a skilled workforce graduating from the University and a group of academics willing to work part time with them. Such is the strength of the cluster and importance of the University that Bill Gates endowed it with sufficient funds to finance new state-of-the-art computer laboratories. Universities generally are seen as an important source of knowledge and therefore important to the development of clusters, hence the various initiatives to encourage them to work more closely with industry. Universities generate 'public knowledge' and this 'spills over' into the commercial world through conferences and seminars, consultants, the personal networks of academics and industrial researchers (MacPherson, 1998), and commercial spin-offs (Mitra, 2000).

💼 Innovative Potential Indicator

Innovation is the prime tool entrepreneurs use to create or exploit opportunity and is one of the two most important distinguishing features of their character. The Innovative Potential Indicator (IPI) was developed by Dr Fiona Patterson based upon research on employees in established companies. It is published by Oxford Psychologists Press. It claims to be the only psychometric test able to identify those people who have the potential to become innovative thinkers.

Dr Patterson identifies ten types of people:

1   The **Change Agent** who thrives on change and is independent, who conjures up the strangest ways to solve problems and who does not stick to what they were told. This is the innovative thinker who embodies one of the most essential characteristics that differentiate entrepreneurs from owner-managers.
2   The **Consolidator**, whose rigidity and independence militates against innovative thinking but is a safety net because of their preference for the status quo.
3   The **Harmoniser**, who likes the challenge but does not disclose good ideas for fear of upsetting people.
4   The **Firefighter**, who flits from one idea to another in an imaginative but unpredictable way.
5   The **Cooperator**, who likes change but `goes with the flow'.
6   The **Catalyst**, who is good at thinking up ideas but soon loses interest.
7   The **Inhibited Innovator**, whose brainwaives could be valuable but lacks the confidence to push it forward.
8   The **Incremental Innovator**, who dreams up radical ideas but likes to implement them in a step-by-step way which can appear inflexible.
9   The **Spice-of-Life**, whose dominant characteristic is the need to be doing something, anything, new.
10 The **Middle-of-the-Road**, who is good at blending ideas but is ambivalent about them.

The IPI questionnaire asks for agreement/disagreement to 36 statements about how you approach change, how adaptable you are and how you stand up to others. Based upon your answers, it scores you on four main areas of behaviour which Dr Patterson's research shows can be used to establish whether a person has innovative potential. Scores can be between 20 and 80 on each dimension. The dimensions are:

▷ Motivation to change (MTC).
▷ Willingness to behave in a challenging way (CB).
▷ Willingness to adapt and use tried and tested approaches (AD).
▷ Consistency of working style which indicates efficiency and orderliness (CWS).

Change Agents have high MTC and CB scores, and low AD and CWS scores. So, for example, Trevor Baylis, the inventor of the clockwork radio, had a MTC score of 70, a CB score of 60, an AD score of 25 and a CWS score of 35 (*The Times*, 14 March 2000).

📖 Case with questions Big companies and new ideas

LEGO – the well known children's building system – has been around for a long time and, in an age when new toys come and go with astonishing rapidity and technology-based toys like video games are reaching astonishing heights of sophistication, it might be difficult to understand the enduring market appeal of these basic building blocks. Well the answer is that LEGO has changed with the market and the company, currently owned by the founder's grandson Kjeld Kirk Christiansen, continues to invest large sums around the world to understand changes in children's tastes and to explore new product developments based around its mission 'to inspire children to explore and challenge their own creative potential'.

Concept and product development take place primarily at the Concept Centre within the company's headquarters in Billund. This creative core is made up of 120 designers representing about 15 nationalities, most of whom trained at art school. The company also has what it calls 'listening posts' – otherwise known as Concept Labs – in Munich, Barcelona, Los Angeles and Tokyo. At these Labs children from four very different countries are encouraged to try out different combinations with the same LEGO pieces and create worlds of their own, which the company can incorporate into its 'play themes'. The Labs try to spot trends in children's play, to understand the motivations behind this and to translate them into what it means for the company and new product development – effectively trying to systematically understand children's creativity by observing them at play. The Labs also take an active role in the product concept and early development phase of any new product.

☐ More information on Lego can be found on their website: www.lego.com

LG – a Korean electronics firm – aims to integrate technological developments with design. Design is a key part of LG's culture. The company's design philosophy for mobile phones is to 'appeal to customers' emotions' a concept originally called 'haptic', meaning the feeling of touch but broadened to include all five senses – 'touch, smell the glowing lights, all the emotional things'. LG's products must be technologically advanced and functionally effective, but then most electronic products are. The reasons why people buy one product rather than another are to do with the intangible elements – and design and brand image have a crucial part to play in this. And whilst the functional elements of any product are usually easy to copy, these less tangible elements are more difficult. LG believes that good design enhances its brand image and this allows it to position its products at the premium end of the market.

Designers are encouraged to do 'town-watching' – visiting the chic streets of Hongdae or Cheongdam-dong to spot new design trends. It was on one of these trips that the trend towards more natural shapes was identified. Eventually this was incorporated into the KG800 mobile phone – the 'Chocolate Phone' – which won a Red Dot award. The phone has nothing to do with chocolate, LG just thought that the name was memorable. This was the first mobile phone in the world to have a touch sensitive key pad. Seventeen months after its launch it had sold 10 million units and spawned a limited edition 'White Chocolate' phone with a lavender-scented keypad which was sold on Valentines Day 2006. The phone model for 2007 was the sophisticated Prada phone.

☐ More information on LG can be found on their website: www.lge.com

Hallmark – the well known greeting cards company – was founded in 1910 when Joyce Clyde Hall started selling two shoeboxes of postcards in Kansas City. Hallmark now design about 19,000 new greeting cards every year. Each card costs about £40,000 to produce and is expected to generate some £85,000 in sales. Hallmark take creativity and innovation seriously. Their philosophy, work environment and development programmes are designed to encourage creative thinking. Their global headquarters is still in Kansas and their 800 in-house creative staff are based there. They have access to the world's biggest creative library with some 20,000 volumes and 175 current periodicals. They also have programme

→

of visiting speakers, including writers, photographers and artists. Their staff development programme is diverse, with courses on working with Hallmark's colour management process but also classes on sculpting and even doll-making. They have a 'creative renewal programme' for staff who feel they are losing their edge which is based at their own 'creativity retreat', Kearney Farm, an old farmhouse set in a 172 acre estate. It boasts its own art studio and regular creative brainstorming sessions are held there. Hallmark also organises research visits to overseas countries so that staff keep in touch with 'emotions' in different countries. However there is a hard edge and slogans on some office walls remind staff how much a card that does not sell will cost.

The company takes trend-spotting seriously and employs staff to constantly scan the environment to monitor new developments. Innovations include e-cards that can be sent via Hallmark's own website. You can even create your own card. The site also has a hugely popular 'Say-it-with-music' line where you can send a CD-quality sound card with a choice of more than 100 music artists as well as dialogue and themes from popular movies and TV shows. With over 250 'designs', they feature the original artists and songs and link to the captions and sentiment of the card. The cards even appear on websites such as YouTube, with people lip-synching along to the cards' 45-second music clips.

☐ More information on Hallmark can be found on their website: www.hallmark.com

QUESTIONS

1 Why is innovation important to each of these companies?

2 How do they link creativity and innovation with market opportunities?

3 What are the lessons for a start-up business?

▷ Summary

▷ Innovation is difficult to define. It is about introducing new products, services or processes, opening up new markets, identifying new sources of supply of raw materials or creating new types of industrial organisation. It can be argued that real innovation is more than that – it is about breaking the mould and doing things differently. That might involve invention or developing a completely new industrial process, as with **McDonald's**. But to be successful it must be linked to customer demand.

▷ However, competitive advantage can equally be gained by frequent, incremental innovations – a strategy that is less risky and from which the majority of commercially significant innovations have come. It is degree or scale and frequency of innovation that combine to produce competitive advantage.

▷ Some innovations can, however, be radical or discontinuous. This can be triggered by technological change like the invention of the world wide web and other dramatic changes in the status quo.

▷ Some inventors, like **Trevor Baylis**, are not necessarily innovators. They need the help of an entrepreneur or an entrepreneurial organisation to link their invention to customer demand. However, others, like **James Dyson**, can be inventor, innovator and entrepreneur all in one. Whilst creativity is at the core of invention and innovation, so too is the ability to spot market opportunities – and this is one very important role of the entrepreneur.

▷ Historically there have been cycles of innovation that disrupted economies, causing rapid growth. These are usually technology-led but facilitated by entrepreneurial activity.

▷ Figure 3.3 shows how invention can be successfully exploited in an entrepreneurial environment. It involves matching an invention or innovation, which comes from a creative idea, to an opportunity in the market place. As in the case of **Swarfega**, there can be more than one opportunity and creativity needs equally to be applied to the search for opportunities.

▷ Innovation in one market might involve 'copying' products or services in another. **Great Ormond Street Hospital for Children** 'copied' how Ferrari organised its pit-stops so as to improve its hand-over from theatre to intensive care unit.

▷ Small firms produce more than their fair share of innovations and seem to do it more efficiently than large firms. However, they tend to do this in sectors where resources, in particular capital, are less important. Dyson would seem to be a notable exception. Innovation is not entirely related to firm size. It also relates to business activity, industry, nature of innovation and the type of company. Small and large firms have advantages in producing different types of innovation.

▷ Geographical proximity facilitates the process of knowledge transfer and hence clusters of small firms can be observed, sharing 'collective learning' either through conscious or unconscious mechanisms. This underlines the importance of networks, a topic to which we shall return.

⏻ **Further resources are available at www.palgrave.com/business/burns**

📄 Essays and discussion topics

1 Is invention good? Is it the same as innovation?
2 Do you agree with Michael Porter that 'invention and entrepreneurship are at the heart of national advantage'?
3 What do you think constitutes innovation? Give examples.
4 Are innovations that 'break the mould' really just inventions?
5 Is incremental innovation better than radical innovation?
6 Can an adaptor also be an innovator?
7 What is the relationship between innovation and change?
8 Why are entrepreneurs interested in innovation?
9 In the real world, can you measure the scale or frequency of innovation?
10 What steps would a 'copier' have to take to become an innovator?

11 What steps would a 'struggler' have to take to become an innovator?
12 What are the threats and opportunities presented by discontinuous innovation? Are small firms better placed to cope with this than large firms?
13 List the advantages and disadvantages small firms have over large firms in introducing innovation.
14 What are the main barriers to innovation in large firms?
15 What are the main barriers to innovation in small firms?
16 Large firms are likely to be more innovative than small firms. Discuss.
17 With the development of the internet geographic clusters of small firms sharing 'collective learning' will become a thing of the past. Discuss.
18 If you want to make a big return, you need to take big risks – that is what entrepreneurship is really about. Discuss.

↻ Exercises and assignments

1 Answer the Innovation Potential Indicator questionnaire and assess your innovative potential. You can get more details of how to obtain it from the website of Oxford Psychologists Press on www.opp.co.uk.
2 Research Dyson. How is the company doing since James Dyson retired? Does it continue to grow? Does it continue to innovate? Have any innovations failed? If so, why? How has its strategy changed over the years? What part does marketing play in the success of Dyson?

3 Write up a case study of successful innovation in a small firm. Analyse why it was successful.
4 Research the commercial reasons for the success of the Mini. How important is good marketing to the success of an innovation?
5 Write up a case study of a 'creative' firm. Analyse the factors that contribute to it being creative.
6 Find out how Britain performs compared to other countries in terms of its ability to innovate.

📖 References

Acemoglu, D., Aghion, P. and Zilibotti, F. (2006) 'Distance to the Frontier, Selection and Economic Growth', *Journal of the European Economic Association*, 4.

Acs, Z.J. and Audretsch, D.B. (1990) *Innovation and Small Firms*, Cambridge, MA: MIT Press.

Acs, Z., Audretsch, D. Braunerhjelm, P. and Carlsson, P. (2004) 'The Missing Link: The Knowledge Filter and Entrepreneurship in Endogenous Growth', *CEPR Discussion Paper 5409*, CEPR London.

Acs, Z., Audretsch, D. Braunerhjelm, P. and Carlsson, P. (2005) 'Growth and Entrepreneurship: An Empirical assessment', *CEPR Discussion Paper 5409*, CEPR London.

Aghion, P. and Howitt , P. (1992) 'A Model for Growth through Creative Destruction', *Econometrica*, 60.

Audretsch, D. (1995), 'Innovation, growth and survival', *International Journal of Industrial Organisation*, 13.

Audretsch, D.B. (2007) 'Entrepreneurship Capital and Economic Growth', *Oxford Review of Economic Policy*, 23(1).

Berkhout, F. and Green, K. (2003) *International Journal of Innovation Management*, 6(3), Special issue on Managing Innovation for Sustainability.

Bessant, J. (1999) 'Developing Continuous Improvement Capability', *International Journal of Innovation Management*, 2.

Bolton, B. and Thompson, J. (2000) *Entrepreneurs: Talent, Temperament, Technique*, Oxford: Butterworth-Heinemann.

Camagni, R. (ed.) (1991) *Innovative Networks: Spatial Perspectives*, London: Belhaven.

Cannon, T. (1985) 'Innovation, Creativity and Small Firm Organisation', *International Small Business Journal*, 4, 1.

Capello, R. (1999) 'Spatial Transfer of Knowledge in High Technology Milieux: Learning versus Collective Learning Processes', *Regional Studies*, 33.

Christensen, C. (1997) *The Innovator's Dilemma*, Cambridge, Mass: Harvard Business School Press.

Deakins, D. and Freel, M. (2009) *Entrepreneurship and Small Firms*, 5th edn, London: McGraw Hill.

Hamel, G. and Prahalad, C.E. (1991) 'Corporate Imagination and Expeditionary Marketing', *Harvard Business Review*, 69(4) (July–August).

Kanter, R.M. (1983), *The Change Masters: Innovation and Productivity in American Corporations*, New York: Simon & Schuster.

Keeble, D. and Wilkinson, F. (1999) 'Collective Learning and Knowledge Development in the Evolution of Regional Clusters of High Technology SMEs in Europe', *Regional Studies*, 33.

Kirton, M. (1976) 'Adaptors and Innovators: A Description and Measure', *Journal of Applied Psychology*, October.

MacPherson, A.D. (1998) 'Academic–Industry Linkages and Small Firm Innovation: Evidence from the Scientific Instruments Sector', *Entrepreneurship and Regional Development*, 10(4).

Mellor, R.B. (2005) *Sources and Spread of Innovation in Small e-Commerce Companies*, Skodsborgvej: Forlaget Globe.

Michelacci, C. (2003), 'Low Returns in R&D due to Lack of Entrepreneurial Skills', *Economic Journal*, 113.

Mintzberg, H. (1983) *Structures in Fives: Designing Effective Organisations*, London: Prentice-Hall.

Mitra, J. (2000) 'Nurturing and Sustaining Entrepreneurship: University, Science Park, Business and Government Partnership in Australia', *Industry and Higher Education*, June.

Morris, M.H. and Kuratko, D.F. (2002) *Corporate Entrepreneurship: Entrepreneurial Development within Organisations*, Fort Worth, TX: Harcourt College Publishers.

Pavitt, K., Robinson, M. and Townsend, J. (1987) 'The Size Distribution of Innovating Firms in the UK: 1945–1983', *Journal of Industrial Economics*, 45.

Porter, M. E. (1990) *The Competitive Advantage of Nations*, New York: Free Press.

Porter, M.E. (1998a) *On Competition*, Boston, MA: Harvard Business School.

Porter, M.E. (1998b) 'Clusters and the New Economics of Competition', *Harvard Business Review*, Nov–Dec.

Rothwell, R. (1989) 'Small Firms, Innovation and Industrial Change', *Small Business Economics*, 1, 51–64.

Schmidt, G.M. (2004) 'Low-end and High-end Encroachments for New Products', *Journal of Knowledge Management*, 4(1).

Schumpeter, J.A. (1934) *The Theory of Economic Development: An Inquiry into Profits, Capital, Credit, Interest and the Business Cycle* (trans. by Redvers Opie), Oxford University Press.

Schumpeter, J.A. (1983/1996) *The Theory of Economic Development*, New Brunswick, NJ: Transaction Publishers.

Simmie, J. (2002) 'Knowledge Spillovers and Reasons for the Concentration of Innovative SMEs', *Urban Studies*, 39, 5–6.

Storey, D.J., Watson, R. and Wynarcyzk, P. (1989) 'Fast Growth Small Business: Case Studies of 40 Small Firms in North East England', Department of Employment.

Tidd, J., Bessant, J. and Pavitt, K. (2005) *Managing Innovation: Integrating Technological, Market and Organisational Change*, 3rd edn, Chichester: Wiley.

Utterback, J. and Acee, H.J. (2005) 'Disruptive Technologies: An Expanded View', *International Journal of Innovation Management*, 9(1).

Van Grundy, A. (1987) 'Organisational Creativity and Innovation', in S.G. Isaksen, *Frontiers of Creativity Research*, Buffalo, NY: Brearly.

Vossen, R.W. (1998) 'Relative Strengths and Weaknesses of Small Firms in Innovation', *International Small Business Journal*, 16(3), 88–94.

4 Social and civic entrepreneurship

▷ **The rise of social entrepreneurship**
▷ **Social enterprise and the social economy**
▷ **Legal forms of social enterprise in the UK**
▷ **The social entrepreneur**
▷ **The growth and development of the social enterprise**
▷ **The civic entrepreneur**
▷ **The dangers of social entrepreneurship**
▷ **Summary**

Case insights
▷ The Maggie Keswick Jencks Cancer Caring Centres Trust
▷ Abs-Kids
▷ Bright Ideas Trust
▷ Seven Stories

Cases with questions
▷ The Big Issue
▷ Ridgeway Primary School
▷ Nin Castle, Phoebe Emerson and Goodone

the way that not-for-profit organisations see themselves, and are funded. Brinckerhoff (2000) actually says that social entrepreneurship is one of the essential characteristics of successful not-for-profit organisations. And an important extra dimension to social entrepreneurship, particularly in the USA, has become fund-raising.

Social entrepreneurship is therefore an emerging but ill-defined concept. It can be loosely defined as the use of entrepreneurial behaviour for social rather than profit objectives. Social entrepreneurs therefore differ from business entrepreneurs in terms of their mission. Their primary purpose is to 'create superior social value for their clients' (Mort et al., 2003). They 'identify under-utilised resources – people, buildings, equipment – and find ways of putting them to use to satisfy unmet social needs' (Leadbeater, op. cit.). They may work in not-for-profit organisations, ethical businesses, government or other public bodies. However, in practice the term social entrepreneurship covers two overlapping activities:

1 Combining an income-generating activity with a social goal – often called a 'social enterprise', but this can also include entrepreneurial fund-raising activities undertaken by charities. Often this is a response to a changing environment of reduced grants.

2 Creating social change at a community level – normally through voluntary or community groups – without necessarily involving income-generating activities. This is also sometimes called 'civic innovation', which Fowler (2000) defines as creating 'something different in the way citizens understand and solve a social problem. It is characterised by a new set of civic institutions or patterns of social relations.' Such hybrid organisations combine economic, environmental and social principles or practices.

There is further confusion. As with business entrepreneurship, the literature on social entrepreneurship often confuses the act of starting a new enterprise, albeit social, with entrepreneurial behaviour. Mort (op. cit.) defines social entrepreneurship as 'leading to the establishment of a new social enterprise and the continued innovation in existing ones'. However, a social enterprise – whether old or new – may not necessarily act entrepreneurially. Continuing innovation is the defining characteristic of entrepreneurship. Some authors recognise this, for example Leadbeater (op. cit.) says that social entrepreneurs 'innovate new welfare services and new ways of delivering existing ones'. However, note in this definition the absence of income-generating activities. Finally, just like business entrepreneurship, there is a strong focus in the literature on the individual rather than the organisation (see, for example, Thompson et al., 2000).

A further distinction is the use of the term 'integrated' as opposed to 'complementary' social entrepreneurship. The term 'integrated social entrepreneurship' is used when surplus-generating activities simultaneously create social benefit, with one objective not getting in the way of the other. The art of integration, according to Fowler (op. cit.), is to 'marry the development agendas with market opportunities and then manage them properly so that they are synergistic not draining.' One example he uses is the Grameen Bank. This bank was set up in Bangladesh in 1976 by Muhammad Yunis (for which he received the Nobel Peace Prize in 2006) and now provides micro-credit – tiny loans – to the poor of 36 countries to help start and grow tiny businesses. (Grameen means 'bank of the villages' in Bangla.) It uses micro-credit to establish a new sort of self-sustaining rural association between women in particular. The examples Fowler uses seek to 'reduce external financial dependency, increase development impact and spread risk.' Today Grameen Bank is owned by the rural poor it serves.

All too often, however, this is not the case and the one agenda 'contaminates' the other, perhaps leading to reduced efficiency and effectiveness on the commercial side or dilution of the social objectives on the other. When surpluses from the commercial activity are simply used as a source of cross-subsidy for the social objectives, rather than producing social benefits themselves, this can more accurately be called 'complementary social entrepreneurship' – which almost takes us back to companies like Lush in the UK and Timberland in the USA.

Social enterprise and the social economy

A social enterprise is a business set up primarily for social objectives whose surpluses are reinvested in the business or in the community for that purpose. They are often formed to address particular social or environmental needs and have led the way in combining ethical trading with commercial success. Many social enterprises operate in the commercial sector. In 2009 it was estimated that there were 55 000 social enterprises in the UK that together generated annual turnover of £27 billion, contributing £8.4 billion to the UK economy (Jonathan Kestenbaum, *The Times*, 23 January 2009). Examples are Jamie Oliver's Fifteen restaurant group and Cafédirect. Social enterprises are frequently the innovative start-up that is the brainchild of the social entrepreneur, and therefore the terms often go hand in hand. As we shall see in the next section, social enterprises can take a number of forms. Definitions do vary, although the primary mission of a social enterprise is always social. In the USA a defining characteristic seems to be the ability to earn revenues and to reinvest them to achieve the social aim. In the UK the emphasis is on community involvement and separation from government.

> There is a gap in the market, and that gap has developed because no matter how much money we have as an economy, public services are never going to be able to fulfil all of society's needs and expectations in terms of health, education and social welfare ... Part of the problem is that socially entrepreneurial behaviour unsettles a lot of people. Social entrepreneurs by their nature are seeing gaps in the market, developing new ways of doing things, and challenging others to do things differently. People are suspicious of that and don't know how to see it as a constructive force.
>
> ☐ Adele Blakebrough, co-founder of Community Action Network Professional Manager, March 2004

Pearce (2003) characterises the social enterprise as:

▷ Having a primarily social purpose, with a secondary commercial activity;
▷ Achieving that purpose by engaging in trade;
▷ Not distributing profits to individuals but reinvesting profits either in the enterprise or new social ventures;
▷ Democratically involving members in its governance;
▷ Being openly accountable to a defined constituency and a wider community.

Pearce tries to explain this myriad of interlinking concepts by talking about three systems of the economy – private, public and social – delineated in two dimensions – trading/non-trading and global/community-based. These are shown in Figure 4.1. The first system is the private sector which concentrates on trading, with the objective of profit maximisation. But even this has its legal and illegal sectors. It operates on anything from a local to a global basis. The second is the public services and government, which operates in a planned, non-trading way. It is characterised as bureaucratic and inefficient. It also operates on anything from a local to a global basis. The third

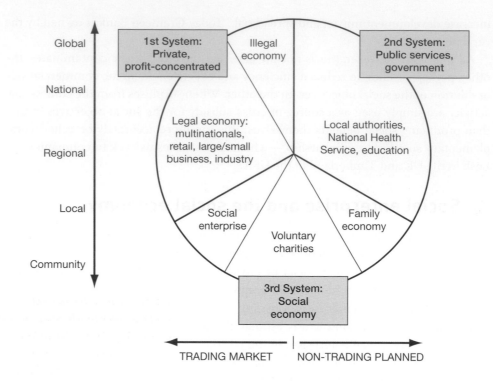

F4.1 The three systems of the economy

Source: Pearce (2003)

system is the social economy that includes social enterprise, voluntary and charity organisations and the family economy. This is far more community-based and can be both planned and based upon market trading. The use of the word 'system', rather than sector, in this context is deliberate as it is meant to imply that each system is not homogenous.

In the UK social enterprise is seen as a way of encouraging local or community involvement. It has been encouraged into public sector delivery of services, such as health and social care, transport, fostering and adoption, recycling and sports and leisure. This is partly because social enterprise is also seen as innovative and efficient, but partly as a way of getting extra funding into the service. Nevertheless combining the advantages of all three sectors has obvious appeal.

♀ Legal forms of social enterprise in the UK

So what precisely is a social enterprise? The answer to this is not straightforward. It is really what the business does with its profits that determines whether or not it is a social enterprise, rather than its specific legal structure. It need not even be registered as a charity to be a social enterprise, although this does offer a number of benefits, not least significant tax relief, albeit with increased regulation and less flexibility. Notwithstanding this proviso, in the UK there are six main forms of social enterprise.

Unincorporated associations

These are informal associations of individuals that can form (and reform) quickly. They enjoy great freedom as they are not regulated. They are not registered with any body, but they can apply for charitable status, which means they have to comply with the regulations of the Charity Commission (www.charity-commission.gov.uk). They can trade but cannot own assets as an association has no legal status. However, it may be possible to set up a trust to legally hold ownership of property and assets for the

📖 Case with questions The Big Issue

The Big Issue is probably the most prominent example of social entrepreneurship in the UK. Initially started up as a non-profit organisation by John Bird in 1991, and then backed by Gordon and Anita Roddick (of Body Shop fame), it is now a limited company that donates its profits to the Big Issue Foundation, a charity that addresses the problems of the homeless. The scheme started in London, based on a similar idea in New York.

The Big Issue produces a magazine of the same name which is sold by homeless people on the streets of many UK towns and cities. Its aim is to allow them to work to earn a living – enabling them to address their personal poverty and retake control of their lives – and to campaign on social exclusion issues. The magazine is sold to consumers on its quality rather than as a means of securing a charitable donation. However, the fact that it is sold by the homeless, exclusively on the streets, rather than in magazine stores or by volunteers, makes the nature of the transaction not altogether straightforward. When they are asked to buy, consumers come face-to-face with beneficiaries and can see that they are trying to help themselves out of their situation. Sellers are first given a small number of magazines and thereafter have to buy copies to sell on. One key aspect of the transaction is that the consumer is asked for a limited and relatively small financial contribution (the cover price was £1.70 in 2010). This legitimises small donations. In this way giving small amounts to a morally justified and legitimate cause is made easy.

The Big Issue drops in on David Cameron

These factors have led researchers to conclude that 'the *Big Issue* is rarely bought for its own sake, simply as a quality product, but that its intrinsic value to the consumer does play a role in whether or not the initiative is supported. In other words, consumers buy it because they believe that they are helping the homeless (to help themselves)' (Hibbert et al., 2002).

☐ Up-to-date information on the Big Issue can be found on their website: www.bigissue.com

QUESTIONS

1 Is this an example of social entrepreneurship? If so, why?

2 Is the Big Issue a social enterprise? If so, why?

3 Is it an entrepreneurial response to a social problem? If so, why?

4 Is it the best response to this social problem? What problems do you see with it?

community they are intended to benefit. Because these associations are unincorporated, each individual in the association is personally liable for any debts or loans.

Trusts

These are run according to the social objectives set out in the trust deed. Many organisations in health care and education are structured as trusts. Trusts are unincorporated bodies. Trustees manage the trust on behalf of the community for which it was set up, which will be laid down, along with the trust's social objectives, in the trust deed. The trust can hold assets but it cannot distribute any profits. However, trustees are personally liable for any debts or loans. Trusts may need to register with Companies House (www.companieshouse.gov.uk) and, since they have social objectives, they can apply for charitable status through the Charities Commission.

Charitable social enterprises

These are set up wholly for charitable purposes that benefit the public. They must be registered with Companies House or the Financial Services Authority (www.fsa.gov.uk). They are regulated by Charity Commission regulations (HM Revenue & Customs in Northern Ireland and the Office of the Scottish Charities Regulator in Scotland). Trusts benefit from tax and rate relief and any surplus must be reinvested. The founder of a charity shapes its creation but not its strategic direction or operation. The charity is run by directors or trustees, who cannot be paid for their work. They shape its strategic direction.

Community benefit societies (BenComs)

These are incorporated industrial and provident societies, set up with social objectives, which conduct business for the benefit of their community. They are run and managed by their members but profits cannot be distributed among members and must be returned to the community. BenComs can raise funds by issuing shares to the public and can be registered as charities. They are regulated by the Financial Services Authority and must submit annual accounts. BenComs different from cooperatives in that cooperatives operate for the mutual benefit of their members – which is not necessarily the same as the community – and therefore cannot be registered as charities.

Community interest companies (CIC)

These are essentially limited liability companies, registered with Companies House or the Financial Services Authority, but with extra requirements. They can be limited by shares or by guarantee. They must demonstrate their social and environmental impact each year by issuing an annual community interest company report alongside the annual accounts. They must operate transparently and not pay directors excessive salaries. Profit distribution is also regulated; companies limited by guarantee may not distribute profits, whereas those limited by shares can do so under certain circumstances. CICs must have an asset lock, which means that profits or assets cannot be transferred for less than their full market value. People who start a CIC can steer the business as they see fit as they will be directors, and this might suit social entrepreneurs best as an organisational form. More information can be found on www.cicregulator.gov.uk.

A CIC cannot be a charity. However, it is common for it to run alongside one. So, for example, it is common for a social organisation to have two forms: a CIC, which runs in a business-like way while giving the community a stake in how it is run, and a charitable social enterprise to which the CIC's profits are transferred and which decides how they are spent. This dual form can maximise tax advantages. It also means that the charity can apply for grant funding that will help to get projects up and running, while the income generated by the CIC means that the organisation is not totally dependent on these grants or the goodwill of donors or government.

Charitable incorporated organisations (CIO)

These are a new form of incorporated organisation that is set up for charitable purposes and therefore reports to the Charity Commission rather than Companies

House or the Financial Services Authority. Like CICs they must benefit local communities and have an asset lock. They are not able to distribute profits or assets to their members. Unlike CICs which have directors, CIOs have charity trustees. CICs and charitable social enterprises can convert into CIOs.

Business Link publish a guide to legal structures for social enterprises that is free to download (www.businesslink.gov.uk). They also provide signposts to specialist institutions providing finance such as the Community Development Finance Institution as well as government-backed funding.

Case insights

Social enterprises come in many forms and many sizes. Here are a few examples.

The Maggie Keswick Jencks Cancer Caring Centres Trust (just called Maggie's Centre) was set up by Maggie Keswick Jencks, a landscape designer with an international reputation, just before her death from breast cancer in 1996. Maggie's has

6 centres and 3 'interim centres' and dealt with 77 000 visitors in 2008. Each centre is located next to a NHS cancer hospital. All of the centres are designed by leading architects, such as Frank Gehry, based upon the belief of the Trust founder that design affects how we feel. Each is unique, being built around a kitchen on an open plan basis – no closed doors – and designed to be friendly and welcoming. Each is staffed by health professionals, including a cancer nurse and a psychologist, and a fundraiser. Maggie's is piloting online support groups, managed by psychologists.

☐ Visit the website on www.maggiescentres.org.uk

After being bullied at school, Abbi Morrall, then aged 12, and her stepfather, Phill Faulkner set up the **Abs-Kids** website in 2005. (Abs stands for Anti-Bullying Shared.) They used £4500 of their own money, which was supplemented by £500 won from the Archbishop of Canterbury's Champions of Respect Awards. The site is child friendly. All incoming e-mails are anonymous and are still answered by Abbi. Her mother deals with website administration. Initially the site was promoted through local press and radio, but a television appearance in 2006 boosted its popularity enormously. Abbi raises money to update the site through t-shirt sales. She plans to produce data packs for schools to buy and download and wants to do more, such as launching the site in different languages

☐ Visit the website on www.abs-kids.co.uk

The **Bright Ideas Trust** was set up by Tim Campbell, winner of the first TV *Apprentice* series in 2005. It was established in 2007 with Richard Morris and Paul Humphries to help 16- to 30-year-olds from socially excluded groups who are not in education, employment or training to set up their own business. Tim invested £2000 of his own money and got the support of the consultancy firm Accenture and law firms Herbert Smith and Taylor Wessing. As well as providing guidance, Bright Ideas takes a stake in the businesses it funds, just like venture capitalists.

☐ Visit the website on www.brightideastrust.com.

The **Seven Stories** children's book museum in Newcastle upon Tyne is the first museum in the UK wholly dedicated to British children's books. It was founded in 2005 by two women who wanted to inspire local children to love books, and is now run by 40 paid workers and some 25 volunteers. It has exhibitions of books, drop-in family activities, storytelling, author and illustrator events – all intended to make books exciting – open to families and school parties. The museum charges for entry. It also has its own bookshop which claims to be the largest independent specialist children's bookshop in Britain with over 50 000 titles. It is a not-for-profit charitable trust governed by a board of trustees.

☐ Visit the website on www.sevenstories.org.uk.

💡 The social entrepreneur

As you might expect, social entrepreneurs seem to enjoy most of the character traits and behavioural characteristics of their business counterparts. Thompson (op. cit.) says:

> They are *ambitious* and *driven*. They have been able to clarify and *communicate* an *inspirational mission*; around this they have *recruited* and *inspired* paid staff, users and partners, as well as an army of volunteers. They have known where they could acquire resources, some of which they have 'begged, stolen or borrowed.' But their vision has been for something which will *add value* for the underprivileged sections of the community. The development of *relationships* and *networks* of contacts has brought *trust*, visibility, credibility and cooperation which has been used as an intellectual base from which the physical and financial capital required to generate social capital could be found. *Creativity* invariably featured. By understanding and managing the inherent *risks* – the projects are often financially fragile with *limited resourcing*; and the targeted beneficiaries may be prone to stray – the social entrepreneurs have been able to overcome the inevitable setbacks and crises. (Italics in original)

Social entrepreneurs are often seen as leaders of public organisations who possess several leadership characteristics with significant personal credibility that allows them to generate followers' commitment in terms of social values which shows itself in strong collective purpose (Waddock and Post, 1991). Leadbeater (op. cit.) would add to the catalogue of characteristics the ability to identify gaps and related opportunity. He describes social entrepreneurs in similar ways to Thompson but with more of an emphasis on the leadership sklls we shall address in Chapter 17:

▷ 'Socially *driven*, *ambitious* leaders, with great skills in *communicating a mission* and *inspiring* staff, users and partners. In all cases they have been capable of creating impressive schemes with virtually *no resources*.'
▷ Creating '*flat and flexible organisations*, with a core of full-time paid staff, who work with few resources but a *culture of creativity*.'

In the UK, the GEM report (op. cit.) claims that the highest level of social entrepreneurial activity is among the youngest age group (18–24 years) at 4.4 per cent – a result that has persisted for a number of years. However it is the oldest age group (55–64 years) that are most likely to be running established social enterprises (1.7 per cent involvement). The report shows no significant difference between women and men, and reports that those most likely to be social entrepreneurs belong to the mixed ethnic origin group (6.3 per cent) and combined black African and black Caribbean group (7.5 per cent) – all higher than the percentage of the white population who play a part in social enterprise. These claims should, however, be treated with caution because the definition of social entrepreneur is so broad that it includes anybody trying to start or managing alone or with others any form of social, community or voluntary activity.

In essence, social entrepreneurs are entrepreneurs in a social or not-for-profit context. The difference is that their prime motivation, aims and mission are social rather than commercial. They still pursue opportunities and continually innovate, but for the purpose of serving their social mission. And in doing this they, perhaps, exhibit a longer-term planning horizon than the typical business entrepreneur. They can become entrepreneurial leaders if they have or can develop the skills, but again their mission and values are social. Perhaps the skills they need to achieve their aims are slightly different. The School for Social Entrepreneurs identifies the basic tools of social entrepreneurship as fund-raising, marketing, finances, charity law and publicity. However, I would add the need for them to have a heightened sense of accountability to the wide range of stakeholders involved in the complexity of a social enterprise. And it is this that sets social entrepreneurs apart.

Not-for-profit organisations are uniquely complex organisations that are set up to provide some sort of exchange which results in increased social value. They often have multiple stakeholders – clients, sponsors, donors, employees, government – and multiple service objectives. In a business the objective is usually far more simple – to maximise the return to the owner. Not-for-profit organisations also face a rapidly changing environment in which they compete intensely with each other and even with other commercial organisations for monetary donations. They therefore must pursue dual strategies that involve commercial success by developing sustainable competitive advantage in order to fulfil their social mission. It is this complexity that the social entrepreneur is somehow able to bind into a vision that affects public attitudes (Waddock and Post, op. cit.).

Mort et al. (op. cit.) use this complexity to argue for the multi-dimensional nature of social entrepreneurship. They conceptualise the social entrepreneurship construct and depict it in Figure 4.2. They argue that, firstly, the social entrepreneur is driven by a mission of 'creating better social value than their competitors which results in them exhibiting entrepreneurially virtuous behaviour.' Secondly, they exhibit balanced judgement and an ability to see through the complexity of the situation they face. Thirdly, in a similar way to business entrepreneurs, they are able to recognise opportunities to create better social value that others cannot. Finally, just like business entrepreneurs, they display innovativeness, proactiveness and risk-taking in their decision-making. Only when these four elements combine is social entrepreneurship created.

Virtue is a key element in the construct. It underpins the social entrepreneur's balanced judgement. The authors define it as 'positively good values such as love, integrity, honesty and empathy, which must be acted upon to become genuine virtues.' The social entrepreneur's attitudes and behaviours must have a virtuous dimension. This influences everything they do and gives them a 'coherent unity of purpose and

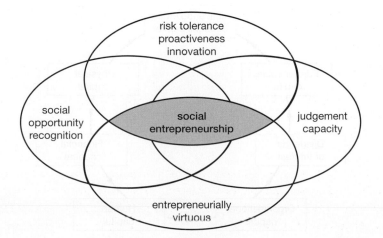

F4.2 Multidimensional social entrepreneurship construct

action in the face of moral complexity.' And of course the similarities with the entrepreneurial leader, with their strong vision built on equally strong underlying values as described in previous chapters, are obvious. Only the context changes.

💡 The growth and development of the social enterprise

Leadbeater (op. cit.) places great store on the development of social capital during the life of the social enterprise. He calls this a 'virtuous circle'. It starts with an endowment of social capital – 'a network of relationships and contracts, which are tied together by shared values and interests.' The trick for the entrepreneur is to lever this up to gain access to more resources – firstly physical capital such as buildings and then financial capital to start the wheel turning and then human resources to start delivering the project. Organisational capital is generated as the project starts delivering its objectives and further resources are attracted, but this will only be achieved with greater formalisation in structures and financial controls and a stronger set of relationships with partners. Finally the project starts to pay dividends, such as the creation of permanent physical infrastructure that can be used by the community – new community centres, hospices or sports facilities. And the increased trust and cooperation generated by a successful project can lead to a fresh injection of social capital as the network of relationships and contacts expands. And so the cycle continues. This is shown in Figure 4.3.

To Leadbeater only the fusion of the public and private sectors produces this chemical reaction:

> The welfare state is blessed with a lot of physical and financial capital. Yet it destroys social and human capital as often as it creates it. It is too bureaucratic to generate the relationships of trust and goodwill, which can start to revive a sense of community and solidarity … The private sector relies on social capital, but all too rarely creates it. Private sector companies depend upon a relationship of trust with their employees, consumers and the communities where they operate. Yet all too often restructuring, delayering and down sizing have destroyed these bonds of social capital.

Leadbeater contends that entrepreneurial social organisations are driven to grow, but, like their commercial counterparts, they can run into a range of problems that

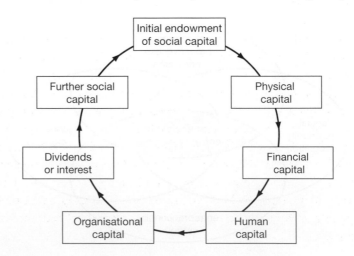

F4.3 The virtuous circle of social capital

Source: Leadbeater (op. cit.), courtesy of Demos (www.demos.co.uk/openaccess)

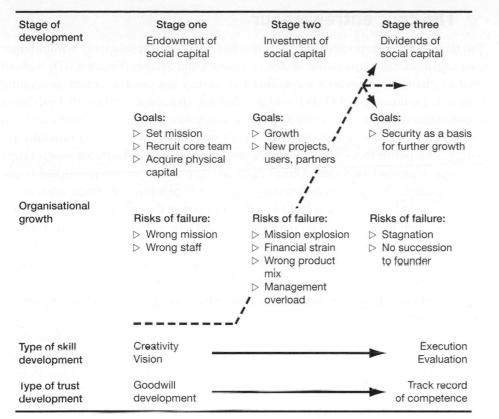

Stage of development	Stage one Endowment of social capital	Stage two Investment of social capital	Stage three Dividends of social capital
	Goals: ▷ Set mission ▷ Recruit core team ▷ Acquire physical capital	Goals: ▷ Growth ▷ New projects, users, partners	Goals: ▷ Security as a basis for further growth
Organisational growth	Risks of failure: ▷ Wrong mission ▷ Wrong staff	Risks of failure: ▷ Mission explosion ▷ Financial strain ▷ Wrong product mix ▷ Management overload	Risks of failure: ▷ Stagnation ▷ No succession to founder
Type of skill development	Creativity Vision		Execution Evaluation
Type of trust development	Goodwill development		Track record of competence

F4.4 The life cycle of the social entrepreneur

Source: Leadbeater (op. cit), courtesy of Demos (www.demos.co.uk/openaccess)

can stunt their growth or even lead to failure at each stage. This three-stage growth model is shown in Figure 4.4. At each stage there are different imperatives and a need for different skills.

Stage one sees the organisation trying to establish itself. The key issue is to set the appropriate mission. But as the organisation grows this may have to be revisited as the scope of its activities expands. This needs to be handled sensitively with all the stakeholders. There is always the danger that one group of stakeholders may hijack the mission and revise it to meet its own ends, thus alienating others. This can be a risk for organisations that are short of funds and the funders therefore are able to set conditions that affect the mission. At the other extreme, too much influence by consumers may result in low prices and financial problems for the organisation that can threaten its survival. These are issues of governance, which become more complex as the organisation grows.

As social organisations grow they may have to change the products or services they offer because of changing social need (Stage two). New products or services may displace existing ones and, without clear criteria for making these decisions, such as profit, the process can become political. This means that the organisation needs to become very adept at evaluating the success of its work – developing appropriate measures of accountability is a significant issue in a not-for-profit organisation. At the same time it needs to become more professional and to develop the entrepreneurial leadership skills outlined in Chapter 17. Effective, efficient delivery becomes increasingly important. The organisation needs to build a reputation based on its track record – in the commercial world it would be called 'developing a brand'. And the final challenge (Stage three) is the same as for its commercial counterpart – how to manage succession.

♀ The civic entrepreneur

The term 'civic entrepreneurship' is concerned with entrepreneurship within larger civic organisations in the public sector, or Pearce's 2nd System (Figure 4.1). It is about creating change in innovative ways. This may or may not involve income-generating activities. Leadbeater and Goss (1998) profiled five civic organisations that exhibited entrepreneurial behaviour: a small school, a police force, a health authority and two local authorities. The school reinvented itself to become more of a community resource. The police force implemented a restorative justice system for youth crime involving a number of different local agencies. The health authority worked to integrate community services by encouraging general practitioners (local doctors) to plan strategically how to meet local health needs rather than concentrating solely on delivering their basic medical services contract. Both local authorities restructured to create more space for entrepreneurship, devolving powers and delegating authority. Leadbeater and Goss noted that 'all these organisations were inspired by a sense of mission, which focused on producing better outcomes rather than merely producing more output. They were guided by a goal of becoming more effective, not merely more efficient.'

Civic entrepreneurship involves a civic manager, head-teacher or other head of an organisational unit acting entrepreneurially. Kirby (2003) likens them to intrapreneurs – entrepreneurs in a large organisation – in the commercial world. According to Ross and Unwalla (1986) the best intrapreneurs are result-orientated, ambitious, rational, competitive and questioning. They dislike bureaucracy – so they are less likely to be found in the 2nd System – and are challenged by innovation but have an understanding of their organisation and a belief in their colleagues. They are adept at politics and good at resolving conflict – and need to be because they will face a lot of it as they smooth the connections with 'conventional' management. Political adeptness cannot be underestimated. Intrapreneurs must be able to focus on the single issue politics of their goal and bring together, perhaps unlikely, partners to make the goal a reality. Often they have a high level sponsor in senior management who facilitates their initiatives. However, ultimately the organisation within which they operate must be tolerant, indeed even encouraging, of their activities. We look at the personal qualities and role of intrapreneurs in large commercial organisation in Chapter 18.

However, intrapreneurs work in the commercial world and civic entrepreneurs in the public sector and Leadbeater and Goss (op. cit.) have a slightly different view of the qualities needed for success. They would add that civic entrepreneurs know that they cannot succeed alone and are keen to involve other individuals or organisations with complementary skills. They are keen to work across traditional boundaries, within and outside their organisation. They also need to be extremely adept at dealing with complex, political situations and communicating with a wide range of stakeholders with differing objectives. To work effectively, a civic entrepreneur either needs to be highly placed or, like an intrapreneur, to have a high-level sponsor to protect them when times are difficult or vested interests are upset, and to help them to unblock the blockages to change as they occur. Sponsors will help secure resources, provide advice and contacts. They will need to nurture and encourage the civic entrepreneur, particularly early on in the life of the project or when things go wrong. They will need to endorse and create visibility for the project at the appropriate time and be good at managing the political and public dimensions of their work, building legitimacy as the project becomes successful. As Leadbeater and Goss (op. cit.) noted in their study of civic entrepreneurship:

> In most cases the process of revitalisation began with a joint effort by political leaders, managers, staff and users to rethink the organisation's goals and purpose. This strategic sense of purpose was not confined to senior managers. They understood that this sense of purpose needed to be shared, ideally from the outset, by politicians, staff and users.

The issue in civic entrepreneurship is the degree of risk that is acceptable within the services offered in the public sector. Many of these services – like health care and education – affect people's lives. Whilst innovation is obviously needed, otherwise organisations will stultify, what scale of innovation, with the related risks, should a civic entrepreneur be allowed to push through? Entrepreneurship involves the risk of failure, but if failure means that a person dies – as it might do in the context of health care – is that risk acceptable? There is also the issue of democratic accountability. Whilst a certain amount of risk might be acceptable to senior managers, is it acceptable to the electorate? And how and when should the issues involved be communicated to them? Failure in the political sense can often degenerate into a witch hunt of who to blame – which is not an atmosphere that encourages creativity and change.

Whilst a private sector entrepreneur may seem very different from a civic entrepreneur in a number of dimensions, particularly with respect to risk, the distinction between the private sector entrepreneur and the social entrepreneur is less clear. Many private sector entrepreneurs have enterprises with a strong social dimension. In the UK some activities, such as schooling, are undertaken both as public and social enterprises. Indeed, schools can also be private enterprises. In that respect Pearce's clearly delineated 'systems' in Figure 4.1 do not show that the boundaries that exist between the three systems can be very blurred. Figure 4.5 attempts to demonstrate this blurring by showing entrepreneurship as a spectrum between private sector entrepreneur, through social entrepreneur, on to civic entrepreneur.

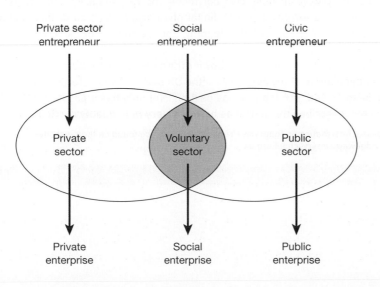

F4.5 The spectrum of entrepreneurship

🖅 Case with questions Ridgeway Primary School

Ridgeway Primary School and Nursery is a large primary school on the outskirts of Croydon in the UK. It is an unlikely place to find an example of civic entrepreneurship but since 1998 it has defied the UK's national curriculum and not implemented the literacy or numeracy hours required of it. Instead it has followed its own strongly held philosophy that a primary curriculum is only made coherent through making creative links between subjects. The school's vision is to have a creative curriculum that inspires both children and teachers to learn. The school wants to create a real learning community based upon a genuine will to learn that encourages creativity in children and teachers alike. The literacy and numeracy hours did not fit with this philosophy.

Head teacher, Anna House, believes creativity is the thread that runs through everything the school does. She believes in motivating people rather than working through hierarchies and structures. Parents, governors and visitors are used as a creative resource. Teachers work in creative teams along with teaching assistants, each learning from the other. Even the school meals organisers are encouraged to think creatively.

There is a detailed 38-page teaching and learning policy which draws on research into effective teaching and learning to justify the school's policies. The school aims to create a holistic curriculum with certain sustained themes like 'spirituality', 'citizenship', 'water' or 'save the planet' running through it so as to create continuity and embed learning, thus avoiding the danger of short-term, easily forgotten experiences. There are three themes each year. The themes build up to provide a view of the world that fires the children's curiosity. There is detailed planning of the curriculum around these themes. Literacy or numeracy is encouraged because of the child's interest in the theme, rather than as an end in itself. So, for example, the theme of 'shoes' was used as the context in year 6 for learning about materials and developing different shoe designs. This 'enquiry-based learning' provides scope for individual creativity and the development of thinking skills. The curriculum is enhanced by lunchtime clubs in areas such as chess, drama and even Japanese (run by a parent). At Key Stage 1 (5–7 years old) there are no set playtimes. Creative activity is linked to opportunities to think, so as to turn the experience into learning. So, for example, children are encouraged to think about how and why certain types of shading on a drawing create the effect of texture. There is also an emphasis on developing independence and self-direction in learning. Children assess themselves against their own learning targets. In year 1 children are given their own Inventions Book in which to design creative solutions to problems. They develop their own portfolios showing achievements in learning. One feature of this is the extensive use of digital photographs to record these achievements. Teachers also enjoy a great deal of autonomy. For example, they can choose when, and if, to take a playtime.

The risks faced by the school in not following the national curriculum were high. Ultimately, if there had been persistently poor Ofsted (the UK schools' inspectorate) reports the school may have been closed. But the risk has paid off. Not only has it passed all its Ofsted visits but Ofsted has described the school as having a 'very high quality curriculum'.

☐ Up-to-date information on Ridgeway Primary School can be found on their website: www.ridgewayprimaryschool.org.uk

QUESTIONS

1 Is this an example of civic entrepreneurship? If so, why?

2 Is this an entrepreneurial response to an educational issue? If so, why?

3 What are the risks posed by this form of action?

♀ The dangers of social entrepreneurship

There are always lessons to be learnt when the activities of one sector are compared to another, as in the 'Third Way' and the 'Big Society'. Eikenberry and Kluver (2004) acknowledge the need for the public sector to work with not-for-profit organisations and community and voluntary organisations: 'They are more than just tools for achieving the most efficient and effective mode of service delivery; they are also important vehicles for creating and maintaining a strong civil society'. Alexander et al. (1999) underline the importance of their role as 'schools or laboratories of democratic citizenship' – training grounds for citizenship that involve people in socially beneficial activities that they would not otherwise engage in.

However, the 'Third Way' has been criticised from many quarters as ill-defined and not something that can be relied upon to deliver social objectives as a matter of policy because it relies too much on the philanthropic motives of individuals. It has also been pointed out that, unlike its commercial counterpart, no economic case in terms of efficiency can be made to support a shift to social entrepreneurship and the market is not a legitimate benchmark to justify changes from a rights-based welfare system (Cook et al., 2003).

The problem then is the mixing of social and economic objectives. There is no accepted framework to measure the two together and, in particular, the trade-off between them. What is efficient economically may be ineffective socially and vice versa, but where does the acceptable trade-off lie, and who decides? Social enterprises can therefore all too easily avoid rigorous monitoring both because of the lack of an accounting framework and because of the complexity of the interests of their diverse stakeholder base. In the commercial world it is simple. Owners generally look to get the maximum financial return on their investment and if a sole owner has different, perhaps lifestyle, objectives, they have no other owners who can object to their decision.

Fowler (op. cit.) also has reservations, noting particularly that it is a risky framework for the development of recipients of international development aid – non-government development organisations (NGOs). These organisations handle large amounts of public money. He doubts that they can handle the conflicts between social and commercial behaviour. He argues that retaining their moral underpinning and inspiration is vital and any involvement in income-generating activities will compromise this. He also fears that the social entrepreneur framework is not sustainable for their survival because they are so dependent on government aid. There is also the concern about what entrepreneurial activities the large amounts of public money they receive might be put to. Fowler is therefore more in favour of 'civic entrepreneurship' which he sees as providing 'civic, as opposed to public, legitimacy and economic viability from a broad base of citizen support.'

Eikenberry and Kluver (op. cit.) are particularly concerned about the problems of what they call 'the methods and values of the market' being applied in both the public and the not-for-profit sector and its detrimental impact upon democracy and citizenship in the USA. They put their point strongly: 'For the public sector, an emphasis on entrepreneurialism is incompatible with democratic citizenship and its emphasis on accountability and collective action for the public interest (King and Strivers, 1998; Box, 1999; deLeon and Denhardt, 2000; Denhardt and Denhardt, 2000; Box et al., 2001). Furthermore, the market model places little or no value on democratic ideals such as fairness and justice (Terry, 1998). For the non-profit sector, marketisation trends such as commercial revenue generation, contract competition, the influence of

🗀 Case with questions

Nin Castle, Phoebe Emerson and Goodone

Nin Castle and Phoebe Emerson met at Brighton University in 2001. Both Nin and Phoebe were doing fashion courses and they talked about setting up a fashion business but were

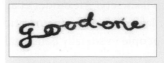

uneasy about some of the ethical and environmental issues relating to the industry. Two million tonnes of clothes are sold annually in the UK of which one million will end up in landfill sites when half of it is reusable. It was whilst at a nightclub in 2003 that they came up with the idea of **Goodone**. The idea was to design and produce innovative, quality, one-off clothing which was made from hand-picked, locally-sourced, recycled fabrics. They wanted to change perceptions of what recycled clothing can be by creating garments which did not look recycled.

Starting with only £1000, in 2005 they made a deal with a local charity shop that allowed them to go through all the bags of textiles that were being sent to the rag factory at the cost of £1 a bag. They also acquired a disused car showroom in Brighton – a large open space into which they put two makeshift beds and a couple of second-hand sewing machines – and started their business:

> 'We had no funding, were living on housing benefit and doing part-time jobs to try and get the business up and running. In 2006 our first customers were local boutiques. We were full of enthusiasm and rather naive as we really thought that our tiny business could make an impact on the huge fashion industry.'

> Nin Castle, *Daily Telegraph* 5 February 2009

Nin did the design work and Pheobe looked after the business side, both working on the manufacturing. Within a few months they decided to go on a three-day 'Creative Business' start-up course run by the National Council for Graduate Entrepreneurship (NCGE) and registered Goodone as a company. After a year in the car showroom, they relocated to Hackney in London so as to be in the 'fashion hub' of the UK. They also set up their own online shop.

In 2007 they won a £15 000 prize from NCGE, much of which was spent on repairing the sewing machines. However, the prize also generated a lot of free PR and articles about the company appeared in the national press. These stimulated sales – Goodone fulfilled orders for clothes from the cult shop 'Side by Side' in Tokyo, Japan – and created more opportunities. They exhibited at the 'Fashion Made Fair' sale in Brick Lane, London, 'The Clothes Show Live' in Birmingham and the 'Margin' trade show in London, and started giving presentations to the London School of Fashion. They were awarded Manufacturing Advisory Service funding to develop the Goodone product line and brand and a London Development Agency SME Innovation Award, which gave them manufacturing consultancy from the London College of Fashion. Normally lengths of cloth are sent to the manufacturer but with recycled fabric every piece is different and that creates special problems. Goodone also began outsourcing some manufacturing to HEBA Women's Project, a London charity.

In January 2008 Phoebe amicably left the company to work in other areas of social enterprise. Nin then went on to produce charity t-shirts by recycling old campaign t-shirts from Greenpeace, Shelter, Amnesty, Liberty and WWF. She spent August 2009 in South Africa working for the Tabeisa Project, designing and producing clothes in a township outside Cape Town for sale in the UK.

Goodone's mission statement is reproduced below:

'Goodone design and produce innovative, quality, one-off clothing which is made from hand-picked, locally-sourced, recycled fabrics. We aim to exceed people's expectations of what recycled clothing can be by creating garments which don't look obviously recycled. Instead of 'reworking' or 'customising' existing pieces we design for production. Using our specialist knowledge in the deconstruction and reconstruction of garments, sustainable sourcing and production we are able to create a limitless amount of new clothing from old, which, dependent on the combination of coloured, patterned and textured fabrics chosen, will inherently always remain unique. This means we are able to mass produce the one-off.

By using these recycled materials we are not only providing a creative and sustainable solution for waste reduction but also minimising energy use and the damage to environment caused by the production of new clothing. It is our goal to continue to build a reputable brand which is internationally recognised for pioneering the production of high-quality, innovative 'recreated' clothing, secondly, provide specialist consultancy, working with, instead of against, existing brands and retailers to solve their own waste issues, consequently impacting the industry on a bigger scale, and thirdly, to educate the next generation of fashion designers, entrepreneurs and consumers on the urgency and methods for designing, producing and consuming sustainably.'

By 2009 Goodone was supplying outlets in London, Manchester, Brighton and Glasgow in the UK and internationally in Berlin, Hong Kong, Melbourne and New York. They were also selling from their website. Turnover was £20 000 and the business employed one part-timer and had a number of interns. Nin also teaches at fashion colleges and Goodone's income gets ploughed back into the business. Goodone is an example of a business with social objectives and one that has made the most of grants and support that are available to young enterprises.

☐ Up-to-date information on Goodone can be found on their website: www.goodone.co.uk

QUESTIONS

1 What do you think might be Nin's personal objectives in running this business?

2 Is this a social enterprise or just a socially ethical business?

3 Is Goodone successful? How do you measure this?

4 What does money measure in this business?

5 Is it right that Nin should be able to make so much use of grants and support?

new and emerging donors, and social entrepreneurship compromise the non-profit sector's civil society roles as value guardians, service providers and advocates, and the builders of social capital.'

There are a number of strategic issues that run through the literature on social entrepreneurship. The first is that the mixing of social and economic objectives within a social enterprise can be dangerous. There are difficulties with accounting for the two objectives and in particular making trade-offs between the two. The range of activities – everything from social services to shops – means that it is imperative to focus on the core business, or mission and realise what is peripheral, a means to the ultimate mission. Unless this happens, social enterprises can avoid rigorous monitoring and democratic accountability. But how do these organisations decide on their core mission, and who decides? And even then, how do they arrive at a clear idea of what is 'performance', and then how it can be measured?

The likely complex nature of the stakeholders' interests in a social organisation mean that an understanding of these dynamics and how they might be influenced is important. With a lack of clear performance criteria, these dynamics take on an added importance. This raises the possibility of political influence leading to economic benefit, otherwise known as political patronage and other less savoury names. How do social enterprises guard against this?

Social enterprise is at the boundary between public and private sectors – and that boundary keeps shifting. There is an inherent conflict in the values and beliefs of the two sectors. It is a conflict we will see in the family firm (Chapter 16). And with an acknowledgement of the conflict can come ways of finding a resolution. The issues relating to social enterprise revolve around its efficiency and effectiveness on the one hand and its democratic accountability on the other. But the argument that the public sector itself – in all its many guises – can learn some lessons from entrepreneurship seems to have been won.

⊳ Summary

⊳ Social entrepreneurship is an ill-defined concept. It can be loosely defined as the use of entrepreneurial behaviour for social rather than profit objectives. Social entrepreneurs therefore differ from business entrepreneurs in terms of their mission. Social enterprises are the organisations that social entrepreneurs set up to achieve their aims. **The Big Issue**, started by John Bird, is probably the best known example of social entrepreneurship in the UK.

⊳ A social enterprise is a business set up primarily for social objectives whose surpluses are reinvested in the business or in the community for that purpose. As we saw with a range of social enterprises, this can take a number of legal forms. A major confusion is whether or not social enterprises need to engage in income-generating commercial activities. If they do, the surpluses should be applied to their social mission.

Integrated social entrepreneurship occurs when surplus-generating activities simultaneously create social benefit. As we saw with **Goodone**, it is a thin line between a social enterprise and a socially ethical company.

⊳ Social entrepreneurship happens when social opportunity recognition combines with risk tolerance, proactiveness, innovation and good judgement, and is applied towards a virtuous objective.

⊳ Social entrepreneurs have many of the same qualities as business entrepreneurs, however they also need a heightened sense of accountability to the wide range of stakeholders involved in a social enterprise.

⊳ The virtuous circle of social capital can lead to its growth and the building of capacity. But as the social enterprise grows it will face different problems, imperatives and the need for different skills (Figure 4.4).

▷ Civic entrepreneurship is concerned with entrepreneurial behaviour in the public sector. It is similar to intrapreneurship in the commercial world, although often the civic entrepreneur is also an existing head of an organisational unit – like **Anna House** at the **Ridgeway Primary School and Nursery**. The issue here is the degree of risk that is acceptable within many of the services offered in the public sector. What scale of innovation, with the related risks, should a civic entrepreneur be allowed to push through – for example in the area of health care or education?

▷ The mixing of social and economic objectives within a social enterprise can be dangerous. There are difficulties in accounting for the two objectives and in particular making trade-offs between the two. Social enterprises can therefore avoid rigorous monitoring and democratic accountability. This is particularly the case when the body is in receipt of large amounts of public money, such as non-government development organisations. It has also been pointed out that no economic case can be made for a shift to social entrepreneurship. Finally there is the fear that the increase in commercialisation of not-for-profit organisations will jeopardise their role as training grounds for democratic citizenship.

☑ Useful websites

☑ www.businesslink.gov.uk
Business Link is probably the most useful website offering practical help and advice for the UK. Search for 'social enterprise'.

☑ www.cdfa.org.uk
Community Development Finance Association for sources of finance for social enterprise.

Others:

☑ www.socialent.org
The Institute for Social Entrepreneurs.

☑ www.sse.org.uk
The School for Social Entrepreneurs (UK).

☑ www.socialenterprise.org.uk
Social Enterprise Coalition is the UK national body for social enterprise.

☑ www.socialenterpriselive.com
Social Enterprise Magazine.

☑ www.changemakers.net
Ashoka Changemakers is a website of resources for social entrepreneurship.

☑ www.setas.co.uk
Social Enterprise Training and Support is another resources website.

☑ www.sel.org.uk/publications.aspx
Social Enterprise London is another resources website.

☑ www.demos.co.uk
Demos is a political 'think-tank' that has articles about social enterprise and the 'third way'.

☑ www.gemconsortium.org
Social Entrepreneurship Monitor – Go to the GEM website and select your country of choice (GEM national teams drop-down in top right hand corner) to find all their 'reports and documents'. In the UK in 2010 the most recent Social Entrepreneurship Report is for 2006.

☑ www.gsb.stanford.edu/csi/
Center for Social Innovation at Stanford Business School.

(⏻) **Further resources are available at www.palgrave.com/business/burns**

🗋 Essays and discussion topics

1 How would you define social entrepreneurship? Is the term misused?

2 Can social and business objectives mix? If so, how?

3 What are the cultures of the private and public sectors? How do they differ and why will they clash? Can this be resolved? If so, how?

4 Can not-for-profit organisations like charities be run entrepreneurially? Should they be?

5 How do you feel about the entrepreneurial – some would say aggressive – fund-raising activities of some charities? Does this affect their ability to meet their mission?

6 Most charities raise money, however little, for their causes. Does this make them social enterprises? What distinguishes the social enterprise? Does how much is raised or how it is raised affect your view?

7 How is a social entrepreneur different from a business entrepreneur?

8 How will social entrepreneurs know they have been successful?

9 'Virtue is in the eye of the beholder.' How might this comment apply to the social entrepreneur?

10 How different is the accumulation of social capital by the social entrepreneur from financial capital by the business entrepreneur at start-up?

11 Which do you think is the most effective legal form of social enterprise? Why?

12 How is a civic entrepreneur different from an intrapreneur?

13 How will civic entrepreneurs know they have been successful?

14 Is risk-taking appropriate in the public sector?

15 How can a social enterprise be held to account?

16 Should public money be given to a social enterprise?

17 Should public money be used to develop a commercial activity as part of a social enterprise? If not, why not? If yes, why and would there be any constraints on this?

18 In subsidising a social enterprise tax payers' money is being used to put other owner-managers of small local firms out of business. Discuss.

19 Where is the boundary between social enterprise and voluntary or charity organisations? Give examples.

20 Where is the boundary between social enterprise and commercial business? Give examples.

⟲ Activities

1 Go to the Demos website and download the report by Charles Leadbeater: *The Rise of the Social Entrepreneur* (it is freely available). It contains five case studies:

> The Bromley-by-Bow Centre
> The Mildmay Mission Hospital
> Kaleidoscope
> The Youth Charter for Sport
> The Eldonians

Select one case and write a report evaluating whether this is a legitimate example of social entrepreneurship. Note any dangers you see in the case. What do you think of the author's argument for civic entrepreneurship?

2 Go to the Demos website and download the report by Charles Leadbeater and Sue Goss: *Civic Entrepreneurship* (it is freely available). It contains five case studies:

> West Walker Primary School
> Thames Valley Police
> Kirklees Metropolitan Authority
> Dorset Health Authority
> South Somerset District Council.

Select one case and write a report evaluating whether this is a legitimate example of civic entrepreneurship. Note any dangers you see in the case. What do you think of the authors' argument for civic entrepreneurship?

3 Review the websites on this topic given in the chapter and prepare a list of resources that are available to someone thinking of setting up a social enterprise.

⊕ Further reading

Brinckerhoff, P. (2000) *Social Entrepreneurship: The Art of Mission-Based Venture Development*, Hoboken, NJ: Wiley.

Dees, J.G., Emerson, J. and Economy, P. (2001) *Enterprising Nonprofits: A Toolkit for Social Entrepreneurs*, Hoboken, NJ: Wiley.

📖 References

Alexander, J., Nank, R. and Strivers, C. (1999) 'Implications of Welfare Reform: Do Nonprofit Survival Strategies Threaten Civil Society?', *Nonprofit and Voluntary Sector Quarterly*, 28(4).

Boschee, J. (1998) *Merging Mission and Money: A Board Member's Guide to Social Entrepreneurship*, Washington, DC: BoardSource.

Box, R.C. (1999) 'Running Government Like a Business: Implications for Public Administration Theory and Practice', *American Review of Public Administration*, 29(1).

Box, R.C., Marshall, G.S., Reed, B.J. and Reed, C.M. (2001) 'New Public Management and Substantive Democracy', *Public Administration Review*, 60(5), September/October.

Brinckerhoff, P. (2000) *Social Entrepreneurship: The Art of Mission-Based Venture Development*, Hoboken, NJ: Wiley.

Cook B., Dodds C. and Mitchell W. (2003) 'Social Entrepreneurship – False Premises and Dangerous Forebodings', *Australian Journal of Social Issues*, 38(1), February.

deLeon, L. and Denhardt, R.B. (2000) 'The Political Theory of Reinvention', *Public Administration Review*, 60(2), March/April.

Denhardt, R.B. and Denhardt, J.V. (2000) 'The New Public Service: Serving Rather than Steering', *Public Administration Review*, 60(6), November/December.

Eikenberry, A. and Kluver, J.D. (2004) 'The Marketisation of the Non-profit Sector: Civil Society at Risk?', *Public Administration Review*, 64(2), March/April.

Fowler, A. (2000) 'NGDOs as a Moment in History: Beyond Aid to Social Entrepreneurship or Civic Innovation?', *Third World Quarterly*, 21(4).

GEM (Harding, R.) (2006) *GEM United Kingdom 2006 Report – Social Entrepreneurship*, www.gemconsortium .com.

Hibbert, S.A., Hogg, G. and Quinn, T. (2002) 'Consumer Response to Social Entrepreneurship: The Case of the Big Issue in Scotland', *International Journal of Nonprofit and Voluntary Sector Marketing*, 7(3).

King, C.S. and Strivers, C. (eds) (1998) *Government Is Us: Public Administration in an Anti-Government Era*, Thousand Oaks, CA: Sage.

Kirby, D. (2003) *Entrepreneurship*, Maidenhead: McGraw-Hill.

Leadbeater, C. (1997) *The Rise of the Social Entrepreneur*, London: Demos.

Leadbeater, C. and Goss, S. (1998) *Civic Entrepreneurship*, London: Demos.

Mort, G.S., Weerawardena, J. and Carnegie, K. (2003) 'Social Entrepreneurship: Towards Conceptualisation', *International Journal of Nonprofit and Voluntary Sector Marketing*, 8(1).

Pearce, J. (2003) *Social Enterprise in Anytown*, Calouste Gulbenkian Foundation.

Ross, J.E. and Unwalla, D. (1986) 'Who is an Intrapreneur?', *Personnel*, 63(12).

Terry, L.D. (1998) 'Administrative Leadership, Neo-Managerialism, and the Public Management Movement', *Public Administration Review*, 58(3), May/June.

Thompson, J., Alvey, G. and Lees, A. (2000) 'Social Entrepreneurship – A Look at the People and the Potential', *Management Decision*, 38/5.

Waddock, S.A. and Post, J.E. (1991) 'Social Entrepreneurs and Catalytic Change', *Public Administration Review*, 51(5).

2 Start-up

5 Developing creativity and the business idea

6 Evaluating the business idea

7 Launching the business

8 International entrepreneurship

9 Running the business

10 Financing the business

5 Developing creativity and the business idea

▷ **Creativity**
▷ **Barriers to creativity**
▷ **The creative process**
▷ **Techniques for generating new ideas**
▷ **Recognising opportunity**
▷ **The business idea**
▷ **The internet**
▷ **Safeguarding your ideas**
▷ **Summary**

Case insights
▷ Martin Dix and Current Cost
▷ Bruce Bratley and First Mile
▷ Tom Mercer and mOma
▷ Adrian Wood and GTI

Cases with questions
▷ Alex Tew and the Million
  Dollar Homepage
▷ eBay
▷ Andrew Valentine and Streetcar

Learning outcomes

By the end of this chapter you should be able to:

▷ Explain what makes an individual creative;

▷ Assess your own aptitude to be creative;

▷ Describe and recognise barriers to creativity;

▷ Describe the creative process;

▷ Use a range of techniques to help generate new ideas;

▷ Use a range of techniques to help spot commercial opportunities;

▷ Generate new business ideas based on these opportunities;

▷ Describe the business opportunities created by the internet;

▷ Safeguard new business ideas.

💡 Creativity

Creativity is at the core of any true entrepreneur. Creativity is important in coming up with completely new ways of doing things, rather than looking for adaptive, incremental change. Parkhurst (1999) defined it as 'the ability or quality displayed when solving hitherto unsolved problems, when developing original and novel solutions to problems others have solved differently, or when developing original and novel (at least to its originator) products'. For the entrepreneur, the focus for their creativity is commercial opportunity leading to new products, services, processes or marketing approaches. It has been estimated that for every eleven ideas that enter the new product development process, only one new product will be successfully launched (Page, 1993). So new ideas are at a premium and it is a numbers game. The more you generate, the more are likely to see the light of day commercially. So how can you stimulate creativity?

> *When you don't have a lot of money you've got to be creative about how you go about things … There's going to be a whole new range of 'clever companies' that set up because creativity is now king, not cash.*
>
> ☐ Will King, founder of King of Shaves, *RealBusiness* 1 July 2009

We are now starting to understand how the creative process works on an individual level. The brain has two sides that operate in quite different ways. The left side performs rational, logical functions. It tends to be verbal and analytic, operating in a linked, linear sequence (called logical or vertical thinking). The right side operates intuitive and non-rational modes of thought. It is non-verbal, linking images together to get a holistic perspective (called creative or lateral thinking). A person uses both sides, shifting naturally from one to the other. However, the right side is the creative side. Creative innovation is, therefore, primarily a right brain activity whilst adaptive innovation is a left brain activity.

Left brain thinkers tend to be rational, logical, analytical and sequential in their approach to problem-solving. Right brain thinkers are more intuitive, value-based and non-linear in their approach. The cognitive styles are also reflected in the preferred work styles with left brain thinkers preferring to work alone, learn about things rather than experience them and having the ability or preference to make quick decisions. By way of contrast, right brain thinkers prefer working in groups, experiencing things (for example, learning by doing) and generating lots of options in preference to focusing on making a speedy decision. People have a preference for one or other approach, but can and do switch between them for different tasks and in different contexts.

Normally the two halves of the brain complement each other, but many factors, not least our education, tend to encourage development of left brain activity – logic. Kirby (2003) speculates that this may well explain why so many successful entrepreneurs appear not to have succeeded in the formal education system. He argues that entrepreneurs are right brain dominant. But he goes even further by speculating that there may be a link between this and dyslexia, observing that many entrepreneurs are dyslexic and language skills are left brain activities. This is an interesting but unproved hypothesis.

However, the point is that most people need to encourage and develop right brain activity if they wish to be creative. And this is possible, with training. To overcome the habit of logic you need to deliberately set aside this ingrained way of thinking. Creative or lateral thinking is different in a number of dimensions to logical or vertical thinking. It is imaginative, emotional, and often results in more than one solution. Edward de Bono (1971) set out some of the dimensions of difference. Figure 5.1 is based on his work.

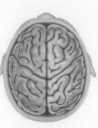

Logical	Creative
Seeks answers	Seeks questions
Converges	Diverges
Asserts best or right view	Explores different views, seeks insights
Uses existing structure	Restructures
Says when an idea will not work	Seeks ways an idea might help
Uses logical steps	Welcomes discontinuous leaps
Concentrates on what is relevant	Welcomes chance intrusions
Closed	Open-ended

F5.1 Dimensions of creative (lateral) vs logical (vertical) thinking

One important aspect of high level creativity is the ability to recognise relationships among objects, processes, cause and effect, people and so on that others do not see, searching for different, unorthodox relationships that can be replicated in a different context. These relationships can lead to new ideas, products or services. So, the inconvenience of mixing different drinks to form a cocktail led to the (obvious?) idea of selling them ready mixed. James Dyson was able to see that a cyclone system for separating paint particles could be used (less obviously?) to develop a better vacuum cleaner; doctors at Great Ormond Street Hospital were able to see that the efficiency of Formula 1 pit stops could help them to improve patient care (Chapter 3). Most creativity skills can be practised and enhanced, but this particular skill is probably the most difficult to encourage. Majaro (1992) believes that, while stereotyping is to be avoided, creative types do exhibit some similar characteristics:

▷ *Conceptual fluency* They are able to produce many ideas.
▷ *Mental flexibility* They are adept at lateral thinking.
▷ *Originality* They produce atypical responses to problems.
▷ *Suspension of judgement* They do not analyse too quickly.
▷ *Impulsive* They act impulsively on an idea, expressing their 'gut-feel'.
▷ *Anti-authority* They are always willing to challenge authority.
▷ *Tolerance* They have a high tolerance threshold towards the ideas of others.

🗂 Creativity test

Find out how creative you are by going to www.creax.com/csa and answering the 40 questions in the creativity quiz. It is free and the analysis assesses you on eight dimensions against answers from others with similar backgrounds. The dimensions are:

▷ **Abstraction** – the ability to apply abstract concepts/ideas.
▷ **Connection** – the ability to make connections between things that do not appear connected.
▷ **Perspective** – the ability to shift one's perspective on a situation in terms of space, time and other people.
▷ **Curiosity** – the desire to change or improve things that others see as normal.
▷ **Boldness** – the confidence to push boundaries beyond accepted conventions. Also the ability to eliminate the fear of what others might think of you.
▷ **Paradox** – the ability to simultaneously accept and work with statements that are contradictory.
▷ **Complexity** – the ability to carry large quantities of information and the capacity to manipulate and manage the relationships between such information.
▷ **Persistence** – the ability to force oneself to keep trying to find more and stronger solutions even when good ones have already been generated.

Mintzberg (1976) makes the interesting suggestion that the very logical activity of planning is essentially a left brain activity whilst the implementation of the plan, that is the act of management, is a right brain activity. He bases this claim on the observation that managers split their attention between a number of different tasks, preferring to talk briefly to people rather than to write and reading non-verbal as well as verbal aspects of the interaction, take a holistic view of the situation and rely on intuition. He argues that truly effective managers are those that can harness both sides of the brain.

♀ Barriers to creativity

People are inherently creative, but most of us stifle it because we find change threatening. We all create rituals and routines that we feel comfortable with and these normally mitigate against questioning the status quo. These routines help us through the day. Being creative often takes people outside of their 'comfort-zone'. They are uneasy with it. Sometimes blocks and barriers need to be attacked. Von Oech (1998) focuses on the blocks to individual creativity. He lists ten that are critical:

> *We learned the importance of ignoring conventional wisdom … It's fun to do things that people don't think are possible or likely. It's also exciting to achieve the unexpected.*
>
> ☐ Michael Dell (1999)

1 The fallacy that there is only one correct solution to a problem.
2 The fallacy that logic is important in creativity.
3 The tendency to be practical.
4 The tendency to follow established rules unquestioningly.
5 The tendency to avoid ambiguity in viewing a situation.
6 The tendency to assign blame for failure.
7 The unwillingness to recognise the creative power of play.
8 The tendency to think too narrowly and with too much focus.
9 The unwillingness to think unconventionally because of the fear of appearing foolish.
10 The lack of belief that you can be creative.

Realising these blocks may exist in yourself can be the first step to dismantling them. It is never easy to change an inherent tendency, but it can be done and the techniques in the next section can help.

♀ The creative process

The creative process has four commonly agreed phases, shown in Figure 5.2. There is wide agreement on their general nature and the relationship between them, although they are referred to by a variety of names (de Bono, 1995).

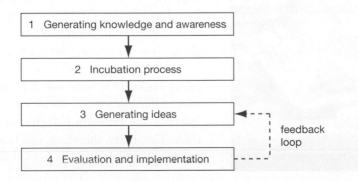

F5.2 The creative process

Phase 1: Generating knowledge and awareness

A prerequisite to all creative processes is the generation of awareness of different ideas and ways of doing things through reading and travelling widely, talking with different

people with different views about the world. You may, for example, see demands being met in one country that are not met in others. You may read about products made in one country that are not yet available in another. This is, of course, to be placed in the context of the issue being addressed. So, in these examples of demand and supply, the opportunities you have spotted in other countries are very relevant to your desire to set up your own business. It is not just about being aware of different approaches or perspectives on the problem, but also about getting the brain to accept that there are different ways of doing things – developing both an open and an enquiring mind. Many people almost have to give themselves permission

Travelling, reading and an open mind are of the utmost importance to the creative processes

to be creative – to think the unthinkable. Carrying a notebook and recording ideas and information can be useful. So too can developing a small library. Look how far Lego, LG and Hallmark went in order to expose their staff to new ideas (p. 78). Some sources of commercial new ideas are shown in Figure 5.3.

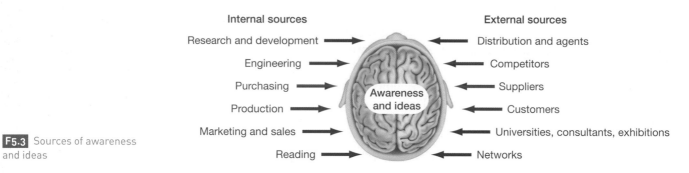

F5.3 Sources of awareness and ideas

Phase 2: Incubation process

Ideas happen unexpectedly, even while you are asleep

People need time to mull over the tremendous amounts of information they generate in Phase 1. This incubation period happens when people are engaged in other

activities (the best are those instinctive activities that do not require left brain dominance) and they can let their subconscious mind work on the problem. Interestingly, sleep happens when the left brain gets tired or bored and during this time the right brain has dominance. Incubation therefore often needs sleep. The old adage, 'sleep on the problem', has its origins in an understanding of how the brain works. It is little wonder that so many people have creative ideas when they are asleep – the problem is trying to remember them. Creativity, therefore, can take time and needs 'sleeping on'.

Phase 3: Generating ideas

Ideas can come up unexpectedly during the incubation period, sometimes while you are asleep. However, often they need encouragement and there are a number of techniques that can help to encourage idea generation. Some of the more widely used ones are explained in the next section.

Phase 4: Evaluation and implementation

The next stage is to select which ideas are the most promising. This is the convergent stage of the process involving discussion and analysis, possibly voting. Some ideas generated in Phase 3 might be easy to discard because they are unrealistic but others might need to be worked up or modified before they can be properly evaluated. Sometimes a return to Phase 3 is required to do this. We shall look at how you might evaluate your business ideas in the next chapter.

💼 Case insight Martin Dix and Current Cost

The big idea came to Martin Dix, founder of Current Cost, on New Years Day 2004 but it was not until 2007 that he started selling it. The idea was a home electricity meter which showed the £ value of electricity being consumed at any point in time and was cheap enough for energy companies to give to customers. He started out by confirming that most people did not know the annual electricity running cost for ordinary household appliances. He then started to research the product, going to China to visit potential manufacturers and investigate logistics. Despite interest from UK government offices Martin was finding it impossible to get financial backing for the idea. Nevertheless he went back to China in 2005 to set up manufacturing partners. It was not until 2006 that he was able to find two partners, who put in £5000 each.

The business really took off in 2007 when OFGEM, Scottish and Southern Electricity gave Current Cost £250 000 to provide them with 5000 meters for a year-long trial. The results were so startlingly successful that four months later they started ordering more as part of one of their regular tariffs. A year later, in 2008 another electricity company, Eon, also started offering Current Cost meters. A new product had been developed for the international market and in the same year this started selling to the USA, France, Australia and New Zealand. December 2008 saw the launch of a second generation display for the UK.

By 2009 Current Cost had a turnover of £6 million and Chris still owned 50 per cent of the business.

☐ Up-to-date information on Current Cost can be found on their website: www.currentcost.com

---

Roger von Oech (1986) has a slightly different view of the creative process, focusing on the changing role of the individual as it takes its course. He outlines four sequential roles:

1 The explorer – searching for new insights and perspectives by sifting through information, being curious, observing other fields, generating ideas, broadening perspectives, following unexpected leads, using difficulties and obstacles and constantly writing things down.

2 The artist – turning information and resources into new ideas by imagining, adapting, reversing, linking, parodying, evaluating and discarding.

3 The judge – evaluating and assessing the merits of a concept and incorporating ideas through objectivity and looking at assumptions, probabilities and timing.

4 The warrior – achieving organisational acceptance and implementation of ideas by being bold, courageous and persistent, developing plans, commanding resources, motivating stakeholders to commit themselves to the project.

In a start-up the entrepreneur may have to fulfil all four of these roles – a considerable achievement, not least because they require different types of left and right brain activity.

Some organisations have created environments designed to facilitate these stages of the creative process. The Royal Mail Group has its own 'Creativity Laboratory'. This is made up of a number of open areas – facilitating groups forming, breaking up and coming together again – all with very informal seating arrangements. Standing and walking are encouraged. There is background music as well as toys, drinks and other distractions for the left brain. All the walls are 'white walls' which can be written on with felt tip pens when ideas are in free flow. Pens are everywhere. There are computer systems that allow ideas to be posted and voted on anonymously. And records are kept of the whole process – even the white walls are photographed – so agreed actions and outcomes can be followed up back in the workplace.

🧳 Case insight Bruce Bratley and First Mile

The business idea developed slowly for Bruce Bratley. Having done a PhD in environmental science he was convinced there were commercial opportunities in waste recycling. He first got a job as commercial director in a start-up firm that recycled packaging materials but in 2002 left to start his own consultancy, advising waste businesses on their strategy. He became convinced that there was a gap in the market for a recycling company that could use internet technology to service business customers who found it expensive and difficult to dispose of their waste and who could not easily recycle. Initially he was looking around for a company to buy as a springboard for this idea, but that came to nothing.

It was not until 2007 that he found a business partner, Paul Ashworth, and they decided to set up their own business, each putting in £20 000. First Mile was launched in 2007 on the back of a £95 000 grant from Enhance, a support service for green enterprises in London. First Mile offers a unique kerbside collection service for waste collection and recycling. Customers buy prepaid sacks which they fill with non-recyclable waste or mixed recycling waste and place on the street for collection at a prearranged time. They can also dispose of confidential and other specialist waste. First Mile takes the waste to depots to be sorted and dealt with. To keep costs low all transactions are handled on the internet (there is a 0800 number for service enquiries). Customers can log on to their account, order sacks – delivered the next day – and payments are collected by direct debit, eliminating paperwork. There is no contract and First Mile guarantee to beat the local council price for waste disposal, so the service is particularly attractive to SMEs.

By 2009 First Mile had spread from London to Leeds, Birmingham and Bristol and had 5500 customers. Turnover was £4 million.

☐ Up-to-date information on First Mile can be found on their website: www.firstmile.co.uk

💡 Techniques for generating new ideas

There are many techniques designed to help encourage the generation of new ideas. Most are directed at generating a higher quality of idea rather than a greater volume. People with different thinking styles will respond differently to each of them. Here are just a few of the more widely used ones.

Brainstorming

This is one of the most widely used techniques. It is practised in a group. In the session you do not question or criticise ideas. You suspend disbelief. The aim is to encourage the free flow of ideas – divergent thinking – and as many ideas as possible. Everyone has thousands of good ideas within them just waiting to come out.

But people inherently fear making mistakes or looking foolish in front of others. Here making 'mistakes' and putting forward ideas which don't work is not only acceptable, it is also encouraged.

You might start with a problem to be solved or an opportunity to be exploited. You encourage and write down ideas as they come by facilitating all the dimensions of creative thinking in Figure 5.1. There are no 'bad' ideas. All ideas are, at the very least, springboards for other ideas. You allow the right side of the brain full rein and only engage the left brain to analyse the ideas you come up with at a later date. It is often best undertaken with a multidisciplinary team so that the issue can be approached from many different perspectives, encouraging the cross-fertilisation of ideas.

Negative brainstorming, thinking about the negative aspects of a problem or situation, can often be used initially to unblock more creative and positive brainstorming. It is particularly useful in getting people to think about what might happen if they do not think more creatively and can be used to help change motivations and behaviour.

🗂 A seven-step guide to running a brainstorming session

1 Describe the outcome you are trying to achieve – the problem or opportunity – BUT NOT THE SOLUTION. This could be a broad area of investigation – new ideas and new markets can be discovered if you don't follow conventional paths.

2 Decide how you will run the session and who will take part. You need an impartial facilitator who will introduce things, keep to the rules and watch the time. This person will restate the creative process if it slows down. The group can number anything from 4 to 30. The larger the number the more diverse the inputs but the slower (and more frustrating) the process – so something around 12 is probably ideal.

3 Set out the room in a participative (i.e. circular) and informal style. Comfortable chairs are important. Refreshments should be available continuously. Make certain there are flip charts, coloured pens and so on or. If you want to be high tech, you can use some of the specialist software that is available (e.g. Brainstorming Toolbox). People should also have a note pad so they can write down ideas.

4 Relax participants as much as possible. The style is informal. The rules of engagement should be posted clearly for all to see and run through so that everybody understands:

 ▷ Quantity counts, not quality – postpone judgement on all ideas;
 ▷ Encourage wild, exaggerated ideas – all ideas are of equal value;
 ▷ Build on ideas rather than demolish them.

5 Open the session by asking for as many ideas as possible. Get people to shout out. Write every idea down on the flip chart and post the sheets on the wall. Encourage and engage with people. Close down criticism. Try to create group engagement.

6 When the ideas have dried up – it might take a little time for it finally to do so – close the session, thanking participants and keeping the door open for them should they have any ideas later.

7 Analyse the ideas posted. Brainstorming helps generate ideas, not analyse them. What happens from here is up to you. Sometimes the people who generated the ideas can also help sort them, but remember to separate out the sessions clearly. Perhaps excellent ideas can be implemented immediately, but do not forget to investigate the interesting ones – no matter how 'off-the-wall'.

☐ For more information on the technique visit www.brainstorming.co.uk.

A variant on brainstorming is called brainwriting, whereby ideas are written down anonymously and then communicated to the group (computer technologies, like those used in the Royal Mail's Creativity Centre, can help with this), thus avoiding the influence of dominant individuals.

🗁 Case with questions

Alex Tew and the Million Dollar Homepage

Alex Tew, a Nottingham Trent University student in the UK was only 21 years old when he had his big business idea in 2005. Within months he had set it up – his website that is – the Million Dollar Homepage, www.milliondollarhomepage.com. By January 2006 Alex was a millionaire.

The Million Dollar Homepage is a single web page that is divided into 10 000 boxes, each 100 pixels in size. Alex sold the space to advertisers at $1 for each pixel, with a minimum of 100 pixels. The result is a montage of company logos each with a hyperlink to the advertiser's website. The site features a web banner with 'a pixel counter displaying the number of pixels sold, a navigation bar containing nine small links to the site's internal web pages, and an empty square grid of 1 000 000 pixels divided into 10 000 blocks of 100 pixels. Alex promised customers that the site would remain online for five years – that is, until at least 26 August 2010.

The idea for the web page originated from brainstorming and came whilst Alex lay on his bed at home in August 2005:

> 'I have always been an ideas person and I have a brainstorming session every night before I go to bed and write things down on a note pad.'
>
> *Sunday Times* 18 December 2005

The site took just two days to set up and cost £50. Alex sold the first blocks of pixels to his brothers and some friends and used that money to advertise the site. The site address began appearing in internet blogs and chat rooms. Following a press release, a BBC technology programme ran a story on the page in September 2005. This was followed swiftly by articles in newspapers around the world, as well as features on national television. As the site caught on, more and more advertisers signed up – after all $100 was not a lot to pay. By January 2006 he had sold all 1 million pixels – the final 1000 pixels were sold by a 10-day auction on eBay – at which point he closed the site to new entrants and left it on the internet. Alex had become a celebrity millionaire ($1 037 100 to be precise) and the homepage had become a phenomenon, all within a year!

> 'From the outset I knew the idea had potential, but it was one of those things that could have gone either way. My thinking was I had nothing to lose, apart from the £50 or so it cost to register the domain and set up the hosting. I knew the idea was quirky enough to create interest ... The internet is a very powerful medium.
>
> The crucial thing in creating the media interest was the idea itself; it was unique and quirky enough to stand out. I only had to push the idea a bit in the first few days by sending out a press release which essentially acted as a catalyst. This interest coupled with traditional word-of-mouth created a buzz around the homepage, which in turn created more interest.'
>
> Ask the Expert: How to make a Million, FT.com 22 February 2006 (www.ft.com)

☐ Visit the website on www.milliondollarhomepage.com

QUESTIONS

1 In your opinion is this a 'one-off' business, or can it be replicated?

2 If you think it can, how would you set about it?

3 What lessons do you learn from Alex's success?

Analogy

This is a product-centred technique that attempts to join together apparently unconnected or unrelated combinations of features of a product or service and benefits to the customer to come up with innovative solutions to problems. Analogies are proposed once the initial problem has been stated. The analogies are then related to opportunities in the market place. Operated in a similar way to brainstorming, it is probably best explained with an example. Georges de Mestral noticed that burdock seed heads stuck to his clothing. On closer examination he discovered the seed heads carried tiny hooks. His analogy was to apply this principle to the problem of sticking and unsticking things and to develop what we recognise today as Velcro.

The first steps to building an analogy are to ask some basic questions:

▷ What does the situation or problem remind you of?
▷ What other areas of life or work experience similar situations?
▷ Who does these similar things and can the principles be adapted?

Often the analogy contains the words 'is like' So you might ask why one thing 'is like' another. For example, why is advertising like cooking? The answer is because there is so much preamble to eating. Anticipation from presentation and smell, even the ambience of the restaurant you eat in, are just as important as the taste and nutritional value of the food itself.

Attribute analysis

This is another product-centred technique which is designed to evolve product improvements and line extensions and is used as the product reaches the mature phase of its life cycle. It uses the basic marketing technique of looking at the features of a product or service which in turn perform a series of functions but, most importantly, deliver benefits to the customers. An existing product or service is stripped down to its component parts and the group then explores how these features might be altered but then focuses on whether those changes might bring valuable benefits to the customer.

For example, you might focus on a domestic lock. This secures a door from opening by an unwelcome intruder. The benefit is security and reduction/elimination of theft from the house. But you can lose keys or forget to lock doors and some locks are difficult or inconvenient to open from the inside. A potential solution is to have doors that sense people approaching from the outside and lock or unlock themselves depending on who is approaching. The exterior sensor could recognise 'friendly' people approaching the door because of sensors they carry in the form of 'credit cards' or keys. This technology is now being applied to car locks. You could even have a reverse sensor on the inside that unlocks the door when anyone approaches (which could be activated or deactivated centrally).

Gap analysis

This is a market-based approach that attempts to produce a 'map' of product/market attributes based on dimensions that are perceived as important to customers, analysing where competing products might lie and then spotting gaps where there is little or no competition. Because of the complexity involved, the attributes are normally shown in only two dimensions. There are a number of approaches to this task.

Perceptual mapping places the attributes of a product within specific categories. So for example, the dessert market might be characterised as hot vs cold and sophisticated vs unsophisticated. Various desserts would then be mapped onto these two dimensions. This could be shown graphically (see alongside). The issue is whether the 'gap' identified between one product and another is one that customers would value being filled – and means understanding whether they value the dimensions being measured. That is a question for market research to attempt to answer.

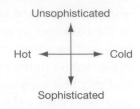

Non-metric mapping maps products in groups that customers find similar and then tries to explain why these groupings exist. A classic example would be the soft drinks market where products might be clustered and then described simply in terms of still vs carbonated and flavoured vs non-flavoured. The key here is also finding the appropriate dimensions that create opportunities for differentiating the product and creating competitive advantage. The mapping of soft drinks on the two dimensions above is unlikely to reveal any gaps in the market.

Repertory grid is a more systematic extension of this technique. Customers are asked to group similar and dissimilar products within a market, again normally in

🗁 Personal Construct Theory and the Repertory Grid

George Kelly was an American engineer who became a highly respected clinical psychologist, best known for the development in 1955 of his own theory of personality known as Personal Construct Theory and a tool to explore people's personalities in terms of the theory, called the Repertory Grid. Kelly believed that the personality theories of the day suffered from three things: an inherent observer bias, a lack of precision and prediction and an over-reliance on the expert.

Kelly believed that we all have our own 'constructs' – views of the world or biases – that help us navigate our way around the world quickly. Certain words will trigger certain preconceptions, be they logical or otherwise. When you open and walk through a door you do so without consciously thinking what you are doing but you are preconditioned to act in a way that has opened a similar door before. The fact that it is locked can often come as quite a sharp surprise. Construct systems influence our expectations and perceptions subconsciously – and introduce bias. This means that one person's constructs are not those of another – and sometimes they can even be internally inconsistent because we never question them.

The Repertory Grid attempts to get rid of this bias. The technique identifies a small set of elements (objects, entities) and the user is asked to define some constructs (attributes, slots) which characterise those elements. All these terms are identified in terms of the user's own language. So, for example, 'good' can only exist in contrast to the concept of 'bad'. Any construct can reasonably be measured by answering the question 'compared to what?' Construct values are given for each element on a limited scale between extreme polar points. The process of taking three elements and asking for two of them to be paired in contrast with the third is the most effective way in which the poles of the construct can be discovered and articulated.

It is beyond this book to explain, in detail, how this technique should be deployed. However, one of the most accessible and short books on the topic is by Devi Jankovicz (2003). It really is 'The Easy Guide to Repertory Grids'.

pairs. They are then asked to explain the similarities and dissimilarities. The sequence is repeated for all groups of similar and dissimilar products. The explanations are then used to derive 'constructs' which describe the way in which customers relate and evaluate the products. These constructs form a grid that can be used to map the products, applying the words used by the customers themselves.

📖 Creativity resources

To find what must be the world largest resource of creativity and innovation resources go to www.creax.net. The website contains hyperlinks to almost 900 other sites around the world. These include: authors, articles, books, basic research, creative environments, creative thinking pioneers, design, e-learning and creativity, education, creativity tools, ideas factories, ideas markets, imagination tools, innovation tools, internet assisted creativity, mind mapping, online techniques, ideas management, tests and puzzles and many, many more.

All the techniques discussed here – and more – are covered in more detail somewhere on this website. There are also tools and resources to help you try them.

💡 Recognising opportunity

Creativity on its own is not necessarily entrepreneurial. As we saw in Chapter 3, it is only entrepreneurial if it is applied to the process of innovation which leads to the development of new products or services that have a value in the market place. And the key to this is linking creativity and innovation to opportunities in the market place. The techniques outlined in the previous sections can be applied directly to commercial opportunity recognition in a systematic way.

Valery (1999) believes that 'innovation has more to do with the pragmatic search for opportunity than the romantic ideas about serendipity or lonely pioneers pursuing their vision against all the odds.' Peter Drucker (1985) takes this further. He believes innovation can be practised systematically through a creative analysis of change in the environment and the opportunities this generates. It is not the result of 'happenstance'. Entrepreneurs can practise innovation systematically by using their creativity skills to search for change and then evaluate its potential for an economic or social return. Change provides the opportunity for innovation. Skills in creativity help identify these opportunities. And it is the actions of the entrepreneur that make this opportunity generate an economic return.

Drucker said 'innovation is the specific tool of entrepreneurs, the means by which they exploit change as an opportunity for a different business or a different service. It is capable of being presented as a discipline, capable of being learned and capable of being practised. Entrepreneurs need to search purposefully for the sources of innovation, the changes and their symptoms that indicate opportunities for successful innovation. And they need to know and to apply the principles of successful innovation.'

> *When I started the Gadget Shop it was from frustration with the difficulties of finding gifts for the family and friends with a love of innovation and gadgets. There are lots of problems in life that could be solved with the right insight leading to a business opportunity: you just have to spot them. Some of the most successful ideas are actually simple.*
>
> ☐ Jonathan Elvidge, founder of Gadget Shop, *The Times* 6 July 2002

> *Our success is due, in part, to not just an ability but a willingness to look at things differently. I believe opportunity is part instinct and part immersion – in an industry, a subject, or an area of expertise ... You don't have to be a genius, or a visionary, or even a college graduate to think unconventionally. You just need a framework ... Seeing and seizing opportunities are skills that can be applied universally, if you have the curiosity and commitment.*
>
> ☐ Michael Dell

He lists seven sources of opportunity for firms in search of creative innovation. Four can be found within the firm itself or from the industry of which it is part and are therefore reasonably easy to spot. They are 'basic symptoms' – highly reliable indicators of changes that have already happened or can be made to happen with little effort. They are:

1 The *unexpected*, be it the unexpected success or failure or the unexpected event. Nobody can predict the future but an ability to react quickly to changes is a real commercial advantage, particularly in a rapidly changing environment. Information and knowledge are invaluable.

2 The *incongruity* between what actually happens and what was supposed to happen. Plans go wrong and unexpected outcomes produce opportunities for firms that are able to spot them.

3 The *inadequacy in underlying processes* that are taken for granted but can be improved or changed. This is essentially improving process engineering – especially important if the product or service is competing primarily on price and therefore costs need to be minimised.

4 The *changes in industry or market structure* that take everyone by surprise. Again, unexpected change, perhaps arising from technology, legislation or other outside events creates an opportunity for the entrepreneur and, as is often the case with all these sources of opportunity, first-mover advantage – making the most of the advantage before others do so – is usually worth striving for.

These changes produce sources of opportunity that need to be dissected and the underlying causes of change understood. The causes give clues about how innovation can be used to increase value added to the customer and economic return.

The other three factors come from the outside world:

5 *Demographic changes* – population changes caused by changes in birth rates, wars, medical improvements etc.

6 *Changes in perception, mood and meaning* that can be brought about by the ups and down of the economy, culture, fashion etc. In-depth interviews or focus groups can often give an insight into these changes.

7 *New knowledge*, both scientific and non-scientific.

Drucker lists the seven factors in what he sees as increasing order of difficulty, uncertainty and unreliability, which means that he believes that new knowledge including scientific knowledge, for all its visibility and glamour, is in fact the most difficult, least reliable and least predictable source of innovation. Paradoxically, this is the area to which government, academics and even entrepreneurial firms pay most attention. He argues that innovations arising from the systematic analysis of mundane and unglamorous unexpected successes or failures are far more likely to yield commercial innovations. They have the shortest lead times between start and yielding measurable results and carry fairly low risk and uncertainty.

```
OPPORTUNITY SCAN
Internal
▷ The unexpected
▷ The incongruity
▷ Inadequacy in underlying processes
▷ Changes in industry or market structure

External
▷ Demographic changes
▷ Changes in perception, mood and meaning
▷ New knowledge
```

⬇

```
BUSINESS OPPORTUNITY
```

F5.4 Generating a viable business idea

🛄 Case insight Tom Mercer and mOma

Tom Mercer was a management consultant with Bain and Co. in London. Before going to work he would blend smoothies with oats for his breakfast in his flat in Waterloo. But it took time and he was often late for work. Then it suddenly struck him that his problem was actually a good business idea – pre-prepare the blend and then sell it to commuters from key points, like stations, around London. And so mOma was born in 2006.

Now you can see mOma's distinctively colourful carts around stations in London. They sell Oaties – smoothies and oats, Jumbles – oats soaked in apple juice and mingled with low-fat yoghurt and fruit, and Hodge-Podge – a layer of fruit cooked with spices, yoghurt and a packet of granola. Tom spent five months developing his recipes. The first products were sold in

used plastic water bottles with labels glued on. Now the breakfasts are prepared in Deptford, South East London, then driven to central London to be sold from mOma's eight carts between 6.15 am and 10.45 am. In 2009 Tom had 25 people working for him, including 10 stall workers who are mainly students wanting to earn extra money. The driver picks up the stall workers and the leftovers at the end of the shift.

mOma products are also sold in Selfridges' food hall and served on Virgin Atlantic flights. Tom plans to open more stalls and extend the company beyond London by selling through Ocado, the internet grocer.

Drucker's Opportunity Scanning process is summarised in Figure 5.4. It can be used with brainstorming and other techniques that encourage creativity to form the basis of a systematic business opportunity scanning process. The next chapter will lay the structure for how the opportunities it generates can be evaluated.

As Drucker's analysis makes clear, gaps in markets come from change. If you are looking for a business idea think of changes that are taking place – in markets, technology, society etc. – and the implications they may have. For example:

▷ Products or services that you have seen but are not available in your area can mean there are opportunities. Experience of overseas countries and markets is always valuable.
▷ Changes in customer demands or fashions can mean needs are not being met.
▷ Changes in markets can lead to opportunities; for example, the opening up of new retail outlets, shopping areas or sales channels such as the internet.
▷ Changes in legislation can create opportunities; for example, changes in Health and Safety regulations and Food Hygiene regulations have created opportunities in the past.

One technique for getting to the root cause of Drucker's 'unexpected events', 'incongruities' or 'inadequacies' is the 'Why? Why?' exercise. This is used to explore options related to the event. Figure 5.5 shows a 'Why? Why?' diagram exploring the reason for a fall in sales (Vyakarnham and Leppard, 1999). From it you can see there are several possible reasons, although the trails have not been taken to completion. The root cause will lie at the end of one of the 'why?' trails.

In the section on Attribute analysis, the 'why? why?' technique could have been used to question why the domestic lock was designed in a particular way, taking nothing for granted. In this way the technique should uncover the prime attributes that users are seeking. An alternative solution to the problem can then be constructed.

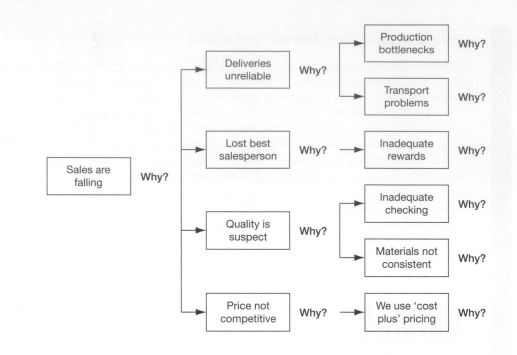

F5.5 Why? Why? diagram

Source: Adapted from Vyarkarnham and
Leppard (1999)

Even after start-up you must continue to work at opportunity spotting. Firms with a good track record for innovation practise it systematically. It does not happen by chance. They look for small changes that can be made to the way they do things. Indeed so systematic can the search for innovation be that some firms have been set up specifically to undertake it. Drucker (op. cit.) advocates a five-stage approach to purposeful, systematic innovation:

1 *Start with the analysis of opportunities, inside the firm and its industry and in the external environment.* Information and knowledge are invaluable – from as many sources as possible. Do not innovate for the future, innovate for now. Timing is everything. The right idea at the wrong time is worth nothing.

2 *Innovation is both conceptual and perceptual.* Therefore look at the financial implications but also talk to people, particularly customers, and analyse how to meet the opportunity.

3 *To be effective, an innovation must be simple and has to be 'focused'.* Keep it as simple as possible. Don't try to be too clever. Don't try to do too many things at once. The slightly-wrong-but-can-be-improved idea can always be developed and still earn a fortune.

4 *To be effective, start small.* Don't be grandiose. Take an incremental approach. Minimise the commitment of resources for as long as possible, thus maximising information and knowledge and minimising risk. This is called 'bootstrapping' and we return to it in Chapter 6.

5 *Aim at leadership and dominate the competition in the particular area of innovation as soon as possible.* This marketing strategy is called niche marketing and we return to it also in Chapter 6 because it is the strategy that is most likely to lead to success.

How innovations, particularly technical innovations, see the light of commercial day is complex. Scientific discoveries do lead to commercial opportunities which entrepreneurial firms can exploit. However, the linkages are not always as you would expect and they can involve a labyrinthine series of inter-relationships and networks

🗂 Case insight Adrian Wood and GTI

Adrian Wood set up GTI, a publishing company, in 1988 whilst at university. Adrian and two friends, Mark Blythe and Wayne Collins, were thinking about their futures and realised they did not know much about the jobs they were considering. The idea was to explain to students what was involved in various occupations. Adrian first thought of the idea in his second year studying economics at Reading University. He decided that he needed to 'sell' the idea to students – and more importantly to advertisers – by attracting some well known business names to contribute articles to the magazine. So he wrote to dozens of people and some, including Sir John Harvey-Jones, agreed to contribute.

Initially, Adrian and his two friends each put £200 into the business and used the university careers adviser as a consultant. Their first publication tackled quantity surveying and property. They took a week off studying and interviewed lecturers in different departments. They even got the backing of the head of education of the Royal Institute of Chartered Surveyors. About half of the publication was devoted to advertising and they personally delivered copies of it around the country. It made £6000 profit.

And so the company was born – 'to produce careers publications and an honest view of life'. The following year five magazines were published and sales came to £120 000. In 1990 GTI bought a barn in Wallingford, Oxfordshire and converted it into offices to accommodate its growing staff numbers.

Today GTI publishes over 100 careers products from offices in six countries. In the UK, their major brands are TARGETjobs, TARGETcourses and TARGETchances. In Ireland, GTI is the official careers publisher for all universities with their gradireland range of products. In Germany GTI operates as Staufenbiel – a highly respected name for graduate careers information. In 2008 GTI bought the UK and German graduate recruitment divisions of Hobsons, part of DMGI. GTI are also publishing partners for some 30 European universities through their Careers Service Guide range.

☐ Up-to-date information on GTI can be found on their website: www.groupgti.com

that we shall explore further in the next chapter. William Shockley had to invent a theory of electrons and 'holes' in semiconductors to explain why the transistors that he and his colleagues at Bell Laboratories in the USA had invented in 1948 actually worked. Even then, in order for the transistor idea to see the light of day, he and his colleagues had to take it to Palo Alto in California and start a company that eventually became Intel.

💡 The business idea

As we have seen, good business ideas can come from spotting good commercial opportunities – linked to market demand. Often the first attempt at putting that product or service together in a marketable way fails, so a series of trial-and-error iterations may be necesary. Howard Head, the inventor of the steel ski, made some 40 different metal skis before he finally made one that would work consistently. Most people base their business upon skills, experience or qualifications that they have already gained from a previous job or through a hobby. Often they think that their employer is not making the most of some opportunity. Sometimes they have an idea but cannot persuade their employer to take it up, so they decide to try it themselves. Often they have contacts in the industry they believe they can exploit to their own advantage.

As we saw in the previous section, you can create your own change and your own opportunity through innovation. This innovation could form the basis for a new business idea. For example, innovation could mean:

▷ *Invention*: Although, as we saw in Chapter 3, this is not necessarily the same thing as innovation. Often inventors are best advised to sell on their idea rather than to try to exploit it themselves.

▷ *Ways of doing things better or cheaper*: Better is good; cheaper, as we shall see, can lead to problems.

▷ *New developments in technology*: Computing, telephonics and the internet are at the forefront of technological change at the moment.

▷ *New ways of getting goods or services to markets*: Direct selling of certain types of goods or services firstly over the telephone and now the internet have created many millionaires in the last couple of decades.

However, there are many other sources of potential new business ideas. They come from an exposure to business and commerce around the world – an inquisitiveness and a constant searching for commercial opportunity. They come, not so much from asking the question 'why?', but rather from asking the question 'why not?'. And many of the techniques discussed in the previous section can be used to generate them. They could come from:

▷ Existing businesses around the world – either what they are offering or what they are not offering;

▷ Existing franchises not offered in certain countries;

▷ Innovations – your own or those belonging to other people;

▷ Patents and licences – your own or those belonging to others that are not yet fully exploited;

▷ Research institutes – where new products may have commercial potential;

▷ Industry and trade contacts yielding insights into gaps in markets;

▷ Industry and trade shows where new products and services are seeking new markets;

▷ Newspapers and trade journals – where new products, services or markets around the world are reviewed and, most importantly, gaps in markets might be exposed;

▷ Business networks and contacts – which might provide the blinding insight that a market opportunity exists;

▷ Television and radio.

'I know everyone wants to think that it is like an act of God – that you sit down and have a brilliant idea. Well, when you start your own business it does not work like that. I remember walking through Littlehampton with the kids, one in a pushchair and one walking beside me. We went into the sweet shop, then into the greengrocer and then to Boots. In both the sweet shop and the greengrocers I had choice. I could buy as much, or as little, as I wanted. I could buy half a pound of gob-stoppers or a kilo of apples, the quantities were up to me. In Boots I suddenly thought "What a shame that I can't buy as little as I like here too. Why am I stuck with only big sizes to choose from? If I'm trying something out and don't like it, I am too intimidated to return it, so I'm stuck with it." That one thought, that single reaction, was me voicing a need, a disappointment with things as they were. But if that's a need I have, lots of other women must have the same need, I thought. Why can't we buy smaller sizes – like in the greengrocers?'

☐ Anita Roddick, founder of Body Shop, Personal interview

One significant factor, of course, will be the sectors and markets in which small firms are currently growing most quickly. It is here that opportunities currently exist. But will you be able to capitalise on these developments as quickly as existing firms? And will those opportunities still exist in five years' time? A good business idea has a window of commercial opportunity. Too early or too late and it is unlikely to be successful. Cecil Duckworth set up his engineering firm to manufacture self-service petrol pumps, but when petrol in the UK was still being served by attendants. He did not sell a single one and the business nearly failed. However, within 18 months he started manufacturing central heating boilers and laid the foundations for the highly successful Worcester Engineering Group that he subsequently sold for over £30 million to the Bosch Group. It took another two or three years before self-service petrol pumps started to become popular and by then Worcester Engineering was no longer interested.

Finally, Bolton and Thompson (2000) suggest that there are three basic approaches to innovation – in many ways taking a different perspective on Drucker's analysis. None of these approaches are mutually exclusive. They can all be used to generate new business ideas.

▷ *Identify a problem and seek a solution.* They cite as an example Edwin Land's invention of the Polaroid camera because his young daughter could not understand why she had to wait to have pictures of herself printed.

▷ *Identify a solution and seek a problem.* They cite 3M's Post-It notes as an example of a product with loosely-sticking qualities that was applied to the need to mark pages in a manuscript.

▷ *Identify a need and develop a solution.* The example they cite is James Dyson's dual cyclone cleaner that he developed because of his frustration with the inadequate suction provided by his existing vacuum cleaner when he was converting an old property.

Your creativity skills can be used in identifying the problem, solution or a need in Bolton and Thompson's approach. You can also use your creativity skills to identify the solution or even the problem. Put another way, you can use your creativity skills to spot an opportunity. You can also then use your creativity skills to develop a product or service to meet the opportunity. Either way creativity is the key to innovation. And innovation is the key to a successful business idea. If all else fails, try the internet for

🗁 Start-up ideas from the USA

The USA is known for its entrepreneurship and here is a selection of some of the weirdest real start-up businesses in the USA. Some may have short life spans but it all goes to show that you can make money out of most things.

▷ **HappyBalls.com** of Cumming, Georgia, makes foam balls with colourful faces to be placed on top of car aerials. Do not mock – this is a million-dollar company.

▷ **Afterlife Telegrams** of New Athens, Illinois, offers to contact the dead. For a fee, they arrange for terminally ill patients to memorise a message that can be relayed to loved ones who have died when they themselves pass on.

▷ **eNthem** of San Francisco writes full length corporate theme songs.

▷ **Lucky Break Wishbone** of Seattle sells plastic wishbones so that all the family can have one despite the fact there is only really one in a chicken or turkey.

▷ **SomethingStore** of Huntington, New York, will, for a payment of $10, send you something, anything – but no telling what.

▷ **WeightNags** of Austin sends mildly abusive weekly messages to dieters, to encourage them to keep dieting.

▷ **Yelo** of New York City offers New Yorkers 20- or 40-minute naps in 'sleep pods'.

▷ **Throx** of San Francisco sells socks in packs of three – think about it.

▷ **Gaming-Lessons** of Jupiter, Florida offers video game lessons and coaching.

▷ **Cuddle Party** of New York City offers 'structured, safe workshops on boundaries, communication, intimacy and affection ... A laboratory where you can experiment with what makes you feel safe and feel good.'

▷ **Neuticles** of Oak Grove, Missouri, offers testicular implants for dogs that have been neutered.

ideas (sites such as www.businessideas.net or www.entrepreneur.com/businessideas/
index.php). They may not always be original but they get you to start thinking.

♀ The internet

The internet was probably the most important innovation affecting business at the end
of the twentieth century. It was a 'discontinuous innovation' that created major opportunities for new and small firms. The 'dot.com' boom in many ways resembled the
'railway mania' of the nineteenth century – another 'discontinuous innovation' – and
the consequences were remarkably similar. The value of many of the internet's new
companies became inflated and over-investment occurred. However, the new means
of communication, just like the new means of transport in the nineteenth century,
soon revolutionised many business functions and changed customers' buying habits
by improving communications and lowering transaction and other costs, particularly
for the service sector. Even the over-investment in the networks laid the basis for the
broadband revolution, which made the internet faster and more powerful and itself
laid the groundwork for the next phase of internet expansion.

The first start-up internet company to attract widespread stock market attention
was Netscape, founded by Jim Clark and Marc Andreessen, who had originally developed a web browser called Mosaic. The company was featured in the first edition of
this book. When Netscape went public in 1995, eighteen months after its launch, the
founders became billionaires and the shares tripled in value on the first day of trading.
Netscape soon disappeared as a rival browser, Microsoft's Internet Explorer, came
to dominate the market. However, the internet boom continued, firstly with portals
like Yahoo, Lycos, and AltaVista. They were set up, they were taken over and the
market consolidated. Then came the telecommunications companies that provided
the internet's hard-wired backbone, like MCI and WorldCom. Even companies that
produced the switchgear, like Cisco Systems, experienced the boom. As customers
learnt to shop online, the internet retailers like eToys and pets.com started to appear.
The boom spread to the UK with firms like Lastminute.com, floating on the London
stock market and a clothing start-up company called Boo.com raising millions of
pounds before it had sold a single garment.

Many new and truly innovative businesses were set up to exploit the unique characteristics of the internet and the advantages it offered. Certainly the internet service
providers came out of the boom. And firms with innovative business models like
eBay – arguably the most successful of the internet business start-ups – prospered
and grew (see Case insight). Community sites, bringing people with similar interests
together from around the world, grew out of the new technology. Many were started
in bedrooms and developed into valuable commercial enterprises.

This hectic dot.com boom probably came to a head with the disastrous merger
of internet portal AOL and the entertainment or content-provider Time Warner in
2000. Between 1995 and 2000, the main US stock market index, the NASDAQ, rose
five-fold. However, these share prices were over-inflated and in 2000 the stock prices
of internet and other high-tech companies plummeted. The dot.com bubble had
burst and reality was beginning to dawn. Firms with weak cash flow (like Boo.com)
went into liquidation, others were forced into mergers. Generally the survivors
consolidated their position and increased their market share of this growing market.
Companies like Amazon, Yahoo, eBay and Google emerged as the dominant companies in their sector.

But the internet did more than just allow innovative businesses to be established. It allowed small firms to compete in a global market place on price, the differentiated qualities of the products or service or by being able to focus even more effectively on market segments – niche marketing. The internet's lasting legacy are the new routes to market that changed the balance of power in the small versus large firm equation of competition. Almost any market on the planet is now accessible by the smallest of firms. With barriers down, competition is likely to intensify.

Much of the cost-saving effect of the internet has happened quietly, inside departments of large companies. The internet encouraged the growth of outsourcing, which led to manufacturing companies moving much of their production to cheaper, overseas locations. It is business-to-business trading that has been the greatest success of the internet so far. Large companies such as Dell Computers showed the way forward for manufacturers. Dell's 'information partnership' and 'fully integrated value chain' link customers, Dell and their suppliers and allow stock to be delivered on a just-in-time basis, thereby minimising inventories and costs. Many back-office service functions, from data processing to personnel, also moved offshore, particularly to India. However, the increasingly symbiotic relationships between these large firms and their small firm suppliers carry many dangers for the supplier.

Business-to-consumer retailing has also expanded dramatically as broadband networks have expanded. There are many opportunities for small firms on the internet that allow them to tap large markets without the overheads associated with the high street. Firms like Amazon, Lastminute.com in the UK, Dangdang.com in China and NCsoft in Korea are all examples of this. For retailers the internet allows them to keep in stock items that would not be available offline – for example, the range of books available from Amazon. However, the big high-street names have now established themselves on the internet and they are capitalising on their established brand and their loyal customer base. And it has become second nature for many people to check out products, prices and availability online before buying – often using price comparison websites. The internet has also allowed markets to be established where none existed before, for example through the online auction house eBay. And the range of goods and services available online continues to expand, for example with digital music and video downloads and voice-over internet calls.

The internet has been a truly discontinuous innovation. However, whilst the internet has become mainstream in the sense that it now permeates all we do, we are unlikely yet to have seen its full potential. Many more entrepreneurial opportunities probably still remain, undiscovered, in the virtual world it has created.

♀ Safeguarding your ideas

If you have an original business idea there are a number of ways you can help safeguard it. They come under the general heading of 'intellectual property' (IP), but they comprise a number of different approaches to giving you certain exclusive ownership rights to a variety of intangible assets broadly described as 'artistic and commercial creations of the mind'. Common types of IP include patents, trade marks, copyrights, industrial design rights and, in some countries, trade secrets.

The justification of these rights is that they encourage the creation of IP and pay for associated research and development. It is claimed that there are substantial benefits in terms of economic growth for countries that encourage IP protection, whether or not it is a form of monopoly. A report by Shapiro and Pham (2007) observes that,

📖 20 internet ideas from around the world

AUSTRALIA	**BestPlace Online** is a web design and hosting service that helps small firms to gain an effective web presence.
CZECH REPUBLIC	**Webnode** is an interactive real-time drag-and-drop website builder.
CANADA	**Octopz** helps creative professionals in fields like advertising, architecture, film, television and radio to work together in real time on a project online.
CHINA	**china-tomb.com** is an online mourning (tomb-sweeping) website.
FRANCE	**MyID.is** is a digital identity certification platform.
GERMANY	**StudiVZ** is a Facebook clone for the German market (many exist in other countries).
INDIA	**Vakow!** is a Web 2.0 subscription-based start-up that allows you to post and share SMS messages in Hindi, Tamil, Telgu or any other language.
IRELAND	**Cmypitch** is a website that enables aspiring start-ups to upload a video pitch which can be viewed by potential investors – a sort of 'Dragons' Den meets YouTube'.
KOREA	**Cmune** creates 3D multi-user social applications and games.
NETHERLANDS	**Myngle** is a global language e-learning market place where teachers and students come together to learn new languages and cultures.
NEW ZEALAND	**PocketSmith** is a web-based calendar that forecasts and allows you to manage your cash flow.
NIGERIA	**NaijaPulse** is Nigeria's version of Twitter.
RUSSIA	**WomanJournal** is a female-orientated online shopping site.
SINGAPORE	**RecordTV** allows users to download free-to-air TV programmes.
SOUTH AFRICA	**Amatomu** is an aggregator of South African blogs with a ranking system based on page views and inbound links with various widgets to facilitate its integration into other blogs.
SPAIN	**Bubok** is a service that allows you to upload your book, give it a professional image and offer it for sale.
SWEDEN	**Storytel** streams audiobooks to your mobile phone.
TUNISIA	**Ekree** (meaning 'rent' in Tunisian Arabic) is a portal for those who want to rent anything or put up anything for rent.
UK	**iSuki** is an online, subscription-based, social and dating agency.
USA	**MyMiniLife** is a new form of entertainment that allows people to design their own personal environment – a sort of virtual Lego Land.

📁 Case with questions eBay

Crucial to success for dot.com firms is the 'business model' – how income will be generated. Arguably the most successful model is that of the online auctioneer eBay. eBay was founded by Pierre M. Omidyar in 1995. The company has now expanded worldwide, claiming hundreds of millions of registered users, over 15 000 employees and revenues of almost $8 billion.

eBay's success comes from being nothing more than an intermediary – software running on a web server. Its customers, both buyers and sellers, do all the work. Sellers pay to set up their own auction, buyers use eBay's software to place their bids, shipping and payment are arranged between the seller and buyer and eBay takes between 7 and 18 per cent of the selling price as commission for letting them use its software. eBay is simply the trading platform. It holds no stocks and its involvement in the trade is minimal. After each transaction the buyer and seller rate each other. Next to each user's identification is a figure in brackets recording the number of positive comments – thus encouraging honesty and trust. It is a truly virtual business which also sells advertising space.

eBay developed a 'virtuous circle' in which more buyers attracted more sellers, which attracted yet more buyers and sellers – called 'network effects'. At the core of eBay's business is software rather than people. The company has bought software companies to gain exclusive use of their technologies and make the auction process more efficient. It therefore faces enormous economies of scale in attracting as many auction transactions as possible and, with that in mind, has moved into new areas such as used cars and hosting storefronts for small merchants where 'buy-it-now' goods are offered. It has also started to sell private-label versions of its service to companies, for a fee.

In 2002 eBay purchased iBazar, a similar European auction website. It also purchased PayPal, the dominant provider of internet payments in the USA. The two companies are complementary but depend on each other. Indeed, auctions account for almost two-thirds of PayPal's business. PayPal allows customers to register details of their credit card or bank account with it so that when they buy something on the internet they just enter an e-mail account and an amount. Like eBay, it is fully automated, relying on software rather than people. Like eBay, it also relies on 'network effects'.

Not all of eBay's new ventures have been successful. In 2005 it bought the internet phone company Skype, expecting to be able to use this medium as a platform for its main business. However it sold a 65 per cent share in 2009 to Netscape co-founder Marc Andreessen and a group of private equity firms, claiming Skype offered 'limited synergies'. In 2006, eBay opened its new eBay Express site, which was designed to work like a standard Internet shopping site for consumers with US addresses. It closed in 2008.

The company's business strategy involves achieving market dominance worldwide. It has already expanded into over two dozen countries including China and India. The only countries where expansion failed were Taiwan and Japan, where Yahoo! had a head start, and New Zealand, where TradeMe is still the dominant online auction site. Another element of its strategy is to leverage the relationship between it and PayPal. eBay's basic business model generates revenues from sellers. Driving buyers and sellers to use PayPal means eBay also turn buyers into clients. It also means that for each new PayPal registration it achieves via the eBay site, it also earns off-site revenues when the PayPal account is used in non-eBay transactions.

QUESTIONS

1 Why is eBay's business model so attractive?

2 How does PayPal enhance this business model?

3 Why does one element of eBay's strategy involve market dominance?

whilst economists trace 30 to 40 per cent of all US gains in productivity and growth over the course of the twentieth century to economic innovation in its various forms, today, some two-thirds of the value of America's large businesses can be traced to the intangible assets that embody ideas, especially the IP of patents and trade marks. They claim that 'IP-intensive industries produce 72% more value added per employee than non-IP-intensive industries and create jobs at a rate 140% higher than non-IP-intensive industries, excluding computers/electronics'. The authors go on to say that 'promoting and protecting new IP should be a high priority for US policymakers'.

However some critics characterise these rights as intellectual protectionism or monopoly and argue that public interest is harmed by protectionist legislation (Levine and Boldrin, 2008). Contrary to Shapiro and Pham's study, Dosi et al. (2006) observed that, despite the doubling of patent registrations and a tripling of related legal costs of enforcement in the USA in the 1990s, there was no observable step-change in the levels of innovation or profitability. From a managerial rather than a policy perspective, strong intellectual property rights (IPR) can also have some significant disadvantages. In particular, where systematic innovation requiring constant input of external knowledge is concerned, for example through various forms of networking, strong IPR gets in the way because it inhibits collaborative working. The argument is that by collaborative working the small firm may have a small part in a very much larger pie and is therefore better off. Indeed, one study concluded that the use of IPR has a *negative* effect on a strategy of long-term value creation, the positive influences being lead time, secrecy and tacitness of knowledge (Hurmelinna-Laukkanen and Puumalainen, 2007). Tidd and Bessant (2009) conclude: 'Firms need to balance the desire to protect their knowledge with the need to share aspects of knowledge to promote innovation ... Theoretical arguments and empirical research suggest that from both a policy and management perspective, *only a limited level of IPR* is desirable to encourage risk taking and innovation.'

So, the message for an existing business is that you should not rely too much on IPR, and certainly do not let it get in the way of networking or collaborative working where external knowledge is an important part of your systematic innovation. Secrecy may be just as strong a tool as IPR. However, for a start-up the IP you have on your business idea may be one of the few real assets available to you and in seeking finance for your idea you will have to expose it to many people, some of whom may be less scrupulous than others. In this case you would be well advised to seek the maximum IPR you can find. Nevertheless being first to market is sometimes more effective in creating competitive advantage than IPR on an idea that has missed its window of commercial opportunity.

Modern use of the term IP goes back at least as far as 1888 with the founding in Berne of the Swiss Federal Office for Intellectual Property, but the origins of patents for invention go back even further. No one country can claim to have been the first in the field with a patent system, although Britain does have the longest continuous patent tradition in the world. Its origins date from the fifteenth century, when the Crown started making specific grants of privilege to manufacturers and traders. They were given open letters marked with the King's Great Seal called 'Letters Patent'. Henry VI granted the earliest known patent to Flemish-born John of Utynam in 1449, giving him a 20-year monopoly on a method of making stained glass.

IP law varies from country to country. It is complex and usually comprises a multiplicity of individual pieces of legislation generated over a number of years. With the exception of copyright, if you want to protect your IP in other countries you will generally need to apply for protection in that country. The World Intellectual Property Organisation, an agency of the United Nations, produces the *Guide to Intellectual Property Worldwide* (available at www.ipo.int). In the UK information on regulations and laws can be obtained from the Intellectual Property Office (IPO) (www.ipo.gov.uk). Detailed UK legislation can be viewed on this site, as well as practical help with searches and registering your IP. Generally, however, four fundamental methods of protection are offered in most countries: patents, trademarks, industrial design rights and copyright. A simplified guide to these is given below, but details may vary from country to country and professional help should always be sought over complex IP issues.

Patent

A patent is intended to protect new inventions. It covers how they work, what they do, how they do it, what they are made of and how they are made. It gives the owner the right to prevent others from copying, making, using, importing or selling the invention without permission. The existence of a patent may be enough on its own to prevent others from trying to exploit the invention. However should they persist in trying to do so, it gives you the right to take legal action to stop them exploiting your invention and to claim damages. And herein lies the problem for cash-strapped start-ups. Can they really afford the legal fees involved in pursuing such a claim? Nevertheless the patent allows you to sell the invention and all the IP rights, license it to someone else but retain all the IP rights or discuss the invention with others in order to set up a business based on the invention.

⬜ Intellectual property protection in the UK

The *Intellectual Property Office* (IPO), an executive agency of the Department of Business Innovation and Skills, became the operating arm of the *Patent Office* in 2007. The Patent Office was set up in 1852 to act as the sole office for the granting of patents, although its origins go back some 400 years. The *Design Registry* was set up in 1839 to protect industrial designs. Its responsibilities were transferred to the Patent Office in 1875. The registration of trade marks became a Patent Office function in 1876.

The IPO say that for the invention to be eligible for patenting it must be *new*, have an *inventive step* that is not obvious to someone with knowledge and experience in the subject and be capable of being *made* or *used* in some kind of industry. If a patent is granted, it lasts for 20 years but must in the UK be renewed every year after the fifth year. Patents are published after 18 months, which makes people aware of patents that they will eventually be able to use freely once the patent protection ceases. This also can be seen as a disadvantage and you should remember that there is no legal requirement for you to file a patent; you can always decide to keep your invention secret. This is undoubtedly cheaper but if the invention enters the public domain then you may lose your rights to it. However, in dealing with individuals you might approach regarding an unpatented invention you may ask them to sign a confidentiality agreement (also known as a non-disclosure agreement) to protect your rights.

The IPO lists some things for which a patent cannot be granted such as:

▷ a scientific or mathematical discovery, theory or method;
▷ a literary, dramatic, musical or artistic work;
▷ a way of performing a mental act, playing a game or doing business;
▷ the presentation of information, or some computer programs;
▷ an animal or plant variety;
▷ a method of medical treatment or diagnosis;
▷ anything that is against public policy or morality.

Trade mark ®,™

A trade mark is a sign – made up of words or a logo or both – which distinguishes goods and services from those of competitors. This is important as part of a strategy of differentiation, explained elsewhere. The IPO says that a trade mark must be *distinctive for the goods and services provided*. In other words it can be recognised as a sign that *differentiates* your goods or service from someone else's. Once registered, trade mark registration must be renewed every ten years.

Once registered a trade mark gives you the exclusive right to use your mark for the goods and/or services that it covers in the country in which you have registered it. You can put the ® or ™ symbol next to it to warn others against using it.

As with a patent, a registered trade mark may put people off using the trade mark without permission and allows you to take legal action against anyone who uses it without your permission. However, in the UK a trade mark also allows Trading Standards Officers or the Police to bring criminal charges against counterfeiters illegally using it. As with a patent, you can sell a trade mark, or let other people have a licence that allows them to use it. In the UK, even if you don't register your trade mark, you may still be able to take action if someone uses your mark without your permission, using the lengthier and onerous common law action of 'passing off'.

It is worth mentioning that, just because a company has its name registered with Companies House in the UK, it does not mean that that name is a registered trade mark – company law is different from trade mark law. Similarly, being the owner of a registered trade mark does not automatically entitle you to use that mark as an internet domain name, and vice versa. This is because the same trade mark can be registered for different goods or services and by different proprietors. Also, someone may have already registered the domain name, perhaps with its use being connected with unregistered goods or services. To search or register a domain name you should apply to an Accredited Registrar (available from the Internet Corporation for Assigned Names and Numbers, www.icann.org).

The IPO say that trade marks cannot be registered if they:

▷ describe goods or services or any characteristics of them, for example, marks which show the quality, quantity, purpose, value or geographical origin of the goods or services (e.g. Cheap Car Rentals or Quality Builders);
▷ have become customary in this line of trade;
▷ are not distinctive;
▷ are three dimensional shapes, if the shape is typical of the goods you are trading, has a function or adds value to the goods;
▷ are specially protected emblems;
▷ are offensive;
▷ are against the law (e.g. promoting illegal drugs);
▷ are deceptive.

Registered design

If you are creating products or articles, which are unique because they look different from anything else currently available, then you might want to protect the look by registering it as a design. A registered design is a legal right which protects the overall visual appearance of a product in the geographical area you register it. The registered design covers the things that give the product a unique appearance, such as the lines, contours, colours, shape, texture, materials and the ornamentation of the product (e.g. a pattern on a product or a stylised logo). It is a valuable asset that allows you to stop others from creating similar designs. It does not offer protection from what a product is made of or how it works.

Registering a design gives you exclusive rights for the look and appearance of your product. This may be enough on its own to stop anyone using your design, irrespective of whether they copied it or came up with the design independently. Once a design is registered you can sell or license it and sell or retain the IP rights.

The IPO say that to be able to register a design it must:

▷ be new – in the UK a design is considered new if no identical or similar design has been published or publicly disclosed in the UK or the European Economic Area;
▷ have individual character – this means that the appearance of the design (its impression) is different from the appearance of other already known designs.

In the UK, Design Right and Community Design Right may also give you automatic protection for the look of your product.

Copyright ©

Copyright allows you to protect your original material and stops others from using your work without permission. It can be used to protect any media:

▷ literary works such as computer programs, websites, song lyrics, novels, instruction manuals, newspaper articles and some types of database;
▷ dramatic works including dance or mime;
▷ musical works;
▷ artistic works such as technical drawings, paintings, photographs, sculptures, architecture, diagrams, maps and logos;
▷ layouts or typographical arrangements used to publish a work (e.g. for a book);
▷ sound or visual recordings of a work;
▷ broadcasts of a work.

Copyright does not protect ideas, only the 'published' manifestation of those ideas, for example in writing. This happens automatically in most countries, which means that you do not have to apply for it so long as it falls within one of the categories of media protected, but it also means there is no official copyright register. Although not essential, you should mark the material with the © symbol, the name of the copyright owner and the year in which the work was created. Copyright owners may also choose to use technical measures such as copy protection devices to protect their material. In the UK, in addition to or instead of copyright protection, a database may be protected by the 'database right'. Trade marks can be both registered designs (for the artwork) and copyright. You can only copy a work protected by copyright with the owner's permission, even when you cross media boundaries (e.g. crossing from the internet to print).

As copyright owner you have the right to authorise or prohibit any of the following actions in relation to your work:

▷ copying the work in any way (e.g. photocopying, reproducing a printed page by handwriting, typing or scanning into a computer, and taping live or recorded music);

▷ renting or lending copies of the work to the public, although in the UK some lending of copyright works falls within the Public Lending Rights Scheme and this does not infringe copyright;

▷ performing, showing or playing the work in public. (e.g. performing plays and music, playing sound recordings and showing films or videos in public);

▷ broadcasting the work or other communication to the public by electronic transmission, including transmission through the internet;

▷ making an adaptation of the work (e.g. by translating a literary or dramatic work, or transcribing a musical work or converting a computer program into a different computer language).

If you have copyright of a work you can sell or license it and sell or retain your ownership. You can also object if your work is distorted or mutilated. As with other forms of IP protection, the existence of copyright may be enough on its own to stop others from trying to copy your material. If it does not, you have the right to take legal action to stop them exploiting your copyright and to claim damages – that is if you can afford to go to court. Copyright infringement only occurs when a whole work or substantial part of it is copied without consent. However, what constitutes a substantial part is not defined and may therefore have to be decided by court action. Copyright is essentially a private right and therefore the cost of enforcing it falls to the individual.

🗑 Case with questions Andrew Valentine and Streetcar

Andrew Valentine studied modern languages and anthropology at Durham University. Whilst there, he and a friend set up a student radio station, Purple FM. After graduating he joined the shipping company P&O and worked for them for six years, doing a part-time MBA. But in 2002 Andrew got itchy feet and decided he wanted to set up his own business, rather than work for other people. The problem was he did not have a business idea. So he and a friend, Brett Akker, became partners and set about searching systematically for the right business. They spent 18 months researching many ideas rom organic food to training courses, meeting twice a week, before coming up with the final idea.

> 'We looked at hundreds of ideas. We were basically trying to identify gaps, so we were looking at how society was changing and what was missing. Our business had to have potential, be capable of being scaled up and play to our strengths. We kept looking until we found something that matched our criteria.'

The final idea came from something Andrew read about in another country – a car sharing club. By 2009 Andrew and Brett's company, called Streetcar, had a turnover of £20 million and some 1300 cars based in six UK cities. The idea is that people in towns and cities can rent a car for as little as half an hour, replacing the need to buy. Cars are parked in residential streets and are ready to drive away using an electronic card to open the door and start up.

> 'I read about a similar business overseas and immediately thought, what an amazing idea. There were a couple of other companies already running this kind of service in Britain but they weren't doing it the way we imagined we would be able to do it. We thought we could be more effective.'

→

Once Andrew and Brett had the idea, they spent four months holding market research focus groups to test out the business model and developing financial projections to estimate the resources they would need.

'We were satisfying ourselves that not only would it work but that there was enough demand for it.'

Initially called Mystreetcar and based in Clapham, South London, the business was finally launched in 2004 on the back of their savings, £60 000 of outside finance and £130 000 of lease finance to purchase the first eight cars. Initially they did everything themselves, working almost a 24-hour day. They handed out leaflets at train and tube stations in the early mornings, eventually getting family and friends to help, they answered the phone and signed up members, meeting them to show how to use the cars. They even washed and maintained the cars themselves. They offered a 24-hour service to members so, to start with, one of them had to be near to a phone all day, every day. After three months they had 100 members, each having paid a membership deposit and joining fee, so they went out and leased 20 more cars at a cost of £300 000.

The business model has changed slightly now. There is no deposit, just an annual membership fee and cars are rented by the hour, which includes 30 miles of petrol. In 2007 Andrew and Brett gave up 43 per cent of the business to Smedvig, a venture capital company, which invested £6.4 million in Streetcar.

'Brett and I share a healthy level of permanent dissatisfaction with the service. This means that we are constantly working at making it better and improving everything. I really enjoy the creativity of growing a business.'

Sunday Times 15 November 2009

☐ Up–to-date information on Streetcar can be found on their website: www.streetcar.co.uk

QUESTIONS

1 How did Andrew and Brett go about getting their business idea?

2 How did they minimise their risks in setting up the business?

▷ Summary

▷ Creativity is the soul of entrepreneurship. It underpins innovation.

▷ Creativity is a right brain activity that involves lateral as opposed to vertical thinking. It is intuitive, imaginative and rule-breaking. It requires interpersonal and emotional skills and is people-focused. Creative types do exhibit certain common characteristics and there are tests that purport to detect them.

▷ The creative process involves four steps and, as with **Current Cost** and **First Mile**, can take time:

1 Generating knowledge and awareness.
2 Incubation.
3 Generating ideas.
4 Evaluation and implementation.

▷ There are blocks to creativity. Realising they exist can be the first step to dismantling them. What is more, there are also techniques that can help in the process such as brainstorming (–the technique used by **Alex Tew** when he set up **The Million Dollar Homepage**), analogy, attribute analysis and gap analysis. A key element is the ability to spot relationships and then replicate them in a different context. Appropriate facilities and environments can help with the process.

▷ You can use creativity skills to spot a commercial opportunity. You can also use them to develop a product or service to meet the opportunity.

▷ Opportunities can be spotted from the systematic analysis of unexpected successes or failures, or the incongruities between what actually happens and what was supposed to happen. Opportunities also come from new knowledge, including scientific knowledge, but this is the most difficult form of opportunity to bring to market. The 'discontinuous innovation' of the internet created an enormous number of commercial opportunities and many companies went bust trying to pursue them. Those that survived consolidated their position, making their founders multimillionaires.

▷ Alternatively, to help you spot opportunities you can adopt a three-stage process:

    1 Identify a problem and seek a solution, like **Adrian Wood** and **GTI**;

    2 Identify a solution and seek a problem;

    3 Identify a need and develop a solution.

▷ The thread that binds this all together is the entrepreneurial firm that links creativity and ideas to a commercial opportunity and, like **eBay**, offers an effective business model with good management that allows the idea to be exploited successfully. Entrepreneurs may have to be creative, but they also have to be good at business.

▷ You can safeguard your business ideas through patents, trade marks, registered designs and copyright, depending on which mechanism is most appropriate. However, being the first to market is sometimes more effective in creating competitive advantage than IPR on an idea that has missed its window of commercial opportunity.

⏻ **Further resources are available at www.palgrave.com/business/burns**

📄 Essays and discussion topics

1 Do you believe people can be trained to be more creative and generate business ideas?

2 What do you think is involved in being creative? Give examples.

3 Compare and contrast creative vs logical thinking.

4 Creativity is a more difficult skill than entrepreneurship to develop. Discuss.

5 Why is creativity the soul of entrepreneurship?

6 Can you think of an entrepreneur who was not creative?

7 Are you a left or a right brain person?

8 Are you comfortable being creative? If not, why?

9 Can one individual undertake the whole creative process without help?

10 Do you see yourself more as an explorer, artist, judge or warrior? Why?

11 Is creativity good in all individuals and organisations? Give examples to support your argument.

12 Can you make a living out of being creative without being entrepreneurial?

13 Over the last ten years what have been the major commercial opportunities that arose? How were they exploited? Were the developments technology-led or market-led? What were the consequences?

14 Over the next ten years, what do you think will be the main commercial opportunities that entrepreneurial firms might be best advised to exploit?

15 Have there been any disruptive events recently that have created commercial opportunities? What were they and what opportunities do they create

16 What makes a good internet business?

17 What lessons do you learn from the dot.com boom and bust?

18 Give some examples of new-to-the-world products that have been successful and some that have not. Why have they been successful or unsuccessful?

19 Why is 'time to market' important?

20 Do you have an idea for a new product or service? Explain why it might be successful.

21 How can government persuade more people to set up their own business? Should it do so?

↻ Exercises and assignments

1 Try assessing your creative potential. You can find many resources by undertaking an internet search on 'creativity'. Tests can be found on:

    ▷ www.creax.com/csa

    ▷ www.angelfire.com/wi/2brains

2 List the barriers that you feel inhibit you from being creative at home and at your college or university. How might they be removed or circumvented?

3 List the sources for awareness and new ideas you have at your disposal. What do you need to do to capitalise on them in a systematic way?

4 Like Alex Tew, try applying brainstorming in a group to the generation of new ideas. Try thinking of a new product/service application. Define an area for review, for example by looking at a problem you face in your everyday life and trying to find a solution to it. If you have problems with the technique, go to www.brainstorming.co.uk for further explanation.

5 Trying to use analogy in a group to come up with innovative solutions to problems can be more difficult – even with a group of friends. Start with a problem to be solved and find the way similar problems might be solved in a different context. Alternatively, find a natural solution to a problem and consider whether it can be applied to a different circumstance.

6 Try using attribute analysis in a group. Again, this can be difficult. Focus the group on an everyday product or service. Select one feature or aspect and ask 'why does it have to be that way – what benefit does it bring to the customer?' Try it a few times with different product/service features.

7 Try using gap analysis. Select an everyday product or service. Characterise the product or service in two dimensions and use perceptual mapping to plot where competing products lie on these dimensions. Is there a gap in the market? Repeat the exercise for another product/service.

8 Try applying some of the creativity techniques to generate new ideas. Try thinking of a new product/service application. Define an area for review, for example by looking at a problem you face in your everyday life and trying to find a solution to it.

📖 References

Bolton, B. and Thompson, J. (2000) *Entrepreneurs: Talent, Temperament, Technique*, Oxford: Butterworth-Heinemann.

de Bono, E. (1971) *Lateral Thinking for Management*, Harmondsworth: Penguin.

de Bono, E. (1995) 'Serious Creativity', *Journal for Quality and Participation*, 18(5).

Dosi, G., Maengo, L. and Pasquali, C. (2006) 'How Much Should Society Fuel the Greed of Innovators? On the Relations Between Appropriability, Opportunities and Rates of Innovation', *Research Policy*, 35.

Drucker, P. (1985) *Innovation and Entrepreneurship*, London: Heinemann.

Hurmelinna-Laukkanen, P. and Puumalainen, K. (2007) 'Nature and Dynamics of Appropriability: Strategies for Appropriating Returns on Innovation', *R&D Management*, 37.

Jankowicz, D. (2003) The Easy Guide to Repertory Grids, New York: John Wiley & Sons.

Kirby, D. (2003) *Entrepreneurship*, London: McGraw Hill.

Levine. D. and Boldrin. M. (2008) *Against Intellectual Monopoly*, Cambridge: Cambridge University Press.

Majaro, S. (1992) 'Managing Ideas for Profit', *Journal of Marketing Management*, 8.

Mintzberg, H. (1976) 'Planning on the Left Side and Managing on the Right', *Harvard Business Review*, 54, July/August.

Page, A.L. (1993) 'Assessing New Product Development Practices and Performance: Establishing Crucial Norms', *Journal of Product Innovation* Management, 10.

Parkhurst, H.B. (1999), 'Confusion, Lack of Consensus and the Definition of Creativity as a Construct', *Journal of Creative Behaviour*, 33.

Shapiro. R. and Pham. N. (2007) *Economic Effects of Intellectual Property-Intensive Manufacturing in the United States*, World Growth, www.sonecon.com/docs/studies/0807_thevalueofip.pdf.

Tidd, J. and Bessant, J. (2009) *Managing Innovation: Integrating Technological, Market and Organizational Change*, Chichester: John Wiley.

Valery, N. (1999) 'Innovation in Industry', *Economist*, 5(28).

von Oech, R. (1986) *A Kick in the Seat of the Pants*, New York: Harper & Row.

von Oech, R. (1998) *A Whack on the Side of the Head*, New York: Warner Books.

Vyakarnham, S. and Leppard, J. (1999) *A Marketing Action Plan for the Growing Business*, 2nd edn, London: Kogan Page.

6 Evaluating the business idea

▷ **What you need to start a business**
▷ **Personal attributes**
▷ **Knowing your customers**
▷ **Knowing your competitors**
▷ **Marketing strategies**
▷ **Resources**
▷ **Capital**
▷ **The importance of networks**
▷ **Planning and evaluation**
▷ **Summary**

Case insights
▷ Quad Electroacoustics
▷ Morgan Motor Company
▷ Alan Pound and Aculab
▷ Richard Branson
▷ Robbie Cowling and Jobserve
▷ Big companies and strategic alliances

Cases with questions
▷ David Sanger and Rollover
▷ Mark Constantine and Lush

Learning outcomes

By the end of this chapter you should be able to:

▷ Explain a framework for evaluating a business idea and understand the knowledge and skills needed;

▷ Describe the personal attributes needed to run your own business;

▷ Explain the importance of identifying and understanding the motivations of potential customers;

▷ Evaluate competitors in a sector or industry and how you might be differentiated from them;

▷ Explain Porter's generic marketing strategies and evaluate which is most appropriate for your business idea;

▷ Explain the basis for economies of scale and economies of small scale;

▷ Explain the wide range of resources needed to start up a business and the phrase 'bootstrapping';

▷ Explain the capital that is brought to a start-up – financial, human and social;

▷ Explain why networks are important;

▷ Describe the planning process that underpins production of a business plan.

What you need to start a business

You need more than just an idea and a trigger to establish a successful business. As we saw from the failure statistics (Chapter 1), too many start-ups fail within the first three years. This chapter will give you a framework to help you evaluate your business idea.

For the idea to be translated into reality with a chance of success you need to have the personal skills and personal character traits to run the business. We looked at these in Chapter 2. Crucially, you also need to find customers that want to buy your product or service. If you are to prosper, you need to understand your competitors and the market place in which you are going to compete. You need to understand how you can attract customers at the expense of these competitors – your marketing strategies. Finally you need to ensure that you have sufficient resources – and that usually means money. These factors are summarised in Figure 6.1.

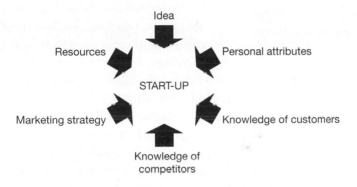

F6.1 What you need to start a business

Pulling these things together means research and that means you will probably have to acquire new skills. To evaluate whether your business idea has a chance of success means that you will have to plan how you might launch the business and how it might grow. Evaluating its potential for success means that you need first to prepare a business plan. Indeed, if you need start-up capital a business plan is essential. Subsequent chapters will give you all the skills you need to draw up and then evaluate a business plan, but we will start with the basics and the elements in Figure 6.1 that you need to start your business.

Personal attributes

It goes without saying that, if certain operating skills are needed to run a business, somebody in the firm must have them. Normally that person will be the founder. You cannot be a carpenter without having the skills of a carpenter. However, if you have six carpenters working for you, the primary skills you might need could be those of a salesperson. In fact a self-employed carpenter probably needs to be a salesperson too, as well as an administrator and a bookkeeper. The smaller the business the more the owner-manager needs to be a jack-of-all-trades, an all-rounder. Only as the business grows can they afford the luxury of buying in specialist help.

However, it is not just relevant operational skills that you need. You are likely to have the character

In those days I employed a girl to help me make the doughnuts. We started making them at midnight and this lasted four or five hours. Then I would load up the van and make the deliveries. After that I had to do the paperwork and snatch a few hours sleep before starting again.

☐ Gary Frank, founder of Fabulous Bakin Boys
Sunday Times 5 September 1999

traits of owner-managers and entrepreneurs that we looked at in Chapter 2 but you also need certain personal qualities which overlap these:

I don't count how many hours I work. I'm always looking for ways to improve my business, so even when I'm relaxing at home I'm ready to get back to work if a great idea occurs to me. A good entrepreneur doesn't just run a business; they live and breathe it.

☐ Martyn Dawes, founder of Coffee Nation
Startups: www.startups.co.uk

I'm often asked what sets successful entrepreneurs apart. It's a difficult question to answer but a couple of key attributes are determination and common sense … anyone can make £100million if they have the commitment and staying power. The beauty of being an entrepreneur is that, if the first idea doesn't work, you can come up with a second, and a third until you hit on a workable concept.

☐ Duncan Bannatyne, serial entrepreneur and Dragon
Daily Telegraph 5 March 2009

▷ *Stamina*: In your own firm you work long hours with few holidays, so you need the stamina for hard work. Robert Wright, who set up a small airline company called Connectair in the 1980s after leaving Cranfield University, called it '90% perspiration, 10% inspiration'. I found out how real this was when I ran my own business. It really is a 24/7 activity and very hard work. You need stamina and, actually, you need to be pretty fit.

▷ *Commitment and dedication*: In order to be motivated to put in that hard work you need to be committed and dedicated. And that can put a strain on relationships. You need to be tenacious and disciplined, willing to make personal sacrifices.

▷ *Ability to bounce back*: It is often said that the most common answer to any question in business is 'no' and this can be very dispiriting. All the more so if you are self-employed. You need to be able to bounce back and ask again and again. You need to be persistent. You need to be cheerful – even when the going gets tough.

▷ *Motivation to excel*: You need to be results-orientated, with high but realistic goals and a drive to achieve them. One thing is for certain; it can be very lonely running your own firm, so you need to be self-motivated, but the point here is that this motivation needs to be directed towards doing the best that you possibly can for your customers.

Finally it is worth stressing two of the key character traits needed to run your own business and how the tools developed in subsequent chapters might enhance them:

▷ *Opportunity perception*: Real entrepreneurs spot opportunities first – and continue doing it. This means taking opportunities almost before they appear – being aware of future possibilities. Whilst you need to be in the right place at the right time, you must make your own luck by playing the odds. The skills you acquired in the previous chapter need to be applied to spot new opportunities as your business grows. The skills you will acquire in subsequent chapters should help you focus your search for opportunities.

▷ *Tolerance of risk, ambiguity and uncertainty*: As we saw, the ability to live with uncertainty and take risks is a key character trait of entrepreneurs. If you crave certainty, regular routine and clear job definitions, do not go into business on your own – I mean it. However, there are ways of measuring and minimising risk – for example a technique called 'break-even analysis', which we shall develop in the next chapter, Subsequent chapters will also develop your understanding of the risks you face, for example in using different forms of external finance or in pursuing different growth strategies. You cannot eliminate risk but by understanding the risks you face you can take steps to mitigate or minimise them. As with opportunity, you can make your own luck by playing the odds.

Running your own business is not an easy option. It needs people with outstanding qualities and they deserve our admiration.

◯ Knowing your customers

Ralf Waldo Emerson once wrote: 'If a man can make a better mousetrap than his neighbour, though he builds his house in the wood, the world will make a beaten path to his door'. Let me tell you – he was wrong. Two further things are essential. Firstly, the world must need the mousetrap. There must be a market demand for a business idea for it to be capable of being transformed into a viable business. Customers will buy a product or service because it solves a problem for them, meets a need they have or adds value to them. Secondly, the world must know about the mousetrap and be persuaded to buy it. Customers must know about a new product or service and be persuaded that it will perform as promised before they will buy it. That can also mean understanding their motives for buying and tailoring the product or service better to meet those needs. The marketing skills you need to do this are developed in the next chapter.

I would have spent more time researching my idea. Although I couldn't afford it at the time, it would have saved me a lot of effort if I had recognised that customers wanted top quality gourmet coffee through machines rather than the instant product that was part of my original business plan.

☐ Martyn Dawes, founder of Coffee Nation
Startups: www.startups.co.uk

Inventors are particularly prone to mousetrap myopia; they tend to focus on the product and not on the market. But market demand is the key to commercial viability, and you need to start with basics:

▷ Who is going to buy the product or service? Name names and describe the customers.
▷ Why will they buy it?
▷ What needs do they want the product or service to meet?
▷ Is the customer reachable? If so, how?
▷ What are the channels of distribution?
▷ Is the market for the product or service new or mature?
▷ Is the market growing or declining?
▷ How big is the market?
▷ Does it have boundaries (for example, geographic location)?
▷ Are there competitors? If so, why should customers buy your product or service rather than that of the competitor?
▷ Is the product or service unique in any way?
▷ Is the market highly concentrated or fragmented?

Many of these things are difficult to assess at start-up, but some market research really is vital. One of the things you are trying to estimate is the sales potential of your product or service. This will, amongst other things, determine the scale and nature of the resources you need. Estimating the size of a completely new market for a completely new product or service can be a daunting task. For example, the market for PCs was completely underestimated when they were first introduced. It was not that market research was neglected, it was just that this was such a new, revolutionary and discontinuous innovation that customers could not foresee how it would be used. Given how ubiquitous the computer now is, this is difficult to believe. Where there are existing markets for similar products or services the task will be easier. Techniques for market research are covered in the next chapter. However, sometimes the quickest and cheapest way of finding out these things is by starting the business anyway, limiting the costs and risks, and closely monitoring the outcomes. This approach is attractive to owner-managers because they are action-orientated and learn by doing. However, all too often it is just an excuse for not undertaking any market research at all.

◊ Knowing your competitors

It is particularly important that a start-up business understands the nature of the competition it faces. This involves undertaking market research to develop a detailed knowledge of competitors and how your product or service compares to theirs. Research indicates that low growth firms have the least understanding of their competitors (Storey et al., 1987). Ultimately you will have to find some form of competitive advantage over them if you are to be successful. A major survey of over 2500 small firms concluded that there was an inverse relationship between the number of competitors and growth performance (Cosh and Hughes, 1998). In other words, as you might expect, the fewer competitors the better. Subsequent chapters will help you understand and develop your competitive advantage.

However, few competitors can be a bad thing in some circumstances. If you are entering a market where there is high concentration, then it may be that these competitors will combine to deter entry. High concentration can also mean bigger, more powerful companies as competitors. You need to think carefully before entering a market dominated by big companies because they will have well established market positions and the resources to fight off new entrants. Finally, it might just be that there are few competitors because the market is so small and/or unattractive.

Location can be an important factor dictating competition. In the UK, as in other countries, there can be marked variations in the sectoral, size and age structures of firms in different regions of the country and at different points in time. Whilst in the past surveys have found that small firms in the UK have tended to grow more quickly in rural rather than urban areas (ESRC, 1992), the 1998 survey (Cosh and Hughes, op. cit.) found the opposite. Of course, some of this may be due to factors other than competition. So for example, whilst firms in the south east of England face fiercer competition than firms in other parts of Britain, the survey also noted that they tended to enjoy higher growth rates. One reason for this might be that the market for their goods or services was growing faster and therefore greater competition could be sustained.

The structure of the market – the customers, suppliers, competitors – and the potential substitutes and barriers to entry determine the degree of competition and therefore the profitability you are likely to achieve. Michael Porter (1985) developed a useful structural analysis of industries which he claims goes some way towards explaining the profitability of firms within it. The aim of any competitive strategy, he says, 'is to cope with and, if possible, change the rules in favour of the company'. Unfortunately, a small firm is unlikely to be able to change those rules, so it pays to understand them. Porter claims that five forces determine competitiveness in any industry. These are shown in Figure 6.2.

1 *The power of buyers.* This is determined by the relative size of buyers and their concentration. It is also influenced by the volumes they purchase, the information they have about competitors or substitutes, switch costs and their ability to backward integrate. Switch costs are the costs of switching to another product. The extent to which the product they are buying is differentiated in some way

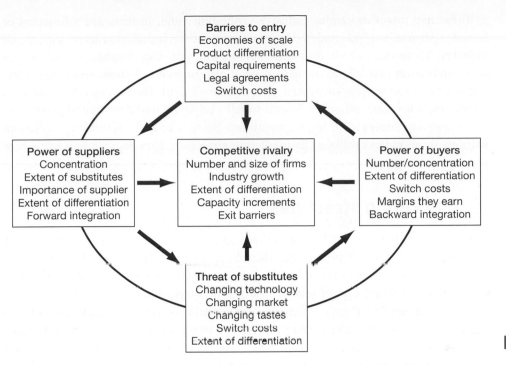

Barriers to entry
Economies of scale
Product differentiation
Capital requirements
Legal agreements
Switch costs

Power of suppliers
Concentration
Extent of substitutes
Importance of supplier
Extent of differentiation
Forward integration

Competitive rivalry
Number and size of firms
Industry growth
Extent of differentiation
Capacity increments
Exit barriers

Power of buyers
Number/concentration
Extent of differentiation
Switch costs
Margins they earn
Backward integration

Threat of substitutes
Changing technology
Changing market
Changing tastes
Switch costs
Extent of differentiation

F6.2 Porter's Five Forces

also affects relative buying power. The greater the power of the buyer, the weaker the bargaining position of the firm selling to them. So if buyers are large firms, in concentrated industries, buying large volumes with good price information about a relatively undifferentiated product with low switch costs they will be in a strong position to keep prices low.

2 *The power of suppliers.* This is also determined by the relative size of firms and the other factors mentioned above. So, if suppliers are large firms in concentrated industries, with well differentiated products that are relatively important to the small firms buying them, then those small firms are in a weak position to keep prices, and therefore their costs, low.

3 *The threat of new entrants.* Barriers to entry keep out new entrants to an industry. These can arise because of legal protection (patents and so on), economies of scale, proprietary product differences, brand identity, access to distribution, government policy, switch costs, capital costs and so forth. For example, a firm whose product is protected by patent or copyright may feel that it is relatively safe from competition. The greater the possible threat of new entry to a market, the lower the bargaining power and control over price of the small firm within it.

4 *The threat of substitutes.* This revolves around their relative price performance, switch costs and the propensity of the customer to switch, for example because of changes in tastes or fashion. The greater the threat of substitutes, the less the ability of the firm to charge a high price. So, a small firm selling a poorly differentiated product in a price sensitive, fashion market should find it difficult to charge a high price.

5 *Competitive rivalry in the industry.* The competitive rivalry of an industry will depend on the number and size of firms within it and their concentration, its newness and growth and therefore its attractiveness in terms of profit and value added together with intermittent over-capacity. Crucially important is the extent of product differentiation, brand identity and switch costs. The greater the competitive rivalry, the less the ability of the firm to charge a high price.

These five forces determine industry profitability and, in turn, are a function of industry structure – the underlying economic and technical characteristics of the industry. These can change over time but the analysis does emphasise the need to select industries carefully in the first place. It also provides a framework for predicting, *a priori*, the success or otherwise of the small firm. For example, a small firm competing with many other small firms to sell a relatively undifferentiated product to a few large customers in an industry with few barriers to entry is unlikely to do well without some radical shifts in its marketing strategies. How many small firms face just such a situation?

♀ Marketing strategies

How you communicate to customers that you have a product or service that meets some need they have is important. The whole area is called 'marketing' and how you pull it all together is called 'marketing strategy'. However, in reality there have only ever been three ways of selling products or services and at the launch of your business you need to decide which one applies to you. You see two of them being used every day in any street market. At one end of the market there is a street trader offering the cheapest goods in the market – fruit, vegetables or whatever; at the other end there is another offering something different – the freshest or organically-grown fruit, vegetables or whatever. The more different you are, the higher the price you can charge. But there is also a third way to charge a higher price – not to go to the market, but rather to take the product to the customer. This is focusing on the customer and their needs.

Michael Porter (op. cit.) gave this piece of common sense the catchy title of 'generic marketing strategies' and argued that there are only three fundamental ways of achieving sustainable competitive advantage:

▷ Low price;
▷ High differentiation;
▷ Customer focus.

These lead to the four market positions, or 'generic marketing strategies', shown in Figure 6.3.

F6.3 Generic marketing strategies

Commodity supplier

This is where the firm sets out to be the lowest priced producer in the industry, appealing to a very broad market with a relatively undifferentiated product. To have the

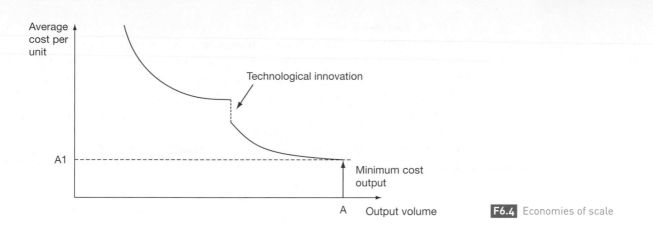

F6.4 Economies of scale

lowest price means you must have the lowest costs. This assumes that costs can be reduced, for example through economies of scale, and that this is important to the customer. If a firm sets up in a market where economies of scale are achievable and are important to customers it must grow quickly, just to survive. A firm can find itself in this situation when the market or product is new and economies of scale have yet to be developed. Firms may not yet have grown to their optimal size to achieve these economies and the battle is on to see who can get there first – it will be a risky battle with many casualties along the way. This is shown in Figure 6.4. Technological change can cause a step change downward in this curve at any time. Minimum cost on this curve is at output A with average cost per unit A1.

This strategy is an inherently unattractive alternative for most smaller firms as they can rarely achieve the economies of scale of large firms and seldom have the capital to invest constantly in new technology. What is more, it is likely that sustainable cost leadership can only be achieved by means of 'substantial relative market share advantage' because this provides the firm with cost advantage through economies of scale, market power and experience curve effects. This means that any firm pursuing this strategy will have to fight competitors hard to sustain its advantage. It will also try to set up as many barriers to entry into the industry as possible. A start-up coming into this established industry will have its work cut out just to survive.

The average size of businesses varies from industry to industry. For example, the average size of a chemical firm is very large, whereas the average size of a retail firm is relatively small. One of the reasons for this is the extent to which economies of scale affect an industry; that is, how total cost per unit produced changes as more units are produced. Generally this can be expected to decline up to some point, for example, as an expensive piece of machinery is used more fully. However, beyond this point unit costs may start to increase, for example, as economies of scale of production become increasingly offset by rising distribution costs. The potential for economies of scale is often greatest in capital-intensive industries like chemicals. This is shown in Figure 6.5. Total costs include production, selling and distribution costs and are therefore dependent upon the state of technology, the size of the market and the location of potential customers. The unit cost for industry A turns up at a relatively low level of output, implying the optimal size of firm is relatively small, in contrast to industry B where there are considerable economies of scale. Porter calls these 'fragmented' industries where economies of scale just do not exist and large firms cannot, therefore, dominate the industry. These are clearly easier industries for a small business start-up. Where economies of scale are considerable, and they are valued by the customer, this is an industry that a small business start-up should avoid.

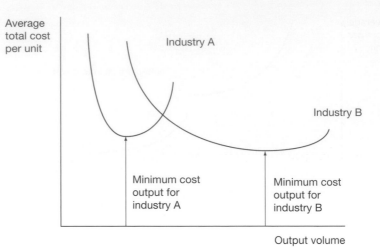

Average
total cost
per unit

F6.5 Economies of scale in two industries

An example of the effects of economies of scale is the personal computer industry. Born in the late 1970s with unknown demand for its products and no established producers, it has grown rapidly. However, the industry offers substantial economies of scale, particularly in R&D for hardware and software. Consequently the market has consolidated, with many small firms going out of business. The survivors have been one of two types of firm. First, there are firms like Microsoft for software and Apple or Dell for hardware which recognised that the industry would eventually be dominated by a few large firms either offering low cost or premium quality products. Apple went for well designed, high quality, high priced products. Dell went for market dominance offering competitively priced machines that are heavily marketed. Similarly Microsoft went for market dominance. Their big break came when IBM chose their operating system for its first PC in 1981, and the company was then able to ride to market dominance on the back of IBM's entry into the PC market. Secondly there were firms like Sun Microsystems which specialised in CAD/CAM equipment and aimed at even smaller specific market segments. Sun Microsystems established an effective market niche for itself and headed off any direct competition with big companies. Customers valued their expertise and economies of scale were less important. As often happens, it has been the middle-sized firm, which pursued neither strategy, which has suffered in this industry.

Market trader

And yet, we do see very small businesses surviving in highly price-competitive markets where economies of scale exist. Just visit your local Saturday market to see some examples. How do they do it? The answer lies in businesses that are classified as market traders.

When an economist draws a production cost curve like Figure 6.6 it is almost assumed that there will be economies of scale and that minimum cost output will be at some point A yielding a unit cost of A1. But have you ever noticed that the curve economists draw never touches the vertical axis? So what happens to the left of the curve? The truth is not something economists discuss. In many industries it is possible to start up with an absolute minimum of overheads, enabling you to compete with bigger companies who achieve the economies of scale. For example, consider the consultant working from home or the 'metal-basher' operating from a low-cost workshop under the railway arches. The average cost of production might then actually be

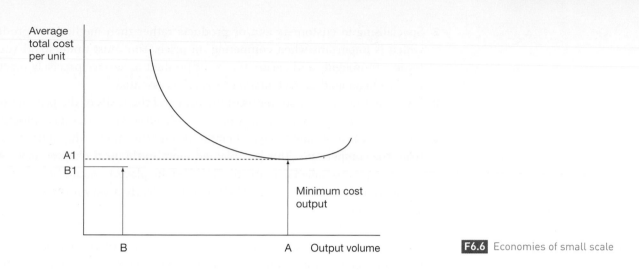

F6.6 Economies of small scale

lower than that of the big firm, for example B1. The problem is that that will only hold true of production levels up to a certain level, say B. To grow the business beyond this size means that the firm must increase its overheads and then it starts to move down the cost curve. In order to increase volume and cross the 'no-man's-land' between B and A the firm will need high investment and it will need to move quickly. The chances of making this dash successfully are relatively low. Businesses in this category are therefore unlikely to see growth.

Small firms, therefore, can compete on price as market traders. They may also compete in industries where economies of scale exist but are either unimportant to the customer or cannot be achieved because of limitations in the size of the market, either in total or geographically. This happens particularly in highly specialist industries. The problem for market traders is that they are unlikely to see growth.

Niche player

Differentiation means setting out to be unique in the industry along some dimensions that are widely valued by customers. This is called developing a unique selling proposition (USP). The firm sets out to establish itself as unique and different from its competitors in some way. It can then charge a premium price.

Where the firm combines this with a focus on a narrow target market segment it is said to be following a strategy of 'focused differentiation', better known as a niche strategy. Economists call this occupying the 'interstices' of the economy. Clear differentiation often goes with well aimed segmentation as it is easier to differentiate yourself in a small, clearly identified market. The key to segmentation is the ability to identify the unique benefits that a product or service offers to potential customers. Thus, for example, there may be two electrical engineers producing similar products but, whereas one is a jobbing engineer producing a range of products for many customers with no particular competitive advantage, the other might differentiate itself on the basis of its market – that it sells to a few large companies with whom it has long-term relationships, being integrated into their supply chains.

Being a niche player involves four things:

1 Finding out what elements in the marketing mix are 'unique' to the business. That means understanding what the customers really want when they buy the product or service and why they buy it from you rather than a competitor. Uniquenesses can be product- or market-based.

2 Specialising in customers and/or products rather than methods of production, which is important when competing on price. You must understand your customers thoroughly and ensure that your product or service precisely meets their needs. Ongoing, thorough market research is essential.

3 Stressing the inherent strengths of the firm and the USPs of the product or service, such as innovation, flexibility or personalised service, over its competitors.

4 Not selling just on low price and emphasising other things that differentiate you from the competition. This is explained more in the next chapter as we start to build up what is called a 'marketing mix'. Niche players should be able to charge a premium price and sustain a high margin, clearly a very attractive option for smaller firms.

It is vital that a firm understands the basis of its competitive advantage. For a firm pursuing a differentiation strategy this means understanding the basis for its differential advantage. This can be based in law (a licence, copyright, patent and so on), upon elements of the product (quality, design and so on), the service offered or intangible things like image. For a shop it may be based on location (the only shop on the estate). The more elements that the firm can claim to set it apart from the competition the better. However, these elements must be of real benefit and add value to the customer. If the firm has elements of differentiation then it should aggressively promote them, usually through a strong brand identity.

Establishing a market niche is most effective when aimed at a narrowly defined market segment. Sometimes this can involve concentrating on gaps in the market place left by larger companies. One problem of a niche market is its very narrowness, which limits it, but what might be limited for larger companies offers smaller firms a range of opportunities. Entrepreneurs often run businesses in different niches, finding growth through diversification. However the environment can change; markets grow or shrink, technology changes and customers move around. As the picture changes, so do opportunities, and what might offer a good niche in one decade may turn into a free-for-all in another.

The general thrust of research strongly suggests that market positioning is a key contributor to growth and that developing a market niche by differentiating a business from its competitors is a strategy that offers smaller firms the best chance of success and possibly sustainable growth. For example, in a survey of some 1500 smaller companies across Europe, it was found that those companies that had seen their sales and/or profit grow in the 1990s were those who had 'better or different products or services', and this led to weak-to-normal levels of competition (Burns and Whitehouse, 1994). Those that had seen sales, but particularly profits,

📖 Case insight Quad Electroaccoustics

One Huntingdon-based family company that has been very successful in differentiating its products and selling to a small but lucrative market segment is Quad Electroacoustics. Originally founded in 1936 by Peter Walker as an 'acoustical manufacturing company' to produce 'public address' systems, today its silvery grey, bizarrely sculptured audio equipment looks like no others. It sounds superb as well. When Japanese 'competitors' bring out new models every year, Quad's stay the same and last forever. Its original electrostatic loudspeaker was in production for 28 years. Quads are a byword for quality, reliability and design originality – but they are not cheap. Current models sell for over £3000 and still 70 per cent of Quad's sales are exported, especially to Europe, USA and Japan.

☐ Up-to-date information on Quad can be found on their website: www.quad-hifi.co.uk

Create something that is unique. The thing that makes Coffee Nation fundamentally successful is the concept is different. It's pioneering … the potential is far greater. If you set up a company selling widgets like the bloke down the road and the only difference is that yours are cheaper, you'll make a living, but that is all you'll achieve. If you can be truly differentiated and unique, then you've really got something.

☐ Martyn Dawes, founder of Coffee Nation
Startups: www.startups.co.uk

decline competed on price and encountered fierce competition. Another survey into 3500 of Britain's 'Superleague Companies' concluded that most of these high-growth companies served niche markets (3i, 1993). Storey et al. (1989) concluded that the owner-managers of the fast-growing firms were much more likely to emphasise competitive advantage as being in areas such as innovation and product or service quality. By way of contrast, the owner-managers of the slow-growing firms emphasised price.

There are, of course, risks with any marketing strategy. The risks associated with a policy of differentiation are that the basis for differentiation cannot be sustained as competitors imitate or if the USP becomes less important to customers. If the premium charged for the product or service is too high, customers may decide not to purchase. The risks associated with a policy of focus are that the segment becomes unattractive for some reason, or that smaller segments start to appear, chipping away at what is already a small customer base, or that the basis for segmentation disappears as the differences between segments disappear. Despite these risks, the niche player stands the best chance of launching and then growing a successful start-up.

Case insight Morgan Motor Company

One company, that arguably could make even higher margins by charging a higher price for its products, is the Morgan Motor Company. Founded in 1909, it is the world's oldest privately owned car manufacturer, making a quintessentially British sports car.

Every Morgan is hand-built and looks like it came from the 1930s. Each car is different, with a choice of 35 000 body colours and leather upholstery to match. It takes seven weeks to build a car and customers are invited to the factory to see the process. Morgan sells only about 500 cars a year, half overseas, and demand exceeds supply, cushioning the company from the vagaries of demand. Morgan is, arguably, a unique car manufacturer and certainly a niche player.

☐ Up-to-date information on Morgan can be found on their website: www.morgan-motor.co.uk

Case insight Alan Pound and Aculab

Back in the 1970s Alan Pound was making sound-mixing equipment in his garage and selling it through trade magazines. But in 1988 he moved into the computer-telephony market and started making hardware and software that is used in voice mail systems. His company, Aculab Plc now provides computer telephony components for integration into high performance communications solutions ranging from call centres and predictive dialers to prepaid services and mobile military communication units. It offers media processing resources, digital network access, protocols and approvals, IP telephony, fax, and speech processing and conferencing products. Companies around the world have adopted their technology.

Aculab remains a privately owned company with over 100 software and hardware engineers based at their headquarters in Milton Keynes and Edinburgh, with sales offices in Boston USA and Munich. They pride themselves on funding their growth through retained profits as opposed to borrowing, which has helped them decide their own destiny in terms of product strategy. The company also has a flat management structure without functional walls, producing a relaxed, empowering environment.

Alan Pound's view of the reasons for his success is simple, to the point and a lesson to us all:

'The company's success stems from picking a profitable niche in an area where there is little competition, high margins and huge barriers to entry.'

☐ Up-to-date information on Aculab can be found on their website: www.aculab.co.uk

Outstanding success

Sometimes firms that differentiate themselves effectively turn out to have a very broad market appeal, and what may have started as a niche business turns out to be an outstanding success and experiences rapid and considerable growth. However, it is unlikely that many businesses will start life here, except perhaps in areas of real innovation. Commodity suppliers try desperately to differentiate themselves, with varying degrees of success. Those companies that succeed in differentiating themselves do so through the effective use of branding.

Eventually even the big company can feel threatened by a large number of extremely effective niche companies. The computer industry as a whole has now fragmented into many different segments and no company now tries to compete in every segment. Based upon these generic marketing strategies, a specific launch strategy for the business needs to be developed. Subsequent chapters will help you draw that up. However, any start-up also needs resources and careful planning.

♀ Resources

The resources you need will depend ultimately upon the size of the business and this is difficult to predict at start-up. Most start-ups need money, but sometimes this can be minimised by borrowing resources or obtaining assets on lease or hire purchase. Certainly in the early days it does not pay to be burdened by high interest payments and flexibility is crucial. A golden rule in start-ups is to keep your fixed costs as low as possible. We shall explain how this can be achieved in the next chapter. Subsequent chapters will also explain how you can draw up a cash flow forecast that enables you to estimate the money you need for your business. We shall also explain how you might go about finding external sources of finance for your business.

Research awards, prizes, free consultancy, anything that will help financially and provide free business knowledge.

☐ Nin Castle, founder of Goodone, *Daily Telegraph* 5 February 2009

However, there are other less obvious resource needs. The business needs customers, suppliers, perhaps employees and a landlord. If it is to borrow the money, it will need a banker. The process of assembling these resources is a difficult one and is crucially dependent on one factor – credibility. The whole process has been likened to the credibility merry-go-round, shown in Figure 6.7, that can be mounted at any point (Birley and Norburn, 1984).

If you go to a banker with an ill thought through proposal, not knowing how much money you need, your credibility in terms of whether you are likely to manage the start-up effectively will be very low. The banker is looking for you to persuade him that your start-up will succeed. He might suggest you go out and get your first customer. But if you go to potential customers and ask them to place an order for your product or service they might ask about reliability or after-sales service. They might also reasonably expect to see the product. They might even ask for evidence of previous satisfied customers. The same problem happens when you approach suppliers or a landlord. They will ask for a bank reference, or look to a trading track record – none of which you have. So how do you get onto the merry-go-round?

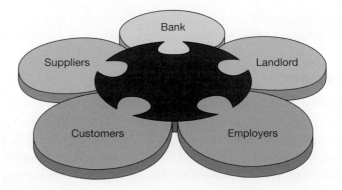

F6.7 The credibility merry-go-round

Deciding what resources are needed, when and how to acquire them are important strategic decisions for a start-up. Entrepreneurs typically seek to use the minimum amount of resources at each stage of the business. The important thing to remember is that you do not have to own a resource to be able to use and control it. Owning a resource normally means buying it and that ties up capital which increases the risk that the business faces. It has even been suggested that entrepreneurs who do not own a resource are in a better position to commit and de-commit quickly, giving them greater flexibility and reducing the risks they face (Stevenson et al., 1985). In the USA, minimising the resources that you own but still use and control is called 'bootstrapping', more formally defined as a 'multistage commitment of resources with a minimum commitment at each stage or decision point' (Bhidé, 1992). Clearly, to bootstrap you need to tap into as wide a network of contacts as possible.

> ### 📁 Case insight Richard Branson
>
> Richard Branson may have been lucky to find someone willing to let him have the premises for his first Oxford Street record shop rent free, but when he launched Virgin Atlantic he showed that he understood that high capital costs lead to high risks. He minimised these risks by leasing everything and then being able to offer a good quality service at attractive prices.
>
> Richard Branson's main skills are said to be networking, finding opportunities and securing the resources necessary for their exploitation.

> ### 📁 Case insight Robbie Cowling and Jobserve
>
> In the early 1990s Robbie Cowling started JobServe in his spare time from his bedroom by finding out what contract work was available locally and sending the list to subscribers. It was the world's first 'Jobs by Email' service delivering a handful of jobs to just over a dozen email addresses. This was followed later in the year by the world's first recruitment website which, very quickly, had some 3000 subscribers. At this point Alan's job as an IT consultant with the Ministry of Defence was relegated to four days a week – he was nothing if not cautious. Soon the business started spilling out of the bedroom. This was the point at which he decided to dedicate himself to it full-time. He also decided that he needed to move to a bigger house, which he also used as an office. Only one year later did he decide that the business had grown sufficiently to warrant taking the risk of moving to a dedicated office of its own.
>
> JobServe currently operate in 17 industry sectors and advertises jobs from all over the world. It employs over 80 staff working from its purpose-built headquarters in Tiptree, Essex as well as offices in Colchester, Hixon and Swindon in the UK and Sydney in Australia. They advertise over 2.5 million jobs a year and 'Jobs by Email' is now sent immediately when requested. They deliver over 800 000 emails a day. JobServe's website receives over 10 000 000 hits a month from over 70 000 unique visitors. And Robbie Cowling is a millionaire – at least on paper.
>
> ☐ Up-to-date information on Jobserve can be found on their website: www.jobserve.co.uk

💡 Capital

When you start a business you bring to it capital in a number of different forms. And we've already seen that the financial capital you bring to a start-up may be limited. But capital is more than just *financial*. It is also *human* – such as previous managerial or sectoral experience and training – and also *social* derived from access to appropriate professional networks. All this is shown in Figure 6.8. Research has established that the more capital you bring to the business, particularly that derived through networks, the more likely you are to succeed (Firkin, 2003).

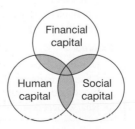

F6.8 Start-up capital

We have already seen that knowledge and experience of a business or sector is an invaluable source of business ideas, but it also gives you an insight into the problems that you will face. It is better to make business mistakes at somebody else's expense rather than your own. If you do not have that experience then education and training can alert you to the problems and give you the skills to overcome them. That is why so many people take start-up courses before they actually set up in business – they improve the chances of success. All these things increase your human capital.

> *Get as much professional training as you can before starting a business. Doing a MBA first really helped me.*
>
> ☐ Andrew Valentine, founder of Streetcar
> *Sunday Times* 15 November 2009

Social capital is built on relationships and relationships are at the core of the entrepreneurial approach to doing business – relationships with customers, employees, suppliers, the bank and landlord. It is social capital that enables you to build your credibility with all these stakeholders in the business. It is the personal touch that distinguishes entrepreneurs from the faceless, grey-suited managers of large firms. For the successful entrepreneur, these relationships build into an invaluable network of contacts and goodwill that can be used whenever the firm needs to change or do something just a little more risky than the average business. And these networks are also proving to be particularly valuable for knowledge-based start-ups.

> *You're constantly reading business books and constantly meeting people ... (taking) advice from all sorts of people. I would recommend that.*
>
> ☐ Mark Constantine, founder of Lush
> *RealBusiness* interview 26 May 2009

Human and social capital also help to establish the credibility you need to get onto the credibility merry-go-round we looked at in the last section. Human capital in the form of education and track record are important. If you can demonstrate achievements, particularly in the industry that you want to start up in, it counts for a lot. Social capital in the form of networks of friends and commercial contacts can also be important. A strong personal relationship can bring with it credibility. Your network of contacts might provide you with your first customer, or provide you with low-cost or free office space. They might even provide you with the cash that the banker is so reluctant to provide.

> *Have great advisers and listen to them. You don't have to take their advice but it's valuable to have other voices.*
>
> ☐ Sara Murray, founder of Confused.com
> *Sunday Times* 1 February 2009

We can combine the process of scanning the environment for opportunities, described in the last chapter and summarised in Figure 5.4, with this process of evaluation. The whole process of generating a viable business idea is summarised in Figure 6.9. The key to the opportunity becoming a viable business idea lies in customer need – identifying a real need that people are willing to pay for and that you are better able than competitors to meet.

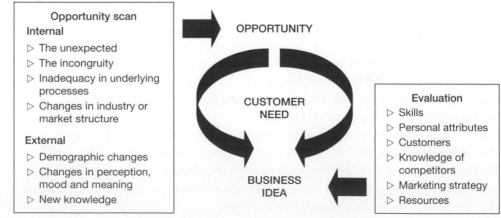

F6.9 Generating a viable business idea

💡 The importance of networks

Commercially, networks are important structures that provide you with information about markets and opportunities for your products or services. Networks can also provide you with professional advice and opinion, often without charge. Formal networks such as Chambers of Commerce, Business Links in the UK, Small Business Development Centers in the USA and trade associations can be invaluable for this. Networks enable entrepreneurs to do five things:

1 Gain customers by developing relationships based upon trust, often based upon reciprocity. Mass marketing can be expensive in terms of money but this form of direct marketing is expensive in time rather than money.

2 Gain knowledge of completely new markets and help find contacts to market the product or service. As we shall see in Chapter 8, it has been shown that international networks are an important stimulant for international start-ups (McDougall et al., 1994; Oviatt and McDougall, 1995; Johnson, 2004).

3 Gain knowledge and information that helps them keep abreast of changes in the market place. Being close to market changes is an important attribute of the successful entrepreneur.

4 Share knowledge and information that helps them keep abreast of innovation in their sector and move forward with partnerships developed in these networks to exploit these opportunities. In that sense the knowledge shared with others is a resource they do not own but can put to good use.

5 Gain confidence in their abilities by mixing with a supportive group of similarly minded individuals. This seems to be particularly beneficial for 'minority' or 'marginal' groups, such as women, who feel particularly uncertain about the entrepreneurial life.

All networks are based on personal relationships and reciprocity, and all relationships are based on trust, self-interest and reputation (Dubini and Aldrich, 1991; Larson, 1992). They are strengthened by increased frequency and depth of interaction. These days networks can be real, based upon physical interaction, and virtual, based upon the internet. Networks on the internet can take many forms; for example the internet is frequently used to build supplier networks, as in the case of Dell. It is a medium that is best used to undertake specific tasks that do not need personal contact or the building of true relationships – in many ways it is best seen as a precursor to personal contact if a deep relationship is required. Because these personal relationships are not developed, internet-based networks are likely to have a shorter life. With this exception, virtual networks of this sort share many of the advantages of the real-world network. Handy (1996) described them as a 'box of contracts' and because of the internet's lack of tangibility it has profound consequences for how we think of organisational forms.

There is growing evidence of the benefits of networking as a way of stimulating innovation and knowledge transfer. At a macro-economic level strategic alliances and supplier networks are said to be crucial for the future success of US manufacturing (Goldhar and Lei, 1991). At a firm level the advantages are just as real, so much so that big firms are now encouraging them. Chesborough (2003) calls this process 'open innovation' – sourcing ideas from outside the company, where links and connections become more important than ownership of the knowledge. Procter & Gamble use the phrase 'Connect and Develop' (C&D) and see collaborative networks as crucial in helping them keep in touch with the research that they do not undertake themselves.

Networks blur the boundaries of the firm, extending them to a community of interest rather than restricting them to a legal or economic unit – which is important if your firm is small. Strong extended networks mean that resources, particularly knowledge, and risks can be shared across economic units so that networks of small firms can compete more effectively against large firms. For knowledge firms – firms whose business involves knowledge, information or innovation in any of its different forms – new forms of organising revolve around social and relational dimensions (Nahapiet and Ghoshal, 1998) and networks can play an important role.

If your business idea involves innovation, the nature of that innovation has implications for the type of networks you might be usefully involved with. How you operate an innovation network depends heavily on the type of network and the purpose it is set up to achieve. Tidd et al. (2005) map some of these different networks onto a simple matrix, differentiating between how radical the innovation outcome and how similar the participating organisations. This relationship is shown in Figure 6.10. Zone 1 has similar firms dealing with tactical innovation issues – 'good practice' fora. Zone 2 has similar firms working together to create new products or processes by challenging existing boundaries, dealing with the issues of knowledge-sharing and risk-taking through the structures of formal joint ventures and strategic alliances. Zone 3 has different firms bringing key pieces of information, perhaps from a wide range of disciplines, to the network. The risks of disclosure can be high so the ground rules for disclosure need to be set well in advance and any intellectual property rights issues resolved. The stakes are even higher in Zone 4 and third-party gatekeepers such as universities can play an important part as neutral knowledge brokers.

Networks can involve more formal structures. Strategic alliances (Zone 2) are longer-term cooperative arrangements between organisations with the aim of achieving certain goals Alliances involving exchanges of resources can be an effective way of sustaining competitive advantage, particularly with respect to radical innovation. They can create economic advantage by leveraging the market presence of individually smaller or less important organisations (Ohmae, 1989; Lewis, 1990; Lorange and Roos, 1992). They can provide vertical integration and scale economies by bringing these organisations together at a greatly reduced cost (Anderson and Weitz, 1992). As with the companies in the strategic alliances Case insight, individual partners bring different things to the alliance. Aside from the explicit strategic and operational motives such as gaining access to new markets, acquiring new technologies, enhancing new product

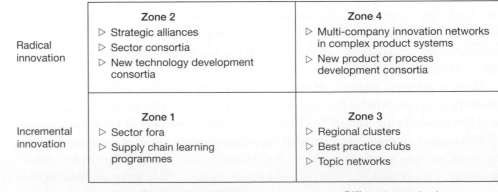

	Similar organisations	Different organisations
Radical innovation	**Zone 2** ▷ Strategic alliances ▷ Sector consortia ▷ New technology development consortia	**Zone 4** ▷ Multi-company innovation networks in complex product systems ▷ New product or process development consortia
Incremental innovation	**Zone 1** ▷ Sector fora ▷ Supply chain learning programmes	**Zone 3** ▷ Regional clusters ▷ Best practice clubs ▷ Topic networks

 **F6.10** Innovation networks

Source: Adapted from Tidd et al. (op. cit.)

development capabilities or leveraging on economies of scale or scope, mutual learning is an important element in many alliances. Alliances evolve and change in nature over time. Firms involved in an alliance often have a mix of emotions involving competition and collaboration in varying proportions as the partnership develops.

Alliances can grow into even more formal strategic partnerships. As can be seen from the Case insight, these are usually designed to create value through synergy as partners achieve mutual gains that neither could gain individually (Teece, 1992). For example, since assets are owned by the constituent individuals or organisations, the financial resources needed and the risk associated with any joint venture are spread and flexibility is increased.

🗎 Case insight Big companies and strategic alliances

In 2007 the **BBC** and **IBM** forged a strategic alliance following the signing of an agreement for a framework outlining several joint projects. One of the first was applying an IBM image/video search technology to CBeebies and CBBC programmes. The IBM research system, called 'Marvel', has the ability to visually analyse images so as to categorise content based upon appearance. This allows images/videos to be more easily searched online for specific content. The project is the first of a number that will allow the BBC to unlock the commercial value of its massive TV and radio archive.

In 2007 **Sun Microsystems** and **Intel** announced a broad strategic alliance that centred on Intel's endorsement of Sun's Solaris operating system and Sun's commitment to deliver a comprehensive family of enterprise servers and workstations based on Intel's Xeon processors. The alliance also included joint engineering, design and marketing efforts as well as other Intel and Sun enterprise-class technologies. The alliance is expected to help with the widespread adoption of Sun's Solaris but, perhaps more importantly, it is expected to move Intel's Xeon-based systems up the server value chain to data-centres and other high performance environments. These are currently dominated by HP, with its range of servers powered by an Itanium chip which itself was co-developed with Intel, and IBM.

💡 Planning and evaluation

Assembling the resources needed to start up a new business needs careful planning. Writing down what you intend to do and what you need helps to ensure that you do things systematically, in a coordinated fashion. It means others can comment upon and help improve your plans. For many people it also adds a touch of certainty to an otherwise highly uncertain activity. For them, the plan represents the vision of what they want the business to become and how they will go about achieving it. It can become a symbol of what they are striving for. Self-employment creates uncertainty about income generation and small firms face greater market uncertainty than large firms. As we saw in Chapter 2, the ability to deal with uncertainty is a central feature of entrepreneurship. Planning helps to address this issue.

What is needed is a business plan, and what goes into that we consider in Chapter 14. However, in broad terms it means that we need to address three issues:

1 *Viability* – customers, competition and marketing strategy, but also the profitability of the business. These are the bare bones of the business plan.
2 *Resources* – people and other resources, but, most important of all, the money needed to finance the start-up, over what period and how it will be repaid. This requires a cash flow forecast.

My advice to start-ups is:

1 Network – find out who your mentors are.
2 Find out what you want to do and look at the competition and decide on how you can improve on the competition.
3 What is your USP? What is it about your business that makes you different from anyone else. And once you have found those little uniquenesses state them time and time again because those little uniquenesses are the things the competition will find difficult to duplicate.

🗎 Anita Roddick, founder of Body Shop, personal interview

3 *Credibility* – track record and experience. This is important if you are to use the plan to assemble the resources you need.

Of course, a plan will not make uncertainty go away or even diminish it. It is simply that planning is the best way man knows of preparing for uncertainty, both practically and psychologically. It is also the best way we have of convincing others that we are prepared and addressing the issue of credibility. It is not that there is any simplistic formula for successfully starting a business. It is just that by planning you give yourself a better chance of avoiding at least some of the pitfalls.

In many ways it is the planning process that is more valuable than the plan itself unless, perhaps, you are seeking finance. So the plan itself needs to be fit for purpose. A plan which seeks to convince others to lend to or invest in a business will be something of a selling document. The more money being sought, the more it needs to convince and, therefore, the longer that plan. A plan which is for your own purposes can be a brief working document. Whatever its purpose, it needs to be flexible because the only thing that is certain in life is that the future is not. So it is quite likely that plans will have to adapt or even change completely.

Networks of friends and colleagues can be an invaluable source of advice and opinion about your business plan. What is more, advice is available from a myriad of more formal sources. Many banks produce free booklets detailing what is needed to set up your own business and how to go about developing a business plan. There are government agencies in many countries that give start-up advice, usually without charge. Further details about sources of help and advice in the UK are given on the website accompanying this book. The more rapid the growth your business will face, the more likely you are to need advice. Indeed, evidence shows that fast-growth firms are more likely to seek out and use advice than average-growth businesses (Cosh and Hughes, op. cit.). However, it cannot be proved directly that the advice they received led to their growth.

🗂 Case with questions David Sanger and Rollover

David Sanger set up his first business in 1991 at the age of 25. Since then he has made enough mistakes to last many people a life-time but has learnt from them and managed, not only to survive, but to prosper.

Using savings of £50 000 and a £50 000 bank loan he opened what he hoped would be the first of a chain of sandwich bars in West London in 1991. Called **Rollover**, it was initially a dismal flop, partly because David had no experience of the industry. He worked in the sandwich bar 16 hours a day, but after three months it was still losing money, so he decided to change tack. If the customers would not come to him, he would go to the customers. He hired a manager to run the shop and went out himself looking for wholesale customers, such as hotels and hospitals, for his sandwiches. Within two months sales had tripled. By 1995 David had eight sandwich bars, using the same business model.

It was whilst on a holiday in Copenhagen that the next stage in Rollover's development came. David kept coming across street traders selling hot dogs. He tried one and thought they were delicious – far better quality than those available in England – and he was also taken by the special machine that inserted the sausage inside the bread roll, completely enclosing it and making it easy to hold and eat whilst on the move. Indeed he was so intrigued that he bought one and took it home where he had it modified so that customers could see what was going on inside, installed it in one of his shops and started importing the high-quality German sausages to go in it. Sales went so well that he installed a machine

→

in each of his sandwich bars. They became known as 'Rollovers with ketchup' by accident because they were wrapped in a napkin with the Rollover name on it. Then his local pub asked if it could borrow a machine to make hot dogs for customers watching an international rugby match. It was so successful that within two weeks the pub chain's area manager hired six machines and Rollover's wholesale hot dog business was born.

This new business went so well that in 1995 David sold the sandwich bars for £350 000 to concentrate on the hot dog business. But then he made his second big mistake. Rather than concentrating on wholesale, he borrowed £750 000 and opened 18 hot dog retail outlets in the space of 18 months. Without proper controls in place the rapid roll-out was a disaster. There were thefts and staff irregularities, which all resulted in mounting losses. David spent the next 18 months closing the worst outlets and franchising the rest. He lost some £1 million.

Fortunately the wholesale operation survived – indeed prospered. Rollover™ now sells some 25 million branded hot dogs a year – 'the best hot dog in the world' – and can be seen at most Premiership football clubs, theme parks and concert halls in England. It offers loan equipment and point of sale packages, from mobile catering karts to new-build kiosks, to those selling its products. The company now also sells burgers, pies, wraps, popcorn and other snacks.

☐ Up to date information on Rollover can be found on their website: www.rollover-uk.com

QUESTIONS

1 What were the mistakes David made? Could they have been avoided?

2 What are the lessons you learn from David's experience?

📋 Case with questions Mark Constantine and Lush

If you walk down any high street in the UK – and many in a wide range of overseas countries – you might suddenly have your attention taken by a very distinctive, honeyed smell that causes you to look around and notice the bright, inviting shop front from which it emanates

– a shop called Lush. You might, in passing, think that the shop front (if not the smell) bears more than a passing resemblance to another shop called Body Shop, originally founded by Anita Roddick in 1976 and sold by her to the multinational L'Oréal (part of the Nestlé group) in 2006 for £652 million. And you would be right, not only the look but also the culture and ethics of the business are similar to Body Shop, at least in its early years. The link is the founder of Lush – Mark Constantine – and his is a very entrepreneurial roller-coaster of a story.

Born in 1953, Mark was thrown out of his home by his mother and stepfather at the age of 17 years and initially lived rough in woods in Dorset, UK before moving to London. He got a job as a hairdresser but started developing natural hair and skin products in his small bedroom. His ambition was to turn this into a business making and selling natural cosmetics, but it was not until he was 23 years old that he stumbled on his first success. He had read about Body Shop in the press and sent Anita Roddick some samples, including a henna cream shampoo 'which looked a bit like you'd just done a poo'. She had just opened her second shop. They met, got on well together and she placed her first order for £1200-worth of products. That was the real start of his first company, Constantine and Weir, set up with his wife, Mo, and Elizabeth Weir, then a beauty therapist and now retail director at Lush. The company became Body Shop's biggest supplier of cosmetics and Mark is credited for many of the elements of the company's ethical brand image, in particular its opposition to animal testing, that Body Shop and Anita Roddick built up over those early years. However, Body Shop became uncomfortable with the formulations of many of its products being owned by another company and, in 1988, it bought Constantine and Weir for £9 million.

→

Mark put the money into Cosmetics to Go, a mail order company he had already started. The company never made a profit in any of its years of trading and went into bankruptcy in 1994. Faced with no money and a family to maintain, Mark started selling the bankrupt stock from a shop in Poole. This was the start of Lush. The company was set up with seven shareholders, including his wife, Mo, and Elizabeth Weir. New finance was injected by Peter Blacker, of British Ensign Estates, and his finance director, Andrew Gerrie, who now sits on the board of Lush. They put in 'modest sums' but, cleverly Mark set the exit value of these investments at the time, so that they could be bought out.

Lush does more than just make and sell cosmetics – hand-made soaps, bubble bar slices and fragrances. The distinctive smell is caused by the lack of packaging. Some products, like 'bath ballistics', are stacked like fruit and others such as soap are sold like cheese, wedges stacked on shelves and sold by weight wrapped in greaseproof paper. The cosmetics are made from organic fruit and vegetables, essential oils, and safe-synthetic ingredients. In addition to not using animal fats in its products, Lush is also against animal testing and tests its products solely with volunteers instead. Moreover, Lush does not buy from companies that carry out, fund or commission any animal testing. The

Lush brand has a strong ethical dimension and it supports many campaigns around animal welfare, environmental conservation, human rights and climate change. It donates around 2 per cent of its profits to charity, supporting many direct action groups such as Plane Stupid, a group against the expansion of UK airports, and Sea Shepherd, a group that takes action against Japanese whaling ships. Often it launches products specifically to support these groups. Profits from the sale of 'Guantanamo Garden', an orange foaming bath ball, were donated to the human rights charity, Reprieve, which helped Binyam Mohamed, a British resident who was held at Guantanamo Bay. It has just launched a Charity Pot moisturiser, giving the entire proceeds to charities such as the Dorset Wildlife Trust and the Sumatran Orangutan Society. The shops seem to be staffed by enthusiastic young people. The firm's mission statement is prominent on its wall, part of which states that 'we believe in the right to make mistakes, lose everything and start again'.

Lush never advertises. Its growth has been organic. It owns its businesses overseas in various joint ventures and now has shops in over 40 countries around the world, including the USA, Japan and Australia. In 2001 Lush tried to buy Body Shop, but the Roddicks turned down the offer. It is listed regularly in the *Sunday Times* 100 Best Companies to work for. By 2009 Lush had sales of £240 million through some 600 shops and Mark Constantine was a multimillionaire. It is still a privately owned company – all seven shareholders work for Lush – and quite a family business. Mo still designs cosmetics, one son, Simon, is head perfumer and another son, Jack, does the online marketing. Their daughter, Claire, works in retail support for the company. The business is still based in Poole, Dorset, run from a small office above the first shop. Production is based at five local factories. The Constantines have lived in the same house for 25 years. Mark does not hold a driving licence and has never owned a car. He often cycles to work. His hobby is bird songs and he recently published a book on the subject.

☐ Up-to-date information on Lush can be found on their website: www.lush.co.uk

QUESTIONS

1 What were Mark's motives in starting Lush?

2 Is Lush an original business idea?

3 What is the role of ethics in Lush?

4 How important is Mark Constantine to the Lush brand image?

5 Why do you think Mark has not floated the company on the stock market?

▷ Summary

- To start a business, not only do you need an idea, you also need certain personal attributes, customers willing to pay for the product or service, an ability to deal with competitors, a marketing strategy to persuade customers to buy from you and finally resources. The motivation to set up your own business can come from deep inside and you can wait a long time to find the best opportunity. The process is not linear or necessarily sequential – and many might say luck is involved.

- To run your own firm you will probably need to have the character traits of an owner-manager and an entrepreneur. You must have stamina and be willing to work hard for long hours. You must be committed and dedicated, willing to make personal sacrifices, be able to bounce back when, like **David Sanger** of **Rollover**, you make mistakes and motivated to excel for your customers. Whilst you need to be opportunistic, opportunity perception can be encouraged. Similarly, whilst you need to take risks, risk can be mitigated and minimised.

- As **David Sanger** found, an idea is of no use unless it is linked to market demand. There must be a need for the product or service in the market place that is capable of being exploited. You need to know who your customers will be and why they will buy from you rather than competitors. Careful research needs to be undertaken into the sector or industry into which you are launching the business. Some entrepreneurs, like **Mark Constantine** of **Lush**, base their business on established business models that they believe they can improve on.

- You are most likely to succeed where there is little direct competition. However, even where there are few competitors, you might still face an uphill struggle if they are large firms. Porter's Five Forces is a useful way of making judgements about the degree of competition in a market. It looks at the power of buyers and suppliers, the threat of new entrants and substitutes and the competitive rivalry within the industry.

- You need a marketing strategy for your business, but you first need to understand that there are only three fundamental ways of achieving sustainable competitive advantage:
  - ▷ Low price;
  - ▷ High differentiation;
  - ▷ Customer focus.

- These combine to provide four generic marketing strategies that have been around since markets began:

  - ▷ *Commodity supplier*, where you are selling a commodity on price alone. You therefore need to be the lowest-cost producer, making the most of any economies of scale that are available.
  - ▷ *Market trader*, where you are still selling on price but using economies of small scale, in particular low overheads, to keep costs low. However, in these circumstances you must be aware of the limitations to the size of your market and the risks you face in trying to grow the business.
  - ▷ *Niche player*, selling a differentiated product or service to a targeted, narrow market segment, like **Quad Electroacoustics** or **Morgan Motor Company**. This strategy offers the best chance of success for a small firm.
  - ▷ *Outstanding success*. Sometimes niche firms become outstanding successes as the market to which they originally sold expands beyond their expectations, as **Alan Pound** and **Aculab** have proved.

- Most business start-ups require a broad range of resources and acquiring them can be a problem because of the lack of credibility of the entrepreneur. It is important for most businesses that overheads and the break-even point are kept as low as possible. **Robbie Cowling** understood this when he started **Jobserve** from his bedroom. Even if you need assets to set up, you do not always have to own them. You can beg and/or borrow them – called 'bootstrapping'. Using informal and formal networks of contacts can be vital in helping you to do this. Even if you need to own assets you do not always need to purchase them outright. You might be able to rent or lease them – which is how **Richard Branson** started his **Virgin Atlantic** airline.

▷ We bring three sorts of capital to a start-up – financial, human and social. Human capital is derived from our knowledge and experience. Social capital is derived from our networks of contacts and the knowledge and goodwill they bring.

▷ Networking is an important way of stimulating innovation and knowledge transfer. It is particularly important for a knowledge-based start-up. Networks blur the boundaries of the firm, extending them to a community of interest. Strong extended networks mean that resources, particularly knowledge, and risks can be shared across economic units so that networks of small firms can compete more effectively against large firms. Networks can be both formal and informal and can evolve into strategic alliances such as the ones between **BBC** and **IBM** and **Intel** and **Sun MicroSystems**.

▷ Finally, the start-up needs to be thought through and the business plan is a vital tool in allowing you to do this. It may be no more than a brief, working document that allows you to marshal your ideas in a systematic way. However, if you need it to raise finance it will have to be more comprehensive and much more of a 'selling document'.

⏻ **Further resources are available at www.palgrave.com/business/burns**

📄 Essays and discussion topics

1 How can government persuade more people to set up their own business? Should they attempt to do so?

2 Do you think you have the personal attributes needed to run your own business?

3 Why do you need to undertake market research before setting up in business? What sort of market research do you need to undertake?

4 Can a lifestyle business still cater for customers' needs?

5 If a business idea is good, is it not the case that there is bound to be competition?

6 Is it better to have big company or small company competitors?

7 Why might many small firms perceive themselves as having no competition?

8 Are there really only three ways to sell a product or service?

9 How might you go about driving down costs if you were a commodity supplier?

10 What are the risks that a market trader faces in growing a business? How might they be overcome?

11 Do you know of any small firms that compete successfully on price? How do they do it? Can they grow?

12 Do you know of any niche players? How do they differentiate themselves? What market segment(s) do they sell to?

13 Can a niche player grow? If so, how and what are the dangers they face in doing so?

14 How important is a brand in communicating differential advantage?

15 Can differential advantage be sustained indefinitely?

16 Why are networks important?

17 How do you generate a network of contacts in a systematic way?

18 How important is 'good luck' in setting up your own business?

19 If the future is uncertain, what is the point of planning?

20 What is meant by 'flexibility' with regard to the business plan? Why is this important?

↻ Exercises and assignments

1 Select a market or industry and, using library data, evaluate the competitive forces within it using Porter's Five Forces.

2 List 10 ways a product or service can be differentiated from competitors. Against each, list how that differential advantage might be sustained.

3 Consider the market for a commodity, for example petrol. List the different market segments this sells to, whether the segments offer the opportunity to develop a differential advantage and if so what these are. Note whether there are pricing differences between the segments.

4 Select a product or service that is clearly differentiated. List the ways it is differentiated, the value to the customer and how these differential advantages are communicated to the customer.

5 Write a mini case study about how an entrepreneur you know who set up their own business managed to assemble all the resources they needed.

6 List the friends, relatives and contacts that might be useful to you were you to set up your own business. Against each name jot down why they might be useful.

📖 References

3i European Enterprise Centre (1993) *Britain's Superleague Companies*, Report no. 9.

Anderson, E. and Weitz, B. (1992) 'The Use of Pledges to Build and Sustain Commitment in Distribution Channels', *Journal of Marketing Research*, 29 (February).

Bhidé, A. (1992) 'Bootstrap Finance: The Art of Start-Ups', *Harvard Business Review*, November/December.

Birley, S. and Norburn, D. (1984) 'Small versus Large Companies: The Entrepreneurial Conundrum', *Journal of Business Strategy*, 6(1), Summer.

Burns, P. and Whitehouse, O. (1994) *Winners and Losers in the 1990s*, 3i European Enterprise Centre, Report no. 12.

Chesborough, H. (2003) *Open Innovation: The New Imperative for Creating and Profiting from Technology*, Boston, Mass: Harvard Business School Press.

Cosh, A. and Hughes, A. (eds) (1998) *Enterprise Britain: Growth Innovation and Public Policy in the Small and Medium Sized Enterprise Sector 1994–97*, Cambridge: ESRC Centre for Business Research.

Dubini, P. and Aldrich, H. (1991) 'Personal and Extended Networks are Central to the Entrepreneurial Process', *Journal of Business Venturing*, 6.

ESRC Centre for Business Research (1992) *The State of British Enterprise: Growth, Innovation and Competitive Advantage in Small and Medium-Sized Firms*, Cambridge: ESRC.

Firkin, P. (2003) 'Entrepreneurial Capital', in A. de Bruin and A.A. Dupuis (eds) *Entrepreneurship: New Perspectives in a Global Age*, Aldershot: Ashgate.

Goldhar, J.D. and Lei, D (1991) 'The Shape of Twenty-first Century Global Manufacturing', *Journal of Business Strategy*, 12 (2).

Handy, C. (1996) 'Rethinking Organisations', in T. Clark (ed.) *Advancement in Organisation Behaviour: Essays in Honour of Derek, S. Pugh*, Aldershot: Ashgate.

Johnson, J.E. (2004) 'Factors Influencing the Early Internationalisation of High Technology Start-ups: US and UK Evidence', *Journal of International Entrepreneurship*, 2.

Larson, A. (1992) 'Network Dyads in Entrepreneurial Settings: A Study of the Governance of Exchange Relationships', *Administrative Science Quarterly*, 37.

Lewis, J.D. (1990) *Partnerships for Profit: Structuring and Managing Strategic Alliances*, New York: Free Press.

Lorange, P. and Roos, J. (1992) *Strategic Alliances: Formation, Implementation and Evolution*, Oxford: Blackwell.

McDougall, P.P., Shane, S. and Oviatt, B.M. (1994) 'Explaining the Formation of International New Ventures: The Limits of Theories from International Business Research', *Journal of Business Venturing*, 9.

Nahapiet, J. and Ghoshal, S. (1998) 'Social Capital, Intellectual Capital and the Creation of Value in Firms', *Academy of Management Best Paper Proceedings*.

Ohmae, K. (1989) 'The Global Logic of Strategic Alliances', *Harvard Business Review*, March/April.

Oviatt, B.M. and McDougall, P.P. (1995) 'Global Start-ups: Entrepreneurs on a Worldwide Stage', *Academy of Management Executive*, 9(2).

Porter, M.E. (1985) *Competitive Advantage, Creating and Sustaining Superior Performance*, New York: Free Press.

Stevenson, H.H., Roberts, M.J. and Grousebeck, H.I. (1985) *New Business Ventures and the Entrepreneur*, Homewood, IL: Irwin.

Storey, D.J., Keasey, K., Watson, R. and Wynarczyk, P. (1987) *The Performance of Small Firms: Profits, Jobs and Failures*, London: Croom Helm.

Storey, D.J., Watson, R. and Wynarcyzk, P. (1989) *Fast Growth Small Business: Case Studies of 40 Small Firms in North East England*, Department of Employment, Research Paper No. 67, London: HMSO.

Teece, D.J. (1992) 'Competition, Cooperation and innovation: Organisational Arrangements for Regimes of Rapid Technological Progress', *Journal of Economic Behaviour and Organisation*, 18.

Tidd, J., Bassant, J. and Pavitt. K. (2005) *Managing Innovation: Integrating Technological, Market and Organizational Change*, 3rd edn, Chichester: Wiley.

7 Launching the business

▷ **Marketing strategies**
▷ **Pricing**
▷ **Differentiation**
▷ **Developing customer focus**
▷ **Entrepreneurial marketing**
▷ **Undertaking market research**
▷ **Developing selling skills**
▷ **Retailing on the internet**
▷ **Legal forms of business**
▷ **Summary**

Case insights
▷ Martin Penny and Good Hair Day
▷ Jean Young
▷ Radio Spirits
▷ Mark Dorman and Black Vodka
▷ Mark Goldsmith and
   Goldsmith's Fine Foods
▷ Gary Frank and The
   Fabulous Bakin' Boys

Cases with questions
▷ The Body Shop franchise
▷ Stephen Waring and Green Thumb
▷ Calypso Rose and Clippy

Learning outcomes

By the end of this chapter you should be able to:

▷ Explain why customers buy products or services and the difference between features and benefits;

▷ Explain what is meant by the term 'marketing mix' and how it can be used to describe elements of the marketing strategy;

▷ Recognise the influences on pricing decisions and explain how the price of a product or service might be set;

▷ Calculate the break-even point for a business;

▷ Explain what is needed to differentiate a product or service;

▷ Explain how markets can be segmented and what is meant by market focus;

▷ Construct an appropriate marketing mix for different market segments;

▷ Describe the different forms of market research and how to go about collecting information;

▷ Develop a market research questionnaire and a market research plan;

▷ Explain what is needed to sell effectively and how selling skills might be developed;

▷ Explain how the internet can be used to help sell a product or service and what is needed to set up an effective retail website;

▷ Decide on the appropriate legal form for a business start-up.

○ Marketing strategies

How do you decide which generic marketing strategy to adopt when you launch the business? This depends upon a thorough understanding of customers (what they want), competitors (how their product or service compares) and the degree of competition in the market (Porter's Five Forces). The fiercer the competition in the industry, the better the product or service competitors have to offer, then the more a start-up will have to compete on price.

However, the first thing to understand is why customers buy a product or service. Take, as an example, why people might buy a mundane item like a drill bit. They do not buy it for its aesthetic qualities, they buy it because they want to drill a hole, perhaps to fix something to a wall. The drill solves the problem of creating a hole or fixing something to a wall. If there happens to be a more efficient or easier way of making holes or fixing things to walls, the drill manufacturer is in trouble. A founder of a successful cosmetics firm once said that in the factory he made perfume but in the shops he sold dreams.

In marketing terms, this is called understanding the benefits the customer is looking for. They do not buy the features that describe the product or service, they buy the benefits it brings to them. You do not buy oil for your car because of its colour or viscosity as such, you buy it because it makes the engine run smoothly, extends its life and reduces repair bills. The features might convince you of the benefits, but it is the benefits you really want. So, different people buying a pen might be looking for different benefits. Of course it must write, but if that were the only benefit they were looking for, why would anybody buy anything but the cheapest pen available? An expensive pen is rarely bought just as a writing implement (for the consumer), but more usually as a gift that reflects warmly on the giver (the customer). If the customer is not the consumer then a product or service must offer benefits to both. The customer is buying intangible benefits such as status or esteem for the recipient. The consumer will derive benefit from a writing implement that is aesthetically pleasing and the fact that the donor held him in such esteem that she went to the trouble and expense of buying the gift. There is a market for both cheap and expensive pens, but to different customers.

Understanding the difference between features and benefits is the cornerstone of marketing. It is important in tailoring the marketing offered to customers, deciding on your competitive advantage and building a growth strategy to sustain it. It is real tangible benefits to the customer that differentiate a product or service and allow a premium price to be charged. Unfortunately, many owner-managers like to define their products in physical terms and therefore think they are selling one thing, only to find customers are buying something else.

Features can be turned into benefits, for example:

Feature		Benefit
Our shop takes credit cards	⇨	You can budget to suit your pocket
Our shop stays open later than others	⇨	You get more choice when to shop
Our shop is an approved dealer	⇨	You can be guaranteed that we know and understand all technical aspects of the product
Our shop is a family business	⇨	You get individual, personal attention from somebody who cares

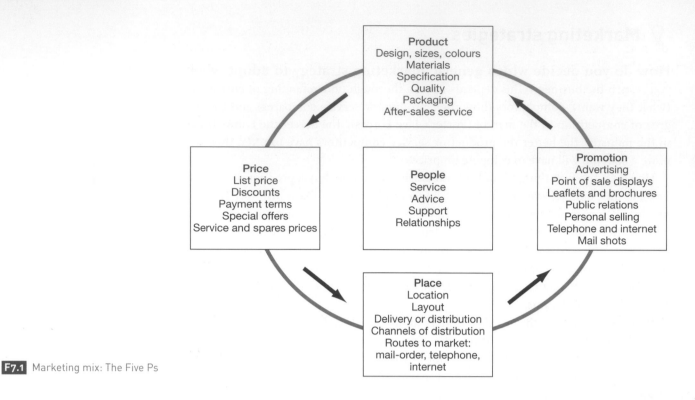

Product
Design, sizes, colours
Materials
Specification
Quality
Packaging
After-sales service

Price
List price
Discounts
Payment terms
Special offers
Service and spares prices

People
Service
Advice
Support
Relationships

Promotion
Advertising
Point of sale displays
Leaflets and brochures
Public relations
Personal selling
Telephone and internet
Mail shots

Place
Location
Layout
Delivery or distribution
Channels of distribution
Routes to market:
mail-order, telephone,
internet

F7.1 Marketing mix: The Five Ps

So, listing the features of a product or service can be the start of the process of understanding the benefits that the customer is seeking from them. However, it is more convincing to start with the benefits that customers are looking for and then construct features that provide those benefits. Which actually comes first is a little like the chicken and the egg.

One technique that is widely used to describe the features of a product or service is called the marketing mix or The Five Ps, a convenient short-hand for a range of sub-elements consisting of product (or service), price, promotion, place and people. This is shown in Figure 7.1.

The customer buys the marketing mix as a package, and the mix must be consistent to reinforce the benefits that the customer is looking for. The marketing mix is only as strong as its weakest link. As we saw in the last chapter, there is a trade-off between price and the other elements of the mix. The stronger or more distinctive and different these elements, the higher the price you are normally able to command. Too many small firms compete primarily on price because they believe the other elements of their marketing mix are insufficiently different from their competitors. However, price is more usually a barrier to sale rather than a positive inducement.

Central to the whole marketing mix are entrepreneurs and their personal approach which will probably, of necessity, involve a very much hands-on, face-to-face way of marketing. They will develop relationships with customers in this way and this in itself can be a distinct form of competitive advantage over large firms.

The appropriate marketing mix depends on the benefits the customer, and consumer, are looking for. Take for example a pen, bought simply as a writing implement. It is sold in many high street shops, with only point of sale display materials (probably self-service), with no promotion and minimum service at a very low price. The benefit is that it writes and can be easily obtained. Other elements of the marketing mix are relatively unimportant, so there is strong price competition. On the other hand, a pen bought as a gift has an expensive looking exterior and is also sold in the high street, but probably from behind locked glass display stands that can be accessed only with the help of an assistant. It comes with a guarantee and is promoted at Christmas time with the realisation that most pens are bought as gifts, not by the consumer. The customer wants to spend, say, £25 on a gift and even a so-called 'rational man' would not consider buying a box of 250 cheap, disposable pens as a substitute gift, even though they are likely to last longer than the expensive pen. The way to go about marketing these two apparently similar products is therefore totally different. The point is that you need to know what the customer and consumer are buying – which may not be the same as you think you are selling.

Customers do not usually sit and wait for a new business to open its doors. They need to be informed of what it has to offer and convinced to try it, and word-of-mouth recommendations can take time. Advertising is only one, very expensive, form of promotion. Many small firms cannot afford it and indeed prefer more personal forms of communication with customers. More recently, large firms have started calling this 'relationship marketing'. Once established, small firms have an advantage in this because the relationship is usually sincere and built on the trust that owner-managers will deliver the product or service they promise. If they do not, they face the risk of going out of business.

Many firms do not advertise because of its expense and because all too often it is not targeted at specific customers. Lush does not advertise, relying instead on its window displays in the high street, because it feels that it is inconsistent with its ethical stand and general brand image. J. Barbour & Sons, the manufacturer of upper-class but utilitarian waterproof jackets, spend very little on advertising, preferring to sponsor outdoor events such as horse trials.

Stokes (1998) makes the point that owner-managers typically prefer 'interactive marketing' – interacting on a one-to-one basis with customers – because they have strong preferences for personal contact rather than impersonal marketing through mass promotions. He points out that this extends to their preference in terms of market research. They prefer to talk to and observe customers, rather than undertake desk or other more formal research. Promotion is often by word of mouth and recommendation – something that can be crucial to purchasing decisions in some consumer and business-to-business markets (Bayus, 1985). One reason for this preference is, of course, cost but the other is that this is something that large firms are not as good at. This preference for interactive marketing also underlines the importance of networking. In small firm marketing the most important P is probably the personality of the entrepreneur.

The term 'place' in the marketing mix encompasses channels of distribution. Not all businesses sell direct to the end users. Many sell through intermediaries – agents, wholesalers, mail order companies, retailers, specialist outlets or other routes. Often these are established routes to particular markets offering the advantage of loyal customers and local knowledge as well as possible savings in terms of distribution costs or reduced stock holding. For a start-up it might be difficult and risky to ignore these established distribution channels, although that is precisely what many internet start-ups are doing – a topic to which we shall return later in this chapter. For example, a designer and producer of novel greeting cards has little practical alternative but to sell his cards through high street shops. However, he might decide to sell directly to selected shops rather than go through wholesalers, selling to small shops rather than chains. Doing things differently can be risky, but the rewards of success can be high. The decision about channels revolves around matching the product or service

F7.2 Generic marketing strategies

to the customer and their needs in a way that provides an adequate return. However, the evidence points towards small firms rarely being adventurous in their choice of distribution channels.

The elements of the marketing mix, related to the customers they are targeted at, together make up the marketing strategy of the firm. The strategy is just a series of related tasks that, taken together, have coherence and give direction to the firm. The strategy adopted at the launch of a new business may change as it becomes more established. For example, special price offers may be appropriate at launch in order to get customers to try the product or service and then repeat buy. On the other hand, if the product or service is sufficiently unique and different, then it may be possible to premium price at launch, particularly if the product or service is unlikely to be repeat purchased quickly. Similarly at launch you need to promote your product/service aggressively to create awareness, explaining its benefits. This can take many forms, including personal selling, advertising, e-mail or mail shots. But for a start-up it is likely to be limited by the resources you have available and certainly later on, word-of-mouth customer recommendation is likely to become increasingly important.

Let us return to the three fundamental ways of achieving sustainable competitive advantage shown in Figure 7.2 – low price, high differentiation and customer focus – and explore what this means for a start-up.

⌁ Pricing

Many start-ups are uncertain about how to set prices. They often feel that they must be cheap to attract customers and feel insecure about charging a premium price compared to the competition. To sustain a low-price strategy you must be a low-cost provider and do whatever is needed to drive costs down. However, there are other approaches to pricing.

The price charged for a product or service ought to reflect the value of the package of benefits to the customer. The value can be different to different customers and in different circumstances. Take, for example, the price charged for emergency, compared to routine, plumbing work. A premium price reflects the benefit to the customer of preventing the house being flooded. However, the features of that emergency service, as reflected in the marketing mix, must reflect the benefits the customer is looking for; for example, ease of telephone call-out, 24-hour fast and efficient service, clear-up, facilitation of insurance claims and so on. Similarly, a railway company is able to charge a range of different prices for what is essentially the same service, transportation from one place to another. Given these things, there is often a 'going rate' for a similar product or service.

🛍 Case insight Martin Penny and Good Hair Day

It is often the case for a start-up that a potential mass market is better ignored in favour of a niche opportunity – at least in the short term. It means that the high fixed costs often associated with mass markets and all too unaffordable by the typical start-up are avoided. It means a premium price can be charged, albeit on a smaller volume. And often that niche is bigger than the founder ever imagined.

Jemella Group, which trades as GHD – Good Hair Day – was started by Martin Penny in 2001. Based in West Yorkshire, the company has revolutionised the hair industry with an iron that straightens hair between two heated ceramic plates. But when Martin first took the idea to his bank, asking for a £50 000 loan, the bank manager was sceptical, seeing the product as 'just another set of hair tongs'. The only way Martin got the money was on the strength of his track record running an environmental consultancy. But Martin decided on two important strategies that were to underpin the subsequent success of his business. The first strategy was not to manufacture the product himself, indeed the product was manufactured in Korea where costs were lower. In this way he could focus on sales and keep his fixed costs to a minimum. The second was not to sell through the high street but to target firstly up-market London West End hair salons and then salons across the UK. The 'hair styling irons' were sold both for salon use and through the salons themselves. Despite keeping costs low the product itself was priced high and, partly in this way, differentiated from 'just another set of hair tongs'. It was seen as professional, special and up-market.

Largely because of these strategies sales have increased from £459 000 in 2001 to £115 million in 2007. In 2007, after being sold to Lloyds Development Capital just 11 months earlier, Jemella was re-sold to management backed by Montagu Private Equity group for £160 million.

The company claims that the iron is now used in more than 10 000 UK salons – 85 per cent of the market. But celebrities such as Madonna, Victoria Beckham, Jennifer Aniston and Gwyneth Paltrow are also happy to pay the high price for the product – which helps to give it a certain exclusive cachet that helps sell the product to the general public. Based on this success the company is now diversifying into other hair-care products such as shampoo, conditioner and styling gel, and has launched a new brand called 'Nu:U', aimed at the mid-price, mass salon market.

☐ Up-to-date information on Good Hair Day can be found on their website: www.ghdhair.com

One factor in the pricing decision is the costs you face in doing business. There are many cost concepts and this book does not intend to go into them in detail. The conventional profit-maximising model developed by economists tends to indicate that price should be set at a point where marginal cost – the cost of producing and marketing one extra unit – is equal to marginal revenue – the income generated by the sale of the additional unit. In practice this is difficult, if not impossible, to apply. This is because the economists' model assumes that price is also determined by demand, whereas in reality this is not always the case.

Many people use what is called 'cost-plus pricing'. This takes the total cost of producing a product or delivering a service and divides it by the number of units produced to arrive at the average cost of production, to which a target mark-up is then added. As well as the notorious difficulties in allocating cost there is the problem of reconciling price with demand. What happens if volumes are not as predicted? Some costs, often called 'overhead costs', are fixed – they do not change with volume – for example, rent and insurance. So if volumes are less than predicted, the same costs have to be spread over smaller volumes – which means that you would have to charge a higher price to recover the overheads from the decreased volume, a strategy that itself is likely to lead to falling sales. The reverse is true if volumes are greater than predicted.

Cost-plus pricing is shown in Figure 7.3. Fixed costs are the horizontal line AB. Producing the product or delivering the service will mean incurring additional variable costs – costs that vary with volume like materials and piece-work labour. Every

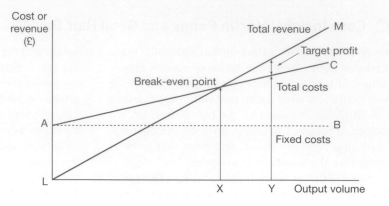

time an additional unit is produced and sold, an additional cost is incurred. Line AC therefore represents the total cost of producing the product or delivering the service – the fixed cost plus the variable cost. Over large volumes, this line may curve downwards as the effects of economies of scale are felt. Line LM represents the revenue generated by sales – sales volume multiplied by unit price. At volume X all costs are covered by revenue. This is called the break-even point. At volume Y a certain target profit is reached. Obviously the problem with this sort of approach to pricing is that it tends to assume that at a given price, a given number of products will be sold, whereas in reality the quantity sold will be linked in some way to the price charged. The break-even point can be easily calculated. To do so requires two further terms to be defined. *Contribution* is the difference between sales price and variable cost. *Total contribution* is the difference between total sales (or turnover) and total variable costs for a specified period. Contribution margin expresses this as a percentage of sales price or total sales. For example (assuming sales of 100 units per week):

	Per unit		*Total*
Sales price	£10	Total sales	£1000
Variable cost	£ 6	Total variable costs	£ 600
Contribution	£ 4	Total contribution	£ 400
Contribution margin	0.40 or 40%	Contribution margin	0.40 or 40%

Break-even (expressed in £ turnover) is defined as:

$$\frac{\text{Total fixed costs}}{\text{Contribution margin}}$$

If total fixed costs were £200 per week, the break-even point would be:

£200/0.40 = £500 or 50 units per week

Verifying:

Break-even sales 50 units @ £10	£500
Variable costs 50 units @ £6	£300
Total contribution	£200
Total fixed costs	£200
Profit	nil

Once above the break-even point, each £1 of sales contributes £0.40 or 40 per cent to profits. So, if the target profit is £400 per week then sales would have to be:

£400/0.40 =£1000 *above the break-even point* = £1500 (150 units)

Verifying:

> On sales of £1500:
> | Total contribution @ 40% | £600 |
> |---|---|
> | Total fixed costs | £200 |
> | Profit | £400 |

As we shall see in the next chapter, break-even is a very important concept for many reasons. However, whilst competitors may know about costs, customers rarely do and, just sometimes, as in the case of prestige pens bought as gifts, they may want to pay a high price. How demand holds up to changes in price is determined by the cross elasticity of demand. The more differentiated the product or service, the more price inelastic is demand – it does not vary greatly with changes in price. The more the product or service is a commodity, the more price will be elastic – it will be affected by price changes. Price elasticity may sound a highly theoretical concept, but the practical applications of it are important.

Table 7.1 shows the increase in sales volume required to maintain the same level of profitability as a result of a price reduction. This depends on the contribution margin before the price cut. If the contribution margin is only 20 per cent and you were tempted to cut prices by 15 per cent, you would have to increase sales volume by a massive 300 per cent, or quadruple sales, just to make the same amount of profit as before. The higher the margin, the less the effect. But even at 40 per cent margin, you would still have to increase sales by 27 per cent. In the face of static or declining sales many owner-managers would be tempted to cut prices. Table 7.1 makes you think twice about that strategy. Of course there may be other important factors influencing the decision, such as reducing stocks or bringing in some much-needed cash. However, seeking to increase profits by increasing sales at low prices is fraught with dangers.

The arithmetic of pricing is even more persuasive when it comes to price increases. Table 7.2 shows the decrease in sales volume that could sustain the same level of profitability in the face of a price increase. The same 20 per cent margin could see a reduction in sales volume of 43 per cent in the face of a 15 per cent price increase and would still achieve the same level of profitability. Of course the effect is less the higher the margin. Nevertheless such deep reductions in volume may see profits actually increase as overheads are cut (why maintain the same level of staff with less work?). Alternatively you might decide to

📁 Case insight Jean Young

When Jean Young set up as a sole trader offering training to the health-care sector she estimated her sales in the first year to be a modest £17 200. Deciding on a daily charge was easy, the market would pay in the range of £300 to £1200 per day. Whilst she was experienced, Jean was a start-up so she reckoned that a safe rate would be £400. She already had some days booked at this rate and she estimated that she could sell 43 days in her first year (£17 200).

With no variable costs she had a contribution margin of 100%. Her fixed costs were reasonable as well since she worked from home. The main element was depreciation on her car and computer equipment. Her fixed costs for the year were estimated at:

Depreciation	£2700
Secretarial wages	330
Transport	430
Telephone	450
Stationery	570
Repairs	350
Other	285
Insurance	100
Total	£5215

She therefore calculated her profit would be £11 985 (£17 200 – £5215) and worked out her break-even point would be £5215 of turnover, and that included the depreciation on her car that she would keep with or without the business. Since she already had firm commitments for training work totalling £17 200, she felt certain the business was viable. What is more, she calculated that she only needed 13 days' work (fixed costs of £5215 divided by her contribution of £400 per day) before she started making a profit – her break-even point. Jean thought this was the salary she could 'take home'. As we shall see in Chapter 9, she was confusing profit and cash flow and this was not correct.

Price reduction	Contribution margin		
	20%	30%	40%
−5%	33%	20%	14%
−10%	100%	50%	33%
−15%	300%	100%	60%

T7.1 Price cuts – percentage increase in sales volume required to generate

Price increase	Contribution margin		
	20%	30%	40%
5%	−20%	−14%	−11%
10%	−33%	−25%	−20%
15%	−43%	−33%	−27%

T7.2 Price increases – percentage decrease in sales volume required to generate the same level of profit after a price increase

improve the level of service offered so as to justify the higher price. What is more, the lower volumes mean that stock holdings and other capital costs are likely to come down, an important consideration if capital is scarce.

The actual effect of price on volumes sold depends on the cross elasticity of demand and a small firm can decrease it by attempting to differentiate itself from the competition as much as possible and, in so doing, charging as high a price for its goods or services as the market will bear. This price must, however, be consistent with the other elements of the marketing mix. Tables 7.1 and 7.2 give you some indication of the price–volume–profit effects – so long as you know the contribution margin.

Pricing, therefore, is a question of judgement. It is certainly not a science. The range of prices that a business can charge is shown in Figure 7.4. At the bottom of the range is variable cost – the cost of producing one additional unit, normally the same as marginal cost (except when additional fixed costs will be incurred by increasing production). In the previous example, variable cost was £6. If the price charged falls below this then any additional sale costs more to produce than the revenue it generates. However, variable cost is likely to be too low a price to charge since, by definition, it does not include any fixed costs. These are only covered when average cost is reached, which depends on volumes. In the previous example, average cost was £10 for 50 units, £8 for 100 units or £7.33 for 150 units. The top end of the range depends totally on the differential advantage the firm enjoys – and how well the firm can capitalise upon it. However, no business can afford to ignore competition. Even products or services that are unique face price resistance and ultimately there will be a price that is 'too high' for the customer. In the previous example the 'going rate' was taken to be £10. At the lower extreme there will be a price that is so low that customers will not believe the product or service can deliver the claims that it makes.

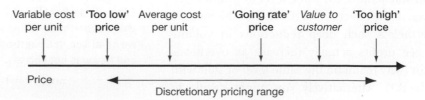

F7.4 The pricing range

Indeed for some products, like the exclusive pen bought as a gift, a high price can be very much part of what the customer is expecting to buy.

So, the longer-term pricing strategy you adopt needs to fall within these parameters. However, at start-up there are two variations on these principles:

1 Pricing high where the product or service is unique or novel, particularly where the purchase is likely to be infrequent. This is called *skimming* and tends to work best when demand is relatively price inelastic, or there are likely to be a number of different groups of customers and you can appeal to those who will pay a higher price first and move on to the rest later, or little is known about the costs of producing and marketing the product or service. So, for example, when large LCD, flat screen TVs were first offered for sale the initial price was high and they were sold very much as an innovative, exclusive product. Prices rapidly fell as they became more of an everyday product. Skimming generates high profits and, as the volume sold is usually low, the capital needed for the business is reduced.

2 Pricing low where the product or service is not significantly different or where you expect customers to be frequent purchasers and it is important to get the customer to try it first, relying on them liking it sufficiently to repeat purchase. This is called *penetration* and tends to work best when demand is relatively price elastic or competitors are likely to enter the market quickly, or there are no distinct price–customer groupings or there is the possibility of achieving economies of scale if volume sales can be achieved. It builds sales quickly where no regular customers exist. So, for example, when a new washing powder is launched there may be special 'two for the price of one' offers to get customers to try it. Special offers of this sort are particularly useful as they benchmark the price at a higher level and create the expectation that the price will rise at some future date. Without that there might be resistance to any subsequent price rise.

♀ Differentiation

Differentiation is about being different and distinctive. It can come from being innovative in some way. However, many firms might not be described as innovative but are still clearly differentiated from the competition. For both a product and a service differentiation can come about through function, design, quality, performance, technology or other tangible characteristics. So, for example, Mercedes Benz and Bang & Olufsen aim to differentiate themselves through quality in their respective sectors. McDonald's does it, in part, through quality of service (speed, cleanliness and so on) – but price is clearly important. Differentiation might come from the other elements of the marketing mix, for example, the channels of distribution. When Amazon started selling books on the internet it was so radically different that it was seen as an innovation in bookselling that had implications for other sectors. And yet the innovation was simply the use of another, much cheaper, channel of distribution.

Differentiation can, however, prove costly if the basis that is chosen subsequently proves inappropriate, for example, DVD compared to BlueRay format. Companies try to protect the basis for differentiation in any way possible. It might be that a product can be patented, the design registered or, for written material, copyrighted.

Differentiation is helped by clear branding. A brand should be the embodiment of the product or service offered to customers. So, for example, the Mercedes Benz, Jaguar and BMW brands all convey quality. Virgin is the embodiment of Richard

Branson; brash, entrepreneurial, different, anti-establishment. Lush is environmentally friendly. The Co-op bank is ethical whereas Coutts Bank is for the wealthy. Many so-called brands, however, fall far short of this instant recognition of values and virtues, being little more than expensive logos. What do the Barclays, Shell or BT brands convey, other than the knowledge of what the firm sells?

In a world where products and services are often all too homogeneous, a good brand is a powerful marketing tool that must be the cornerstone of any strategy of differentiation. Not only can it help turn prospects into customers, if everything else is right it can turn them into regular customers. What is more, as shown in Figure 7.5, it can help turn them into supporters – regular customers who think positively about the brand – or even advocates – who are willing to recommend the product and bring in new customers. This is an approach far more in tune with interactive marketing, one that is easier to achieve with the personal touch.

F7.5 The customer loyalty ladder

Branding and things like patents and copyrights are about securing differential advantage for as long as possible and creating barriers to entry into the market. The bigger the market, the more difficult and expensive this is to achieve. That is why differentiation is most successful when combined with a strategy of customer focus.

💡 Developing customer focus

Focus involves breaking down markets into different groups of customers; these are called segments – groups of customers who have similar characteristics or needs. The key for most start-ups is to focus their attention and resources on just three or four clearly defined market segments, tailoring the marketing mix to the needs of customers in those segments and communicating the benefits to them in an appropriate way and through an appropriate medium. This is the starting point of niche marketing discussed in the last chapter. Studies show that there is a relationship between profitability and gaining a high market share of a particular segment.

There are many ways of segmenting markets. You are looking for groups of customers with similar needs that can be identified and described in some meaningful and useful way. For consumer markets these include personal characteristics (demographics) such as age, gender, socio-economic group, occupation, location of home, stage in family life cycle, and so on. If the group can be identified in this way information on their buying habits is relatively easy to obtain and it is also possible to find out the best media through which to reach them. For example, ACORN (A Classification of Regional Neighbourhoods) breaks down the whole of the UK into about 40 different neighbourhoods, each identified by postcode. So, for example, large inner-city Victorian houses near universities may, reasonably, be assumed to house a lot of university students, which could be important if that is your target market.

💼 Case insight Radio Spirits

Radio Spirits Inc. is certainly a niche business. Based in Illinois, USA, it sells old-time radio shows such as 'The Lone Ranger', 'Dragnet', 'The Jack Benny Show' and 'The Burns and Allen Show'. Collecting these shows started as a hobby for its founder, Carl Amari. It now has a catalogue of over 4000 shows that it mails to 350 000 potential customers across the USA. It also has a pay-per-listen website. Despite being a niche business the company still manages sales that run into the millions of dollars.

☐ Up-to-date information on Radio Spirits can be found on their website: www.radiospirits.com

For business markets, segments might include type of business, size, location, nature of technology, creditworthiness and so on. The most commonly used classification is the official standard industrial classification (SIC), which breaks down all businesses into broad groups and sub-groups according to activity.

Market segments can be any one – or a combination of – descriptive factors associated with the product or service, the customer, channels of distribution, sales territories and so forth. There are no prescriptive approaches to segmentation. It requires creative insight into customers' buying habits as well as an understanding of the unique benefits offered by the product or service to these groups. This means understanding the market and competitors, but most of all the customers. Brassington and Pettitt (2006) list four 'absolute requirements' for any segmentation to be successful:

1   The segment must be distinctive and significantly different from any other segment. Without this the segment boundaries are likely to be too blurred.
2   The segment must be of sufficient size to make it commercially attractive. It may be that a gap in the market exists because it is not commercially attractive.
3   The segment must be accessible. The gap in the market might not exist in reality because the segment cannot be reached.
4   The segment must be defendable from competitors.

The slimmer the market segment that the product or service is tailored to suit, the higher customer satisfaction is likely to be. We all like personal service and the ultimate market segment comprises just one customer. However, this might not be a viable segment economically. The trend is towards slimmer and slimmer market segments. The danger facing firms selling to slim market segments is their over-reliance on a small customer base. If tastes change the segment might disappear. It is vital therefore that niche businesses keep in close touch with the changing needs of their customers.

One small firm producing motor components found itself competing unsuccessfully against a large multinational that undercut it on price. It decided to rethink its whole marketing strategy and found there were many opportunities for products manufactured to a high technical specification in which quality and supplier reputation were more important than the price charged. By focusing its marketing strategy on these segments, the company was able to establish itself as a niche player in what was otherwise a highly competitive industry.

Once you understand what your customers or market segments are looking for, you can start to tailor the product or service that you offer. Once you understand your competition, you will start to understand the strength or otherwise of your competitive advantage. With this in mind you can decide which of Porter's generic marketing strategies is most appropriate to each product/market offering. From that you start to understand the imperatives you face and what tasks need to be addressed in your marketing plan. The advantages of developing a market niche can be considerable. If done properly it is profitable and avoids confrontation and competition.

Research indicates that small firms often go about the process of niche positioning in a 'bottom-up' sort of way (Dalgic and Leeuw, 1994). Often they start by pursuing an opportunity through matching innovative ideas to their resources, testing it by trial and error in the market place. The entrepreneur does not always use formal research at this stage, relying perhaps more on intuition. If the idea attracts customers (whether or not they conform to an expected profile), the entrepreneur gets to know them through regular contact. Expansion then comes by looking for more customers with the same profile. Often this is, again, a gradual process of self-selection with some encouragement from the entrepreneur rather than a process involving formal research and deliberate choice.

💡 Entrepreneurial marketing

One dimension in which entrepreneurial marketing differs from conventional marketing is its heavy reliance on relationships. More recently this has been recognised and christened 'relationship marketing', which can be contrasted to the more traditional transactional marketing. Supporters of this 'new' approach – in fact, long used by small firms – believe that it can deliver sustainable customer loyalty (Webster, 1992). The two approaches are contrasted in Table 7.3. This approach may not be viable with all products or services, but it does add yet a further dimension to Porter's generic marketing strategies. Relationship marketing can be mixed with any of the four strategies to create a relationship hybrid that implies a different set of strategic imperatives from those implied by a transactional marketing approach.

Relationship marketing	Transactional marketing
▷ Encourages close, frequent customer contact	▷ Limited contact
▷ Encourages repeat sales	▷ Orientated towards a single purchase
▷ Focus on customer service	▷ Limited customer service
▷ Focus on value to the customer	▷ Focus on product/service benefits
▷ Focus on quality of total offering	▷ Focus on quality of product
▷ Focus on long-term performance	▷ Focus on short-term performance

T7.3 Relationship vs transactional marketing

However, a reliance on relationships may not in itself be sufficient to mark out the entrepreneurial firm. Chaston (2000) says that truly entrepreneurial firms have a distinctively different approach to marketing which he defines as 'the philosophy of challenging established market conventions during the process of developing new solutions'. The entrepreneurial marketing process is essentially simple, involving understanding conventional competitors and then challenging the approach they adopt. The process of 'rational entrepreneurship' is shown in Figure 7.6. In essence, he is suggesting that marketing is judged to be entrepreneurial by its degree of innovation. Since this is the essence of entrepreneurship, it is difficult to dispute.

As Chaston points out, even relationship marketing can be copied, although larger firms may find it more difficult to sustain than smaller firms. Here again he encourages the entrepreneur to do things differently. For example, many internet businesses foster relationships with their customers by generating a sense of community on their website. Chaston's approach is deceptively simple as he points out that there are many conventions that can be challenged. He suggests three categories:

1 Sectoral conventions are the strategic rules that guide the marketing operations of the majority of firms in a sector such as efficiency of plants, economies of scale, methods of distribution and so on. The advent of the internet caused many firms to rethink their distribution channels and opened up worldwide markets to smaller firms without the need to appoint agents.

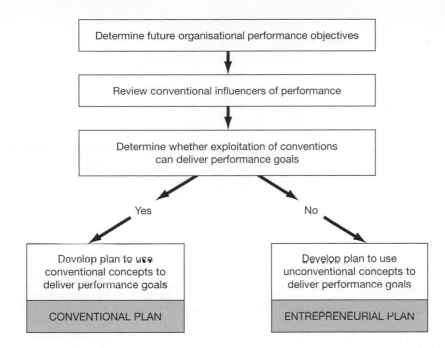

F7.6 Entrepreneurial vs non-entrepreneurial planning pathway

Source: Chaston (2000)

2 Performance conventions set by other firms in the sector such as profit, cost of production, quality and so forth. The low-cost airlines changed the terms on which airlines competed and the way passengers viewed air travel. As a result, the market expanded dramatically.

3 Customer conventions which make certain assumptions about what customers are looking for from their purchases, for example price, size, design and so on. Lush and The Body Shop redefined the cosmetic industry's 'feel-good factor' to include environmental factors.

In most sectors there are factors that managers believe are critical to the success of their business. Chaston encourages entrepreneurs to ask 'why?' These conventions are all worth questioning and doing things differently is what entrepreneurship is about, but doing things differently is risky and Chaston is the first to say it takes careful research and analysis, matching opportunities to the firm's capabilities. He proposes a somewhat different approach to marketing planning which he calls 'mapping the future'. This eight-stage process is shown in Figure 7.7. Although shown as linear and sequential, the process is interrupted as new market information is discovered and earlier decisions are revisited. The process also includes small-scale market entry and trial to gain further information.

The process starts with the development of a detailed understanding of sector conventions. Stage two involves assessing the performance gap between aspirations of future performance and the level of performance currently being delivered. If the size is sufficient to attract an entrepreneurial approach (that is, an incremental approach is not warranted), then the opportunity is investigated using an innovative approach that questions all current assumptions about delivery. Whatever that approach is, it must next be matched to the ability to deliver. If the firm has the capability, then the remaining processes are more straightforward; defining performance objectives, defining strategy, developing a detailed plan and specifying control systems. All these will be considered in greater detail in subsequent chapters and pulled together into a detailed business plan in Chapter 14.

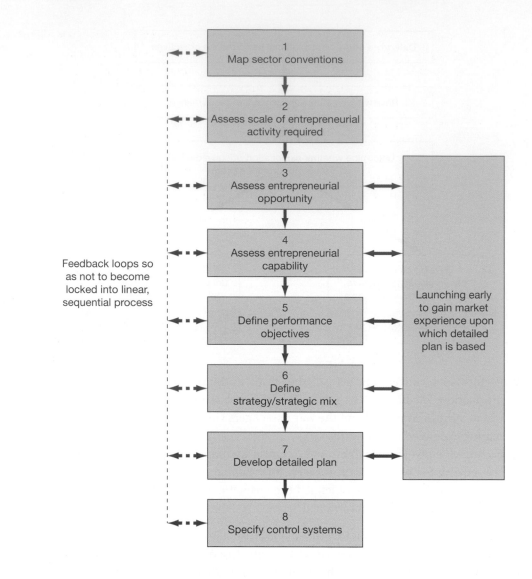

F7.7 The entrepreneurial marketing planning process

Source: Chaston (2000)

💡 Undertaking market research

The President of Harvard Business School once said that if you thought knowledge was expensive, you should try ignorance. Some market research is essential before a business is started. It helps minimise risk and uncertainty and provides some basis on which to make the decisions about marketing strategy. Collecting information and making judgements on it are key entrepreneurial competencies (Carson et al., 1995). Market research involves getting information about customers and competitors. For a start-up any information is probably of value, but the key question that needs to be answered is – why should anyone buy from you rather than from your competitors? To answer this question, break it down into four elements:

1 Who will buy?
2 What are they buying?
3 Who are your competitors?
4 Why do people buy from them?

Clarifying who the customers are likely to be will enable the firm to focus on those that will give it most business. Knowing as much as possible about them and why they might buy will enable the firm to fine-tune its marketing better to suit their needs and help it to identify both new customers and, eventually, new products or services.

Knowing who the competitors are is just as important. A pizza restaurant may face competition from a whole range of other local restaurants, not just those offering pizza. Understanding why customers buy from competitors gives a further insight into the needs of customers and ideas about how you may combat competition.

Market research, therefore, might involve estimating the size and nature of the market including profiling of consumers or industrial customers. A consumer profile might include age, sex, income, occupation, social status, geographic location and so on. An industrial profile might include sector, size, geographic location and so forth. It might involve understanding why, where and when customers buy, the nature of distribution channels and the nature of economic and other environmental trends that might affect the business. It might involve analysing competitors in terms of their product/service offering, size, profitability, operating methods. If a new product or service is involved, it might involve some testing to get customers' reaction. The important thing is to start by specifying what market information is needed.

If you ask me how we find new markets, the answer is research, research, research ... For us research is critical when it comes to opening new outlets. We put a lot of work into demographics and social indicators and really know our business. But they can fail: we put a store in Dewsbury, West Yorkshire, four years ago, everything looked good, we did the groundwork, but what the figures didn't show was that our site was in the middle of the town's devoutly Muslim centre. They ate only halal meat, and they certainly weren't eating pizza. We got it wrong and we had to shut the store.

☐ Stephen Hemsley, Chief Executive, Domino's Pizza, *Sunday Times* 23 May 2004

There are two ways to research a market (Table 7.4):

1 Field research;
2 Desk research.

Field research can involve conducting face-to-face individual or group interviews, telephone surveys or administering postal questionnaires. Simple observation and discussion will go a long way without costing much other than time. Asking questions of potential customers face to face, by mail shot or by telephone will provide a lot of valuable information. Visiting competitors at their place of business, perhaps buying their product or service and talking to other customers will give an insight into how they operate.

Research based on interviewing has to ensure that a representative sample of respondents is seen and that, where a structured interview is used, the subject areas are covered comprehensively. When questionnaires are used, the questions must be clear and unambiguous. They should not 'lead' respondents by implying an answer to the question. Their design should facilitate interpretation and possible data processing.

	Field research	Desk research
Advantages	▷ Reflects your needs	▷ Cheap
	▷ You control quality	▷ Quick
	▷ Up-to-date	▷ Good for background information
Disadvantages	▷ Expensive	▷ Not specific to your business
	▷ Takes time	▷ Can be incomplete or inaccurate
	▷ Can tell competition what you are up to	▷ Can be out-of-date

T7.4 Advantages and disadvantages of field vs desk research

🖹 Case insight Mark Dorman and Black Vodka

Mark Dorman was an advertising executive who had worked for 20 years in the business. In 1995 he was sitting in a hotel bar in the USA feeling jet-lagged. The barman offered him a vodka or a coffee, black or white, to help him come round. Something registered in his mind – what a brilliant idea if you could really have black vodka. It would be completely unique and instantly branded as it was poured into the glass.

When he got back to the UK he decided to investigate the idea. He asked for help from a friend, Christopher Hayman, who worked for Beefeater Gin. After some experimentation they found that it could be done by colouring the vodka with black catechu, a Burmese herb. There was also the added advantage that if you put a mixer in first, as the Americans do, the vodka floats to the top, giving a distinctive cocktail. He also found out that there was a lucrative market in the USA with more than 350 million cases of vodka sold annually.

By 1997 Mark had invested some £750 000 of his own money in the idea, a third of which was simply the legal costs of registering the product in different countries. He had a company, imaginatively called the Black Vodka Company. However, he had run out of money and was still unable to produce the vodka in volume.

The story has a happy ending. Mark was able to find a private backer who shared his faith in the product and bought a share of the company. In 1998 black vodka went on sale in Britain and the USA. It was a success. In 1999 Francarep, the capital development arm of the Rothschild family, bought a 27 per cent stake in the company. The company went on to be listed on AIM and then obtained a full listing ahead of merging with a US drinks company to become known as Blavod Extreme Spirits. Although Mark no longer has anything to do with the company, it wasn't a bad idea from a barman!

For retailers, location is obviously very important. Once prospective premises have been identified, check out the local trade. Find out how many and what type of customers pass by the location. Standing outside the location and counting will tell you how many potential customers pass it at any time of day. Are shops in the immediate vicinity an advantage or disadvantage? Location can be important for other businesses, for example proximity to customers or a workforce. Many start-ups locate where the owner-manager happens to live. It is not a positive decision. Some lifestyle businesses also locate where the owner-managers want to live. The advantages of different types of field research are shown in Table 7.5.

Desk research can provide information quickly and cheaply. Information on markets, sectors and industries is published in newspapers, trade magazines, industry surveys and reports, trade journals or directories, many of which will be available at the local business library. There will be websites that provide information. Desk research can provide information on product developments, customer needs or characteristics, competitors and market trends. However, for many start-ups local information is of far more importance than regional or national information and that might come from Chambers of Commerce and other local sources of help and advice.

For many start-ups the easiest and cheapest way to undertake market research is to test-market and launch the business in a low-cost way, constantly reviewing what is happening and how customers react and refining the product or service offered to

	Personal interview	Telephone interview	Postal questionnaire
Quality of data	Very good	Good	Good
Quantity of data	Very good	Fair	Poor
Speed	Good	Very good	Poor
Response rate	Good	Good	Poor
Cost	High (your time)	Fair	Fair

T7.5 Advantages and disadvantages of different types of field research

them. However, this can be a very expensive way of doing market research if things go wrong, and some basic market research is essential for just about any start-up. The bigger the start-up, the more important is proper market research.

Whilst any and all information is probably worth having, we need to know what we are looking for. The vital need is to understand why customers buy and how they might be influenced. We need to understand how to go about matching what the firm is capable of producing with what the customer needs – and that is called marketing. Marketing is first and foremost an attitude of mind about always putting the customer first. Understanding customer needs and motivations is central to marketing.

💡 Developing selling skills

Whatever the 'theory' of marketing might be, the practical reality is that most owner-managers will have to do at least some of their own selling at start-up. The first thing to do is to identify the customer. It sounds obvious but, particularly for business-to-business products or services, the consumer or user of the product or service is not always the buyer. Indeed to get a sale you might have to persuade a range of people – called the 'decision-making unit' (DMU) – each with different interests. The DMU tends to increase with the size of firm you are selling to. The DMU might involve, say, two engineers, a buyer and somebody from the finance department, each looking for different things. Each one has to be satisfied.

It is important to plan a sales interview so as not to waste time or create a bad impression. This starts with knowing as much as you can about the prospective customer and being clear about what you want from the interview. It is important to evaluate the business potential from each customer so as to make the most of your time. The other variable here is their attitude towards you but, whilst you can affect attitude, you are unlikely to be able to affect business potential. Figure 7.8 shows a selling potential matrix that salesmen can use to improve their use of time. Most time should be spent with friendly customers with high potential. Salesmen tend to spend time with any and all friendly customers. In fact they must husband their time between these and the high business potential customers, so as to move these from less friendly to more friendly over time.

It is important to gain the customer's attention, arouse their interest and build confidence. All the time you are trying to find out three important things:

1   What they want.
2   How to match this to the product or service you have to sell.
3   How to build up agreement that it does indeed meet their requirements.

and fourth:

4   How to close the sale.

		Business potential of customer		
		High	Medium	Low
Attitude	Friendly	Most time	Increasing time	Some time
	Indifferent	Increasing time	Some time	Perhaps
	Unfriendly	Some time	Perhaps	Opportunistic

F7.8   The selling potential matrix

The sales interview is the ideal opportunity to bridge the gap between a customer's needs and the benefits offered by a product or service. If you can do that, and convince the customer that the product or service does indeed meet their requirements, you have a sale. Sales interviews can be started in a number of ways:

▷ *Question*: You might ask a question to ascertain that the customer buys these sorts of products or services.
▷ *Statement*: You might state the benefits of the product or service directly, for example 'our service will save the average household 20% on their phone bills'.
▷ *Reference*: You might give a personal reference like 'Mr Smith in your other factory was impressed with our service and said you might be interested …' You can equally use impersonal references like an article in the trade or national press.
▷ *Sales aids*: You might launch straight into looking at photographs, brochures and so on.
▷ *Demonstration*: If you have the product with you, a demonstration may be the best way to get going.
▷ *Link to earlier contact*: You may have phoned or made contact earlier and agreed to the meeting.

Once you have opened, your aim should be to state the features and benefits of the product and start matching them to the needs of the customer. There are various techniques to help get your message across. Visual stimuli like support materials, demonstrations or presentations all help. Building the relationship is vital. Small things can be important to help achieve this in the short space of time available. For example, dressing appropriately, being punctual, keeping eye contact, being confident and enthusiastic about the product or service, listening to the customer and trying to see things from their point of view, being courteous and polite, and avoiding negative body language like looking bored. The most important advice of all, particularly if the interview goes wrong, is to let the customer talk and to really listen to what he is saying. All the time he is giving you information which should enable you to match the benefits of your product or service to his needs. This entails understanding how to turn features into benefits, as discussed earlier. Relationships are built on over time and networks of contacts can be developed through good customer relationships, so pressurising a customer is unlikely to pay off in the long run.

Selling benefits means understanding both the product or service and the needs of the customer, being able to match the two and then convince the customer that he should buy. That often means avoiding jargon and talking the customer's language.

As the sales interview progresses the customer may show a lack of interest. If this is the case, then the opening was probably not sufficiently interesting and you need to discover what other areas of need – if any – the product or service might meet.

📋 Case insight

Mark Goldsmith and Goldsmith's Fine Foods

Goldsmith's Fine Foods was set up by Mark Goldsmith in Manchester immediately after leaving university. It was a wholesaler that sold savoury snacks and cakes to a range of customers, but mainly small restaurants and snack bars. Early on Mark realised that he was not just selling snacks and cakes – too many other companies were doing that. To the owners of these outlets he was selling the opportunity to make additional income from their customers by tempting them with something they might not otherwise buy – this was the benefit to them. An additional feature to enhance this benefit was the advice Mark gave on the positioning of various products, including his own, so as to maximise the spend from each of their customers. These small outlets were inexperienced at doing this. Offering this service allowed Mark to differentiate himself, for this particular target market segment, from other wholesalers and develop close relationships with his customers. At its height Goldsmith's employed 35 people in Manchester and London before it was taken over.

In other words you need to ask questions. If the customer raises an objection – which is more than likely at some point in the interview – then at least he is showing an interest and in raising the objection he is providing additional information. If the customer has a fundamental objection, for example, you are trying to sell double glazing and it turns out to be a new house, then it may be time to move on. But just sometimes this is not the case and it may be worth asking why he does not see the need for the product or service. It may just be worth trying to convince him of the benefits it offers over what he already uses, even if the time to change is some way in the future. There are six other types of objection, some of which can be dealt with. They are:

▷ *Feature objection* – some of the features do not meet the customer's approval. This can be dealt with by emphasising the positive reasons for these features.
▷ *Information-seeking objections* – the customer is not fully convinced by some aspect of the presentation. This provides the opportunity to give relevant information and tailor it to the customer's requirements.
▷ *Price objections*: These may be fundamental but often the objection can be made in the hope of negotiating a lower price. Benefits should be restated and compared to the price difference in competing products. Value for money needs to be stressed and a discount only offered as a last resort, perhaps using it to secure a larger order.
▷ *Delay objection* – the customer wants to put off making a decision. This is difficult if the delay is genuine. Arranging a return visit when the time is right may be all you can achieve.
▷ *Loyalty objection* – the customer may have an established relationship with a competitor. Stress the benefits of the product or service and never 'knock' the competitor. Try to find reasons why they should change supplier, for example, are they being taken for granted in terms of the service they receive? Always keep contact as it may just take time to convince them to try you.
▷ *Hidden objection* – the buyer prevaricates for no obvious reason. This is another difficult situation. It is important to get to the unstated objection and deal with it, so ask questions.

Some people have problems recognising buying signals and can continue relentlessly through their presentation long after the customer actually wanted to buy the product or service. Buying signals can be many and various; the customer becoming interested and animated, positive body language such as leaning forward or wanting to pick up or try the product. If interest is confirmed by asking a few questions, the whole process can be short-circuited and you can go to the most important stage of all – closing the sale.

There are six well-known techniques used for closing the sale:

▷ *The trial close*: You can try this one immediately you see a buying signal. This close uses the opportunity of an expression of interest to ask a further question which implicitly assumes a sale. For example, 'You will want to take our extended credit, won't you?' or 'It is the quality of the product that has convinced you, hasn't it?' Notice the trial close ends with a question and if the answer is positive then you can proceed straight to close the sale.
▷ *The alternative close*: This forces the customer to a decision between options. For example, 'Do you want 1000 or 5000?' or 'Can we deliver next month or would you prefer next week?'

▷ *The summary close*: This is useful if the buyer is uncertain about the next step. It summarises what has been said and sets out the next steps. For example, 'So those are the advantages our service offers over the one you are using at the moment and I think you would agree we are better in every respect. Do you agree?'

▷ *The concession close*: Concessions are usually on price. They may secure orders but should not be given away too soon, only at the end of the interview when you judge it necessary to tip the balance in your favour. For example, 'And if you place an order in December, there is a special 5% discount.'

▷ *The quotation close*: Often you have to provide a formal quote at the end of the sales interview. If this is the case, then it should be followed up with another visit to the customer to clarify the main points, answer any queries and secure the sale.

▷ *The direct close*: Just sometimes it is actually necessary to ask for the order directly – and then remain silent and listen to the answer. If the answer is 'no' at least it should provide some objections that you might be able to overcome.

Successful selling means knowing your product or service inside out and understanding the needs of your customers. It is not just about winning orders, it is about building relationships – vital for a small firm that does not have the advertising and promotion budget that a large firm might have. Relationships are built on trust and respect and, if you cannot get these from the customer, then you are simply an order-taker and the business could easily disappear at any time.

♀ Retailing on the internet

According to IMRG, the industry body for global e-retailing, in 2006 consumers spent £30.2 billion on online goods and services, and this is growing rapidly. Selling on the web offers the opportunity to do business 24 hours a day, seven days a week – worldwide. It also offers you the chance to build relationships and develop an understanding of individual customer's buying patterns. The pure internet firm does not require the major fixed costs of a retail business like the high street site and the shop-floor staff – but many traditional bricks-and-mortar business are now also trading on the internet, trying to offer customers the best of both worlds. At the moment internet-based retail is most successful for branded products where the features are already understood, or for 'low touch' products or services such as music downloads, books, airline or theatre tickets where, once again, customers understand precisely what they are buying. However, even here the nature of trading is changing as media is increasingly downloaded directly rather than being delivered through the post.

The key to successful trading on the internet is a good website – one that gets people to visit and then revisit. You can spend as much as you want to set up a website. A basic one might cost as little as £500 but a good one could easily cost £20 000. If you do not want to build your own website you can search for web designers online, or ask friends and colleagues for recommendations.

The website should enable customers to order quickly and easily. A site with a difficult sales process is likely to lose customers before they reach the checkout. It should also be easy to navigate so customers do not get frustrated and leave without even attempting to make a purchase. Security should also be a priority, and potential customers should be assured that their details will be kept safe. The website's content needs to be updated regularly so as to maintain customer interest. It should also present a 'human face' and, better still, build a community of interest that encourages the visitor to communicate with you, ideally leaving their email address. You can then communicate with them directly. This generates web loyalty and customer trust.

You need to get customers to visit your site in the first place. Internet business often seems to forget this. You can create awareness of your site by advertising – in print media or on other websites. Sites such as Google AdWords can be cost-effective. These operate on a 'pay per click' basis, so you only pay when someone clicks through to your website. Chatrooms and discussion forums can be cheap ways of getting customers to become aware of your website – a technique called 'viral marketing'. You might even email friends and family and ask them to do the same. Search engine optimisation (SEO) ensures that you catch any potential customers searching for your type of product on search engines such as Yahoo or Google, but this can be expensive if you employ a company to do it. On the other hand you can learn how to do it yourself with the help of a good book, an online course and some specialist software such as Google Analytics, which helps you monitor the traffic on your website.

The types of program that you plan to use and the volume of usage will dictate exactly what type of connection and hardware you will need. You may decide to have a 'hosting account' with a company that hosts your web files, and then transfer files between your own computer and the account. This will keep hardware costs down.

🗂 Useful links for search engine optimisation

Google.com/analytics	A free tool for analysing your website traffic
Compete.com	A keyword research tool
Seochat.com and Seoforum.com	Guides and tips for SEO
Seolite.com	SEO tools for downloading

🗂 Case insight Gary Frank and The Fabulous Bakin' Boys

Gary Frank understands the importance of image and branding, particularly for a small firm trying to carve a niche in the market. The company he set up in 1989, the Delicious Doughnut Company, was turning in lacklustre performance. It did not even produce doughnuts any more. So in 1997 he decided to create a new image and re-brand the company with the name Fabulous Bakin' Boys. He invested £300 000 in the name change and recruited a marketing manager. It had an immediate impact, with sales increasing by 50 per cent. This growth continued and in 1999 the company moved to a new factory in Witney near Oxford, employing 150 staff. Because of the new branding, and after improvements to the packaging, the products were taken on by the big supermarkets – initially Tesco, Safeway and Sainsbury's and, since 2002, Asda and Somerfield.

The Fabulous Bakin' Boys have specialised in internet marketing. Their website contains a database of jokes, cheeky postcard advertisements and online games such as Muffin Munchin' and Cake Invaders that can be downloaded or 'mailed to a mate' as part of a viral campaign. However you can only do all this after you have registered. Once registered you receive regular mail-outs. Online ordering is also possible. The Fabulous Bakin' Boys have now become one of Europe's leading muffin makers.

☐ Up-to-date information on The Fabulous Bakin' Boys can be found on their website: www.bakinboys.co.uk

Indeed some small businesses avoid most hardware and software costs simply by trading through other trading sites such as eBay.

Brady (1999) argues that success for a purely internet start-up depends on several factors, although, interestingly, all but the last factor could apply to any business:

▷ Providing something different.
▷ The business must be clearly focused but be sufficiently flexible to change quickly to sustain growth.
▷ The management must be good with a good plan, a grasp of critical issues and credibility in the eyes of financiers.
▷ The business must develop a strong brand and, on the back of this, create and maintain very high levels of service.
▷ Delivery must be on time.
▷ The site must be readily accessible, orders must be simple to place and easily tracked whilst they are in the system.

E-business is not just a new element to be added into the marketing mix. It is a fundamental and dramatic change in the way we do business which increases the degree of competition and makes us reinterpret some of the fundamentals of marketing.

Legal forms of business

Nothing, in the over-regulated world of today, is ever simple. Before a new business is launched some thought should be given to the legal problems that need to be dealt with. There is a checklist on the website accompanying this book setting out the regulations to be met in starting up a business in the UK. It also contains sources of information, help and advice in the UK. The first issue is the legal form for the business. The three most popular are: sole trader (almost 60 per cent of businesses), partnership and limited liability company.

Sole traders

This is the business owned by one individual. The individual is the business, and the business is the individual. The two are inseparable. A sole trader is the simplest form of business to start – all that is needed is the first customer. It faces fewer regulations than a limited company and there are no major requirements about accounts and audits, although the individual will pay personal taxes which are based upon the profits made by the business.

There are two important limitations, however. The first is that a sole trader will find it more difficult to borrow large amounts of money than a limited company. Lending institutions prefer the assets of the business to be placed within the legal framework of a company because of the restrictions then placed upon the business. It is, however, quite common for a business to start life as a sole trader and incorporate later in life as more capital is needed.

The second disadvantage is that the sole trader is personally liable for all the debts of the business, no matter how large. That means creditors may look both to the business assets and the proprietor's assets to satisfy their debts. However, this disadvantage should not be over-emphasised because of the widely adopted practice of placing some family assets in the name of the spouse or another relative and because, even as a limited company, a bank is likely to ask for a personal guarantee from the proprietor before giving a loan.

Partnerships

Some professions, such as doctors and accountants, are required by law to conduct business as partnerships. Partnerships are just groups of sole traders who come together, formally or informally, to do business. As such it allows them to pool their resources; some to contribute capital, others their skills. Partnerships, therefore, face all the advantages of sole traders plus some additional disadvantages.

The first of these disadvantages is that each partner has unlimited liability for the debts of the partnership, whether they incurred them personally or not. Clearly partnerships require a lot of trust. The second disadvantage is that the partnership is held to cease every time one partner leaves or a new one joins, which means dividing up the assets and liabilities in some way, even if other partners end up buying them and the business never actually ceases trading.

Generally, if you are considering a partnership you would be well advised to draw up a formal partnership agreement. It is very easy to get into an informal partnership with a friend, but if you cannot work together, or times get hard, you may regret it. If there is no formal agreement, then in the UK the terms of the Partnership Act 1890 are held to apply. Partnership agreements cover such issues as capital contributions, division of profit and interest on capital, power to draw money or take remuneration from the business, preparation of accounts and procedures when the partnership is held to 'cease'. Solicitors can provide a model agreement which can be adapted to suit particular circumstances.

Limited companies

A company (registered in accordance with the provisions of the Companies Acts in the UK) is a separate legal entity distinct from its owners or shareholders, and its directors or managers. It can enter into contracts and sue or be sued in its own right. It is taxed separately through Corporation Tax. There is a divorce between management and ownership, with a board of directors elected by the shareholders to control the day-to-day running of the business. There need be only two shareholders and one director, and shareholders can also be directors.

The advantage of this form of business is that the liability of the shareholders is limited by the amount of capital they put into the business. What is more, a company has unlimited life and can be sold on to other shareholders. Indeed there is no limit to the number of shareholders. Therefore a limited company can attract additional risk capital from backers who may not wish to be involved in the day-to-day running of the business. Also, because of the regulation they face, bankers prefer to lend to companies rather than sole traders, although they may still require personal guarantees. Clearly this is the best form for a growth business that will require capital and will face risks as it grows.

Nevertheless there are some disadvantages to this form of business. In the UK under the Companies Acts, a company must keep certain books of account and appoint an auditor. It must file an annual return with Companies House which includes accounts and details of directors and shareholders. This takes time and money and means that competitors might have access to information that they would not otherwise see. Advantages and disadvantages of different forms of business are summarised in Table 7.6.

The easiest and cheapest way to set up a company is to buy one 'off the shelf' from a Company Registration Agent. This avoids all the tedious form-filling that is otherwise

	Sole trader	Partnership	Limited company
Advantages	▷ Easy to form ▷ Minimum of regulation	▷ Easy to form ▷ Minimum of regulation	▷ Limited liability ▷ Easier to borrow money ▷ Can raise risk capital through additional shareholders ▷ Can be sold on ▷ Pays Corporation Tax (which can be lower than personal tax)
Disadvantages	▷ Unlimited personal liability ▷ More difficult to borrow money ▷ Pays personal tax	▷ Unlimited personal liability for debts of whole partnership ▷ More difficult to borrow money ▷ 'Cease trading' whenever partners change ▷ Pays personal tax	▷ Must comply with Companies Acts ▷ Greater regulation ▷ Greater disclosure of information

T7.6 Advantages and disadvantages of different forms of business

required. It also saves time. Agents will also show you how to go about changing the company's name if you want to. To find out more simply Google 'Company Registration Agent'.

Franchises

These are not so much a legal form of business as a way of doing business. They are increasingly popular, particularly with individuals who are less entrepreneurial but wish to run their own business. A franchise is a business in which the owner of the name or method of doing business (the franchisor) allows a local operator (the franchisee) to set up a business under that name. The local operator may be a sole trader or a limited company.

In exchange for an initial fee (anything from a few thousand to hundreds of thousands of pounds) and a royalty on sales, the franchisor lays down a blueprint of how the business is to be run; content and nature of product or service, price and performance standards, type, size and layout of shop or business, training and other support or controls. Since the franchise is usually a tried and tested idea, well known

	Franchisee	Franchisor
Advantages	▷ Business format proved; less risk of failure ▷ Easier to obtain finance than own start-up ▷ Established format; start-up should be quicker ▷ Training and support available from franchisor ▷ National branding should help sales ▷ Economies of scale may apply	▷ Way of expanding business quickly ▷ Financing costs shared with franchisees ▷ Franchisees usually highly motivated since their livelihood depends on success
Disadvantages	▷ Not really your own idea and creation ▷ Lack of real independence ▷ Franchisor makes the rules ▷ Buying into franchise can be expensive ▷ Royalties can be high ▷ Goodwill you build up dependent upon continuing franchise agreement; this may cause problems if you wish to sell ▷ Franchisor can damage brand	▷ British Franchise Association rules take time and money to comply with ▷ Loss of some control to franchisees ▷ Franchisees can influence the business ▷ Failure of franchisee can reflect on franchise ▷ May be obligations to franchisee in the franchise agreement

T7.7 Advantages and disadvantages of being a franchisee or franchisor

to potential customers, the franchisee should have a ready market and a better chance of a successful start-up. Indeed only about 10 per cent of franchises fail.

There are hundreds of franchises in the UK as well as tens of thousands of franchisees. Most established franchisors are members of the British Franchise Association, which has a code of conduct and accreditation rules, based on codes developed by the European Franchise Association. One key principle is that the franchisor shall have operated the business concept with success for a reasonable time, and in at least one pilot unit before starting the franchise network. Table 7.7 summarises the advantages and disadvantages of being a franchisee and a franchisor.

💼 Case with questions The Body Shop franchise

Although now owned by L'Oréal, the first The Body Shop store was opened by Anita Roddick in a back street in Brighton in 1976. It sold only about a dozen inexpensive 'natural' cosmetics, all herbal creams and shampoos, in simple packaging. Anita thought it would only appeal to a small number of customers who shared her values. Her husband, Gordon, even went off to ride a horse across the Americas about a month after it opened. But Anita was wrong. It proved to be a huge success. However, whilst this idea was novel at the time, it was easy to copy. The firm's initial roll-out owed much to Anita and Gordon Roddick's clear focus on where their competitive advantage lay. They realised that their idea could be easily copied and success would only come from developing the brand and a rapid expansion. Unfortunately they had little cash to do either. It was Gordon who had the idea of making The Body Shop a franchise, which meant that franchisees purchased the rights to open a The Body Shop® store and managed the shop themselves. The Roddicks initially decided not to manufacture their products or even invest in a distribution system, but rather to concentrate on getting the franchise formula right, developing the brand and protecting it from imitators.

Today, The Body Shop remains an international franchise chain of shops. The Body Shop International Ltd is the franchisor. Traditionally, franchisees paid an initial fee plus an annual operating charge for a fixed term, for a renewable franchise. Franchisees would buy a 'turn-key' system with a tightly controlled retail format providing shop fitting and layout, staff training and a stock control system, even help with site identification. The Body Shop International, of course, would also make a margin on the products it sold to the franchisees. Franchisees receive regular visits from company representatives who provide assistance with display, sales promotion and training. Information packs, newsletters, videos and free promotional material are made available and franchisees return a monthly report on their sales. This enables the company to monitor both trading results and the local sales performance of individual products. The company closely monitors the use of the The Body Shop trade mark in all franchisees' literature, advertising and other uses.

Even today the The Body Shop® brand is inexorably linked with its values and culture, which in turn is grounded firmly in its ethical and environmental beliefs. Based very much around Anita Roddick's original views that business can be a vehicle for social and environmental change, the firm has championed numerous causes including 'against-animal-testing', 'trade-not-aid' and 'protect-the-environment'. These not only show themselves in window displays, they also underscore everything the company does. Franchisees are selected partly upon their 'fit' with these ideals. Employees receive regular newsletters and videos concentrating on The Body Shop campaigns and are given time off to work on local social projects as a paid 'volunteering day'. This ethical dimension has been broadly copied by Mark Constantine and his company, Lush, which is hardly surprising since he was, at one point, a supplier of their cosmetics.

☐   Visit the website on: www.thebodyshop.com

QUESTIONS

1   Why was The Body Shop's decision to franchise its shops an important part of its success?

2   What are the dangers for the franchisor of franchising?

3   What are the dangers for the franchisee?

📋 Case with questions Steven Waring and Green Thumb

The motivation to set up your own business can come from deep inside and wait a long time to find the best opportunity. The process is not linear or necessarily sequential – and many might say luck is involved. Stephen Waring's entrepreneurial instinct kicked in at the age of 14 when he started framing old prints and selling them at local fetes around his home town in North Wales in his spare time. Stephen's father was the sales director for a loft insulation firm and by the age of 16 he was helping canvass potential customers by knocking on doors.

He was good at selling, and so when he left school at 17 he set up his own loft insulation firm – it came naturally. He was so successful he even persuaded his older brother to come and help him. When his brother married an American girl in 1985, Stephen went to the USA for the wedding. There he met his new sister-in-law's uncle who owned a lawn treatment company. He found out that 24 per cent of homes in the USA hired someone to treat their lawns in some way.

Despite the scepticism of his parents, Stephen researched the idea. First he set out to find competitors by looking through the Yellow Pages telephone directories, but he could not find anybody offering the same service in the UK. The question was whether nobody else had thought about this idea or whether there was no demand for this sort of service. Stephen could not believe that a service that sold to millions of people in the USA would not sell in the UK so he decided to persevere. Next he set out to find the best mix of fertiliser ingredients for the UK. He experimented on his parents' lawn, turning it orange and black in the process. Having perfected a suitable mix, Stephen next spent £64 on printing 1000 leaflets and hand-delivered them around housing estates near his home. Then he went around doing what he did best – knocking on doors and selling. In this way he secured 70 customers.

Thus, Green Thumb was born. Stephen quickly developed a routine of visiting customers four or five times a year to treat their lawns, as in the USA. The treatment worked and word-of-mouth brought in more customers, so Stephen brought in his younger brother to help him. By 1995, Green Thumb had several thousand regular customers and that was when the next stage in the business's development came about. A customer asked him to sell him a Green Thumb franchise. By 2009 Green Thumb was the largest lawn treatment service in the UK with 90 per cent of the market, operating through almost 200 franchisees.

> 'When people ask me if I ever imagined that my business would be as successful as it has turned out to be, I have to say yes. And we are still embryonic in our growth … The challenge was developing an industry from scratch as opposed to jumping on the bandwagon of somebody else who was already doing it … It helps to have a strong belief in your abilities and not to feel insecure.'

Sunday Times 2 October 2005

☐ Up-to-date information on Green Thumb can be found on their website: www.greenthumb.co.uk

QUESTIONS

1 In what ways did Stephen minimise his start-up and growth costs?
2 How much of Stephen's success was down to luck?
3 Would Stephen have succeeded in any business?

📋 Case with questions Calypso Rose and Clippy

Calypso Rose graduated from a technical theatre course at a drama school and got a job in television production. It was whilst she was working in this job that she made the first see-through bag with pockets to display her collection of photographs of family and friends. She never intended to start up a business. However, so many people kept asking where they could buy something similar that she started thinking about the possibility. When, in 2004, her parents offered to lend her £2000 to make the first 250 bags she decided to take the plunge, aged just 22, and Clippy was born.

Calypso decided to work from home to keep her overheads low. Her mother, Clare, also helped with the business. She found a UK manufacturer through Kelly's online directory (www.kellysearch.co.uk), deciding that this was better than going to China to find a supplier. The UK manufacturer could turn around orders more quickly and, once she established a track record, would offer normal trade terms for payment, thereby helping her cash flow. Initial sales were mainly to family and friends – many of the people who had asked where they could buy the first bag. But the official launch of the company – then called Clippykit – was at Olympia's Spirit of Christmas Fair in 2004. She established a website, customised a large bag with a sign saying 'stop me and buy one' and took a small market stall on the Portobello Road in London. She sold all 250 bags in the first month. Working from home and only using the initial £2000 she managed to build a turnover of £180 000 in the first year. At the age of 22 she was voted London Young Business Person of the Year.

Calypso was worried from the start that the idea could be easily copied – after all it was just a plastic bag with pockets for photographs – and that a bigger company with more resources could roll out an imitation product more effectively than her. So the idea was to push sales as quickly as possible, but also to establish a fashion brand. A major break-through came when the fashionable Notting Hill boutique Coco Ribbon decided to sell her bags. Things got even better when celebrities such as Helena Bonham Carter, Jools Holland and Jamie Oliver started carrying Clippy bags. The bags have even been used as a 'goody bag' at the Brit Awards and the Orange Prize.

It also became clear early on that the concept behind the bags was flexible and could be applied to other products like make-up bags, lamp shades, wallets and umbrellas. Another development was in personalising the products and Calypso started offering kits to help people do that.

Calypso has been very adept at promoting the product herself. For example, in 2009, working with an enterprise organisation called Make Your Mark, 650 girls in London took part in a competition to personalise a Clippy bag with an issue that was relevant to them.

By 2009 the range of Clippy products had grown. The company now has a turnover of £500 000 and employs two full-time and one part-time staff. The bags are sold through conventional wholesale and retail markets – through about 250 independent boutiques. They are sold as fashion items and promotional products, often customised for the promotion event. However, about a quarter of sales come from the website which shows how the products can be used, hosts competitions and has a Calypso blog. You can also sign up for a regular newsletter. In 2010, with the help of UK Trade & Investment, she started exporting to Japan.

→

QUESTIONS

1 What was the launch strategy for this business?

2 Why did Calypso decide to have her bag manufactured in the UK? What are the pros and cons of this decision? Do you think it was the right one? Is it the right one as the business matures?

3 What is the growth strategy for this business?

4 How sustainable is this business?

Calypso is ambitious for Clippy: 'In the long term, it would be great to have a lifestyle brand and then sell the company'. She has some tips for other start-ups:

'Stay positive and have faith in your product.

Keep your costs to a minimum. If you can work from home and do your own PR in the beginning this will give you the cash to develop the product.

Vary your markets. Think about how your product could fit into different markets. Clippykit works for retail, the promotions industry and education.

Optimise your website. Keep driving customers to your website using PR and marketing and make your site sticky. It's your portal to world markets.

Don't expect it (your business) to be a short cut to prosperity. Profit made equals business development not personal wages.'

Daily Telegraph 6 February 2009

☐ Up-to-date information on Clippy can be found on their website: www.clippykitlondon.co.uk

▷ Summary

▷ Customers buy products or services to obtain benefits. Sometimes there are separate customers and consumers for the product or service, both looking for benefits. It is important to understand what benefits they are looking for. All too often owner-managers focus just on the features of the product or service.

▷ One way of describing the features is the marketing mix, or The Five Ps:

  ▷ *Product*: the tangible characteristics of the product or service;
  ▷ *Price*: the price, including discounts or special offers;
  ▷ *Promotion*: advertising, point of sale displays, PR, selling and so on;
  ▷ *Place*: location, layout, channels of distribution and so on;
  ▷ *People*: the service, advice, support and relationships, particularly important to owner-managed businesses.

▷ The marketing mix must be consistent, reinforcing the benefits the customer is looking for. It is only as strong as its weakest link. The stronger, more distinctive and different the other elements of the marketing mix, the higher the price that can be charged. The elements of the marketing mix, related to the customers they are targeted at, together make up the marketing strategy of the firm.

▷ Owner-managers prefer 'interactive marketing' – doing things themselves and using one-to-one contact with customers for anything from market research to promotion. For them the fifth P in the marketing mix is their personality.

▷ Too many small firms sell on price because they fear competition. The price charged ought to reflect the benefits customers obtain from a product or service. Therefore similar products or services might be able to command different prices with different target markets. There is a pricing range available to most firms with a number of other benchmarks: variable cost, average total cost and, important for **Jean Young**, the going rate. Also important is the break-even point. Many firms 'cost-plus' price based upon break-even and a target level of profitability.

▷ Whether it is possible to charge a higher price like **Good Hair Day** depends on the elasticity of demand which in turn depends, in part, on the uniqueness of the product or service. There are considerable benefits to being able to charge a higher price and, for many firms, small increases can more than compensate for relatively large reductions in the volume of sales. In setting price, information on the variable and average cost of production is relevant, but there will be a going rate that is influenced by the value to the customer and the price charged by competitors. Ultimately however, for any product or service, there will be a price that is too low for credibility and one that is too high. Variations in pricing strategy at start-up might include skimming or penetration, depending on product–market characteristics.

▷ Differentiation is about being different or distinctive in some way. It does not necessarily involve innovation but can be made up from a myriad of small distinguishing features. Differentiation is helped by clear, effective branding – and can be safeguarded by patents, design registrations and copyrights. A brand should be the embodiment of the product or service offering to the customer. A good brand can help turn prospects into customers and move customers up the loyalty ladder. It helps a business to secure differential advantage.

▷ Customer focus involves breaking markets down into segments that have similar characteristics or needs. For a start-up this allows resources to be focused on segments where there is the highest possibility of making a sale. It can also lead to niche positioning, which can be very profitable. The slimmer the market segment, the easier it is to defend against competition, but slim segments carry the danger that customers' tastes might change and the market disappears.

▷ As we saw with **Radio Spirits**, there are many different market segments and there is no prescriptive way of segmenting a market. It requires creative insight into customers' buying habits as well as an understanding of the unique benefits offered by the product or service. If you want to be entrepreneurial in your approach to marketing you need to understand what the conventions are in your market place and try to do things differently if you have the capabilities.

▷ Constructing a marketing mix for different market segments is called a marketing strategy and, as in the case of **Clippy**, this can be tailored to meet the challenges and resources of a start-up.

▷ Market research is important for a start-up. It minimises risk and uncertainty and provides information on which to build a marketing strategy. The key question to be answered is why someone should buy from you rather than from competitors. As we saw with **Black Vodka**, the range of information needed can vary enormously. There are two approaches to getting information;

field research and desk research. Field research involves discussions and interviews. It might use postal questionnaires or telephone surveys. It might involve simple observation. Desk research involves getting published information from a variety of sources. It is quick and cheap and can provide invaluable background information. It helped **Euravia Engineering** decide on the location for the business.

▷ Many start-ups do not undertake formal market research, treating the launch as market research and constantly reviewing customer reaction. However, if things go wrong this can be an expensive form of research.

▷ As **Stephen Waring** from **Green Thumb** knew, the ability to sell is important at start-up. Selling is about matching the benefits of the product or service to the needs of customers and then convincing them to buy. As with **Goldsmith's Fine Foods**, the benefits customers are looking for are not always obvious, but the sales role is important in finding out what they are. Over time the salesperson can build a relationship of trust and respect that can lead to new customer networks being developed. Selling skills can be developed with practice. There are a number of ways to start a sales interview; there are sales aids that can be used in the interview itself. There are techniques to handle objections and to help close a sale.

▷ The internet offers new opportunities for innovative businesses – and new routes to a global market for small firms generally. It increases competitive pressures and emphasises the need to understand what you are selling, to whom and why your customers continue to buy from you. The key to effective retail marketing is a good website, like that of **The Fabulous Bakin' Boy**s, and effective advertising of the site.

▷ Businesses may be organised as sole traders, partnerships and limited liability companies. Sole traders are easy and quick to set up but, if the business is to grow, it is probably best to form it into a limited company sooner rather than later.

▷ Franchise is a popular, low-risk way of setting up in business using the ideas, expertise and systems of an established organisation like **Body Shop**. It can help small firms with limited resources like **Green Thumb** to grow quickly.

⏻ **Further resources are available at www.palgrave.com/business/burns**

📄 Essays and discussion topics

1 Are customers logical?

2 Why are people willing to pay quite high prices for bottled water?

3 Why do owner-managers prefer interactive or personal marketing?

4 Why is it said that the three most important elements of the marketing mix for a retail business are location, location and location?

5 Advertising is the most expensive way of one person talking to another. Discuss.

6 What is marketing?

7 What is the difference between marketing and selling?

8 Why is marketing important?

9 Costs determine prices. Discuss.

10 Is there really a limit to the price you can charge for a product or service?

11 Can you really sell less and make more profit?

12 How can you charge different prices for the same product or service?

13 How different does a product or service have to be to mean that you are following a strategy of differentiation?

14 Every product or service is different. Discuss.

15 Why is branding so important?

16 Is creating a brand easier or more difficult for a small firm?

17 What makes a good brand?

18 We spent most of the twentieth century creating mass markets and will spend most of the twenty-first breaking them down. Discuss.

19 Is market segmentation an art or a science?

20 Is market research worthwhile?

21 Do most small firms set about market positioning in a haphazard sort of way with the result that success or failure is really just luck?

22 The cheapest way to research a really new business is to start up and monitor progress. Discuss.

23 If you think knowledge is expensive, try ignorance. Discuss.

24 How do you go about undertaking market research prior to starting a business?

25 How do you find out who your customers might actually be?

26 Describe the sorts of customers that might not be interested in the service that Goldsmith's Fine Foods provides. What elements of the marketing mix might they be more interested in?

27 Selling is not an honourable profession. Discuss.

28 What are the particular problems facing a small firm wanting to sell on the internet and how might they be overcome?

29 What are the particular problems facing a purely internet start-up and how might they be overcome?

30 Are there any good business opportunities left using the internet?

31 What are the good things about the website for The Fabulous Bakin' Boys?

32 What really annoys you about a retail website?

33 Why are franchises an attactive business opportunity?

34 What is the best legal form of business?

⏱ Exercises and assignments

1 Select five products or services.

▷ List their features and translate these into benefits for the customer. Alongside this list any proof that might be needed to convince the customer that the benefit is real.

▷ Place the five products or services in each of the four boxes of Porter's Generic Marketing Strategies. Explain why you place them where you do.

▷ Select one product or service and write up its history – how it got to be where it is, what strategies the firm followed and how competitors reacted.

▷ Select one product or service. Team up with two other students, one as a customer, another as an observer. Conduct a role-playing sales interview with the customer lasting 10 minutes. Make certain each of you understands the role you are playing. Plan your interview using the outline contained in this chapter. When it is finished, get the observer to give you feedback on how you performed.

2 List as many generic ways to differentiate a product or service as you can think of. Alongside them jot down what you need to do to sustain these differences.

3 Develop a market research questionnaire to find out what benefits existing customers of a health club are looking for from their membership.

4 Develop a market research plan to evaluate the commercial potential of opening a shop selling sportswear in a small market town.

📖 References

Bayus, B.L. (1985) 'Word-of-Mouth: The Indirect Effects of Marketing Efforts', *Journal of Advertising Research*, 25(3), June/July.

Brady, G. (1999) 'New Rules for Start-ups', *e-business*, December.

Brassington, F. and Pettitt, S. (2006), Principles of Marketing, London: Prentice Hall.

Carson, D., Cromie, S., McGowan, P. and Hill, J. (1995) *Marketing and Entrepreneurship in SMEs*, London: Prentice Hall.

Chaston, I. (2000) *Entrepreneurial Marketing: Competing by Challenging Convention*, Basingstoke: Macmillan – now Palgrave-Macmillan.

Dalgic, T. and Leeuw, M. (1994) 'Niche Marketing Revisited: Concept, Applications and Some European Cases', *European Journal of Marketing*, 20(1).

Stokes, D. (1998) *Small Business Management: A Case Study Approach*, London: Letts Educational.

Webster, J.E. (1992) 'The Changing Role of Marketing in the Corporation', *Journal of Marketing*, 56, October.

8 International entrepreneurship

- ▷ **Globalisation and international entrepreneurship**
- ▷ **The international start-up**
- ▷ **The stage model of internationalisation**
- ▷ **The influence of networks and learning theory**
- ▷ **Export strategies**
- ▷ **The agency dilemma**
- ▷ **Summary**

Case insights
- ▷ Michael Ross and Figleaves
- ▷ John and Julie Gilbert and Hop Back
- ▷ Julie Diem Le and Zoobug

Cases with questions
- ▷ B&Q
- ▷ Hightech Components

Learning outcomes

By the end of this chapter you should be able to:

▷ Explain what is meant by the term 'international entrepreneurship';

▷ List the global influences and trends encouraging it and the factors that inhibit it;

▷ Explain the factors that encourage the international start-up;

▷ Explain the 'stage model' of internationalisation and the reasons why, although it may be logically appealing, it has been criticised;

▷ Describe the influence of network and learning theory on the process of internationalisation;

▷ List the practical problems related to exporting and explain how they might be overcome.

💡 Globalisation and international entrepreneurship

The phrase 'international entrepreneurship' can mean different things. On the one hand it has been used to describe entrepreneurial behaviour in different countries and cultures. On the other hand, it has been used to describe entrepreneurial behaviour across national boundaries – how you might start up a business in a country other than your own, export into it or import out of it. Arguably the first articles on the internationalisation of small firms appeared in the 1970s (Johanson and Wiedershheim-Paul, 1975; Johanson and Vahlne, 1977; who popularised the stage model of internationalisation). Since then the field has broadened to include international start-ups, exporting, alliances and joint ventures, market entry modes, knowledge management and network theory.

In many ways it is surprising that the area took so long to develop. After all, entrepreneurship is about exploiting commercial opportunities and these are likely to exist where there are distant countries with different resources, different needs and different markets. Entrepreneurs are quick to realise that there is profit to be made from trading between different markets. Arguably European colonisation was just one example of international entrepreneurship. Indeed, before that Columbus might be characterised as an international entrepreneur, financed by venture capitalists who happened to be Spanish royalty. However, it has been the internet that has really opened up international opportunities and made the possibility of trading a reality for SMEs across the world.

The area has become increasingly topical with the trend towards globalisation. Competition is becoming increasingly global as barriers to international trade are dismantled and international communication and information networks improve. The world's markets and economies are becoming increasingly integrated and this can affect the smallest of businesses. Accompanying this is a general loss of national sovereignty, a homogenisation of cultures and a democratisation of many aspects of life. All this has been hastened by ever-improving communication links through television, telephone and the internet. What happens on one side of the world can be seen on the other, instantly. What is available in one market can be communicated to another almost as quickly. Few national markets are now insulated from the effects of other national markets. Technology – in particular the internet – has therefore been a key element in the trend to globalisation. Technology and globalisation have become mutually reinforcing with the global market also enhancing the profitability of the new technologies (Aggarwal, 1999).

Global markets, products and brands have appeared. At the same time market niches have fragmented and become ever smaller in terms of product or service specification, making them economically viable only on a global basis. However, new technology and new forms of communication have enabled many of these niches to be exploited globally. The internet has made global sourcing a reality both for consumers and business customers. Dell is well known for its 'fully integrated value chain' – B2B2C – linking customers and their orders with suppliers around the world in real time via the company's extranet. Dell organises the supplies of components and assembles the computers. At the other extreme of size, Mansfield Motors, a small Land Rover garage set up in Essex, England in 1993, sells Land Rover parts around the world from its website, boasting a quicker delivery time than many local authorised Land Rover dealers.

Nevertheless, the reality is that most small firms are not in any way international. One study (Carson, 1990) suggested that only 6 per cent of small firms in the UK, across all sectors, export. Most small firms still serve predominantly a local market – never mind a regional, national or international one. Indeed it is generally accepted that there continues to be a 'home country bias', with both personal and business consumers preferring to buy from their home country if at all possible. But actually setting up business in a foreign country can bring with it enormous risks. The roll of large British companies that have failed to establish themselves in foreign markets is

📁 Case with questions B&Q

Not all British retailers fail in overseas ventures. B&Q, the UK do-it-yourself (DIY) store chain, is hardly a small business but its experience in setting up in China is interesting. B&Q opened its first store in China in 1999. Up until 2005, when China joined the World Trade Organization, foreign retailers were prevented from opening more than three stores in any one city and some towns were completely off limits. What is more, they had to work with Chinese partners. B&Q did deals with a number of Chinese organisations, normally giving them a 35 per cent stake in the business, but making it very clear that B&Q intended to buy them out at soon as it could – which it typically did in 2005. Also in 2005, it acquired 13 stores of OBI China for an undisclosed sum, all of which have been converted to the B&Q format.

The stores were a huge success and the Beijing store now boasts the highest average customer spend of any store in the world (over £50). But it is the cultural similarities and differences and how they affected the retailer that are really interesting. The stores look very similar to those in the UK, although they are usually considerably bigger. At 20 000 sq ft, the Beijing Golden Four Season store is the largest of its kind in the world. Like their UK counterparts, staff wear orange overalls. The products offered are also very similar, although the space devoted to garden products is considerably smaller and the Chinese B&Q also sells soft furnishings.

But the big difference is that Chinese customers do not want to 'do-it' themselves at all, they prefer to get others to do it for them. The Chinese customers are typically middle class and wealthy. They come to the store to select what they want and get it installed by a professional. The reasons for this are partly cultural and partly economic. Labour is significantly cheaper than in the West but also things like painting would be regarded as a major DIY job in China. What is more, if you buy one of the thousands of apartments being built in Beijing you buy a concrete shell – with no garden – and customers will then purchase everything else they need – plumbing, lighting, kitchens, bathrooms and furnishings – from one store. B&Q therefore started to offer more services to customers – designers and contractors to install its products. The Beijing store has a room full of designers working at computer terminals, ready to design the customer's living room, kitchen or bathroom. Teams of workers then deliver and install the products. Twenty-five per cent of all B&Q sales in China now involve some kind of B&Q service.

B&Q is now the market leading DIY chain in China. However, in 2008/09 sales at B&Q China fell dramatically. B&Q claimed this was the result of the world recesion and in particular the decline in building activity in China. Losses totalled £80 million in 2008/9 and, after reorganisation and a reduction in the number of shops from 83 to 43, losses fell to £34 million in 2009/10. B&Q said its turnaround strategy remained on track to break even in 2011 – but only time will tell if this is accurate..

☐   Up-to-date information on B&Q can be found on their website: www.kingfisher.com

QUESTION

What lessons can be learned from the experience of B&Q in China?

as long as it is distinguished: Marks & Spencer, Sainsbury's and Boots. And that rings warning bells for small firms.

But the world has changed. And there are many positive reasons for SMEs to think international. They can increase sales and therefore profits. If theirs is a unique product or service selling to a niche market, that niche could be very large internationally. And with increased volumes may come economies of scale. In fact this is even more important if the product is perceived as a commodity and cost leadership is dependent upon achieving those economies. Whether a niche or a commodity product, speed of market roll-out and 'first-mover advantage' can be important in new product development. Another reason for thinking international might be that a company's key competency lies with the product it produces, for example with capital goods like cars, and therefore the preferred and logical route for expansion is the continued exploitation of the product by finding new markets in which to sell it. Most capital goods companies follow this strategy – opening up new overseas markets as existing markets become saturated – because of the high cost of developing new products.

There are also reactive reasons for internationalising. By way of contrast, many service businesses such as accounting, insurance, advertising and banking have been pulled into overseas markets because their clients operate there and their clients demand an international service. Some firms enter overseas markets because there is over-capacity or stiff competition at home. Indeed it might be that the product or service is nearing the end of its life cycle in the existing market and their home market is in terminal decline. This was the case with McDonald's and its entry into the East European markets in the 1990s. Hamburgers were a mature product in the West but an exciting new one in Eastern Europe after the fall of communism.

So, there are many attractive advantages to internationalisation. But how do most SMEs do it and why do some do it at start-up?

♀ The international start-up

Alfred Weber was probably the first economist to propose a location theory for the firm, based upon lowest cost. He argued that a firm would locate where transport and labour costs were lowest, and that these costs would be reduced where there was a concentration or cluster of several producers in a single location. Proximity of customers and suppliers is crucial. However this theory tried to explain specific location rather than lack of location implied by an international start-up.

The increasing number of new ventures that establish as international start-ups generally do so because they derive some other significant form of competitive advantage from going international (Oviatt and McDougall, 1994). These firms start with an international business strategy, for example at the outset making international product/market offering decisions or making use of international sourcing of components. They deploy their assets internationally. Typically they use alliances and networks to overcome resource deficiencies – a topic to which we shall return later in this chapter.

One strand to the literature is the 'resource-based' perspective, with the firm seen as owning certain valuable assets that can be exploited in or transferred to a foreign location (Oviatt and McDougall, op. cit.). The new technology or innovation upon which the start-up is based is one example of this. However, it could also be the international experience and contacts possessed by the founding team (Oviatt and

McDougall, 1995). In this way they can capitalise on international market imperfections by linking resources from around the world. The systematic and effective exploitation of this key asset is seen as the prime reason for early internationalisation.

Aggarwal (op. cit.) observes that many of these international start-ups conduct business in high technology niche markets worldwide. Empirical studies indicate that they do this through necessity (Litvak, 1990; Coviello and Munro, 1995; Oakley, 1996). They need to internationalise early because the high cost of R&D precludes a purely domestic orientation if costs are to be recouped and profits made. Economies of scale are important. What is more, the ever accelerating pace of technological innovation means that product life cycles (see Chapter 12) are shortening and first-mover advantage in all markets becomes vital. Rapid international expansion is designed to counter competitive reaction. High technology, in particular, seems to be a highly competitive, fast-moving, global market place, even for the start-up venture.

In a review of the literature and a study of twelve high technology international start-ups, Johnson (2004) found many factors influencing the decision to internationalise. These are summarised in Figure 8.1. However, he concluded that the principal factors influencing this decision were:

▷ The international vision of the founders;
▷ Their desire to be international market leaders;
▷ The identification of specific international opportunities;
▷ The possession of specific international contacts and sales leads.

Internal factors
▷ International vision of the founders
▷ International experience of the founders
▷ Alert international entrepreneurs
▷ Need to gain foreign financing
▷ Additional market opportunities
▷ Exploitation of proprietary technology internationally
▷ Avoidance of domestic inertia within the firm
▷ High R&D costs

External factors
▷ International nature of industry
▷ 'Borderless world'
▷ Economies of scale, necessitated by industry
▷ International niche markets
▷ Homogeneity of international markets
▷ International market imperfections
▷ Accelerated pace of worldwide technological innovation
▷ Competitive nature of international industry
▷ Need to respond to competitor initiatives
▷ Need to pre-empt competitors
▷ Intense domestic competition
▷ Small domestic market
▷ Short product life cycles
▷ Setting a world standard
▷ Influence of network partners
▷ External 'pull' from domestic and international customers

International start-up

Facilitating factors
▷ Advances in international communications
▷ Advances in international transportation
▷ Advances in information technology
▷ Advances in process technology Integration of the world's financial markets

F8.1 Factors influencing the early internationalisation of international start-ups

Source: Johnson (2004)

These basic entrepreneurial qualities can be summarised as vision, drive, opportunity perception and relationship development. It is interesting to observe that they remain so important for high technology start-ups.

The stage model of internationalisation

The international start-up is a relatively modern, but still infrequent, phenomenon reflecting the increasingly global nature of all markets. It has been argued that most small firms progress through specific stages of export development. Vernon (1966) characterised the process of internationalisation using a product life cycle of domestic product development, followed by exporting as overseas demand grows, and finally foreign production as the home market matures and cost reduction becomes more important. Eventually the foreign producers may start to export themselves as cost becomes a driving force for competitiveness and production shifts to low-cost countries.

Dicken (1998) also envisaged a sequential process, starting with the firm serving its domestic market, and moving through stages, first starting to export as its home market is saturated and finally moving into overseas production. These stages are shown in Figure 8.2. In this model expansion into overseas markets may take a number of different forms. Exports may start by using the services of an agent. However, if this is successful, the firm may seek a more permanent presence by setting up its own sales outlets. It may also consider licensing other manufacturers in the country to produce the product, particularly where it is able to safeguard its intellectual property right through patents for inventions or trademarks for brands.

However, it was Johanson and Vahlne (op. cit.) who looked in detail at this process, trying to explain where firms export to and how they extend their process of internationalisation beyond export. They popularised what has become known as the stage model of internationalisation, also called the Uppsala model because it was based upon studies of Swedish manufacturing firms in that region. The model proposes

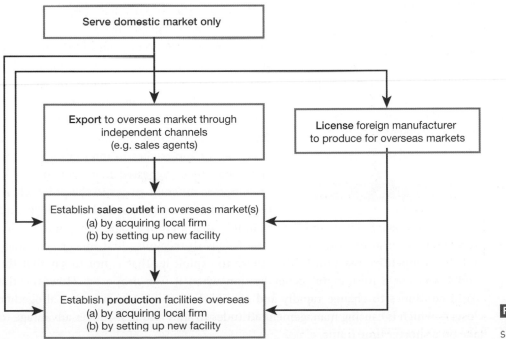

F8.2 International development

Source: Dicken (1998)

that small firms take an incremental stepwise approach to internationalisation over time. They target psychically close markets – ones that they feel mentally comfortable with – initially using market entry methods that require limited commitment, such as exporting. As they gain knowledge and experience from their market involvement over time, so they increase their commitment. This process is repeated from market to market. This form of creeping international incrementalism is called 'graduated entry'. Small firms start with low-cost, low-risk entry modes and then, if the experience is rewarded, they move to more complex, often higher-risk, modes.

Leonidou and Katsikeas (1996) characterise this as having three stages – pre-engagement, initial and advanced. The pre-engagement phase is when the firm is active in its domestic market but not in an export market. The initial phase is when it has sporadic or exploratory export activity. The advanced phase is when it is actively and consistently involved in exporting and internationalisation of its activities. If these phases are successful the firm builds confidence, eventually embedding internationalisation into the mainstream of its activities. However, should it experience failure then it can retrench and re-evaluate its growth options without endangering its core markets and activities.

The model is appealing, not least because of its inherent risk-minimising logic. It also mirrors the way entrepreneurs 'learn by doing'. In addition, the stepwise progression towards internationalisation mirrors the incremental approach entrepreneurs have towards business development and decision-making. It is also conditionally compatible with the 'resource-based' view of internationalisation. As the firm develops its resource base over time, so too will it develop its export capability.

However, the model has been criticised (Leonidou and Katsikeas, op. cit.). Whilst firms seem to fit into different stages of the model at any point of time (using cross-sectional data), there is no empirical evidence of dynamic progression based upon longitudinal studies over time. Indeed the existence of international start-ups suggests that this model is but one of a number of approaches to internationalisation and it has been suggested that firms may skip or compress different stages to the point where the model becomes meaningless (Welch and Loustarinen, 1988; Sullivan and Bauerschmidt, 1990). From a logic viewpoint, graduated entry can also be criticised because it fails to recognise first-mover advantage and the competitive reaction to the failure to exploit it. That is not to say that the model was not a meaningful generalisation when it was proposed. However, the world continues to change rapidly and once-distant markets now seem altogether closer – which is causing management attitudes to shift and first-mover advantage to take on a shorter time frame.

📁 Case insight Michael Ross and Figleaves

The internet has made it easier for many small firms to sell their products overseas. Michael Ross, Chief Executive of Figleaves, a UK online retailer of women's lingerie, has managed to penetrate one of the most difficult markets in the world – the USA. Launched in 1999 as easyshop.co.uk, the company changed its name the following year after it decided to focus on lingerie. But the secret for Figleaves was that, when it launched in the USA, it was already its second largest market because it sold on the internet and American women were not concerned that the lingerie they ordered came from Britain.

Figleaves have negotiated a number of online marketing deals and web links to maximise the exposure their site enjoys. US deals are negotiated by somebody who flies out once a month from the UK. The company even has a concession within Amazon.com. Its 'Shock Absorber' bra was launched in the USA together with Amazon, by holding a tennis match between Amazon's founder, Jeff Bezos, and the tennis star Anna Kournikova. One feature of the Figleaves website is the facility to purchase in a number of different currencies. Figleaves now claim to be the global leader of 'multi-brand intimate apparel etailers'. The figleaves.com website features 250 brands and more than 30 000 items of lingerie, swimwear, sleepwear, active-wear, menswear and hosiery.

☐ Up–to–date information on Figleaves can be found on their website: www.figleaves.com

One important factor in the timing of internationalisation is management. Management with international experience seem to be a key ingredient in early internationalisation (Reuber and Fisher, 1997). This seems to be a key resource that allows small firms access to markets that they would otherwise avoid – which takes us back to the 'resource-based' strand of literature. But it may be useful to draw a distinction between type of resource and volume of resource. Type and quality of resource is probably more important than volume as volume can always be levered using external resources. Hence, very small firms need not feel resource-constrained because of size. The pattern of internationalisation they follow is likely to be far more determined by the type and quality of the resource they control, in particular the experience of the founders.

The influence of networks and learning theory

As we saw in Chapter 6, networking is an important entrepreneurial skill and it gives us some insights into internationalisation. SMEs can use their networks to identify international opportunities (for exporting and importing), gain access to resources, improve their strategic position, learn new skills, gain market knowledge, establish credibility and control transaction costs. Both Johnson (op. cit.) and Oviatt and McDougall (op. cit.) identified strong international business networks or contacts as one of the most important characteristics of successful international start-ups. McDougall et al. (1994) explained that networks helped international start-ups to identify international business opportunities and that the networks influenced country choices more than psychic distance. Coviello and Munro (op. cit.) added that these network contacts also influenced market entry initiatives in such a way that the resulting strategies appeared 'random and somewhat irrational, when in fact the span of activities can be linked to opportunities emerging from the network of relationships'. The conclusion is clear: networks are a vital influence on small firm internationalisation. They produce the knowledge that helps identify opportunities and the community of resource that enables their exploitation.

As we observed in Chapter 6, networks are based on personal relationships and reciprocity, and all relationships are based on trust and reputation (Dubini and Aldrich, 1991; Larson, 1992). However, organisational networks can develop based upon multiple networks of individuals. In these networks relationships may be multi-level rather than flat, formed by clusters of coalitions at different hierarchical levels. These complex networks can facilitate many forms of organisational relationships such as strategic alliances or joint ventures. The many links in these networks are strengthened by increased interaction and can be further strengthened by an entrepreneurial leader pulling the network together and giving it stability and direction. Since assets are owned by the constituent individuals or organisations, the financial resources needed and the risk associated with any joint venture are spread and flexibility increased. These organisational networks can create distinctive capabilities based on trust and mutual self-interest.

This might explain why first generation immigrants can have such a competitive advantage in starting up a business in a new country. They can have strong local networks in both their country of origin and the country they settle in. This can give them not only information on local customer needs, wants or tastes that are not being met – business ideas – but also information on suppliers and how customers' needs might be better met.

Learning theory also has a role to play in the literature on international entrepreneurship. The need to acquire local knowledge is important – it mitigates risk. This applies to both knowledge of customers and suppliers. Learning helps overcome the barrier of 'foreignness' and lack of local market knowledge (Lord and Ranft, 2000). Thus learning was central to Johanson and Vahlne's (op. cit.) stage model of internationalisation. Organisational learning is complex, particularly when taking place across national boundaries involving different languages, cultures and corporate governance structures and relevant to this is the concept of the learning organisation (see Chapter 18).

But knowledge can also form the basis of competitive advantage, particularly for the international start-up. To conduct business successfully in another country, a firm needs knowledge of:

▷ the needs and tastes of local customers;
▷ the general demand conditions in the local market;
▷ local competitors;
▷ how the marketing mix might be adapted to better suit local needs – product, price, promotion and distribution.

Related to this, Autio et al. (2000) put forward the interesting proposition that there is competitive advantage in newness because new organisations find it easier to learn than older ones and this helps them grow in new environments, including foreign markets. New firms, therefore, have an advantage over old, and by implication small over large firms. However, this is not borne out by statistical evidence that shows exporting to be most likely to be undertaken by large (and therefore older) organisations. Selassie et al. (2004) conclude that within small firms the proportion of firms engaged in exporting increases with firm size: 'The larger the firms the higher the export intensity and the more the experience in internationalisation.' Burns (2005) broadens the debate by placing learning and relational networks at the centre of the entrepreneurial architecture needed to develop larger entrepreneurial organisations. To him these are key entrepreneurial components in any context or arena, including age and size.

♀ Export strategies

Chapter 13 addresses what strategies to employ to help your business grow, once established. Exporting is an example of one of these growth options, called 'market development'. Namiki (1988) suggests that small firms pursuing export markets adopt one of four competitive patterns of actions, and that strategies 3 and 4 better suit most small firms' resource capabilities:

1 *Competitive pricing; branding; control over distribution; advertising; and marketing innovation.* This pattern requires a sophisticated understanding of marketing. Both brand development and control over distribution networks take time and an intimate knowledge of marketing. Innovation in marketing takes entrepreneurial flair. In that sense this pattern is more likely to be seen in a mature small firm that has had time to develop its resource base. However, remember always that type of resource is probably more important than volume.

2 *Capability to manufacture speciality products for customers, broad range of products; and new product development.* This pattern requires significant capability and experience in tailoring products, to make broad product offerings available and to innovate. Again this pattern is more likely to be seen in a mature small firm that has had time to develop its resource base.

3 *Technological superiority and product innovation.* This includes new-to-the-market products and innovations that can just as easily be marketed by start-ups based upon their uniqueness rather than their resource base.

4 *Customer service and high quality products.* Again this uniqueness of product, possibly coupled with a narrow target (niche) market means it is a pattern that can be adopted by start-ups or very small firms.

But as we have observed, few small firms actually export. This may be because they do not want to – they are a lifestyle business – or because internationalisation may seem impractical to a 'market trader' such as a window cleaner.

Even if there is the potential and a will to internationalise, there can be disincentives. This may be because the owner-manager has a lack of knowledge and experience in the target market, coupled with a lack of information. Risk based upon ignorance is an important factor. We always know more about our own world rather than those of others and information asymmetry – a topic covered in Chapter 10 in respect of financing small firms – is a factor.

Owner-managers may fear lengthy payment terms or the possibility of bad debts. They face economic and financial risks such as currency fluctuations, cycles in economic activity and changing or punitive tax laws. They face political risks such as unstable governments, ideological differences and wars and other conflicts. They face social risks arising from religious or class differences, high disparities in wealth distribution, union militancy and riots or other forms of disorder.

🛄 Case insight
John and Julie Gilbert and Hop Back

Hop Back Brewery was set up by John and Julie Gilbert in 1987 in the cellar of their pub near Salisbury in Wiltshire, England. In 2001 it started exporting its best known cask beer, Summer Lightning, to Italy where the brewery now supplies over 50 bars in Rome, Milan and Turin. Having sought advice initially from the government-backed organisation UK Trade and Investment, it now exports about 2700 gallons each year through Food from Britain in Italy, a marketing-development consultancy for British food and drink producers.

☐ Up-to-date information on Hop Back can be found on their website: www.hopback.co.uk

---

🛄 Help and advice on exporting in the UK

There are a number of schemes providing help and assistance for those firms wanting to follow this route in the UK. For example, UK Trade and Investment has an interactive checklist that enables you to assess your readiness to export. It provides information on trading with most countries (over 200 countries across 34 market sectors) through their various country desks. It provides training, planning, trade missions and support. It is also able to put potential exporters in touch with the British embassy, high commission or consulate in their target country and help identify potential partners.

The British Chambers of Commerce issue export documentation and often, together with local Business Links, provide advice; the Central Office of Information offers export publicity information; and the Export Credits Guarantee Department of the DTI can arrange insurance against the possibility of non-payment. This can be assigned to a bank or other lending institution in order to obtain export finance.

☐ For more information visit the following websites:
UK Trade and Investment: www.uktradeinvest.gov.uk
British Chambers of Commerce: www.britishchambers.org.uk
Business Link: www.businesslink.gov.uk

To some extent the decision not to internationalise reflects simple patriotism – a softer term than jingoistic nationalism – whereby both owner-manager and customers prefer to trade with local suppliers. Hence, given a straight choice, we will often buy the local product because we know how it was produced and, if it fails, we know where we can return it to obtain a refund. But cultural differences can also create significant barriers to trade in terms of taste, communication, lifestyles and values.

In the past the costs of international participation – such as transport, communication and taxes imposed as tariff barriers – were high, so prices of international products and services were also high, thus weakening demand. There was (and still is) exchange rate volatility. There is also political volatility. Who could have predicted the events of 9/11 and their effects on world trade?

Governments try to address these barriers by offering a range of support to firms wishing to export. However most of the literature is sceptical about generic programmes to motivate SMEs to export, pointing to certain behavioural characteristics that need to be addressed first (Karagozoglu and Lindell, 1996; Crick and Choudhry, 1997).

Two further factors affecting market attractiveness are entry and exit barriers. These are shown in Figure 8.3. The most attractive market from the point of view of profitability is likely to be one with high entry barriers and low exit barriers – few firms can enter but poor performers can easily exit. With high entry barriers but high exit barriers, poor performers are forced to stay on, making the returns more risky as they fight for market share. Unfortunately, a firm seeking to enter these markets has to overcome the high entry barriers, whatever they may be. For example, this could involve overcoming legal barriers or high investment costs. If entry barriers are low, returns are likely to be low, but stable if exit barriers are low and unstable if exit barriers are high, and poor performers are forced to stay on if the market worsens.

Whilst, as we have seen, personal knowledge and the existence of personal relationships is likely to be a major element in selecting the overseas markets to try to exploit, underlying this must be sound commercial opportunities and legal realities. Exporting can be expensive and the margins in the export market must therefore be sufficient to justify it. All the risks and disincentives must be outweighed by the potential economic gain if the owner-manager is to internationalise.

Owner managers are faced with political risks; who could have predicted the effect 9/11 would have on trade?

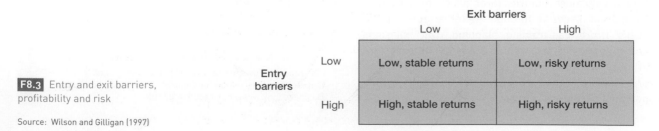

F8.3 Entry and exit barriers, profitability and risk

Source: Wilson and Gilligan (1997)

🛍 Case insight Julie Diem Le and Zoobug

Julie Diem Le was a successful 29-year-old eye surgeon with the NHS and a member of the Royal College of Ophthalmogists when she decided to start up her own business. The idea came when she tried to buy a pair of sunglasses for her niece. She regularly saw young eyes damaged by bright sunshine and yet she could not find a pair that provided maximum protection from the harmful rays of the sun. She also realised that few were both fashionable and comfortable to wear. Julie therefore formed the idea of producing an up-market, fashionable but ophthalmically correct range of sunglasses for children. Having attended courses run by her local Business Link in Birmingham, Julie wrote a business plan and, on the back of the plan, obtained a £35 000 loan from NatWest Bank. She found an Italian designer to help create the first glasses for children aged 7 to 16, and eventually launched her company, Zoobug in 2006 at the Premier Kids trade exhibition in Birmingham.

Within a year she was selling more than 2000 pairs of sunglasses a month through up-market opticians and stores like Selfridges. But things rarely go according to plan and she had to adjust both her prices and target age range downwards as she discovered what the market actually wanted. Also, two summers of poor weather in the UK convinced her that she needed to sell the sunglasses overseas if she was to do well. She funded this with another £60 000 loan. In 2008 she added a range of optical frames for children aged 2 to 12 to her product portfolio, launching them at an exhibition in Milan.

By 2009 sales of optical frames outstripped those of sunglasses and Julie was selling sunglasses and optical frames in 20 countries, 8 through official distributors. France is her biggest market, ahead of the UK. The sunglasses are now made in Italy and the Far East.

'It was helpful that I started with sunglasses because it meant I had to look overseas for new business because there wasn't any sun in Britain. So I already had distributors in place overseas when the recession began. If we just relied on the British market, we wouldn't exist.

It is really hard work. When you first approach it, it is fun and you don't really know what is involved so you go in there with a lot of bravado. When you get down to the nitty-gritty, this industry is all about building relationships, and you have to fulfil your promise every time in stock, distribution and supply... I'm glad I did it. The experience has taught me a lot about business which I could never learn in a book.'

Sunday Times 24 May 2009

☐ Up-to-date information on Zoobug can be found on their website: www.zoobug.co.uk

💡 The agency dilemma

For many small firms, exporting often means finding a distributor or sales agent in the country to which they wish to export, an organisation that understands the local distribution channels and variations in customer needs (Dicken's model in Figure 8.2). In such situations the firm is very dependent upon the distributor. The distributor might influence changes in the product or other elements of the marketing mix to suit local needs. The firm might be expected to finance advertising and promotion themselves and with no certainty of a profitable return. Finding a distributor can be difficult enough but if, for whatever reason, the distributor does not push the firm's products then there is little the firm can do other than seek to change distributors. The only alternative would be to set up a sales outlet of their own in the country – and that can be both expensive and risky.

However, the relationship is not all one-sided. The sales agents – often themselves small firms – also face risks. Firstly, they are likely to be paid on a commission-only basis – no sales, no commission. They may have an exclusive contract but it will relate to a specified geographic area, so they cannot expand without the agreement of the exporter. Nor are they likely to be able to sell competing products. What is more, the contract will be time-limited so that if they are too successful exporters may be tempted to distribute the product themselves and save paying the commission. Agents may be expected to finance advertising and promotion themselves but they are likely to be dependent on the exporter for a range of sales and promotional information and materials. All of these things will be set out in the contract and, when the contract comes to an end, its terms can be renegotiated. Finally, the agent is completely dependent on the exporter for product and product range development. If the exporter does not invest in this the agent may have difficulties, no matter how good their sales skills.

So SMEs seeking to export will probably have to use local agents, at least initially. However, overseas companies seeking to import their products into a local market will probably need local agents, who are likely to be SMEs. There are commercial opportunities on both sides of the relationship. However, the role of agent is a delicate one. If the balance of power or dependency shifts too far from one party to the other the relationship may be threatened.

A variation on the agency model is the franchise model. In this model the franchisee pays the franchisor to use the brand and sell the products or services. The details of this were covered in Chapter 7. Franchisees may be appointed in any country, although a more usual model is to appoint a head franchisee in a country with the power to appoint sub-franchisees. Commissions are then shared with the head franchisee. In this way local knowledge is used to roll out the franchise in that country.

To be effective the agent, distributor or head franchisee must have a symbiotic relationship with the firm that appointed them, one based upon mutual trust and with effective incentives on both sides to ensure success. However, over time this relationship may well break down.

If, eventually, the firm decides to set up its own production facility, it may consider a joint venture with a local partner. Sometimes this is required by local law, sometimes it is simply a prudent way of gaining local knowledge of the business environment. The joint venture will probably involve setting up a new entity in which both partners acquire an ownership stake. However, it is the local firm that will typically control and manage the joint venture and that gives it the upper hand. As with distributors, a good deal of trust is required to make a success of a joint venture, especially given the likely cultural differences between partners (Hoon-Halbauer, 1999). And that is where personal relationships, rather than legal agreements, can be important for small firms.

🗀 Case with questions Hightech Components

Hightech Components started life as a representative agent in the UK for Inland Motors, a US manufacturer of high quality precision servo components for closed loop control systems. It was set up by Roger Lacey, who had initially worked for Precision Systems, the UK subsidiary of Inland Motors, as a salesman. However sales were disappointing and Inland decided to close its subsidiary, instead offering Roger an exclusive contract to operate as UK sales representative for Inland Motors on a commission-only basis.

→

A servo is a system in which the main mechanism is set in operation by a subsidiary mechanism and is able to develop a force greater than the force communicated to it. It is used in a wide variety of specialist applications such as radar systems and robotic arms where mechanisms need to rotate or move in different directions simultaneously. The servo components and systems Hightech sold were very high quality, precision instruments and the company quickly became an approved supplier for a large number of military, aerospace and industrial applications on land, sea and in the air. It also became an approved supplier to the Ministry of Defence in the UK.

Ten years after start-up the company had seven employees and a turnover of £2 million. It had over 200 active accounts, mainly with blue-chip customers. Hightech now exclusively represented five companies in the UK including three divisions of Inland Motors – Speciality Products, Defence Products and the Sierra Vista Division – as well as three other US companies – Inductosyn International, Sequential Electronic Systems Inc and Airflyte Electronics Company – and Thomson CSF of France. In acting for these companies Hightech was able to offer its customers a full range of servo products, including drives, controls, position and velocity transducers and amplifiers. Few UK competitors offered the comprehensive range of components that Hightech now offered. This meant that customers could obtain all the servo components that they needed to build systems without needing to go to other suppliers.

Hightech had a very professional approach to selling, following through on leads in a systematic manner, researching companies and their applications before approaching them and building close relationships once they became customers. It presented itself as a professional organisation helping engineers solve difficult technical problems. It offered seminars either in-house or at the premises of client companies. Rather than advertise, staff devoted time to writing technical articles for magazines, always mentioning the Hightech name. The only advertising space the company bought was in the trade reference manuals used by engineers looking for Hightech's type of equipment. The company only exhibited once or twice a year. It had high-quality sales literature, using bright colours which would stand out on an engineer's cluttered desk. In this way the company achieved a conversion rate of enquiries to orders, of around 15 per cent compared to the industry average of about 5 per cent.

Hightech had found a comfortable market niche for itself, but growth prospects were limited. This incremental growth was mainly based on finding new customers, particularly as new applications for servo mechanisms emerged, but also based on making the most of the excellent relationships they already had with their existing customers to try to sell more to them. To help with this strategy Hightech continued to try to find new companies to represent in the UK. However, the problem was that these would have to be complementary products and be acceptable to the companies Hightech currently represented – particularly Inland Motors.

Hightech continued with this successful strategy. Five years later it had over 300 active accounts and turnover had topped £3 million. Hightech was also representing two new companies; Astro Instrument Corporation of the USA, which manufactured a unique brushless motor gearhead range that produced very high torque, and PMI Technologies of the USA, a sister company to Inland Motors producing low inertia printed circuit motors.

Relationships with the companies Hightech represented, particularly Inland Motors, were always good. Roger Lacey paid regular visits to them and Hightech made extensive use of the company's promotional material, suitably rebranded. However, Hightech's continuing success was not going unnoticed. Two year later, Kollmorgen Motion Technologies Group, owners of Inland Motors, purchased the assets and liabilities of Hightech and Roger Lacey became Director of European Business Development at Kollmorgen, responsible for improving the company's market penetration in Europe. Both parties were happy with the outcome.

QUESTIONS

1 Why was Hightech successful? How would you describe its marketing strategy?

2 What were the continuing business risks that Hightech faced as an agent during its seventeen years of independent life?

3 Was Hightech's approach to growth sensible? What other options did it have and why might they not have been pursued?

▷ Summary

- ▷ International entrepreneurship is a term used to describe entrepreneurial activities across national boundaries. The trend towards globalisation has encouraged interest in the area.

- ▷ Most small firms are local in orientation, not international. The reasons for this may be simply that most small firms are lifestyle businesses that do not wish to internationalise. However there are real barriers to and risks associated with international trade. These range from cultural differences, legal, political and financial disincentives to lack of knowledge of the markets (information asymmetry). **B&Q** is still trying to decide whether it has understood these differences in the Chinese market.

- ▷ A small but increasing number of start-ups are international from inception. These are often high-technology firms that need to exploit this advantage as quickly as possible. But a more important advantage is the international experience, networks and knowledge of the founders.

- ▷ Figure 8.1 summarises the influences on the decision to internationalise but the principal factors are:

  - ▷ The international vision of the founders;
  - ▷ Their desire to be international market leaders;
  - ▷ The identification of specific international opportunities;
  - ▷ The possession of specific international contacts and sales leads.

- ▷ The stage model of internationalisation sees small firms progressing through an incremental, sequential process of serving domestic markets, exporting, opening sales outlets and finally setting up production outlets – also called graduated entry. They target psychically close markets initially using market entry methods that require limited commitment, such as exporting. As they gain knowledge and experience from their market involvement over time, so they increase their commitment. This process is repeated from market to market. Although appealing, this model cannot be proved using longitudinal research and ignores the increasing importance of 'first-mover advantage'.

- ▷ As in the case of **Figleaves**, the internet has made exporting easier for many small firms.

- ▷ Networks produce the knowledge that helps identify opportunities and the community of resource that enables their exploitation. Learning underpins the stage theory of internationalisation and is key to the successful exploitation of any overseas market whether you agree with this model or not.

- ▷ In most countries government agencies have been set up to help small firms, like **Hop Back Brewery**, wishing to export. However most of the literature is sceptical about generic programmes.

- ▷ Many firms use a commission-only agent to distribute their products in international markets. To be effective the firm and the agent or distributor must have a symbiotic relationship, one based upon mutual trust and with effective incentives on both sides to ensure success. However, over time this relationship may break down. Either the company's products are not 'pushed' as hard as they would hope or, as **Hightech Components** found, the agents are too successful and are taken over by the exporter.

☑ Useful websites

- ☑ The International Monetary Fund (IMF) has a range of briefs on its website: www.imf.org.

- ☑ The World Trade Organization website: www.wto.org.

- ☑ The World Bank website: www.worldbank.org.

- ☑ The United Nations Conference on Trade and Development publishes a World Investment Report annually. Highlights can be found on its website: www.unctad.org.

☑ The International Chamber of Commerce has a world business organisation website: www.iccwbo.org.

☑ The Peterson Institute for International Economics website contains numerous resources and links related to trade issues: www.iie.com.

☑ The International Forum on Globalization has a website: www.ifg.org.

⏻ **Further resources are available at www.palgrave.com/business/burns**

📄 Essays and discussion topics

1 Why are most small firms not interested in internationalising?

2 What are the advantages to a small firm of thinking about internationalisation sooner rather than later?

3 What are the global trends that push small firms towards internationalising? Which are the strongest and which are accelerating fastest?

4 What are the disincentives faced by small firms which internationalise?

5 What is a 'global brand'? How likely is a small firm to achieve a global brand presence?

6 What are the problems facing a service business internationalising? How might they be overcome?

7 What are the problems facing a retail business internationalising? How might they be overcome?

8 What is the role of e-business and the internet in internationalisation?

9 Few dot.com start-ups were really international from inception. Discuss. Try to provide examples of those that were and those that were not and the reasons for this.

10 What are the barriers to an international start-up? How can they be overcome?

11 Why are high-technology start-ups more likely to be international from inception?

12 Do you agree with the stage model of internationalisation? Explain.

13 How important to internationalisation is network theory?

14 How important to internationalisation is learning theory?

15 Why might 'real' entrepreneurs – not necessarily just owner-managers – find that they are really good at internationalisation?

16 Why might immigrants find that they are really good at international entrepreneurship? Is there any evidence to suggest that they are?

17 The most important issue in the business plan is management. The most important issue in internationalisation is management. The most important issue in business is management. Discuss.

18 Can education and training help the process of internationalisation? If so, how can this be achieved?

19 Is the degree and speed of internationalisation related to the age and size of the firm?

20 Is increasing internationalisation good for everyone?

⟳ Activities

1 Find an example of an international start-up and write a report explaining what it did and why it did it.

2 Each year the United Nations Conference on Trade and Development (UNCTAD) publishes its World Investment Report on its website (see list above). Access the most recent report. What does this tell you about the most recent trends? What does this tell you about the role of SMEs? Write a report assessing the current position.

3 Using the websites listed above, examine the trends in globalisation and write a report assessing their impact on the international business environment.

⊕ Further reading

Dicken, P. (1998) *Global Shift: Transforming the World Economy*, London: Paul Chapman Publishing.

Giddens, A. (2000) *Runaway World: How Globalisation is Reshaping our Lives*, Andover: Routledge.

Leonidou, L.C. and Katsikeas, C.S. (1996) 'The Export Development Process: An Integrative Review of Empirical Models', *Journal of International Business Studies*, no. 27 (Third Quarter).

Zahra, S.A. and George, G. (2000) 'International Entrepreneurship: The Current Status of the Field and Future Research Agenda', in M.A. Hitt, R.D. Ireland , S.M. Camp and D.I. Sexton, *Strategic Entrepreneurship: Creating a New Mindset*, Oxford: Blackwell.

📖 References

Aggarwal, R. (1999) 'Technology and Globalisation as Mutual Reinforcers in Business: Reorienting Strategic Thinking for the New Millennium', *Management International Review*, 2 (1).

Autio, E., Sapienza, H.J. and Almeida, J.G. (2000) 'Effects of Age at Entry, Knowledge Intensity, and Limitability on International Growth', Academy of Management Journal, 43.

Burns, P. (2005) *Corporate Entrepreneurship: Building an Entrepreneurial Organisation*, Basingstoke: Palgrave Macmillan.

Carson, D. (1990) 'Some Exploratory Models of Assessing Small Firms' Marketing Performance', *European Journal of Marketing*, 24(11).

Coviello, N.E. and Munro, H.J. (1995) 'Growing the Entrepreneurial Firm: Networking for International Market Development', *European Journal of Marketing*, 29(7).

Crick, D. and Choudhry, S. (1997) ' "Small Business" Motives for Exporting: The Effect of Internationalisation', *Journal of Marketing Practice: Applied Marketing Science*, 3(3).

Dicken, P. (1998) *Global Shift: Transforming the World Economy*, London: Paul Chapman.

Dubini, P. and Aldrich, H. (1991) 'Personal and Extended Networks are Central to the Entrepreneurial Process', *Journal of Business Venturing*, 6.

Hoon-Halbauer, S.K. (1999) 'Managing Relationships with Sino-Foreign Joint Ventures', *Journal of World Business*, 34.

Johanson, J. and Vahlne, J.-E. (1977) 'The Internationalisation of the Firm: A Model of Knowledge Development and Increasing Foreign Market Commitments', *Journal of International Business Studies*, 4.

Johanson, J. and Wiedershheim-Paul, F. (1975) 'The Internationalisation Process of the Firm: Four Swedish Cases', *Journal of Management Studies*, 12 (October).

Johnson, J.E. (2004) 'Factors Influencing the Early Internationalisation of High Technology Start-ups: US and UK Evidence', *Journal of International Entrepreneurship*, 2.

Karagozoglu, N. and Lindell, M. (1996) 'Internationalisation of Small and Medium-sized Technology-based Firms: An Exploratory Study', *Journal of Small Business Management*, 36(1).

Larson, A. (1992) 'Network Dyads in Entrepreneurial Settings: A Study of the Governance of Exchange Relationships', *Administrative Science Quarterly*, 37.

Leonidou, L.C. and Katsikeas, C.S. (1996) 'The Export Development Process: An Integrative Review of Empirical Models', *Journal of International Business Studies*, 27 (Third Quarter).

Litvak, I.A. (1990) 'Instant International: Strategic Reality for Small High-Technology Firms in Canada', *Multinational Business*, 2 (Summer).

Lord, M.D. and Ranft, A.L. (2000) 'Organisational Learning about New International Markets: Exploring the Internal Transfer of Local Market Knowledge', *Journal of International Business Studies*, 31.

McDougall, P.P., Shane, S. and Oviatt, B.M. (1994) 'Explaining the Formation of International New Ventures: The Limits of Theories from International Business Research', *Journal of Business Venturing*, 9.

Namiki, N. (1988) 'Export Strategy for Small Business', *Journal of Small Business Management*, 26 (April).

Oakley, P. (1996) 'High-Tech NPD Success through Faster Overseas Launch', *European Journal of Marketing*, 30(8).

Oviatt, B.M. and McDougall, P.P. (1994) 'Towards a Theory of International New Ventures', *Journal of International Business Studies*, 25 (First Quarter).

Oviatt, B.M. and McDougall, P.P. (1995) 'Global Start-ups: Entrepreneurs on a Worldwide Stage', *Academy of Management Executive*, 9 (2).

Reuber, A.R. and Fisher, E. (1997) 'The Influence of the Management Team's International Experience on the

Internationalisation Behaviours of SMEs', *Journal of International Business Studies*, 28 (Fourth Quarter).

Selassie, H., Mathews, B., Lloyd-Reason, T. and Mughan, T. (2004) 'Internationalisation Factors and Firm Size: An Empirical Study of the East of England', in F. McDonald, M. Mayer and T. Buck (eds), *The Process of Internationalisation: Strategic, Cultural and Policy Perspectives*, Basingstoke: Palgrave Macmillan.

Sullivan, D. and Bauerschmidt, A. (1990) 'Incremental Internationalisation: A Test of Johanson and Vahlne's Thesis', *Management International Review*, 30 (January).

Vernon, R. (1966) 'International Investment and International Trade in the Product Cycle', *Quarterly Journal of Economics*, 80.

Welch, L. and Loustarinen, R. (1988) 'Internationalisation: Evolution of a Concept', *Journal of General Management*, 14(2).

Wilson, R.M.S. and Gilligan, C. (1997), *Strategic Marketing Management: Planning, Implementation and Control*, Oxford: Butterworth-Heineman.

9 Running the business

▷ **Cash flow and Death Valley**
▷ **The profit statement**
▷ **The balance sheet**
▷ **Planning and control**
▷ **Financial drivers**
▷ **Break-even**
▷ **Decision-making**
▷ **Summary**
▷ **Appendix 1: Forecasts and budgets – an example**
▷ **Appendix 2: Accounting records – an example**

Case insights
▷ Jean Young 1
▷ Jean Young 2
▷ Jean Young 3
▷ Chris Hutt and the Newt & Cucumber
▷ David Speakman and Travel Counsellors
▷ Flitwick Manor Hotel
▷ Penforth Sofa Beds

Learning outcomes

By the end of this chapter you should be able to:

▷ Explain the difference between profit and cash flow;

▷ Draw up a cash flow forecast;

▷ Describe the information conveyed in a profit statement and balance sheet;

▷ Draw up a profit statement;

▷ Prepare a detailed budget for a medium-sized business;

▷ Identify and explain why the key financial drivers of a business are important;

▷ Record the financial information needed to effectively control a small firm;

▷ Use profit–cost–volume information for decision-making;

▷ Recognise the need for a start-up to minimise its fixed overhead costs and maximise its contribution margin.

♀ Cash flow and Death Valley

Cash flow is the lifeblood of a business; it pays the bills and the wages, but most small firms are short of it. A start-up may spend cash on premises, equipment, stock and so on even before the first customer walks through the door. Even that first sale might be on credit and it can take time before debts are collected. During this time the business will have a negative cash flow. It is called the Death Valley curve and is shown in Figure 9.1. The depth of Death Valley depends on how much you need to invest in premises, equipment and stocks. The length and depth of Death Valley varies from firm to firm and industry to industry. The length can be affected by the trading cycle – how long it takes to turn £1 of investment into £1 (hopefully more) of cash from sales. It is affected by the time it takes to get a product or service to the market place – a long time for a new drug, less than 24 hours for some market traders. Every start-up faces the challenge of the Death Valley curve.

Be warned – many firms do not survive to come through to the other end of Death Valley, so you need to plot its course and plan how to navigate it. Just about every firm that fails runs out of cash but to do so at the start of a new venture – one that might have been very successful – just because you have not planned for this very predictable challenge is just plain stupid.

Death Valley may not be a problem if you have sufficient capital – your own or borrowed – so that you can trade all that time when no cash is coming in. But you need to map out Death Valley to see what you face. Work out its depth – how much cash is needed – and its length – how long you will need the cash. Death Valley might be deeper and longer than you expect. Indeed if you get some unexpected orders and sales really take off, Death Valley could get longer or deeper, or both because you need to buy and pay for extra stocks, perhaps even hire extra staff to cope with the demand – all before the cash starts rolling in.

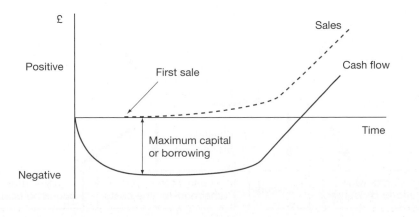

F9.1 The Death Valley curve

The way to chart a path through Death Valley is by preparing a cash flow forecast which lists the estimated cash receipts and payments of the business. This can be done on a daily, a weekly or, more normally, a monthly basis. The total cash receipts minus the cash payments in any period is called cash flow. In Death Valley cash flow is negative. Cash flow is added to (or, if negative, subtracted from) the cash balance at the end of the previous period to show the cash balance at the end of this period. If the cash balance is negative, you will need to seek external funds, possibly from a bank – and we shall explain how that can be done in a later chapter. For now, we shall concentrate on generating that vital piece of information – the cash flow forecast.

♀ The profit statement

We start with profit. It is important to realise that profit is not the same as cash. Total profit is the difference between total sales and total costs. You may not have received payment for your sales nor indeed paid your costs. Profit per unit is the difference between unit selling price and unit cost. Total profit tells you how **all** the assets of a business have grown (or shrunk) through trading – not just about changes in cash. You can make a profit but have no cash, for example because the person who has bought the good or service has not yet paid for it. It is true that eventually the profit should turn into cash but, meanwhile, bills and wages need to be paid, and if you do not have the cash to pay them you may go out of business. Figure 9.2 shows how profit is made and, at the same time, money flows around the business. Start at 1 and work through the diagram in the sequence detailed below.

1 A business starting up needs to find capital in the form of cash. This could be a sole trader's own money or, for a company, shareholders contributing share capital, both perhaps supplemented by bank borrowings.

2 This is now invested in assets to be used in the business. The assets will comprise long-term or fixed assets such as plant and machinery, office equipment, computers, vehicle and so on, and assets for use on a day-to-day basis. They will also include stocks of goods for resale, stocks of consumables to be used in the office, and, of course, cash to pay the bills – usually called current assets. The

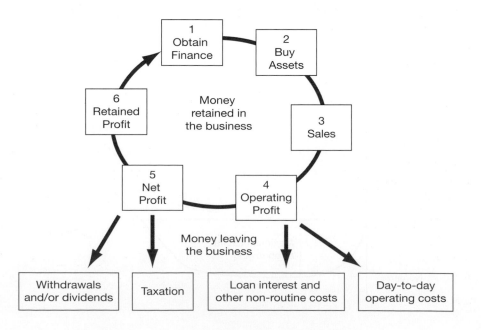

F9.2 The flow of money

💼 Case insight Jean Young 1

Jean Young is the start-up sole trader offering consultancy and training to the health sector that we had as a Case Insight in Chapter 7 (page 175). She charges a daily rate of £400 and estimates annual sales as £17 200. Her estimated total annual sales are below the VAT threshold, so she does not have to account for VAT, but that means she cannot reclaim any VAT charged on goods or services. She is working from home, so her overheads are low – estimated at £5215 in the Case insight in Chapter 7. She also has a working husband so they have agreed that she does not have to withdraw cash from the business until March. Her best estimates of the cash in-flows and out-flows the business will face during its first year of trading are given below, and these are summarised in the cash flow forecast in Figure 9.3, using a pro forma cash flow worksheet.

Month:	Nov	Dec	Jan	Feb	Mar	Apr	May	Jun	Jul	Aug	Sept	Oct	Total
SALES													
Volume: days	1	1	2	2	3	4	5	5	5	5	5	5	43
Value	400	400	800	800	1200	1600	2000	2000	2000	2000	2000	2000	17200
CASH RECEIPTS													
Sales – cash													
Sales – debtors		400	400	800	800	1200	1600	2000	2000	2000	2000	2000	15200
Capital introduced	2000												2000
Grants, loans etc.													
TOTAL (A)	2000	400	400	800	800	1200	1600	2000	2000	2000	2000	2000	17200
CASH PAYMENTS													
Materials													
Wages/salaries Sec	10	120	20	20	20	20	20	20	20	20	20	20	330
Rent													
Heat/light/power													
Advertising													
Insurance		100											100
Travel – petrol	10	10	20	20	30	40	50	50	50	50	50	50	430
Telephone	120			100			100			100			420
Stationery/postage	130	40	40	40	40	40	40	40	40	40	40	40	570
Repairs/renewals		200						150					350
Local taxes													
Other Prof. fees	50											125	175
Other		10	10	10	10	10	10	10	10	10	10	10	110
Capital purchases	2000												2000
Loan repayments													
Drawings/dividends					820	850	1000	2000	2000	2000	2000	2000	12670
TOTAL (B)	2320	480	90	190	920	960	1220	2270	2120	2220	2120	2245	17155
CASH BALANCES													
Cash flow (A) – (B)	(320)	(80)	310	610	(120)	240	380	(270)	(120)	(220)	(120)	(245)	
Opening balance	-	(320)	(400)	(90)	520	400	640	1020	750	630	410	290	
Closing balance	(320)	(400)	(90)	520	400	640	1020	750	630	410	290	45	45

F9.3 Cash flow forecast for Jean Young 2011/12

1 Sales estimates are the key to any business plan. In most cases sales at start-up are overestimated. It takes longer for a start-up to gain customers than the owner-manager usually appreciates. In this case, however, Jean Young plans a modest build-up of her training days, selling only one day at £400 in November. In the forecast she has set out the number of days she expects to work each month and the value of the work she will therefore undertake. This she will invoice immediately and she assumes the invoice will be paid one month later, which are her normal terms of trade. The cash receipts therefore show a one-month lag behind the issuing of the invoice.

2 £2000 is the capital introduced into the business in the form of cash to pay for the capital purchases below.

3 She estimates she will pay £2000 (including VAT) immediately for capital equipment – computer and software, printing and other presentation equipment. She will, however, also be using her own car, valued at £13 000, for business purposes.

4 Payments are estimated cash payments in appropriate months. Notice that these are not always the same as the fixed costs shown in the profit statement in Chapter 7.

5 Jean plans to start taking money out of the business in March and in June she plans to start taking £2000 a month out of the business because that is what she is invoicing to her clients.

If you look at the final three rows in the cash flow forecast (under the heading cash balances) you can see the effects these plans will have on her cash flow and cash balances. Because of the low level of overheads and her decision not to take any money out of the business until March her cash flow is initially positive, except for the first two months and then in March when she starts withdrawing money. However, once she starts taking £2000 a month out of the business her cash flow becomes negative and her cash balance starts decreasing.

The initial overdraft reaches a maximum of £400 in December and the maximum balance in her bank account reaches £1020 in April. However, after May she is withdrawing more cash each month than she is generating and the cash balance decreases month on month. This level of drawings is not sustainable if she does not want to go into overdraft again and must be reduced.

cash has now turned into other assets, but all these funds are still retained in the business.

3 The assets are then used to generate sales. Goods are resold, services are rendered. This is the first stage on the way to making profits.

4 Of course, making sales is not enough to guarantee profits. Sales might be high, but if day-to-day business costs are higher, then a loss rather than a profit will emerge. So there is a need for management to control day-to-day costs and produce an operating profit. Other non-routine costs, such as loan interest, might also have to be deducted.

5 The result is net profit. This is still not, necessarily, cash since customers might owe you money or you might not have paid all your bills. However, it does represent an increase in the total assets – or funds – of the business. If the business is established as a sole trader, money may now be withdrawn. If the business is a limited company, corporation tax is deducted, and then dividends may be paid to shareholders. Sole traders pay income tax on the profits of the business and shareholders pay income tax on their dividends.

6 The balance of retained profits represents another injection of capital into the business. However, this capital is not, necessarily, cash. This is important as any

business will need a constant flow of capital to replace existing assets which are used up and/or to expand or grow. As we know, many small firms prefer to finance their expansion using their own money rather than borrowing or giving equity away.

Boxes 3, 4, 5 and 6 are reported in the profit statement, but boxes 1 and 2 are reported in the balance sheet. The cash flow statement tells you how one asset – cash – has changed over the period. The profit statement, therefore, does not tell you about new capital you might introduce into the business nor the assets that the business might have and use to generate profit. It tells you about how the business goes about using its assets to increase their value. If those assets are being used in the business the profit statement needs to recognise that there is a cost associated with this as the asset wears out and reduces in value. Whereas the cash cost of the asset is recognised in the cash flow statement when the cash is spent, the cost of the asset needs to be allocated, somehow, over its life to the profit statement. Therefore, when you sell a good or service you recognise its cost when you make a sale. But how do you allocate the cost of a long-term, fixed asset over its life? Depreciation is a way of showing this in the profit statement and is a major difference between profit and cash flow.

The simplest method of depreciation is called 'straight-line depreciation' which writes off the fixed asset in equal amounts over its life. For example, if there was an asset that cost £5000 and has a working life of 5 years, at which time it could be sold off for £1000, the annual depreciation shown as a cost would be:

$$\frac{\text{Initial cost} - \text{final or residual value}}{\text{Working life}} = \frac{£(5000 - 1000)}{5} = £800$$

The value of the asset would go down each year by £800. At the end of year one it would have a value of £4200, year two £3400 and so on, until year five when it would be £1000. Depreciation is a cost in the profit statement. It does not represent any cash expenditure. That takes place when the asset is purchased

Successful businesses sell their goods or services for more than they cost to produce, so this flow of funds will continually increase as more and more profits are retained. However, the hidden ingredient in this is time. By speeding up the flow of funds you can decrease the amount of capital you need – or simply take more out of the business.

The key to this is debtors and creditors. Debtors are those customers that owe you money because they have not paid immediately and creditors are those suppliers that you owe money to. By getting debtors to pay quickly you speed up the flow of funds. You can speed up the collection of debts by:

▷ Choosing customers carefully to start with and invoicing them immediately upon sale. In choosing credit customers always ask for, and check up on, trade references: ask for a bank reference, make credit checks with other suppliers, check any published information (such as accounts) about the customer and, if possible, visit their premises.
▷ Setting appropriate credit limits and making payment terms clear. Once the customer's references are checked they can be set a credit ceiling that must be kept. This minimises exposure to any bad debts. Bad debts are expensive. If you are making a 20 per cent margin, you need to increase sales by £4 to recover each £1 of bad debt.

▷ Taking the right measures to speed up payments. These include sending statements, following up outstanding debts by telephone – it could be that there is a problem with the delivery or the cheque has gone astray, offering discounts for prompt payment or charging interest on overdue accounts, withholding supplies, threatening to reclaim your goods, taking legal action or using debt collectors when all else fails.

By getting creditors to wait for payment you also speed up the flow of funds because you have the use of their money. But you must always handle creditors carefully because, if you get a reputation for late payment, you may find it difficult to get credit at all. If you make an arrangement, then stick to it. Always try to agree good terms at the beginning, try for part payment of large orders or buy in small quantities, do not pay early and, if in trouble, keep talking to your creditors – silence is often taken as a sure sign of bad news.

The profit statement tells you how the assets – all the assets – of the business are growing through trading. As we have seen it does not tell you about cash. Profit is not an exact figure since it involves elements of judgement, for example in the calculation of depreciation or an estimated liability. However, there are also some other things it does not do. It does not tell you about the profitability of individual product lines – your business might have many. Nor does it tell you, on its own, how well you are doing. If you make a profit of £5 000 from a capital investment of £250 000 you are making a return of only 2 per cent (£5 000 divided by £250 000) and would probably be better off putting your money in a bank. So it does not tell you about capital investment – for that you have to go to the balance sheet.

It is one thing to realise that profit is not the same as cash flow, but it is altogether more difficult to reconcile the two figures. Let us go back to the example of Jean Young.

🗀 Case insight Jean Young 2

Jean is forecasting that she will have £45 in her bank account at the end of October. But this is not the same as profit. Her projected profit statement, reproduced from Chapter 7, is shown below. Her estimated profit was £11 985. However, after her proposed drawings of £12 670 this means that she is taking more out of the business than she is earning as profit, and so she is actually draining her capital by £685.

Sales		£17 200
Overheads:		
Depreciation	£2 700	
Secretarial wage	330	
Transport	430	
Telephone	450	
Stationery	570	
Repairs	350	
Other	285	
Insurance	100	
Total		£ 5 215
Net profit		£11 985
Drawings		£12 670
Profit (loss) retained in business		£(685)

So rather than retain anything in the business Jean has drained her capital by £685, But what does this mean, and how does it reconcile to her closing cash balance of £45 – the cash generated in her first year of business? The reconciliation is shown below. However because she now has some assets and liabilities, the total picture will not emerge until we draw up Jean's balance sheet.

Profit statement		Cash flow forecast		Difference
Income		Receipts		
Sales	£17 200	Cash from sales	£15 200	£2000 is still owed to Jean – an asset
		Capital introduced	2 000	£2000 cash was introduced by Jean. This is not trading income and therefore not shown in the profit statement
		Total cash receipts	£17 200	
Expenses		Payments		
Depreciation	£2 700			Depreciation is a way of showing in the profit statement how assets wear out – allocating their cost over their life. There is no cash flow. This depreciation is on Jean's car and computer equipment
Secretarial wage	330	Secretarial wage	330	
Transport	430	Transport	430	
Telephone	450	Telephone	420	£30 is still owed by Jean for the telephone charges in September and October – a liability
Stationery	570	Stationery	570	
Repairs	350	Repairs	350	
Other	285	Other	285	
Insurance	100	Insurance	100	
		Capital purchases	2 000	£2000 cash was paid for equipment – this will be allocated over the life of the asset and shown as depreciation in the profit statement
Total expenses	£5 215			
Net profit	£11 985			
Drawings	12 670		12 670	
		Total cash payments	£17 155	
Profit (loss) retained in business	£(685)	**Increase(decrease) in cash – closing balance**	£45	

♀ The balance sheet

The balance sheet is a snapshot at a point in time that shows two things:

▷ Where the money in a business is invested;
▷ Where this money came from.

Money initially comes from the capital the owner puts in (called 'share capital' if it is a limited company) and loans. It is increased by the profits that are retained in the business. This money is invested in the assets of the business – fixed assets; things the business means to keep such as vehicles, machinery and so on, and working capital; things the business means to sell or turn over. Working capital comprises current assets such as stock, debtors or cash less current liabilities such as creditors and accrued expenses. In other words, the balance sheet gives details of all the money retained in the business as shown in Figure 9.2.

There are two sides to a balance sheet and they always balance. If £1000 were put into a business as cash the balance sheet would balance:

This would be shown as:

Where money is invested:	Cash	£1000
Where it came from:	Capital introduced	£1000

If £500 of this is spent on machinery and £500 on stock the balance sheet would not change much:

Machinery	£ 500
Stock	£1500
	£1000
Capital introduced	£1000

Only when the business starts trading do additional funds start to be generated in the form of profit as you can see from Figure 9.2; if the stock was sold for £1000 cash, a profit of £500 would have been made and the balance sheet would still balance:

Machinery	£ 500
Cash	£1000
	£1500
Capital introduced	£1000
Retained profit	£ 500
	£1500

If the balance sheet does not balance then either assets are missing or there is an arithmetical mistake.

As with profit statements, you can have forecasted balance sheets or historic balance sheets – ones that explain what actually happened. A start-up will prepare forecasted cash flows and profit statements, possibly forecasted balance sheets. Once the business starts running it needs to monitor how it is doing against these forecasts to make certain things are going as planned. Historic profit statements and balance sheets are derived from the books of account that are used to control a business.

📦 Case insight Jean Young 3

We have constructed a cash flow forecast and a profit statement for Jean Young. The final element in the jigsaw puzzle is her balance sheet.

Jean's car was valued at £13 000 at the start of the year and the computer equipment cost £2000 (both of which she introduced to the business). If we say these are expected to last five years at which point only the car would have a residual value of £1500, and the other equipment would have no value, then her depreciation charge would be:

$$\frac{(13\,000 + £2000) - £1500}{5} = £2700$$

And these fixed assets at the end of the year would have a value of:

$$(£13\,000 + £2000) - £2700 = £12\,300$$

From this and the information in the previous Case insight we can draw up her balance sheet as a sole trader at the end of October:

Fixed assets			
	Car		£13 000
	Computer and other equipment		2 000
			£15 000
less:	Depreciation		2700
			£12 300
Current assets			
	Debtors	£2 000	
	Cash	45	
		£2 045	
less:	**Current liabilities**		
	Telephone	£30	
Net current assets			£ 2 015
Total assets			**£14 315**
Represented by:			
Capital introduced			
	Cash		£2 000
	Other asset introduced (car)		£13 000
			£15 000
Net profit for year			£11 985
less:	Drawings		£12 670
Total capital			**£14 315**

The cash flow forecast and forecasted profit statement and balance sheet tell us the full story for the year:

▷ The business is certainly commercially viable. We can tell that from the £11 985 net profit it generates.
▷ We know it is low risk. We can tell that from the low break-even point of 13 days' work calculated in Chapter 7.
▷ The cash requirements are modest, with a maximum overdraft requirement of only £400.

However, because of the high level of drawings from June onwards the business is forecast to make a retained loss of £685 (retained earnings) for the year – which is clearly not sustainable in the long run as Jean will be continually depleting her capital rather than building it up. Jean will also end the year with only £45 cash in the bank – clearly a small sum and probably insufficient to guard against things going wrong (for example, payment of the £2000 owed to her being delayed a further month, or worse still the client not paying at all). To be safe Jean needs to rethink her level of drawings – or bring in more work. And since these are forecasts she can do just that and plan ahead accordingly, reworking these forecasts as required. However, these are just forecasts and the next step is to monitor actual performance against them. Only if her actual performance is as good as or better than her forecasts will she really be able to withdraw the money she wants from the business.

💡 Planning and control

Rapid growth can be every bit as dangerous as the start-up itself. It can lead to the danger of over-trading – the Death Valley curve getting longer and deeper. Proper planning and management of cash flow is therefore vital. If cash is needed to finance growth, bankers like to be forewarned so that facilities can be made available in advance. It also makes sense to negotiate from a position of strength rather than weakness. Planning and good management might also allow a firm to minimise its cash flow requirements. Just as the preparation of financial plans are important at start-up, it is also important for a growing firm.

Plans and budgets are an invaluable tool to control and monitor performance of the business. By comparing actual financial results to the budget on a timely basis, the entrepreneur can 'manage by exception', only intervening when performance deviates from plan. This can free up time to concentrate on strategy or dealing with real problems. The budget provides a framework against which the performance of the firm can be judged. For a larger firm, the detail involved in pulling together a complicated budget can be time-consuming, but by this stage it is certain that the firm will have its own accountant who can undertake the task. Nevertheless the appendix to this chapter contains a detailed example of how to go about drawing up a comprehensive budget for a manufacturing firm – cash flow forecast, profit statement and balance sheet.

As the firm grows, budgets can be prepared at the department and division level, rather than just at the company level. This has the advantage of encouraging the entrepreneur to delegate responsibility for planning and decision-making to other managers, whilst at the same time providing the entrepreneur with sufficient information to satisfy themselves that everything is running as planned. The budgeting process can then be used as a tool for communicating and coordinating the activities of responsible managers. It can become a systematic tool for establishing standards of performance, providing motivation and assessing the results managers achieve. An essential element in this process of making managers accountable is that each knows exactly what they are held responsible for, and each does indeed control this aspect of the firm's operations. Responsibility cannot be assigned without authority. A clear management structure is a fundamental necessity. The principle is to make every manager responsible for the costs and revenues they control, even if they, in turn, delegate responsibility down the line.

Of course, if managers are going to be held responsible for the costs and revenues they control, they are going to want to be involved in the budgeting process. The advantage of this is that often they know more about certain aspects of the business than the owner. Also, if budgets are to motivate staff, they have to 'buy into' them and believe that they are realistic and achievable. Once they accept the standards of performance against which they are to be judged, they will normally try hard to achieve them. Imposing budgets from above normally causes resentment and leads to a lack of commitment.

The basics of sound financial control remain the same as a business increases in size, the difference is just one of scale. However, most firms now operate computerised accounting and budgeting systems. The most popular is produced by Sage. These speed the processing of transactions and the production of financial information. They also help with the management of trade credit. Almost all business transactions are on credit terms and it has been estimated that trade debtors represent 28 per cent of total assets in small firms whilst trade creditors are equivalent to 11 per cent, and yet managing trade debtors seems to be the Achilles heel of most small firms – they are just bad at it (Chittenden et al., 1998). Before embarking on a growth path a company needs to have in place robust financial planning and control mechanisms.

💡 Financial drivers

Accounting systems can provide enormous amounts of information, including full profit statements, balance sheets and details of outstanding debtors, creditors and stock-holding levels. Sometimes they produce so much information that owner-managers cannot cope and prefer to ignore them. In fact, most small firms can be controlled by monitoring, on a timely basis, just six pieces of information that tell the owner-manager different, but vital, information on the performance of the business. These are called financial drivers. They are like the instruments on a car dashboard. They tell you different things about the engine of the business and different pieces of information are important at different times and in different circumstances. On a road with a speed restriction you watch your speedometer. When changing gear at speed you watch your rev-meter. When low on petrol your eye never strays from the petrol gauge. The financial drivers tell you all you need to know about driving the business. The six financial drivers are:

1 Cash

As we have already seen, it is vital to monitor cash. Without cash the bills cannot be paid. For a start-up or when it is in short supply cash may have to be monitored on a daily basis, but most small firms need to keep an eye on it at least on a weekly basis. Actual balances need to be compared to forecasts.

2 Sales

This tells the firm about the volume of activity it is experiencing. This should also be compared to forecasts. If sales are running ahead of forecasts, does the firm have the resources to meet these demands? Current sales may be a good indicator of future sales, but if not, then order books may also have to be monitored. It is sales that always drive cash flow and profitability. It should be monitored on a daily or weekly basis for most start-ups and at least monthly even for an established business.

3 Profit margins

In the process of setting prices in line with projected costs, the owner-manager will also be setting profit targets. These can only be achieved if the sales volume targets are met, at the appropriate prices, and costs are controlled. Profit margins give the owner manager this information. They should be compared to original forecasts and kept as high as possible. Margins probably need only be monitored on a monthly basis. It might be that it is sufficient simply to monitor contribution margin. This would be the case if fixed overheads are unlikely to change dramatically or quickly. In the example of Jean Young, there are no variable costs and in this case it is therefore more appropriate to monitor net profit margins. The net profit margin is net profit expressed as a percentage of total sales. In the previous example of Jean Young this is:

$$\frac{\text{Net profit} \times 100}{\text{Sales}}: \quad \frac{11\,985 \times 100}{17\,200} = 70\%$$

4 Margin of safety or break-even

Break-even is an important reference point and we shall be looking at this important concept in more detail in the next section. However, as a business grows the break-even point is likely to increase. That is a fact of business. In order to grow most businesses must, at some point, take on more fixed overheads. This increases the break-even point. What is important is not so much the absolute level, but rather how much above it the firm is operating. The margin of safety is a measure of how far sales are above break-even, expressed as a percentage of total sales. In the example of Jean Young, because she has no variable costs, this happens to be the same as the net profit margin and is:

$$\frac{(\text{Total sales} - \text{Break-even sales}) \times 100}{\text{Total sales}} = \frac{(17\,200 - 5215) \times 100}{17\,200} = 70\%$$

📔 Case insight Chris Hutt and the Newt & Cucumber

When Chris Hutt set up Unicorn Inns he was hoping to sell it on as a going concern within ten years. When he discovered the successful Newt & Cucumber formula he believed that rigorous, centrally applied financial controls were the key to profitable operation and a successful sell-on. (We will look at his marketing plan in Chapter 14.) One of the first things he did was appoint a Finance Director to provide the Board with in-house financial management skills. As part of Chris's emphasis on control, the company ensured the following checks were in place:

▷ Daily checks on cash takings and banking, carried out by telephone and direct computer input to the company's bank account.
▷ Weekly sales and profit performance measured within 16 hours of each week ending. Results were reviewed immediately by management and priorities for action identified.
▷ Weekly stocktaking to ensure there were no stock losses and gross margin targets were attained.
▷ Labour costs, as a percentage of sales, monitored through monthly management accounts, mailed to all affected parties no later than ten working days after each period.

All of these factors were linked to targets set for each pub manager and tied into their bonus scheme.

Chris believed that two of the key pieces of financial information any growing business needs to monitor are the break-even point and the margin of safety. He monitored this data monthly and above his desk he kept a graph showing sales against break-even point (the margin of safety). It makes interesting reading, showing the gradual improvement in the margin of safety because of the high margins and low fixed costs as Unicorn Inns rolled out the Newt & Cucumber concept. Chris eventually sold his pub chain to the brewer, Moorland, for over £13 million. Monitoring his financial drivers closely really did pay dividends!

The higher the margin of safety the better, because that makes the firm safer in terms of maintaining its profitability should sales suddenly decline. Margin of safety is therefore a measure of operating risk. However, it reflects a number of factors: level of sales, ability to maintain contribution margins and ability to control fixed overheads. It is therefore a powerful piece of information and needs to be checked monthly.

The margin of safety is of great interest to bank managers. If you start up in business manufacturing, say, umbrellas and anticipate sales reaching 2000 per month shortly after the factory opens, and at this level of sales your margin of safety will be 10 per cent, banks would be worried about granting a loan with such a small margin of safety. They know from bitter experience that sales forecasts, particularly for new ventures, are notoriously unreliable. On a risky lending proposition most bank managers would be looking for a margin of safety of at least 50 per cent. However, realistically, if sales were actually to start falling and the company was approaching its break-even point, a prudent businessman would try to cut their fixed costs – particularly discretionary ones that they control – and thus reduce the break-even point and perhaps restore the margin of safety. In other words the break-even point, and therefore the margin of safety, are not set in concrete, they can be engineered to minimise the risks.

5 Productivity

For most firms the single largest and most important expense they face is their wage costs. It therefore needs to be controlled carefully. However, as with break-even, as a firm grows its wage costs are likely to increase. Wages are therefore best measured in relation to the productivity that they generate. For many firms this is most easily measured by the simple percentage of wages to sales. Often there are industry norms that can be used to measure productivity. For example, in the licensed trade the benchmark for this is 20 per cent. Wages of bar staff should be about 20 per cent of sales. If higher, the pub is over-staffed, if lower, it is under-staffed – a crude but simple and effective measure that needs to be checked weekly or monthly.

6 Debtor or stock turnover

Similarly most firms will have one important current asset on their balance sheet that represents over 50 per cent of their total assets. For a service business this will be debtors. For a retail business it will be stocks. For a manufacturing business it could be both. This asset needs to be monitored on a monthly basis. However, as with previous figures, as the firm grows it is likely to increase, so what is important is not its absolute size but rather its relationship to the level of activity or sales of a business. Two statistics are widely used:

1 Debtor turnover: $\dfrac{\text{Sales}}{\text{Debtors}}$

   If sales were £120 000 per year and debtors stood at £20 000, debtor turnover would be 6. This means that debtors turn over six times a year. In other words, debtors pay after every 2 months. This can be compared to the plan, the terms of trade and the industry norm to judge whether debtors are being controlled effectively. If they are not, the firm will be having problems with its cash flow.

2 Stock turnover: $\dfrac{\text{Sales}}{\text{Stocks}}$

   If sales were £120 000 and stocks stood at £30 000, stock turnover would be 4, meaning that stock turns over four times a year, equivalent to every 3 months. This can be compared to the plan and the industry norm to judge whether stock is being controlled effectively. If not, the firm is likely to be having problems with its cash flow.

It is important for a growing firm to have appropriate and relevant financial information that can be produced promptly and on a timely basis, at an acceptable cost. The financial drivers give the owner-manager simple, understandable information. They can be reproduced on a single piece of paper. They provide the headline information on how the business is doing. If they disclose a problem then more information might be needed to decide on the appropriate course of action. For example, if debtors are not being controlled effectively then a detailed list of debtors and when the debts were due for payment (called an aged listing of debtors) will provide the information needed so that action can be taken.

💡 Break-even

Figure 9.4 reproduces the familiar cost–profit–volume chart introduced in Chapter 7. However, the simplified profit–volume chart in Figure 9.5 is far easier to interpret and use and emphasises the two most important financial principles of start-up:

1 Keep fixed costs as low as possible.
2 Keep contribution margins as high as possible.

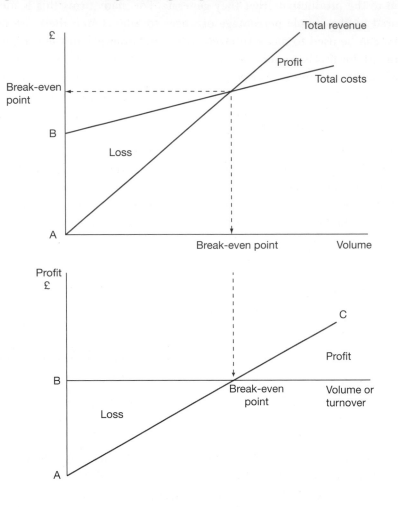

F9.4 Cost–profit–volume chart

F9.5 Profit–volume chart

Keep fixed costs as low as possible

The lower the fixed cost AB, the lower the break-even point and therefore the lower the risk. If fixed costs AB can be reduced, line AC in Figure 9.5 moves upwards – and therefore the break-even point and risk are lower. High fixed trading or operating costs are called high operating gearing or leverage. This can be measured as the proportion of total costs represented by fixed costs. This percentage should be kept as low as possible, particularly at start-up. Remember, higher fixed assets also mean higher depreciation charges and therefore higher fixed costs. Investment in fixed assets can therefore increase a business's break-even point.

High borrowings – perhaps to finance investment in fixed assets – mean high interest costs, which are fixed and over which there is little discretion. If turnover goes down, interest payments stay the same. Indeed, sometimes interest rates, and therefore interest payments, can go up when turnover, and therefore profit, goes down. This is the classic situation that is created when interest rates go up in order to decrease overall demand in the economy. The small firm faces a squeeze with higher costs and lower turnover. High financing costs are called high financial gearing or leverage.

Businesses with high operating or financial gearing (or both) need to make certain they achieve their sales targets. They have very little day-to-day influence over their fixed costs so their business imperative is to attract a sufficient volume of customers – and that is about marketing and sales. They can afford to offer special price deals if their margins are high, so as to attract different market segments at different prices. For example, running a train from London to Manchester incurs mainly fixed costs and the train operator must fill the train as full as possible. The company does this by offering a range of fares with all sorts of different terms and conditions or facilities to a range of different customers. In that way a business man might pay eight times as much as an off-peak student traveller on the same train and yet not feel that he is getting a bad deal.

As we saw in Chapter 7, the lowest price at which a product or service can be offered is its variable cost. Above this every £1 is extra contribution to fixed costs or, if the business is operating above its break-even point, extra profit. If, in addition to high fixed costs, a firm faces low variable costs, then it is able to offer its product or service at a very low price in order to attract marginal business – extra business it would not otherwise have. So, for example, our railway company may offer a £1 special offer fare, possibly linked to other conditions or purchases, and would still make £1 extra profit. The only problem with this is that, unless you are able to make this product or service sufficiently different from the normal product or service you offer, all your regular customers might be attracted to it and sales might never be high enough to meet fixed costs.

🛄 Case insight
David Speakman and Travel Counsellors

David Speakman is a serial entrepreneur. But when his second business, a restaurant, failed losing him ££500 000 he decided to list the prime attributes of the ideal business. He wrote: 'no fixed labour costs, commission only sales, large volume and low overheads'.

He was already running a small travel agency with a turnover of £548 000, but the experience of failure made him decide to re-jig it. The result was Travel Counsellors, started in 1994. The firm has a small head office handling marketing, billing and supplies. However, it relies mainly on some travelling counsellors equipped with portable computers and mobile phones who visit customers' homes mapping out itineraries, online counsellors working from their own homes, fielding telephone and internet enquiries and arranging visits to customers.

The idea proved to be both successful and profitable but with 540 counsellors and only 100 staff in the head office in Bolton, Lancashire, the emphasis was still very much on keeping fixed costs as low as possible:

'The ideal business has no fixed overheads, commission only sales, large volume and low overheads.'

David Speakman, founder of Travel Counsellors
Sunday Times 6 December 1998

☐ Up-to-date information on Travel Counsellors can be found on their website: www.travelcounsellors.co.uk

🛄 Case insight Flitwick Manor Hotel

Flitwick Manor Hotel is a country house hotel in Bedfordshire. Some years ago it had a turnover of £922 000 per annum, with high fixed costs of £426 000, of which 34 per cent represented permanent staff and 20 per cent loan interest; 82 per cent of its variable costs represented consumables such as food and wine. The hotel lets out rooms and sells food and drink and therefore the average contribution margin can be used to calculate its break-even point:

Turnover (ex VAT)	£922 000	
Total variable cost	£326 000	
Contribution	£596 000	64%
Fixed costs	£426 000	
Profit	£170 000	

$$\text{Break-even} \quad \frac{£426\,000}{0.64} = £666\,000$$

Margin of safety = 27.8%

With the high fixed costs and high contribution margin it is important that Flitwick keeps its beds and restaurant full. It therefore spends heavily on promotion. It also has a luncheon club, offering cheap lunches to regular customers, who receive regular promotions from the hotel.

Marginal business can be very attractive, particularly to businesses with high fixed costs, such as railways, airlines and hotels. The railway has to run its trains to a predetermined timetable and so the marginal cost of an extra passenger is very, very low – hence all of the special schemes and discounts to encourage people to travel on the off-peak services. Standby tickets for air flights are a similar case, as are weekend bargain breaks in hotels. The danger, of course, is that all the customers end up wanting cut-price fares and you end up not making a profit at all.

Keep contribution margins as high as possible

Do not sell just on price, find a differential advantage. Higher margins increase the angle of line AC in Figure 9.5, pivoting it in an anticlockwise direction about A, and lowering the break-even point. Once past the break-even point every £1 of sales revenue yields even higher profits. However, high contribution margins generally mean high differential advantage.

Businesses with low contribution margins cannot afford to cut their prices (see Table 7.1). What is more, their business imperative must be to control these high variable costs. For them, a 1 per cent reduction in the contribution margin can have disastrous effects on their profitability, so cost control and cost minimisation is a vital day-to-day activity for the owner-manager. This is the case for Penforth Sofa Beds (opposite).

♀ Decision-making

Break-even analysis is a powerful tool. As we have seen, it gives you the tools you need to make decisions about pricing and how the finances of a business should be structured. These are basic, important principles. However, it also gives you the tools to answer four other sorts of important business questions:

1 'How well is the business doing?' questions;
2 'What if?' questions;
3 'Which product or service is more profitable?' questions;
4 'Where should I focus limited resources?' questions.

How well is the business doing?

The break-even point is a benchmark above which the business starts to make a profit. But if you know the break-even point and the contribution margin, it is very easy to estimate the level of profitability – given the level of sales – without needing to resort to an accounting system. The formula to use is:

$$\text{Profit} = \frac{(\text{Sales} - \text{Break-even sales})}{\text{Contribution margin}}$$

So, we saw in the Case insight, when Jean Young had sales of £17 200, her net profit was £11 985. This can be calculated simply and quickly using the formula, given that we know her break-even point was £5215 and her contribution margin was 100%:

$$\frac{(£17\,200 - £5\,215)}{1} = £11\,985$$

Similarly, if break-even were £500 a week and contribution margin were 40 per cent, at sales of £1500 the profit would be:

$$\frac{(£1500 - £500)}{0.4} = £400$$

What if?

The most asked question in business, particularly for a start-up, is 'what if?' What if I invest in a van? What if I place that expensive advertisement in the newspaper? Contribution analysis can help answer the question by giving information about the additional sales needed to make sufficient profit to recoup the cost. This may not make the decision about what to do, but it does provide invaluable information on which to base it. So, for example, if the advertisement costs £1000 and the contribution margin is 40 per cent, the extra sales needed would be £2500. This can be calculated using a simple formula:

$$\text{Extra sales needed} = \frac{\text{Increase in fixed costs}}{\text{Contribution margin}}$$

$$= \frac{£1000}{0.40}$$

$$= £2500$$

Contribution analysis can also be used to answer 'what if' questions about price. Suppose that a competitor to a business selling skateboards wholesale at £20 each (retail is £50–£60) starts price-cutting, selling equivalent boards at just £16 wholesale. The problem is to decide whether to match the price reduction, or to seek a more profitable alternative strategy. Look at the calculation overleaf.

📖 Case insight Penforth Sofa Beds

As its name implies, Penforth Sofa Beds made sofa beds. Selling to large retail outlets, its margins were squeezed and, despite low fixed costs of £102 000, it made a contribution margin of only 17 per cent on a typical sofa bed.

Selling price (ex VAT)	£200
Variable cost	£166
Contribution	£ 34 17%

$$\text{Break-even} \quad \frac{£102\,000}{0.17} = £600\,000$$

Seventy-eight per cent of the variable costs represent materials and 12 per cent represent piecework labour. With this cost structure and because Penforth cannot influence the price it charges, it is vital that all variable costs are tightly controlled. Materials must be sourced from the lowest-cost provider and labour costs kept down to a minimum.

Penforth Sofa Beds sold between 4000 and 5000 sofas a year, giving it a turnover of £800 000 to £1 million and a profit of £34 000 to £68 000. John Douglas, the owner-manager, was also the company salesman. He did think about hiring another salesman. If he paid a basic salary of £15 000 with a 5% commission, to justify hiring he would have to increase sales by:

$$\frac{£15\,000}{(0.17 - 0.05)} = £125\,000$$

$$= 625 \text{ sofas}$$

Since he was far from certain he could get a good salesman for this salary package, and because in a good year the company is pretty near to full capacity, he decided against trying to recruit anybody.

	1 Current position	2 Competitor lowers price and we hold price	3 Competitor lowers price and we lower price
Price	£20	£20	£16
Variable cost	£12	£12	£12
Contribution	£8	£8	£4
Sales volume	3 000	2 000	3 000
Total contribution	£24 000	£16 000	£12 000
Fixed costs	£16 000	£16 000	£16 000
Profit	£ 8 000	£ –	£(4 000)

Column 2 shows the effect on profits if prices are maintained with the result that there is a one-third fall in sales. Column 3 shows the effect on profits if prices are reduced in order to maintain the level of sales.

As we see from column 3, the business will actually lose money (£4000 per month) if it follows the price lead of the competitor. If it maintains its prices, the position is rather better, although it will still not make a profit (column 2). However, there may also be the opportunity in this situation to reduce overheads to reflect the lower sales, or even to spend more on advertising to persuade customers that the board is better and worth £20. Despite the evidence that an analysis of this kind often reveals, many companies automatically cut prices as a 'knee-jerk' reaction to competitive pressures, without appreciating the real costs or evaluating the alternatives.

Which product or service is more profitable?

For any business producing more than one product or service the question as to which is the more profitable, and therefore the one which is to have its sales 'pushed' hardest, is an interesting one, and one to which the answer is not as straightforward as you might think. However, it is a fundamental question in deciding upon the mix of sales.

Suppose the skateboard company can produce three versions; 'Standard', 'All-terrain' and 'Freestyle', and the costs and margins are as follows:

	Standard	All-terrain	Freestyle
Price	£25	£32	£50
Variable cost	£10	£16	£30
Contribution	£15	£16	£20
Contribution margin	60%	50%	40%

This shows that Freestyle gives the highest £ contribution per board, but that Standard has the best contribution margin. So which is the one that the firm should encourage the sales of most? The answer depends on the market that the different products are selling to.

Let us say that the total market for skateboards is limited and selling more of one reduces demand for the others. In this case, as can be seen below, for every £500 spent the company can make a bigger profit from selling the Standard board, with its higher contribution margin.

	Standard	All-terrain	Freestyle
Price	£25	£32	£50
Variable cost	£10	£16	£30
Contribution	£15	£16	£20
Contribution margin	60%	50%	40%
Contribution from £500 sales	£300	£250	£200

However, where the products or markets are independent, that is if the Freestyle board is sold to one customer, the Standard to another and the All-terrain to a third, then selling one does not reduce the budget available for the others. In this case, you sell as much as you can of the Freestyle board first, moving on to the All-terrain board and finally the Standard board.

The general rule therefore is:

▷ where you are selling products or services which compete with each other in the same market, push the sales of those products which have the highest contribution margin;

▷ where you are selling independent products which do not compete against each other, first sell the items that give the highest £ per unit contribution.

In the case of the customer with a limited budget, the firm has to take account of a limiting factor, the amount of money available to buy their products. This is a special case of the next situation.

Where should I focus limited resources?

All businesses face some form of limiting factor. For example, think about possible constraints which might limit the launch of a new product or service. Apart from the obvious constraint of demand, there can be several other factors that limit an organisation's ability to expand, such as a lack of skilled labour, limited machine capacity, shortage of raw materials, lack of management expertise, or shortage of money. Retailers often regard available shelf space as being their main limiting factor, while for a fast-growing manufacturing business the limiting factor may well be the availability of cash to finance their working capital needs.

Where a limiting factor exists, then a business will maximise its profits by making the best use of the limiting resource. For example, retailers need to make the best use of their available shelf space.

Assume that the skateboard company has a shortage of machinery which reflects itself in availability of machine hours. It needs to decide how to use the machine hours available to maximise its profits. This is done by looking at the contribution per machine hour:

	Standard	All-terrain	Freestyle
Price	£25	£32	£50
Variable cost	£10	£16	£30
Contribution	£15	£16	£20
Machine hours needed per 100 boards	1	0.5	2
Contribution per machine hour	£1500	£3200	£1000

As we see, the contribution per machine hour is greatest from the All-terrain boards. Every hour of machine work produces 200 boards and yields £3200 contribution. Therefore, if machine hours really is the key limiting resource, the company should produce All-terrain boards first, until demand is satisfied, followed by Standard boards, until demand is satisfied, and make up any unfilled capacity finally with the Freestyle board.

The general rule, where a limiting factor exists, is that the business should give priority to those products or services (or to those customers and markets) which generate the highest contribution per unit of limiting factor.

As always, the real world doesn't behave quite like a mathematical formula. If a supermarket filled its shelves entirely with small, high margin items it might find it had a lot of dissatisfied customers unable to find bread, sugar and washing powder. Similarly, a manufacturer may prefer to sell to reliable large customers rather than to take greater risks selling to small traders, even though the contribution per sale may be higher in the latter case.

One practical problem when a company has a range of products, each with different contribution margins, is interpreting just what the break-even point means. The calculation is easy. It does not change. But what does the result mean in terms of the sales mix? The answer is that the mix of sales at break-even is identical to the mix of sales that yields the average contribution margin. The problem is that if the sales mix changes, so too does the break-even point.

If the fixed costs for our skateboard company were £190000 and the sales were as detailed below, producing an average contribution margin of 50 per cent, we could go on to calculate the break-even point using the usual formula:

	Standard	**All-terrain**	**Freestyle**		**Total**
Sales volume	8000	2000	4000		
Price	£25	£32	£50	Turnover	£464000
Variable cost	£10	£16	£30	Variable cost	£232000
Contribution	£15	£16	£20		
Total contribution	£120000	£32000	£80000		£232000
Margin	60%	50%	40%		(50%)
				Fixed costs	£190000
				Profit	£ 42000

$$\text{Break-even} = \frac{£190\,000}{0.50} = £380\,000$$

The problem is that this break-even point only holds if the mix of sales always remains the same, that is for every eight Standard boards sold we always sell two All-terrain boards and four Freestyle boards. Should the mix change, then the break-even point will change.

Notwithstanding this, an understanding of which products, customers or markets generate the best contributions, and of the optimal way to utilise limited resources, can make a significant difference to the overall profitability of the business. You will be in a much better position to optimise the sales mix if you know which products are most profitable. It is also essential to know the break-even point, together with its limitations and manage it in the appropriate way.

🗁 10 Practical tips for a successful start-up

1 Don't run out of cash – plan your cash flow so that you can chart the length and depth of Death Valley and find the funds you need to start up.
2 Understand the mechanics of the business – what it takes to make the product or service, and make certain you can deliver.
3 Understand yourself – what your strengths and weaknesses are, and make sure you play to your strengths and avoid (or compensate for) your weaknesses.
4 Understand your customers – who they are (name names), and why they should buy from you.
5 Understand your competitors – who they are (name names), and why customers will buy from you and not them.
6 Don't be afraid to be different – but understand why customers value it.
7 Don't be afraid to charge as high a price as possible – but be able to justify doing so and make certain customers agree.
8 Keep your fixed costs as low as possible – and for as long as possible.
9 Plan ahead – but any plan should not constrain you, it should allow you to think through and plan for contingencies, and don't be afraid to change it if circumstances change.
AND
10 Don't run out of cash.

▷ Summary

▷ Cash flow is the lifeblood of a business. You can be making a profit and still run out of cash which means that bills go unpaid. Start-ups face the danger of Death Valley; they need to chart its length and depth by producing a cash flow forecast and using it to plan to meet their financing needs.

▷ Money flows around the business and it is important to make sure it keeps flowing as quickly as possible. That means making sure debtors pay as quickly as possible – choosing credit customers carefully, invoicing promptly, setting credit limits and following up promptly on late payment. Stocks should be kept to a minimum, buying only the minimum needed, and all available supplier credit should be taken.

▷ Profit represents the growth in the assets of a business that comes about through trading. Profit can be represented in any asset, not just cash. The balance sheet is a snap shot at a point in time that tells you where the money in a business comes from and where it is invested. Fixed assets, such as equipment and vehicles, are things the business means to keep. Working capital, which comprises current assets such as stocks and debtors and current liabilities such as creditors, is the thing the business means to sell or turn over.

▷ Start-ups like **Jean Young** need to forecast cash flow, profit statements and balance sheets at least for the first year of trading. This allows them to plan ahead to meet their financial results and needs.

▷ As a business grows effective planning and control becomes even more essential. Growth eats into cash and the financing needs of the firm during its growth need to be anticipated and planned. Comprehensive budgets need to be prepared – cash flow, profit statement and balance sheet. These help in the management of the firm and can be a useful tool to encourage the entrepreneur to delegate control to the managers they have recruited. Increasingly from here the firm will start to look more professional with formal organisation and control systems. It is about to stop being a 'small firm' – by any definition.

▷ Most businesses, like the **Newt & Cucumber** pub chain, can be controlled by monitoring six important financial drivers on a regular and timely basis. These drivers are:

1 Cash;   4 Margin of safety;
2 Sales;   5 Productivity;
3 Profit margins;   6 Debtor or stock turnover.

▷ Companies like **Travel Counsellors** understand that it is vital to keep fixed overhead costs as low as possible, particularly at start-up. It is also important to keep contribution margins as high as possible. Whilst **Flitwick Manor Hotel** had high operating and financial gearing, it also had high contribution margins. When operating gearing is high it is important that sales targets are met. A high contribution margin gives some discretion on pricing, allowing very low prices to be charged based upon the low marginal cost involved. However, this should only be tried when differential pricing – charging different prices to different customers – is practical. **Penforth Sofa Beds** has low fixed costs but also low

contribution margins. Low contribution margins make it imperative that variable costs are closely monitored. They also make it dangerous to drop prices any further.

▷ Contribution and break-even analysis are powerful tools. They tell you about the risk the business faces and the imperatives for management. Break-even is a benchmark above which a business starts to make profit. If you know how much above your break-even you are operating at, and your contribution margin, then it is easy to estimate your profitability.

▷ Contribution analysis can also be used to answer 'what if?' type questions, such as the question for **Penforth Sofa Beds** as to whether to recruit a new salesman or not. It tells you the value of extra sales needed to cover the increased fixed costs. Contribution analysis tells you which products or services are most profitable and, when some critical resource is limited, which to push the sales of. All in all, contribution analysis is a vital tool for the owner-manager.

ⓘ **Further resources are available at www.palgrave.com/business/burns**

📄 Essays and discussion topics

1 Why is cash flow not the same as profit?
2 What would you do to ensure your start-up makes it through Death Valley?
3 There is no such thing as certainty, therefore there is no point in trying to forecast the future. Discuss.
4 The most important three pieces of advice for a start-up are:
   ▷ Think customer;
   ▷ Plan ahead;
   ▷ Don't run out of cash.
   Discuss.
5 Profit is just something that an accountant constructs. The amount of profit depends on the assumptions the accountant decides to make. Therefore profit is not objective and means nothing. Discuss.
6 Why do you think owner-managers are not interested in accounting and control?
7 Do you think computer-based accounting systems make the task of controlling a small business easier?

8 What steps would you take in your start-up business to ensure debtors are kept to a minimum?
9 What steps would you take in your start-up business to ensure stocks are kept to a minimum?
10 Do you really think you can control a business by monitoring six financial drivers?
11 Entrepreneurs make decisions by instinct and not by using financial analysis. Discuss.
12 Cost–profit–volume analysis reflects the way owner-managers think. Discuss.
13 The margin of safety tells you about the long-term viability of a business, the risks it faces and the earning quality of each £ of turnover. Discuss.
14 Behind every successful entrepreneur there is an accountant. Discuss.
15 Why is budgeting so important at the take-off stage?
16 Budgeting helps entrepreneurs to delegate effectively. Discuss.

☉ Exercises and assignments

1 Work through the budget setting process for the PC Modem (Appendix 1). Make certain you understand the calculations and processes.

2 Work through the accounting process for ACE Computers (Appendix 2). Now check your understanding. Using the Accounting Worksheet below, record the following transactions and draw up the balance sheet and profit statement.

A £1000 cash from share capital received. £500 cash from bank loan received;

B Fixed assets purchased on credit for £1100;

C Stock purchased on credit for £550;

D Some stock sold on credit for £500;

E Pay creditors £1250;

F Receive £1250 from debtors;

G Pay cash expenses (no invoices) of £30;

H Depreciation of fixed assets charged at £110;

I Stock at the end of the period is £350;

J Repair work to the value of £40 undertaken, still awaiting invoice.

3 Arrange for a presentation of the Sage accounting system. Visit the company's website on www.sage.com and investigate the range of packages available.

Accounting worksheet

	Assets £				=	Capital £		Liabilities £	
	Cash	Debtors	Stocks	Fixed assets		Shares	Profit	Bank loan	Creditors
A					=				
A					=				
B					=				
C					=				
D					=				
E					=				
F					–				
G					=				
H					=				
I					=				
J					=				
					=				

📖 References

Chittenden, F., Poutziouris, P. and Michaelas, N. (1998) *Financial Management and Working Capital Practices in UK SMEs*, Manchester Business School.

Appendix 1: Forecasts and budgets – an example

Preparing forecasts or budgets can be complicated, particularly for a manufacturing company. This is a comprehensive example for just such a company. This company is already in business, producing two specialist computer modems (A and B). The year-end (31 December 2015) balance sheet for the company is shown as Table 9.1. We shall prepare the budget for 2016 only. The budgeting process would be easier for a start-up company, since there would be no balance sheet at the beginning of the period, and easier for a service business, since there would not be a manufacturing process to complicate the costing. This business is also registered for Value Added Tax (VAT) and accounting for that is an added complication.

The company has been fairly successful so far and the owner is looking for a return (profit before interest and tax) on his net assets of 15 per cent per annum. So far it has funded its fairly rapid expansion by a long-term loan of £100 000, which is not due for repayment until 2018, and an overdraft which, this year, reached its maximum permissible level of £30 000. Because of the highly cyclical nature of demand, the company has experienced difficulty with supplies of modems at certain times of the year. Since the modems are always required for immediate delivery, if an order cannot be met within a few days, it will be lost. The company would like to rectify this problem by increasing its stock of finished modems.

Sales budget

The sales manager sees the 2016 market as continuing to be extremely good for the company. He is aware that this is an expanding market but equally aware that costs are going up ahead of inflation. He feels that a 5 per cent increase in selling price can easily be accommodated and sales volume would still increase by an estimated

	£	£	£
FIXED ASSETS			484 000
CURRENT ASSETS:			
Stock			
– Finished goods: modem A (400)	30 400		
modem B (360)	19 800		
	50 200		
– Raw materials base stock	10 000		60 200
Debtors		VAT	
– estimated payment January	66 000	13 200	
– estimated payment February	78 000	15 600	172 800
			233 000
CREDITORS DUE WITHIN ONE YEAR:			
Overdraft			(30 000)
Creditors		VAT	
– due for payment January	20 880	4176	
– due for payment February	20 880	4176	(50 112)
Corporation tax (due September)			(27 500)
			(107 612)
NET CURRENT ASSETS (WORKING CAPITAL)			125 388
NET ASSETS (FIXED ASSETS *plus* NET CURRENT ASSETS)			609 388
CREDITORS DUE AFTER MORE THAN ONE YEAR:			
Long-term loan			(100 000)
			509 388
CAPITAL AND RESERVES:			
Share capital			10 000
Profit-and-loss account			499 388
			509 388

T9.1 Balance sheet, 31 December 2015

20 per cent. Looking at the pattern of last year's sales and noting the requirements of existing major customers, he arrives at his first estimate of sales, broken down by month, as shown in Table 9.2. Since he knows that his budget exceeds the productive capacity of existing plant, before proceeding further he passes it on to the managing director and the production manager for consideration.

Units	Jan	Feb	Mar	Apr	May	June	July	Aug	Sep	Oct	Nov	Dec	Total
Modem A	400	400	440	280	100	100	80	80	200	360	360	440	3 240
Modem B	600	660	520	320	160	160	120	120	360	660	780	780	5 240

T9.2 Preliminary sales budget

Production budget

The company would like to be able to meet the tentative sales budget and to build up finished modem stocks. However, demand is cyclical, whereas production needs to be kept fairly stable throughout the year, since skilled labour cannot be hired and fired at will. Also, even if new machinery were to be purchased in January, it could not be installed and working effectively until March. An added problem is works holidays: one week in December and January and two weeks in August. In those months production is always down, pro rata.

Based upon the production schedule, the production manager decides how many new machines to purchase. These machines will cost £120 000 (+ VAT @ 20% = £24 000) and can be installed in January. Like all creditors, payment can be delayed by two months. These machines will increase production of modem A from the normal 240 to 320 per month and of modem B from 400 to 520 per month from March onwards.

The budgeted production schedule is shown in Table 9.3. Opening stocks of modem A were 400 and of modem B 360. The new production schedule will indeed result in higher year-end stocks of 640 and 830 respectively. The lower production in January, August and December reflects the works holidays. Monthly stock levels were computed to compare with the provisional sales budgets to ascertain whether demand will be met. Unfortunately this is not always so, and it is estimated that sales of 100 A modems and 200 B modems will be lost in March and February respectively. However, our investment appraisal tells us it is not worth installing extra productive capacity to satisfy demand in these months. Thus budgeted annual production, sales and stock figures are agreed:

	Units	Modem A	Modem B
	Stock 31 Dec 2015	400	360
plus	Production	3380	5510
minus	Sales	−3140	−5040
	Stock 31 Dec 2016	640	830

The costs of production, after taking into account inflation in material prices and wage increases, are shown overleaf. These are derived from the company's detailed costing record.

Units	Jan	Feb	Mar[1]	Apr	May	June	July	Aug[2]	Sep	Oct	Nov	Dec[3]	Total
Modem A													
Start stocks	400	180	20	0	40	260	480	720	800	920	880	840	
+ production	180	240	320	320	320	320	320	160	320	320	320	240	3380
– sales	400	400	340	280	100	100	80	80	200	360	360	440	3140
= End stock	180	20	0	40	260	480	720	800	920	880	840	640	
Modem B													
Start stocks	360	60	0	0	200	560	920	1320	1460	1620	1480	1220	
+ production	300	400	520	520	520	520	520	260	520	520	520	390	5510
–sales	600	460	520	320	160	160	120	120	360	660	780	780	5040
= End stock	60	0	0	200	560	920	1320	1460	1620	1480	1220	830	

[1] sales = lower of budgeted sales (Table 9.2) or stock in hand.
[2] 50% production.
[3] 75% production.

T9.3 Production budget

Cost per unit (£)		Modem A	Modem B
Direct labour (fixed cost)		24	15
Direct materials (variable cost)		22	18
Variable factory overheads		15	12
Fixed factory overheads (depreciation)		15	10
		76	55

Workers are on fixed weekly wages. The current wage bill is £10 290 per month. With wage increases due in March and the new operatives needed in that month, this will jump to £14 319 per month (a total of £163 770 for the year). This level of direct labour will be sufficient to meet the planned range of production. Direct material and variable overheads are paid under normal trade terms, on average delaying payments by two months. Fixed factory overheads is depreciation of plant and equipment. This totals £105 800 (£15 × 3380 + £10 × 5510). These unit costs give the following estimates of production costs, cost of sales and stock costs:

	Modem A		Modem B	
	Units	£	Units	£
Stock 31 Dec 2015	400	30 400	360	19 800
+ Production (costs)	3380	256 880	5510	303 050
− Sales (costs)	−3140	−238 640	−5040	−277 200
Stock 31 Dec 2016	640	48 640	830	45 650

The company keeps a tight control over raw material stocks, and the current base stock of £10 000 will be maintained in value terms.

		Jan	Feb	Mar	Apr	May	Jun	Jul	Aug	Sep	Oct	Nov	Dec	Totals
Modem A														
Production (units)		180	240	320	320	320	320	320	160	320	320	320	240	
Direct materials @ £22	£	3960	5280	7040	7040	7040	7040	7040	3520	7040	7040	7040	5280	
Variable overheads @ £15	£	2700	3600	4800	4800	4800	4800	4800	2400	4800	4800	4800	3600	
Labour @ £24	£	4320	5760	7680	7680	7680	7680	7680	3840	7680	7680	7680	5670	
Modem B														
Production (units)		300	400	520	520	520	520	520	260	520	520	520	390	
Direct materials @ £18	£	5400	7200	9360	9360	9360	9360	9360	4680	9360	9360	9360	7020	
Variable overheads @ £12	£	3600	4800	6240	6240	6240	6240	6240	3120	6240	6240	6240	4680	
Labour @ £15	£	4500	6000	7800	7800	7800	7800	7800	3900	7800	7800	7800	5850	
Totals														**Totals**
Direct materials & variable overheads	£	15 660	20 880	27 440	27 440	27 440	27 440	27 440	13 720	27 440	27 440	27 440	20 580	290 360
Related VAT @ 20%	£	3132	4176	5488	5488	5488	5488	5488	2744	5488	5488	5488	4186	58 072
Quarterly VAT totals	£			12 796			16 464			13 720			15 092	
Labour	£	10 290	10 697	14 319	14 319	14 319	14 319	14 319	14 319	14 319	14 319	14 319	14 319	163 770

T9.4 Budgeted purchases, overheads and wage payments

Purchasing budget

The next task for the company is to prepare the monthly purchasing budget. This is shown in Table 9.4. The unit variable costs of direct material and overheads and fixed direct labour costs are applied to the production schedule shown in Table 9.3 to arrive at estimated purchases each month.

Notice that VAT at 20 per cent has been added to purchases of materials and overheads, assuming all purchases are chargeable. A company acts as a collector of VAT for HM Revenue and Customs. Although it will have to pay VAT on purchases and charge VAT on most sales, it can reclaim the VAT paid and must repay the VAT it collects to the Customs and Excise on a quarterly basis. Therefore, while VAT does not affect a business's profitability (except in so far as it may deter customers), it can cause cash flow problems, as the business pays and collects VAT at different times from its payments to HM Revenue and Customs.

Revised sales budget

The original sales budget could not be met and therefore it will have to be revised, in line with Table 9.3. The revised sales budget is shown in Table 9.5. Modem A is priced at £90, and modem B at £75, excluding VAT. Notice that, once more, VAT chargeable is shown separately. This will only affect the cash flow budget.

To achieve this level of sales it is estimated that selling, distribution and general costs will have to rise to £24000. Let us assume, for simplicity, that these costs incur VAT at 17.5 per cent (£4200), they accrue evenly over the year, and that they are paid monthly.

		Jan	Feb	Mar	Apr	May	June	July	Aug	Sep	Oct	Nov	Dec	Total
Modem A @ £90 each	units	400	400	340	280	100	100	80	80	200	360	360	440	3140
	£	36000	30600	30600	25200	9000	9000	7200	7200	18000	32400	32400	39600	282600
Modem B @ £75 each	units	600	460	520	320	160	160	120	120	360	660	780	780	5040
	£	45000	34500	39000	24000	12000	12000	9000	9000	27000	49500	58500	58500	378000
Total	£	81000	70500	69600	49200	21000	21000	16200	16200	45000	81900	90900	98100	660600
Related VAT @ 20%	£	16200	14100	13920	9840	4200	4200	3240	3240	9000	16380	18180	19620	132120
Quarterly VAT totals				44220			18240			15480			54180	

T9.5 Final sales budget

Budgeted income statement

The budgeted income statement is shown in Table 9.6. Sales are as shown in Table 9.5 and cost of sales was calculated from the costing records detailed previously. The budgeted profit before interest and tax payments is £120760: a margin of 18 per cent on sales. Notice that this calculation excludes VAT.

	Modem A	Modem B	Total
Sales	£282600	£378000	£660600
Cost of sales	238640	277200	515840
Gross profit	£ 43960	£100800	£144760
Selling, distribution and general costs			24000
Profit before interest and tax			£120760
Estimated corporation tax			24000
Profit before interest but after tax			£ 96760

T9.6 Budgeted income statement, 2016

Cash flow forecast

The cash flow forecast is shown in Table 9.7. This shows the cash flow surplus or deficit each month and the resulting effect on the cash balance or overdraft of the business. Sales receipts and related VAT are lagged by two months. In other words, sales in January (see Table 9.5) do not generate cash receipts until March. Obviously this means sales in November and December will not have been collected by the year-end. Similarly, purchases and related VAT are lagged by two months. January purchases (see Table 9.4) are not paid until March, and November and December purchases are not paid by the year end. Selling, distribution and general costs and related VAT are paid in the month incurred, as are direct labour costs. The capital expenditure and related VAT is paid in March, and the corporation tax bill shown in last year's balance-sheet is paid in September.

VAT payments to HM Revenue and Customs are quarterly, at the end of March, June, September and December. There are various schemes for VAT, including cash accounting which is based simply on VAT received *less* VAT paid. However, once turnover exceeds a certain limit, as in this case, the company must apply invoice accounting which is based upon the VAT you have charged *less* the VAT charged to you during the period, irrespective of whether or not you have received or paid it. Budgeted VAT payments have been calculated in Table 9.8. VAT receivable is taken from Table 9.5 and VAT payable on materials and variable

£	Jan	Feb	Mar	Apr	May	Jun	Jul	Aug	Sep	Oct	Nov	Dec	Total
RECEIPTS													
Sales receipts	66000	78000	81000	70500	69600	49200	21000	21000	16200	16200	45000	81900	615600
Related VAT @ 20%	13200	15600	16200	14100	13920	9840	4200	4200	3240	3240	9000	16380	123120
Total receipts A	79200	93600	97200	84600	83520	59040	25200	25200	19440	19440	54000	98280	738720
PAYMENTS													
Direct materials and overheads	20880	20880	15660	20880	27440	27440	27440	27440	27440	13720	27440	27440	284100
Related VAT @ 20%	4176	4176	3132	4176	5488	5488	5488	5488	5488	2744	5488	5488	56820
Selling, general etc	2000	2000	2000	2000	2000	2000	2000	2000	2000	2000	2000	2000	24000
Related VAT	400	400	400	400	400	400	400	400	400	400	400	400	4800
Direct labour	10290	10290	14319	14319	14319	14319	14319	14319	14319	14319	14319	14319	163770
Capital expenditure			120000										120000
Related VAT @ 20%			24000										24000
VAT payments			6224			576			560			3788	45248
Corporation tax									27500				27500
Total payments B	37746	37746	185735	41775	49647	50223	49647	49647	77707	33183	49647	87535	750238
CASH FLOW A – B	41454	55854	–88535	42825	33873	8817	–24447	–24447	–58267	–13743	4353	10745	–11518
Brought forward	–30000	11454	67308	–21227	21598	55471	64288	39841	15394	–42873	–56616	–52267	
CASH BALANCE	11454	67308	–21227	21598	55471	64288	39841	15394	–42873	–56616	–52267	–41518	

T9.7 Cash flow forecast 2016

	Mar	Jun	Sep	Dec	Total
VAT receivable	£44220	£18240	£15480	£54180	£132120
minus					
VAT payable					
Materials and overheads (Table 9.4)	–12796	–16464	–13720	–15092	–58072
Selling and general (Table 9.7)	–1200	–1200	–1200	–1200	–4800
Capital expenditure (Table 9.7)	–24000	—	—	—	–24000
Quarterly payments	£6224	£576	£560	£37888	£45248

T9.8 VAT quarterly returns summary

overheads from Table 9.4. Selling and general costs and capital expenditures are as detailed. This complication is unfortunate, but essential, since VAT can make an enormous difference to the cash flows of any business and often a small business can experience difficulty meeting these quarterly bills.

The budgeted cash flow statement is essential for short-term planning. The business started the year with an overdraft of £30000, which was the maximum facility offered by the bank. This overdraft limit will not be exceeded until September, when an overdraft of £42873 will be required. This will increase to £56616 in October, and even at the end of the year will be £41518 (cash flow for the year is –£11518). Obviously the business must either arrange to increase its overdraft facility in advance for these months or arrange for a term loan to inject the necessary cash. But would the banks lend to the business? To find this out, we need to look at the business's profit and its balance sheet. Alternatively the business can look to leasing or hire purchase to fund the new equipment purchase. These options will be reviewed in the next chapter.

Budgeted balance sheet

The budgeted balance sheet is shown in Table 9.9. Debtors and related VAT represent November and December sales, and creditors and related VAT represent November and December purchases of materials and overheads. Finished goods stock was calculated in the production schedule and the raw materials base stock is maintained at £10 000. The overdraft was calculated from the budgeted cash flow statement. Corporation tax is estimated at £24 000.

Fixed assets are calculated below:

	brought forward 31 Dec 2015 (net)	£484 000
plus	purchases	120 000
minus	depreciation	−105 800
	carried forward 31 Dec 2016 (net)	£498 200

Depreciation is calculated by writing off assets over an estimated 10-year life. The company does this by charging depreciation of 10 per cent on the gross cost of the asset over a 10-year period.

Net assets for the company total £709 592, an increase of £102 760 over last year, which represents the profit the business has made this year since our budget shows no increase in share or loan capital. For those readers with a more detailed knowledge of accounts, Tables 9.9

and 9.10 analyse the movement on key balance sheet accounts.

The business is making a return on net assets of:

$$\frac{120\,760}{706\,148} \times 100 = 17\%$$

This is well above the target set by the owner, and above current interest rates. However, this return does exclude interest and taxation. The capital gearing is

$$\frac{(41\,518 + 100\,000)}{606\,148} \times 100 = 23\%$$

This is well below the maximum level of security that many lenders require. In other words, the business would probably be able to support more loan capital to enable it to meet the cash flow deficit. The owner now has all the information he requires either to approach the bank manager or another source of funds. The options will be reviewed in the next chapter.

	£	£	£
FIXED ASSETS (NET)			498 200
CURRENT ASSETS:			
Finished goods: modem A (640)	48 640		
modem B (830)	45 650		
	94 290		
Raw materials base stock	10 000		104 290
Debtors		VAT	
– November sales	90 900	18 180	
– December sales	98 100	19 620	226 800
			331 090
CREDITORS DUE WITHIN ONE YEAR:		VAT	
Overdraft			(41 518)
Creditors			
– November materials and overhead purchases	(27 440)	(5 488)	
– December materials and overhead purchases	(20 580)	(4 116)	(57 624)
Corporation tax (estimate)			(24 000)
			(123 142)
NET CURRENT ASSETS			207 948
NET ASSETS			706 148
CREDITORS DUE AFTER MORE THAN ONE YEAR:			
Long-term loan			(100 000)
			606 148
CAPITAL AND RESERVES:			
Share capital			10 000
Profit-and-loss account			
– brought forward 2015	499 388		
– 2016 profit after tax	96 760		596 148
			606 148

T9.9 Budgeted balance sheet, 31 December 2016

Debtors

brought forward 2015	£144 000
+ sales	660 600
– cash received	–615 600
carried forward 2016	£189 000

Creditors		**Stock**	
brought forward 2015	£41 760	brought forward 2015	£60 200
+ purchases	290 360	+ purchases	290 360
– cash paid	–284 100	+ depreciation allocation	105 800
		+ labour costs	163 770
		– cost of sales	–515 840
carried forward 2016	£48 020	carried forward 2016	£104 290

VAT

Brought forward 2015: debtors (Nov & Dec)	£28 800	
– creditors (Nov & Dec)	– 8 352	£20 448
– collected from sales		–123 120
+ paid on purchases (materials and overheads)		56 820
+ paid on selling and general costs		4 800
+ paid on capital expenditure		24 000
+ VAT paid quarterly to C & E		45 248
Carried forward 2016: debtors (Nov & Dec)	£37 800	
– creditors (Nov & Dec)	– 9 604	£28 196

T9.10 Analysis of accounts

Appendix 2: Accounting records – an example

The Companies Acts require that all companies keep certain accounting records to show and explain the company's transactions:

1 A record of day-to-day cash receipts and expenditures;
2 A record of assets and liabilities;
3 A statement of stock at the end of each financial year, and a statement of stocktaking from which it was prepared;
4 Except for ordinary retail trade, statements of all goods sold and purchased showing the goods and the buyers and sellers.

Whilst sole traders and partnerships are not required formally to keep all these records, they would be well advised to do so. After all, without adequate accounting information it is impossible to monitor the performance of the business.

It is reckless to run a business without any accounting records and yet many smaller firms do just that. The simplest accounting system can be very cheap and relatively easy to operate. It can provide regular and timely financial information. As the size of a business grows, so too does the complexity of the task of controlling it. However, computers have come to the rescue, providing an increasingly cheap way of processing a lot of data. Nevertheless, any system, manual or computerised, is only as good as the information entered into it. If you put garbage in, then you will get garbage out.

Let's start with the simplest accounting system, where the only accounting record is a cash book showing receipts and payments. This is the barest essential for any business since it needs cash to pay the bills and, without a record of it, there might be nothing in the bank account to pay them. Cash books take many forms. The simplest comprise four columns:

One column to describe the transaction;
One column to record amounts deposited;
One column to record amounts spent;
The final column to record the resulting balance in the account.

Only slightly more complicated are the books that separate out receipts and payments and provide some detailed analysis of where the cash came from and where it is going. An example of this is given in

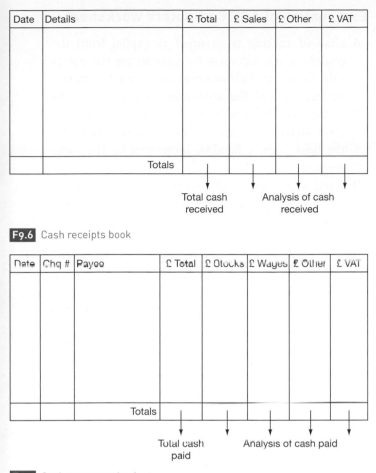

Date	Details		£ Total	£ Sales	£ Other	£ VAT
		Totals				

Total cash received   Analysis of cash received

F9.6 Cash receipts book

Date	Chq #	Payee	£ Total	£ Stocks	£ Wages	£ Other	£ VAT
		Totals					

Total cash paid   Analysis of cash paid

F9.7 Cash payments book

Figures 9.6 and 9.7. Typically, the cash book records the cash held in the bank rather than actual cash on hand in the business. The balance in the bank is the difference between total receipts and total payments, plus or minus any amounts brought forward in the account. As you might expect, this does not always agree with the balance shown on your bank statement as being in your account. This is because transactions may be recorded in your accounting system at different times to the bank's. These are called 'timing differences'. However, other differences could arise because of recording errors, bank errors – or theft! Because of these differences, it is important that any cash book is reconciled with the bank statement regularly.

Most firms will also have some cash, however small an amount, actually on hand. This is normally called 'petty cash'. The easiest way to control and account for this if it is a small amount is through what is called an 'imprest system'. You start with a cash file with, say, £100 in it. Every time cash is needed to purchase something the cash is replaced with either an invoice or a properly authorised petty cash voucher describing what was purchased. At any time that total value of cash plus invoices plus vouchers will always be £100. At the end of every week or month, or simply when the cash runs out, the vouchers are replaced with cash from the bank account and the invoices and vouchers written up in the normal way. If the volume of cash transactions is too great for this system then a separate cash book for the cash on hand will have to be kept.

Cash books can form part of accounting systems and all accounting systems are based on the idea of double entry book-keeping. You will recall the earlier comment that the balance sheet should balance. This means that the idea of liabilities and assets balancing may be viewed as being an equation. If one part of such a balancing equation were to change, then another corresponding change should be recorded to ensure that the equation, and thus the balance sheet, remains in balance. For example, if the asset cash decreases because a bill is paid, so the liability of creditors should also be reduced. This leads to the idea of double entry book-keeping. Double entry is a system of book-keeping which ensures that the accounting equation shown below is always kept in balance:

$$\text{Capital} = \text{Assets} - \text{Liabilities}$$

or

$$\text{Assets} = \text{Capital} + \text{Liabilities}$$

Capital comprises the capital introduced – in a limited company this is by way of share capital – and retained profit. The process of recording is simple: every time an additional asset is created or purchased for the organisation, recognition of where it came from must also be made. For example, if you put £1000 in cash into the business, recognition of its source must be made, let us say, by showing £1000 increase in capital. If for any reason the accounts do not 'balance', then some aspect of the transaction has not been properly recorded.

The illustration below shows how the process of double entry works. The transactions below relate to a fictitious business, ACE Computers Ltd, which buys and resells software. The details relate to its first year of operations.

A The owners contributed £25 000 in cash as share capital. A bank loan for £10 000 was obtained, repayable in five years with an interest rate of 10% per cent.

B Fixed assets costing £20 000 were purchased for cash.

C Sales totalled £60 000, being 50 per cent for cash and 50 per cent to account customers on credit.

D Depreciation on fixed assets amounted to £5000.

E Sundry operating expenses totalled £10 000 of which £1000 remained unpaid at the year end.

F Loan interest of £1000 was paid.

G Stock costing £25 000 was purchased on account.

H Trade creditors were paid £20 000 in cash.

I Debtors paid £25 000 in cash.

J Stocks at the end of the year had cost £10 000.

These details were used to construct an accounting worksheet for ACE Computers, shown in Figure 9.8.

Explanation of ACE Computers worksheet

A Cash of £25 000 is obtained as capital from the owners. Cash increases by £25 000 on the assets side; on the capital/liabilities side capital increases by £25 000 and the accounting equation remains in balance. A bank loan of £10 000 is obtained. Cash increases by £10 000 on the assets side with the bank loan, a liability, increasing by the same amount.

B Fixed assets are purchased for £20 000. Cash decreases on the assets side by £20 000. This is one asset being exchanged for another so fixed assets increase by £20 000

C Here, the sales figures are recorded. On the assets side, cash goes up by £30 000 (50 per cent of the

	Assets £				=	Capital £		Liabilities £	
	Cash	Debtors	Stocks	Fixed assets		Shares	Profit	Bank loan	Creditors
A	+25 000				=	+25 000			
A	+10 000				=			+10 000	
B	−20 000			+20 000	=				
C	+30 000	+30 000			=		+60 000		
D				−5 000	=		−5 000		
E	−9 000				=		−10 000		+1 000
F	−1 000				=		−1 000		
G			+25 000		=				+25 000
H	−20 000				=				−20 000
I	+25 000	−25 000			=				
J			−15 000		=		−15 000		
	+40 000	+5 000	+10 000	+15 000	=	+25 000	+29 000	+10 000	+6 000

F9.8 Accounting worksheet for ACE Computers

sales for the year) with debtors also increasing by £30 000 (the other 50 per cent). All of the £60 000 is recognised as a sale even though some of the cash from debtors may not have been received. This is an important accounting idea – sales can be recorded as sales and thus increase profits whether or not the cash inflow has taken place. In this case the increase of £60 000 on the assets side of the accounting equation is balanced by an addition to profits of £60 000 on the capital side.

D Depreciation is calculated as being £5000 for the year. This results in, on the assets side, fixed assets being reduced by £5000, with profits on the capital side being decreased by the same amount.

E Here, the sundry operating expenses are recorded. As with the accounting idea of cash not having to be received to be recognised as a sale, so we see an illustration of cash not having to be paid to be recognised as a charge against profits. Although only £9000 of the £10 000 sundry operating charges has been paid, accountants charge all of the £10 000 against profits, recognising the unpaid £1000 as creditors. Thus on the assets side cash goes down by £9000; on the capital/liabilities side profit decreases by all of the £10 000 with creditors increasing by £1000 (under creditors in liabilities). The entries recorded keep both sides of the accounting equation in balance – a decrease of £9000 on the assets side and a net decrease of £9000 on the capital/liabilities side.

F The loan interest paid results in cash on the assets side going down by £1000 with profits going down by £1000 on the liabilities side.

G Stocks being purchased on credit for £25 000 is reflected in stocks on the assets side increasing by £25 000, with the same increase in creditors on the liabilities side.

H The payment of £20 000 to creditors results in both cash and creditors decreasing by that amount.

I Here the payment of some of the sums owed by debtors is recorded. Cash increases by £25 000 and debtors decreases by £25 000. Note that, although this sum is associated with sales, there is no impact upon profit. This is because we recorded the debtors' impact upon sales earlier (the £30 000 in line C)

J This line relates to the fact that stocks costing £10 000 are left at the year end. We know (from line G) that stocks costing £25 000 were purchased. If stocks costing £10 000 are left then stocks costing £15 000 must have been sold (hopefully not stolen). Thus on the assets side stocks decreases by £15 000 with a corresponding decrease against profits on the liabilities side.

The final row shows the totals for each column. We see that, at the end of the year:

▷ There is £40 000 in the form of cash and in the bank;
▷ Debtors owe £5000;
▷ There are unsold stocks to hand which had cost £10 000;
▷ Fixed assets, having originally cost £20 000, are now valued at £15 000;
▷ £5000 is owed to trade creditors and £1000 to other creditors in respect of accrued sundry operating expenses, whilst £10 000 is still owed to the bank in respect of the bank loan;
▷ No further capital has been introduced BUT, as a result of operations, profits of £29 000 have been made. This amount is shown as capital as it is held on behalf of the owners by the organisation, owed back to them. Until such time as the owners take back some or all of the profits, the profits are retained and shown on the balance sheet as capital.

A simple accounting worksheet like this can be used to record the transactions of a very small business but proper books of account will soon be needed. Indeed, these days computer-based accounting systems such as Sage are so cheap that more and more start-ups are using them from day one. Computers are excellent at dealing with large volumes of repetitive tasks quickly and accurately. However, they often do not reduce the time taken to keep the records, rather they improve the information generated by them. Most small firms still need a book-keeper to run the computerised system. However, one option is to out-source the book-keeping function and either have a professional come in to undertake the accounting work, say one day a week, or take details of the transactions to them on a regular basis.

The worksheet in Figure 9.8 contains all the information needed to construct the financial statements. The profit statement details are contained in the profits column. These are represented in the form of a profit statement:

ACE Computers: profit statement for the year

		£000s	£000s
Sales	for cash	30	
	on account	30	60
less:			
cost of stock sold			15
Gross profit			45
less:			
operating expenses			10
depreciation		5	15
Operating profit			30
less:			
bank loan interest		1	1
Net profit			29

The profit statement is divided into sections. The first section determines the gross profit. This is the profit ACE Computers makes on buying and reselling stock. It is important as it is this gross profit figure from which other expenses are deducted. If the gross profit is low but other expenses are high a loss will result. In Jean Young's profit statement she did not have a gross profit line because she did not buy and sell goods.

For ACE the remaining expenses and charges are sundry operating expenses (£10 000), depreciation (£5000) and bank loan interest (£1000). Not all of these other items are charged in one section – the bank loan interest is kept apart from the operating expenses and the depreciation charge. By grouping these latter items together and deducting them from the gross profit we arrive at a profit figure which reflects the surplus – the operating profit – of £30 000 made on day-to-day activities. The bank loan interest is not an operations expense; rather it is a cost of financing. Although the loan interest (£1000) is deducted from the operating profit to give the net profit of £29 000, the day-to-day performance of management teams is normally related to the generation of operating profits.

Since ACE Computers is a limited company, the final net profit figure is the figure from which dividends can be paid. In their case there are no dividends so this is also the profit retained in the business. Compare this to Jean Young's profit statement. She also had net profit from which her drawings as a sole trader were deducted to arrive at the profit retained in the business. The balance sheet at the end of the first year for ACE Computers is shown below. It comes directly from the worksheet.

ACE Computers: balance sheet at end of first year

	£000s	£000s
Fixed assets		
at cost	20	
less: depreciation to date	5	15
Current assets		
cash/bank	40	
debtors	5	
stocks	10	55
less:		
Current liabilities		
creditors	(5)	
accruals	(1)	(6)
Net current assets		49
Total assets		64
less:		
creditors falling due after one year		
bank loan	(10)	(10)
Net assets		54
Represented by:		
Shareholders' funds		
share capital	25	
retained profit	29	54

This balance sheet shows the company's assets and liabilities at the year end. However, the balance sheet also reveals whether shareholders' funds have increased or decreased over the year with a resulting change in the net worth of the organisation. In this case the shareholders' funds (and so the net assets) have increased from the original investment of £25 000 to £54 000 as a result of the profit made and retained of £29 000. Notice, however, that cash increased only by £15 000 from £25 000 to £40 000. The difference is represented in the other assets shown in the balance sheet which increased by £14 000, net of liabilities.

10 Financing small firms

▷ **Money**
▷ **Bank finance**
▷ **The bank's perspective**
▷ **Banking relationships**
▷ **Venture capital institutions and business angels**
▷ **The equity investor's perspective**
▷ **Stock market floatation**
▷ **Is there a financing gap?**
▷ **Gender, ethnicity and finance**
▷ **Summary**

Case insights
▷ Martyn Dowes and Coffee Nation
▷ Peter Kelly and Softcat
▷ Andrew Barber, Robin Hall and FBS Engineering
▷ Fred Turok and LA Fitness
▷ Bob Holt and Mears Group
▷ Elizabeth Gooch and EG Solutions

Cases with questions
▷ Specsavers
▷ NDT

Learning outcomes

By the end of this chapter you will be able to:

▷ List the principles of prudent financing;

▷ Describe the sources of finance available to small firms and their appropriate uses;

▷ Explain how small firms in the UK actually are financed;

▷ Recognise the perspective of bankers in assessing lending opportunities and monitoring a firm's performance;

▷ Recognise the perspective and priorities of venture capitalists in assessing an investment opportunity;

▷ Describe the options available when floating a company;

▷ Explain what is meant by the 'financing gap' and form an opinion as to whether it really exists for small firms;

▷ Form an opinion as to whether women and ethnic minorities are discriminated against in the provision of finance.

♀ Money

The availability (or lack) of finance and its cost is often cited by owner-managers as a barrier to growth. This is not new. Back in 1931 the Macmillan Committee believed it was extremely difficult for smaller firms to obtain long-term capital in amounts of less than £200 000 (a figure probably equivalent to about £5 million today; Macmillan, 1931). Since then there has been much debate about whether a 'financing gap' really does exist. More recently the debate has been broadened to include the question of discrimination against women and ethnic minorities.

The adequate provision of finance is vital if small firms are to grow and make the most of their potential, but the topic raises paradoxes resulting from the ambiguous attitudes of owner-managers towards its provision. On the one hand, they want outside finance in order to grow but, on the other hand, they do not want to lose independence or control. At the same time they want both maximum flexibility and maximum security – objectives that are not easily reconciled – at the lowest price.

The first thing to realise is that not all money is the same. Different sorts of money ought to be used for different purposes and not all types of money are available to all small firms. In fact many owner-managers, particularly at start-up, try to avoid using money at all by borrowing or using other people's resources wherever possible. Where this fails, they might borrow money from friends or relatives. Friends and relatives can be flexible, perhaps agreeing to lend at a low or zero interest rate and without any guarantees because they know and trust the person they are lending to. They might even help with running the firm and bring valuable experience with them. However, rather than relying on informal agreements, most advisors would recommend that more formal loan agreements are drawn up so as to avoid misunderstandings and arguments later. Many owner-managers make extensive use of personal credit cards, particularly at start-up, because of the problems they face in securing other sources of finance. Inevitably, however, most firms will need to obtain some form of external finance at some point in their life.

Table 10.1 summarises the major forms of finance and how they ought to be used, in theory. The principle is that the term-duration of the source of finance should be matched to the term-duration of the use to which it is put. Fixed or permanent assets should be financed by long-term sources of finance and only working capital should be financed by short-term finance.

The owner-manager is likely to have to put some personal equity into the business, whatever its size. For a limited company this takes the form of share capital. Over time these funds grow as profits are retained in the business. The majority of

	Source of finance	Use of finance

Long-term	▷ Equity
	   – personal investment
	   – other people's money
	▷ Medium- and long-term bank loans
	▷ Leasing
	▷ Hire purchase
		Fixed or permanent assets (land, buildings, furniture, equipment, plant, vehicles and so on)

Short-term	▷ Factoring ▷ Short-term bank loans and overdraft	Working capital (debtors and stocks)

T10.1 Sources and uses of finance

Most firms use a range of financing to suit their differing needs and circumstances. The flowchart in Figure 10.1 attempts to guide the small firm through the process of deciding upon a suitable financing package. The advantages and disadvantages of these different methods of financing a business are summarised in Table 10.2.

Source	Advantages	Disadvantages
Family loans	▷ Security unlikely to be required ▷ Profit stays in the family	▷ Can strain family relationships if repayments are not made as expected ▷ If business fails, all the family suffers ▷ Family members may interfere in the business
Bank overdraft	▷ Flexible – once agreed, available on demand ▷ Cheap in that you only pay interest when you use it ▷ Good solution to short-term financing needs	▷ Repayable on demand ▷ Usually secured against business assets ▷ Can be refused because of lack of security ▷ Rate of interest charged is usually higher than loans
Bank loans	▷ Term of loan is fixed – not repayable on demand ▷ Interest and capital repayments fixed and known in advance ▷ Rate of interest usually lower than for an overdraft	▷ Usually secured against business or personal assets ▷ Can be refused because of lack of security ▷ Requires good cash flow to pay interest and meet capital repayments
Factoring/ invoice discounting	▷ Security is on debts generated by sales – as sales grow, so too does available finance ▷ Interest and charges deducted from balances paid to firm – no chance of non-payment	▷ Expensive compared to rates of interest charged on loans ▷ Certain conditions imposed, including checks on new customers
Lease/HP	▷ Security is on assets purchased	▷ Expensive compared to rates of interest charged on loans ▷ Requires adequate cash flow to meet regular payments
Equity/shares	▷ Good, secure long-term finance ▷ No interest or capital repayments	▷ Dividends may be expected ▷ Selling shares to outsiders dilutes your stake in the business and may lead to loss of control ▷ Outsiders providing equity may want to interfere in the business
Business angels (equity)	▷ Smaller amounts of equity available ▷ Investment based on business plan rather than security ▷ Investment usually made for 5 to 10 years ▷ Often offers hands-on expertise ▷ No interest or capital repayments	▷ Only really available to businesses with growth prospects ▷ A significant proportion of the profits of the business will go to the investors ▷ Dividends may be expected ▷ Investors will want to sell on their stake in the business at some point in the future to realise their profit ▷ Hands-on expertise may be seen as interference in the business
Venture capital (equity)	▷ Investment based on business plan rather than security ▷ Investment usually made for 5 to 10 years ▷ Can offer longer-term strategic advice ▷ Not normally involved in day-to-day running of business ▷ Should be able to arrange loans to go with equity investment, if required ▷ No interest or capital repayments, unless loans are part of the package	▷ Only really available to businesses with significant growth prospects ▷ A significant proportion of the profits of the business will go to the investor ▷ Dividends may be expected ▷ Investors will want to sell on their stake in the business at some point in the future to realise their profit ▷ Will require very detailed information about the company ▷ Takes time to arrange

T10.2   Advantages and disadvantages of different forms of finance

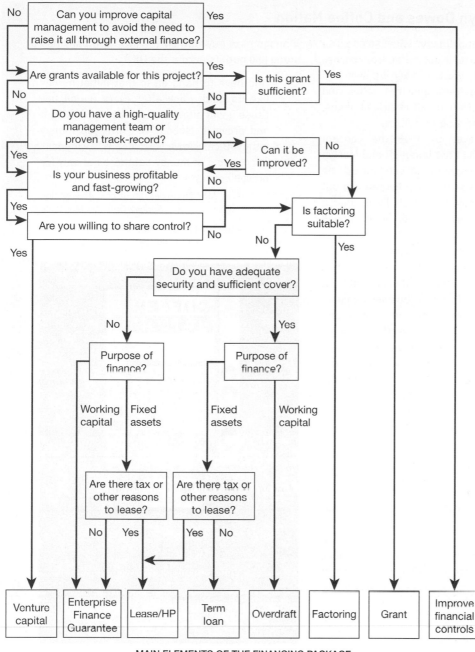

MAIN ELEMENTS OF THE FINANCING PACKAGE

F10.1 How to finance the entrepreneurial business

Source: Adapted from DTI (1997) and updated

💡 Bank finance

Bank finance is the main source of external finance for the vast majority of small firms in the UK. The 2006 membership survey by the Federation of Small Business reported that the main sources of finance were (in order): bank overdraft (49% of companies), own savings (42%), retained profit (36%), bank loans (30%) and personal credit cards (21%). The older and larger the firm, the more likely it is to use bank finance. Because of their importance, banks are a constant cause for complaint about their unwillingness to lend, high charges and poor service. The recession caused by the banking crisis of 2008/9 saw bank finance almost dry up, with the result that many small firms failed. Despite complaints, few customers actually change banks (perhaps as few as

💼 Case insight Martyn Dowes and Coffee Nation

Martyn Dowes set up Coffee Nation in 1996 with £50 000. The original idea was to sell ready-to-drink coffee from corner shops, but the idea only really worked when he switched from selling instant coffee to fresh gourmet coffee and started securing contracts from national chains of shops, garages and hotels, rather than small retailers.

However by 1998 the concept still had not taken off and Martyn was considering winding up the business because he had run out of money. Unexpectedly he met a contact from his previous job as a consultant who offered to invest £30 000 in the business. Buoyed by this, eventually he was put in touch with Great Eastern Investment Forum – a forum of business angels. He prepared a business plan and made a pitch to the forum offering members a 20 per cent equity stake in the business for £100 000 – effectively valuing the business he had previously thought of closing at £500 000. Martyn's plan was good, he was convincing and he got the money. Lloyds Bank matched the amount he raised with £90 000 in the form of a government-backed small-firm loan. Suddenly Coffee Nation was back on track.

In 2000 Martyn started looking for further expansion money, with guaranteed contracts from the Tesco and Somerfield supermarkets and the Welcome Break hotel chain. He found a firm of accountants to help him put together a further business plan and, after extended negotiations, secured £4 million from Primary Capital as part of a management buy-out to roll out the business. On the back of this and with the track record of meeting every target set by Primary Capital, Martyn's next approach was to the banks, eventually securing additional loan capital.

In 2008 Primary Capital sold the business to Milestone Capital and Coffee Nation's management in a secondary management buy-out. By then the company had some 550 outlets across the UK.

'You have to hang on to that initial money like its gold. Look after every pound because it will allow you to get your idea right and prove it. Nobody will give you money until you can prove your idea is a winner ... There's lots of money out there but only for proven concepts.'

Martyn Dowes, founder Coffee Nation
Sunday Times 23 May 2004

☐ Up-to-date information on Coffee Nation can be found on their website: www.coffeenation.com

5 per cent each year), although this might be because they do not perceive another bank as being any better than the one they are with or because of the high switch costs associated with changing banks. All of which begs the question of the degree of competition between banks in the UK.

However, banks face significant problems in lending to small firms. Banks lend a sum of money in return for agreed interest payments and the repayment of the sum borrowed. They do not share in the profits of a highly successful firm. And if a firm fails, the bad debt is expensive to recoup. So, if banks make a 4 per cent margin on a loan (the difference between the rate they can borrow at and the rate they can lend at), then every £100 lost as a bad debt will need a further £2500 to be lent for the margin to cover it (100/0.04). Put another way, the bank has to make a further 25 loans to cover this one bad debt. Not surprisingly, therefore, bankers are risk averse and will do all they can to avoid a bad debt. What is more, they are all too aware of the failure statistics for business start-ups, which explains why it is often difficult to obtain start-up finance.

Even existing firms seem a risky lending proposition to a banker looking for security against their loan. Table 10.3 shows the aggregate balance sheet structure of small and large companies in the UK. A comparison of the two would lead you to conclude that small firms, compared to large firms:

1 Overinvest in debtors and stock;
2 Underinvest in fixed assets;
3 Are over-reliant on creditor finance – money that is probably due for payment in the very near future;
4 Are over-reliant on short-term, particularly overdraft, finance;
5 Have insufficient capital and reserves and are undercapitalised.

As a banker you would see the small firms as the riskier lending proposition – higher, mainly short-term, gearing (particularly if creditors are taken into account) and fewer fixed assets to offer you security in the event of a bad debt. What is more, there is evidence of wide variability in gearing. Putting this in a European context, one survey in 1995 found that 56 per cent of small firms in Britain, France, Germany, Spain and Italy (52 per cent in Britain) had gearing levels of 50 per cent or less (gearing defined here as all loans divided by shareholders' funds) but 21 per cent had levels over 100 per cent (21 per cent also in Britain) (Bank of England, 1998). This had changed little since a previous survey in 1992 (Burns, 1992). Gearing levels tended to be lowest in Germany and highest in Spain, with Britain about average, although Britain was notable for its heavy reliance on overdraft finance – 42 per cent of debt compared to 17 per cent in Germany. It was this heavy reliance on overdraft finance that caused so many small firms to have problems in the recession that started in 2008, when banks called in these overdrafts.

However, banks do not just lend on the strength of the balance sheet. They are interested in the general prospects of the business they are lending to, and here the issue of information asymmetry – one party having better information than the other – arises. Where asymmetric information favours the small firm – the owner-manager

	Small companies	Large companies
Fixed assets	32	57
Stock	20	14
Debtors	39	19
Cash	9	10
	100	100
Overdraft	13	8
Creditors	47	24
Long-term loans	9	15
Shares and reserves	31	53
	100	100

Source: *Business Monitor MA3 Company Finance*, various issues, and Burns (1985)

T10.3 Balance sheet structures – small and large companies

having more or better information than the bank – the bank is likely to be more wary about lending because of greater uncertainty. This is less of a problem with larger firms because there is so much more public information about them and many independent analysts reviewing them for investment purposes. For owner-managers it means that they have an uphill task convincing the bank manager of the viability of their project. It underlines the importance of effective communication. For the bank, it means that they are likely to incur extra costs in getting the information they need to make and then monitor a loan, and it is worth noting that these costs do not rise or fall pro rata with the size of the loan. This is one reason why banks so often ask for collateral against a loan. Where sufficient collateral can be made available, the bank may feel that less information is required because the debt is more likely to be recovered in the event of default. What is more, bankers may also feel that the provision of collateral gives the owner-manager a strong incentive to see the business succeed. If the firm's balance sheet cannot provide it, the owner-manager may be asked to guarantee the loan, secured on their personal assets.

Interestingly, it has been argued that information asymmetry (unequal possession of information by the parties) favours the bank for a start-up (Jovanovic, 1982). The bank manager may have a broader experience on which to base a judgement of whether or not a start-up will succeed than the owner-manager, who will probably learn mainly from the experience of trading. It is only by surviving that successful owner-managers distinguish themselves from the less successful ones.

One of the things that banks do to deal with the problem of information asymmetry is to create a portfolio of loans, combining a spectrum of different risk–return lendings across all the sectors of industry. The portfolio will always have firms that will fail but they will be more than balanced by those that survive and the risks the portfolio faces reflect those facing the whole economy.

The natural response of banks to the problem of information asymmetry is likely to be to charge higher rates of interest and to ask for collateral. However, it can be shown that charging higher rates of interest may not be to a bank's advantage because this discourages low-return but low-risk businesses (Stiglitz and Weiss, 1981). High-return but high-risk firms may continue to borrow but the banks do not share in their success – only their failure. The rational response to information asymmetry should therefore be to ration credit in some way rather than to raise interest rates., Indeed, whilst small firms typically do pay higher interest rates than larger firms, the

Asset	% value that can be borrowed	
Freehold land and buildings	70	
Long leasehold	60	
Specialist plant and machinery	5–10	100% can be obtained by leasing but APR may be more
Non-specialist plant and machinery	30	100% can be obtained by leasing but APR may be more
Debtors	30–50	Depends on age and quality
Stock	25	Depends on age and quality and the significance of any retention of title clauses. Raw materials will be worth more than part processed stock.

Source: DTI (1997) Financing Your Business: A Guide to Sources of Finance and Advice

T10.4 Asset security values

difference is usually only a couple of points. If credit rationing is indeed taking place, then it leads to the question whether some borrowers are being excluded from access to credit, even though they might be willing to pay higher rates of interest. It therefore raises the question once more of the existence of a financing gap for riskier, growing firms.

In valuing collateral the bank assumes that the assets will be sold on a second-hand market and this typically leads to far lower values being put on assets than many owner-managers would expect. Table 10.4 gives a guide to what to expect. Given these asset security values, it is clear that growing firms wishing to purchase new plant and equipment will have to spend more than the assets add to their collateral base. Because the business collateral base is insufficient for their needs they may well turn to lease, hire purchase and factoring as ways of financing their growth and, if all else fails, the owner-manager may have to provide personal guarantees, perhaps using their house as collateral. However, this once more raises the question of debt gaps, particularly for growing firms, as it has been argued that a heavy reliance on collateral, particularly personal collateral, may effectively create such a gap because of the resultant erosion of limited liability status (Binks et al., 1990). Many owner-managers observe that this frequent requirement to give personal guarantees means that the separation between a limited liability company and their own finances is little more than theoretical.

One solution to this problem, widely used in Europe but little seen in the UK, is the mutual guarantee scheme. Hughes (1992) points to their extensive use in Europe in 'pooling their private information about project riskiness and entrepreneurial quality, and developing mutual schemes to guarantee individual loan applications to banks by members of the group, after group screening based upon pooled information'. The problem is that, whilst individuals may benefit by easier access to finance and lower rates of interest, they also face the possibility of having to make good the bad debts of others in the mutual guarantee scheme.

📁 Case insight Peter Kelly and Softcat

Peter Kelly never finished his degree, instead he travelled the world before returning to the UK. He worked for Rank Xerox in Sales and Training for 7 years before starting Software Catalogue, a mail-order software business, in 1993. This became Softcat Limited and is now based in Marlow, UK. Peter is still Chairman. Softcat employs over 200 people and has a turnover in excess of £100 million It has become a leading supplier of software licensing, hardware, security solutions and related IT services to companies.

Success brought unexpected problems early in Softcat's life. Initially Peter drew up a business plan, put in £35000 of his own money and found two external investors willing to each put in a further £10000. The mail-order software market was virtually untapped at the time and it was the firm's success that caused the problem. Within a year it had run out of cash and had reached the end of its ever-increasing overdraft limit as debtors were increasing at an alarming rate. The firm was overtrading – the classic example of success causing Death Valley to go on and on. Peter's response was to factor his debts – relying on the one asset in his balance sheet for security. It might have been more expensive than overdraft finance, but it helped the company to survive, grow and become the success it is today.

□ Up-to-date information on Softcat can be found on their website: www.softcat.com

💡 The bank's perspective

Banks are in business to make as much money as possible with the least risk. Above all they want to avoid bad debts; they do not share in the profits of a successful firm, so they do not want to share in the risks. Notwithstanding this, in the UK 89 per cent of small business loan applications are successful (Fraser, 2005). Bank managers are employees, they work in a highly regulated environment, and they have limited, and probably declining, discretion. Two high-street banks use a computer-based expert system which produces a lending recommendation for existing firms based upon

is evidence that the closer the relationship, the greater the owner-manager's perception of the quality of banking service and the less likely they are to want to change banks (Binks and Ennew, 1996). It would therefore appear that working to improve the banking relationship benefits both sides. In recent years the banks have invested enormous amounts in training managers about both the problems facing small firms and how to analyse them, and also about how to approach the issue of developing relationships. There are grounds for believing that a better relationship would prevail if owner-managers showed a greater willingness to participate in it (Hughes, 1992).

Venture capital institutions and business angels

Venture capital institutions provide equity and loan finance to businesses with substantial growth potential. Typically they invest larger amounts – over £2 million and expect to see a significant return within three years. About half of all investments goes to help established companies expand and about a third goes into management buy-outs (the management of a firm buying it) or buy-ins (external managers buying a firm and normally replacing the management).

Venture capitalists provide risk finance and the annualised rate of return they expect on their investment is high – from 30 per cent to 60 per cent, depending on the risk involved (Murray and Lott, 1995). They are therefore looking primarily for high-growth firms to invest in. They reject some 95 per cent of the approximately 5000 applications made to them each year (Bannock, 1991; Dixon, 1991). The financing structure they put together varies from deal to deal. Usually they do not want to take control of the business away from the entrepreneur initially, so the deal involves a mixture of equity (less than a 50 per cent stake), preference shares and loans. However, many studies have found that founders are replaced post venture capital funding. For example a UK study found that 32 per cent of founders were replaced when the business moved into the initial commercialisation phase (Cressy and Hall, 2006).

Preference shares are normally non-voting, allowing the venture capitalist to take equity without taking control of the business. They give a preferential claim to the profits and assets of the business over ordinary shareholders. The dividend on them is limited to a fixed percentage of the face value and there is no right to a dividend if the directors do not declare one, but they always have priority over ordinary shareholders if dividends are paid. Most preference shares are 'cumulative' which means that unpaid dividends must be accumulated and made good before ordinary shareholders are paid. They also have preference over ordinary shareholders in the event of liquidation. Some preference shares are 'redeemable', normally at their face value at some specified future date. Others are 'convertible' into ordinary shares, normally at the shareholder's option. A 'convertible preferred ordinary share' is a hybrid form of share capital much loved by some venture capitalists. They carry the right to either fixed or variable dividends and allow the company to pay dividends on them without obliging ordinary shareholders to take a dividend which might, for tax reasons, be unattractive. When converted into ordinary shares, the right to these fixed dividends is lost and the shares become 'ordinary'.

Start-up investments by venture capitalists usually involve an investment in excess of £100 000 in a business capable of generating profits in excess of £250 000 within four or five years. The BVCA produces a free annual Directory of Members, which gives a full list of venture capital institutions and their investment criteria. It has also produced a very useful *Guide to Private Equity* (2004) which explains and offers advice on the venture capital raising process and outlines what should be included in a business plan intended for venture capitalists.

Smaller amounts of equity, between about £10 000 and £250 000, are also available from individual investors – called 'business angels' – either on their own or as part of an informal syndicate. These have been popularised in the BBC series called *Dragons' Den*, with one of the Dragons, Duncan Bannatyne, featuring as a serial entrepreneur in this book. Often this investment helps take the investee business to a point at which it is attractive for a venture capital firm. The typical UK business angel makes only one or two investments a year. Many are former entrepreneurs. Many have preferences about sectors or stages (seed, start-up, early stage, expansion, management buy-out or buy-in) of investment based on their personal knowledge. Most prefer local investments, in companies within, say, 100 miles from where they live or work. Most also prefer to stay anonymous. However, over the past few years a number of business angel networks have been established which act as 'introduction services'. Some of the networks can also provide help in raising finance from other sources and in preparing a business plan for a fee. Many business angels belong to the British Business Angel Association. It has a code of conduct for its members and a directory of members is available on its website. Local business angels can also be contacted through the local Business Link or Enterprise Agency, who also have their own Local Investment Network Company (LINC) that seeks to match small firms seeking funds with potential investors. Investors receive a monthly bulletin of opportunities available, submitted to LINC as business plans from small firms seeking finance. LINC Scotland is the national association for business angels in Scotland.

Venture capital is a cyclical business. In the UK, the 1980s saw recession followed by several years of increased economic growth, only to be replaced by recession at the start of the 1990s. The increasing economic growth of the late 1990s led to massive investment in technology, and in particular dot.com businesses, only to be followed by a shake-out in 2000. Specialist venture capitalist networks have also evolved for sectors such as high technology. Big players have consolidated their position. Elsewhere there has been increased competition for the good investments that are available. All this came to an abrupt end when the recession, caused by the banking crisis of 2008/9, saw the virtual drying up of venture capital markets. Despite this we can say that provision has tended to grow more rapidly than the UK economy over the last two decades.

📖 Case insight Andrew Barber, Robin Hall and FBS Engineering

Andrew Barber and Robin Hall left Rover, where they were design engineers, to set up their own company producing a specialist sports car – but only after they had taken the advice of their local Business Link. Originally they thought the car would sell to a mass market at a competitive price, but advisors convinced them to pitch it to a specialist market niche and charge £30 000 for the vehicle. In this case lower volume also meant higher price and lower capital needs. Business Link also advised them on where to get finance – the pair did not even have equity in their houses to offer a bank – and helped them develop and present a business plan. The company, called FBS Engineering, secured £240 000 from a business angel which it invested in premises in Brackley, Northamptonshire and tooling for its first car, called Census.

But nothing in business is certain and getting start-up funding is just the start of the real work. It took the company two-and-a-half years to build just eleven vehicles – three prototypes and eight customer vehicles (which were all sold). However, by that time the cash had run out. The company went into administrative receivership in August 2003.

Case with questions Specsavers

Specsavers was founded in 1984 by Doug and Mary Perkins. They started the business in their spare bedroom in Guernsey and opened their first stores in Guernsey and Bristol, followed rapidly by stores in Plymouth, Swansea and Bath. The couple had moved to Guernsey after selling a small chain of West Country opticians. In the early 1980s the UK Government deregulated professional services, including opticians, allowing them to advertise for the first time. Doug and Mary seized the opportunity to try to launch a national chain of opticians. They wanted the company to establish its brand so that it would be seen as offering a wide range of stylish, fashionable glasses at affordable prices. They wanted Specsavers to be seen as trustworthy, locally based but with the huge buying power of a national company that meant savings could be passed on to the customer. Specsavers is now the largest privately owned opticians in the world and, as well as being seen on every UK high street, has expanded overseas.

Specsavers has used an interesting joint venture approach to grow its business. It enters into joint ventures with individual opticians, meaning that each joint venture is a separate legal entity. When the new company is formed, an equal number of 'A' shares and 'B' shares are issued. All the 'A' shares in the company are issued to the practice partners. All the 'B' shares are issued to Specsavers Optical Group. If there is more than one director in the business, for example an optometrist and a dispensing optician or retailer, then the 'A' shares are divided between the two parties. 'A' shareholders are delegated responsibility for the day-to-day running of the store. As 'B' shareholder, Specsavers provides supporting services, expertise, experience and information. As the number of practices has grown, so has the range of support services provided to practices, so that partners receive full support in all aspects of their business, tailored to their requirements. These can include property services, practice design, practice start-up, buying and distribution, retail training, professional recruitment as well as support in producing accounts, audits and tax returns. Individual opticians can sell on their 'A' shares, subject to certain conditions.

A typical joint venture start-up may cost in excess of £150 000, depending on location and practice size. In an equal partnership between two optician partners, each would be expected to provide the business with a loan of at least £20 000. Specsavers will match this loan. Specsavers Finance will provide a further 5-year loan for the remainder of the capital. Personal collateral is not required by Specsavers Finance to secure this loan. Specsavers and the partners sign a specific finance agreement. Loans are repaid from practice profits, sometimes within three years.

Specsavers claim the following advantages to this joint venture approach:

▷ A lower level of financial commitment from the opticians than a franchise;
▷ If targets are met the initial loan can be repaid from operating surpluses;
▷ Unlike a brand partnership, a joint venture partnership gives the partner the possibility of selling their shares in the future;
▷ The partner can end the relationship when they want.

☐ Up-to-date information on Specsavers can be found on their website: www.specsavers.co.uk

QUESTIONS

1 What are the advantages to both Specsavers and partners of this form of joint venture?

2 How is this different to a franchise?

The equity investor's perspective

Whilst venture capital institutions and business angels may look at the same range of criteria as a banker, their perspective is very different since, unlike the banker, they are sharing in the risk of the business. If it fails, they stand to lose everything. Consequently they are interested in risk and return. In particular, they are interested in the return they will make on their investment rather than the security they can obtain from the entrepreneur. Because of this, the business plan is far more important to them and they pay far greater attention to the quality of management and experience of the entrepreneur and management team. When looking at the business plan they will apply the full range of performance criteria and profitability ratios outlined in the next chapter to both past and projected future performance. In assessing risk the margin of safety is particularly important, but so too is a detailed assessment of the business risks. They will also want to be assured that they can sell on their investment at some time in the future and realise their profit. We shall expand on the venture banker's and venture capitalist's different perspectives on a business plan in Chapter 14.

Most venture capital institutions will want to appoint a non-executive director to the board. Some, particularly business angels, may also expect a more a 'hands-on', day-to-day involvement in the business. However, others take a far more 'hands-off' approach and will only intervene in the management of the firm in exceptional circumstances. This is because they take a portfolio approach to their investments, diversifying the risks they face across industries and sectors. The role of the venture capitalist has been described as (Sapienza and Timmons, 1989):

▷ Offering support;
▷ Providing a strategic overview;
▷ Providing access to a larger network of business contacts.

As with bank managers, it is important to develop a close personal relationship with a venture capitalist – particularly a business angel. Ultimately they invest in people rather than businesses and, since they face more risk than the banker, they need to be convinced that the entrepreneur and the management team can make the business plan actually happen. Since they only make money if the firm succeeds, they are highly committed to helping the growing firm through the inevitable problems it will face. Many have valuable business experience, sometimes in the same business sector, and they can bring with them a wealth of business contacts. In short, used properly they can be a real asset to the firm.

Stock market floatation

Venture capitalists may expect high returns but they realise that their main reward will come in the form of a capital gain, rather than dividend or interest payments. Consequently they normally seek to realise their investment within 10 years. Often this means going for a public listing on a stock exchange – called a stock market floatation. A stock market floatation involves selling a percentage of the business in the form of shares on one of the stock markets. To do so requires a track record of solid profitability and good growth potential. Different criteria are required for each stock market which means that this form of finance is unlikely to be suitable for most businesses – a trade sale is far easier and cheaper. A floatation can be expensive and may mean a loss of management control. It certainly means that the business will then have to comply with a whole range of new regulations and disclosure requirements designed to make trading in their shares fairer – and this in itself has led some entrepreneurs to 'delist' their companies by buying back their shares.

There are three stock markets in the UK on which a business can be floated: the OFEX market, the Alternative Investment Market (AIM) or a full listing on the Stock

📁 Case insight Fred Turok and LA Fitness

Fred Turok was born in Cape Town, South Africa, in 1955. His father was a white African National Congress activist who was twice imprisoned by the apartheid regime and forced to flee to Britain. Fred's time at school was troubled. He was dyslexic – a characteristic shared with Richard Branson – and was shunted around different schools. Whilst he was branded as stupid, his two brothers were very bright and both went on to become professors. Fred retreated into sport. He became a PE teacher in London, but that did not work out so he took a job at a David Lloyd centre as a swimming coach. David Lloyd saw the potential in Fred and made him a manager. It was here that he learnt about the fitness business.

Fred decided there was a gap in the market for a smaller club, so in 1990 he remortgaged his house to buy a loss-making private gym in a basement in Victoria in London's West End for £150 000. In the first year he turned a £30 000 loss into a £150 000 profit. Two years later he bought his second club in Kingston-upon-Thames and then a third in the Minories on the fringes of the City. The fourth club that he bought in Isleworth in 1996 gave him the name for his business – LA Fitness. He paid for that in cash, but it used up every penny he had. So far all the acquisitions had been paid for by cash flow or borrowings but the business was doing very well and the fifth gym, a new-build in Golders Green, was also funded from cash flow.

At this point Fred saw an opportunity to raise some money for growth by going to the stock market but the £3 million float (valuing the firm at £8 million) was only 50 per cent subscribed because a similar firm, Fitness First, floated just two weeks before it. Fred pulled the float and instead went to the venture capitalists 3i who put in £1.5 million in exchange for 30 per cent of the

equity. After this he just kept building the chain. By the time LA Fitness had secured a Main Listing on the stock market in October 1999, 3i had put in another £1.5 million, enabling the firm to grow to 15 clubs. The float valued LA Fitness at £55 million, including £15 million of new money. In 2000 the firm made a £10 million rights issue with a view to increasing the number of clubs even further. It also secured new bank facilities of £15 million with a further £25 million promised. By 2005 LA Fitness had 67 clubs with over 200 000 members and 3500 employees. Fred Turok had become a paper millionaire, worth over £20 million.

In May 2005 it was announced that the company would exit the London stock market and return to being a private company through its sale to MidOcean Partners, a private equity fund, and top management – including Fred Turok. The deal was worth £90 million (£141 million including debt) and Fred is estimated to have made £14 million on it. Since then LA Fitness has continued to grow, buying the Dragon chain of gyms. It now has more than 88 clubs and over a quarter of a million members all over the UK. Fred's formula remains the same today as in the 1990s – medium-sized club, always with a gym and pool, costing about £37 a month to join.

> 'Yes I have banked the money but I also have a percentage of the institutional investment in LA Fitness which invests pari passu with MidOcean. My equity component is realised only on the success of the business, which is typically how venture capital works.'
>
> *Sunday Times* 21 August 2005

☐ Up-to-date information on LA Fitness can be found on their website: www.lafitness.co.uk

Exchange Main Market. OFEX is aimed at smaller companies seeking to raise up to £10 million. It is the most 'junior' of the markets and, whilst it is regulated, the regulations are not as stringent as AIM or the main market. Costs are also lower but the pool of investors is limited and it is seen mainly as a vehicle for private investors rather than the public.

AIM was launched in 1995 by the London Stock Exchange with the aim of giving smaller firms access to the stock market without imposing on them the rigorous reporting and control requirements demanded for a listing on the Main Market. An increasing number of companies seek a floatation on AIM with one survey claiming that it was the most popular market for those considering floatation, with the main market suffering a significant drop in popularity (HLB Kidson, 2000). To obtain a listing a firm simply needs to be incorporated and have a broker and nominated advisor who must be available at all times. Typically it takes at least six months to obtain a listing. Brokers ideally want two non-executive directors on the board to ensure a system of checks and balances. They also want some evidence of a track record that can assure them of good corporate governance. They are looking for quality of earnings – assurance that earnings will continue in the future with some degree of predictability – and prefer firms that offer some unique selling proposition rather than 'me too' companies.

The costs of an AIM floatation vary widely. However, with lawyers', accountants' and brokers' fees plus commission, together with the AIM joining fee and annual charge, firms with a valuation below £1 million are likely to find membership costs prohibitive. The disadvantage of membership is the exposure to greater outside scrutiny and the dilution of control and decision-making. Any owner-manager looking for an AIM quotation simply as a badge of success must realise that there is a high price to pay for it.

The two key reasons for floating on AIM were cited in the survey as raising funds for growth and giving investors and the entrepreneur the opportunity to release personal equity. This underlines the fact that AIM – and OFEX – can also act as the first stage in the exit route that an entrepreneur may put in place to harvest the return from their years of personal investment in their business. OFEX and AIM are also the first steps on the route to a listing on the Main Market and by the time that happens the firm probably will have become large by any criteria.

> ## 🗂 Case insight Bob Holt and Mears Group
>
> Mears Group started life as a small, private building contractor in 1988. It is now a leading UK PLC. In 1992 Mears was awarded its first multidisciplinary maintenance and repairs contract from a local authority. Since then it has grown to become the leading social housing repairs and maintenance provider in the UK. In 1996, with a turnover of £12 million and 83 employees, its Chairman and Chief Executive Bob Holt floated the company on AIM, raising £950 000 with a market capitalisation of £3.6 million. Over the following years it grew partly through organic growth and partly through acquisition, moving into the domiciliary care market. In 2008 it moved to the Main Market of the London Stock Exchange, with a turnover of £420 million and over 8000 employees. In 2009 Mears Group won the PLC Award for New Company of the Year on the LSE Main Market. Mears is listed on the FTSE4Good Index in recognition of its Community and Social Responsibility activity.
>
> ☐ Up-to-date information on Mears Group can be found on their website: www.mearsgroup.co.uk

💡 Is there a financing gap?

Notwithstanding the recession caused by the banking crisis of 2008/09, the question remains as to whether there is a long-term financing gap for small firms – defined as an unwillingness on the part of suppliers of finance to supply it on terms and conditions that owner-managers need. Owner-managers who are unsuccessful in obtaining finance will always say there is. Survey after survey of owner-managers will reveal this to be a major 'barrier to growth'. However, just because the owner-manager might want finance – on specific terms – does not necessarily mean that it should be provided – either for the good of the owner-manager, the financier or the economy as a whole.

Economists would criticise the use of the word 'gap' and prefer to use the term 'market failure' or 'credit rationing' because there may be a 'gap' even in a perfect market simply because, for example, an owner-manager is unwilling to pay higher rates of interest or investors judge a project to be too risky. The preceding analysis has shown that 'gaps' can easily arise, largely as a result of information asymmetry, the fixed costs of providing small amounts of capital, in terms of assessing the project and monitoring the investment, and the requirement of bankers for small firms or owner-managers to provide collateral. Also there is the inherent reluctance of the owner-manager to share equity in their business. The question is, however, whether there is evidence that the gap actually exists.

💡 Gender, ethnicity and finance

In Chapter 2 we raised the issue of why women are less likely to start up a business than men and why women-owned businesses are likely to perform less well than male-owned businesses. The answer seems to lie in the capital women-owners bring to their start-up business. This capital takes three forms: *financial capital, human capital* – such as previous managerial or sectoral experience and training – and *social capital* – derived from access to appropriate professional networks. Human and social capital are linked to the performance of an entrepreneurial business, just as much as financial capital (Firkin, 2003), and research indicates that women-owned businesses are under-capitalised in all three areas (Brush, 1992; Bodden and Nucci, 2000).

For many people, self-employment reflects experiences from prior employment which give them both social capital – experiences and networks – and economic capital – savings. In the workplace women face a range of barriers in gaining these resources because of their gender. People talk about a 'glass ceiling' for promotion. Women are likely to be less well paid, even for doing the same job as men. They therefore have less savings than men and present less collateral for bank loans. This translates into less financial capital being available to invest in the business. This can constrain both the scale of the start-up and the sectors that they might set up in. What is more, the sectors in which women work are more likely to be low-pay, low-skill sectors which may constrain their entrepreneurial vision. Women also tend to have lower status positions in the workplace, often with lower skills, than men. This constrains the networks within which they operate. All this can leave women with less human and social capital to put into their business than men. And the combination of all these factors in turn can translate into women setting up businesses in low-profit, poorly-performing segments of the service sector, which struggle to survive or grow.

I don't think there is any lack of talent among female entrepreneurs, quite the opposite, it's just that they often have a different mentality to men. In my view, women are inclined by nature to be nest-builders so, when they have constructed a successful business from scratch, in general they remain faithful to the business rather than sell up and move on. It would be great to see more women found and run fast-growth businesses that turn into large companies but it's easier to do that when you have several bites at the cherry. I have no problem with loyalty to one company. Commitment and dedication are invaluable in the business world and women who display those qualities get nothing but admiration and respect from me. A prime example was Dame Anita Roddick, a fantastic entrepreneur who built up a successful business empire (Body Shop) spanning more than 2,000 shops in 53 countries. Men tend to be less emotionally attached and are therefore happy to move on and look for the next project. Hence, they are more likely to be serial entrepreneurs.

☐ Duncan Bannatyne, serial entrepreneur and Dragon
Daily Telegraph 17 June 2009

> Overall, the manner in which women are segregated and subordinated in waged labour underpins their position in self-employment. Issues such as sectoral concentration, credibility gaps, access to finance and networks, and hence firm performance, are directly related to their subordination within prevailing gender systems and then reinforced by their positioning in waged and domestic labour.
>
> Carter and Marlow, 2003

But this is not the natural order. Research has also shown that, given the same starting capital, women- and men-owned businesses perform equally well (Watson, 2002; Johnsen and McMahon, 2005). So, many scholars argue that women are 'disadvantaged' by this lack of financial, human and social capital and should therefore have special training and development, even financing resources, focused upon them. In the UK, organisations like PROWESS (Promoting Women's Enterprise Support (www.prowess.org.uk)) recognise these issues and have put in place a wide range of support structures.

The issue of networks is an interesting one since different types of networks generate different types of information and relationships. Like males, women tend to have networks based on work, family and social ties. However, research shows that women are more likely to have both women and men in their networks but men are more likely to have just men in theirs (Aldrich, 1989). Women are also likely to have fewer entrepreneurs in their networks (Allen, 2000). These are interesting if inconclusive findings since all these networks might generate entrepreneurial information, albeit from a different source. It is more likely that the issue about networks has more to do with the nature and 'level' in the hierarchy of the contacts they generate.

Women-owned businesses, then, tend to attract less outside funding than male-owned businesses. Studies have repeatedly found that women-owned businesses start with significantly less financial capital (typically only one-third) than men-owned start-ups (Hisrich and Brush, 1984; Carter and Rosa, 1998; Coleman, 2000). They are also more likely to rely on personal savings, however limited, and are rarely given access to venture funding (Green et al., 2000; Marlow and Patton, 2003). The question of whether there is active discrimination against women in the provision of finance or the existence of a supply-side finance gap therefore needs to be addressed. Firstly, research has reported no differences in bank loan rejection rates by gender (in the UK: Fraser, 2006; in the USA: Treichel and Scott, 2006; in Australia: Watson et al., 2009). It has also failed to unearth evidence of a supply-side finance gap for women (in the UK: Fraser, 2006; in the USA: Levenson and Willard, 2000; in Australia: Watson et al., 2009). Indeed Watson et al. (op. cit.) concluded that they could find no evidence of actual discrimination by financial institutions and suggested that other demand-side factors were at play. Although not conclusive, other researchers broadly concur, which takes us back to deficiencies in human and social capital.

Lack of confidence is one of the factors cited as influencing women's willingness to approach banks for finance. It is also cited as influencing the low rates of female entrepreneurship (Morris et. al., 2006). Another factor influencing growth is that women entrepreneurs start up their businesses for different reasons to men. According to the ISBE Enterprise Matters, Women's Enterprise Dataset (2009), 21 per cent do so because of 'family commitments' compared to only 2 per cent of men. The influence of family on female entrepreneurship is, however, complex and more likely to be negative for both men and women. For example, Morris et al. (op. cit.) suggest that many women deliberately keep the size of their business small so as to balance their family and business priorities. Indeed more women than men use the home as a base for their business. What is more, many women set up businesses whilst continuing with other occupations, almost as a side-line. About one in five are pushed into self-employment through unemployment, compared to one in fifteen for men. This UK database quotes an average first-year turnover for a female start-up as £150 000, compared to £360 000 for a male start-up.

> *I want to be a mother but also successful, so there has to be some kind of balance. There are times that I have realised I have not spent enough time with my husband or children all weekend because I have been doing business related things … There are more opportunities to start a business from home; something that suits women who are juggling careers and parenthood … I think women have the ability to be multi-skilled – ironing and being on the phone at the same time – which gives them an advantage in balancing work and life.*
>
> ☐ Ruth Coe, founder of Bespoke Beauty. Startups; www.startups.co.uk

Finally, women's conception of firm performance and their approach to success appear to be different from men's (Marlow, 1997; Cliff, 1998; Ahl, 2006; Shaw et. al., 2009). They appear more risk averse, striving for a more controllable and manageable rate of growth (Cliff op. cit.). Shaw et. al. (op. cit.) highlighted that performance might be indicated by 'personal development and a sense of independence rather than numbers of employees and turnover'. More broadly these reflect differences in personal motivations and goals, but existing research does not seem to have developed a clear understanding of what these are. They might also reflect the influences of the family and culture within which entrepreneurial ambitions are nurtured. Gender–power relationships within families continue to exist and changes in family composition and the roles of family members over time have been shown to influence opportunity recognition, the decision to set up a venture and access to finance (Aldrich and Cliff, 2003). In a more recent UK survey it was concluded that families do indeed influence the growth of businesses run by women entrepreneurs – both positively and negatively, depending on the family situation (Roomi et al., 2009).

Shaw et. al. went on to observe that their conclusion regarding how women conceive of performance 'is supported by the feminist analyses of entrepreneurship which argue that the entrepreneurship scholars' neutralisation of gender has created a discourse which reflects male experiences while ignoring female experiences', and they argue that the different contribution that women entrepreneurs make to society is not fully appreciated.

In a large-scale survey of high-growth women-owned businesses Gundry and Welsch (2001) found that these women did indeed have a different approach to management. They had a more structured approach to organising their business suggesting a more disciplined approach to management. They characterised these

🗁 Case insight Elizabeth Gooch and EG Solutions

Elizabeth Gooch was named as the seventh leading female entrepreneur in the UK by *Management Today* in 2006.

About a quarter of the Top 100 Entrepreneurs list are female. Elizabeth is founder and CEO of EG Solutions. Here are her thoughts on being a female entrepreneur in the financial services sector.

'Initially, when I was first starting the business and approaching the big five banks for a corporate bank account, it was quite challenging. Their response to me becoming a consultant for improving financial services was to pat me on the head like a dog, saying 'there, there, little girl'.

Overall I've found that being a woman in the financial services sector has actually helped me greatly. If a man is trying to give improvement advice to another man there's often potential for conflict, whereas if you're a woman putting that advice across it can be done in a style that's a bit more acceptable or perhaps more cheeky.

That approach has stood me in good stead because I am still to this day one of the very few women at this level of the financial services industry. That's not really changed at all over the last 18 years in the City, so I'm quite a novelty in many respects and I use that to my advantage as best I can.'

Venture online 12 April 2007
(www.venturemagazine.co.uk)

☐ Up-to-date information on EG can be found on their website: www.eguk.co.uk

high-growth women entrepreneurs as having the following distinctions: 'strategic intentions that emphasise market growth and technological change, stronger commitment to the success of the business, greater willingness to sacrifice on behalf of the business, earlier planning for the growth of the business, utilisation of a team-based form of organisation design, concern for reputation and quality, adequate capitalization, strong leadership, and utilisation of a wider range of financing sources for the expansion of the venture.' All these are admirable qualities which are often missing in entrepreneurs of either sex. Perhaps it is time to move on from researching *whether* gender shapes entrepreneurship but rather focus on *how* it does so and why.

Turning to ethnic minority businesses, these appear no different from white businesses in their dependence on bank finance, although this is significantly less for black African and black Caribbean business (Bank of England, 1999). Specialist banks have grown up to cater for the needs of different ethnic groups; for example, specialist Islamic banks which allow Muslim businesses to bank according to their principles and faith. There is also evidence of a strong preference for informal sources of finance (Ram et. al., 2002). This study found the reliance on informal finance was most significant in South Asian-owned businesses. These informal sources are usually accessed from a wide network of family, friends and others within the ethnic community, thus combining social with financial capital. Many of these sources are not available to white entrepreneurs.

Nevertheless, as with female entrepreneurs, there is a strong feeling of prejudice from traditional banks. However, the Bank of England (1999) could find no evidence of this, citing sectoral concentration, failure rates and lack of business planning for rejection rates. A large-scale study of ethnic minority business and their access to finance broadly supported this (Ram et al., op. cit.) noting, however, that the issue was 'complex'. It did find evidence of diversity of experience from bank manager to bank manager and between different ethnic minority groups, confirming the existence of particular problems for Africans and Caribbeans. Not surprisingly, it found that best practice was where the bank manager had built up trust with their local minority community through close contact and stable relationships. More recently, Fraser (2009) used econometric analysis on a large-scale survey of UK small business finance to look for evidence of ethnic discrimination (loan denials, interest rates and discouragement). He concluded firstly that there were large differences across ethnic groups – black and Bangladeshi businesses experiencing poor outcomes compared to white and Indian businesses. For example, from the finance provider's perspective, black African firms were significantly more likely to miss loan repayments or exceed their agreed overdraft limit. He also noted that many from the ethnic minorities felt they were discriminated against. However, he concluded very firmly that there was no evidence of discrimination. He felt that many in these groups needed to tackle fundamentals like a lack of financial skills and advice and poor levels of financial performance rather than just addressing cultural differences and the effects they might have.

▷ Summary

▷ The basic principle of prudent financing is to match the term-duration of the source of finance with the term-duration of the use to which it is put. Fixed or permanent assets should be financed with equity, medium- and long-term bank finance, leasing or hire purchase. Working capital should be financed by short-term loans and factoring, with fluctuations financed by overdraft.

▷ Start-ups and fast-growing firms have particular problems raising finance. To get round this, they often 'borrow' resources and, where all else fails, they borrow cash from family and friends. Where they do not have the track record or security to obtain bank finance they may be eligible for the Enterprise Finance Guarantee. However, most small firms prefer to rely on their own internally generated funds to finance their growth and development rather than to seek outside finance, which explains why **Martyn Dowes** was so careful in using it when he set up **Coffee Nation**.

▷ Leasing can be a particularly effective way for growing firms to finance fixed assets, matching finance with the security of the asset it purchases. Similarly, as **Softcat** found, factoring, although expensive, can sometimes be the only way a growing firm can finance its way through Death Valley. **NDT** realised that if there is insufficient finance available to undertake a contract, even with factoring, then the company may have to walk away from it, however lucrative.

▷ Bankers are very risk averse. They do not share in the success of the business but stand to lose all their capital if the business fails, and therefore they will do all they can to avoid a bad debt. Small firms present a riskier lending proposition than larger firms because they have higher, mainly short-term, gearing and fewer fixed assets to offer as security in the event of a bad debt.

▷ Information asymmetry is where one party in the lending transaction has more information than the other. Where this exists, it can be expensive for banks to get the information they need to make the lending decision and then monitor the loan. Banks' reaction to this problem is to seek collateral from small firms which will offer them security in the event of default. Since the asset base of a small, growing firm is unlikely to be able to provide this, bankers often ask for personal guarantees from the owner-manager. Financing gaps can arise as a result of information asymmetry, the fixed costs of providing small amounts of capital and the requirement of bankers for small firms or owner-managers to provide this collateral.

▷ Bankers look at a range of financial indicators in arriving at their investment decisions but they are particularly interested in the cash flow forecast because this shows the ability of the firm to make its interest payments and repay capital. However they are also interested in a range of business and personal factors, summed up in the acronym CAMPARI. It is important to have a good working relationship with the banker – it helps the owner-manager obtain and maintain finance and bridge any financing gap that might exist.

▷ Venture capital is a mix of equity and loan finance for businesses with growth potential. Whilst the UK industry is the largest after the USA, it mainly invests in established companies and management buy-outs and buy-ins. Most investments are over £2 million. It rarely invests sums of less than £100 000 and is not keen on start-ups unless they are capable of generating profits in excess of £250 000 within four or five years. There are some venture capital organisations investing smaller sums, but most of these investments come from 'business angels'. 'Partnering' with larger organisations, like **Specsavers**, can also make obtaining capital easier.

▷ Venture capitalists and business angels share in the success of the firm. As **FBS Engineering** found, they also share in failure. Consequently, they look at the full range of performance criteria that will be explained in the next chapter. They are particularly interested in the quality and experience of the entrepreneur and the management team. They rarely take a controlling interest in the firm but typically ask to place a director on the board, although some ask for a more 'hands-on' involvement in terms of day-to-day management than others. Typically they are looking for a 30 per cent to 60 per cent annualised return on their investment, normally taken as a capital gain in about ten years' time. As in the case of **LA Fitness**, often their capital gain is realised by taking the business to a stock market such as AIM and then on to a full stock market float. However, sometimes the entrepreneur ends up buying back their company.

▷ Despite numerous 'growth constraints' surveys, it has been impossible to objectively establish that a long-term financing gap for SMEs – indicating market failure or credit rationing – exists in any systematic way in the UK. This probably changed during the recession caused by the banking crisis of 2008/09 when companies of all sizes failed because of a lack of credit.

▷ The poor performance of women-owned businesses seems to be related to a lack of capital at start-up – financial, human and social. Despite the fact that women-owned businesses do not receive the same amount of financial support as male-owned business, there is no evidence of discrimination or a financing gap. **Elizabeth Gooch** of **EG Solutions** even thinks that being a woman has worked to her advantage. What is lacking is social and human capital. However, there is little understanding of how and why gender shapes entrepreneurship.

▷ There is also no evidence of a financing gap for ethnic businesses.

▷ Companies like **LA Fitness** and **Mears Group** have used most of the sources of finance outlined in this chapter to finance their growth at different stages. The appropriate source depends on what it will be used for and the business that will use it.

☑ Useful websites

☑ www.businesslink.gov.uk provides a practical guide to all forms of business finance and useful hyperlinks to related sites.

☑ www.fairinvestment.co.uk provides an independent comparison of business banking services.

☑ www.bbaa.org.uk: The website of the British Business Angels Association.

☑ www.growthbusiness.co.uk provides a guide to UK venture capital funds.

☑ www.venturesite.co.uk: virtual network of business angels on which investment opportunities can be posted.

☑ www.bvca.co.uk: The website of the British Venture Capital Association.

☑ www.evca.eu: The website of the European Private Equity & Venture Capital Association.

⏻ **Further resources are available at www.palgrave.com/business/burns**

🗎 Essays and discussion topics

1 Does the financing gap still exist? If so, why, and what are the likely consequences? If not, explain why.

2 What can or should the government do to improve the provision of finance to small firms?

3 How can banks improve the service they offer small firms?

4 If there is a financing gap, it is more the fault of the owner-manager than the banker. Discuss.

5 How can banking relationships be enhanced and how can they be hindered?

6 It is not fair to ask the owner-manager for personal guarantees. Discuss.

7 There is no such thing as limited liability for the owner-manager. Discuss.

8 What are venture capitalists looking for from their investments?

9 Why are management buy-outs and management buy-ins such attractive investments for venture capitalists?

10 Why do venture capitalists not invest more in start-ups?

11 What are the advantages and disadvantages of having a Business Angel invest in a company?

12 Why do entrepreneurs take their companies off the stock market?

3 Growth

11 Planning for growth

12 New products and services

13 Growing the business

14 Developing the business plan

15 Exit: failure and success

11 Planning for growth

▷ **Ingredients of success**
▷ **A framework for developing strategy**
▷ **Sustainability and corporate social responsibility**
▷ **Vision and mission**
▷ **Values and ethics**
▷ **The SWOT analysis**
▷ **Financial performance analysis**
▷ **Value chains**
▷ **SLEPT analysis**
▷ **Strategic intent**
▷ **Securing competitive advantage**
▷ **Successful entrepreneurial strategies**
▷ **Developing entrepreneurial strategies in the real world**
▷ **Summary**

Case insights
▷ Jordans
▷ Dale Vince and Ecotricity
▷ Abel & Cole
▷ J. J. Cash
▷ Dell Computer Corporation

Cases with questions
▷ Dmitry Kotenko and Nitrol Solar
▷ Lastminute.com
▷ easyJet

Learning outcomes

By the end of this chapter you should be able to:

▷ Describe the ingredients of success for a growing firm;

▷ Describe the strategic planning process;

▷ Explain why corporate social responsibility must be at the heart of any growth strategy;

▷ Explain what is meant by vision and values – what they entail and how they can be communicated effectively;

▷ Write a vision or mission statement;

▷ Undertake a SWOT analysis;

▷ Undertake a financial appraisal of a small firm using ratio analysis;

▷ Explain the concept of a value chain and describe how it can be used;

▷ Undertake a SLEPT analysis and explain how it can be used;

▷ Explain which strategies are most likely to lead to successful growth.

💡 Ingredients of success

In the turbulent world of business, survival – over a longer period – is a badge of success. But entrepreneurs like Bill Gates and Richard Branson have managed to do more than just survive – they managed to grow their businesses and grow them extremely quickly and with enormous success. Despite being few in number, high-growth businesses – companies that go on to the take-off phase in our growth models – are important to national economies. Even in 1999 the market capitalisation of Microsoft, Dell, Cisco and MCI, all under 20 years old, was equivalent to 13 per cent of US GDP (Jovanovic, 2001). It has been estimated that, whilst 15 000 medium-sized businesses represent just 1 per cent of all businesses in the USA, they generate a quarter of all sales and they employ a fifth of all private sector labour (Harrison and Taylor, 1996). For the UK, Storey et al. (1987) have asserted that 'out of every 100 small firms, the fastest growing four firms will create half the jobs in the group over a decade.'

So, is there such a thing as a recipe for success? The answer is that we know the ingredients, but the precise recipe can vary from situation to situation. The ingredients of success are shown in Figure 11.1; they comprise:

▷ *The entrepreneurial character.* This is the vital ingredient. Growth rarely happens by chance. The owner-manager must want it and possess all the characteristics of the entrepreneur. What is more, as we discuss in Chapter 17, they must be able to adapt and change as the business grows.

▷ *The business culture.* This is an important tool for effective leadership of an entrepreneurial firm. Having the right culture is probably more important than the right structure. What is more, part of the culture must be the ambition to grow. Companies which have risen to positions of global leadership over the last 20 years invariably began with ambitions that were out of proportion to their size or resources. They maintained an obsession with winning long enough to succeed. In Chapter 17 we see how the entrepreneur can build the culture in their firm.

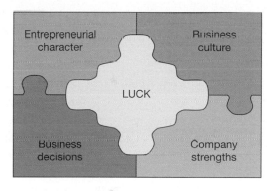

F11.1 The ingredients of success

▷ *Company strengths.* For successful growth a company needs a good management team and good financial control systems. It needs to understand who its customers are and why they buy from them rather than competitors. This chapter will show you some frameworks that help you evaluate both the strengths and weaknesses of the company. It will show you how to undertake the SWOT analysis so beloved by most business schools – an analysis of the Strengths and Weaknesses of an organisation and the Opportunities and Threats it faces – and introduces some tools to help with this process.

▷ *Business strategies.* Having no business strategies can be just as disastrous as having bad strategies. We've already introduced you to the concept of strategy, But which strategies are more likely to lead to success and growth and how might they be developed? This chapter will outline some of the strategies that research has shown to be most likely to lead to success.

All of which leaves the question of luck. Whether success is due to luck or good judgement or good timing is a difficult question to answer. Timing is everything and a good product or service, launched before its time, with insufficient demand is likely to fail. How many failed start-ups would have survived if the banking crisis of 2008/9 and the subsequent recession had not happened?'

💡 A framework for developing strategy

Developing the strategy either for a start-up or for further growth can be undertaken in a systematic way. That is not to say that the strategy should then become a constraint if unexpected entrepreneurial opportunities present themselves. Strategies develop and evolve. They are a constant work in progress. For many entrepreneurs, in their rapidly changing markets, as soon as they are written down they are out of date and obsolete. However, the strategic frameworks that will be explained in the next three chapters allow you to think through the issues facing your firm in a logical, common sense way. They replicate good practice – they way business people talk to each other – and an understanding of them is essential if you want to write a good business plan, which you will need if you require external finance. However, reality is often not as simple as this framework and we shall return to the issue of how strategy is developed in the real world later in this chapter. For now we need to understand the frameworks.

Figure 11.2 sets out a process for how strategy might be developed in a systematic way. Strategy should be more than a wish list driven by the entrepreneur's vision – what they want the business to become. As we shall see in a later section, a vision must be realistic and credible and the leader's job involves developing 'creative tension' by contrasting the vision to the reality of the current situation. So, too, with strategy. Effective strategy must be rooted in the distinctive capabilities of the business. It starts with a thorough understanding of its strengths and weaknesses. It then goes on to contrast this with the opportunities and threats it faces in the environment. This is the classic SWOT analysis (strengths, weaknesses, opportunities and threats). What is more, other tools have been developed to help this analysis be undertaken in a systematic and rational way.

The second element in the strategic process is strategy formulation. A strategy is just a linked pattern of actions. First you identify the strategic options, evaluating each one in terms of fit with the strengths and weaknesses of the organisation and finally selecting the most appropriate option. As we saw in Chapter 6, there are some

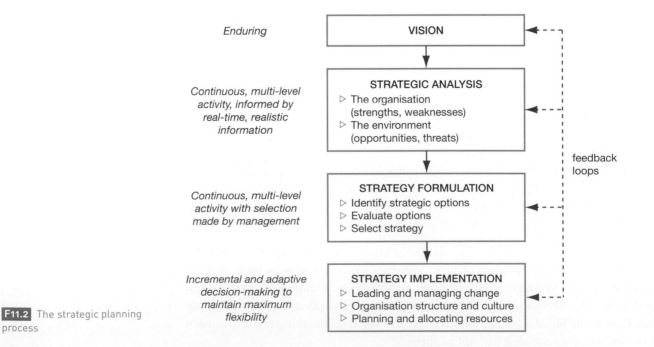

F11.2 The strategic planning process

common or generic marketing strategies that a business might consider, and we shall return to these later. Strategy formulation should be a continuous process. In a start-up you might do this yourself (with advice from friends and professionals) but in an existing entrepreneurial organisation it should be undertaken at many different levels with varying degrees of formality. The 'right' strategy will emerge as part of these consultative processes but it should never be sufficiently rigid to inhibit the pursuit of opportunity – and that means generating strategic options and evaluating them.

The final element is strategy implementation. This involves leading and managing the process, developing the organisational structure and culture to sustain it as it grows and planning and allocating resources to make it happen. In fact, in the hands of a skilled strategist, strategy formulation and implementation are inextricably linked, because the likelihood of the strategy being successfully implemented, given the organisational capabilities, is part of the formulation process. What is more, the process of implementation will feed back on both the analysis and formulation stages, particularly in an entrepreneurial organisation. The success or otherwise of implementation will even affect the vision. The whole process is, therefore, inextricably interlinked and never-ending.

Sustainability and corporate social responsibility

Before moving on to consider this process in more detail it is worth introducing the concept of sustainability – for both the business and society as a whole. It is not just social entrepreneurs who have a role within society and, as with social enterprises, money can be made from being socially responsible – wherever it is reinvested. It is now widely accepted that many business practices have negative social and environmental side effects. Growing pressures are leading firms to give careful consideration to sustainable development and how it might contribute to the sustainability of competitive advantage and growth of the organisation. These pressures come from:

▷ *Environmentalists* – who see companies rapidly using up the valuable but limited resources of the planet and at the same time contributing to global warming, which may ultimately cause the destruction of the planet. Green issues and the corporate 'carbon footprint' are rapidly becoming the most important issues facing business today.

▷ *Social reformers* – who see companies behaving in ways that they object to, for example by 'exploiting' cheap labour in developing countries, or providing poor working conditions. Trade unions and consumer groups have both focused on social issues in the past, often with the result that legislation limiting the activity of companies has been enacted (e.g. the minimum wage in Europe).

▷ *Social activists* – who see companies as having a broader social role in the community beyond the boundaries of the working environment. Corporate citizenship programmes, in which employees undertake charitable work in the community, for example, have become a trendy outlet for many companies, whilst others like Body Shop and Timberland have practised this for years.

▷ *Ethical activists* – who see companies (such as Enron) behaving in ways which are ethically unacceptable, usually by trying to mislead stakeholders. There is, of course, an overlap here with the agendas of the other groups. Nevertheless, business ethics has risen up the agenda of society as a whole and shareholders, in particular, and companies are responding.

☐ Case insight Jordans

Specialist cereals producer Jordans is a family company tracing its origins back to 1855 with milling and the supply of animal feed. However, when Bill and David Jordan were travelling through California in the late 1960s they discovered the natural goodness of wholegrain food. When they returned to the family mill in the UK, they decided to create all-natural cereals and champion the nutritious benefits of wholegrains. In the 1960s the company switched from producing white to wholemeal flour in the face of fierce price competition from big conglomerates. It also started producing small quantities of oat-based cereals, which it sold to health food stores.

Jordans Cereals was born in 1972. Based in Biggleswade, UK, their first organic wholegrain breakfast cereal was called 'Crunchy G' and became a hit, despite the trend at the time for highly processed foods. By the 1970s health foods had really caught on and Jordans was selling to the supermarkets. Two keys to their growth since then have been product quality and innovation, although to this day, wholegrain oats are still at the heart of all their products. Quality, backed with a respected brand identity, have allowed them not to be drawn too far into the vicious food-price wars. All products are made from cereals sourced from selected local farms and grown to high environmental standards, without artificial colours, flavours, preservatives or genetically modified organisms. Innovation has kept them one step ahead of the big-company competition. They were among the first to introduce 'food on the run' cereal bars. They were also one of the first to introduce freeze-dried fruits to their breakfast cereals, even innovating in the packaging by introducing cellophane bags. They pioneered the introduction of 'conservation grade' ingredients which are cheaper than organically grown but contain few pesticides.

Jordans has also entered the own-brand market and 20 per cent of its £50 million turnover comes from this source. Even here it trades on its 'brand integrity' – its ability to produce tasty and nutritious cereals in an environmentally-friendly way. But it has had to control costs. It is also entering the adult savoury market with its low-fat cereal-based oven-crisped chips. It now plans a major expansion into Europe.

☐ Up-to-date information on Jordan's can be found on their website: www.jordanscereals.co.uk

Often these issues are bundled together under the broad umbrella of corporate social responsibility (CSR). More and more companies are engaging seriously in CSR, and over 500 in the UK issue annual CSR reports on their performance. Much of the CSR literature is highly moralistic in nature, reflecting the idealism of scholars who question the profit maximisation objective of companies (Wood, 2000). However, Burke and Logsdon (1996) argue that there are sound business reasons for following a strong CSR policy and organisations can expect six strategic outcomes:

▷ *Enhanced customer loyalty*: Certainly a strong CSR profile can reinforce and enhance brand image (see the Abel & Cole Case insight). Customers are increasingly drawn to brands with a strong CSR profile and CSR has become an element in the continuous process of trying to differentiate one company from another. In 20 developed countries a survey of 20 000 people showed CSR-related factors collectively accounted for 49 per cent of a company's image, compared to 35 per cent for brand image and just 10 per cent for financial management (Environics International, 2001).

▷ *Increased future purchases*: Whilst any product must first satisfy the customer's key buying criteria – quality, price etc. – a strong CSR brand can increase sales and customer loyalty by helping to differentiate it. On the other hand a bad CSR image can damage sales quite severely. The Environics survey (op. cit.) showed 42 per cent of consumers in North America would punish companies for being socially irresponsible by not buying their product – a factor BP was very concerned about after the Gulf of Mexico oil spill in 2010. This fell to 25 per cent in Europe but collapsed to 8 per cent in Asia where CSR issues are seen as less important.

▷ *Reduced operating costs*: Many environmental initiatives can reduce costs (e.g. reducing waste and recycling, having better control of building temperatures or reducing use of agrochemicals). Many social initiatives can increase employee motivation and cut absenteeism and staff turnover, and an increasing number of graduates take CSR issues into consideration when making employment decisions.

▷ *Improved new product development*: Focus on CSR issues can lead to new product opportunities. For example, car manufacturers are striving to find alternatives to fossil fuels, whilst developing conventional engines that are more and more economical. Innovation linked to sustainability often has major systems-level implications, demanding a holistic and integrated approach to innovation management. The commitment of the retailer M&S to be completely carbon-neutral by 2012 has required them to completely re-engineer many of their operations, leading to opportunities for specialist suppliers. Berkhout and Green (2003) argue for a systems approach to innovation, linking it with sustainable research, policy and management, and concluding that 'greater awareness and interaction between research and management of innovation, environmental management, corporate social responsibility and innovation and environment will prove fruitful'.

> ### 🧳 Case insight Dale Vince and Ecotricity
>
> Dale Vince was once a New Age hippie who toured Britain and the Continent in a peace convoy. These days he is better known as a millionaire entrepreneur who owns the fast-growing company Ecotricity, which he founded in 1995. Ecotricity generates electricity from its wind turbines around the UK, as far apart as Dundee and Somerset, and sells the 'green' energy to domestic and corporate customers, including Sainsbury's, Tesco and Ford. The idea came to Dale on a hill near Stroud in Gloucestershire where his home – a former army lorry - was powered by a small wind turbine. Why not build a full-sized permanent wind turbine in the field, he thought?
>
> These days the company is still based in Stroud but employs some 170 'co-workers'. It is very much a family business. Dale's sons Dane, 25, and Sam, 20, work in the office whilst his brother Simon helps design the turbines and his sister, Sharon, deals with customers' inquiries. Ecotricity made a profit of almost £2 million in 2008 and reinvested most of this in renewable energy sources. It has some 90 turbines and supplies about 12 per cent of the UK's on-shore wind energy.
>
> ☐ Up-to-date information on Ecotricity can be found on their website: www.ecotricity.co.uk

▷ *Access to new markets*: A strong CSR brand can create its own market niche for an organisation. For example, the Co-operative Bank in the UK has a long history of CSR. It has set itself up as an ethical and ecological investor with an investment policy that is the most frequently cited reason that customers choose the bank. It also has been at the forefront of social auditing practices and has produced an independently audited 'Social Report' since 1997 that measures the impact and identifies improvements the company could make in social responsibility areas.

▷ *Productivity gains*: Actions to improve working conditions, lessen environmental impact or increase employee involvement in decision-making can improve productivity. For example, actions to improve work conditions in the supply chain have been seen to lead to decreases in defect rates in merchandise.

Not surprisingly, therefore, strong CSR performance seems to be linked to financial performance. A 2002 study showed that the overall financial performance of the 2001 *Business Ethics* Best Citizen companies in the USA was significantly better than that of the remaining companies in the S&P 500 Index (Verschoor, 2002). There is growing awareness that incorporating CSR into mainstream corporate strategy translates into bottom-line performance. In the short term it, at least, avoids negative consumer or activist publicity, in the medium term it delivers better performance for investors and the community, and in the long term, by encouraging consideration of abiding social and environmental interests, it can give management a broader, long-term perspective on the sustainability of the company's performance.

Certainly companies like Abel & Cole have used CSR as a major plank in their branding. But CSR predates Abel & Cole by over a century. In the UK Cadbury, Wilkin & Sons (maker of Tiptree Jams) and the Co-op are all early examples of businesses with a CSR dimension. Today many large organisations, like the UK retailers Marks & Spencer (M&S) and John Lewis, and the US company IBM and outdoor-

🧳 Case insight Abel & Cole

Abel & Cole may be the UK's largest organic food delivery company with sales of more than £30 million in 2008 and over 50 000 regular customers, but that was not how it started. In 1985 where Keith Abel was studying history and economics at Leeds University, and selling potatoes door-to-door to make some money. He was a good salesman and that meant he could charge more for the potatoes than the supermarkets. Keith went on to City University, London, to study law. Unfortunately he failed his bar exams and decided he might as well team up with a friend, Paul Cole, and start doing the same thing to make some money – no notion of organic food, just making money. A Devon-based farmer, Bernard Gauvier, approached them to sell his organic potatoes. They cost more, but after a week of selling them Keith realised that nobody asked the price. He decided to investigate the differences between organic and non-organic products, and went to see what his regular supplier was spraying on his potatoes. Keith was 'pretty appalled' at what he saw. The organic idea slowly started to creep into his consciousness and he started to 'push' the organic side of the business – after all he was good at selling, and he was delivering the produce to the door of the customers. They responded by buying more and asking for other things. Bernard persuaded Keith and Paul to start putting together organic vegetable boxes and by 1991 they converted to selling only organic vegetables, buying them directly from farmers. Sales took off in the 1990s and they started to employ people. Unfortunately, whilst sales increased, the result was mounting losses.

By 1999 Abel & Cole had 1500 regular customers but things came to a head when unpaid debts caused the Inland Revenue to threaten them with bankruptcy. Paul decided to leave and set up his own wholesale company, while Keith decided to resit his bar exams

– and passed. Then Keith realised that he could not practise law if he was declared bankrupt. Threatened with losing the family house, Keith's father-in-law, Peter Chipparelli, then chairman of Mobil Oil in South America, decided to bail him out. This may have focused Keith's mind because he started taking advice, first from his father-in-law then from social entrepreneur and author of *The Natural Advantage*, Alan Heeks. He brought with him his 22-year-old daughter, Ella, who stayed to do work experience and went on to become Managing Director three years later. She must take a lot of the credit for the success of Abel & Cole.

In 2007 the private equity firm Phoenix Equity Partners bought a stake in Abel & Cole, valuing it at over £40 million. The success of the company is due to the consistency of its marketing mix. Its ethical, eco-conscious profile is assiduously nurtured. Vegetables are organic, local (never air-freighted), seasonal, and ethically farmed. They are delivered in a recycled cardboard box by a yellow bio-fuel van, together with a newsletter which includes lively vegetable biographies and hints on how to deal with some of the more obscure vegetables in the box. The company prides itself on employing the formerly long-term unemployed and offers them bonuses for cutting waste. It gives to charity. Customers can deposit keys with the company so that vegetable boxes are left safe and sound indoors. Prices are high, but not outrageously so since the 'middle-man' has been cut out of the distribution chain. Customers are middle class and shopping from Abel & Cole is definitely fashionable. The medium- to long-term question is whether these factors will outweigh the need to economise following the 2008/9 banking crisis and subsequent recession.

☐ Up-to-date information on Abel and Cole can be found on their website: www.abelandcole.co.uk

ware manufacturer Timberland, have extensive CSR programmes ranging from community involvement (staff working on community projects in company time) through to ethical sourcing (from humans and animals) and into environmental issues (such as M&S' objective to become completely carbon neutral). M&S' 100-point 'Plan A' is generally seen as a model for today's socially responsible large companies.

There is also growing investor pressure to implement CSR. The Environics survey (op. cit.) showed that over a quarter of US share owners bought or sold shares because of a company's social performance and a similar pattern emerged in Britain, Canada, Italy, Canada and France (Environics International, op. cit.). There are now CSR stock market indices, like the *Dow Jones Sustainability Index* and the *FTSE4Good*, and, increasingly, mainstream investors see CSR as a strategic business issue and raise it in annual meetings. Activist groups also buy shares in targeted companies to give them access to these annual meetings so that they can raise CSR issues.

CSR can be integrated into the strategic planning process outlined in Figure 11.2:

▷ *Strategic analysis*: Firms need to be aware of legislation and should compare themselves to competitors (Epstein and Roy, 2001) and find out about the expectations of external stakeholders (Smith, 2003). Similarly companies should find out the expectations of their internal stakeholders (Smith, op cit) with a view to assessing the adequacy of their organisational capacity – their resources and processes (deColle and Gonella, 2002; Epstein and Roy, op cit). The firm should then be able to assess the fit between the CSR commitments it might aspire to and its central business objectives (Burke and Logsdon, op. cit.; Smith, op. cit.), which may or may not result in changing the vision and mission for the business.

▷ *Strategy formulation*: This is usually demonstrated as a list of commitments. According to Smith (op. cit.), this should reflect 'an understanding of whether (and why) greater attention to CSR is warranted by that particular organisation.'

▷ *Strategy implementation:* This requires concrete actions to be undertaken but also it is important to publicise this to internal and external stakeholders to demonstrate commitment and attainment (Burke and Logsdon, op. cit.). These may have to be audited or evaluated (de Colle and Gonella, op. cit.).

Sustainability and CSR can therefore be integrated into the strategic planning process. Indeed they should be at the heart of any growth strategy. CSR encourages a long-term view and reflects the concerns of the society in which the company is embedded. However, it also makes good business sense, providing market and brand opportunities that translate into bottom-line profits. CSR is set to become more important in the future and is likely to be an essential element of strategy for all companies of every size.

♀ Vision and mission

A vision is a shared mental image of a desired future state – an idea of what the enterprise can become – a new and better world. It must be a realistic, credible and attractive future and one that engages and energises people (Nanus, 1992). It is usually qualitative rather than quantitative (that is the role of the objectives). Vision is seen as inspiring and motivating, transcending logic and contractual relationships. It is more emotional than analytical, something that touches the heart. It gives existence within an organisation to that most fundamental of human cravings – a sense of meaning and purpose. As Bartlett and Ghoshal (1994) explain:

> Traditionally top-level managers have tried to engage employees intellectually through the persuasive logic of strategic analysis. But clinically framed and contractually based relationships do not inspire the extraordinary effort and sustained commitment required to deliver consistently superior performance … Senior managers must convert the contractual employees of an economic entity into committed members of a purposeful organisation.

Visions, then, are aspirational but they can take many forms. They can be intrinsic, directing the organisation to do things better in some way, such as improving customer satisfaction or increasing product innovation. They can be extrinsic, for example, beating the competition. But what do you do when you have beaten the competition?

Entrepreneurs have to make their own decisions and follow their vision. They must motivate their team, get them to ignore shaky markets and a possible war and look positively to the future, to keep exploring uncharted territory. To do that they have to subscribe to the entrepreneur's vision – but they don't necessarily have to agree with it.

☐   Derrick Collin, founder and managing director of Brulines Ltd
The Times 10 October 2001

Vision is formally communicated through a vision statement or as part of a mission statement. A mission statement is a formal statement of the purpose of the business. It says what the business aims to achieve and how it will achieve it. It is a way of formalising the vision, articulating how the vision might be achieved. It encourages this analysis, subjecting the vision to scrutiny as to whether it is realistic and achievable. It usually defines the scope of the business by including reference to the product or service (basis for competitive advantage, quality, innovation and so on), customer groups and the benefits they derive, or competitors. This stops the entrepreneur straying into markets where they have no competitive advantage, clarifies strategic options and offers guidance for setting objectives. Often it encompasses the values upheld by the company. Any mission

Where any three people within an organisation will give the same answer to a question on the company's mission statement. That reflects total coherency and a focused workforce.

☐   Gururaj Deshpande, serial entrepreneur and founder of Sycamore Networks, *Financial Times* 21 February 2000

statement should be short, snappy and as memorable as possible. Like the vision, mission statements are qualitative. Some examples are given in the box below.

💼 Dell mission

Dell's mission is to be the most successful computer company in the world at delivering the best computer experience in markets we serve. In doing so, Dell will meet customer expectations of:

▷ Highest quality;
▷ Leading technology;
▷ Competitive pricing;
▷ Individual and company accountability;

▷ Best-in-class service and support;
▷ Flexible customisation capability;
▷ Superior corporate citizenship;
▷ Financial stability.

💼 easyJet mission

To provide our customers with safe, good value, point-to-point air services. To effect and to offer a consistent and reliable product and fares appealing to leisure and business markets on a range of European routes. To achieve this we will develop our people and establish lasting relationships with our suppliers.

Wickham (2001) suggests a generic format for a mission statement:

> (*The company*) aims to use its (*competitive advantage*) to achieve/maintain (*aspirations*) in providing (*product scope*) which offers (*benefits*) to satisfy the (*needs*) of (*customer scope*). In doing this the company will at all times strive to uphold (*values*).

As a start-up, articulating your own individual vision is relatively easy. But as the business grows you will find that building a shared vision with your staff is no easy task – it is not about simply going off and writing a vision or mission statement. We shall return to this in Chapter 17 when we look at the role of the entrepreneur as the business grows.

💡 Values and ethics

Values are the core beliefs upon which the organisation is founded. They underpin the vision and the mission of the organisation. They set expectations regarding how the organisation operates and how it treats people. Often these values have an ethical dimension, and, as we saw in the previous section, ethics have underpinned business for many years. Not only do they form a strong bond between all the stakeholders in the business, but also using them to underpin the business can make good commercial sense.

The vision and mission of the organisation must be consistent with its values. All three go hand-in-hand, one reinforcing the other. In a start-up they reflect the values of the founder. As the organisation grows they often develop to represent a wider community but then face the risk of being diluted to the point where they are not clear. Organisations with strong values tend to recruit staff that are able to identify with those values and thus they become reinforced. So a strong set of values at start-up will help you attract the right sort of staff and also create a bond with customers and suppliers alike.

Values are important because they create a constant framework within which to operate in a turbulent, changing environment. They help you develop the business beyond the start-up phase. As represented in Figure 11.3, whilst strategies and tactics might change rapidly in an entrepreneurial firm, vision and values are enduring. They form the 'road map' that tells everyone in the organisation where it is going and how it will get there, even when one route is blocked. Values form part of the cognitive processes that help shape and develop the culture of the organisation. They guide strategy and help delegate authority

🗄 The Body Shop

Values

▷ We consider testing products or ingredients on animals to be morally and scientifically indefensible;
▷ We support small producer communities around the world who supply us with accessories and natural ingredients;
▷ We know that you are unique, and we'll always treat you as an individual. We like you just the way you are;
▷ We believe that it is the responsibility of every individual to actively support those who have human rights denied to them;
▷ We believe that a business has the responsibility to protect the environment in which it operates, locally and globally.

Mission

▷ To dedicate our business to the pursuit of social and environmental change;
▷ To creatively balance the financial and human needs of our stakeholders, employees, customers, franchisees and shareholders;
▷ To courageously ensure that our business is ecologically sustainable: meeting the needs of the present without compromising the future;
▷ To meaningfully contribute to local, national and international communities in which we trade, by adopting a code of conduct which ensures care, honesty, fairness and respect;
▷ To passionately campaign for the protection of the environment, human and civil rights, and against animal testing within the cosmetics and toiletries industry;
▷ To tirelessly work to narrow the gap between principle and practice, whilst making fun, passion and care part of our daily lives.

Values, vision, strategy and tactics

– telling people the 'right' thing to do. Shared values form a bond that binds the organisation together – aligning and motivating people. They help develop a high-trust culture that cements long-term relationships.

Values need to be articulated and taught by the entrepreneur through 'walking-the-talk' – practising what they preach. It therefore follows that it is very difficult to pretend to have values that are not real – you'll be caught out when you fail to practise them. Values are not negotiable and need to be reinforced through recognition and reward of staff. They need to be embedded in the systems and procedures of the organisation, so that everybody can see clearly that the organisation means what it says. Nonaka (1991) recommends the use of language, metaphor and analogy in promoting values, which he sees as promoting the special capabilities of the organisation that enable resources to be leveraged internally, thereby creating competitive advantage.

> *One of the most important aspects of any business is its ethical code, a statement of the principles governing the way it operates and its employees behave.*
>
> ☐   Duncan Bannatyne, serial entrepreneur and Dragon
> *Daily Telegraph* 5 August 2009

💡 The SWOT analysis

We can break the planning process down into further detail and show how it leads to the development of, first, a marketing plan and then a financial plan. Together these form the basis for a coherent and consistent business plan which is an important tool in seeking external finance. We shall explain in detail what should go into the business plan in Chapter 14. Broadly, it explains where the business is going, how it will get there and the resources it needs to make it happen. This amplified planning process is shown in Figure 11.4.

As you can see, the basic tool of strategic analysis is the SWOT analysis. This is just a shorthand way of looking at you and the business – strengths and weaknesses – and the market environment in which the business operates – opportunities and threats. This is partly to do with your personal strengths and weaknesses, in relation to the business, but it is also to do with the product or service and its fit with the market place. The SWOT allows you to link your vision to customer needs through an analysis of your capabilities. Because of their subjective nature, it is easy to under or over-estimate the importance of elements of the SWOT and it is often a good idea to ask the opinion of a friend or colleague when you draw one up. But it is equally important to remember always to challenge the conventions of the market place, to find ways of turning a weakness into a strength, of finding opportunities by being unconventional.

What the SWOT process is seeking to achieve is an overlap between the business environment and the firm's resources. In other words, a match between the firm's strategic or core competencies and a market opportunity. This match, as such, may not create sustainable competitive advantage – it may be copied – and may change over time. The secret to success, therefore, starts with identifying this unique set of competencies and capabilities. This portfolio of resources can be combined in various

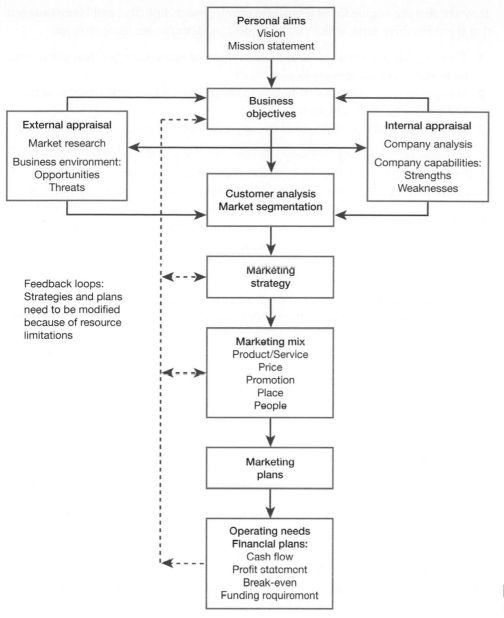

F11.4 The business planning process

ways to meet opportunities or threats. They could, for example, allow a firm to diversify into new markets by reapplying and reconfiguring what it does best. But, what is more, it is the continuing process of analysis, positioning and repositioning that is important. In other words, the value of planning is really as a continuing process, repeated regularly in either a formal or informal way. Indeed if you talk to successful entrepreneurs you get the feeling that they are continually reviewing their strategies – often called strategising – and reviewing the options generated in the continually changing market and environment they thrive in.

Two of the chief proponents of this approach are Prahalad and Hamel (1990). They see core competency as the 'collective learning of the organisation, especially how to coordinate diverse production skills and integrate multiple streams of technology … [through] … communication, involvement, and a deep commitment to work across organisational boundaries … Competencies are the glue that binds existing businesses.

They are also the engine for new business development.' Prahalad and Hamel suggest that there are three tests, which can be applied to identify core competencies:

1 They provide potential access to a wide variety of markets rather than generating competitive advantage only in one.
2 They make 'a significant contribution to the perceived customer benefits of the end-product' – they add value.
3 They are difficult for competitors to copy. Products are easier to copy than processes.

The SWOT analysis is also the basis for undertaking customer analysis and deciding on market segmentation. It informs marketing strategy but equally must be interpreted in the context of a particular market, taking into account both customers and competitors. Strengths can be transformed into weaknesses in a different market and vice versa. The market context is crucial. Thus a SWOT analysis on the fast-food chain McDonald's in the context of the US market would yield completely different results to one undertaken in the context of the market of a developing economy. In the USA it is a mature product, facing declining sales amidst severe competition. In a developing economy it is still a novel product in high demand.

A strength, when used to excess, can be a weakness.

□ Michael Dell

The whole process is an art rather than a science. There is no prescriptive approach. Successfully pursuing opportunities is about identifying attractive business opportunities which, given the firm's capabilities, have a high probability of success. This probability is influenced by the firm's strengths, in particular how its distinctive competencies match the key success requirements to operate in the market, given the existing competition. Most opportunities also carry associated threats. Threats may be classified according to their seriousness and probability of occurrence. A view of the overall attractiveness of a market is based upon the opportunities it offers balanced by the threats that it poses. In making this judgement it is often useful to list the factors – whether you control them or not – that are critical to the success of the venture.

To undertake a SWOT you have to be brutally honest about yourself and your business. That means not pretending that something is a core competency when really it is not. As Gary Hamel urges, it means listening to people with different opinions and judging what is the prevailing wisdom in the company. Treacy and Wiersema (1995) pose five questions about the status quo that need to be answered honestly:

▷ What are the dimensions of value that customers care about? They claim there are only three value disciplines:
  – *Operational excellence.* A good product/market offering (e.g. McDonald's or Dell);
  – *Product leadership.* The best quality, most innovative product (e.g. Quad Electroacoustics or Rolls Royce);
  – *Customer intimacy.* Understanding and developing relationships with customers (e.g. Lush and Abel & Cole).
▷ For each dimension, what proportion of customers focus on it as their primary or dominant decision criterion?
▷ Which competitors provide the best value in each of these value dimensions?
▷ How does the firm compare to the competition on each dimension?
▷ Why does the firm fall short of the value leaders in each dimension of value?

From the answers to these questions, realistic options can be listed and choices made. But, once again, honesty is essential because this means being realistic about the options even if some of them are not very pleasant.

A number of techniques can help in a SWOT analysis. These are summarised in Table 11.1. We have covered some tools and techniques already. For example, the generic marketing strategies are relevant to the internal appraisal and market research, knowledge of economies of scale and Porter's Five Forces analysis of industry competitiveness are relevant to the appraisal of the external environment.

Internal appraisal (strengths, weaknesses)	External appraisal (opportunities, threats)
▷ Benchmarking	▷ Market research (see Chapter 7)
▷ Financial ratio analysis	▷ Economies of scale (see Chapter 6)
▷ Value chains	▷ Porter's Five Forces industry analysis (see Chapter 6)
▷ Generic marketing strategies (see Chapter 6)	▷ SLEPT analysis
▷ Life cycle analysis (see Chapter 12)	
▷ Portfolio analysis (see Chapter 12)	

111.1 Tools of the SWOT analysis

Central to a SWOT analysis are the concepts of benchmarking and market research. Benchmarking performance has been around in one form or another since the 1960s. It usually involves developing performance ratios. These can be compared over time, measuring improvement or deterioration, or compared to other companies in the same industry or used as absolute measures of performance. Financial ratios are important. These can be judged against budgets, trends over time or against industry norms, based on published financial data produced by organisations like the Centre for Interfirm Comparison or ICC Business Ratios.

📋 Case insight J.J. Cash

J.J. Cash, a Coventry based textile manufacturer dating back to 1846 has a history of change. Then it was a leading manufacturer of silk ribbon. Now it manufactures name labels, name tags, clothing labels and personalised luggage straps and badges. The textile industry has always been competitive and J.J. Cash pride themselves on the introduction of new work methods and new technologies to keep costs down and product quality up. When they undertook a benchmarking exercise they got some surprising results. They knew they had good product quality and thought they had excellent labour relations. However, the exercise showed that the customer satisfaction rate was not good. Despite good product quality, the speed of response, vital in the fashion-led clothing industry, was not fast enough. Where they had lead times of four to six weeks, other firms could manage two. What is more, a set of key indicators such as accident rates, absenteeism and staff turnover revealed that the workers were suffering from a lack of motivation.

What followed was nothing short of a complete culture change in the company. The old assembly-line production methods were dropped and new team-working structures were implemented across the entire organisation, underpinned with a generous training budget. Teams were given more authority and new 'two-way' communications procedures were put in place. As a result delivery-on-time rates increased from 60 per cent to 90 per cent, prototypes leave the factory in 48 hours, stock waste has fallen from 6.5 per cent to 2 per cent, stock turnover has increased and staff absenteeism and turnover rates have gone down.

☐ Up-to-date information on J.J. Cash can be found on their website: www.jjcash.co.uk

♀ Financial performance analysis

No SWOT analysis would be complete without an analysis of the company's financial position. Chapter 9 set out many of the elements of this – break-even and margin of safety remain important measures of risk. However, once established, investors and other backers of a firm start to look for other things and make use of a technique called 'ratio analysis'.

This starts by assuming that owners (shareholders) of the firm want to maximise their investment. Whatever they invest in, investors are ultimately interested in the final return they receive, after all expenses, in relation to their investment. If they invest £10 and receive £1, after all expenses, they receive a 10 per cent return which can then be compared to other investment opportunities. Shareholders, who own all the profits of the firm, want to maximise the return they receive on the shareholders' funds they have invested (share capital + retained profit). The critical performance ratio, that must be kept as high as possible, is therefore:

$$\text{Return to shareholders (\%)} = \frac{\text{Profit after interest (and all other costs)}}{\text{Shareholders' funds}}$$

This is expressed as a percentage. To maximise it means operating profit should be as high as possible, interest should be as low as possible and shareholders' funds should also be as low as possible. And here lies the dilemma. One way of keeping shareholders' funds low is to borrow (shareholders' funds = total assets – loans), but this increases interest payments. So the question is, how much to borrow? The following example should provide the answer. The business makes a return on all the money invested in it, both shareholders' funds and loans. Let us say that the shareholder puts £50 into the business and then obtains a bank loan of £50 on which interest of 10 per cent is payable. The business makes a return of 25 per cent on the total £100 invested in it. The situation is set out below:

Investment:		Return:	
Total assets	£100	Business @ 25%	= £25
comprising:		less:	
Loans	£ 50	Interest @ 10%	= £ 5
Shareholders' funds	£ 50	Balance for shareholder	= £20

The shareholder therefore gets to keep £20 – a 40 per cent return on investment. This is above the 25 per cent return the business is making because the shareholders are willing to take the risk of borrowing money on which they only pay a 10 per cent rate of interest. They get to keep the additional 15 per cent. However, this is a risk. If the business were only able to make a 5 per cent return (return = £5) then all the money would go to pay interest, leaving nothing for the shareholders. Similarly, in the unlikely event of interest rates rising above 25 per cent, the return to the shareholders would suffer.

As long as the return the business is making is above the rate of interest charged, the shareholders' return will be increased by maximising borrowing. However, in doing this the riskiness of the business increases because fixed interest costs increase. The appropriate level of borrowing, called gearing or leverage, is the classic risk/return trade-off decision – it is a question of judgement. However, bankers do have some benchmark ratios to inform their lending decisions, as we shall see later in this section.

Therefore, as far as the business is concerned, the critical performance ratio, that must be kept as high as possible, is:

$$\textbf{Return on total assets (\%)} = \frac{\text{Net operating profit (before interest)}}{\text{Total assets (fixed + current assets − current liabilities)}}$$

This is also expressed as a percentage. It is a measure of the operating efficiency of the business, the return operations make as opposed to the way the business is financed. It should be as high as possible, but be aware that the owner will also be taking a salary out of the business which is deducted in arriving at operating income. The measure can therefore be distorted if salaries are unrealistically low or high. The ratio, in turn, depends on two further ratios that when multiplied together yield the above ratio:

↓

Profit margin (%)

$$-\frac{\text{Net operating profit}}{\text{Sales}}$$

This measures the profit margin the firm is able to command and is expressed as a percentage. The ratio should be as high as possible.

↓

This ratio in turn depends upon how its constituent parts perform:

Gross profit margin (%)

$$= \frac{\text{Gross profit}}{\text{Sales}}$$

Gross profit is the difference between sales or turnover and the costs to produce the goods sold. The ratio should be as high as possible.

In addition, there are some key cost ratios, also expressed as percentages, that should be kept as low as possible:

$$\frac{\text{Cost of materials}}{\text{Sales}}, \frac{\text{Cost of labour}}{\text{Sales}},$$

$$\frac{\text{Overhead costs}}{\text{Sales}}$$

↓

Total asset efficiency $= \dfrac{\text{Sales}}{\text{Total assets}}$

This measures how efficiently the total assets are being used in relation to the level of activity, measured by sales, and is expressed as a number. It should be as high as possible.

↓

This ratio in turn depends upon how its constituent parts perform:

Debtor turnover $= \dfrac{\text{Sales}}{\text{Debtors}}$

This number tells you how many times debtors turn over each year. If sales are £3 million and debtors are £0.6 million, they turn over 5 times a year, equivalent to every 1.2 months. You can compare this to the credit terms offered to customers.

There may be other costs that are high and sensitive to changes in the market place that can be usefully measured against sales in this format.

Stock turnover $= \dfrac{\text{Sales}}{\text{Stock}}$

Fixed asset turnover $= \dfrac{\text{Sales}}{\text{Fixed assets}}$

These ratios are expressed as numbers and should be as high as possible.

Ratios are useful because they measure one number against another – they therefore allow for growth. So, for example, debtors are bound to increase as the business grows and sales increase, but what is important is not the absolute value of debtors but rather its relationship to sales, measured by debtor turnover. Similarly, there is no way of knowing whether a £2 million profit in one company is better than a £1 million profit in another unless you know how much was invested in each to achieve it.

To obtain a high return to the shareholder, a firm needs effective profit management and efficient asset management. Put crudely, margins need to be as high as possible and assets should be kept as low as possible. Systematic calculation of these ratios can give you clues about how profit might be increased and where assets might be reduced. Of course to do this you need some benchmarks. One fundamental benchmark is the rate of interest. The return on total assets should never fall below this, otherwise you are better off closing the company and putting the money in the bank. Another benchmark is your payment terms against which debtor turnover can be judged. All the others are a question of judgement, but you can judge them against:

▷ *Projected budgets.* Ratios can be based on projected as well as actual financial information. Comparing actual to budgeted financial performance is part of effective financial control.
▷ *Trends over time.* Ratios do change over time and trends can give both good and bad news.
▷ *Industry norms.* Industry-based ratios, often based on published financial statements, are produced by organisations like the Centre for Interfirm Comparison and ICC Business Ratios.

There are also two ratios that measure the liquidity of a business. These are of particular interest to bankers and people offering credit to the business as they measure the firm's ability to repay them. These ratios are all expressed as numbers:

$$\textbf{Current ratio} = \frac{\text{Current assets}}{\text{Current liabilities}}$$

Current ratio is expected to be greater than 1, indicating that current assets exceed current liabilities.

$$\textbf{Quick ratio} = \frac{\text{Current assets excluding stock}}{\text{Current liabilities}}$$

This is expected to be near to 1, perhaps as low as 0.8.

The level of borrowing is called gearing or leverage. High gearing or leverage is risky. It is measured by a number of ratios that are of particular interest to bankers:

$$\textbf{Gearing (\%)} = \frac{\text{All loans + overdraft}}{\text{Shareholders' funds}}$$

Bankers like this ratio to be under 100 per cent, indicating that shareholders have put in more money than the banks. Frequently for growing firms this is not the case. Above 400 per cent is considered very high risk and the business likely to fail. However, some management buy-outs can have gearing above this level.

$$\textbf{Short-term borrowing (\%)} = \frac{\text{Short-term loans + overdraft}}{\text{All loans + overdraft}}$$

Long-term loans give greater security than short-term loans. Therefore the higher this ratio, the riskier the firm. The ratio must be read alongside gearing. Low gearing means the percentage short-term borrowing can be higher.

$$\textbf{Interest cover} = \frac{\text{Operating profit}}{\text{Interest}}$$

This measures how secure interest payments are. The higher the number the better.

The margin of safety remains an important ratio for measuring the riskiness of the business due to its level of fixed costs. A financial ratio checklist which includes the margin of safety is shown as Figure 11.5. You may wish to revisit Chapter 9 where many of these terms and some of these ratios were explained.

Performance

Return on shareholders funds (%): $\dfrac{\text{Net profit (after interest)}}{\text{Shareholders funds}}$

Return on total assets (%): $\dfrac{\text{Net operating profit (before interest)}}{\text{Total assets}}$

Profitability

Net margin (%): $\dfrac{\text{Net profit}}{\text{Sales}}$

Gross margin (%): $\dfrac{\text{Gross profit}}{\text{Sales}}$

Cost of materials (%): $\dfrac{\text{Cost of materials}}{\text{Sales}}$

Cost of labour (%): $\dfrac{\text{Cost of labour}}{\text{Sales}}$

Overhead cost (%): $\dfrac{\text{Overhead costs}}{\text{Sales}}$

Asset efficiency

Capital/Total asset turnover: $\dfrac{\text{Sales}}{\text{Total assets}}$

Debtor turnover: $\dfrac{\text{Sales}}{\text{Debtors}}$

Stock turnover: $\dfrac{\text{Sales}}{\text{Stock}}$

Fixed asset turnover: $\dfrac{\text{Sales}}{\text{Fixed assets}}$

Liquidity

Current ratio: $\dfrac{\text{Current assets}}{\text{Current liabilities}}$

Quick ratio: $\dfrac{\text{Current assets excluding stock}}{\text{Current liabilities}}$

Gearing

Gearing ratio (%): $\dfrac{\text{All loans + overdrafts}}{\text{Shareholders funds}}$

Short-term debt ratio (%): $\dfrac{\text{Short-term loans + overdrafts}}{\text{All loans + overdraft}}$

Interest cover: $\dfrac{\text{Trading profit}}{\text{Interest}}$

Risk

Margin of safety: $\dfrac{\text{Sales} - \text{Break-even sales}}{\text{Sales}}$

F11.5 Financial ratio checklist

◌ Value chains

In order to deliver value to a firm's customers real advantages in cost or differentiation need to be found in the chain of activities that it performs. Michael Porter (1985) says that the value chain, shown in Figure 11.6, should be the start of any strategic analysis. He identifies five primary activities:

1 Inbound logistics (receiving, storing, disseminating inputs)
2 Operations (transforming inputs into a final product)
3 Outbound logistics (collecting, storing and distributing products to customers)
4 Marketing and sales
5 After-sales and service

and four secondary or support activities:

1 Procurement (purchasing consumable and capital items)
2 Human resource management
3 Technology development (R&D and so on)
4 Firm infrastructure (general management, accounting and so on)

Porter argues that each generic category can be broken down into discrete activities unique to a particular firm. The firm can then look at the costs associated with each activity and try to compare it to the value obtained by customers from the particular activity. By identifying the cost or value drivers – the factors that determine cost or value for each activity – and the linkages which reduce cost or add value or discourage imitation, the firm can develop the strategies that lead to competitive advantage.

This is a way of focusing on the drivers of value in a business that ought to influence the strategy of the firm. For example, the low-cost supply situation may be linked to being close to a key supplier and could therefore disappear if the firm decides, as part of its expansion plans, to move to another location. The value chain is also a useful way of thinking about how differentiation might be achieved. For example, a high-quality product might be let down by low-quality after-sales service – the value to the customer not being matched by the investment. In other words, differentiation is likely to be achieved by multiple linkages in the value chain – a consistent marketing mix. If multiple compatible linkages can be established, they are more difficult to

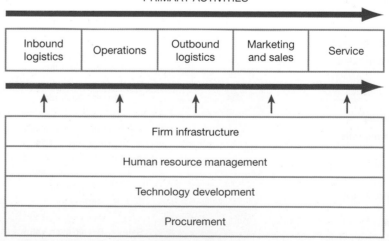

F11.6 The value chain

imitate than single linkages. Similarly, building switch costs into the value chain can also enhance competitive position. However, the advent of e-commerce has generally made it easier to disaggregate the value chain, establishing markets at different points along it, allowing firms to radically rethink or 're-engineer' the way their product/market offering is put together.

Entrepreneurs can add value to customers in a number of ways, not least by developing the close relationships they are so good at. A particularly effective entrepreneurial strategy is to identify a sector in which relationships are weak and create value by tightening them up.

SLEPT analysis

SLEPT analysis can be useful in thinking about future developments in the environment and how they might affect the business, but not necessarily the firm's position in the environment. The analysis looks at the changes that are likely to occur in the areas spelt out by the acronym SLEPT:

Social   Social changes such as an ageing population, increasing work participation often from home, 24-hour shopping, increasing crime, increasing participation in higher education, changing employment patterns, increasing number of one-parent families and so on.

Legal   Legal changes such as Health and Safety, changes in employment laws, food hygiene regulations, patent laws and so on.

Economic   Economic changes such as changes in interest rates, growth, inflation, employment and so on.

Political   Political changes like local or central government elections; political initiatives, for example on green issues, subcontracting of public services to the private sector, new or changed taxes, merger and take-over policy and so on.

Technological   Technological developments such as the internet, increasing use of computers and chip technology, increasing use of mobile phones, increasing use of surveillance cameras and so on.

The trick is to brainstorm and think outside the square about how these developments might affect the business. For example, the ability to download films and music on the internet might be thought to bring into question the future viability of shops selling DVDs and CDs. The availability of cheap teleconferencing via the internet might be seen as a threat to those firms providing business travel over long distances, such as airlines. The development of internet shopping might cause developers to rethink the purpose and structure of our town centres as well as causing individual shops to re-engineer the way they meet customer needs – most shops have websites and many offer internet shopping alongside conventional shopping. The future may be uncertain, but it cannot be ignored.

Another technique used sometimes to help think about the future in a structured way is called 'futures thinking'. Futures thinking tries to take a holistic perspective, avoiding a rigid approach to strategic planning: a vision about a desired future state is developed and planning then takes place, backwards, from that state to where the firm is at the moment. Current constraints to action are ignored and in this way the barriers to change are identified. Some barriers may be permanent, but some might not be.

Similar to this is 'scenario planning', which can be a valuable tool for assessing a firm's environment in conditions of high uncertainty over a longer term, say five years or more. With this technique, views of possible future situations that might impact on the firm are constructed. Often major trends in the environment are identified from the SLEPT analysis and built into scenarios. These situations must be logically consistent possible futures, usually an optimistic, a pessimistic and a 'most likely' future, based around key factors influencing the firm. Optional courses of action or strategies are then matched to these scenarios. In effect, the scenarios are being used to test the sensitivity of possible strategies. They also allow assumptions about the status quo of the environment in which a firm operates to be challenged. So, for example, a company planning overseas expansion may be uncertain about factors like exchange rate fluctuations or tariff barriers and might construct possible futures that help it decide whether to manufacture in the UK and export or to set up a manufacturing base in the country.

Scenario planning takes the firm away from the short-term, day-to-day imperatives and helps it think about long-term trends and changes in its environment. Most entrepreneurs, however, prefer to learn by doing and take a short-term, incremental approach to decision-making, reacting to events as they occur. However, in a risky environment, or one where high capital costs are involved, scenario planning has a lot to recommend it – and it is a lot cheaper than making mistakes.

💡 Strategic intent

Of course the SWOT analysis may lead the firm to conclude that their strengths and resources do not match their high aspirations. Based upon a study of firms that have challenged established big companies in a range of industries, Hamel and Prahalad (1994) say that, in reconciling the mismatch, successful firms use something they call 'strategic intent', which is about developing a common vision about the future, aligning staff behaviour with a common purpose and delegating and decentralising decision-making. They argue that 'the challengers had succeeded in creating entirely new forms of competitive advantage and dramatically rewriting the rules of engagement'. Managers in these firms could imagine new products, services and even entire industries that did not exist and then went on to create them. They were not just benchmarking and analysing competition, they were creating new market places that they could dominate because it was a market place of their own making. Hamel and Prahalad claim that the trick is to answer three key questions:

▷ What new types of customer benefits should we seek to provide in 5, 10 or 15 years?
▷ What new competencies will we need to build or acquire in order to offer these benefits?
▷ How will we need to reconfigure our customer interface over the next few years.

Whilst these managers may be revolutionaries, they have their feet firmly on the ground because they understand very clearly the firm's core competencies – that is, the skills and technologies that enable the company to provide benefits to customers. This brings us back to understanding our marketing strategies and reworking our SWOT analysis.

💡 Securing competitive advantage

The distinguishing feature of entrepreneurs is that they recognise what works and replicate it quickly before competitors can react. So, the first thing that a growing firm needs to understand is why it has been successful so far. It needs to revisit the generic marketing strategies in relation to the SWOT analysis in order to be certain it can answer four key questions that enable it to understand the basis of its competitive advantage and capitalise on the relevant factors:

1 Who are our customers?
2 What benefits are they looking for when they buy our products or services?
3 Why do they buy from us rather than our competitors?
4 What strengths do we have and how can they be used to build advantage?

Each of the generic marketing strategies (reproduced in Figure 11.7) has certain strategic decision-making implications. These are actions that you would expect the firm to be undertaking in order to secure its competitive advantage for as long as possible. After the initial success of a start-up it is good to just pause to consider how this will be achieved.

F11.7 Generic marketing strategies

A company that is selling on price needs to maintain cost leadership. This means imposing tight cost controls and being aware of how cost savings might be achieved, for example through economies of scale, the introduction of more efficient ways of working or the introduction of new technology. To be market leader implies being the lowest-cost provider and doing whatever it takes to achieve this. This means constantly moving down the cost curve and keeping all costs as low as possible, for example by moving production to countries with low-cost labour, changing the materials used in manufacture or minimising sales and distribution costs. To sustain cost leadership can be a constant struggle and to help in this, wherever possible, companies develop patents and copyrights on their processes and procedures. Accountants play an important part in running this sort of company. The commodity supplier needs to have a strategy for doing all these things.

As we discussed in previous chapters, it is vital for a company following a policy of differentiation that it understands the basis of its differential advantage very clearly and then does whatever is needed to reinforce and build it. Differentiation involves being different and distinctive in some way. It often involves innovation. Branding has a vital role to play for a company trying to differentiate itself. A brand should be the embodiment of the product or service offering to customers. It takes time to build as it is based upon trust that the product or service will consistently deliver what it promises. A good brand is a valuable business asset and a firm following a differentiation strategy will need to invest time and money in developing it.

📁 Case insight Dell Computer Corporation

Dell Computers' market place is highly competitive. Dell prides itself on good marketing of quality products but, most important, speedy delivery of customised products. Nevertheless, whilst it might not sell the cheapest computers in the market place, the price it asks must always be competitive and that means costs must be kept as low as possible.

Dell decided early on that its competitive advantage lay in the computer-based processes it used to keep costs low and to build to order, quickly. In the 1990s,

in order to sustain these competitive advantages, Dell started applying for patents, not for its products, but for different parts of its ordering, building and testing processes. It now holds about 80 such patents. However good, the machines it sells have become commodities using homogenous components from hard disk drives to microprocessors – mostly from Intel – but the processes Dell uses to build them allow the company to achieve competitive advantage and to sustain it.

If a firm is focusing on a narrow market, then it needs to be undertaking regular market research to monitor changes in that market segment. Are tastes changing? Should the firm be adapting its offering to reflect these tastes? After all, the strength of the business should be its knowledge of and close relationship with the narrow market segment that it sells to. One danger is that the smaller the number of customers in a segment, the greater the risk that the changing buying patterns of just a few will have a dramatic impact on the firm. However, these days focusing on a narrow market segment can go hand in hand with having a global market of millions of customers.

Basically any brand is an assurance to customers. It is an assurance of quality, an assurance of consistency. There is an immediate recognition, when you see the Cadbury signature on the front of the chocolate bar or box of Milk Tray, all those things are guaranteed.

☐ Sir Adrian Cadbury, *The Times* 8 July 2000

📁 Case with questions Dmitry Kotenko and Nitol Solar

Dmitry Kotenko and a group of friends set up Nitol in 1998. A graduate of Baumann Technical Institute in Moscow, Dmitry left a career in science in the 1990s for a career in banking and then set up Nitol as a chemical trading company. However, the company changed completely when it acquired a ramshackle, 70-year-old, chemical factory, near the remote Siberian city of Irkutsk, at a knockdown price. What really attracted Dmitry was a small plant that produced a chemical called trichlorosilane, used in various industrial processes but, most importantly, a key ingredient in polysilicon, which is used in the production of solar panels. Solar panels were becoming big business at this time. Between 2003 and 2008, solar electricity production increased tenfold. The European Photovoltaic Association predict that it will quadruple again by 2013, if there is further government support. By 2008 global sales of solar energy equipment was $37.1 billion.

Dmitry set about refocusing the business, changing the name to Nitol Solar. The company invested $700 million to build modern production facilities, expanding the Irkutsk factory output and moving up the value chain into production of polysilicon itself. Raising the finance was not easy. Despite the fact that the company had some $1.66 billion in long-term contracts and had received $100 million in prepayment financing, a planned initial public offering on the London Stock Exchange in 2008 was cancelled. Instead, other investors stepped in, including Suntech Power Holdings, a leading Chinese solar cell manufacturer, that took a $100 million minority equity stake in the company, $75 million from the International Finance Corporation (IFC), part of the World Bank, and Rusnano (Russian Corporation of Nanotechnologies, a Russian Government financing corporation), which provided $140 million in credits and $94 million in guarantees.

➡

Most of the new plant is of foreign origin, but the basics existed in the old plant because pioneering solar technologies were developed by the Soviet space programme. The Irkutsk factory also had its track record of making trichlorosilane – described as 'the toughest part' of the manufacturing process. Full capacity was reached in 2010. Two other significant competitive advantages are low energy costs, based upon Russia's plentiful supplies of cheap gas, and low labour costs. Manufacturing costs for polysilicon in Russia in 2009 were around $30–$40 per kilogram compared to the market price of $80 per kilogram.

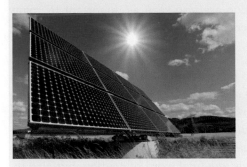

Today Nitol Solar is Russia's largest producer of polysilicon but it relies heavily on exports. It has customers around the world. One of the largest is Evergreen Solar, a Massachusetts-based US company, and a leading maker of solar products. However the Russian market remains very small because it has plentiful supplies of cheap fossil fuels, so Nitol's success has certainly not been based upon local market demand for its product.

☐ Up-to-date information on Nitol Solar can be found on their website: www.nitolsolar.com

QUESTIONS

1 Upon what is Nitol's success based?

2 How important and how sustainable are its competitive advantages?

3 If you were Dmitry, what would you do ensure the long-term viability of the business?

4 If you were Dmitry, what would your personal strategy be? Explain why.

♀ Successful entrepreneurial strategies

So, Porter wants you to select one of his generic strategies – cost leadership, differentiation or focus. Hamel and Prahalad want you to focus on core competencies. On the other hand, Treacy and Wiersema want you to select operational excellence, product leadership or customer intimacy. Which theory do you choose? The key theme is that strategy should emphasise something that makes the firm as unique as possible and delivers as much value to the customer as possible today and, more importantly, tomorrow. And we might add that, whatever you do, you must do it quickly so as to seize the market opportunity and that means, inevitably, that your strategy cannot be spelt out in detail. You need a firm idea of your general direction – your vision – and the rest of the firm will have to deal with the detail on a day-to-day basis.

And what does research tell us are the specific strategies that are most likely to ensure growth? In their survey of 179 supergrowth companies, Harrison and Taylor's (op. cit.) entrepreneurs identified five 'winning performance factors', most of which can be supported by other research:

1 *Compete on quality rather than price.* Competing on the quality of a product or service rather than price is an important element of success for entrepreneurial firms across Europe (Ray and Hutchinson, 1983; Storey et al., 1989; Burns, 1994). By way of contrast, slow growing firms tend to emphasise price (Burns, op. cit.).

2 *Dominate a market niche.* Many surveys support this conclusion about niche marketing (Solem and Steiner, 1989; Storey et al., 1989; Birley and Westhead, 1990; Macrae, 1991; Siegel et al., 1993; 3i, 1993). There is also a strong relationship between market share and financial return (Boston Consulting Group, 1968, 1972; Buzell et al., 1974; Buzell and Gale, 1987; Yelle, 1979).

3 *Compete in areas of strength.* This relates particularly to the previous point since the ability to differentiate effectively is a considerable strength.

4 *Have tight financial and operating controls.* Researchers often link strong financial control with planning (3i, 1991).

5 *Frequent product or service innovation* (particularly important in manufacturing). Innovation and new product introduction are also seen as important by many researchers (Dunkelberg et al., 1987; Solem and Steiner, op. cit.; Storey et al., 1989; Woo et al., 1989; Wynarczyk et al., 1993).

The conclusion is obvious. If you want to play the odds, *the strategy with the best chance of generating the highest profits is to differentiate with the aim of dominating that market and to do it effectively and quickly, then continue to innovate based on your differential advantage.*

> *We learned to identify our core strengths ... The idea of building a business solely on cost or price was not a sustainable advantage. There would always be someone with something that was lower in price or cheaper to produce. What was really important was sustaining loyalty among customers and employees, and that could only be derived from having the highest level of service and very high performing products.*
>
> ☐   Michael Dell (1999)

There is one final word of caution, but also reinforcement. Nohria and Joyce (2003) report the results of a ten-year study of 160 companies and their use of some 200 different management techniques. They conclude what we all suspect; that it does not matter so much which technique(s) you apply but it matters very much that you execute it flawlessly. They claim flawless execution is something too many management theorists have forgotten. Attention to detail is important. They also highlight three other things that distinguish successful companies over time:

1   A company culture that aims high.
2   A structure that is flexible and responsive.
3   A strategy that is clear and focused.

💡 Developing entrepreneurial strategies in the real world

We have talked very much as if strategy can be developed in a systematic, logical way. To a large extent strategy can be developed in this way. However, many entrepreneurs develop strategy instinctively – often they call it 'gut feel'. They do not know the jargon, do not use the frameworks we have developed – and justified with empirical evidence – but instinctively they arrive at the right decision. There is nothing wrong with this. These words and frameworks give meaning and logic to what they do. Many excellent musicians or athletes were not taught what they do. They picked up the skills instinctively. Explaining why they do what they do can give confidence to replicate their successes and even improve.

Strategic frameworks replicate what is good practice. They ought to be logical, common sense. They are not in the nature of a scientific discovery. They are, to quote a colleague, 'a glimpse of the blindingly obvious', something you knew all along but were never quite able to express it in that simple way. As John Kay (1998) explained:

> An organisational framework can never be right, or wrong, only helpful or unhelpful. A good organisational framework is minimalist – it is as simple as is consistent with illuminating the issues under discussion – and is memorable ... The organisational framework provides the link from judgement through experience to learning. A valid framework is one which

focuses sharply on what the skilled manager, at least instinctively, already knows. He is constantly alive to strengths, weaknesses, opportunities, threats which confront him ... A successful framework formalises and extends their existing knowledge. For the less practised, an effective framework is one which organises and develops what would otherwise be disjointed experience.

Some entrepreneurs may claim to have achieved their success through luck. Never underestimate luck, we all need it, but remember that entrepreneurs have a strong internal locus of control which means that they may believe in luck, but they do not believe in fate. They believe they can, and will, shape their own destiny and that may mean working to create more opportunities than most people. By creating more strategic options and opportunities, they improve their chances of successfully pursuing at least one. Make no mistake, entrepreneurs to a large extent create their own luck.

And yet there is always the nagging doubt that perhaps entrepreneurs are more opportunistic and adaptive, rather than calculating and planning in the way strategy is laid out in books. In fact this view is as old as strategy itself and was called by Lindblom (1959) 'the science of muddling through'. The implications of this for strategy were developed by Mintzberg (1978) who contrasted deliberate with emergent strategy. As he put it: 'The strategy-making process is characterised by reactive solution to existing problems ... The adaptive organisation makes its decisions in incremental, serial steps.' And here we do catch reflections of how the entrepreneur, in their spider's web of influence, approaches decision-making in a risky, uncertain and rapidly changing environment. But then there is nothing wrong with strategy that is incremental and adaptive, and that does not mean that strategy cannot be analysed, managed and controlled. The frameworks are just as useful. And successful entrepreneurs are constantly strategising – thinking about the future and analysing their options. Indeed many businessmen have gone so far as to suggest that formalised strategic planning is inappropriate in today's changing environment. What is needed instead is more strategising and the development of strategic options – options that lead the firm in the general direction it wants to go – with decisions on which option to select depending upon market conditions and opportunities (Mathewson, 2000). The greater the number of strategic options open to the firm, the safer it is in an uncertain environment.

So, for some firms, strategy development may be systematic and deliberate but for many entrepreneurial firms it is likely to be emergent. It is likely to be incremental and adaptive. 'Strategic intent' is still needed to give the firm clear direction, only the path to achieving these goals is not always clear. In these circumstances the process of strategising or strategy development is vital. The development of multiple strategic options is the key to success, with decision-making based upon opportunistic circumstances at the time.

What holds this all together is a strong vision of where the organisation is going. Thus entrepreneurs need to know the goal they are ultimately seeking and need to have the frameworks to make those incremental, adaptive decisions. There is nothing wrong with having a map with a planned route, but it makes sense to find a way around any road blocks you encounter rather than going headlong into them.

One interesting research study indicates that the strategy development process for growing SMEs actually changes from emergent to deliberate as they go through recurrent crises followed by periods of consolidation (McCarthy and Leavy, 2000). The study suggests that the strategy development process in small firms is both

GROWTH   CRISIS

EMERGENT   DELIBERATE
STRATEGY   STRATEGY
FORMULATION   FORMULATION

CONSOLIDATION

F11.8 The strategy formulation cycle

deliberate and emergent in nature and the degree of deliberateness in the early phase of development is influenced most by the personality of the entrepreneur and the nature of the business context. Over time strategy formulation follows a phase pattern, moving from an early fluid phase to a more defined phase, usually triggered by a crisis or defining episode, so that the degree of deliberateness is also a function of history, with firms oscillating between emergent strategy development, when learning is taking place, and deliberate planning modes over time. Rather than entrepreneurs having only one style, they would seem to adopt both, depending on circumstances. In this way the well documented process of growth to crisis to consolidation parallels a process of emergent to deliberate to emergent strategy formulation, represented in Figure 11.8.

🛍 Case with questions Lastminute.com

Lastminute sells travel (flights, hotels, holidays etc.), gifts (chocolates, lingerie, gourmet foods, fun experiences etc.) and leisure (theatre, concert, sports tickets etc.). It was set up in 1998 by Brent Hoberman (then 30 years old) and Martha Lane Fox (then 26) after raising £600 000 in venture capital. In 1999 it had a turnover of £195 000 and did not make a profit. By early 2000 the company was operating in the UK, France, Germany and Sweden, had 162

employees and 800 000 registered subscribers, and generated sales of £30 million. In the same year it was floated on the Stock Market at a valuation of more than £400 million. Lastminute has been one of the dot.com survivors, indeed successes, and both its founders have now left, having become millionaires.

Back in 2000, apart from the general dot.com frenzy of the time, there were four main reasons for the high float valuation of Lastminute.com, which together led commentators at the time to think the company would be a success:

1 *Brand*   Lastminute.com claimed early on to be the most recognised e-retailer in the UK after Amazon. This is partly as a result of a very 'old-media' advertising and promotion campaign. Branding recognition is vital to dot.coms, without it nobody visits their sites. Even today its aim is to be the Number 1 independent online travel and leisure group in Europe.

2 *Timing*   It was first in the market place and, only by 2000, were there signs of real competition. First movers have a distinct advantage in e-commerce – as the success of other dot.coms such as eBay and Amazon has proved. But the company decided that, whilst it had first mover advantage, economies of scale were important in this market and it needed to continue to grow quickly simply to survive as competition started to emerge. It therefore decided on a policy of aggressive acquisition to help it achieve scale in either a product category or in a relevant geographic market. Early on it purchased Dégrif-tour, France's biggest online travel company and, more importantly because of the name, Lastminute.de in Germany, which created the largest online travel company

→

in Germany. It also purchased the Destination Holdings Group, a direct-selling international tour operator. Throughout the first decade of its life Lastminute.com continued to have an aggressive acquisition strategy, taking over potential competition and consolidating its brand across Europe.

3 *Innovation* The products/services it offers are tailor-made for the internet. Not only are its partners eager to sell off their products at a discount to customers who have forgotten to buy them in the first place, it is also attempting to create a last minute market place in its own right, in which people can leave decisions about holidays etc. until a time that suits them. It is not just selling on cheapness, it is about getting its partners to provide a sufficient supply to make buying at the last minute a viable and reliable option. Hotel chains and airlines were generally receptive to the idea as it was a low-risk venture for them. No investment was required, all they had to do was allocate a certain amount of their product. As a result Lastminute.com developed an established supply chain very quickly. By 2004 it started to expand down its supply chain through strategic acquisitions such as Med Hotels, First Option, Gemstone.

4 *Track record* Although young, the founders grew the company with determination and a clear vision. Both had worked for Spectrum Strategy, a company that wrote business plans for technology firms, which gave them the opportunity to study the sector and understand what was needed for a successful dot.com start-up. They also recruited a strong, experienced management and directorial team from the very beginning. At various times the Board included Peter Bouw, former chairman and chief executive of KLM, Bob Colliers, vice president of Intercontinental Hotels, Linda Fayne Levinson, who ran Amex Travel, and Allan Leighton, former CEO of Wal-Mart and Chairman of Royal Mail Group. All have enormous experience and credibility with funding institutions. How did they attract such a strong management team? Martha Lane Fox explains:

> 'We decided not to be greedy about equity but to recruit a highly talented and experienced management team by selling them a dream – a stake in lastminute.com.'
>
> *The Times* 24 March 2000

> 'You try to attract the best person for the job, usually far too qualified for the stage that the company is at, but you hope it will grow to accommodate them. If as founders you think you can do better than everyone else, you are in big trouble, because you never can.'
>
> *Sunday Times* 28 July 2002

The success of Lastminute.com's business model depends on the number of site 'hits' it receives, how many convert into registrations for its weekly e-mail newsletters and how many then actually buy something. The company sees the newsletter, along with other relationship marketing techniques, as a very cost effective and quick way of building the brand personality and loyalty, demonstrating to potential customers the breadth of product range it offers and generally stimulating demand. The content is based upon a profile from the customer database which ensures that the content reflects their past purchases and therefore appears more tailored to their personal interests than normal 'junk mail'. The customer database is, therefore, a valuable strategic asset which grows organically with the company, accumulating data on every customer.

> 'We knew that if we had special offers we would get people onto the site, sign up for the e-mail, and forward it to someone who would take up the offer to go to New York for £100. The idea is to convert lookers into bookers. Our customer conversion rate is 19 per cent and we want to get it even higher. Small percentage points have a huge impact on sales. That is critical to the business. It's all about the cost of attracting customers and how much we have to spend to attract them balanced by what they're spending. We still need to build our customer base.'

☐ Up-to-date information on Lastminute can be found on their website: www.lastminute.com

QUESTIONS

1 Why has this company been successful when most dot. coms have not?

2 What advantages does it have over 'bricks-and-mortar' companies?

3 Why is size important for Lastminute?

4 What advantages does Lastminute offer consumers of its goods/services?

5 What advantages does Lastminute offer suppliers of its goods/services?

6 Why has its business orientation evolved since its launch?

7 In what direction would you take the firm now?

📋 Case with questions easyJet

One firm that has successfully followed the low-price strategy is easyJet. It was founded by Stelios Haji-Ioannou, a graduate of London Business School, in 1995 with £5 million borrowed from his father, a Greek shipping tycoon. Copying similar operations in the USA and Ryanair flying out of Ireland, easyJet was one of the first 'low-cost' airlines in the UK, flying from Luton to Scotland. He then launched similar low-cost, no-frills services to continental Europe. The company has transformed the European air travel market and has beaten off many rival imitators. easyJet was floated on the Stock Market in 2000 at 310p a share, making Stelios £280 million profit.

> 'You start the business as a dream, you make it your passion for a while and then you get experienced managers to run it because it's not as much fun as starting. I think there's a lot to be said about starting a business and a lot to be said about running a business when its mature.'
>
> *Sunday Times* 29 October 2000

A central strategy of being low-price is being low-cost and that has a number of implications for the way easyJet and its rivals are run. Low costs come from two driving principles – 'sweating' the assets and high operating efficiency. easyJet flies its Boeing 737s for 11 hours a day, 4 hours longer than BA. Their pilots fly 900 hours a year, 50 per cent more than BA pilots.

In terms of operating efficiency, it means:

▷ Aircraft fly out of low-cost airports. These are normally not the major airport serving any destination and can be some distance from the destination.
▷ Aircraft are tightly scheduled. They are allowed only 25 minutes to off-load one set of passengers and load another, less than half the time of its scheduled full-fare rivals.
▷ Aircraft must leave and arrive on time (they will not wait for passengers), and if there are delays they can have horrendous knock-on consequences for the timetable. Nevertheless punctuality is varied, with the low-cost carriers just as good as full-fare airlines on some routes.
▷ There is no 'slack' in the system. easyJet admits to having 'one and a half planes' worth' of spare capacity compared with the dozen planes BA has on stand-by at Gatwick and Heathrow. If something goes wrong with a plane it can lead to cancellations and long delays.
▷ There are fewer cabin crew than full-fare rivals and staff rostering is a major logistical problem.

In terms of customer service, it means:

▷ No 'frills' such as free drinks, meals or assigned seats.
▷ There is no compensation for delays or lost baggage.
▷ The low-cost airlines do not guarantee transfers as the planes could be late.
▷ The low-cost airlines concentrate on point-to-point flights, whereas the full-fare airlines tend to concentrate on hub-and-spoke traffic.

easyJet is aggressive in promoting its brand and running advertising promotions to get more 'bums on seats'. It realises that its planes must have a high seat occupancy to be economic. To this end it is particularly inventive with pricing, encouraging real bargain hunters onto the less popular flights during the day and promoting early bookings with cheaper fares.

easyJet has been at the forefront of the use of the internet for virtual ticketing, to the point where it now sells most of its tickets over the web. This means it does not have to

→

pay commission to travel agents and check-in can be quicker and more efficient. Its website has been held up as a model for the industry and many have copied it.

However, easyJet does have competition and some airlines are cheaper. Whilst easyJet claim an average price of £45 per 600 kilometres, Ryanair claim £34. This compares to British Airways' price of £110. Interestingly Ryanair has so little faith in its timetable that it advises passengers not to book connecting flights.

One of the fears about low-cost airlines has been that they will be tempted to compromise on safety for the sake of cutting costs. The British Airline Pilots Association has claimed that pilots of low-cost airlines have been tempted to cut corners to achieve flight timetables. Stelios himself fuelled the safety debate by expressing doubts about Ryanair's use of 20-year-old planes on some of its routes, pointing out that though they might improve profits in the short term, they put the future of the whole airline at risk in the event of an accident. Ryanair has phased these planes out and does have an unblemished safety record. But the industry is all too aware that the low-cost US airline, Valuejet, went bankrupt after one of its planes crashed in 1996, killing all 110 people on board. As the *Economist* said (17 August 2002): 'the low cost airline business is not for the faint-hearted'.

Only seven years after founding the company, in 2002, and still owning 29 per cent of easyJet Stelios realised that he was not suited to managing an established public company and was better suited to being a serial entrepreneur, so he resigned as Chairman, aged only 35. He was to be replaced by Sir Colin Chandler, aged 62, part of London's financial establishment as chairman of Vickers Defence Systems, deputy chairman of Smiths Group and director of Thales.

> 'Running a company that is listed on the Stock Exchange is different from building up and running a private company. The history of the City is littered with entrepreneurs who hold onto their creations for too long, failing to recognise the changing needs of the company. I am a serial entrepreneur ... It is all part of growing up. I've built something and now it is time to move on.'
>
> *The Times* 19 April 2002

Shortly after Stelios' departure easyJet took over Go, the low-cost airline set up by British Airways and sold off to its management. Newspaper comment at the time suggested Stelios had been blocking such a deal and this might have been one reason for his departure.

Go had been in fierce price competition with easyJet on certain routes, to the point where tickets were being given away with only airport tax to pay. One of the first things easyJet did was to close the Go flights on these routes and restore prices. As well as eliminating competition, the purchase of Go had other strategic reasoning behind it. easyJet were purchasing market share in a fast-growing market (in 2002 it grew 60 per cent) where there are economies of scale. They were also buying new routes and landing rights, which can be difficult to secure.

Stelios still has many other 'easy' ventures to grow. These include easyCar – a car rental business, easyEverything – a chain of internet cafes and cinemas, and easyValue – which provides impartial comparisons for online shopping. He still has everything to play for, doing something he enjoys more and possibly does better.

☐ Up-to-date information on easyJet can be found on their website: www.easyjet.com

QUESTIONS

1 Based upon this information, undertake a SWOT analysis on easyJet

2 Compared to Ryanair and British Airways, where would you place easyJet in terms of Porter's generic marketing strategies? Is this sustainable?

3 What is the underlying strategy behind all of Stelios' 'easy' ventures? Can this strategy be replicated in any market? What is required for it to work?

19 If you are being really innovative – revolutionary – you are venturing into the unknown and you cannot plan for that. What form might planning take in these circumstances?

20 How can futures thinking and scenario planning help you think about the future?

21 How do you think music will be sold in the future? How can firms make a profit from it?

22 A firm needs two plans – one for the provider of capital that 'sells' the business idea to them and a second that is a true evaluation of how the firm might perform. Discuss.

23 How would you go about undertaking a SWOT on an established small firm?

24 In an uncertain world, planning is a waste of time and developing strategy a meaningless activity. Discuss.

25 How do entrepreneurs develop strategy? Explain and give examples.

26 Are entrepreneurs lucky?

⮌ Exercises and assignments

1 Select a successful entrepreneur such as Bill Gates or Richard Branson and research their backgrounds, showing how their business developed, and analyse why they have been so successful.

2 Undertake a financial analysis on the forecast results of PC Modem (Appendix 1, Chapter 9) using the Financial Audit Checklist in Figure 11.5.

3 For a selected set of published financial statements, undertake a financial analysis using the Financial Audit Checklist in Figure 11.5.

4 Undertake a SLEPT analysis on your university, college or department. Based upon this, try scenario planning on one major trend that you identify.

5 Undertake a SLEPT analysis on a selected firm. Based upon this, try scenario planning on one major trend that you identify.

6 Undertake a SWOT analysis on your university, college or department. Draw up a list of action points that follow from your analysis.

7 Undertake a comprehensive SWOT analysis on your course. Draw up a list of action points that follow from your analysis.

📖 References

3i European Enterprise Centre (1991) *High Performance SMEs: A Two Country Study*, Report no. 1, September.

3i European Enterprise Centre (1993) *Britain's Superleague Companies*, Report no. 9, August.

Bartlett, C.A. and Ghoshal, S. (1994) 'Changing the Role of Top Management: Beyond Strategy to Purpose', *Harvard Business Review*, November/December.

Berkhout, F. and Green, K. (2003) *International Journal of Innovation Management*, 6(3), Special issue on Managing Innovation for Sustainability.

Birley, S. and Westhead, P. (1990) 'Growth and Performance Contrasts Between "Types" of Small Firms', *Strategic Management Journal*, II.

Boston Consulting Group (1968) *Perspectives on Experience*, Boston, MA: Boston Consulting Group.

Boston Consulting Group (1972) *Perspectives on Experience*, Boston, MA: Boston Consulting Group.

Burke, L. and Logsdon, J.M. (1996) 'How Corporate Social Responsibility Pays off', *Long Range Planning*, 29(4).

Burns, P. (1994) *Winners and Losers in the 1990s*, 3i European Enterprise Centre, Report no. 12, April.

Buzell, R.D. and Gale, B.T. (1987) *The PIMS Principles – Linking Strategy to Performance*, New York: Free Press.

Buzell, R.D., Heany, D.F. and Schoeffer, S. (1974) 'Impact of Strategic Planning on Profit Performance', *Harvard Business Review*, 52(2).

de Colle, S. and Gonella, C. (2002) 'The Social and Ethical Alchemy: An Integrative Approach to Social and Ethical Accountability', *Business Ethics: A European Review*, 11(1).

Dunkelberg, W.G., Cooper, A.C., Woo, C. and Dennis, W.J. (1987) 'New Firm Growth and Performance', in N.C. Churchill, J.A. Hornday, B.A. Kirchhoff, C.J. Krasner and K.H. Vesper (eds), *Frontiers of Entrepreneurship Research*, Boston, MA: Babson College Press.

Environics International (2001) *Corporate Social Responsibility Monitor 2001: Global Public Opinion* on the Changing Role of Companies, Toronto, Canada: Environics International (now Globescan).

Epstein, M.J. and Roy, M.J. (2001) 'Sustainability in Action: Identifying and Measuring the Key Performance Drivers', Long Range Planning, 34.

Hamel, G. and Prahalad, C.K. (1994) Competing for the Future: Breakthrough Strategies for Seizing Control of your Industry and Creating the Markets of Tomorrow, Boston, MA: Harvard Business School Press.

Harrison, J. and Taylor, B. (1996) Supergrowth Companies: Entrepreneurs in Action, Oxford: Butterworth-Heinemann.

Jovanovic, B. (2001) 'New Technology and the Small Firm', Small Business Economics, 16(1).

Kay, J. (1998) Foundations of Corporate Success, Oxford: Oxford University Press.

Lindblom, L.E. (1959) 'The Science of Muddling Through', Public Administration Review, 19, Spring.

Macrae, D.J.R. (1991) 'Characteristics of High and Low Growth Small and Medium-Sized Businesses', paper presented at 21st European Small Business Seminar, Barcelona, Spain.

Mathewson, Sir G., (2000) Keynote address, British Academy of Management Annual Conference, Edinburgh.

McCarthy, B. and Leavy, B. (2000) 'Strategy Formation in Irish SMEs: A Phase Model of Process', British Academy of Management Annual Conference, Edinburgh.

Mintzberg, H. (1978) 'Patterns in Strategy Formation', Management Science, 934–48.

Nanus, B. (1992) Visionary Leadership: Creating a Compelling Sense of Direction for your Organization, San Francisco: Jossey-Bass.

Nohria, N. and Joyce, W. (2003) 'What Really Works', Harvard Business Review, July/August.

Nonaka, I. (1991) 'The Knowledge-Creating Company', Harvard Business Review, November/December.

Porter, M.E. (1985) Competitive Advantage: Creating and Sustaining Superior Performance, New York: Free Press.

Prahalad, C.K. and Hamel, G. (1990) 'The Core Competence of the Corporation', Harvard Business Review, 68(3), May/June.

Ray, G.H. and Hutchinson, P.J. (1983) The Financing and Financial Control of Small Enterprise Development, London: Gower.

Siegel, R., Siegel, E. and MacMillan, I.C. (1993) 'Characteristics Distinguishing High Growth Ventures, Journal of Business Venturing, 8.

Smith, N.C. (2003) 'Corporate Social Responsibility: Whether or How?', California Management Review, 45(4).

Solem, O. and Steiner, M.P. (1989) 'Factors for Success in Small Manufacturing Firms – and with Special Emphasis on Growing Firms', paper presented at Conference on SMEs and the Challenges of 1992, Mikkeli, Finland.

Storey, D.J., Keasey, K., Watson, R. and Wynarczyk, P. (1987) The Performance of Small Firms: Profits, Jobs and Failures, London: Croom Helm.

Storey D.J., Watson R. and Wynarczyk, P. (1989) Fast Growth Small Business: Case Studies of 40 Small Firms in Northern Ireland, Department of Employment, research paper no. 67.

Treacy, M. and Wiersema, F. (1995) The Discipline of Market Leaders, Reading, MA: Addison Wesley.

Verschoor, C.C. (2002) 'Best Corporate Citizens have Better Financial Performance', Strategic Finance, January.

Wickham, P.A. (2001) Strategic Entrepreneurship: A Decision-Making Approach to New Venture Creation and Management, Harlow: Pearson Education.

Woo, C.Y., Cooper, A.C., Dunkelberg, W.C., Daellenbach, U. and Dennis, W.J. (1989) 'Determinants of Growth for Small and Large Entrepreneurial Start-Ups', paper presented to Babson Entrepreneurship Conference.

Wood, D. (2000) 'Theory and Integrity in Business and Society', Business and Society, 39(4).

Wynarczyk, P., Watson, R., Storey, D.J., Short, H. and Keasey, K. (1993) The Managerial Labour Market in Small and Medium-Sized Enterprises, London: Routledge.

Yelle, L.E. (1979) 'The Learning Curve: Historical Review and Comprehensive Survey', Decision Sciences, 10.

12 New products and services

▷ **Product life cycles**
▷ **Product portfolios**
▷ **Portfolio strategies**
▷ **Managing the product life cycle**
▷ **Financial implications of the product portfolio**
▷ **Implications for the entrepreneur**
▷ **Summary**

Case insights
▷ Heineken

Cases with questions
▷ Cadbury 1
▷ Barbie and Mattel Corporation

Learning outcomes

By the end of this chapter you should be able to:

▷ Explain the effect of product life cycles on marketing strategy;

▷ Explain how the life cycle can be lengthened through product expansion and extension;

▷ Use the Boston matrix to present marketing strategies for a portfolio of products;

▷ Describe the effects of the product portfolio on cash flow and profitability;

▷ Describe the implications of the product portfolio on management styles and the problems this creates for the entrepreneur;

▷ Explain how the concept of life cycle can be extended to companies and industries and what the implications of this are for management.

💡 Product life cycles

As they grow most firms become more complex organisations. They introduce new products or services as original ones age. After a few years most companies find themselves selling a range of different products or services into a range of different markets, each with a different strategy. These are called different 'product/market offerings'. The same product can even be sold to different market segments with a slightly different strategy. Slightly different products might also be developed to better meet the needs of different market segments. The permutations are endless.

One important influence on the marketing strategy for a product or service is the point it is at in its life cycle. This can be used to identify the different market segments attracted to the product and the degree and nature of competition it faces. From this comes another set of 'routine patterns, based on experience', which can be used either as a strategy checklist or as a benchmark to assess how different you dare to be – but remember the odds! This concept can, in turn, be used to better understand the complexity of the portfolio of different product/market offerings and how that portfolio can be managed. The concept of the product life cycle is based on the idea that all products or services have a finite life cycle and that, to some extent, the appropriate marketing strategy is dictated by the stage it is at in this life cycle. Life cycles can vary in length from short for fashion products, such as clothing and other consumables, to long for durable products like cars. Often the life cycle can be extended by a variety of marketing initiatives. Figure 12.1 shows a four-stage product life cycle with the implications for marketing strategy at the different stages. The simplicity of the model has much to recommend it. However, these broad generalisations must be treated with caution because all products are different, as are different market segments and the customers that comprise them.

At the introductory phase the objective should be to make potential customers aware of the product and to get them to try it. The benefits need to be explained and the relevance to the customer needs to be underlined. Early customers are likely to be 'innovators', that is people who think for themselves and try things. It has been estimated that they make up some 2.5 per cent of the population (Rogers, 1962) although, with fashions or fads, the proportion can be higher. Entrepreneurial firms launching innovative new products are particularly interested in this phase, and where novelty or uniqueness is high, as it was with the iPad, prices charged can be high.

At the growth phase the objective should be to grab market share as quickly as possible because competitors will be entering the market. This means that prices will have to be competitive, depending on the uniqueness of the product and how well it can be differentiated. The promotion emphasis should shift to one of promoting the brand and why it is better than that of competitors. By this stage 'early adopters' will be buying the product. These tend to be people with status in their market segment and opinion leaders. They adopt successful products, making them acceptable and respectable. These have been estimated to represent some 13.5 per cent of the population. The product range should start to be developed at this stage so as to give customers more choice and gain advantage over competitors.

The 'middle and late majority' next start buying the product and take it into the mature phase of its life cycle. The middle majority (comprising some 34 per cent) are more conservative, with slightly higher status and are more deliberate purchasers. They only adopt the product after it has become acceptable. The late majority (also comprising some 34 per cent) are typically below average status, are sceptical and

Sales

Introduction	Growth	Maturity	Decline
Low sales	High, rapidly increasing sales	Static but high sales	Declining sales
Low growth	Higher profits as costs come down	Static but high profits	Declining profits or losses
Low profits or losses as costs are high	Competitors emerging and competition intensifying	Focus on cost reduction	Competitors exit
Few competitors		Fight for market share	
		Established competitors	

Time

| *Innovators* | *Early adopters* | *Middle and late majority* | *Laggards* |

Elements of marketing strategy

Basic product	Develop product extensions and service levels	Wide range in place but expansion slows down or eventually ceases	Range narrows
Price low for repeat purchase products where trial is important	Price competitively to combat competition and penetrate market	Modify and differentiate	Weak products are dropped
Price high where novelty or uniqueness is valued, particularly if purchases are infrequent	Promote actively and aggressively	Develop next generation	Price high if reducing number of competitors means demand still high
		Price defensively – meeting or beating competitors – to ensure maximum return	
	Build brand	Emphasise brand	Price low to dispose of stocks at end of life, in line with declining demand
Promote actively and aggressively	Intensive push on distribution	Differentiate	
Explain product benefits	Limited trade discounts	Selective marketing, based around special offers or promotions	Minimum promotion required to maintain loyalty
Build awareness, encourage early adoption		Intensive push on distribution	
		Trade discounts offered	Emphasis on low price
Selective distribution			Distribute selectively
			Phase out weak outlets

F12.1 The product/service life cycle

adopt the product much later. In this phase competitors are becoming established as some companies fall by the wayside. In order to maintain market share, pricing tends to be defensive at, or around, the level of competitors. There should be an emphasis on cost reduction so that profits are as high as possible. The accountant's influence should be evident at this stage in the life cycle. It is at this point that products tend to get revamped – by changing designs, colours, packaging and so on – in order to extend their life cycle. Toward the end of this period, price reductions may be hidden by offering extra elements to the product for the same price. Cars, for example, often get this treatment with limited edition models offering many extras for the same price.

'Laggards' (comprising some 16 per cent) tend to view life through the rear view mirror and will continue buying products because of habit. The interesting thing about the decline phase of the life cycle is that there may still be the opportunity to charge high prices and make good profits, at least in the short term, because competitors may be exiting the market quicker than demand is tailing off. Exactly when to exit is therefore a matter of careful judgement.

The problem with this concept is one of trying to establish where a product might actually be. Firms plotting their own product sales are not recording the product's life but their ability to manage it. Bad management can lead to an early downturn in sales which is not necessarily the mature phase of the life cycle, and vice versa. What is more, products can be at the mature phase of their life cycle in one market but at the introductory phase in another. You only have to see the queues and check the prices for McDonald's hamburgers in many emerging markets to realise that the product has a long way to go in these, never mind where it is in the mature Western markets. Not only can the length of the life cycle vary from country to country and product to product or new technology to new technology, but the length of each phase can also vary. The take-off phase comes when slow initial sales accelerate towards a mass market. This introductory phase can take a number of years but is becoming shorter and shorter as time goes on. 'White goods' – refrigerators, washing machines, freezers and so on – have generally taken longer. 'Brown goods' – TVs, CD and DVD players, iPods and so on – have generally taken less time. But the average 'time-to-take-off' also varies from country to country.

Tellis et al. (2003) studied 137 new product launches across 10 consumer durable categories in 16 European countries and found that, despite the Common Market, there were considerable differences, summarised in Table 12.1. Scandinavian countries tended to have the shortest 'time-to-take-off' – for example 3.3 years in Denmark. This was well ahead of the largest EU economies of France, Germany, Italy, Spain and the UK. The average time in Scandinavian countries was 4 years, compared to 7.4 years in Mediterranean countries. They concluded that cultural factors partly explain the differences. In particular, the probability of take-off increases in countries that are placed high in an index of achievement and industriousness and low in uncertainty avoidance. Economic factors were found not to be strong or robust explanatory variables. They also found that the probability of a new product's take-off in one country increased with prior take-offs in other countries. The authors therefore recommend that managers adopt a 'waterfall' strategy for product introduction in Europe, putting them first into the countries that are likely to have the shortest 'time-to-take-off'.

The consulting firm Arthur D. Little linked the life cycle to competitive position within a product/market sector to produce the resulting implications for strategy based upon Porter's generic strategies. Figure 12.2 summarises their analysis. In many

Upper quartile: 8 to 10 years	Greece UK
Upper-middle quartile: 6 to 8 years	France Spain Italy Germany
Average 6 years	
Lower-middle quartile: 4 to 6 years	Finland Sweden
Lower quartile: up to 4 years	Norway Denmark

T12.1 New products: average time-to-take-off in Europe

Life cycle stage

	Start-up	Growth	Maturity	Decline
Dominant	Grow fast	Grow fast Attain cost leadership	Defend position Attain cost leadership Review	Defend position Renew Grow with industry
Strong	Differentiate Grow fast	Grow fast Catch up Differentiate	Reduce costs Differentiate Grow with industry	Find and hold niche Grow with industry Harvest profit
Satisfactory	Differentiate Focus Grow fast	Differentiate Focus Grow with industry	Harvest profit Find niche Grow with industry	Consolidate Cut costs
Weak	Focus Grow with industry	Harvest, catch up Find and hold niche Turn around	Harvest profit Turn around Find niche Consolidate	Divest
Very weak	Find niche Grow with industry	Turn around Consolidate	Withdraw Divest	Withdraw

Competitive position (vertical axis label)

F12.2 The life cycle and competitive position

ways it is an over-simplified version of Figure 12.1, but it does, once more, act as a checklist that allows you to focus on the imperatives for the business. At the two extremes it emphasises that if you dominate a market at start-up, it pays to grow fast, whilst if you are in a very weak position with a product at the end of its life cycle you might as well cut your losses and get out of the market as quickly as possible.

♀ Product portfolios

As already outlined, if a company has more than one product or service, then it might be following different strategies for each of the different product/market offerings it has and one important reason for this is that each of these offerings might be at a different stage of its life cycle in the particular market. So, for example, McDonald's may have a different marketing mix for its products in emerging markets, where it is at the introductory or take-off phase of its life cycle, compared to the USA, where it is a mature product – although the length of the life cycle in these emerging markets is likely to be a lot shorter than it was in the USA.

This added complexity of having a portfolio of product/market offerings can be handled using a technique adapted from the 'Boston Matrix', which derives its name from the Boston Consulting Group that developed it. The original matrix was adapted by McKinsey so as to have more realistic multidimensional axes. Figure 12.3 shows the adapted matrix. Market attractiveness – the strengths and resources that relate to the market – is measured on the vertical axis. The strength of product or service offering in the market – sales, relative market share and so on – is measured on the horizontal axis. When a product or service offering is first developed it will be launched into an attractive market (otherwise why do it?), but the firm is unlikely to have a great deal of strength. This is called a problem child and is equivalent to the introduction phase of the life cycle. Sometimes the market proves to be unattractive – then the life cycle is

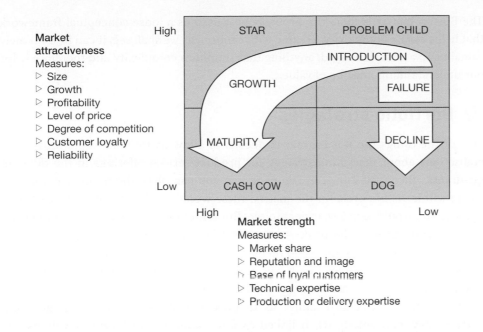

Market
attractiveness
Measures:
▷ Size
▷ Growth
▷ Profitability
▷ Level of price
▷ Degree of competition
▷ Customer loyalty
▷ Reliability

Market strength
Measures:
▷ Market share
▷ Reputation and image
▷ Base of loyal customers
▷ Technical expertise
▷ Production or delivery expertise

F12.3 The Boston matrix

very short. This is called a dog. More often, if the market is attractive, sales will grow and the product or service offering will become more established and will strengthen in the market. This is called a star. Eventually, however, the market will mature and the product or service will become a cash cow. These are market leaders with a lot of stability but little additional growth because they are at the end of their life cycle.

There are many problems with the framework at an operational level, centring around measurement of the elements on the two axes. For example, defining the market a firm is in so that you can measure market share or market growth. You can use just one factor on each axis or, indeed, a number of them weighted appropriately using some sort of simple scale. Nevertheless the problem of measurement remains.

🧳 Case insight Heineken

Heineken is Europe's largest brewer and is second only to the US brewer Anheuser-Busch world-wide. The brand is recognised around the world. However, its dominant market position, particularly in Europe where 40 per cent of the world's beers are consumed, is maintained by actually having a portfolio of brands that allow it to adjust its marketing mix to suit the tastes and needs of local markets. It also allows it to create the necessary distribution network and achieve high levels of economies of scale in production. Heineken typically has three core brands in each European country:

▷ A local brand aimed at the largest market segment, offered at a competitive price. In France it has '33', in Spain it has Aguila Pilsner and in Italy it has Dreher.
▷ A brand aimed at the upper end of the market such as Amstel or the locally produced Aguila Master in Spain.
▷ The premium Heineken brand itself where every effort is made to maintain quality and brand integrity. In the UK the product itself has been developed (called product expansion) into Heineken Export Strength, a stronger version more like the usual Heineken found throughout the rest of Europe.

☐ Up-to-date information on Heineken can be found on their website: www.heineken.com

The Boston matrix is therefore probably best used as a loose conceptual framework that helps clarify complexity. Treated with caution, as we shall see, it can be extremely valuable. In a complex world, anything that simplifies complexity and therefore helps our understanding must be of value.

💡 Portfolio strategies

One of the things the Boston matrix does is to allow us to make some broad generalisations about marketing strategy for product/service offerings in the different quadrants. These are shown in Figure 12.4. If you can place the product/market offering within its life cycle on the matrix, these would be the elements of marketing strategy you would, *a priori*, expect to see. But remember that, whilst this framework reflects product life cycles, it does not reflect Porter's generic marketing strategies, which need to be superimposed on them. Having said that, as a product nears the end of its life cycle and becomes a cash cow, it is more likely to be on its way to becoming a commodity and therefore having to sell on price.

The Boston matrix also allows us to present complex information more understandably, particularly when linked to forecasting future market positions and strategies involved in getting there. For example, Figure 12.5 represents a hypothetical three-product portfolio for a company. The size of each circle is proportionate to the turnover each achieves. The lighter circles represent the present product positions, the darker circles represent the positions projected in three years' time. The portfolio looks balanced and the diagram can be used to explain the strategies that are in place to move the products to where they are planned to be. Again, one essential added complexity is the generic marketing strategies. If products A and B are commodities, selling mainly on price, with low margin under intense pressure, it has implications not only for strategy but also for the cash flow available to invest in product C. This is particularly applicable if this is a niche market product needing heavy investment.

	STAR	PROBLEM CHILD
High	*Objective*: Invest for growth ▷ Penetrate market ▷ Expand geographically ▷ Sell and promote aggressively ▷ Differentiate ▷ Promote brand, if possible ▷ Accept moderate short-term profits ▷ Extend product range	*Objective*: Develop opportunities ▷ Be critical of prospects ▷ Invest selectively in products or services ▷ Specialise in strengths ▷ Shore up weaknesses
Low	*Objective*: Maintain market position and manage for earnings ▷ Maintain market position with successful products or services ▷ Prune less successful products in range ▷ Differentiate ▷ Promote brand, if possible ▷ Stabilise prices, except where temporary aggressive pricing is required in the face of competition CASH COW	*Objective*: Either kill off or maintain and monitor carefully ▷ Minimise expenditure ▷ Improve productivity ▷ Maximise cash flow ▷ Live with declining sales until the best time to kill off product DOG

Market attractiveness (vertical axis), Market strength High–Low (horizontal axis)

F12.4 The Boston matrix – strategy implications

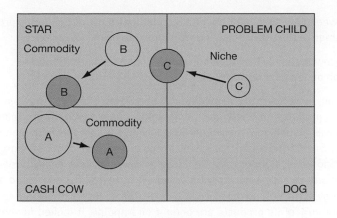

F12.5 Boston matrix for hypothetical company

🗂 Case with questions Cadbury 1

Cadbury is a very well known British confectionery company. Originally a family firm started by John Cadbury and grounded in Quaker values and ideals, it started life in 1824 as a shop selling chocolate as a virtuous alternative to alcohol. It went on to become a large-scale manufacturer of chocolate based at the now legendary Bournville factory, built in 1879, and its picturesque workers' village with its red-brick terraces, cottages, duck ponds and wide open parks. Over the next 100 years Cadbury developed the products that have become so familiar: *Dairy Milk* in 1905, *Milk Tray* in 1915, *Flake* in 1920, *Creme Egg* in 1923, *Roses* in 1938 and more.

From 1969 it traded as Cadbury Schweppes plc until, in 2008, it separated its global confectionery business (which retained the name 'Cadbury') from its US beverages business, which was renamed Dr Pepper Snapple Group Inc. Cadbury Schweppes had already sold off most of its beverages businesses in other countries around the world, a process started in 1999 and concluded in 2009 with the sale of its Australian beverages business. The reason for the exit from the beverages business was to enable Cadbury to focus more clearly on what it saw as its core strengths in confectionery, and better enhance shareholder value. Beverages had become the 'poor sister' in the relationship, with a separate management structure but delivering growth below the targets for the company.

In 2008 the newly de-merged Cadbury set as its goal maintaining its market leadership position, and leveraging its scale and advantaged positions so as to maximise growth and returns. Its vision was to become 'the biggest and best confectionery company in the world' and its governing objective was 'to deliver superior shareholder returns'. To this end, Todd Stitzer, Cadbury's Chief Executive, developed the company's 'Vision into Action' plan for 2008 to 2011 which aimed to deliver six financial targets:

▷ Organic revenue growth of 4%–6% every year;
▷ Total confectionery market share gain;
▷ Trading operating margins improvement from around 10% to mid teens by 2011;
▷ Strong dividend growth;
▷ An efficient balance sheet growth in return on invested capital (ROIC).

By 2009 Cadbury was the second largest confectionery company in the world after Mars-Wrigley. It had a 10% share of the global market and held the number 1 or 2 positions in over 20 of the top 50 world confectionery markets, with strong brands in the markets for chocolate (Cadbury, Fry, Bournville, Green & Black's and Jaffa), gum (Trebor, Trident and Hollywood Chewing Gum) and candy (Bassett's and Maynards). It also generated 38% of its sales from new 'emerging' markets. Confectionery revenues grew by almost 6%, on

➡

average, between 2004 and 2009, despite the fact that most of Cadbury's products were at the mature stage of their life cycle. This growth came from two sources:

▷ organic growth, mainly through finding new channels of distribution;
▷ acquisition of new brands.

The company was also very focused on making cost and efficiency savings, as aging products were produced at lower costs and supply chain savings were made. As a result the business was also hugely cash generative, giving the company between £300 and £400 million a year. So how did it use this cash surplus to generate continuing growth?

As a starting point, Cadbury was looking for new markets for its products but most of these products already sold around the world. It, therefore, developed a two-pronged growth strategy, with both strands reliant upon the company's strong cash flow. First, because about 70% of its products are bought on impulse, it looked for new channels of distribution so as to encourage sales, or 'indulgence opportunities' as they were called. Chocolate bars are now sold anywhere from petrol stations to off-licences and from restaurants to pubs. Vending machines selling them can be found anywhere from factory floors to train stations.

The second strand to the company's strategy was buying into other related high-growth segments where the company can capitalise on its existing distribution chains or use new distribution chains to sell more of its existing products. The company has followed an acquisitions strategy for many years, in part to get into the fast-growing chewing gum market. In 2000 Cadbury bought *Hollywood*, the French gum maker, and *Dandy*, the Danish gum maker. In 2002 it purchased the US company, Adams, from Pfizer. Adams' brands include *Halls*, *Trident*, *Dentyne*, *Bubbas*, *Clorets*, *Chiclets* and *Certs*. It also purchased *Intergum* in Turkey and *Kandia-Excelent* in Romania. By 2008 gum and other 'better for you' products accounted for some 30% of confectionery sales. But there were other confectionery acquisitions such as *Green & Black's* in 2005. These acquisitions made Cadbury the market leader in non-chocolate confectionery, including gum and 'functional' products such as sore throat remedies, and gave it a foothold in markets such as Japan and Latin America.

The company managed each confectionery category – chocolate, gum and candy – on a global basis, focusing on markets where it saw itself as having a competitive advantage. It focused its resources on its top 13 brands, which accounted for around 50% of confectionery revenue in 2008. These brands grew at 10% in 2007 and 8% in 2008. Within this group, five brands were judged to have the strongest potential in existing and new markets on a global basis – Cadbury, Trident, Halls, Green & Black's and The Natural Confectionery Co. The remaining eight brands in the top thirteen were: Creme Egg and Flake in chocolate; Hollywood, Dentyne, Stimorol, Clorets and Bubbaloo in gum; and Eclairs in candy.

Cadbury also focused on a limited number of markets in each category, based on their size or their potential for future scale and growth. Six countries – USA, UK, Mexico, Russia, India and China – were judged to have strong growth opportunities across all confectionery categories. Growth opportunities in other countries were more varied: chocolate in South Africa and Australia; gum in Brazil, France, Japan and Turkey; and candy in Brazil, France, South Africa and Australia. The company also focused its efforts on seven leading customers and three trade channels which, together, accounted for 14% of confectionery revenue in 2008, showing growth of 8%.

Its approach to entry into new markets was to use existing distribution strengths wherever possible. So, for example, the launch of gum in the UK market under the Trident brand complemented an existing strong presence in chocolate and candy. Cadbury's ultimate aim is to have a strong position in all three confectionery categories in all the markets in which it operates.

When it came to innovation, the number of smaller, 'non-advantaged' innovations were reduced. Instead resources were focused on larger innovations from which the company could derive competitive advantage.

So has the strategy been successful? The 2009 results showed sales up once more by 5% (11% on actual currency base), with emerging markets showing growth of 9% and developed markets 2%. Chocolate represented 46% of revenues, gum 33% and candy 21%. Emerging markets represented 38% of revenues and developed markets 62%. Cadbury had held or gained market share in markets that generated over 70% of its revenues. Operating margins also improved to 13.5% due to both an improved gross margin and a reduction in sales, general and administrative costs. Recommended dividends were up 10% on 2008.

However, we may never know whether the Vision into Action plan delivers its 2013 objectives because in 2010, following an acrimonious take-over battle, the US food giant, Kraft Foods, bought Cadbury for £11.5 billion, and de-listed the company from the UK stock exchange. Todd Stitzer, architect of Cadbury's strategy, resigned as Chief Executive following 27 years of service with the company, as did the Cadbury Chairman, Roger Carr.

In a press release on 14 January 2010 Todd Stitzer commented:

> 'Our performance in 2009 was outstanding. We generated good revenue growth despite the weakest economic conditions in 80 years. At the same time, our Vision Into Action plan drove a 160 basis point improvement in margin to 13.5%, on an actual currency basis, delivering over 70% of our original target in half the time.'

- Investor information on Cadbury can be found on: www.cadburyinvestors.com
- Product information can be found on: www.cadbury.com

QUESTIONS

1 Research the Cadbury products that are available in your country and position them on the Boston matrix.
2 Are most of Cadbury's products at the mature stage in their life cycle in your market? Give examples of how they can be mature in one market but different in another.
3 Using the Boston matrix, explain how Cadbury manages its product portfolio.

Managing the product life cycle

Product innovation is not just about entirely new product/market offerings. Every product has a life cycle and that cycle can be managed in a way that expands and extends it and grows the market. Early adopters are the customers characterised as buying products in the growth phase of the life cycle. This is the point when the company can start expanding the product offering and start meeting the needs of selected market segments in order to counter the threat of competition moving in. Expanding the offering means developing product variations. So, for example, a car manufacturer might start offering sports, estate or fuel-efficient variants of a model. A soft drink manufacturer might start to offer 'light' variants or new flavours of a successful brand. The original product might also be modified in terms of quality, function or style so as to address any weaknesses or omissions in it. In many cases service levels will be improved.

At the same time the company might want to try to find new distribution channels so that more customers gain exposure to the product. Sometimes they move from a selective distribution network to a more intensive network. Associated with this is a more aggressive promotion and pricing strategy that encourages further market penetration ahead of the rapidly emerging competition. Building the brand is important and this will be a vital part of the advertising message.

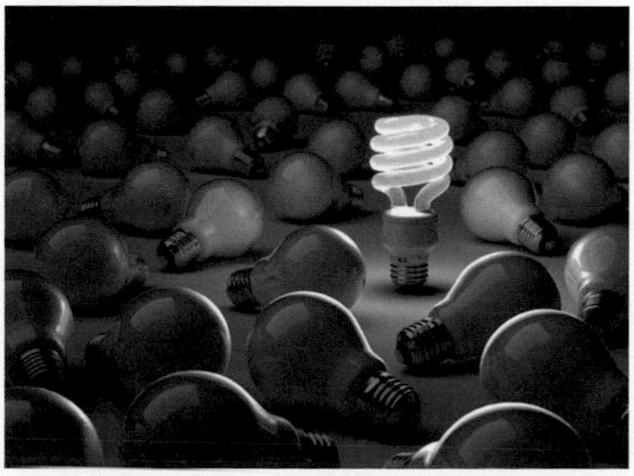

Further growth may even be possible in the mature phase of the life cycle. In many cases a mature market presents opportunities to start segmenting the market and tailoring the product range that was expanded in the previous phase through product modification, so as to better meet the different needs of the different market segments that purchase them. This might lead to further expansion of the range

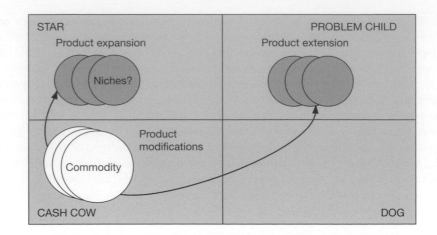

Product life cycle management

and further product modification in terms of quality, function or style. In this way, using the terminology of the Boston matrix, the cash cow product can be 'reinvented' to become a series of smaller star products, all of which are highly profitable.

Another technique is called product extension. In this way a successful brand can be extended to similar but different products that might be purchased by the same customers. In this way a number of chocolate bars , successfully extended their brand into ice cream. The key to success here is having a strong brand – one that actually means something to customers – with values that can be extended onto the other products. Thus Timberland, a company well known for producing durable outdoor footwear, extended its product range to include durable outdoor clothing. Many so-called new products are in fact line extensions. This strategy is generally a less expensive and lower-risk alternative for firms seeking to increase sales. The cash cow product can therefore also be 'reinvented' to become a series of smaller problem children. However, these will face all the challenges of a problem child and may face stiff competition from existing companies in the market. Risk is, however, mitigated compared to a completely new product launch because of customer loyalty to the brand.

Product modification, extension and expansion opportunities can be represented in the Boston matrix. Again this is a useful visual aid to understanding strategy options. An example of this is shown in Figure 12.6.

⌂ Case with questions Barbie® and Mattel Corporation

Barbie was born in 1959 but she has never aged because she is a doll. To date over 1 billion Barbies have been sold by the US company that own her – Mattel Corporation. Ruth Handler, who founded the company along with her husband, Elliot, modelled the doll on an 11.5 inch plastic German toy called Lilli sold to adult men. She named the adapted doll after her daughter, Barbara. It is estimated that the average girl aged between 3 and 11 in the US owns ten Barbies, in Britain or Italy she owns seven and in France or Germany she owns five. With annual sales of over $1.6 billion, it is little wonder that the Barbie brand is valued at some $2 billion – making it the most valuable toy brand in the world. But how has this plastic doll endured for so long in an industry notorious for its susceptibility to fickleness and fashion? Surely it must have come to the end of its life cycle? The answer lies in innovative marketing and product extension.

→

When originally introduced into the market Barbie was competing with dolls that were based on babies and designed to be cradled and cared for. By way of contrast, Barbie, with her adult looks – exaggerated female figure normally with blonde hair and pouting lips – was seen as adult and independent – a child of 'liberated' times, one that could become anything or anyone the child wanted. But Mattel describe Barbie as a 'lifestyle, not just a toy … a fashion statement, a way of life'. Barbie was not only innovative, she was intended to be more than just a doll

Every year Mattel devises some 150 different Barbie dolls and 120 new outfits. She has always been trendy and continues to reinvent herself. She was a 'mod' in the 1960s and a hippie in the 1970s. Her hair style has changed through ponytail, bubble-cut, page boy, swirl to side-part flip. She has various roles in life – from holidaying in Malibu to being an astronaut, soldier, air force pilot, surgeon, vet, doctor, dentist, engineer, fire fighter, diplomat, fashion model, Olympic athlete, skier, scuba diver, ball player, TV news reporter, aerobics instructor, rock star, rap musician and presidential candidate. Each role has numerous accessories to go with it – from cars to horse and carriage, from jewellery box to lunch box – and including a partner called Ken.

Dressing and undressing, grooming and making-up is what Barbie is made for. You can even buy a 'Make-me-pretty talking styling head' play set. And Mattel has worked hard to generate brand extension – more add-ons to the basic Barbie doll. The 2002/03 Rapunzel Barbie came with a handsome prince not to mention a computer animated video and 14 product tie-ins. By 2006 the company had produced the sixth Barbie movie, The 12 Dancing Princesses, each accompanied by special dolls. By wearing a motion-sensor bracelet and shoe clip, the Let's Dance Barbie! allows the doll to follow the child's dance steps. A previous video based on Barbie in the Nutcracker grossed $150 million in sales, including associated products. In addition, Mattel license production of hundreds of different Barbie products including make-up, pyjamas, bed clothes, furniture and wallpapers.

Mattel also continue to segment the market – trying to find new markets to sell the doll and its accessories to. The product extensions attempt this, but selling beyond the basic market, for example to older girls, is problematic. The main problem is that 'age compression' – girls getting older sooner – means that it is increasingly hard to hang on to the basic market, let alone try to extend it. One variation launched in 2002, called My Scene, attempted to sell three Barbie variants, with an older, more 'hip' look, together with perfume, cosmetics and music to this older group. This doll had a moveable face feature that allowed girls to create expressions on the doll's face like frowns, pouts, smirks and smiles.

Over the years Barbie has become a cult. There are Barbie conventions, fan clubs, magazines, websites and exhibitions. She is seen by many as the ideal vision of an American woman. In 1976 the USA included Barbie in the bicentennial time capsule. There are sociology courses in the USA based upon her, speculating on this image and what it implies. Mattel has cultivated these images. They have also worked hard to defend Barbie's image (or reputation). In 1997 they prosecuted (unsuccessfully) the pop group Aqua who produced the satirical song 'Barbie Girl'. Nevertheless, Barbie seems now to have become something of a gay icon. Whether gay or not, collectors have been known to pay up to $10 000 for a vintage model. The question is whether young girls will continue to want the Barbie fantasy world.

The problem remains that Barbie is getting old and must be nearing the end of her product life cycle. Sales peaked at $1.8 billion in 1997. Since then they have fallen continuously every year. Worldwide sales remained 'flat' in 2006, and this included a 1% benefit from changes in currency exchange rates. So the question is how long can innovations sustain Barbie? And how much longer can life stay fantastic?

☐ Up-to-date information on the Mattel Corporation can be found on their website: www.mattel.com

QUESTIONS

1 Why has Barbie been so successful?

2 Barbie is hardly a high-tech product, but has Mattel been innovative in how it has developed the product and extended its life cycle?

3 What are the lessons for product innovation?

♀ Financial implications of the product portfolio

The concept of product portfolios and the need to manage each product/market offering differently has a number of implications for corporate entrepreneurship. The first relates to the cash flow likely to be generated by product/market offerings in each of the different quadrants of the Boston matrix (Guiltinan and Paul, 1982). This is shown in Figure 12.7.

The problem child consumes cash for development and promotional costs at a rate of knots, without generating much cash by way of revenues. This is the situation you are likely to face when you start up a business – Death Valley curve – and underlines the importance of producing a cash flow forecast. The star might start to generate revenues but will still be facing high costs, particularly in marketing, to establish its market position against new entry competitors. It is therefore likely to be, at best, cash neutral. Again, if you are successful at start-up the Death Valley curve may actually get longer and possibly deeper. Only as a cash cow are revenues likely to outstrip costs and cash flow will be positive. There are two kinds of dogs. One is a cash dog that covers its costs and might be worth keeping, for example if it brings in customers for other products or services or it shares overheads. The other is the genuine dog which is losing money – both in cash flow and profit terms – and should be scrapped. It is from this model that phrases like 'shoot the dog', 'invest in stars' and 'milk the cow' came.

Ideally entrepreneurial companies have a balanced portfolio of product/service offerings so that the surplus cash from cash cows can be used to invest in the problem children. However, that situation may take many years to achieve. These funds can be used almost as venture capital to invest, selectively, in new products and services. This 'ideal' firm – if it exists – is self-financing. The problem that arises with an unbalanced portfolio is that there is either a surplus of cash (no new products) or a deficit (too many new products). If the entrepreneurial firm has too many problem children and stars in its portfolio (too many good, new ideas) then it will require cash flow injections which will only be forthcoming if it can either borrow the capital – and that largely depends on the strength of the balance sheet – or raise more equity finance. The challenge is to develop and then effectively manage a balanced portfolio using the different structures available.

Remember, however, that cash flow is not the same as profit. Whilst the analysis above refers to cash flow, the following technique uses profitability. The ABC Sales/Contribution analysis measures success in terms of the profitability of a product

STAR		PROBLEM CHILD	
Revenue	+ + +	Revenue	+
Expenditure	– – –	Expenditure	– – –
Cash flow	neutral	Cash flow	negative
Revenue	+ + +	Revenue	+
Expenditure	–	Expenditure	–
Cash flow	positive	Cash flow	neutral
CASH COW		DOG	

F12.7 Cash flow implications of the Boston matrix

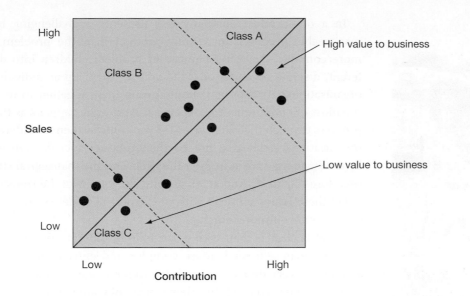

F12.8 ABC analysis contribution chart

in relationship to its sales within the overall product portfolio. High sales and high contribution are the ideal combination. It helps identify those products that are of longer-term value to the company – really successful products. An example is shown in Figure 12.8. Sales are measured on the vertical axis and contribution on the horizontal axis. The 45-degree diagonal line from bottom left to top right is the optimum, but of course most products will fall either side. Class 'A' products are the ideal. They have high sales and make a large contribution to the firm. Class 'B' are less attractive and class 'C' least attractive.

This analysis highlights attractive products – where contribution and sales are high – but it can also be used to identify attractive customers or markets. If sales are low but contribution is high, it shows where a sales push, even if margins are eroded, would yield the greatest reward. Similarly it identifies products, customers or markets where sales are high but contribution is low. Cash flow may be good, but contribution and hence profitability are not helped. Cash flow and profitability measure different things – like a rev meter and speedometer on a car. Ideally, but rarely, they go hand in hand. How the portfolio is managed when they are out of phase is a question of judgement. You need profit for long-term return and growth, but you need sufficient cash flow for survival. If cash flow is insufficient you need to be able to borrow to tide you over the short-term problem.

💡 Implications for the entrepreneur

The product life cycle has some important implications for the entrepreneur. Entrepreneurial skills are most valued in the problem child phase – the start-up. Once the product is in its mature phase it needs to be managed as a cash cow – milked for all the cash flow it can generate. That means high levels of efficiency are needed, probably achieved through a high degree of control and direction. If the problem child is best managed by an entrepreneur, the cash cow is probably best managed by an accountant. And, if we are to characterise the management discipline needed to manage the star, it would probably be marketing. In other words, as the product works its way through its life cycle the approach to management needs to change from entrepreneurial to a more marketing orientation to one of greater emphasis on control and efficiency – much like the firm itself.

In a one-product company this presents a challenging but manageable problem. In a multi-product firm the problem is more complex. Do you separate out problem children into different, discrete organisations? Do you set them up as individual organisations? Perhaps you should group them together to make the most of entrepreneurial expertise? And what happens as they progress through their life cycle? Do you transfer them to different organisations, delineated not by their product specification but by the stage they are at in their life cycle and the managerial style therefore required? And at what point do you make the transfer? All of these issues are dealt with in Chapter 18 under the heading of 'corporate entrepreneurship'.

What is clear is that, with a portfolio of different products or services, management is more complex and entrepreneurs may well find it very difficult to span the different range of skills and temperaments required. In other words they are certain to need an effective team to help them undertake this task – a management team with complementary skills to their own, and one to which they have to provide overall leadership (Chapter 17). They may also have to look to more complex organisational structures. These are reasons why many entrepreneurs prefer to sell a successful business before it grows too large and too complex – they do not have the skills to manage this complexity and do not want to develop them, perhaps preferring instead to start up another business. How they can exit their business is dealt with in Chapter 15.

▷ Summary

▷ Products and services face a predictable life cycle that has implications for marketing strategy at different phases. Most firms, like **Heineken** and **Cadbury**, have a range of products and services at different stages of their life cycle. These can be represented in a Boston matrix – a loose conceptual framework that helps clarify the complexity of the portfolio. The two axes of the matrix represent market attractiveness and market strength. Products at different points in the matrix have different strategic imperatives and different marketing strategies.

▷ You can manage the product life cycle through product modification, expansion and extension. By using these strategies, the **Barbie** doll has been around for over 40 years but may now be at the end of its life cycle. **Cadbury** is very good at managing its product/market portfolio on a global basis. The company plays to its strength, using surplus cash to reinvest in gaining market share or product expansion or extension.

▷ The Boston matrix has cash flow implications; problem children use cash, stars are cash neutral, generating but also using large amounts, and cash cows generate cash. Only when the portfolio is balanced will cash flow be stable. However, cash flow is not the same as profitability. The ABC analysis allows you to analyse products in terms of sales and contribution – those with high levels of both are very attractive (class A products). But equally it can be used to adjust other elements of the marketing mix, such as price, so as to maximise sales.

▷ Problem children are best managed by entrepreneurs – or entrepreneurial firms – and cash cows by accountants – or administrative firms. Where a business has a balanced portfolio of products, the challenge is to find a form of organisation that allows them all to flourish. There are many different approaches to this.

⏻ **Further resources are available at www.palgrave.com/business/burns**

📄 Essays and discussion topics

1 Some products – basic necessities such as food and water – do not have a life cycle. Discuss.
2 How useful are the labels of 'innovators', 'early adopters', 'late adopters' and 'laggards' for referring to customers at different stages of the life cycle?
3 In practical terms it is impossible to find out where a product is at in its life cycle. Discuss.
4 What is the relationship between marketing mix and the product life cycle?
5 How useful is the Boston matrix?
6 How would you go about creating a scale for each axis of the Boston matrix that reflects a range of factors? Give a practical example.
7 In what circumstances might you not want to 'shoot a dog'?

8 Give some examples of product expansions and extensions.
9 Can a problem child be profitable? How and why?
10 Is a star always likely to be a 'class A' product? Explain.
11 In what circumstances might you have a cash cow that is unprofitable? What would you do with it?
12 What are the pros and cons of the take-over of Cadbury by Kraft?
13 Every product in a different market requires a different strategy. Discuss.
14 How can a company become a dominant market force by the mature stage of its product life cycle, other than through mergers and acquisitions?

↻ Exercises and assignments

1 Select a well known product that is now in the mature phase of its life cycle and chart how the marketing strategy has changed over that life cycle.
2 For a selected company, analyse their product portfolio using the Boston matrix. What are your conclusions?

3 Select a mature industry. Research the three major companies in this industry and find out how they gained their market dominance.
4 Research the strategy adopted by Apple to launch and roll out the iPad since 2010. Where is the product now at in its life cycle? Have these strategies been effective? If so why? How does the iPad fit into the portfolio of other Apple products?

📖 References

Guiltinan, J.P. and Paul, G.W. (1982) *Marketing Management: Strategies and Programs*, New York: McGraw Hill.
Rogers, E.M. (1962) *Diffusion of Innovation*, New York: Free Press.

Tellis, G.J., Stremersch, S. and Yin, E. (2003), 'The International Take-off of New Products: The Role of Economics, Culture, and Country Innovativeness', *Marketing Science*, 22(2).

13 Growing the business

- ▷ **Growth options**
- ▷ **Market penetration**
- ▷ **Product/service development**
- ▷ **Market development**
- ▷ **Diversification**
- ▷ **Risk**
- ▷ **Buying growth**
- ▷ **Summary**

Case insights:
- ▷ Wilson & Sons
- ▷ Virgin
- ▷ Tim Slade, Julian Leaver and Fat Face
- ▷ Wing Yip

Cases with questions
- ▷ Jim Ratcliffe and Ineos Group
- ▷ George Brian Boedecker Jr. and Crocs
- ▷ Cadbury 2

Learning outcomes

By the end of this chapter you will be able to:

▷ Describe the growth options facing a firm, the reasons for pursuing them and the advantages and risks associated with each;

▷ Explain the consequences of selecting particular strategies and the factors that are important to make each strategy work;

▷ Describe the different types of diversification and explain the degree of risk faced in pursuing each one;

▷ Describe the different types of acquisitions and mergers, the reasons for following this strategy and the risks involved;

▷ Pick out the strategies that are most likely to lead to successful and sustained growth.

⚬ Growth options

Growing a business is dangerous and, without a clear understanding of what has made the business successful in the first place, there is no sound foundation for the move forward. Some entrepreneurs understand what they are doing, what works and what does not, as they do it, sometimes almost instinctively. Others are more reflective and need time to analyse the situation. Getting the right people and putting the right systems in place can take time. Some situations are more complex than others. Once entrepreneurs understand the basis for their successful survival, so far, they can start to plan their take-off, the growth that will eventually make them leaders of the very small number of high-growth businesses upon which whole economies are so dependent for their growth. This is the point where the small business caterpillar, having become a butterfly, will try to fly.

In general terms, to achieve growth a company should build on its strengths and core competencies, shore up its weaknesses and develop a marketing strategy for each product/market offering that reflects:

▷ the appropriate generic marketing strategy;
▷ the stage a product/market offering is at in its life cycle;
▷ all placed in the context of its portfolio of product/market offerings.

In that context, research tells us that the strategy that is most likely to lead to success comprises a product/service innovation leading into a niche marketing strategy, involving selling a differentiated product or service not selling primarily on price, that allows the company to dominate its market niche. The unique elements of the differentiation strategy are likely to be based on distinctive capabilities that, applied to a relevant market, become a competitive advantage. This will become the firm's core market, the one in which it has a distinct advantage by adding the greatest value for its customers. A focus on core business was emphasised in the 1980s (Abell, 1980) and popularised by Peters and Waterman (1982) as 'sticking to the knitting'. However, core competencies may be relevant to other markets and, even if they are not directly relevant, can often be leveraged by entering other markets in which, although the firm may not have the same distinctive competitive advantage, it can use economies of scale or its channels of distribution to gain market share – which is the strategy of Cadbury. Although firms following other strategies do, of course, succeed, the importance of this research-based finding cannot be over-emphasised. Business, like life, is about playing the odds. You ignore these odds at your peril.

Businesses need solid roots to grow

Whilst the objective of entrepreneurial strategy is growth, its essence is that it is opportunity driven. Stevenson and Gumperter (1985) describe the entrepreneur as 'constantly attuned to the environmental changes that may suggest a favourable chance.' However, in order to start planning the growth phase, there is one further tool that we need. It helps analyse how growth can be achieved in a systematic fashion: the Product/Market Matrix. It was originally devised by Igor Ansoff (1968), and is shown in Figure 13.1. This simple conceptual framework uses existing/new products on one axis and existing/new markets on the other. It then goes on to explore the options within the four quadrants of the matrix and how the options might be achieved.

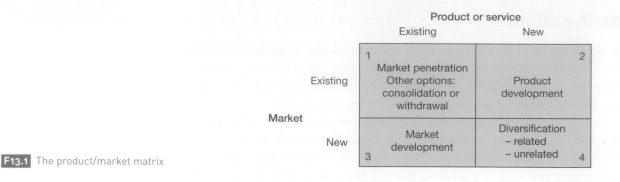

Like all useful business frameworks it is attractively simple and intuitively logical. To achieve growth a company has four options:

1 Market penetration – staying with existing products/services and existing markets and customers;
2 Product development;
3 Market development;
4 Diversification.

To use this framework we need to explore each option systematically in greater detail, find out what it entails and weigh up the risks and returns associated with each one. Empirical research tells us a lot about which are likely to work and which are not.

♀ Market penetration (quadrant 1)

Market penetration involves selling more of the same product/service to the same market – just selling more to existing customers. If the firm has strong relationships with its existing customers this may be possible. It can also involve finding new customers from the same market segment. In the last chapter we saw that Cadbury achieve this by constantly improving their channels of distribution and giving customers more 'indulgence opportunities' for their impulse buy products. Using the Boston matrix, this is how you move from 'problem child' to 'star'. The best way of finding new customers is to understand existing customers – assuming that they are happy with the product/service offering – and try to find more of the same. This involves understanding why they buy and being able to describe the customers' common characteristics – effectively describing the market segment(s) buying the product or service. In a growth market there may be ample opportunity to achieve further growth in this way. Figures 12.1 and 12.4 in the previous chapter set out some ways this can be achieved. The previous chapter also underlined the importance of gaining market dominance as quickly as possible in these circumstances. However, the ease with which a business can pursue this policy will depend on the nature of the market and the position of competitors. In a static or declining market it is much more difficult to pursue this option, unless competitors are complacent or are leaving the market. To attract customers from an established competitor, they must be convinced that the alternative product or service offers greater perceived value, and that might involve price reductions – not always an attractive strategy.

Market penetration is an essential part of gaining market dominance. However, once the market is mature there is unlikely to be significant sales growth. At this point consolidation should generate profit growth, but this strategy inherently starts to go against the entrepreneurial grain and is not one that an entrepreneurial firm is designed or inclined to follow. Inevitably the entrepreneurial firm will start to look at the other quadrants of the matrix to achieve its aims.

There are also a couple of other options in this quadrant. Firstly, the entrepreneur might decide to withdraw, perhaps selling the business to capitalise on the growth so far. Richard Branson did this in 1982 when he sold his original business, Virgin Records, to concentrate on the airline business. It might also be just the right time to get a very good deal, for example because of consolidation in the industry. Withdrawal might be triggered, very simply, by the product or service offered coming to the end of its life cycle. In a declining market, when the firm has low market share and there is little chance of improvement, then a timely withdrawal may minimise future losses. Similarly entry into the market might have been a mistake in the first place, so withdrawal is the least worst option. Alternatively the entrepreneur might simply not see themselves as being able to change and develop in the way that is needed to lead a growing firm. They might prefer to go into another start-up.

Secondly, there is the option to consolidate, that is keeping products/services and markets the same, but changing the way the firm operates. Often this is not a sensible option in a growing market as it leaves competitors free to take market share, which might then affect the firm's competitive cost base. In a mature market it is common for companies to place increasing emphasis on quality, marketing activity or reducing their cost base so as to create barriers to entry for new competitors. In a declining market, consolidation may involve cost reduction, volume reduction and ultimately selling off part or all of the business.

Staying in this quadrant can be attractive for a number of reasons particularly for the 'lifestyle' owner-manager. Essentially it involves staying very much the same so there are none of the risks associated with developing new products or markets. It allows the firm to focus on what it is doing and to do it better, rather than always having to run in order to stand still. Customers may appreciate better service and may even be willing to pay for it. Staying the same also allows the firm to develop its reputation. It might allow the firm to do what it is doing more efficiently and therefore cut costs. It is said that it costs five times less to sell to existing customers than it does to new ones. However, there are also dangers with this approach. As we have seen, the strategy is operationally difficult in a static or declining market where there is the additional question of how much life is left in the product/service. Similarly, it could be risky in a growing market when it may be important to grab market

> ### □ Case insight Wilson & Sons
>
> Established in 1899, the family bakery business of Wilson & Sons based on the south coast of England has had to adapt to some radical market changes in order to stay in business. A hundred years ago families would buy two or three crusty loaves each day from one of a dozen bakers in close proximity to their shop. Charles Wilson introduced doorstep delivery to combat that competition. The First World War saw bread rationing, which at least made demand very predictable, and government subsidies to cushion prices. But it was the arrival of low-priced, factory-produced bread that did most to threaten the business.
>
> Today, families often shop only once a week and prefer soft bread. Competition comes from supermarkets who offer loaves for as little as 30 pence. And the economics of breadmaking have changed. Today's loaf costs 110p, equivalent to less than 10 minutes work in the bakery. In the 1950s the loaf cost 6 pence, equivalent to 15 minutes work, and in the 1920s the loaf cost only 2 pence, but this was equivalent to 30 minutes work.
>
> Andrew Wilson runs the bakery helped by his sister, brother and wife. They offer a wide variety of bread including sunflower, seeded and wholemeal, all baked in the traditional way, free of chemical additives. However, they rely far more for their profits on cakes, fresh sandwiches, pizzas and other take-away food. They also have coffee shops and sandwich bars in their four retail outlets.
>
> □ Up-to-date information on Wilson & Sons can be found on their website: home.btconnect.com/wilson-sons

share as quickly as possible just to compete effectively, for example where price and hence economies of scale are important. There is also the danger of complacency in just doing the same thing and perhaps ignoring changes in customer needs and the market that can lead to you becoming uncompetitive.

♀ Product/service development (quadrant 2)

We have already seen that product/service innovation is one of the key characteristics of successful growth companies. In Ansoff's framework the first option is to do this for existing markets. It may be that completely new products are introduced into the portfolio because market opportunities are spotted. These might be completely new, innovative products to either replace or sell alongside the existing product range. It might involve product development or extension of existing products where the changes are small and evolutionary, or it might entail developing 'me-too', copied products where another firm has successfully pioneered the product in the market. This may be necessary when a product is in its growth phase – through product extension. It may be necessary at the mature phase when the product is nearing the end of its life cycle – product replacement. It may also be necessary as other firms produce a 'better' product and the firm is forced to react. This can be a particular problem for small firms pioneering a product in a market with low barriers to entry, especially if the product develops into a commodity.

One justification for following this growth path is that the company's existing customers are loyal and demand is growing. However, probably the most important reason for following this path is that the firm has a close relationship with customers – a customer focus – and a good reputation for quality or delivery that can be built upon. If there is a relationship of trust, customers are more likely to try the new product, provided of course they perceive a need for it and that means the company must also be good at communicating with customers in whatever way is most appropriate. In developing new products the customer-focused firm will have an advantage because, if it understands how its customers' needs are changing, it ought to be able to develop new products that meet them. The key to this strategy, therefore, is building good customer relationships, often associated with effective branding. Thus Cadbury leverages its brand reputation and channels of distribution for, say chocolate products, to sell gum and candy.

One advantage of this approach is that it is frequently far more cost-effective to increase the volume of business with existing customers than it is to go out looking for new ones. What is more, good relationships often result in customers bringing

🛍 Case insight Virgin

Virgin is one of the best known brands in Britain with 96 per cent recognition and is well-known worldwide. It is strongly associated with its founder, Sir Richard Branson – 95% can name him as the founder. The company has pioneered the concept of a branded venture capitalist, mirroring a Japanese management structure called 'keiretsu', in which different businesses act as a family under one brand. The Virgin Group is made up of more than 20 separate umbrella companies, operating some 200 companies worldwide.

Virgin now uses its brand as a capital asset in joint ventures. Virgin contributes the brand and Richard Branson's PR profile, whilst the partner provides the capital input – in some ways like a franchise operation. The brand has been largely built through the personal PR efforts of its founder.

According to Richard Branson:

> 'Brands must be built around reputation, quality and price ... People should not be asking 'is this one product too far?' but rather, 'what are the qualities of my company's name? How can I develop them?'

According to Will Whitehorn, director of corporate affairs at Virgin Management:

> 'At Virgin, we know what the brand name means, and when we put our brand name on something, we're making a promise. It's a promise we've always kept and always will. It's harder work keeping promises than making them, but there is no secret formula. Virgin sticks to its principles and keeps its promises.'

in new customers through word of mouth or referral. However, developing new products, even for existing customers, can be expensive and risky. Development must be grounded firmly in the needs of the existing market. And even then, if done too rapidly, it can mean resources are spread too thinly across an unbalanced portfolio.

Virgin and Saga are good examples of brands that have been applied to a wide range of diverse products, mainly successfully, linking customers and their lifestyle aspirations. Virgin, however, rarely undertakes 'production', relying instead on partners with developed expertise. On the other hand Mercedes Benz is a brand that has a strong association with quality and the company has capitalised on this by producing an ever wider range of vehicles, always being able to charge a premium price for its product. This has allowed it to move into new and different segments of the vehicle market.

♀ Market development (quadrant 3)

Market development is the natural extension of market penetration. Instead of selling more of the same to your existing customers, you find new customers for those products or services. One reason for finding new markets is to achieve economies of scale of production – particularly important if the product is perceived as a commodity and cost leadership is dependent upon achieving those economies. Another reason might also be that a company's key competency lies with the product, for example with capital goods like cars, and therefore the continued exploitation of the product by market development is the preferred route for expansion. Most capital goods companies follow this strategy – opening up new overseas markets by exporting as existing markets become saturated – because of the high cost of developing new products. By way of contrast, many service businesses such as accounting, insurance, advertising and banking have been pulled into overseas markets because their clients operate there. Finally, another reason to find new markets for a product or service might be simply that it is nearing the end of its life cycle in the existing market. This was the case with McDonald's and its entry into the East European markets.

Any growing firm will have to find new customers and the key to doing so is to understand the customers it has – who they are and why they buy – and then try to find more customers with similar profiles. Many firms start out by selling locally and gradually expand their geographic base by selling regionally and then nationally. However, it is one thing to find new customers in a market that you are familiar with, but it is quite another to enter completely new markets, even when you are selling existing products or services that you are familiar with. Nevertheless, if a firm wants to grow it will have to do so. These new markets might be new market segments or new geographical areas. In seeking new overseas markets the lowest risk option is to seek out segments similar to the ones the firm already sells to. Cadbury has entered the confectionery market in some countries by buying established brands. Issues associated with 'going international' were covered in Chapter 8. However it is true to say that the internet has opened up international markets for small firms like never before.

Trying to sell the same product or service to new market segments usually involves reconfiguring the marketing mix in some way. Simply lowering the price will attract new customers who would not otherwise buy. However, as we have seen, this is not always a sensible way to maximise profits. More likely to be successful is finding new or different channels of distribution, or altering the promotional strategy in some way. However, there is always the danger that by seeking to attract different market

📁 Case insight
Tim Slade, Julian Leaver and Fat Face

Tim Slade and Julian Leaver began selling their own printed t-shirts in a shop in the ski resort of Meribel, France in 1988. They were skiers, but had run out of money and sold their belongings, including a Volkswagen camper van, to purchase plain t-shirts on which to print logos. The whole idea was to finance their lifestyle as 'ski-bums'. The first Fat Face store was opened in the UK in 1993. It has now become a cult brand for sports enthusiasts and the company has over 160 shops worldwide with a turnover of over £120 million. In 2000 Julian Leaver explained what they were trying to achieve:

> 'When you buy a Fat Face product, you are not just buying the fleece, you are buying the experience – the chat in the shop about the snow in Val d'Isère – or surfing in Cowes. Staff are selected because they are passionate about the lifestyle.'

Sunday Times 27 February 2000

In 2000 the company raised £5 million expansion capital from Friends Ivory & Sime Private Equity to finance their expansion but they were careful to manage the brand as they did so. Julian Leaver explained once more:

> 'We could easily wholesale the hell out of it and be in every ski and surf shop and department store inside a year. Within two years, we would have trashed the brand.'

Slow, planned expansion came through increasing the number of shops in Britain and Europe and eventually the rest of the world, making certain that the right sort of staff, with the right sort of personality, were recruited. Initially Fat Face entered new markets based upon intuition and on an experimental basis, later they undertook more professional market research. Their typical customer is a well-off professional in their mid-30s who enjoys skiing or water sports. And they try to keep close to their customers by getting feedback by email and face-to-face and regular panel meetings. Fat Face have also extended their product range into shoes, bags and jewellery, but all with the same lifestyle, sporty image. The key to expansion is brand management, ensuring all the new products have the same lifestyle, sporty image and the shops continue to have the same 'fun' feel.

In 2005 Tim and Julian sold the major shareholding in the company to Advent for £100 million. Advent in turn sold it on to Bridgepoint Capital in 2007 for £360 million. Tim and Julian maintain a minor stake in the company. They both still enjoy skiing.

☐ Up-to-date information on Fat Face can be found on their website: www.fatface.com

segments you will lose market focus and lose your grip on existing customers – particularly if you are following a niche marketing strategy.

💡 Diversification (quadrant 4)

The final growth option is to sell new products into new markets – called diversification. The rationale for this is normally one of 'balancing' the risk in a firm's business portfolio by going into new products and new markets. However, since this strategy involves unfamiliar products and unfamiliar markets, it is actually a high-risk strategy, with too many unknowns in the equation. Reflecting this, most conglomerates formed by this process of diversification seem to be unattractive to stock markets, commanding a discount on their constituent parts.

Of course, market development and product development might go hand-in-hand, since the move into a new market segment may involve the development of variants to the existing product offering by altering the marketing mix or even changes to the product range. Product extension and expansion may similarly be viewed as incremental diversification, in that they involve elements of both new product development and seeking new market segments. However, the risk is mitigated because of the incremental movement in one or other element and it can be further mitigated if these developments are associated with a strong brand with values that are attractive to customers.

Risk is therefore dependent upon the extent of the diversification. The literature distinguishes between related and unrelated diversification and entrepreneurial firms face a distinct opportunity in the former.

1 **Related diversification**   This happens where development is beyond the present product and market, but within the confines of the 'industry' or 'sector' that the firm operates in. There are three variants of this:

▷ Backward vertical integration, where the firm becomes its own supplier of some basic raw materials or services or provides transport or financing.

▷ Forward vertical integration, where the firm becomes its own distributor or retailer, or perhaps services its own products in some way. In this way Timberland, the boot and shoe maker, has opened a number of prominently sited retail outlets selling Timberland branded products.

▷ Horizontal integration, where there is development into activities which are either directly complimentary or competitive with the firm's current activities, for example, where a video rental shop starts to rent out video games. In this way Ford now earn more from financial services related to car purchase than from the manufacture of the vehicles themselves.

In an entrepreneurial firm the portfolio of core competencies can be combined in various ways to meet opportunities. So it can re-apply and reconfigure what it does best in a way best suited to meet the opportunities in new markets. In this way the entrepreneurial firm can have an advantage over others in applying this strategy. So, for example, Mercedes Benz uses new products to move incrementally into new markets and market segments, leveraging on its reputation for quality, for example with its small 100 Series. All of this has been within the industry it knows best. The primary competency lies in product development – it builds good quality cars which appeal in terms of aesthetics and emotions but are leveraged by an excellent brand. In this way it has a competitive advantage over other new entrants to the market, although not necessarily existing ones.

2 **Unrelated diversification**   This is where the firm develops beyond its present industry or sector into products and markets that, on the face of it, bear little relationship to the one they are in. This tends to work better for service rather than manufacturing business where there is strong brand association. Some of Virgin's ventures into new product areas might be described as unrelated diversification except for the fact that Virgin never produces the product or service themselves. In reality this is just brand extension. Unrelated diversification is considered high risk because the firm has no experience of either the market it is entering or the product it is proposing to produce.

'Synergy' is often used as a justification for both related and unrelated diversification, particularly when it involves acquisition or merger. Synergy is concerned with assessing how much extra benefit can be obtained from providing linkages between activities or processes which have been previously unconnected, or where the connection has been of a different type, so that the combined effect is greater than the sum of the parts. It is often described as 'one plus one equals three'. Synergy in related diversification is mainly based upon core product or market characteristics. The claimed synergy in unrelated diversification is normally based on financing – the positive cash flows in one business being used for the funding requirements of another. Another often-claimed synergy is based on the managerial skills of the head office.

Research indicates that most successful entrepreneurial firms follow a strategy of incremental, mainly internal, growth (Burns, 1994). They move carefully into new markets with existing products or sell new products to existing customers. Whilst Johnson and Scholes (1993) claim that attempts to demonstrate the effects of diversification on performance are inconclusive, they also admit that successful diversification is difficult to achieve in practice. However, many researchers have found that more focused firms perform better than diversified ones – conglomerates (Wernerfelt and Montgomery, 1986). This is reflected in their higher share price. What is more, it has been demonstrated that smaller firms that diversify by building on their core business – related diversification – do better than those that diversify in an unrelated way (Ansoff, op. cit.). This was established for a broader range of firms in the 1970s (Rumelt, 1974) and used as part of Porter's (1987) argument for firms that build on their core business doing better than those that diversify in an unrelated way. The conclusion must be that diversification generally is risky and therefore requires careful justification.

🛍 Case insight Wing Yip

Wing Yip came to Britain from Hong Kong in 1958 with only £10 in his pocket and got a job as a waiter in a Chinese restaurant. Within a few years he had his own small chain of Chinese restaurants but he had trouble getting the food supplies he needed. Nobody stocked everything and he had to spend valuable time travelling to a number of different suppliers. This led him to realise that other Chinese restaurants were facing the same problem. And so, in 1970, he decided to set up a cash-and-carry business for Chinese restaurants with his brother Sammy Yap, based in Birmingham. A third brother, Lee Sing Yap, joined them in 1977 to open a second store in Manchester. A third store was opened in London in 1988 and a fourth in Croydon in 1995.

Today the Wing Yip Group operates from four freehold sites covering 16.3 acres and employs 300 staff. The main site, now covering 7 acres in Nechells, Birmingham, houses the head office, a central distribution warehouse, a Business Centre, Chinese medical practice, travel agency and law firm – all serving the Chinese community – together with a 250-seater restaurant called Wing Wah. The company acts as agents for Hong Kong suppliers and sells to other cash-and-carries such as Booker. They also now make their own range of Chinese sauces which they sell to most of the big supermarket chains.

☐ Up-to-date information on the Wing Yip Group can be found on their website: www.wingyipcom

💡 Risk

Ansoff's analysis gives us a valuable insight into the risks associated with growth. Bowman and Faulkner (1997) added an extra dimension to Ansoff's analysis by considering core competency and method of implementation. They pointed out that any move into new markets or new products/services becomes riskier, the further the firm strays from its core competencies. Combining these approaches we can see that:

▷ The lowest risk strategy of all is market penetration, but in growth markets, where gaining market share as quickly as possible is important, security might be short-lived.

▷ Market development is most successful for firms whose core competencies lie in the efficiency of their existing production methods, for example in the capital goods industries, and which are seeking economies of scale, or for firms adept at sales, marketing and developing close customer relationships – the very qualities of an entrepreneurial firm.

▷ Product and process development are most successful for those firms whose competencies lie in building good customer relationships, often associated with effective branding. However, of equal importance could be the ability to innovate. Innovation is a core characteristic of an entrepreneur.

▷ The highest risk strategy of all is diversification, with unrelated diversification being extremely high risk. This can be likened to the introduction of new-to-the-world products. Related diversification is safest for companies that are adept at both innovation and developing close customer relations. Thus it was just as well that the Mini – truly a mould-breaking innovation in car design – was produced by a car manufacturer.

At the extreme, entrepreneurial innovation – introducing new products or services to a new market – is radical and risky. But whilst this may be risky, the returns can be equally large. As Cannon (1985) points out: 'The ability of the entrepreneurial mouldmaker to break free from bureaucratic rigidities, fan the flames of innovation and create new situations has been the basis of the growth of many of today's great corporations. Ford, Durant, Kellogg, Singer, Krupp, Eastman, Courtauld, Daimler, Biro, Siemens and Daussault all built giant enterprises which are virtually synonymous with their industries'. Building on the Ansoff matrix, this is the equivalent of diversification. These developments are represented in Figure 13.2.

With the exception of the 'no innovation' option where risks are minimal in the short term but high in the long term, risk gets progressively higher as the firm moves to the bottom right hand corner of Figure 13.2 in terms of its strategy. This is indicated by the increasingly darker shading. However, risk is not a linear relationship. In the 'twilight zone' – marked by the dotted circle at the centre of the matrix – risk

All diversification in business involves risk

can be lowered. This is the zone where continuous, small incremental changes in product and market can greatly expand the product/service offering and its market place and this is where risk can be lowest. It is the zone where the entrepreneurial firm may have the greatest competitive advantage and therefore face lower risk than other firms in related diversification or developing new products for slightly different markets. The growth of Wing Yip by diversification into new markets and new products has been incremental in this way.

The riskiest strategy of all is to introduce a new product or service into a completely unknown market – 'new to the world', with a completely new invention. For example when PCs were introduced in the late 1970s, IBM refused to enter the

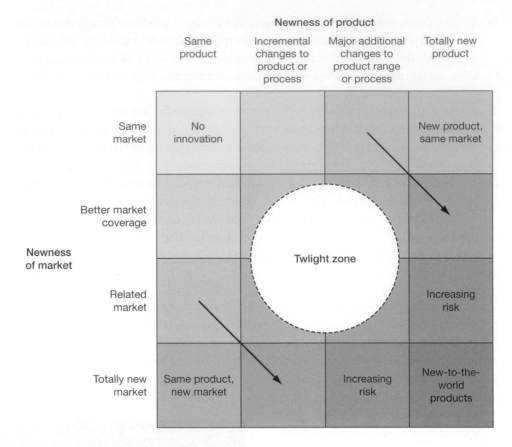

Newness of product

	Same product	Incremental changes to product or process	Major additional changes to product range or process	Totally new product
Same market	No innovation			New product, same market
Better market coverage				
Related market		Twlight zone		Increasing risk
Totally new market	Same product, new market		Increasing risk	New-to-the-world products

Newness of market

F13.2 Growth and risk

Source: Ward (1968)

market, partly because market research could not identify a demand for the product. Potential domestic customers could not understand the product or, more particularly, what it would do for them – how it would add value. Existing applications were commercial. Why would families want a machine to 'do sums'? Why was it better than a typewriter? Of course the PC took off when the domestic applications such as games and the internet were identified, and now most homes in the Western world have (at least) one. But investment in the early-stage development of PCs was a leap of faith.

Of course this is not to say that a company should not take risks, but rather that growth involves risks and it is as well to understand the degrees of risk associated with different strategies. As already noted, research indicates that successful entrepreneurial firms follow a strategy of incremental, mainly internal, growth (Burns, op. cit.). They move carefully into new markets with existing products or sell new products to existing customers. Related diversification only works when based on core competencies. The strategy of unrelated diversification – or real innovation – is high risk and only to be adopted after careful consideration. Entrepreneurial firms must consider carefully whether this is really appropriate to their needs.

One way of mitigating the marketing risk is through joint ventures or strategic alliances, particularly in moving into overseas markets (see Chapter 8). Both can be set up relatively quickly. In these circumstances the partner may possess much needed competencies or expertise, such as market knowledge. It even works with product development. This was the basis of the relationship Mercedes had with Swatch when the Smart car was developed. Swatch offered fashion design. Mercedes offered engineering and production quality. With such relationships the risks can then be compartmentalised and failure will not therefore endanger either core business. What is more, the strategy avoids high set-up costs. And it relies on what an entrepreneurial firm should be good at – building relationships. On the down side, it does mean that the profits must be shared and control is lost to some extent – which is why firms also consider mergers and acquisitions as a way of diversifying or indeed buying a foothold in a new market.

One further important point; for a small firm with limited resources, pursuing all four strategies within any one time frame is likely to be extremely risky. Assuming market penetration will always continue, it is best advised to follow only one other strategy at a time, perhaps alternating the strategy over time. Making the right choice is an important decision, but one that has to be made by a conscious choice rather than by drift or force of circumstance.

One very practical application of these techniques is to help evaluate sales projections or targets. The projections can be broken down into the constituent elements of the product/market matrix (Figure 13.1) or the growth and risk matrix (Figure 13.2). Probabilities of achieving these projections or targets can then be attributed to each constituent element of the matrix. Any projection based largely on market penetration, *a priori* unless the market is saturated, has a high probability of being achieved. Any projection heavily dependent on diversification is, *a priori*, not only highly risky, but also has a low probability of being achieved. Sales people can also use these matrices to have sales targets set with commission rates in the various elements of the matrix reflecting the different levels of risk, for example, basic commission for sales of existing products to existing customers, higher rates for further market penetration and higher rates still for sales of new products. As the probability of achieving sales targets decreases, sales commissions can be increased.

💡 Buying growth

Acquisitions and mergers are frequently used by entrepreneurs as a tool for achieving rapid growth and also as a short-cut to diversification. The compelling reason for this tactic is the speed at which it allows the entrepreneur to enter a new product/market area. Another reason might be that the firm lacks a resource, such as R&D or a customer base, to develop a strategy unaided. Often, particularly when a market is static, it is seen as the easiest way to enter a new market, for example overseas – a strategy used by Cadbury. Sometimes the reason for buying out a competitor is to buy their order book, perhaps related to shutting down their capacity, cutting costs and gaining economies of scale.

However, this tactic can be time-consuming, expensive and risky. By distracting the entrepreneur, it can also damage short-term business performance. In fact there is no evidence that commercial acquisitions or take-overs (other than in a distress sale or a move overseas) add value to the firm. Many studies show that mergers and acquisitions suffer a higher failure rate than marriages, and business history is littered with stories of failed mergers of titanic proportions such as AT&T's purchase of NCR in 1991, the second largest acquisition in the history of the computer industry, or the merger of AOL (America Online) and Time Warner in 2001. Both resulted in shareholders' value being greatly reduced.

The great conglomerate-merger wave of the 1960s did not generally lead to improvements in performance for the firms involved, and was reversed by the large-scale selling of unrelated businesses in the 1980s. Porter (op. cit.), in his study of 33 major corporations between 1950 and 1986, concludes that 75 per cent of unrelated acquisitions were subsequently sold off rather than retained, and the net result was dissipation of shareholder value. And yet companies of all sizes persist in following this strategy.

All too often acquisitions have too much of the entrepreneur's ego tied up in the deal and that can lead to a loss of business logic. It is important that there is a clear logic to the acquisition, related to the product/market matrix; for example:

▷ As a defensive acquisition to maintain market position, perhaps to gain economies of scale, or as a result of aggressive competitive reaction from rivals (Ineos);
▷ As part of a strategy to develop new products when the firm does not have the capability to do so, for example because of R&D or technology (pharmaceuticals);
▷ As part of a strategy to develop new markets, for example overseas (Cadbury);
▷ As part of a strategy of diversification, although this must be seen as the highest of high-risk growth strategies.

In searching for companies to acquire, it is first necessary to decide on the industry. Related diversification will normally be into the same industry. If it is unrelated diversification, then the industry should be one where the acquiring company has the core competencies required for success in the sector and, where there is a deficiency, they should be addressed by being present in the target company. The attractiveness of the industry will depend to some extent on the strategic direction of the company, informed by an analysis of the industry (perhaps using Porter's Five Forces and a SLEPT analysis). The acquisitions that are most likely to succeed are those where an attractive market presents itself to a company with a good 'mesh' between the acquiring company's core competencies and the sector's required key competencies.

Of course, some acquisitions are simply opportunistic. For example, when a rival firm or a firm in a related area goes into receivership, the temptation to buy it out cheaply and quickly from the receiver might be irresistible and might also make sound commercial sense. Ineos has made many such successful purchases (see Case insight). Most acquisitions take three to nine months to complete but a sale from a receiver can be completed in as little as three weeks. Whether buying a trading company or one in receivership, it is always important to take professional advice although fees can amount to 5–7 per cent of the value of the business. Accountants undertake what is called 'due diligence' work, which ensures that the assets on the balance sheet are as stated, there are no undisclosed liabilities and that profit projections are put together in a logical and consistent way, based upon reasonable and explicit assumptions. Accountants can also undertake searches for acquisition prospects and most of the major firms keep informal 'books' of companies that they believe might be available for purchase.

The major reason mergers and acquisitions fail is because of failure of implementation. Claimed synergies may not be achieved, perhaps rationalisation is insufficiently ruthless, possibly because clear management lines and responsibilities are not being laid down. However, one of the major reasons for this failing boils down to the clash of organisational cultures that does not get resolved. This can arise because of many factors, but it results in the merged organisations being unable to work together effectively. This was the major reason for the seemingly logical, but ultimately disastrous, take-over of NCR by AT&T in 1991, and the merger of AOL with Time Warner, in 2001. Not only could the staff not work together, but the claimed synergies never materialised. For whatever reason, one common outcome of mergers or acquisitions is that many managers in the acquired company will leave within a short space of time. They may, of course, be 'pushed' rather than leave of their own volition, but nevertheless this means that the time scale for proactive management of change can be very short.

Company valuation in mergers and take-overs is crucial but problematic for smaller firms, especially if they operate in new areas of business such as e-commerce where growth may be rapid but profits have not yet materialised. A company with a high value placed on its current level of earnings can use this to its advantage in buying out a company with a low valuation, particularly if the deal is based upon shares rather than cash. The issue of company valuation is dealt with in Chapter 15.

🗀 Case with questions Jim Ratcliffe and Ineos Group

The Ineos Group was founded in 1998 when Jim Ratcliffe led a £91 million management buy-out of Inspec's chemicals division from BP. Jim is a chemical engineer and a qualified accountant with a MBA who had previously worked for the US private equity house Advent. Ineos has now grown to become the world's third largest petrochemical company (after BASF and Dow Chemicals). Jim's strategy to achieve this was simple. He went out to buy undervalued subsidiaries from global oil and chemical giants, financed almost entirely by debt – high yield bonds and bank debt. Ineos has purchased most of its assets in auctions, frequently competing against private-equity capital companies. The purchases have been made regardless of whether they have synergies with existing operations. The company has developed strict criteria for acquisition targets, so that the purchase enhances Ineos' value, measured by earnings before interest, taxes, depreciation and amortisation (EBITDA). Ineos aims to double the average EBITDA of a business over a five-year period.

The company has bought businesses from ICI, Dow Chemicals, Degussa, BASF, Cybec, BP and Norsk Hydro. It was Ineos' purchase of BP's petrochemical arm Innovene for £5.1 billion in 2006 that catapulted the company into the world rankings of the petrochemical industry. The deal quadrupled the company's turnover and signalled a move away from specialist compounds to the simpler chemicals from which they are made. Following a £1.6 billion bond issue in 2006 to refinance the purchase of Innovene, Ineos continued its acquisition strategy with the £76 million purchase of BP's German ethylene oxide business followed by the £460 million purchase of Norsk Hydro's polymers business in 2007. In 2007 Ineos formed a joint venture with Lanxess and created Ineos ABS, comprising Lanxess's activities in acrylonitrile butadiene styrene production, located in Tarragona.

Ineos sees itself as a leading global manufacturer of petrochemicals, speciality chemicals and oil products. It believes its strengths lie in its:

▷ High quality, low cost production facilities – keeping costs to a minimum is a key operational imperative. The company has been accused of buying assets then cutting costs through the introduction of new working practices, lower wages and so on. In 2008 it was at the centre of a major industrial relations dispute with the Unite union over its decision to close the final salary pension scheme at its Grangemouth refinery.
▷ Well located, well invested, large plants that allow it to benefit from economies of scale – again keeping costs as low as possible.
▷ Leading market positions that allow it to be the supplier of choice for many large customers – large volume sales are essential for the economies of scale to be achieved.

→

▷ Experienced management – Ineos runs operations with minimal on-site management, using what it calls 'work teams', which it claims are better suited to handling day-to-day workflows than middle management,.

▷ Operating diversity in products, customers, geographic regions, applications and end-user markets.

In 2008 the company had a turnover of some £18 billion and had some 15 000 employees across 64 manufacturing sites. It was ranked the largest private company by the *Sunday Times* – with a turnover three times that of its nearest rival, the John Lewis Partnership. Jim Ratcliffe himself is a fairly low-profile entrepreneur, but he still owns about 75% of the business, giving him a paper fortune of some £2.3 billion. Ineos is split into 18 companies, headed by Ineos Capital, which is run by Jim and three lieutenants; Jim Dawson, Andy Currie and John Reece, his finance director. Every Monday morning the four host a conference call, with each of the 18 divisional heads giving a short report.

Because of the nature of its business and its high level of gearing, Ineos has been vulnerable to the recession of 2008/09. In September 2008, Jim ordered his divisional heads to cut 10% of their cost base and to destock. Six months later, he did the same thing again. Salaries were frozen, bonuses stopped and outside contractors dismissed. In total, some £340 million of costs were cut in the space of a year, despite this being a high fixed cost business. In addition Ineos cut capital spending from some £680 million to £210 million. In 2009 Ineos reported a 30% fall in sales to £16.1 billion. It restructured its debt of £6 billion and moved its tax residency to Switzerland.

☐ Up-to-date information on Ineos Group can be found on their website: www.ineos.com

QUESTIONS

1 Why has Ineos' strategy of growth by acquisition worked?

2 What risks does Ineos face and how have they been mitigated?

3 How secure is the personal fortune of Jim Ratcliffe and what steps might he take to secure it further?

💼 Case with questions George Brian Boedecker Jr. and Crocs

The ubiquitous Crocs™ can be found in over 125 countries, having sold more than 100 million pairs by 2009. And that means about 1 person in every 700 on the entire planet has bought a pair. The Colorado-based company was founded only in 2002 by George Brian Boedecker Jr. to produce and distribute a plastic clog-like shoe now available in all the colours of the rainbow at a relatively cheap price. It was an instant success at the Florida Boat Show, where it was launched. Crocs are made from Coslite, a soft, lightweight, non-marking and odour-resistant material originally manufactured by Foam Creations, a Canadian company Crocs purchased in 2004. Crocs are now manufactured in Mexico, Italy, Romania and China, having closed their Canadian facility in 2008.

And it's a 'rags to riches' entrepreneurial story if the press were anything to go by at the time. According to *Business 2.0* magazine (3 November 2006): 'Three pals from Boulder, Colorado, go sailing in the Caribbean, where a foam clog one had bought in Canada inspires them to build a business around it. Despite a lack of venture capital funding and the derision of foot fashionistas, the multicoloured Crocs with their Swiss-cheese perforations, soft and comfortable soles, and odour-preventing material become a global smash. Celebrities adopt them. Young people adore them. The company goes from $1 million in revenue in 2003 to a projected $322 million this year [2006]. Crocs Inc.'s IPO (Initial Public Offering) in February was the richest in footwear history, and the company has a market cap of more than $1 billion.' The company went public in 2006 with a hugely successful $200 million stock market float (the biggest float in shoe history). Its strategy can be summarised as selling a relatively cheap product to as many people as possible, as quickly as possible.

The company also used the money to diversify and acquire new businesses, such as Jibbitz, which made charms designed to fit Crocs' ventilating holes, and Fury Hockey,

→

which used Croslite to make sports gear. It built manufacturing plants in Mexico and China, opened distribution centres in the Netherlands and Japan, and expanded into the global market place. A foray into Croslite clothing in 2007 fell flat and was quickly scaled back. The company liquidated Fury Hockey in 2008. By 2009 it produced a range of different products mainly plastic clogs and sandals but also including 'Bite', aimed at the golf market.

And herein lies the paradox. Popularity breeds contempt in the fashion business. Arguably, the backlash started in 2006, almost as soon as the company went public, with a *Washington Post* article that said: 'Nor is the fashion world enamored of Crocs. Though their maker touts their "ultra-hip Italian styling," lots of folks find them hideous.' A blog named 'I Hate Crocs.com' follows Croc opponents periodically. The shoes and those who wear them – from US ex-President Bush to Michelle Obama and stars such as Al Pacino, Steven Tyler (Aerosmith) and Faith Hill – have become objects of satire on US television shows since then, and, by 2009, over 1.4 million people had joined a Facebook group which has the sole purpose of eliminating the shoes. The site even features a ritual burning – all of which should start sounding warning bells for a company so dependent on the fickle fashion market.

Nevertheless in 2008, Crocs was ranked the number one casual brand in the athletic specialty sporting goods channel for men, women, and children by the NPD Market Research Group. However that did not stop the company making a $185 million (£113 million) loss and having to cut 2000 jobs in that year. By 2009 the company was stuck with a surplus of shoes it could not sell and a mountain of debt. The share price had plummeted. In May 2010 *Time Magazine* rated Crocs as one of the world's 50 worst inventions. The question is whether it will survive and in what form?

The problem is that the shoes are hitting a saturation point. With a nearly indestructible product and about one in every seven hundred people owning a pair, how many more can the company sell? And the company had invested enormous amounts into meeting a demand for a product that then seemed endless but now seems ridiculous as the shoe's ubiquity put off even the most ardent Crocophile. The new business lines it purchased – often at a premium – failed to prosper. Add to that the effects of a recession in 2008/9 and the logic of that ambitious expansion founded on mounting debt looks dubious. Some say the company failed to understand that it was in the fashion business and that it should have moved to extend the brand more quickly and keep a tighter control on distribution.

In late 2008 the company replaced chief executive Ron Snyder, who went to college with the company's founders, with John Duerden, an industry veteran who ran a consulting firm focused on brand renewal. He believes there is life yet in Crocs and plans to market them for their comfort to caterers, medical workers and people who spend a lot of time on their feet.

☐ Up-to-date information on Crocs can be found on their website: www.crocs.eu

QUESTIONS

1 What went wrong with Crocs?

2 Is a high-growth strategy always good? What are the alternatives?

3 What should Crocs do now?

4 What lessons have you learnt from the experience of Crocs?

☐ Case with questions Cadbury 2

Throughout this chapter we have highlighted how Cadbury used many growth strategies to help it grow, particularly in different countries, up to its take-over by Kraft Foods in 2010. Together, these made up the 'Vision into Action' plan developed by Todd Stitzer, the Chief Executive. Cadbury has consistently extended its existing channels of distribution (market penetration and market development) and also used them to offer more 'indulgence moments' to customers for its full product range – chocolate, gum and candy (product development). In this way it has strived to improve sales and also to achieve even greater economies of scale. Cadbury has also bought overseas confectionery firms to

→

1 Using the Ansoff matrix, explain how Cadbury goes about achieving its growth targets.

2 Explain why the company has 'focused' its strategic efforts in the ways it has.

3 How has Cadbury used its product portfolio to help it achieve its growth targets?

4 Research the progress of Cadbury under Kraft ownership.

gain entry into these new markets simultaneously, both increasing its product range and buying established channels of distribution for its existing products in these new markets (acquisitions leading to market and product development).

The merger with Kraft presented an opportunity to gain further synergies in terms of cost reduction and more effective distribution and market penetration as well as market and product development across the world. However, the Chief Executive and Chairman of Cadbury, the architects of this strategy, both resigned very shortly after the take-over. Many cynics saw the take-over simply as a way for Kraft to put some sparkle into its otherwise uninteresting product portfolio and to prop up its ailing share price. Will the take-over really add value? Only time will tell.

Re-read the Cadbury Case insight in Chapter 12 (pp. 333–335).

☐ Investor information on Cadbury can be found on: www.cadburyinvestors.com

☐ Product information can be found on: www.cadbury.com

▷ Summary

▷ To achieve growth, a company should build on its strengths and core competencies, shore up its weaknesses and develop a marketing strategy for each product/market offering that reflects:

> ▷ the appropriate generic marketing strategy;
> ▷ the stage the product/market offering is at in its life cycle;
> ▷ all placed in the context of its portfolio of product/market offerings.

It has four options:

1 Stay with existing products/services and existing markets and customers;
2 Product development;
3 Market development;
4 Diversification.

▷ Any start-up must focus initially on market penetration – selling more to existing customers. If a company wants growth, staying with the existing products/services and existing customers usually means further market penetration, rather than just selling more to existing customers and the best way of finding new customers is to understand your existing ones and then try to find more of the same. This strategy can be difficult in a static or declining market but also, if the market is growing, you run the risk of being left behind.

▷ Product/service development involves developing new products or services and selling to your existing market, like **Wilson & Sons** have done. This is often a successful strategy for firms that have a strong relationship with their customers – a customer focus – and a strong reputation. The firm can develop products that customers want and their loyalty means they will try them. Getting existing customers to buy more is also often very cost-effective. Often associated with this strategy is a strong brand identity. **Virgin** is probably the best known brand in Britain today, but the company has evolved into a branded venture capitalist, using its brand as a capital asset in joint ventures.

▷ Market development is about finding new markets for existing products or services – like **Fat Face** – thus benefiting from economies of scale or capitalising on the firm's product knowledge competency. In deciding on which markets to enter, consideration should be given to entry and exit barriers. The classic example of market development is into overseas markets, either opening overseas ventures or by exporting. **Crocs** followed this strategy very successfully but eventually markets, at home and overseas, can become saturated.

▷ Diversification is the riskiest of the four options. – Related diversification is about staying within the confines of the industry through either backward vertical integration – becoming your own supplier; forward vertical integration – becoming a distributor or retailer; or horizontal integration – moving into related activities. Unrelated diversification is the riskiest strategy of all and involves developing beyond the firm's present industry, normally because of the claimed benefits of synergy. **Wing Yip** may be seen as doing this, but in fact their growth into new markets and new products is more incremental.

▷ The product/market matrix is a useful tool to help evaluate the risks associated with a growth strategy and the probabilities attached to the related sales estimates. For small firms with limited resources pursuing all four strategies

within any one time frame is likely to be extremely risky. Assuming market penetration will continue, they should select only one other strategy within any time frame, otherwise they risk spreading themselves too thinly.

▷ Acquisitions and mergers are frequently used as a means of achieving rapid expansion. **Ineos** has based its growth on opportunistic purchases of chemical plants without apparent synergies. However, the tactic can be risky. The frequent failure of mergers arises because of failure of implementation, with claimed synergies not being realised.

⏻ **Further resources are available at www.palgrave.com/business/burns**

📄 Essays and discussion topics

1 Penetrating the market is just about selling more. Discuss.
2 Penetrating the market is a low-risk option and therefore always the most attractive option. Discuss.
3 In what circumstances might product development be a lower-risk strategy than market development, and vice versa?
4 How might a small firm go about exporting so as to minimise the risks that it faces?
5 Exporting is expensive and risky. It is therefore not an attractive growth option. Discuss.
6 How do you go about minimising your exposure to currency fluctuations?
7 What business is Virgin in?

8 Diversification is the 'Wally Box' of the product/market matrix. Discuss.
9 Under what circumstances might diversification be an attractive option?
10 Diversified companies underperform 'focused' companies. Discuss.
11 Why might a small firm be looking for another to acquire?
12 Under what circumstances might an acquisition or merger be attractive?
13 What is synergy and how might it be achieved?
14 Why do so many mergers or acquisitions fail? Give examples.
15 What advice would you give to a company taking over another?

↻ Exercises and assignments

1 For your own department in your university or college, use the product/market matrix to list the growth options that it faces for the courses on offer.
2 If you have an idea for business, list as many ideas as you can for increasing sales under the four headings of the product/market matrix.

3 Research the history of a merger or acquisition and analyse the reasons for its success or failure.
4 Research the background to Virgin. Write a report explaining:
   ▷ how Virgin creates wealth for shareholders;
   ▷ whether or not it is a conglomerate; and
   ▷ what risks it faces and how these may or may not differ from those facing a conglomerate.

📖 References

Abell, D.F. (1980) *Defining the Business*, Hemel Hempstead: Prentice Hall.

Ansoff, H.I. (1968) *Corporate Strategy*, London: Penguin.

Bowman, C. and Faulkner, D. (1997) Competitive and Corporate Strategy, London: Irwin.

Burns, P. (1994) *Winners and Losers in the 1990s*, 3i European Enterprise Centre, Report no. 12, April.

Cannon, T (1985) 'Innovation, Creativity and Small Firm Organisation', *International Small Business Journal*, 4(1).

Johnson, G. and Scholes, K. (1993) *Exploring Corporate Strategy*, Hemel Hempstead: Prentice-Hall International.

Peters, T.J. and Waterman, R.H. (1982) *In Search of Excellence*, London: Harper & Row.

Porter, M.E. (1987) 'From Competitive Advantage to Competitive Strategy', *Harvard Business Review*, 65(3).

Rumelt, R.P. (1974) *Strategy, Structure and Economic Performance*, Boston, MA: Harvard University Press.

Stevenson, H.H. and Gumperter, D.E. (1985) 'The Heart of Entrepreneurship', *Harvard Business Review*, March/April.

Ward, A.J. (1968) *Measuring, Directiing and Controlling New Product Development*, London: In Com Tec.

Wernerfelt, B. and Montgomery, C.A. (1986) 'What is an Attractive Industry?', *Management Science*, 32, 1223–9.

14 Developing the business plan

▷ **Why you need a business plan**
▷ **The planning process**
▷ **What a business plan looks like**
▷ **Using the plan to obtain finance**
▷ **The bankers' view**
▷ **The investors' view**
▷ **Presenting a case for finance**
▷ **Pro forma business plan**
▷ **Summary**

Case with questions
▷ Chris Hutt and the Newt & Cucumber

Learning outcomes

By the end of this chapter you should be able to:

▷ Explain the importance of the business plan;

▷ Describe the business planning process;

▷ Develop your own start-up business plan to suit different purposes;

▷ Recognise the information needs of bankers and the providers of equity finance;

▷ Use a plan to assess the need for appropriate finance;

▷ Critically analyse a business plan.

♀ Why you need a business plan

One of the most important steps in setting up any new business is to develop a business plan. It is equally important for a growing firm. It allows the owner-manager to crystallise their business idea and to think through the problems they will face before they have to cope with them. It allows them to set aims and objectives and thereby give themselves a yardstick against which to monitor performance. Perhaps of more immediate importance, it can also act as a vehicle to attract external finance.

Success, for businesses of all sizes, is positively correlated with planning. Timmons (1999) claims that the vast majority of *INC.* magazine's annually-produced 500 fastest-growing companies had business plans at the outset. In a research study, Woo et al. (1989) found that those firms which claimed to spend time in planning activities were those that experienced rapid growth. Kinsella et al. (1993) concluded that 93 per cent of fast-growth firms in their study had written business plans, compared to 70 per cent of matched firms. So, the evidence is there – planning improves the probability of success at start-up and later on. At a more pragmatic level, just try raising finance for your business without a plan and you will realise how essential it is.

Write a business plan – and get advice on doing it properly. I belong to Craft Central, which runs one-day seminars on 'Into Business'. I needed a business plan when applying for funding and it's the most useful thing I've done.
☐ Julie Spurgeon ceramics designer of Material Pleasures
Sunday Telegraph 12 July 2009

Business plans do not have to be long and elaborate. In many ways the process of thinking through how to go about setting up the business is far more important than the final document that is produced and for that reason internal plans can be informal, working documents. Only when they are used to obtain external finance do they need to become a more elaborate 'selling document'.

♀ The planning process

The previous chapters have given you all the tools you need to write a business plan. They have also taken you through the planning process. Essentially planning is a three-stage process:

1 Understanding where you are;
2 Deciding where you want to go;
3 Planning how to get there.

The business plan is just like a road map and the planning process is just like map-reading; decide on where you are and the town you want to go to, and then you can start to plan your route. You might decide not go in a straight line because there are longer but faster routes; you might be forced to take diversions because unexpected road works upset your plans; you might not get to your destination as quickly as you expect because the car breaks down. Indeed it is just possible that you will never reach your destination at all because of an accident. If you cannot decide where you are or where you want to go, the map is of little use. If you know where you are and where you want to go, a good map increases the chance of getting there. And planning the route will also help you estimate the petrol you need and the money you will therefore need to buy it. The business planning process is simple but systematic.

The business plan can be just like a road map

1   *Understanding where you are*

▷ Understanding your product or service and how it is better and worse than that of your competitors – your competitive advantage:

- How do you compete in terms of price, quality and so on?
- Is the product or service differentiated in any way?
- Do you have a 'unique selling proposition' (USP)?
- How can this be reinforced?
- Can the product or service be easily copied?
- Can you discern any patterns in successful or unsuccessful competitors?

▷ Understanding who your customers are and why and how they will buy from you:

- Can you identify market segments and can you get to them?
- Are your existing customers happy with the product or service?
- What is good and bad about your marketing mix?
- Can more customers be found who are similar to your existing customers?
- Are you selling to a niche market?

▷ Understanding your own and your firm's strengths and weaknesses (SWOT):

- What are your own aims, your own strengths and weaknesses?
- How good are your people and your facilities?
- Are you good at leadership and communication?
- What are the critical success factors – those things that it is crucial that you get right if you are to grow?
- What will be the critical problem areas if you grow?
- Do you have money of your own to put into the business?

▷ Understanding the opportunities and threats that the market might present you with (SWOT):

- Are market tastes changing?
- Is the market growing?
- Are there changes in the social, legal, economic, political or technological environment that are likely to affect you in the future (SLEPT analysis)?
- How easy is it for competitors to come into your industry (Porter's Five Forces)? Do you have new product or service ideas?

2   *Decide where you want to go*

▷ Decide the general aims you have for your business and for you. Do you want a lifestyle or do you want to go for growth? For some firms, aims become 'vision and mission statements – statements of what the owner-manager wants the business to become. For example, a medical general practice came up with the mission 'to provide the best possible health care for patients at all times by responding to needs, providing accessible medical and anticipatory care of the highest quality and doing all that is possible to improve the social environment of the community'.

▷ Set some specific objectives that signal you have achieved your aims. Objectives must be quantified, bounded in time and realistically achievable. They can then serve as useful goals and yardsticks against which to judge your performance. For example, an objective might be to achieve profit growth of 10 per cent with a minimum return on capital of 15 per cent. Objectives are the milestones on your journey. They tell you where you are going and let you know when you have arrived.

3   *Planning how to get there*

▷ Strategies need to be developed to enable you to achieve your objectives. Strategies are 'how to' statements. They are not complicated, they are just 'joined-up' tasks. Their development involves coordination of the different management functions – marketing, operations, people and finance.

▷ In particular, you will need to develop a marketing plan that produces a consistent and coherent marketing mix to address how to sell the product or service to the different customers. The generic marketing strategies help with this, but bear in mind where the product or service is in its life cycle.

▷ You may need to draw up different strategies for each of your portfolio of products and then pull these together.

▷ You may need to consider some strategic options, should barriers to your plans emerge over time.

▷ You will need to draw up financial budgets – profit and cash flow forecasts – to see what financial resources are needed to undertake the plan. Do you need to attract bank finance or equity investors? Can you? If not, your plans might have to be modified.

Previous chapters have given you all the tools you need to write a business plan. The whole business planning process was summarised in Figure 11.4. This is reproduced as Figure 14.1, showing relevant chapters. The process starts with the aims of the owner-manager, reflected in the vision or mission for the business, which was covered in Chapter 11.

The next element is a SWOT analysis (strengths, weaknesses, opportunities and threats) which gives a realistic appraisal of the options open to the business, also covered in Chapter 11. The SWOT analysis should be short, succinct and easy to read. However, it is by definition a summary of the key issues emanating from the marketing audit and should contain clear indicators of the key determinants of success rather than just being a smorgasbord of apparently unrelated points. A useful discipline in writing a SWOT is to continually ask yourself what each point means for the business.

What is the right plan? It's the one that helps you identify what you need to do to ensure success. It's the one that rallies your employees around a few common goals – and motivates them to achieve them. It's the one that involves your customers' goals and suppliers' goals and brings them all together in a unified focus.

☐   Michael Dell

The SWOT, in turn, informs the business objectives – covered earlier in this chapter. Business objectives should be quantified, realistic and set within a specified time frame so that they can be measured in order to know when they are achieved. Whereas a mission statement may endure for a number of years, the objectives of a business will change every year in line with commercial conditions. Objectives plot the route towards the aspirations for the firm, which are encapsulated in its mission statement. So, for example, if you aim to be the fastest-growing firm in a sector, your objectives need to reflect this.

The SWOT also informs the analysis of customers (market segmentation) – covered in Chapters 6 and 7. The generic marketing strategies help with this but bear in mind where the product or service is in its life cycle (Chapter 12). The marketing strategy is then developed into a detailed marketing plan, which involves constructing

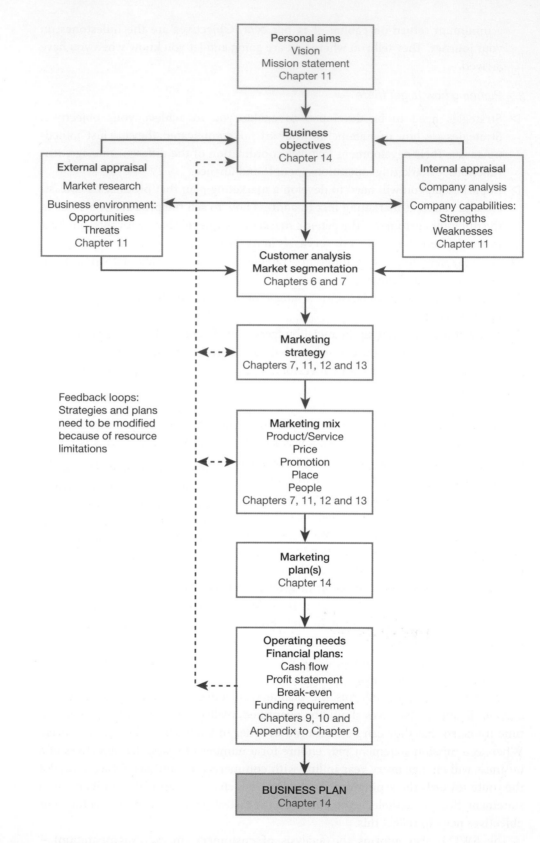

F14.1 The business planning process

a marketing mix to suit each of the different segments the firm is targeting. You may need to draw up different plans for each of your portfolio of products and then pull these together into a coherent growth strategy. You may also need to consider some strategic options, should barriers to your plans emerge over time. All these issues are covered in Chapters 7, 11, 12 and 13. And finally do not forget issues of sustainability and corporate social responsibility (Chapter 11).

Finally, these plans are costed and developed into a detailed set of budgets known as a financial plan. The financial plan should contain a cash flow forecast, a profit statement, calculations of break-even and a clear statement of funding requirement. This was covered in Chapters 9 and 10 and there is a comprehensive example of financial forecasting in the Appendix to Chapter 9.

Notice the numerous feedback loops where plans, strategies or even business objectives have to be modified because of resource limitations or other constraints. The business plan must be realistic. It is worth spending a few minutes thinking through how Figure 14.1 works and, if necessary, referring back to previous chapters to remind yourself of the component parts of this planning process.

Figure 14.1 sets out what Chaston (2000) would call a 'conventional plan' (see Figure 7.6). This is certainly what financial backers will be looking for. In the context of entrepreneurial marketing and the process Chaston proposed, this marketing plan can be described as the detailed plan in step 7 of Figure 7.7. The essential difference with Chaston's process is its emphasis on analysing the market, challenging conventional marketing approaches and trying to develop new approaches, within the capabilities of the business. This is a slightly different approach to the conventional SWOT analysis.

The great advantage of a business plan is that it forces you to think systematically and in detail about the future of the business. It forces you to think through the options that are open to you and justify the decisions you take, whilst thinking through the consequences of your actions. That is not to say you will anticipate all the problems you will face, but it will mean that you are better able to meet these challenges because you have a thorough understanding of the business and its market place. Remember, it is the process that is really important and a true entrepreneur is constantly refining or modifying their plan – strategising and developing strategic options – to meet changing opportunities and threats.

> *Get advice and do not be afraid to ask for help. Start with a business plan and see what develops. Do your research on markets and products. Be positive.*
>
> ☐ Ruth Coe, founder of Bespoke Beauty,
> Startups: www.startups.co.uk

There are many sources of help and advice to assist in developing a business plan. Most banks provide free resource packs that include computer disks with pre-formatted cash flow forecasts. Once developed, it always pays to get feedback on your plan, particularly if you intend to use it to raise finance for the business. The more rapid the growth your business will face, the more likely you are to need advice. Indeed, evidence shows that fast-growth firms are more likely to seek out and use advice (Cosh and Hughes, 1998). However, it cannot be proved directly that the advice led to growth.

♀ What a business plan looks like

There are no set rules that can be used to create a 'perfect business plan'. Each plan is particular to its business and will be different to others. Whilst later in the chapter we give a pro forma plan, even this will be adapted to say more or less about each heading, depending on the particular circumstances. One important point about the plan is that, as well as information about markets and finances, it must also convince the reader that you understand the operation of the business – how to do whatever needs to be done. If it is a retail business, do you understand retailing (for example, the importance of location)? If it is in manufacturing, do you understand the manufacturing process required? If a service business, do you know how that service is delivered? Do you know what laws and regulations you need to comply with for your particular business? Some of the assurance needed will come through the track record of key people involved – their background in a particular industry – but usually it is a fine balance between including sufficient detail in the plan to convince the reader that you know what you are talking about, but not so much that they lose interest. Indeed, too much focus on the operations may convince investors that you are product- rather than market-focused – and that will definitely turn them off.

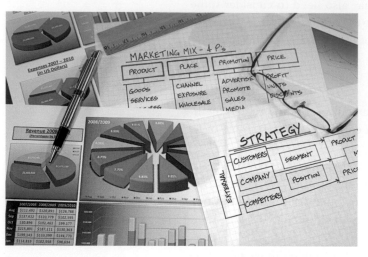

There are no set rules as to what a business plan should look like

The pro forma at the end of this chapter is intended for a relatively straightforward, small-scale start-up. It covers the following areas:

1 Business details – name, address, legal form, business activity.
2 Business aims and objectives.
3 Market information – size, growth, competitors.
4 The firm's strengths and weaknesses as well as competitive advantage (who are your competitors and why are you different?).
5 Details of customers perhaps with details of secured contracts – names, if selling to large industrial or commercial customers – or market segments, if selling to consumers. You need to assure the financier that you really know who will buy your product or service and why.
6 Marketing strategy – how the marketing mix ties together.
7 Premises and equipment needs. For retail business location is vitally important. Remember also that a banker might be looking for security from these assets.
8 Key people, their functions and background. Remember that investment is really in people, not bricks and mortar.
9 Financial highlights – turnover, profit, break-even, funding details.
10 Detailed profit forecast.
11 Detailed monthly cash flow forecast.

Plans that are intended for internal use only can be very short, almost acting as an 'aide memoire'. Those intended for external use – usually for businesses requiring bank or equity finance – tend to be longer and more 'formal'. The larger the start-up, the greater the need for external finance and consequently the longer the plan is likely to be – giving more detailed information and possibly covering forecasts for three years or more. A page showing key targets, with deadlines may be useful in these circumstances. For an existing business seeking additional growth finance, it is important to establish credibility. Brochures and financial statements from past years might be appended. In these circumstances an executive summary at the front of the plan is essential – for a venture capitalist it may be all they ever read. A long plan will also need a contents page.

Here are some further considerations:

▷ It is essential that your 'unique selling proposition' is clearly and simply articulated. Why will customers buy your product or service?

▷ Do not exaggerate or over-estimate the importance of your business idea. You do not need a great idea to start a business (but it does help); you need common sense, perseverance and time. Few businesses are based entirely on new ideas and a new idea is often harder to sell to financiers than an existing one, simply because they are unsure how it will work.

▷ Have clear in your mind who your audience is and what they are looking for in the plan. If it is just for yourself, it can be brief, almost in checklist form. If you are trying to raise funds it will have to be longer. A proposal for venture capital funds may be 50 pages long, including appendices, but must have a clear concise summary explaining what is in it for the investors and how their risks are minimised. Some plans list major risks and how they might be mitigated.

I see business plans so complicated that you need to set aside a week to read them but it is the ability to identify a simple solution that continues to set apart the best entrepreneurs.

☐ Duncan Bannatyne, serial entrepreneur and Dragon
Daily Telegraph 30 July 2009

▷ Keep it as short and simple as possible. Do not pad it out. The plan should be sufficiently long to cover the subject adequately but short enough to maintain interest. To do this you need to be able to prioritise and focus on the important things for your business. Use appendices to provide necessary support information. Use action plans – which are not necessarily part of the business plan – to remind you of who has to do what and by when.

▷ Ensure you are clear and specific. Are market segments clearly identified? Are objectives concrete and measurable? Are targets and deadlines clear?

▷ Ensure the plan is realistic. Are sales targets, costs, milestone deadlines and so on realistic?

▷ Check spelling, grammar, punctuation and, most important of all, financial accuracy. Errors damage your credibility and can throw you off when noticed as you present your plan. Word processors have a grammar and spelling check – use it. A spreadsheet package can be used for the cash flow forecast and that will ensure arithmetic accuracy.

If you type 'business plan' into a Google search you will come up with, literally, hundreds of millions of sites, most offering help, advice and products to help develop a business plan. There are books devoted solely to the topic and there is software to help you develop the plan. There are also a number of sites that offer you free specimen plans for a wide variety of different businesses. Try:

▷ www.bplans.com
▷ www.businessplanarchive.org
▷ www.morebusiness.com
▷ www.businessplans.org
▷ www.teneric.co.uk

▷ Ensure the plan is functional, clearly set out and easy to use. It does not have to be over-elaborate or expensively produced.

Using the plan to obtain finance

Initially you need to decide who you are writing the plan for – bankers, equity investors or yourself. If you are writing the plan for bankers and investors, you need to decide whether you need equity or bank finance, or both. You need to decide how much and what sort of finance you need, so that you can decide who might provide it.

Start by working through Figure 10.1. This will give you a guide to the main elements of the financial package you need. Next, review your cash flow forecast for the planning horizon (say 3 to 5 years). Remember to show the money you take out of the business in this. The forecast will tell you how much cash you need – the maximum and the minimum. The cash flow forecast will also give you some clues about what

📁 Case with questions Chris Hutt and the Newt & Cucumber

When Chris Hutt set up Unicorn Inns he did not think he would sell it ten years later to Moorland Brewery for over £13 million. But it was not until five years later that he analysed and started to understand the appeal of his most successful pub, the Newt & Cucumber, and start to develop it as a formula.

Newt & Cucumber is a prime-sited town- or city-centre free house close to offices, shopping centres and focal points of entertainment, feeding off continuous pedestrian flow. It has a 'traditional but trendy' atmosphere and serves regional real ales alongside national lagers and premium bottled beers. It is open all day and offers food. It is designed to appeal to a wide and varying target market according to the time of day and time of week. It has a large floor space which allows it to have different areas with an informal, basic and unpretentious decor. These areas combine hard-floored, stand-up drinking areas and soft-carpeted, sit-down eating sections. There are large open vistas but there are also intimate corners. It is meant to display 'traditional' pub values – the primacy of beer over any elaborate and frivolous decoration. In this way it is meant to appeal to a wide range of customers. It needs heavy pedestrian flows to generate the customers to fill the large floor space. A Newt & Cucumber free house offers:

▷ A wide range of premium liquor brands;
▷ Tasty, filling, value-for-money lunch-time meals, served fast;
▷ Competitive pricing, including at least one low-priced beer;
▷ A warm, traditional and lively atmosphere;
▷ Efficient, friendly service by motivated staff;
▷ A safe, secure, well managed environment with no games of pool or juke boxes.

➝

Newt & Cucumber's business plan

Segments:	Shoppers	Office/professionals	Pensioners/low paid	Unemployed
Time	12–5	12–2	12–2	2–5
Male/female split	10/90	40/60	90/10	90/10
Marketing mix:				
Product:	Coffee/tea, soft drinks	Choice of good food	Cheap beer	Cheap beer
Service:	Friendly	Fast	Low priority consideration	Low priority consideration
Price:	Competitive	Food under £5.00	Worthington Bitter @ 40% discount	Worthington Bitter @ 40% discount
Place:				
– environment	Safe, sit down, clean toilets	Clean, comfortable	Warm	Music/TVs
– convenience in choice of pub	90%	80%	50%	50%
Critical sucess factors	Safe, clean environment	Rapid delivery of tasty, filling, good value meals	Cheap beer	Cheap beer

Most drinks in the Newt & Cucumber deliver a margin of 65–70%. It is a formula very similar to the Wetherspoon chain of pubs, but at the time it was developed Wetherspoon was also in its infancy.

Chris Hutt planned an exit strategy almost from the first day he started rolling out his Newt & Cucumber chain. He wanted to sell his shareholding either through a trade sale or stock market floatation and his experience of the trade told him that there were four critical success factors that would maximise its value so that when he sold the business it would continue to prosper in a highly competitive industry:

1 Finding suitable sites to roll out the Newt & Cucumber pub formula so that the company could get to an appropriate size to benefit from bulk purchase discounts and to be sufficiently attractive to potential buyers.
2 Recruiting and motivating good pub management. To this end he put in place training programmes, appraisal systems and an attractive bonus package that rewarded managers who achieved targets (based upon key financial drivers outlined on page 234).
3 Putting in place strong financial controls (also based upon the key financial drivers outlined in the Case insight on page 234).
4 Promoting the brand, not only to customers, but also to the trade by writing articles for the trade press and getting free PR, for example, by winning the Multiple Operator of the Year trade award.

Each of these critical success factors was built into his business plan on a year-by-year basis. An extract from this business plan, showing the target markets at different times of the day and the marketing mix for each of these markets is shown below. The objective of this marketing strategy is to ensure that the pub appeals predominantly to different market segments at different times of the day, thus ensuring that it is always as full as possible – important for a business which has high fixed costs.

QUESTIONS

1 Why is the marketing strategy so informative? Can this formula succeed in filling the pub all day? Does this format present the strategy well?

2 How important is the size and location of each outlet?

3 Why is it important to maximise sales in a high fixed cost business?

4 What reservations might you have if you were purchasing or investing in a pub chain of this sort? How far has Chris dealt with these reservations?

Office/professionals	Students	Regulars	Pre-clubbers
6 7	any time	7–11	7–11, Fri/Sat
60/40	50/50	60/40	60/40
Wide range of quality drinks	Wide range of quality drinks	Wide range of quality drinks	Fashionable brand leaders
Friendly	Low priority consideration	Friendly	Fast
20% discount	Competitive	Competitive	Low priority consideration
Upbeat atmosphere	Relaxed, safe	Home from home	Lively, 'in place'
80%	70%	50%	80%
Cheap drinks and upbeat atmosphere after work	Relaxed atmosphere and used by other students	Good service and atmosphere	'In place' reputation

sort of finance you need. For example, if the cash flow swings in and out of negative but shows no long-term negative trend, you may need only overdraft finance. If Death Valley only lasts a year or so before cash flow becomes positive you may only require short-term bank finance. But if major initial investment is required in plant or buildings causing Death Valley to be dramatic and long, you may require long-term finance such as a mortgage or a long-term loan or equity finance.

Finally, analyse your financial performance using the financial ratios outlined in Chapter 11, remembering to review contribution margins, break-even points and margins of safety. What do they tell you about the business? How profitable is the business? Venture capitalists are only interested in ventures that are very profitable, producing a return that is sufficient to double or triple their investment in three to five years. Does the planned profitability meet this criterion? Remember also to look at the key ratios that interest bankers. How will the banker react to them? This financial ratio analysis will tell you how successful others will consider your venture and how attractive it is as an investment. It will also inform them about the riskiness of their potential investment.

If your business is demanding of capital you've got to have a very clear business plan ... because people will only lend you money to make money. They'll want a three times return on their investment within a three to four year window.

☐ Will King, founder of King of Shaves,
RealBusiness interview 1 July 2009

Whether you are trying to borrow money from a bank or seek equity finance from an investor, ultimately you will need to do two things:

1 Present them with a business plan;
2 Establish a relationship of trust and respect.

Whilst each is looking at the same elements of information from the business plan, as you might have concluded from Chapter 10, each places a slightly different importance on the individual elements. However, the reality is that both banks and equity investors ultimately invest in individuals, not in businesses or plans. The plan is just one way, albeit very important, of communicating with them. It must therefore reinforce the perceptions the banker or investor has of the individual(s) seeking finance. That perception must be that they know what they are talking about and that the business proposal has a good chance of success.

♀ The bankers' view

Banks are in the business of lending money; in that respect they are just like any other supplier of a commodity. However, about two-thirds of external finance for small firms comes from banks, which makes them an important supplier. The lending criteria banks adopt were set out in Chapter 10. The thing to remember about banks is that they are not in the risk business, they are looking to obtain a certain rate of interest over a specified period of time and see their capital repaid. They do not share in the extra profits a firm might make, so they do not expect to lose money if there are problems. What is more, the manager stands to lose a lot if he lends to a business that subsequently fails.

Bank managers represent a set of values and practices that are alien to many owner-managers. They are employees, not independent professionals, and increasingly lend only within very strict, centrally dictated, guidelines. They often talk 'a different language' and are subject to numerous rules and regulations that an owner-manager would probably find very tedious. Since they trade in money, they often cannot make decisions on their own without getting approval from 'up the line'. In these circumstances the business plan is an essential weapon in helping them get authorisation for a loan. Any manager will only be able to lend within the bank's own policies, at acceptable levels of risk and with adequate security to cover the loan. However, each of these three constraints requires the exercise of judgement and can therefore be influenced, not least through the style and content of the business plan.

A business plan prepared for a bank needs to demonstrate how the interest on the loan can be paid, even in the worst possible set of circumstances, and the capital can be repaid on the due date. In this respect the cash flow forecast is something that the bank manager will be particularly interested in. As well as cash flow, they are also particularly interested in two important financial ratios:

▷ Break-even – which tells the banker about the operating risk the business faces;
▷ Gearing – which tells the banker about the financial risks the business faces from borrowing.

In an ideal world, they would like both of these to be as low as possible. Your business plan should address these issues head on, by showing the calculations.

Bank managers are trained to examine business plans critically. So expect to be questioned. Make explicit any assumptions that the plan is based on. The plan should seek to identify and then reassure the bank manager about the risks the business faces. All businesses face risks, so the manager will expect to see them identified. Bank managers tend to dislike plans that they see as over-ambitious, since they will not share in the success, so the plan needs to be conservative. Bank managers will always ask questions about some of the claims in the plan, so you must always be able to back them up. Avoid any tendency to generalise in order to disguise a weakness in your knowledge.

For a start-up it is particularly important to establish the credibility of the owner-manager and other key managers. Summarising skills and previous experience, particularly in a related field can do this. For an existing business the bank manager will be more interested in the firm's track record, particularly its financial performance, so previous financial statements will need to go with the plan. Where a long-term loan for R&D or capital expenditure is being sought, where there is little prospect of loan repayment in the short term, the plan must emphasise the cash-generating capacity of the business and take a perspective longer than one year.

However good the business plan, bankers are still likely to ask for a personal guarantee from the owner-manager. After all, if they don't ask, they certainly won't get it. And it does make any loan more secure from their perspective. But be prepared to haggle and shop around. This is just a sales negotiation like any other and the banker is trying to 'sell' you a loan, albeit at a certain price and with certain conditions.

💡 The investors' view

Individuals and institutions investing in unquoted companies are becoming increasingly sophisticated. Who these individuals and institutions are and their investing criteria were explained in Chapter 10. Most business people submit investment proposals to more than one institution for consideration. However, on the other side of the coin, most investment institutions are inundated with proposals. It has been estimated that less than 1 in 20 will ever reach negotiation stage. To a large extent, therefore, the decision whether to proceed beyond an initial reading of the plan will depend crucially on its quality. The business plan is the first, and often the best,

A leading venture capitalist once admitted that, whilst discussions with the owner-manager centred on the business plan, the final decision whether or not to invest really was a result of 'gut feel' – a personal 'chemistry' between them and the owner-manager. At the end of the day, that chemistry must lay the foundation for a long-term relationship based, as with all relationships, on trust and respect.

Pro forma business plan

The pro forma business plan outlined below is a description of the business and what the owner-manager wants it to become, in this case, over the next 12 months. The business plan should contain targets, estimates and projections and describe how they will be achieved. It should help the owner-manager think ahead systematically and raise finance. It is an invaluable route map to help their business succeed. This pro forma plan is meant as a guide for how one should look. It is intended for a modest start-up. Notes are included in the relevant sections. A copy is available on the website accompanying this book.

Specimen plans for three businesses (retail, service and manufacturing) based on this pro forma are available on the website for this book. They are intended to be used for discussion only and not as examples of good or bad plans.

Business plan

Business name and address:

Proprietor's name and address:

Business form: [Sole trader/partnership/limited company]

Business activity:

[Enter here a description of the business, including product/service details. Obviously this is the core around which the plan revolves. It should describe it as thoroughly as possible, but can be supplemented with samples, photographs and so on. It should also give details of any intended future product/service developments.]

Aims:

[Aims for the business and the owner-manager should go here. For example, the aim might be to provide secure employment and an adequate income for the owner-manager and their spouse. The aims are broader than the objectives.]

Objectives:

[The objectives are the specific targets. For example, the objective might be to achieve sales of £150 000 in the first year and a gross profit margin of 40 per cent.]

Market size and growth:

[Market research information can go here. Try to estimate the size of the market the business is aiming for (either locally or nationally) and the share it hopes to capture, the growth in the last few years and any other characteristics. For example, it could be that there are many small competitors without the competitive advantage you have. A good product/service will sell only if a market for it exists or can be created.]

Competitors:

Names   *Strengths*   *Weaknesses*

[List major competitors together with their strengths and weaknesses. For example, there may be a major national competitor but they cannot deliver the personal service this firm offers. The aim is then to develop these advantages but also to counter any advantages competitors might have.]

Your business:

Strengths   *Weaknesses*

[In listing the strengths and weaknesses, the aim is to build on the strengths, particularly when they generate a competitive advantage. Weaknesses will need to be addressed in the marketing plan.]

Competitive advantages:

[Competitive advantage should come from the business strengths and weaknesses. This section also needs to address how the advantage will be maintained. For example, is there a patent or copyrights? Remember that if a new idea proves successful others will copy it.]

Proposed customers:

[This should describe the customers the business intends to sell to, if possible, naming names. For example, the business might intend selling to farmers in a particular geographic area. Try to quantify the number of customers.]

Marketing strategy:

(Describe the marketing strategy making certain to cover all elements of the marketing mix.)

– Product

(Explain the product/service in terms of benefits to the customer.)

– People

(Describe the service, advice or support that will enhance the product offering.)

– Price

(Explain what the pricing policy is and why. Does the firm intend to be cheapest, most expensive or just take the 'going rate'. If relevant, it might describe how the price for a customer is arrived at.)

– Promotion

(Describe how the business will communicate with the proposed customers. For example, by telephone or mail shot. Will it be by advertising? If so what form might it take (for example, notice-board, newspapers, radio and so on).)

– Place

(Describe size, location and any other special characteristics) the type of premises the business will operate from – private house, shop, workshop and so on. Note should be made of planning permissions required and cost – lease, rent or purchase.)

Equipment:

[Any special equipment needed should be described here together with cost and proposed method of acquisition – lease, hire or purchase. Will more equipment be needed in the future?]

Key people and job functions:

[Key people, including the owner-manager, and their roles and responsibilities should be described here.]

Background details of key people:

[The background of the key people should be described here – qualifications, training, previous industry experience and personal strengths and weaknesses. If the plan is used to obtain finance, the owner-manager may need to give fuller background details. This helps establish credibility.]

Financial highlights

12 months to:

Turnover:

[This section summarises information from the profit and loss account.
Sales is the value of goods or services estimated to be sold in the year. It represents the value invoiced to customers and NOT the amount of cash received.]

Profit:

[Net profit (or loss) represents the difference between sales and direct variable and fixed costs. Out of this a sole trader would take drawings. On the other hand, the owner-manager of a limited company will pay themselves a wage or salary (shown in costs) but if they want to take more out of the business they might decide to do so by way of dividends.]

Break-even:

[The break-even calculation should be shown here. This is a measure of the operating risk facing the business. It should be as low as possible.]

Funding requirement:

[This should disclose any funding required and the months it is required, taken from the cash flow forecast. Remember, always to add something as a contingency against the plan going wrong. It should also describe where these funds are expected to come from.]

Source of funds:

[Here indicate the expected source and nature of funding (for example, overdraft for 8 months).]

Forecast profit and loss account

Business:

Period:

Sales:		£	(A)
Less direct (variable) costs:			
Materials	£		
Direct wages	£		
Other	£		
Total direct (variable) costs:		£ _____	
Gross profit/contribution:		£ _____	(B)
Fixed costs (overheads):			
Wages/salaries (including taxes)	£		
Rent	£		
Heat/light/power	£		
Advertising	£		
Insurance	£		
Transport/travel	£		
Telephone	£		
Stationery/postage	£		
Repairs/renewals	£		
Depreciation	£		
Local taxes	£		
Other _____	£		
Other _____	£		
Total fixed costs		£ _____	(C)
Net profit		£ _____	
Less drawings or dividends		£ _____	
Profit retained in the business		£ _____	

Direct (variable) costs are the costs of materials, labour and other expenditures that vary directly with sales activity. It represents the costs associated with the goods or services sold. It does not necessarily represent the total goods or services purchased, since some of these might have been purchased for stock. Nor does it represent the cash spent, as some goods might have been purchased on credit terms.

Fixed costs are the overhead costs of the business that do not vary with sales activity; for example, rent of premises. They do not represent the cash spent, as goods might be purchased on credit or services might be paid for in advance. Furthermore, items like depreciation represent an allocation of the cost of a fixed asset, not the cash spent on it.

$$\text{Break-even point} = \frac{(C) \times (A)}{(B)}$$

Cash flow forecast

Month:												
SALES												
Volume:												
Value:												
RECEIPTS												
Sales – cash												
Sales – debtors												
Capital introduced												
Grants, loans, etc												
Total (A)												
PAYMENTS												
Materials												
Wages/salaries												
Rent												
Heat/light/power												
Advertising												
Insurance												
Transport/travel												
Telephone												
Stationery/postage												
Repairs/renewals												
Local taxes												
Other _____												
Other _____												
Capital purchases												
Loan repayments												
Drawings/dividends												
Total (B)												
CASH BALANCES												
Cash flow (A) – (B)												
Opening balance												
Closing balance												

Cash flow is the lifeblood of a business. The cash flow forecast shows where the cash will be coming from and where it will go. Each monthly column should show the actual amounts the business expects to receive and pay out. But remember, sales made in January may not generate cash until February or later if terms of trade are 30 days. Cash receipts, therefore, show cash coming in, including capital introduced and any loans or grants. Similarly, cash payments include loan repayments, withdrawals or dividends. They do not include depreciation, which is an allocation of the capital cost of an asset over its expected life.

The cash increase (or decrease) is the difference between total cash receipts and total cash payments. This is added to (or subtracted from) the opening balance to give the closing balance that month – that is, the surplus of cash in any month – which is carried forward into next month's column as the opening balance.

⋈ Summary

⋈ Developing a business plan is important to help you crystallise your business idea, think through the problems you might face and to develop a yardstick against which to measure your performance. It is also essential if you need to raise external finance. The planning process is more important than the written business plan itself and a true entrepreneur is constantly refining the plan to meet changing opportunities and threats – even if this is not written down. Planning is a three-stage process:

▷ Understanding where you are;
▷ Deciding where you want to go;
▷ Planning how to get there.

⋈ Starting with your personal aims and ambitions, you develop a business mission that leads to business objectives that are quantifiable, realistic and bounded in time. These are based upon an appraisal of your business capabilities and the opportunities it faces – the SWOT analysis. You go on to identify your customers and develop a marketing strategy based upon your marketing mix that will enable you to sell your product or service in the appropriate volumes to meet your business objectives. This is detailed in a marketing plan, one example of which we looked at for the **Newt & Cucumber** chain of pubs. This plan is then translated into financial and operating budgets – including a cash flow forecast – which together are called the financial plan. The marketing and financial plans together form your business plan.

⋈ There is no standard format for a business plan; however, a typical one might contain the following:

1 Business details – name, address, legal form, business activity;
2 Business aims and objectives;
3 Market information – size, growth, competitors;
4 The firm's strengths and weaknesses as well as competitive advantage;
5 Customers;
6 Marketing strategy – advertising, promotion, pricing and so on;
7 Premises and equipment needs;
8 Key people, their functions and background;
9 Financial highlights – turnover, profit, break-even, funding details;
10 Detailed profit forecast;
11 Detailed monthly cash flow forecast.

⋈ The business plan should only be as long as it needs to be. Keep it as short as possible, whilst delivering all relevant information.

⋈ A business plan presented to a bank needs to demonstrate how interest on the loan can be paid and the capital repaid on the due date. Particular attention, therefore, needs to be paid to the cash flow forecast. Bank managers are risk averse. To obtain a loan you need to gain their trust and develop their respect in your business ability. Credibility is vital.

⋈ A business plan developed for an equity investor needs to demonstrate that a business opportunity exists that can earn a high return in a five- to ten-year time frame and that, as in the case of the **Newt & Cucumber**, the management team are capable of exploiting the opportunity. Issues of control and ownership need to be thought through.

⏻ **Further resources are available at www.palgrave.com/business/burns**

🗋 Essays and discussion topics

1 How can computer-based systems help develop a business plan? What advantages do they offer? Are there any drawbacks?

2 What form do you think a business plan should take for your own, internal use?

3 In a rapidly changing world, is planning really of any use?

4 In a world 'turned upside down' and in chaos, full of uncertainty, how can you plan?

5 Are entrepreneurs congenitally incapable of planning?

6 Every business graduate can produce a good business plan, but not even one per cent can become entrepreneurs. Discuss.

7 The best business plan is a short business plan. Discuss.

8 How realistic is the entrepreneur's 'pitch' in the *Dragons' Den*?

⟳ Exercises and activities

1 List the contents of a business plan that is drawn up:
   (1) For planning purposes within the firm;
   (2) For raising external finance.

   How are they different?

2 Draw up a report for your superior in a bank outlining the criteria you recommend the bank to use in making a loan to:
   (1) A start-up business;
   (2) An established firm.

   How are they different? How much of the necessary information can come from the business plan?

3 An 'elevator pitch' is where you have 3 minutes only to explain your start-up idea to a potential investor/lender and persuade them to see you again to find out more. (It is so called because you might be trapped in the elevator with them for

3 minutes.) It requires you to know exactly what is unique about your product or service and what the investor/lender is interested in. Pair up with other students and practise your pitch. Give each other scores out of 10 but, more importantly, be prepared to explain your score. You should improve with practice.

4 Select one of the three specimen business plans on the website and review it. Critically evaluate the business proposition. Does the business require finance? If so, what form would you recommend?

5 Visit any of the websites that contain specimen business plans, select one and critically evaluate the business proposition.

6 Obtain another pro forma business plan by visiting the website of a major bank. Compare and contrast this to the one in this chapter.

📖 References

Chaston, I. (2000) *Entrepreneurial Marketing: Competing by Challenging Convention*, Basingstoke: Macmillan – now Palgrave Macmillan.

Cosh, A. and Hughes, A. (1998) *Enterprise Britain: Growth, Innovation and Public Policy in the Small and Medium-Sized Enterprise Sector 1994–1997*, ESRC Centre for Business Research, University of Cambridge.

Kinsella, R.P., Clarke, W., Coyne, D., Mulvenna, D. and Storey, D.J. (1993) *Fast Growth Firms and Selectivity*, Dublin: Irish Management Institute.

Timmons, J. A. (1999) *New Venture Creation: Entrepreneurship for the 21st Century*, Singapore: McGraw-Hill International.

Woo, C.Y., Cooper, A.C., Dunkelberg, W.C., Daellenbach, U. and Dennis, W.J. (1989) 'Determinants of Growth for Small and Large Entrepreneurial Start-ups', paper presented at Babson Entrepreneurship Conference.

15 Exit: failure and success

▷ **Stagnate and die**
▷ **Failure**
▷ **The ingredients of failure**
▷ **Predicting failure**
▷ **Dealing with failure as an individual or a sole trader**
▷ **Dealing with failure as a company**
▷ **Success – selling the business**
▷ **Company valuation**
▷ **Summary**

Case insights
▷ Nick Kenton, Rob Taub and Sportbase
▷ Nicholas Hall
▷ Tech board
▷ ZedZed.com
▷ Alex Meisl and Taotalk, then Sponge
▷ Peter Durose and the English Grocer
▷ Kristian Segerstrale and Playfish
▷ Vivid Imaginations
▷ The Body Shop
▷ Julian Harley, Ian West and Harley West Training
▷ Anne and Simon Notley and Feather and Black

Case with questions
▷ Cobra Beer

Learning outcomes

By the end of this chapter you should be able to:

▷ List the ways an owner-manager can exit their business;

▷ Explain what constitutes business failure;

▷ Recognise when a small firm is most at risk of failure and explain what contributes to it;

▷ Explain what options are open to an individual or sole trader struggling to pay their debts;

▷ Explain what options are open to a company struggling to pay its debts;

▷ List the options open to owner-managers in order to harvest their investment in their business and explain what needs to be done to get the best deal;

▷ Explain how company valuations are arrived at.

💡 Stagnate and die

Most small firms are born to stagnate or die. As we saw in Chapter 1, in the UK most do not grow to any size – almost two-thirds of businesses comprise only one or two people, and often the second person is the spouse. Some 95 per cent of firms employ fewer than 10 employees and 99 per cent fewer than 50 employees. Half of businesses cease trading within three years of being set up, although, as pointed out, this does not necessarily mean that the closure has left creditors unpaid, and it can be viewed in a positive light as part of the dynamism of the sector as it responds to changing opportunities in the market place. What is more, when the number of start-ups increases, the number of businesses ceasing to trade tends to do so as well. The pattern is broadly similar internationally, although the USA has an even higher closure rate (Bannock and Daley, 1994). A cynical observer might conclude that, in such a turbulent environment, mere survival is a badge of success.

The exit of an owner-manager can be a thing of sadness or joy, depending on how it is achieved. Ceasing to trade can be a sadness if creditors are left unpaid. For a sole trader this might lead to their personal bankruptcy (which can only be discharged by a court of law) as creditors pursue their debts by claiming their personal assets. Only a tiny number of business exits involve bankruptcy. For a limited company an inability to pay creditors can lead to insolvency and then liquidation, when a liquidator is appointed to dispose of the assets of the business, with their value going to the creditors. Statistically, total insolvencies are defined as all liquidations of insolvent companies plus all personal bankruptcies. These are what most people would agree to call business failures. So, an inability to pay one's debts does not always lead to what is called 'failure'. We deal more fully with the practical and legal options open to sole traders and companies unable to pay their debts later in this chapter.

Even with this definition there are problems of interpretation. It is not uncommon for a bank to foreclose on its debt, forcing a company into liquidation, knowing that it will secure repayment of its preferential debt at the expense of other creditors, and then to provide support for a 'new' company set up by the owner-manager undertaking exactly the same type of business. Is this a business failure?

The liquidation of a company, in itself, may be a natural way of bringing the business to an end. This is called a voluntary liquidation. If there are surplus assets then the company is not insolvent and the owner-manager may make a capital gain after creditors are paid. But perhaps the most attractive exit for owner-managers is to sell the firm as a going concern. If they can achieve this they will reap the harvest of their years of investment in the business. But, even with a sale, definitions are not straightforward because it could be that the sale was prompted by the business making continuing losses which could ultimately have led to failure. Nevertheless, even this form of 'distress sale' may still yield a capital gain for the owner-manager.

One of the first things I learned though was that there was a relationship between screwing up and learning: the more mistakes I made, the faster I learned.

☐ Michael Dell

Whilst in the USA business failure can be seen as a worthwhile experience for entrepreneurs, provided they are seen to learn from it, in the UK there is still a stigma attached to it. Being associated with a failed company can lead to problems when it comes to raising cash for another start-up. Bankers, in particular, need some convincing to persuade them to give an entrepreneur a second chance – particularly if they lost money on the first attempt.

♀ Failure

Notwithstanding these definitional problems, in his review of the literature Storey (1998) identified a number of factors that influence the probability of business failure. These are not necessarily independent of each other. The factors he identified as having the strongest influence were:

▷ *Age of business*: simply reviewing the statistics tells you that young firms are more likely to fail than older firms. Half of firms cease trading within their first three years of existence. The longer a firm survives, the less likely it is to fail. One study estimated that a 1 per cent change in age leads to a 13 per cent improvement in the probability of survival (Evans, 1987).

▷ *Size of business*: similarly, the likelihood of failure is greater the smaller the firm. Size is, of course, related to age but it is easier to close a small firm than a large one. Also, as we saw in a previous chapter, large firms have more assets than smaller firms and are therefore better able to weather adversity in the short term. Evans' survey estimated that a 1 per cent change in firm size leads to a 7 per cent improvement in the probability of survival.

▷ *Past growth*: firms that grow within a short period after start-up are less likely to fail than those that do not.

▷ *Sector*: failure rates vary from sector to sector with the construction and retail sectors showing the highest level of failures. Storey concludes, however, that the influence of sector is not as great as the first three factors.

Storey also considered a number of factors which he concluded had a less certain influence on failure. These were:

▷ *Management*: most people would accept that the character and skills of the owner-manager as well as the team they draw around them influence the probability of either success or failure. Storey reviewed studies that tried to gauge the influence of work history (for example prior business ownership, management experience, unemployment), family background, personal characteristics (age, gender and ethnic background) and education but found the influences 'complex and difficult to predict' and failed to detect any patterns.

▷ *Economic conditions*: small firms are traditionally thought to be vulnerable to changes in economic activity with business failures expected to increase in times of recession. However, studies have failed to establish a clear relationship because of the influence of other factors such as previous levels of start-up.

▷ *Type of firm*: there is evidence that, unsurprisingly, franchises have a lower chance of failure than other businesses. More surprisingly, Storey concluded that limited companies are somewhat more risky than either self-proprietorships or partnerships, presumably due to the potential for unlimited personal liability.

▷ *Location*: there are clear regional variations in failure rates, however, these tend to correspond to high rates of start-up. High start-up rates – for example, in London – go hand in hand with high levels of failure. The influence is, therefore, unclear.

▷ *Ownership*: the influence of ownership is less clear but it is suggested that larger firms with more than one plant are more likely to close a plant when facing difficult trading conditions than single-plant firms.

▷ *Business in receipt of state subsidies*: because state subsidy is often given to the weakest businesses, this influence is also difficult to verify.

Storey's review tells us little about the process of failure and, therefore, how it might be avoided. It implies that failure is mainly influenced by factors outside the owner-manager's control, many being the inevitable consequences of start-up. He points out that failure is endemic in the small business sector which has probably always been characterised by high levels. His overall conclusion – that 'the young are more likely to fail than the old, the very small are more likely to fail than their larger counterparts, and that, for young firms, probably the most powerful influence on their survival is whether or not they grow within a short period after start-up' – may be statistically accurate, but it is of hardly any use to owner-managers.

> *A recession is essentially a time for rebalancing … If you've got a business with either a great product or great brand or offering a great service, all that happens is a lot of things come to challenge you … But if your business has momentum it can help in a way in that lots of businesses that were set up in times of boom which simply got access to cash to launch an average idea or develop an average service simply fell away.*
>
> □ Will King, founder of King of Shaves, *RealBusiness* 1 July 2009

In an extensive review of some 50 articles and five books on the subject of small business failure, Berryman (1983) focused more on the managerial causes of failure. He listed some 25 causes, categorised under six headings, although he noted that many of the items in categories 1 to 4 are probably symptoms rather than causes:

1 *Accounting*: accounting problems such as debtor and stock control or inadequate records were cited most frequently.

2 *Marketing*: marketing problems came a close second. These can be many and various, from a lack of understanding of customer needs or failure to identify target customers to poor selling skills.

3 *Finance*: financing a firm that is failing is bound to be a problem. Cash flow will be poor and further finance may be unavailable. However, this is simply an obvious symptom of the problem rather than a root cause. Nevertheless, as many firms have found, undercapitalisation at start-up can be a significant factor in subsequent failure. Firms that are highly successful almost from start-up can face the danger of overtrading if they are undercapitalised.

4 *Other internal factors*: for example excessive drawings, nepotism or negligence.

5 *Behaviour of owner-manager*: Berryman lists such personal problems as inability to delegate, reluctance to seek help, excessive optimism, unawareness of the environment, inability to adapt to change and thinness of management talent as reasons for failure.

6 *External factors*: the effects of the economic environment or changes in the industry or market. Personal problems can also be significant.

🛄 Case insight Nicholas Hall

Nicholas Hall is President of the Silicon Valley Association of Start-up Entrepreneurs in the USA. He has been involved in six start-ups himself including a brewery and a business network website. His latest venture is Possibility Productions, an online deal broker of media, entertainment and technology conferences. But he is probably best known in the USA for starting the website startupfailures.com, a community website that 'chronicles the challenges of the entrepreneurial journey'. This was born out of his own failure and the need to write about it and learn from it. He found this helped him and he believes it will help others. As he says:

> 'Nobody wants to be a failure. At the same time there is no better education for an entrepreneur than failure.'

Business Week Online 22 June 2005

☐ Visit the website on: www.startupfailures.com

💡 The ingredients of failure

Building on Berryman's classic work and using the model outlined in Figure 11.1 to help us understand business success, we can now start to understand the influences on business failure. Just as with business success, there is a recipe for business failure. This recipe is shown in Figure 15.1. It comprises flaws in the entrepreneurial character, poor business decisions, company weaknesses that combine to make challenges from the external environment too great to deal with ... and of course there is always an element of luck. Whilst the precise recipe varies from situation to situation, we know the ingredients. It is

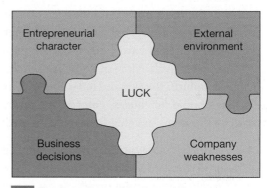

15.1 The ingredients of business failure

a coincidence of a number of factors that is likely to lead to failure, as in a complex chemical reaction.

Entrepreneurial character

Referring back to Chapter 2, we recall that certain of the character traits of owner-managers and entrepreneurs can have very negative effects. For example, the strong internal locus of control can lead to 'control freak' behaviour such as meddling, an inability to delegate, a mistrust of subordinates or an unwillingness to part with equity in the business. Similarly, the strong need for public achievement might lead to unwise overspending on the trappings of corporate life, or the 'big project' that is too risky. The strong self-confidence can, *in extremis*, become 'delusional' behaviour evidenced by an excessive optimism, an exaggerated opinion of their business competence and an unwillingness to listen to advice or seek help. On top of this can be layered the problems associated with family firms that we look at in the next chapter. These combine to produce a potent set of behavioural ingredients which might become underlying causes of failure.

Beaver and Jennings (2005) found evidence of 'non-rational' behaviour contributing to business failure. Larson and Clute (1979) listed eight personal characteristics to be found in owner-managers of failed firms. It is interesting how many of these factors are the negative sides of the character traits of entrepreneurs that we have already noted. The characteristics were:

▷ Exaggerated opinion of business competency based upon knowledge of some skill;
▷ Limited formal education;
▷ Inflexibility to change and not innovative;
▷ Use of own personal tastes and opinions as the standard to follow;
▷ Decisions based upon intuition, emotion and non-objective factors;
▷ Past not future orientation;
▷ Limited reading in literature associated with the business;
▷ Resistant to advice from qualified sources but, paradoxically, accepts it from the less-qualified.

Business decisions

Bad and untimely business decisions have been shown to contribute to business failure in SMEs (Gaskill et al., 1993). By definition, bad business decisions are the opposite of good ones. They often stem from a lack of reliable information and research, or an unwillingness or inability to understand it. For example, bad marketing decisions feature regularly in the literature on causes of failure and these often stem from a lack of understanding of what customers are really buying (benefits), who customers are (market segmentation) and why they do not buy from competitors (competitive advantage). This is basic marketing. Many researchers have indicated that it is lack of business competency in owner-managers that has underpinned business failures (Kiggundu, 2002; Knots et al., 2003). However, the timing of decisions is crucial and a study by Stokes and Blackburn (2002) found that the inability to make difficult decisions on a timely basis was a significant factor in 14 per cent of their sample of 306 failed businesses.

You feel a lot of shame. I had 200 staff. You feel you've let them down.

☐ Mark Constantine, founder of Lush, on the bankruptcy of his Cosmetics to Go business *RealBusiness* interview 26 May 2009

Some of the points when an entrepreneur is most likely to make bad management or personnel decisions are predicted by Greiner's growth model (covered in Chapter 17). These crises are predictable and the problems of dealing with them are anchored in the entrepreneurial character. Hence, for example, an unwillingness to bring in an outside manager may be related to the entrepreneur's unwillingness to delegate, or their unwillingness to give up equity (control) to attract a suitably experienced manager, or because of the mistrust of non-family managers. Many bad decisions stem from the character traits of entrepreneurs. For example, the decision to undertake the risky 'big project' that eventually brings the company down may have been influenced by the entrepreneur's need to demonstrate achievement and receive public applause and recognition.

One study analysed the events that threatened the survival of small firms and found that 38 per cent were marketing-related, 32 per cent finance-related, 14 per cent management-related, 13 per cent personnel-related, 10 per cent were 'acts of God' and 18 per cent had no associated crisis (Watkins, 1982).

Larson and Clute (op. cit.) listed nine 'managerial defects' of failed firms. Many of these we would call bad decisions, but some we would classify under 'weaknesses'. They were:

▷ Inability to identify target market or customers;
▷ Inability to delineate trading area;
▷ Inability to delegate;
▷ Belief that advertising is an expense, not an investment;
▷ Only rudimentary knowledge of pricing strategy;
▷ Immature understanding of distribution channels;
▷ No planning;
▷ Inability to motivate;
▷ Belief that the problem is somebody else's fault and a loan would solve everything.

Company and management weaknesses

Much of the literature on SME failure suggests that it is the result of significant inadequacies in management (Kiggundu, op. cit.; Knotts et al., op. cit.). Weaknesses and bad decisions are closely related, like chicken and egg. Many company weaknesses stem from bad decisions in the past. For example, high gearing may be due to a decision not to dilute the equity of the firm by going to a venture capitalist. In this case the decision may again have stemmed from the character of the entrepreneur and their wish to retain control of the business. On the other hand, many bad decisions stem from poor information caused by inadequate systems.

A frequently cited weakness that is a contributory cause of failure is poor financial control – poor, infrequent information, lax debtor control and/or high stock holding (Haswell and Holmes, 1989; Wichmann, 1983). Poor financial control inevitably leads to the reappearance of Death Valley and a cash flow crisis. If you couple that with poor cash flow planning, then you have the potential for failure.

A major weakness cited by a number of studies is the typical overdependence of small firms on a small number of customers for too high a proportion of their sales (Cosh and Hughes, 1998). Another angle on this is the size of the product range. Some studies have shown that the wider the range, the lower the likelihood of failure (Reid, 1991).

🗀 Case insight
Tech Board and Imperial Board Products

Tech Board, a hardboard maker in Ebbw Vale, South Wales, was Britain's biggest venture capital backed start-up when it began trading in 1995. It was a £40 million project with £25 million of funding from a consortium of private equity houses, led by 3i. Its history in many ways reflects what has been happening to UK manufacturing since then. In 1998 it went into receivership and was rescued by Enron, the American energy and power firm (that itself failed in 2001). The new company, called Imperial Board Products, was sold in April 1999 to a management buy-out team. The purchase was funded by a combination of a loan from Enron, invoice discounting and some state aid. The management buy-out was very highly geared and probably undercapitalised from the start. In August 2000 the firm went into liquidation.

External environment

Firms must cope with an ever-changing market place. Although direct effects cannot be proved statistically, small firms appear particularly vulnerable to macroeconomic variables – after all, they have less financial 'fat' than larger firms. Changes in overall consumer demand, interest rates and inflation can have a disproportionate effect on smaller firms. Many dot.com start-ups that received first-round finance in 1999 failed to obtain second-round finance in 2000 because the market had changed so dramatically, forcing them to cease trading. The 'Credit Crunch' of 2008/09, caused by the reckless lending of many Western banks, saw many smaller companies cease trading because of the combination of a down turn in trade and a drying up of finance

Case insight ZedZed.com

'This is a story with an unhappy ending about my dot.com company ZedZed.com, a site for independent travellers, which went into liquidation in 2000. ZedZed.com was meant to be called ZigZag.com but that name had already gone. We raised £800{tsp}000, which was no mean achievement, but it wasn't enough. In February we encountered dot.com envy from our friends. In March we were winning awards and being asked to speak at conferences in Paris. In June we achieved 1800 user reviews per week. In August we were calling in the liquidators.

Mistakes are always easier to see with the benefit of hindsight, and our worst error was to believe that internet businesses should be valued by the number of subscribers rather than the transactions that they make ... Today you have to be profitable or else you are not going to get funded again. They say that internet speed is fast but three months is a short period of time to reverse your whole raison d'être.

I think we did a lot right too. We built a site in six weeks on a very complicated back-end platform. We chose a content management system that would make us a serious force in the market, and we successfully leveraged that asset with larger organisations who might otherwise have ignored us. We devised a very successful low-cost user subscription campaign without the help of an expensive marketing agency like so many dot.coms. We kept our non-essential expenditure to a minimum, which allowed us to return 20 per cent of the initial subscription to investors. We employed 19 people on low salaries who genuinely loved their daily work. Being a chartered accountant, I knew where our financial position was on a daily basis and knew when the time had come to close the door.

Setting up a dot.com business has been the most exciting, rewarding experience of my life, and of the lives of the team that I had around me. We did something new, different and useful to other people. Sadly for us and our investors, the capital markets have changed to such a degree that we have had to end our quest early. In doing so we are showing that there is sanity amid the madness. Don't pity the pioneers – envy us for our experience. Oh, and pay us well for them too!'

Edward Johnstone, co-founder of ZedZed.com
Daily Telegraph 17 August 2000

to support them. Many start-ups could not obtain the finance they needed. The banks were so big they could not be allowed to fail. Small firms were not in the same position. There are also the 'acts of God' – the strike, the fire, the loss of the major customer – which a larger company might weather but the smaller firm cannot. Some external influences are clearly due to bad luck but some are due to bad judgement – the wrong place at the wrong time – and luck can have a disproportionate effect on smaller firms. And the impact is large. Everett and Watson (2004) estimated that external economic factors to be associated with between 30 per cent and 50 per cent of SME failures.

In reality the effect of the environment depends upon the time period, geographic area, and market sector in which the firm operates. Perhaps the most significant effect on smaller firms is the degree of competition within its industry and therefore Porter's Five Forces influence not only profitability, but, in extremis, the likelihood of failure. A small firm operating in a highly competitive market is more likely to fail than one operating in a market with low levels of competition.

This model gives us an insight into the process of failure. It also reinforces many of the lessons of success. These four ingredients of failure interact. Individually they are present in many firms, but it is only when they combine that the potential for failure is created. What makes the small firm different to the large one is the disproportionate importance of the influence of the owner-manager. Many bad business decisions stem from the entrepreneurial character. Many weaknesses stem from bad business decisions, which in turn may stem from the entrepreneurial character. However, the crisis that triggers the decline into failure is often brought about by some outside factor such as an unexpected change in the market place,

Case insight Alex Meisl and Taotalk, then Sponge

Alex Meisl's first company Taotalk, a telecoms business that offered a real-time internet chat and voice messaging service, failed after a potential investor had a last minute change of mind. Alex lost half a million pounds of his own money, but found the hardest part was telling his 12 employees that they would be made redundant and would not be paid their month's salary. He felt guilty – a very common emotion.

'I felt a huge guilt towards the staff. They had trusted me because I said it would be all right. They missed out on their last month's salary and they didn't get any redundancy other than the statutory minimum.'

When a business fails many people feel depressed and embarrassed and just want to get away from everything and everyone. However, Alex felt it was important to tell all creditors – customers and suppliers, as well as employees – what was happening, personally, either face to face or by phone. He was trying to maintain a personal relationship with creditors and keep at least some of their trust and respect and scotch any unfounded gossip that might develop in the industry.

Alex set up his second business, Sponge, a year later in 2002. Sponge offers voice and mobile applications for agencies and their brands and media groups using a platform called TG³ which allows integration of mobile, web and email in a digital campaign. This time Alex approached things differently. Firstly, instead of going it alone as with Taotalk, he set up Sponge with an experienced business partner, Dan Parker. Secondly, they wrote a business plan together and approached every business deal more systematically. This more considered approach seems to have worked. It is now the UK market leader with clients such as Autotrader, IPC, News International, Vodaphone and over 50 agencies such as Oglivy and BBH. Sponge was responsible for Europe's largest mobile campaign for Walkers crisps. By 2009 it could demonstrate over 20000 applications using TG³.

The experience of failure changed Alex:

'It hardened me and it made me slightly more cynical, in a constructive way. If someone comes through the door and says I am sure we have got a deal with company X, I don't believe it until I have seen the signature on the bottom of the document.'

Sunday Times 17 February 2008

☐ Up-to-date information on Sponge can be found on their website: www.spongegroup.com

customer tastes, competition or distribution channels. This may lead to further bad decisions being made by the owner-manager, for example a decision to overtrade or borrow too much. These, in turn, result in symptoms of failure such as running short of cash or declining profitability. The paradox is that the asset of the entrepreneurial character can become a liability in certain circumstances.

⚲ Predicting failure

It is one thing to understand the process of failure, but it is quite another to try to predict it. Nevertheless this has been of considerable interest to academics over the last four decades. Beaver (1966), Altman (1968) and Taffler (1982), for example, were pioneers in this area of study, mainly using financial ratios as relevant variables. Today distress forecasts are widely used for a range of purposes, including the monitoring of business solvency, assessment of loan security and going-concern evaluations by auditors. Most studies have looked at large public companies because of the ready availability of this information. Financial information in smaller businesses tends to be less reliable, with the profit figure more easy to manipulate, less complete, since they do not have to disclose the same amount of information as public companies, and less timely, since they do not face stock market pressures. However, it has been argued (Keasey and Watson, 1991) that, because of these factors, if predictive models could be developed they would be extremely valuable, not only in terms of their predictive ability but also in terms of their information value or usefulness. This is not surprising given the problems of information asymmetry facing bankers in particular. For this reason trying to predict failure in small firms using models that employ publicly available information has attracted just as much interest as trying to pick winners.

Most of these studies use multiple discriminant analysis on a sample of failed and non-failed firms to select financial ratios that best discriminate between the two groups and then combine them into a simple number, or 'Z score', which indicates the likelihood of failure. Companies are matched by industry and size. Most studies then go on to test the predictive ability of the 'Z score' on a hold-out sample which includes failed and non-failed firms. Studies have used the full range of ratios discussed in Chapter 9 – performance, profitability, asset efficiency, liquidity, gearing and risk – in an attempt to see which best predict failure. For example, one study looked at small firms in the construction and civil engineering sector (Love and D'Silva, 2001). It tested 25 ratios and the final 'Z score' was calculated as shown below, with companies scoring below 0.36 having a high probability of failure:

$$Z = -0.143 + 1.608a + 0.001b + 0.461c + 0.352d - 0.007e$$

where: a = net profit margin
b = debtor days
c = profit before tax divided by shareholders' funds
d = profit before tax divided by current liabilities from the previous year
e = total sales over working capital from the previous year

In this study 72.9 per cent of the predictive ability came from the simple net profit margin ratio.

Studies like these have been criticised on many counts, not least because they look at symptoms rather than root causes of failure. In this respect the major practical problem with them is their timeliness. It is quite probable that by the time these symptoms manifest themselves in published accounts, the company will already have filed for bankruptcy. What is more, the effect of the external environment, particularly for smaller firms, is likely to be very high. For example, profit margins are likely to decline in most firms at times of recession and therefore any bank using this as a predictive tool might be tempted to foreclose on a large number of loans, thus creating a self-fulfilling prophecy. One major UK clearing bank tested 'Z scores' extensively in the 1980s and decided not to use them.

Banks, of course, have a major piece of information at their fingertips that gives them an immediate insight into what is happening within the firm. This is the firm's bank account. From this, banks can monitor cash inflows and outflows as well as balances and this can give them invaluable information about current performance long before it finds its way into published financial information. Notwithstanding this, two major UK clearing banks started using an expert system called Lending Advisor in the 1990s to help them make lending decisions and monitor loans. This computer-based system combines 'hard' financial data with 'soft' judgmental data using weightings that can be adjusted to produce a lending 'recommendation'. The 'hard' financial data includes a range of historic as well as projected financial ratios. The 'soft' data includes a range of judgements about the management of the firm as well as its competitive advantage within its industry. In many ways the system simply attempts to make lending decisions more rational and consistent. The danger with it is that it masks the areas of judgement that are inevitably involved and focuses attention on the simple, final lending recommendation.

♀ Dealing with failure as an individual or sole trader

For an individual struggling to pay their debts – as a sole trader or a partner or as a director of a limited company who has personally guaranteed the company's debts – there are a number of courses of action open to you in England and Wales (Scotland has different rules). Most other countries have similar legal arrangements, but these should be checked. In all cases it is essential that the advice of a professional accountant or lawyer is sought before proceeding.

If you cannot pay your business debts when they fall due, or if your business assets are less than your debts, your business is technically insolvent and this may lead to your business being wound up, with the assets sold off to pay its debts, and you personally being declared 'bankrupt'. If you face this danger, you have several options.

Informal 'family' arrangements

This is where family or friends agree to provide funds on a short-term basis and creditors agree not to take action. However, getting other members of the family involved in the business may present other problems (see the next chapter).

Formal voluntary arrangements

This is where all the creditors agree to a proposal you and your advisors (which must include a licensed insolvency practitioner) put forward. This proposal will typically specify the amount (or proportion) of debt to be repaid and the timescale. If accepted, the creditors are bound by the proposal.

Partnership voluntary arrangements

Partnerships can propose this arrangement. It is similar to the individual arrangement above but to remove the individual partners' joint and several liability to meet the partnership debts the partners will either have to pay off the whole partnership debt or propose an individual voluntary arrangement.

Bankruptcy

If you are unable to pay your debts you can be made personally bankrupt. You or your creditors can apply to the courts for this to happen. The court will appoint an official receiver to take over your affairs (an insolvency practitioner may later take over) and sell off any assets – both your own personal assets and those within the business – so as to discharge your debts as soon as possible. Until discharged the receiver will manage all your affairs and there are restrictions on the financial arrangements you might enter into. As a sole trader or partner your business will normally be closed down and the assets sold off. Until you are discharged as a bankrupt you cannot be a director of a company. Unless you are seen as not cooperating with the receiver, you will usually be discharged from bankruptcy within a year; however you may not regain full control of your own finances straight away. A major consequence of bankruptcy is that your personal credit rating will be badly affected for some years to come, which means that obtaining credit will become more difficult and more costly. Most individuals would seek to avoid bankruptcy.

🛍 Case insight Peter Durose and the English Grocer

In 2006 Peter Durose decided to leave his £250 000 job running the fresh produce section at the supermarket chain Tesco. He was fed up with the early starts and long days and wanted to spend more time with his wife and two young daughters. The mortgage was almost repaid so he felt he could indulge his dream and open a gourmet corner shop in the village of Buntingford. He invested £100 000 of his savings in the venture, called the English Grocer, which opened its doors to business early in 2007.

The English Grocer stocked high-quality, traditional food targeted at up-market customers – good breads, hams, cheese from Neal's Yard dairy, pickles, teas, coffee, olive oils etc. Sales grew steadily and at the Christmas of 2007 one of its most popular lines was its luxury £100 Christmas hamper. But starting up a business was harder than either Peter or his wife believed. Because planning to open the shop took time and they needed the money, Peter started a small consultancy with a friend advising growers on how to find the best market for their produce. That continued once the shop was opened, leaving his wife, Marion, to work in the store.

'I found it difficult to organise my time. I quickly found I was doing seven days a week again. It's easy to lose that balance and you have to stop and think – remember what you are doing here.'

Things only got worse when Marion became pregnant with their third child. As she observed:

'We both did a lot of work in the evening. We would put the kids to bed and then at 8.00 pm we would be sat with our laptops.'

In 2008 the recession hit. At first sales remained buoyant but by November, just as Marion gave birth to a son, sales started to decline as families economised. Peter tried leafleting but with little effect. Customers bought £30 hampers in place of the £100 hampers they had bought the year before. In January 2009 Peter was forced to inject more cash into the business. He even persuaded his landlord to accept a 25 per cent cut in the shop rent. But things did not improve.

'I kept thinking that maybe trade would pick up when the weather got better. But it didn't get better – it snowed in March.'

The final blow came when the Council started work in the high street, erecting bollards and restricting parking. The high street was closed for three weeks and when it reopened the browsers did not reappear. In April Peter and Marion decided to close the business. They reassigned the shop lease to a coffee shop within three weeks and sold off the remaining stock. Peter is philosophical:

'I don't regret any of it, not at all... We had a lot of fun setting up the shop. I learnt more in the past three years than in the previous ten. There is something all-encompassing about starting a business ... The hardest part, I guess, was that we could have carried on. It wasn't just a commercial decision – it was an emotional decision. There may be green shoots [of recovery] out there, but I am not sure anyone agrees ... We found we were consistently talking about the year after next year – and for a small business that is a heck of a gamble In our hearts we don't think the English Grocer is over for ever. Maybe, another time, another place.'

Sunday Times 26 April 2009

💡 Dealing with failure as a company

For a limited liability company struggling to pay its debts and facing possible failure there are a number of courses of action open in England and Wales (Scotland has different rules). Again, most other countries have similar legal arrangements, but these should be checked. In all cases it is essential that the advice of a professional accountant or lawyer is sought before proceeding. The company has several options.

Refinancing

This involves bringing in new debt and/or equity finance to support the business. This may mean that the owner-manager will lose some of their equity in the business and

7 What is compulsory liquidation? What are its consequences?

8 How is a CVA different to administration?

9 How is a CVL different to liquidation?

10 Is a pre-packaged sale fair?

11 If you are trying to predict failure does it matter if you measure symptoms rather than causes?

12 Do entrepreneurs make their own luck?

13 The entrepreneurial character is as much a liability as an asset. Discuss.

14 You cannot distinguish between bad business decisions and managerial or business weaknesses. Discuss.

15 What do you think would be your emotions if the business you set up faced failure? What do you think of the insights by Edward Johnstone (ZedZed.com) and Peter Durose (English Grocer) regarding their business failures?

16 How might planning to sell the business affect the plans that you make and the strategies you follow?

17 There is no such thing as company valuation, only a willing buyer and a willing seller negotiating a price. Discuss.

18 How are small firms different from large ones when it comes to facing possible failure?

☍ Exercises and assignments

1 Find a business that has recently failed and try to fit the circumstances of its failure into the framework of the failure model shown in Figure 15.1.

2 Using desk research, write a case study of a failed business.

📖 References

Altman, E.I. (1968) *Financial Ratios, Discriminant Analysis and the Prediction of Corporate Bankruptcy*, 23(24), September.

Bannock, G. and Daley, M. (1994) *Small Business Statistics*, London: PCP.

Beaver, W.H. (1966) *Financial Ratios as Predictors of Failure, Journal of Accounting Research, Supplement on Empirical Research in Accounting*, pp. 71–111.

Beaver, G. and Jennings, P. (2005) 'Competitive Advantage and Entrepreneurial Power: The Dark Side of Entrepreneurship', *Journal of Small Business and Enterprise Development*, 12(1).

Berryman, J. (1983) 'Small Business Failure and Bankruptcy: A Survey of the Literature', *European Small Business Journal*, 1(4).

Burns, P. and Whitehouse, O. (1996) *Family Ties*, 3i European Enterprise Centre, Special Report no. 10.

Cosh, A. and Hughes, A. (eds) (1998) *Enterprise Britain: Growth Innovation and Public Policy in the Small and Medium Sized Enterprise Sector 1994–97*, Cambridge: ESRC Centre for Business Research.

Evans, D. (1987) 'The Relationship between Firm Growth, Size and Age', *Journal of Industrial Economics*: 567–82.

Everett, J. and Watson, J. (1989) 'Small Business Failure and External Risk Factors', *Small Business Economics*, 11(4).

Gaskill, L.A.R., Van Auken, H.E., and Manning, R.A. (1993) 'A Factoral Analytic Study of the Perceived Causes of Small Business Failure', *Journal of Small Business Management*, 31(4).

Haswell, S. and Holmes, S. (1989) 'Estimating the Small Business Failure Rate: A Reappraisal', *Journal of Small Business Management*, 27.

Houghton, K.A. and Woodliff, D.R. (1987) 'Financial Ratios: The Prediction of Corporate Success aqnd Failure', Journal of Business Finance and Accounting, Vol. 14 (4). Keasey, K. and Watson, R. (1991) 'The State of the Art of Small Firm Failure Prediction: Achievements and Prognosis', *International Small Business Journal*, 9.

Larson, C. and Clute, R. (1979) 'The Failure Syndrome', *American Journal of Small Business*, iv(2), October.

Love, N. and D'Silva, K. (2001) *A Model for Predicting Business Performance in SMEs: Theory and Empirical Evidence*, Paper presented at the British Accounting Association Conference, March 26–27, University of Exeter, England.

Reid, G.C. (1991) 'Staying in Business', *International Journal of Industrial Organisation*, 9.

Storey, D.J. (1998) *Understanding the Small Business Sector*, London: International Thomson Business Press.

Taffler, R.J. (1982) 'Forecasting Company Failure in the UK using Discriminant Analysis and Failure Ratio Data', *Journal of Royal Statistical Society*, 145, part 3.

Watkins, D. (1982) 'Management Development and the Owner-manager', in T. Webb, T. Quince and D. Watkins (eds), *Small Business Research*, Aldershot: Gower.

4 Maturity

16   The family firm

17   From entrepreneur to leader

18   Corporate entrepreneurship

16　The family firm

▷ **The advantages of family**
▷ **Family business is big business**
▷ **The conflict between family and business cultures**
▷ **Succession**
▷ **Points of conflict**
▷ **The introvert firm**
▷ **Resolving conflict: the family constitution**
▷ **Succession planning**
▷ **Summary**

Case insights
▷ Doreen Lofthouse and Fisherman's Friend
▷ Adidas vs Puma
▷ Values and beliefs
▷ Ferrero Rocher
▷ Noon Products
▷ Littlewoods
▷ Alex Ramsay
▷ J&B Wild
▷ Everards Brewery

Cases with questions
▷ Timberland
▷ Wates Group
▷ Mars Inc.

Learning outcomes

By the end of this chapter you should be able to:

▷ Explain the significance of family firms in the business world;

▷ List the advantages and disadvantages of being part of a family firm;

▷ Describe and explain the conflict of cultures between family and business;

▷ Use a framework that helps identify points of conflict within the family firm and explain how they arise and how they might be resolved;

▷ Explain what is meant by an introvert firm and appreciate the dangers it faces;

▷ Use a framework that helps explain the problems of succession within family firms;

▷ Use a framework for planning succession;

▷ Describe what goes into a family strategic plan and how it might be developed;

▷ Describe what goes into a succession plan and explain how it might be developed.

💡 The advantages of family

Starting up a business on your own can be a stressful, lonely way to make money. Many people start up a business with friends – they are known and trusted and may well possess complementary skills. So why not start up a business with the family? Trust is something that there is in abundance – particularly between husband and wife – and if all the family's income depends on the success of the venture then there is no doubting that the motivation to succeed will be strong, although this should be tempered with the recognition of the risk of having only one source of family income. There is the added advantage for husband and wife of giving each other support and friendship and working long hours may not be such a grind when with your partner. What is more, getting the whole family to help with the work brings an added resource to the firm – and one that may not have to be paid a wage.

Husband and wife teams, like Anita and Gordon Roddick who established the original Body Shop chain, can work very successfully. For some couples being together all the time can help in their personal as well as business relationship; for others it might be a recipe for divorce and business failure. As with many issues relating to the family firm, there are few hard and fast rules. Conflict is most likely to arise in making decisions and here clear role definition and a separation between work and home are important. Based upon interviews with husband and wife teams in the USA, Nelton (1986) suggested that the successful teams shared the following characteristics:

▷ Marriage and children came first;
▷ The partners had enormous respect for each other;
▷ There was close communication between partners;
▷ Partners' talents and attitudes were complementary;
▷ Partners defined their individual responsibilities carefully;
▷ Partners competed with other companies, not each other;
▷ Partners kept their egos in check.

There is no theoretical justification for or clear evidence that family firms outperform non-family firms. Nevertheless, family firms have their advantages. Leach (1996) lists seven:

1 *Commitment*: family enthusiasm and family ties can develop added commitment and loyalty;
2 *Knowledge*: special ways of doing things in the business can be coveted and protected within the family;
3 *Flexibility in time, work and money*: putting work and time into the business when necessary and taking money out when the business can afford it rather than according to the dictate of a contract;
4 *Long-range planning*: because the firm is seen as the family's main store of value, something to be passed on to the next generation, family firms are better than others at taking a long-term view, although this may not involve formal planning processes;

Inevitably when you are talking about family businesses there is a sense of generation. There has to be something to hand down, which is the greater shareholder argument of the long-term view. Other sorts of business may have different time horizons.

☐ Sir Adrian Cadbury, *The Times* 8 July 2000

5 *A stable culture*: relationships in family firms have had a long time to develop and the company's ethics and working practices are therefore stable and well established;

6 *Speedy decision-making*: like owner-managed companies, family firms can make decisions quickly because of the short lines of responsibility;

7 *Reliability and pride*: because of the commitment and the stability of their culture family firms can be very solid and reliable structures that, over time, build up good reputations with customers, reputations that the family guard with fierce pride.

Traditionally family businesses have been important in many primary sectors, such as farming. They also tend to thrive in areas such as hotels and restaurants, where high levels of personal service are required. The retail sector – butchers, bakers, florists, corner stores and so on – also boasts a large number of family firms. Family firms are also to be found in the cash generating food-processing industry. Finally there are many in the supply industries like transport and distributorships, especially in the motor sector.

📋 Case insight Doreen Lofthouse and Fisherman's Friend

Back in 1865 a pharmacist called James Lofthouse, who lived in the fishing village of Fleetwood in Lancashire, England, made a few jottings in his recipe book for a lozenge that cleared the nose and throat when blocked with mucus from colds and flu. For the next 100 years the lozenge was sold to the fishing community in Fleetwood and it was the fishermen that coined the name 'Fisherman's Friend'. But when Doreen Lofthouse married into the family things started to change. She was the driving force behind Fisherman's Friend, now a global brand worth £165 million and selling over 5 billion lozenges a year in more than 120 countries. Almost all (97%) of production is exported and the firm has won the Queen's Award for Export Achievement three times. Still based in Lancashire, in 2008 turnover rose by 5 per cent to £33.5 million and the company employed some 280 staff.

The lozenge's strong distinctive taste comes from its blend of liquorice, menthol and eucalyptus oil. The 'inventor', James, never made much of the lozenge and the book of recipes passed to his son, Charles, and then to Charles's son, James, who married Frances, daughter of a Yorkshire miner. Tony was their only child. The family ran a small pharmacy in Lord Street in Fleetwood and, in the summer, they would open a seafront gift shop for the visitors from nearby Blackpool. It was here that the lozenges became popular, so much so that people would write to the shop ordering more. These were sent off by Frances Lofthouse, Tony's mother, complete with a hand-typed label. Tony was working in the gift shop when he met Doreen. It was Doreen who, seeing that so many people went to the trouble of ordering the lozenges by post, realised that there was an untapped market beyond the town. She went to the nearby towns and persuaded shops to stock it. The breakthrough came when Doreen persuaded Boots, the high street pharmacy chain, to stock the lozenges. It was actually Doreen that registered the name 'Fisherman's Friend', although the family had been using it for some time.

These days the lozenge comes in eleven flavours from blackcurrant to mandarin (popular in the Far East) as well as the distinctive original, although only seven can be found in the UK.

The company remains a family firm with all the shares held by the Lofthouse family. Doreen is Chairman and shares an office with her husband, Tony, who is Joint Managing Director and supervises production. (Doreen's first husband was Tony's uncle.) Doreen's son, Duncan, is Financial Director and his wife, Linda, runs the accounts department. Duncan is the youngest of the Lofthouse family and, like Tony, has no heir. What will happen to the famous brand when the family retire remains an unanswered question.

☐ Up-to-date information on Fisherman's Friend can be found on their website: www.fishermansfriend.com.

💡 Family business is big business

It is estimated that as many as 70 per cent of all UK businesses are family owned and they employ 50 per cent of the country's workforce (Institute for Small Business Affairs, 1999). In the European Union the proportion of family firms is claimed to be 85 per cent, whilst in the USA the proportion is as high as 90 per cent (Poutziouris and Chittenden, 1996). What is more, the stereotypical image of the family living above the shop does not do the sector credit. They are not all small, lifestyle firms. Family-owned companies account for a substantial proportion of the value of the stock market. In the USA, family firms – where family members own more than a quarter of the shares – represent more than a third of the *Fortune* 500 (Leach, op. cit.). In Europe the pattern is similar. But most family firms – of any size – are privately owned.

Family firms have some of the strongest brands in business today. Mars, Lego and Levi Strauss are global brands and remain private, family companies. In Britain many family firms are household names – R. Griggs Group (maker of the famous Doc Martens boots, founded 1901), J. Barbour & Sons (maker of the very British waxed jackets, founded in 1894), Wilkin & Sons (maker of the famous Tiptree jams, founded in 1885), Morgan Motor Company (maker of Morgan sports cars, founded in 1909 and the world's oldest privately owned car manufacturer) and Quad Electroacoustics (maker of distinctive hi-fi equipment, founded in 1936). Not only have these firms been around for a long time, but also the values and beliefs on which they were established are well known and respected. Familial brands build consumer trust over long periods and can be very valuable assets.

The continued strength of the Baxter's brand springs from the knowledge, involvement, passion and standards of the Baxter family. We determine the priorities and destiny of the company and so ensure that our family values are always reflected in all the products bearing the Baxter name.

☐ Audrey Baxter, MD, Baxter's Soups, *The Times* 8 July 2000

Indeed, many of the best-known brands today started out as family firms before becoming public companies. For example, the H.J. Heinz company was in family hands until 1946, when it went public. It was founded in 1888, although Henry J. Heinz started producing bottled condiments from 1869. Similarly the chocolate maker, Cadbury, founded in 1924, started out as a family business based on strong Quaker values. Many companies still have links with the founding family. For example, the Ford Motor Company was launched by Henry Ford in a converted wagon factory in Detroit in 1903. His great grandson, William Ford Jr, was appointed chairman in 1998. The Disney Corporation is the largest entertainment conglomerate in the world. Roy E. Disney, a descendant of the original Disney family and the principal shareholder, was Vice Chairman until 2003 and is now Consultant and Vice Chair Director Emeritus.

The family firm has been the backbone of many continental European economies for decades. None more so than in Italy where names like Agnelli, Pirelli and De Benedetti have long controlled large parts of Italy's industry. Because of the historically strong family networks, Italian owner-managers have been loath to surrender even part of the equity capital of their firms to investors, and non-family managers have rarely received shares or share options.

But all this begs the question of what constitutes a family business. Essentially a family business is one that is owned or controlled by one family, although researchers have suggested many more precise definitions, for example:

1 An owner-managed enterprise with family members predominantly involved in its administration, operations and the determination of its destiny. Family

members may include parents, children and grand-children; spouses; brothers, sisters and cousins (Poutziouris, 1994).

2   A company in which majority ownership (in terms of shares) or control lies in a single family and in which two or more family members are, or at some time were, directly involved in the business (Rosenblatt et al., 1985).

3   For a quoted company, one in which 25 per cent of voting shares are controlled by the family (Nelton, op. cit.).

The search for a precise definition could be endless and rather fruitless. Probably the real answer is to ask the family. If family members are involved in the firm and feel a responsibility for it, then that is a good indication that it is a family business. They will probably say it is anyway. One of the over-riding characteristics of the family business is the atmosphere of belonging and common purpose. Just as the small firm has the personality of the owner-manager imprinted on it, so the culture of the family is imprinted on the family firm. Rather than 'two arms, two legs and a giant ego', you have many arms, legs and egos. It is no wonder that the *Spectator* magazine once described the family business sector as 'an endless soap opera of patriarchs and matriarchs, black sheep and prodigal sons, hubris and nemesis'. And there you have the problem.

📁 Case insight Adidas vs Puma

On 21 September 2009 two football teams came together in the town of Herzogenaurach in Bavaria, Germany to play a game of football. The game was preceded by what was described as a 'historic hand-shake' in support of the 'Peace One Day' organisation, which was celebrating its annual day of non-violence. The teams were from the footwear companies Adidas and Puma – whose commercial rivalry is famous – and the story behind the game is a remarkable tale of how family businesses can break up and, in this case, split a town in two.

For over 60 years Herzogenaurach has been a town split into two factions, separated by a river and two major employers – Adidas and Puma. Townsfolk were either 'Adidas' or 'Puma' people, even if they did not work for either firm. Stores and trades people proclaimed their loyalty to one brand or the other. Two soccer teams emerged – ASV Herzogenaurach and FC Herzogenaurach – each sponsored by one of the firms. Rival gangs fought each other and inter-marriage was out of the question. This curious split

in the town can be traced to a family squabble in the 1940s between two local shoemakers – brothers Adolf and Rudolf Dassler. They had made shoes together since the 1920s, starting in their mother's kitchen, and had set up a family business called the Dassler Brothers Shoe Factory. For some reason that has melted into the mists of time the pair fell out and set up rival companies on either side of the town's river. Rudolf set up Puma, and Adolf renamed the company Adidas. It was this falling out that spawned decades of fierce business rivalry, split a town in two, and led to the establishment of two of the best-recognised sporting brands in the world. Once the Dassler brothers died in the 1970s and the companies gradually fell out of the control of the founding families, the tensions between the two firms started to ease. However, the handshake on 21 September 2009 was important for Herzogenaurach residents, whose psyche has been shaped for years by their choice of footwear and its consequences.

💡 The conflict between family and business cultures

At the heart of the family firm are its distinctive values and beliefs – its culture. Often the family culture can strengthen the business. For example, many successful family firms such as Cadbury and Wilkin & Sons were originally built around strong religious ethics whereby the success of the firm was shared with the workforce. In many ways the workforce becomes an extended family and relationships are cemented with trust and respect for the founding family. Families can display their values and beliefs in all sorts of quirky ways in the family firm. Sometimes these are good for the firm. They can bring clear values, beliefs and a focused direction. However, they can also bring a lack of professionalism, nepotism rather than meritocracy, rigidity and family conflict or feuding into the workplace. Any consultant who has worked with family firms realises how important it is to understand the family politics if they are to understand how the business operates.

Whilst family culture can be a tremendous asset for the firm, it can also create the potential for conflict. The problem arises when there are differences between the family and business cultures. Families exist primarily to take care of and to nurture family members, whereas firms exist to profitably generate goods and services. Represented in Figure 16.1, the family culture is based on emotion emphasising loyalty, caring and sharing. It is inward-looking and lasts a lifetime. In contrast, business culture is unemotional, task-orientated and based on self-interest.

> ### 📋 Case insights Values and beliefs
>
> **Cadbury** may be owned by Kraft today but the original family business was very much based on Quaker values and ideals. Founded by John Cadbury in 1824, the original shop sold drinking chocolate as a virtuous alternative to alcohol. In 1834 the firm started manufacturing drinking chocolate and cocoa.
>
> John Cadbury's sons, George and Richard, saw the real expansion of the business. Whilst Richard concentrated on marketing, including the box designs for their chocolates, George concentrated on production. It was he who founded the now legendary Bournville factory and the picturesque village with its red-brick terraces, cottages, duck ponds and wide open park lands. Not only were workers given a fair day's pay, they were also rewarded with homes and education for their children.
>
> **Wilkin & Sons** is still a family-owned business which was founded in 1885 and is best known for its luxury Tiptree jams which sell to over 50 countries. The more esoteric jams such as 'Little Scarlet Strawberry' have attained almost a cult status among jam lovers.
>
> The company is committed to sharing success with its workforce. At the company's 450-hectare estate at Tiptree in Essex, managers and directors test products as well as man the production lines when required. More than 100 of the 180 workforce live in houses owned by the firm. It has operated a non-contributory pension scheme for over a century. The firm has also created a trust which will eventually leave employees with a 51 per cent shareholding in the firm.
>
> There is another ethical dimension to the firm. It has never borrowed and does not want to.

It is outward-looking, rewarding performance and penalising lack of performance. Conflict between the two cultures is unlikely at start-up but, as the firm grows and time passes, the potential for conflict increases.

The emotion-based family culture operates at a subconscious level. There are deep emotional ties that create love, trust and loyalty; but equally there can be disruptive influences like divorce, rivalry between brothers or conflict between son and father. Whilst families are based on permanence and stability, entrepreneurial firms are based on opportunity and change. Even the positive influences of the family may be bad for the business, for example, when parental pride and loyalty gets in the way of objectivity and a son or daughter is appointed to a management position they do

Family
Emotional
Loyal
Caring
Sharing
Inward-looking
Lifetime membership

Potential for conflict

Business
Unemotional
Self interest
Task-based
Reward performance
Perform or leave
Outward-looking

F16.1 Family vs business cultures

not have the skills to undertake. If there is a conflict of interest between the family and the firm, for example in making the dividend payment that the family expects but the firm can ill afford, whose interest comes first? And the very closeness of the family can create an impenetrable barrier for the non-family manager who might feel 'passed-over' for promotion in favour of family or feel left out of the decision-making that seems to take place 'around the kitchen table'.

Family culture even influences the management style within a family firm. Research by Ram and Holliday (1993) suggests that family firms tend to adopt a style of 'negotiated paternalism'. Because of the relationships between family members, family businesses tend to use fewer formal management techniques. Family influence acts to dilute managerial power and discretion, with family members often able to negotiate their duties. In the researchers' opinion this can constrain operating efficiency and lead to management practices that are 'sub-optimal'.

What is more, business can influence the culture within the family. Indeed business can exact a toll on family life. The separation between the two can become very blurred in a family firm. Building a successful business can become an obsessive, single-minded occupation that drives family life into the shadows, creating tensions at home as well as at work. Married couples working together may feel unable ever to 'get away from the shop' and let the stress and tension of growing a business damage their personal relationship. Conflict at work – and there will be conflict in any growing business – may continue at home, feeding on itself and intensifying. A husband and wife team that divorce will find it difficult to continue working together. To survive, a family must learn to separate family and business life. Business and family issues need to be addressed directly, but in an open and balanced way that allows the business to be run properly whilst not disrupting family harmony. This is not always easy.

🗀 Case insight   Ferrero Rocher

Ferrero Rocher is a truly European family firm. It was founded by Pietro Ferrero and his wife Piera in the Italian Alba region in Piedmont in the immediate post-war years. They produced a chocolate bar which included nougat and hazel nuts and called it *pasta gianduja*. The same basic recipe is used today, except the current head of the firm, octagenarian Michele Ferrero, added liqueur.

The company is the fifth-largest sweet maker in the world. It is registered in Amsterdam but has 16 factories across Europe. The family has lived in Brussels for the past 30 years. They are obsessively secretive and Michele has been described as an autocrat with a paternalistic management style. Every 29 June, Ferrero executives must attend church in San Domenico to honour the day the company was founded. Every three years Ferrero organises a pilgrimage to Lourdes for all its 13 000 workers.

🗀 Case with questions   Timberland

Timberland is a third-generation family firm which started life as a small shoe company in south-east Boston, USA. Today Jeff Swartz leads an international company as President and Chief Executive, with his father Sidney still in post as Chairman. Timberland has extended its product range from durable outdoor footwear to include outdoor clothing as well as opening a number of prominently-sited retail outlets selling its boots and other branded products. In 2008 the company had an annual turnover of over $1.3 billion and profits of $42 million.

Whilst Timberland is a strong retail brand, the business is also based on strong ethical foundations. Like his family, Jeff Swartz is an orthodox Jew and the values of the business reflect those of the family and its religion. It has a motto: 'Doing good by doing well.' And Timberland believes that these values reinforce the brand, because customers care about the same things as the company.

→

Timberland has a strong commitment to corporate social responsibility (CSR) which it says 'is grounded in the values that define our community: humanity, humility, integrity and excellence'. It goes on: 'For over 30 years, "community" has been synonymous with the ethic of service – the desire to share our strength for the common good. Our approach to building and sustaining strong communities includes civic engagement, environmental stewardship and global human rights.'

Timberland has a long-term CSR strategy for 2008–2015 focused on four strategic goals, or 'pillars', each supported by several key initiatives with quantitative targets which were vetted through a stakeholder engagement process:

1 To become carbon neutral by 2015. Its California plant now runs on 60 per cent solar energy and, in the two years to 2009, it had reduced its footprint by 27 per cent.

2 To design only recyclable products which are free of toxins and use 100 per cent renewable resources. Boots now only come with recycled rubber soles.

3 To provide fair, safe and non-discriminatory workplaces. Timberland has carved out a role as an industry leader in setting high working standards in its factories and in those of its suppliers. In part this stems from an accident Jeff's grandfather had when working late the night before his wedding in which his hand got caught in a machine and his fingers were severed.

4 To engage employees in community service focused on community greening. For many years Timberland has had a volunteering programme which allows employees to spend up to 40 hours paid-time a year on community projects. 95 per cent of employees use some portion of this time.

> 'Investment in the community is important to me because this is a family company. It's not just because my grandfather and my father grew up on the factory floor but because I did too. Workers' health and safety, for instance, isn't just an ideal. It's as visceral to me as the missing fingers on my grandfather's hand.'
>
> *The Times* 29 May 2004

> 'I have faith in the entrepreneurial system, we will innovate or perish … There are health and safety standards, those too have costs. And you know what? Business has figured out a way to make profits while respecting that social policy. The same is true about the cost of carbon … You can hide behind an economic crisis and say that business can't afford any more pressure but first of all it's not true, second it's disingenuous.'
>
> *Sunday Times* 22 November 2009

☐ Up-to-date information on Timberland can be found on their website: www.timberland.com

QUESTIONS

1 How important is ethical underpinning to the vision, values and culture of a business as well as its brand? Do you believe in Timberland's ethical underpinning, or is it all just 'window-dressing'?

2 Go to the company's website and review its financial performance. What commercial factors have influenced this in recent years? Is there any indication of the impact of its ethical stance?

💡 Succession

The old adage 'from clogs to clogs in three generations' – meaning you might find wealth but you return to poverty in three generations – is definitely true in relation to family firms. With each successive generation the chances of surviving autonomously diminish. Poutziouris and Chittenden (op. cit.) observe that:

> Four out of five family businesses are managed by the first generation, which benefits from the entrepreneurial drive of the founder. However, less than one third of founders successfully pass ownership and management control of the family business to the second generation. Only 10 per cent of second generation family firms are transferred to third generation and less than 5 per cent ever reach beyond the third generation of family management.

However, not all owner-managers want to establish a dynastic family firm. A large scale survey by Burns and Whitehouse (1996) found that only 32 per cent of British owner-managers wanted to pass their business on within the family, with most (68 per cent) preferring to sell the firm, most commonly to a trade buyer, in order to make a capital gain. This contrasted strongly with Germany (57 per cent), Italy (62 per cent) and Spain (74 per cent) where most owner-managers wanted to keep the firm in the family. The same study showed that most owner-managers who inherited their firm wanted to pass it on to their children.

> *It's an Asian way of working. We are all focused on what we are doing and we are working for succession. It's all in the family. We are not growing the business for an exit route.*
>
> ☐ Bharat Shah, founder of Sigma Pharmaceuticals
> *Management Today* May 2004

Figure 16.2 shows a life cycle framework originally developed by Churchill and Hatten (1987) to aid the understanding of family business dynamics during the process of succession and transfer of power. The model suggests that changes in management, strategy and control can be planned and executed but are shaped by family relationships and driven by the inexorable human life cycle. In the model the life cycle of two generations is expressed as the level of influence a family member has on the strategic orientation and operations of the business, during the phases of family business development. Essentially it is a four-stage model that repeats, with increasing complexity as new generations join the firm.

▷ Stage 1 *Owner-managed business.* This is the early stage, beyond start-up, when the founder is in control but a son or daughter is introduced into the business on a permanent basis.

▷ Stage 2 *Training and development of the new generation.* This is the stage where decisions are made, although not always formally, about passing the business on to the son or daughter and a process of training and development should be taking place to groom them for their role.

▷ Stage 3 *Partnership.* This is the stage when the son or daughter shows sufficient business acumen and expertise that the founder starts to loosen the reins of control, delegates authority and starts to share responsibility with them.

▷ Stage 4 *Power transfer.* This is the phase when strategic planning, management control and operational responsibility shifts from one generation to another. The succession process accelerates as the founder begins the retirement process and reduces their active participation in the business.

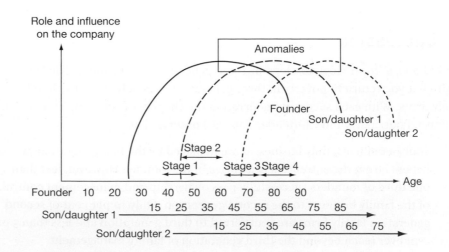

F16.2 The family business life cycle

💼 Case insight Noon Products

Noon Products produces Indian, Thai, Oriental and Mexican food for a range of customers including Birds Eye, Sainsbury's, Waitrose and Somerfield. It was founded by Sir Gulam Noon in 1989 and both his daughters, Zeenat and Zarmin, work in the firm as well as his brother, Akbar, and nephew, Nizar.

> 'You have to work with the family in a professional way. The most important thing ... is to give them the job and resist interfering ... If someone doesn't come up to expectation, then you get rid of them, don't allow it to drag on.'

Zeenat was originally responsible for packaging of temperature-controlled food. More recently she was the driving force behind the introduction of the Bombay Brasserie range. She is the eldest daughter, has a management qualification and joined the firm at the start, having worked with a hotel chain in India and just had a baby. She is on the board.

'You have to prove yourself more when it's a family business. You have to show that you are serious about your job and about your career. You only get respect by working alongside people and not being just the boss's daughter.'

Zarmin has a degree and worked for a travel firm before joining the business. She is director of Noon Restaurants, a separate enterprise.

'It was quite a culture shock coming into the family business. My father lets you get on with it, but he likes to see the figures. You're not expected to go to him with small problems ... unless you come up against a brick wall. But even then he'd prefer you to break through it yourself.'

Family Business, The Stoy Centre for Family Business, 8(1), 2000

☐ Up-to-date information on Noon can be found on their website: www.noon.co.uk

💡 Points of conflict

Would that succession were usually so systematic and trouble-free. It is not. The problems arise as one generation hands over to another – the areas marked as 'anomalies' in Figure 16.2. Although daughters are being brought increasingly into the family business, the most common relationship revolves around father and son. Many father–son relationships can work extremely well but psychologists tell us that this relationship has a unique potential for conflict. If you revisit the personal qualities likely to be present in the entrepreneurial founder, detailed in Chapter 2, you will realise that he is likely to have a very close emotional link with the business. He is likely to see it as an extension of himself, a symbol of his achievement, even an extension of his masculinity. He may guard power jealously and have problems with delegation. He may want to facilitate his son's succession but he may also want to control it. Subconsciously he may feel the need to be stronger than, and in control of, his son and succession may be seen as a 'threat' to his masculinity. This can result in rivalry between father and son, each trying to be the dominant character.

From the son's perspective things are different. We are told that rebellion is natural in youth but, although it is tolerated and sometimes encouraged at home, at work it is something that is normally repressed. Even in its mildest form, this natural tendency will show itself in an increasing drive for independence from father. But if father is also the boss, there is potential for conflict, particularly if father is himself having problems delegating control. So the scene is set with a rebellious son, pressing for more power within the firm, seemingly opposed by a father who, at the same time, is saying that he wants to pass the business on to the son. To the son, the father may appear to be hanging on to power and he may begin to doubt whether father really will retire. In fact he may even begin to distrust his father, and that is the start of the end of the relationship. At the very least, the contradictory signals from the father are likely to lead to frustration in the son. What is more, for the son the option of leaving

📁 Case insight Littlewoods

The one-time UK national retail chain and pools operator Littlewoods was set up by Sir John Moores and his brother, Cecil, in Liverpool in the 1920s. Sir John died in 1993. By then the Moores family had multiplied and, now into the third generation, there were some 40 family shareholders. After his death bitter arguments broke out within the family which are credited with damaging the expansion of the business. In 1996 family relationships deteriorated so much that an external chairman and chief executive was brought in to try to save the business. The rows finally came to an end in 2002 when the business was sold off to the Barclay brothers for £750 million. In 2005 it was sold off again and broken up. Today the name no longer exists on UK high streets.

📁 Case insight Alex Ramsay

In 1965 Alex Ramsay invited his three sons to work for the manufacturing firm he had set up in Sussex. He gave them and his three daughters large shareholdings in the business. But Alex did not find sharing control easy and the eldest son, William, left in frustration. Alex died in 1988. At this point William returned, insisting that, as the eldest son, he should become managing director. The others, reluctantly, complied but his management style and free spending ways soon brought conflict. And when evidence of 'sharp business practice' came to light his brothers used their shareholdings to suspend him. One of the other brothers, Charles, explained what happened next:

> 'William decided that if he wasn't to run the company, then nobody would. My elder sister sided with William and they demanded to be bought out – in cash – assuming that the business would have to be sold or split up as a result. But we remortgaged the company's property, sold some assets and managed to save the company ... It's sad. There were lots of things we could have done to stop the tensions becoming so damaging. We just got it badly wrong.'

Since then the business has recovered but the two sides of the family are still not speaking.

Sunday Times 25 May 2003

the business is problematic as it might be seen as disloyalty to the family.

Family businesses have a high potential for conflict, and the ability to resolve this conflict is important. We shall address this in the next chapter. Levingson (1983) describes how fathers often try to avoid conflict. For example, they might cultivate an atmosphere of ambiguity in decision-making where rules and boundaries are unclear and they can 'meddle' – in this way avoiding any overt conflict. Alternatively they may defer decisions until the last possible moment, continually putting off the time for conflict. The father seeks to avoid the business conflict because he does not want to harm his family relationship with his son. But as we shall see in the next chapter, conflict is rarely best handled through avoidance, and putting off an important business decision is usually a very bad idea.

Leach (op. cit.) claims that father–daughter relationships are less problematic. Fathers seem more able to accept advice about the business and some criticism from daughters, and they often say that they would react to sons saying the same thing as if it were a personal attack. He observes that fathers do not feel threatened by daughters, and daughters are more accommodating, being brought up to be more nurturing, attuned to emotional needs and giving priority to family harmony. Perhaps that is changing.

Nevertheless this may give us an insight into mother–son relationships in the family firm, about which there is little research. There is even less research into mother–daughter relationships. Indeed the assumed relationship in most of the literature is that of a patriarchal hierarchy within the family firm. We know next to nothing about the influences of an extended family, except in the context of ethnicity, or the development of new forms of families, such as those based upon gay relationships. Perhaps the future will see a redefinition of the term 'family firm'.

There can be yet another layer of complexity to the problems facing the family firm, this time caused by sibling rivalry. Sibling rivalry is normal, but some parents actively encourage it, particularly in the context of the family firm. If a number of sons and/or daughters work in the firm there may be rivalry between them as they vie for favour in the eyes of the father or mother. The custom of favouring elder sons with respect to inheritance, although in decline, still shows itself when it comes to succession in the family firm.

Elder sons may be favoured at the expense of daughters or younger sons who may be more able. This can lead to the best talent leaving the family business or the brothers or sisters trying to carve out niches for themselves in the business to establish their independence. Even if the business is split equally between the children, there is the danger of sibling rivalry becoming institutionalised in the firm.

♀ The introvert firm

All businesses must adapt and change to meet the demands of a changing market place, but there is a danger that family firms will become moribund and unable or un-willing to respond with each succeeding generation. Many firms do, of course, adapt. However some family firms become increasingly introvert. They become inward-looking, unresponsive to messages from the market place and unreceptive to new ideas; they might even become unwilling to recruit managers from outside the firm or, worse still, from outside the family. How does this come about?

Families can become distracted from business for a number of reasons. Disagreement between family members might paralyse decision-making within the firm. Avoidance behaviour in the extreme might lead to important business issues not being addressed. Damage done to the firm and relationships within it by the traumatic succession from one generation to another might leave it weak and, like the rabbit caught in the headlights of the car, traumatised. The past success of the firm which has led to increased prosperity for the family might itself cause problems. The family might start to regard the firm as their main store of wealth, demanding regular dividends when the firm can ill-afford them, imposing restrictions on commercial decisions that reflect their risk aversion or vetoing capital investment decisions because it would drain cash flow. The family might also start to view the firm as a milk cow draining the cash away through expense accounts, pensions, cars and other perks or 'jobs for the family'. Borrowings might be vetoed because the family do not want their main store of wealth and source of income to be exposed to any form of risk or the possibility that they might lose control. All of these things damage the business and can mean that it is not doing what it is supposed to do, that is, profitably generate goods and services.

This can be compounded by a sense of alienation felt by non-family members as they see cash being squandered, and no decisions or bad decisions being made. The continuous conflict may make them feel uneasy and unsure about the future direction of the firm. They may feel forced to take sides when they do not wish to. They may feel that they are not part of the decision-making at all or that family considerations are always paramount. They may feel passed over for promotion in favour of less able family members. They might feel that there is no system for adequately rewarding them for the good work they do, for example, by taking some equity in the firm, because the family would not countenance losing control. Indeed the family might actively discourage or prohibit the employment of non-family managers.

🗀 Case insight J&B Wild

The family business of J&B Wild has had a stall in Manchester's New Smithfield Fish Market for 100 years. However, it has had to adapt and change in order to stay in business. Originally, it sold British white fish, made popular with the growth of fish and chip shops. Today British white fish is hard to find, fish and chip shops are in decline and the family has had to develop new products and find new customers just to survive.

Many years ago it started selling chicken, mainly to Indian restaurants in the area. It still sells fish, but most fish is now foreign, flown in from around the world. Most fish is now sold filleted. J&B Wild has developed a reputation for stocking a wide variety of 'exotic' fish which are sold mainly to Chinese restaurants. Fish has now become a food that is susceptible to fashions and fads and the family have to keep on top of market trends.

Many of these issues come down to the business no longer having clear leadership. Second-generation firms might have a board comprising three brothers or sisters each with equal shareholdings and none with clear control. Perhaps none of them possess the entrepreneurial spirit of the founder. To compound the problem, they may all hate each other and be unable to agree on anything. To avoid this catastrophe family firms need ways of resolving family conflict and managing succession. They also need to reward and promote family employees strictly in line with their contribution to the firm and regularly and objectively evaluate the performance of all staff. Delegation outside the family should be taking place and being a member of the family should not be part of the criteria for promotion or appointment. In other words, family business management needs to be seen to be objective for the good of the firm and its family and non-family employees alike.

♀ Resolving conflict: the family constitution

Arguably, the only real way to resolve conflict in the family firm is to resolve conflict in the family – a very tall order indeed. However, confining ourselves to business, the key to conflict resolution is communication and, as we shall see in the next chapter when we look at how conflict might be best resolved (Thomas–Kilman conflict modes), the appropriate style is one of 'collaboration' or 'compromise'. Admitting and, most importantly, understanding the nature and cause of the problem is a good first step. Understanding that many of the problems come from our genetic make-up should help to defuse the situation and make it less personal. Understanding how individuals naturally react to conflict using the Thomas–Kilman framework – can help to explain why arguments happen. With a will, behaviours can be modified. With particularly difficult situations a third-party facilitator – a friend or professional mediator or counsellor – might help. However, the British are known for avoiding sensitive personal and family issues and difficulties.

Leach (op. cit.) advocates the development of a family strategic plan which should be articulated in a written constitution that sets out the family's values and policies in relation to the business. He advocates a four-stage process:

1 Addressing the critical issues relating to family involvement in the business. This involves looking critically at the business and the family and how they relate. How are conflicts between family and business interests to be resolved?
2 Establishing a family council to provide a forum in which members can air their views and participate in policy-making. The council should develop ground rules as to how it should operate.
3 Drawing up a family constitution which involves developing a written statement of the family's values and beliefs and going on to develop policies and objectives. Does the family have any shared values and beliefs in relation to the business? What does the family want from the business? What is the involvement of family to be? Does the family wish to retain control of the firm? What should be the criteria for family entry into the firm? What is the management succession policy? Should family members who are active in the business be treated differently from those who are not? Who might own shares in the business and how might shares be disposed of? What should the dividend policy be? A checklist of what might go into a family constitution is shown in Table 16.1.
4 Monitoring the family's progress and maintaining communication within the family through regular council meetings.

▷ Family values, beliefs and philosophy

▷ Family objectives in relation to the business

▷ Family involvement in the business – share ownership and disposal, voting and control

▷ Family involvement in the business – board membership, voting

▷ Family involvement in the business – selection of chairman and managing director

▷ Family involvement in the business – jobs and remuneration

▷ Family council meetings

▷ Procedures for changing the constitution

T16.1 Family constitution checklist

Leach also advocates giving sons or daughters managerial autonomy within part of the business to help them grow and mature; separating out roles for other members of the family so as to minimise sibling rivalry. Many writers advocate the use of non-executive directors on the boards of family companies. They can be the insurance against a company becoming too introvert. They can bring balance to board-room discussions and should be relied on to put the firm, not the family, first. In that sense they bring independence to meetings and can help resolve family squabbles. Alongside this they bring their own particular expertise and a new network of contacts.

🗂 Case insight Everards Brewery

Everards Brewery is a family company that was founded in Leicestershire in 1849. It brews beers such as Tiger Best Bitter, Beacon Bitter and Original from its Castle Acre site near Leicester, and has a pub estate of over 170 units.

The fifth-generation chairman is Richard Everard. He sees himself as the 'custodian' of the family assets in the business. The family objectives are the driving force behind the philosophy and

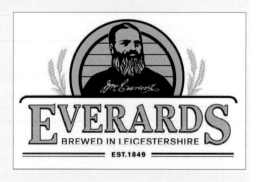

resulting strategy of the firm. When Richard became chairman he sat down with the family, outlined the objectives and set about changing the business strategy to reflect them. Now the emphasis is on property and brewing accounts for only 30 per cent of turnover.

> 'After five generations, 90 per cent of the shares are held by only two family members ... There is a rule that only one family member can have an executive position on the board in any one generation ... We do not offer share options to attract senior people. That would be against our philosophy ... I see my custodianship lasting another twenty years, but should anything happen to me I have left clear instructions on how the next generation should be trained for the position. This would include at least four years of external training.'

> *Family Business*, The Stoy Centre for Family Business, 7(3), 1999

☐ Up-to-date information on Everards can be found on their website: www.everards.co.uk

🗎 Case with questions Wates Group

Wates Group, based in Leatherhead Surrey, is a fourth-generation family construction and land trading business that was established in 1897 by Edward and Arthur Wates. It now has 11 offices in the UK and a turnover of over £1 billion with over 2000 employees.

The company can boast of both commercial success and longevity as a family business. This longevity is based upon a well thought-out and well structured approach to family governance. This includes a family charter that forms the basis of the relationship between the voting shareholders and regular meetings of a family forum. As Andrew explains:

> 'Our success has been achieved by the ability to get an alignment between the professional management and the family. We have been in business for 110 years and have developed a family strategy as well as a business strategy.'

> *This Money* 10 June 2007 www.thismoney.co.uk

Wates Group (WG) is now owned by Wates Family Holdings (WFH), having recently bought back 40 per cent of the shares in WG from two branches of the family. There is a clear legal separation between the two companies and WFH also has some business interests other than WG.

The WG board comprises seven members, including two family members and three non-executives. It is chaired by a non-family member, Paul Drechsler, who is Chief Executive and joined WG in 2004.

The WFH board comprises six family members, two non-executive members and the Director of the Wates Family Office. Five of the six family members also have roles with WG:

▷ Timothy Wates – Chairman of WFH
▷ Andrew Wates – former Chairman of WFH and WG
▷ James Wates – Deputy Chairman of WG
▷ Jonathan Wates – Marketing Director and board member of WG
▷ Andy Wates – Managing Director of Wates Interiors
▷ Charlie Wates – Joint Managing Director of Needspace, a WG-managed workspace business

To achieve these structures, the Wates went through a strategy development process, spread over six months, involving all family members and professionally facilitated. The results started with a vision: 'Wates will be a world-class, family-owned and professionally managed enterprise, generating long term stakeholder value.' To achieve this vision, the family focused on four things – the interface with WG, finance, co-investment and the family 'modus operandi'. At the heart of this was the need to diversify the wealth and income of the family away from WG and at the same time insulate WG from the worst influences of the family. The family tackled the issue of effective family governance structures by setting up a family council that meets regularly, a shareholder management committee that operates through WFH and a charter that governs the family's relations with its trading activities through WFH. Succession planning is based upon encouraging the best of the next generation to succeed within WG. Progression is based on psychometrics, team building, personal development and coaching, supported by outside advisors.

→

'The family ... have grappled with their changing role from owner-managers to just owners – they have invested an enormous amount of time and effort into defining their roles and getting the transition just right. Through shunning the easy options they have developed a prescriptive governance model, which makes it easier for all parties to understand and execute their roles. We behave as a plc. Our governance structure looks and feels like that of a plc, with independent non-executive directors, an established audit, remuneration, nominations and risk committees. Although there is no legal or regulatory reason for organising ourselves in this way, it underpins our focus on growing shareholder value.'

Huw Davies, Chief Financial Officer, Wates Group,
JP Morgan Family Business Honours Award for Overall Excellence, 2006

☐ Up-to-date information on Wates can be found on their website: www.wates.co.uk.

QUESTIONS

1 Why has the family separated ownership and management of Wates Group by setting up Wates Family Holdings?

2 What areas of dispute within the family might you anticipate?

3 Will Wates Group always be effectively insulated from these disputes? If not, how might they be handled?

♀ Succession planning

The usual approach to managing succession is to ignore the issue and do nothing. It is almost as if owner-managers, particularly founders, are in denial about ever leaving the firm. It is a blind spot that they do not wish to discuss – a little like death. They are reluctant to relinquish power and control; they fear that doing so will somehow reflect on them, diminishing their status, identity and masculinity. Sometimes planning involves making unwelcome decisions that might upset the family, particularly if it means selecting a successor from members of the family. Founders often fear retirement – the lack of activity, purpose, status, independence – and often typical entrepreneurs are so single-minded that they do not have other outside interests. However, if succession is not planned and managed it can be a traumatic and stressful event which might threaten the very existence of the firm.

Actually passing on the business within the family is just one of the options open to the founder. The other options are:

▷ *Trade sale.* Competitors may be interested in buying the business as a going concern, generating cash or shares for the founder and the family. This may be attractive if cash is needed for retirement or other family reasons. It might also be just the right time to get a very good deal, for example because of consolidation in the industry. It might simply be that the business has become less attractive or more risky than when the founder set it up and there are better new opportunities for children.

▷ *Management buy-out.* If there is a strong management team in the firm they might be interested in bidding for the firm if they can arrange funding.

▷ *Management buy-in.* An external management team might be persuaded to bid for the firm, again as a going concern.

▷ *Appoint a professional manager.* With this option the family remain as shareholders and probably non-executive directors, receiving dividends and hoping to see the value of the business grow,

▷ *Appoint a caretaker manager.* If the founder wishes to pass on the firm but the son or daughter is too young or inexperienced, they may appoint a caretaker manager to see the firm through until such time as the next generation is ready to take on the role.

▷ *Liquidate.* This is usually the least attractive option as the price for the assets will not reflect any goodwill.

If succession really is the chosen option it will need careful planning. Who should be the successor? Do they possess the necessary skills and temperament? If not, can they be developed through training and experience within the available time frame? What are the financial, tax and pension consequences? The issues that need to be addressed may seem endless. To help approach the task systematically, Leach (op. cit.) proposes the following approach:

1 *Start planning early.* The most successful successions are those that involve the next generation early in the process so as to allow them to grow into the role rather than coming as an unexpected 'event'.

2 *Encourage inter-generational teamwork.* It is important that all issues surrounding the succession are addressed and agreed by all the next generation, not just the chosen successor.

3 *Develop a written succession plan.* This is an action plan setting down what has to be done, by whom and when. It will include details of the founder's reducing involvement and the successor's expanding role and responsibilities. It should also address the structure of the management team.

4 *Involve the family and colleagues in your thinking and, when complete, show them the succession plan.* This is about communication and getting commitment from everybody to the plan.

5 *Take advantage of outside help.* Succession has important financial, tax and pension consequences for the founder and the family. Consulting the firm's accountant and lawyer early in the process is vital.

6 *Establish a training process.* The plan should lay out how the successor is expected to develop the skills needed to take over the firm and over what time frame. This might involve education and training as well as job or work experience.

7 *Plan for retirement.* The owner-manager needs to be prepared financially and emotionally for retirement. Retirement will bring lots of free time and entrepreneurs, particularly, like to keep on the go.

8 *Make retirement timely and unequivocal.* When the timetable for succession is set, it is important to stick to it and not hang on in the job. Sonnenfield (1988) characterised the founder as typically having four exit styles, the last two having a more positive effect on the business:

▷ *Monarchs*: who do not leave the business until they are forced out through ill-health, death or a palace revolt;

▷ *Generals*: who leave the business, but plot a return and quickly do so 'to save the business';

▷ *Ambassadors*: who leave the business quickly and gracefully, frequently to serve as post-retirement mentors;

▷ *Governors*: who rule for a limited term and turn to other activities then to gain fulfilment.

Case with questions Mars Inc.

Mars Inc. is the seventh largest private company in the USA. The company is home to global food brands such as Mars, Milky Way, Snickers, Twix, M&Ms as well as Whiskas, Pedigree and Uncle Ben's. It is a second- (arguably third-) generation family firm – a family that is one of the richest in the world. Founded by Forrest Mars Snr, who died in 1999, it is now governed by a board of directors made up of Mars family members and advisors and run by a global management team led by President and CEO, Paul S. Michaels. Forrest Mars Snr was born into a confectionery-making family in 1904. His father, Frank, ran a modestly successful business in Minnesota where he made butter-cream candies overnight and his wife, Ethel, sold them from a trolley the next day. They had two main products, the Mar-O-Bar and Victoria Butter Creams, which became successful in 1923 when Woolworths started distributing them.

Forrest Mars Snr claimed that the idea for the family's first really successful product, the Milky Way, came to him whilst sitting drinking a chocolate malt drink in a cafe and he suggested to his father that he should put it into a chocolate bar. Some time later, his father did just that, putting caramel on top and chocolate around it. Milky Way was a huge success with sales of $800 000 in its first year. The family moved to Chicago and Frank built a mansion in Wisconsin. However, relations between father and son deteriorated as Forrest wanted further growth and expansion but Frank wanted to settle for an easy life.

In 1932 Forrest left to set up a one-room chocolate business in Slough, England. He quickly produced a similar product to Milky Way, calling it a Mars Bar, using creamier milk chocolate and a sweeter toffee filling. The Mars Bar is a very British product, unknown in the USA. The company returned to the USA in the late 1930s with the hugely successful M&Ms, the candy-coated chocolate 'that melts in your mouth, not in your hand'. Also in this period the company made the first moves into the European pet food industry by combining modern manufacturing techniques with nutritional science. In 1946 it applied modern manufacturing techniques to parboil rice and launched Uncle Ben's rice.

Mars Inc. is committed to remaining under private ownership. It is also a very secretive company. The founder, Forrest Mars Snr, was a recluse and his sons shun public life. They also live and work with a frugality that is in stark contrast to many modern firms. There are no company perks such as cars, reserved parking or executive toilets. Indeed, no one even has a private office. Memos are against company policy. Meetings take place 'as needed'. Elaborate presentations are seen as a waste of time. All employees must do their own photocopying, make their own telephone calls and travel economy class on planes. John and Forrest Jr even share a secretary with their sister, Jacqueline. All employees are known as 'associates' and are on first name terms. Everyone from the top to the bottom has to punch their time-cards daily and receives a 10 per cent bonus for punctuality.

A visit to the company website gives an impression of the strong culture within the organisation. Words like 'ethical', 'honest', trust', 'pride', 'passion', and 'support' abound, as do phrases like 'we like being the best at what we do', 'we are passionate about how we do things and about quality' and 'I know that as a Mars associate I am ethical and have high standards'. The company is run according to a 24-page booklet which codifies Forrest Snr's management philosophy. These are called 'The five principles of Mars':

Quality – 'The consumer is our boss, quality is our work and value for money is our goal'.
Responsibility – 'As individuals, we demand total responsibility from ourselves; as associates we support the responsibility of others'.
Mutuality – 'A mutual benefit is a shared benefit; a shared benefit will endure'.
Efficiency – 'We use resources to the full, waste nothing and do only what we do best'.
Freedom. – 'We need freedom to shape our future; we need profit to remain free'.

☐ Up-to-date information on Mars can be found on their website: www.mars.com

QUESTIONS

1 What are the benefits of the Mars philosophy to both the company and to its employees?

2 In your opinion, does the Mars philosophy replicate itself in its retail brand? How does this compare to the Timberland brand?

3 Mars is a US company but its products are sold in over 100 countries. Does the Mars philosophy resonate in your country? Explain why or why not.

4 How important is the Mars family in generating this philosophy? If Mars were to move out of family control, would its philosophy have to change?

It could be that the future will see a decline in the importance of family businesses. The breakdown of family networks, increasing demands for capital that families cannot supply, a booming stock market which makes obtaining a listing attractive – all these factors may mean that more and more companies are sold on. Certainly the survey by Burns and Whitehouse (op. cit.) indicated this trend was under way in Britain in the 1990s. However, the high proportion of owner-managers still wishing to pass businesses on to the next generation contrasts strongly with the proportion actually succeeding in doing so.

▷ Summary

▷ Starting up as a family firm can be attractive because of the emotional support and helping hands that may not expect to be paid. As they grow, family firms can foster loyalty, responsibility, long-term commitment, not least to ethical standards, and a pride in 'the family tradition'. These virtues are often welded into a desire to transfer the firm from one generation to the next and to preserve it in difficult financial times, as in the case of **Fisherman's Friend**. Seventy per cent of UK businesses can be described as family firms, many with household names like **Mars** and **Cadbury**. Many of today's best-known public companies started life as family firms and still have relationships with the founding family. Familial brands like **Baxter's Soups** and **Timberland** build consumer loyalty over long periods and can be a very valuable asset.

▷ At the heart of the family firm is the family culture – its values and beliefs. These can be based upon ethical convictions, as in the case of **Timberland**, or they can be based on religious beliefs, as in the case of **Cadbury** and **Wilkin & Sons**. They can be quite quirky, as in the case of **Mars**. Sometimes they enhance the brand, sometimes these affect the terms and conditions of employment and the culture of the firm. That culture can mean that the firm is managed in an autocratic, paternalistic fashion like **Ferrero Rocher**.

▷ There is, however, the potential for conflict because family culture is essentially based on emotion. This caused the start-up of rival firms **Adidas** and **Puma**. However, families also emphasise loyalty, caring and sharing, whereas business culture is unemotional, task-orientated and based on self-interest. The emotion-based family culture operates subconsciously and can get in the way of business, as it did in the case of **Littlewoods**. For example, family firms can suffer from nepotism and a lack of professionalism. Managers who are not family members can feel alienated and isolated, believing that important decisions are being made without their involvement, 'over the kitchen table' rather than in the office. Family conflict and politics can result in the firm being neglected or business decisions being made for other than commercial reasons – the introvert firm which tries to ignore commercial reality. It can also mean that the firm is used as a milk cow for the family and loses its commercial edge. As we saw with **J&B Wild**, all firms need to change and adapt, but introvert firms sometimes do not see the need to do so.

▷ Succession in the family firm is often problematic and can itself lead to conflict, as it did at **Littlewoods**. Founders tend to ignore succession until the last minute. Many of the problems stem from the entrepreneurial characteristics of the founder that make him reluctant to relinquish control of the business. Added to this there may be father–son rivalry as the son rebels or strives for independence within the firm. If there are more sons or daughters, then sibling rivalry can intensify the problem, as in the case of **Alex Ramsay**. As we saw with **Noon Products**, introducing the founder's children into the business needs to be handled with care.

▷ Resolving conflict in a family business is often difficult. It requires accommodation or compromise. It might help to understand the nature and underlying cause of the conflict. But ultimately the best approach is to develop a family strategic plan and a family council to monitor it – like **Wates Group**. Setting family objectives led **Everards Brewery** to change their business strategy to emphasise property more.

▷ Succession can be managed. Planning needs to start early and needs to be inter-generational, building in consultation with the firm's accountants and lawyers. A written succession plan should be developed which shows how the founder will exit and how the new generation will take over. It will detail any training and development needed and help the founder plan for retirement. Finally, when it is time to go, go!

⏻ **Further resources are available at www.palgrave.com/business/burns**

🗎 Essays and discussion topics

1 What are the advantages and disadvantages of starting up a business with your partner or spouse?
2 What are the advantages and disadvantages of being part of a family firm?
3 Familial brands build consumer trust over long periods and can be very valuable assets. Discuss.
4 Family firms are more common on continental Europe than in Britain. Why do you think this might be?
5 In the future family firms will decline in importance. Discuss.
6 Does it matter how you define a family firm?
7 How might family and business cultures clash?
8 Why are there so many examples of successful family firms which are based on strong religious or ethical bases?
9 What are the problems you might face in being in charge of running a family firm?
10 What are some of the underlying causes of conflict in a family and how might these show themselves in a family firm?
11 The family business sector is an endless soap opera of patriarchs and matriarchs, black sheep and prodigal sons, hubris and nemesis. Discuss.
12 What are the advantages and disadvantages of being a non-family employee in a family business?
13 What are the problems you might face in being the son or daughter of the founder employed in their firm?
14 How would you get on if you were working for your mother or father?
15 What is an introvert firm? How might a business avoid becoming one?
16 How can succession be managed?
17 What do you think would be a good training programme for a son or daughter intending to take over the running of the family firm?
18 In what circumstances might it be wise not to pass on the firm to a member of the family?
19 What should go into a succession plan?
20 What problems might an entrepreneur encounter in facing retirement?

↻ Exercises and assignments

1 List the questions you would ask members of the family working in a family firm in order to highlight the advantages and problems of working there. Based upon these questions, interview members of the family and write an essay highlighting the advantages and problems of working in the family firm.
2 List the questions you would ask the manager of a second- or third-generation family firm in order to highlight the problems they encountered in taking over the firm. Based upon these questions, interview the manager and write an essay highlighting the problems they encountered.
3 Research by Ram and Holliday (1993) suggests that a leadership style of 'negotiated paternalism' is to be found in many family firms. Referring back to Chapter 8, in what circumstances is this likely to be appropriate? In what circumstances is it likely to be ineffective?
4 Write a specimen family constitution.
5 Find out what are the tax consequences of succession in the family firm.

📖 References

Burns, P. and Whitehouse, O. (1996) *Family Ties*, 3i European Enterprise Centre, Special Report no. 10.

Churchill, N. and Hatten, K. (1987) 'Non-Market Transfers of Wealth and Power: A Research Framework for Family Business', *American Journal of Small Business*, Winter.

Institute for Small Business Affairs (1999) *All in the Family, Policy and Research Issues*, no. 1, August.

Leach, P. (1996) *The BDO Stoy Hayward Guide to the Family Business*, London: Kogan Page.

Levingson, H. (1983) 'Consulting with Family Business: What to Look Out For', Organizational Dynamics, Summer.

Nelton, S. (1986) *In Love and in Business*, New York: John Wiley & Sons.

Poutziouris, P. (1994) 'The Development of the Familial Business', in A. Gibb and M. Rebernick (eds), *Small Business Management in New Europe, and Proceedings of 24th ESBS – September*, Slovenia, in New Europe.

Poutziouris, P. and Chittenden, F. (1996) *Family Businesses or Business Families*, Institute for Small Business Affairs and National Westminster Bank Monograph 1.

Ram, M. and Holliday, R. (1993) 'Relative Merits: Family Culture and Kinship in Small Firms', *Sociology*, 27(4).

Rosenblatt, P.C., de Mik, L., Anderson, R.M. and Johnson, P.A. (1985) *The Real World of the Small Business Owner*, San Francisco: Jossey-Bass.

Sonnenfield, J. (1988) *The Hero's Farewell: What Happens when CEOs Retire*, New York: Oxford University Press.

17 From entrepreneur to leader

▷ **Growth and crises**
▷ **Changing skills**
▷ **Coping with crises**
▷ **The role of leader**
▷ **The evolving vision**
▷ **Leadership style**
▷ **Building the management team**
▷ **The board of directors**
▷ **Entrepreneurial structures**
▷ **Traditional large firm structures**
▷ **Structure, change and task complexity**
▷ **Creating culture**
▷ **Entrepreneurial leadership skills**
▷ **Summary**

Case Insights
▷ David Poole and DP&A
▷ Gary Redman and Now Recruitment

Cases with questions
▷ Michael Dell

Learning outcomes

By the end of this chapter you will be able to:

▷ Describe how the entrepreneur must change as the business grows;

▷ Explain the implications of growth models of business development for the entrepreneur, their style of management, the organisation of the firm and the practical application of the functional aspects of management;

▷ Explain what the job of a leader entails;

▷ Evaluate your preferred leadership style and recognise what is appropriate for a growing firm;

▷ Evaluate how you and other people handle conflict;

▷ Evaluate your preferred team role;

▷ Explain why some teams work and others do not;

▷ Describe the role and importance of the board of directors and the skills they need to undertake their job effectively;

▷ Explain how an entrepreneurial organisation is likely to be structured, the advantages and disadvantages of this structure and appreciate how it might have to change as the firm grows;

▷ Recognise the importance of culture for the success of a firm, describe the elements of culture that go towards making a successful entrepreneurial firm and how it can be created;

▷ Explain what is required to become an entrepreneurial leader.

○ Growth and crises

As the business grows the entrepreneur needs to change and adapt.
The qualities and skills they need to manage the business successfully change. The
more rapid the growth of the business, the more difficult this is. The entrepreneur
needs to metamorphosise into a leader. The business itself also needs to change the
way it operates – its structure and its culture – and become more formal without
becoming more bureaucratic. And these changes need to be properly managed if the
firm is to grow successfully. It is little wonder that so few firms grow to any size, and
little wonder that many fail because the entrepreneur is unable to make the necessary
changes.

Chapter 2 gave some clues about the background of the entrepreneurs who make
this metamorphosis successfully. Research shows what their antecedent influences
generally are:

▷ They were well-educated;
▷ They start the business for positive motivations;
▷ They leave a managerial job in an established company to start the business;
▷ Historically they tend to be middle-aged but there is some evidence that there
is a new generation of very young entrepreneurs, particularly in the e-business
sector;
▷ They are willing to share ownership of the business with other key managers.

These qualities impact upon the process of change and how the entrepreneur han-
dles them. There are a number of growth models that seek to describe the changes
that the entrepreneur faces and, by inference, how the changes need to be managed.
One of the most widely used models was developed by Greiner (1972). This is shown
in Figure 17.1; it offers a five-stage framework for considering the development of
a business, but more particularly the managerial
changes facing the founder. Each phase of growth
is followed by a crisis that necessitates a change
in the way the founder manages the business if it
is to move on and continue to grow – the classic
process of growth, crisis and consolidation that
we have already observed. If the crisis cannot
be overcome then it is possible that the business
might fail. The length of time it takes to go through each phase depends on the industry in which the company operates. In fast-growing industries, growth periods are
relatively short; in slower-growth industries they tend to be longer. Each evolutionary
phase requires a particular management style or emphasis to achieve growth. Each
revolutionary period presents a management problem to overcome. Only phases one
to four really apply to smaller firms.

> *You start the business as a dream, you make it your passion
> for a while and then you get experienced managers to run
> it because it's not as much fun as starting. I think there's
> a lot to be said about starting a business and a lot to be
> said about running a business when it's mature. I think I'm
> capable of making the distinction and coping with both.*
>
> ☐ Stelios Haji-Ioannou, founder, easyJet, *Sunday Times* 29 October 2000

▷ *Phase 1* Growth comes through entrepreneurial creativity. However, this constant seeking out of new opportunities and the development of innovative ways
of doing things leads to a crisis of leadership. Staff, financiers and even customers
increasingly fail to understand the focus of the business – where it is going, what
it is selling – and resources become spread too thinly to follow through effectively
on any single commercial opportunity.
▷ *Phase 2* Growth comes from the direction given by effective leadership in this
phase. The entrepreneur must become more of a leader and give the business the

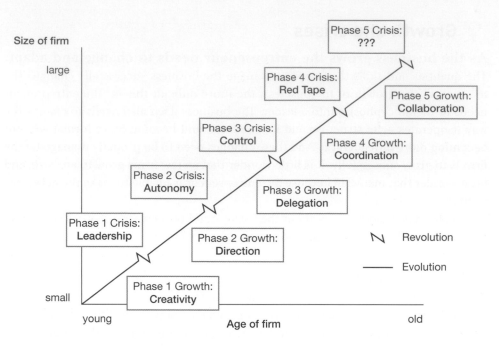

F17.1 The Greiner growth model

direction it needs. However, entrepreneurs have a strong internal locus of control, which means that there is a danger that they will be unable to delegate responsibility to their management team. The leader then faces a crisis of autonomy that will only be addressed by putting that management team in place and delegating work to it.

▷ *Phase 3* Growth in this phase comes because the team is in place and effective delegation is taking place. The business is no longer a one-man-band. However, there is always the danger that delegation becomes abdication of responsibility and, as the firm continues to grow, there is a loss of proper control. Entrepreneurs are notorious for not being interested in the detail of controlling a business.

▷ *Phase 4* Growth now comes from effective coordination of management and its work force. Controls are in place and are working effectively. By this stage the firm will have ceased to have many of the characteristics of an owner-managed firm because there are set procedures and policies for doing things. The danger now is that it might lose its entrepreneurial drive and the next crisis it might face is one of red tape or bureaucracy. Greiner says this can only be overcome by collaboration – making people work together through a sense of mission or purpose rather than by reference to a rule book. This means developing corporate entrepreneurship – a topic we return to in the next chapter.

To address each of these crises entrepreneurs need to adapt and change. In particular, they need to develop into leaders. They need to put in place a management team and work as part of this team – difficult when you consider many of the strong personal characteristics exhibited by entrepreneurs. Alongside this the organisational structure of the firm will need to adapt and change, and an appropriate business culture will need to be created. These then are the four challenges entrepreneurs face as the business grows:

▷ Giving direction through leadership;
▷ Delegation and the encouragement of team-working;

▷ Coordination and control through appropriate organisation structures and culture;

▷ Developing corporate entrepreneurship so as to avoid the bureaucracy that threatens to stifle enterprise in large firms.

💡 Changing skills

As the business grows and the scale of activities increases, the entrepreneur has to recruit managers and learn to delegate. The business will need to take on a more formal structure and the structure will need to be adhered to, by everybody. The entrepreneur has to learn to control the business by monitoring information rather than by direct physical intervention – which is their preferred approach. They have to rely on collecting information in different ways, at appropriate times. This information comes in different forms but it generally relates to the business functions of people management, marketing and financial control. Information then has to be translated into action, and again the processes have to become more formalised. In other words, at the same time as the role of the founder is changing, so too are the skills they require.

The Churchill and Lewis (1983) model, shown in Figure 17.2, is often used to link marketing, people and financial management issues. The five stages are identified as follows:

1 *Existence* The business strategy is to stay alive, and the company needs to find customers and deliver products/services. Everything has a short-term time horizon. The organisation is simple – typically the spider's web which is explained later and shown in Figure 17.10 – with one-to-one relationship management and direct supervision. The owner does everything, or at least is involved in doing everything. Planning is minimal, sometimes non-existent.

2 *Survival* The business imperative is to establish the customer base and product portfolio. The company has to demonstrate that it has sufficient products and customers to be a viable business. It has to control its revenues and expenses

	Stage 1	Stage 2	Stage 3(1)	Stage 3(2)	Stage 4	Stage 5
	Existence	Survival	Success: Disengagement	Success: Growth	Take-off	Maturity
Management style	Direct supervision	Supervised supervision	Functional	Functional	Divisional	Line and staff
Organisation	Simple	Growing	Growing	Growing	Growing	Sophisticated
Extent of formal systems	Minimal to non-existent	Minimal	Basic	Developing	Maturing	Extensive
Major strategic imperative	Existence	Survival	Maintaining profitable status quo	Obtain resources for growth	Growth	Return on investment

F17.2 Churchill and Lewis growth model

to maintain cash flow. The organisation is still simple and planning is, at best, short-term involving cash flow forecasting. The owner is still 'the business'. The spider's web still exists, with one-to-one relationship management and direct supervision.

3 *Success* By this stage the company is big enough and has sufficient customers and sales to establish itself with confidence. The owner has supervisors or managers in place and basic marketing, financial and operations systems are operating.

Planning is in the form of operational budgets. At this stage the company has two strategic options:

▷ Option 1 is disengagement. If it can maintain its market niche or adapt to changing circumstances, it can stay like this for a long time. If not, it will either cease to exist or drop back to the survival stage. This is what we described in an earlier chapter as a lifestyle business.

▷ Option 2 is growth. If this is a viable and desirable option then the entrepreneur must consolidate, clarify the vision and ensure that resources are diverted into growth. This is where they must start to give clear leadership, based upon the vision they have for the firm and a clear strategy as to how the vision might be achieved. However, throughout all this the business must remain profitable.

4 *Take-off* This stage is dangerous and therefore critical. The entrepreneur must ensure that satisfactory financial resources and good management are in place to take the company through it. If this stage is handled properly the company can become very successful and large.

5 *Maturity* The business now begins to develop the characteristics of a stable, larger company with professional management and formal information systems, and will have established strategic planning.

Churchill and Lewis also developed a simple summary of the key factors which affect the success or failure of a business in the different stages of its life. These are split between the attributes of the owner-manager and resources. Table 17.1 shows

	Stage 1 Existence	Stage 2 Survival	Stage 3 Success	Stage 4 Take-off	Stage 5 Maturity
Owner's attributes					
Own goals	☆☆☆	☆	☆☆☆	☆☆☆	☆☆
Operational ability	☆☆☆	☆☆☆	☆☆	☆☆	☆
Management ability	☆	☆☆	☆☆	☆☆☆	☆☆
Strategic ability	☆	☆☆	☆☆☆	☆☆☆	☆☆☆
Resources					
Financial	☆☆☆	☆☆☆	☆☆	☆☆☆	☆☆
Personnel	☆	☆	☆☆	☆☆☆	☆☆
Systems	☆	☆☆	☆☆☆	☆☆☆	☆☆
Business	☆☆☆	☆☆☆	☆☆	☆☆	☆

Critical ☆☆☆   Important but manageable ☆☆   Not very important ☆

T17.1 Churchill and Lewis's growth stage imperatives

	Top management role	Management style	Organisational structure
Inception	Direct supervision	Entrepreneurial and individualistic	Unstructured
Survival	Supervised supervision	Entrepreneurial and administrative	Simple
Growth	Delegation and coordination	Entrepreneurial and coordination	Functional and centralised
Expansion	Decentralisation	Professional and administrative	Functional and decentralised
Maturity	Decentralisation	Watchdog	Decentralised and functional/product

T17.2 Scott and Bruce growth model

the factors and their relative importance. The important point is the move from the owner's operational ability to their strategic ability as the business grows. This is one of the key qualities of leadership. Lifestyle businesses can survive on high levels of operational ability and relatively lower levels of managerial and strategic ability. This changes at the take-off stage. Even when the business is mature, in the final stage, the ability of the owner to think strategically is still critical to its development. The other point to notice is the increasing importance of personnel and systems resources at the take-off stage. In lifestyle businesses these are less important, although some lifestyle businesses do have strong systems that allow them to 'tick over' with the minimum intervention of the owner-manager.

Drawing heavily upon the work of Greiner and Churchill and Lewis, there have been a number of other growth models. Scott and Bruce (1987) proposed the five-stage model summarised in Table 17.2. This shows the appropriate management role, style and organisational structure at different stages. As can be seen, once into the expansion phase the firm loses many of the characteristics of the entrepreneurial firm.

The four-stage model in Table 17.3 (Burns, 1996) summarises the main business imperatives as a firm grows in terms of the orientation of the firm and then the main functional disciplines of management, marketing, accounting and finance. It also emphasises the drift from informal to more formal structures. In this model, lifestyle businesses that never go beyond the survival stage can exist using an informal, tactical orientation on a day-to-day basis. Once they go into the success phase they need to take on a far more strategic orientation, with more formalised procedures and structures. They also start to recruit managers to the business. Managers coming from other, often larger, firms is associated with successful growth. Perhaps this is related to the changes in culture that are taking place in the firm at this stage.

An interesting feature of this model is the way it describes the changes in the functional disciplines. For example, marketing changes from simply getting customers, developing relationships and finding out why they buy from you into developing a unique selling proposition (USP) based upon what is working (called 'emergent strategy formulation'), and then using relationships and networks to get repeat sales. In the growth phase this becomes the basis of defining and developing some form of competitive advantage which will allow the firm to attack the competition.

These models are often used as predictors of the crises that the firm is likely to face as it grows. However, they have four problems associated with them:

1 Most firms do not experience growth and never get beyond the first stage, many dying shortly after start-up.
2 If they do experience growth, it is not quite in the same way or sequence as the models predict. There are so many variables that it is unlikely all will come

	Existence	Survival	Success	Take-off
Orientation	▷ Tactical	▷ Tactical	▷ Strategic	▷ Strategic
Management	▷ Owner is the business and is 'jack of all trades' ▷ Spider's-web organisation ▷ Informal, flexible systems ▷ Opportunity driven	▷ Owner is still the business ▷ Still spider's web organisation ▷ Some delegation, supervision and control	▷ Staff start to be recruited ▷ Organisation starts to become formalised ▷ Staff encouraged and motivated to grow into job ▷ Delegation, supervision and control ▷ Strategic planning	▷ Staff roles clearly defined ▷ Decentralisation starts ▷ Greater coordination and control of staff ▷ Emergence of professional management ▷ Operational and strategic planning
Marketing	▷ Get customers ▷ Undertake market research ▷ Develop relationships and networks	▷ Generate repeat sales ▷ Develop unique selling proposition (USP) and select market segmentation ▷ Use relationships and networks	▷ Generate repeat sales and find new customers ▷ Develop competitive advantage based upon USP and target markets ▷ Use relationships and networks	▷ Select new customers and generate repeat sales ▷ Aggressively attack competition ▷ Use relationships and networks
Accounting	▷ Cash flow	▷ Cash flow ▷ Accounting controls ▷ Break-even and margin of safety	▷ Cash flow ▷ Accounting controls ▷ Break-even and margin of safety ▷ Balance sheet engineering	▷ Cash flow ▷ Accounting controls ▷ Break-even and margin of safety ▷ Balance sheet engineering
Finance	▷ Own funds ▷ Creditors, HP, leasing ▷ Bank loans	▷ Own funds ▷ Creditors, HP, leasing, factoring ▷ Bank loans	▷ First phase venture capital ▷ Creditors, HP, leasing, factoring ▷ Bank loans	▷ First phase venture capital ▷ Creditors, HP, leasing, factoring ▷ Bank loans

T17.3 Burns growth model

together at the same time. For example, the owner-manager's managerial style might be inherited from their previous employment and be out of phase with the organisational structure.

3 Often firms reach a plateau in their development at certain stages of the model – particularly survival – and do not progress beyond that phase, preferring to remain a lifestyle business. Indeed, most firms do not survive the recurrent crises they face.

4 The actual sequence of issues or imperatives predicted by the models is not supported by empirical research. This is particularly true of Greiner's model.

Because of these issues the models are probably best used as checklists of the imperatives that an entrepreneur and a firm ought to face up to if they wish to grow through the different stages of development. The models should not be applied mechanistically, but rather with judgement and discretion, particularly in relation to sequence and timing. However, they provide an invaluable description of the changing role of the entrepreneur and the skills they need.

💡 Coping with crises

One of the reccurring themes in these models is the need to change as the business grows. And failure to change sufficiently rapidly leads to the crises identified by Greiner. This process of growth leading to crisis, followed by consolidation, which repeats itself over time, is well documented. We first noted it in Chapter 11. The process is represented in Figure 17.3. However this simple presentation glosses over the considerable problem of coping with successive crises. As the company passes through each crisis, the entrepreneur encounters a roller coaster of human emotions as they find themselves facing a different role with new demands.

GROWTH   CRISIS

CONSOLIDATION

F17.3 The growth process

The classic change/denial curve shown in Figure 17.4 illustrates these emotional changes very well and can offer insights into the attitude of the entrepreneur at each stage of the crisis (Kakabadse, 1983). At each stage in the growth curve the entrepreneur must learn to become more effective in their new role and to adopt new attitudes and skills. As with any change, this can take time.

▷ *Phase 1* The unfamiliarity of entrepreneurs with their new roles makes them feel anxious about their contribution and so their effectiveness drops slightly. They need to get used to the new circumstances. Within a short time, having become used to the role using previously successful skills, and finding support to help them, their effectiveness improves and they start to believe that they do not have to change. This is the denial phase.

▷ *Phase 2* Real demands are now being made and entrepreneurs experience real stress as they realise that they do have to develop new skills to keep up with the job. They need to relearn their role. Although they may eventually learn how to do their new job, a period of anxiety makes them less effective because they can no longer rely on their old skills and they may believe that they can no longer cope. In fact this 'low' indicates that the person is realising that they have to change and then, at some point, they abandon the past and accept the future. However, it is the most dangerous point in the change cycle as the entrepreneur feels really stressed and may be tempted to give up.

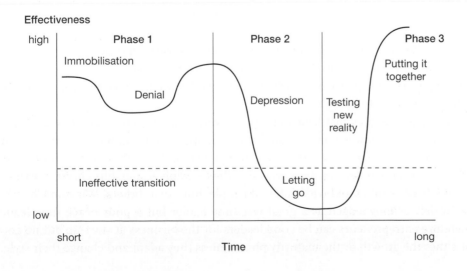

F17.4 Work effectiveness through change

▷ *Phase 3* This testing period can be as frustrating as it can be rewarding. Mistakes can recreate the 'low', but, as the newly learnt skills are brought into play effectively, the entrepreneurs' performance improves and they achieve a higher level of effectiveness than at the beginning of the stage. They now have a set of new skills alongside their old ones. However, this transition is not inevitable and some people fail to acquire new skills or cannot pull themselves out of the 'low'. The risk is that entrepreneurs may give up.

☿ The role of leader

Leading and managing an entrepreneurial organisation is a challenge that requires some distinctive skills and capabilities. Management and leadership are different and distinct terms, although the skills and competencies associated with each are complementary. Management is concerned with handling complexity in organisational processes and the execution of work. It is linked to the authority required to manage, somehow given to managers, within some form of hierarchy. Back in the nineteenth century Max Fayol defined the five functions of management as planning, organising, commanding, coordinating and controlling. Today, these sound very much like the skills needed to lead a communist-style command economy. Fayol's work outlined how these functions required certain skills which could be taught and developed systematically in people. Management is therefore about detail and logic. It is about efficiency and effectiveness.

A well-managed organisation must produce the results for which it exists. It must be administered, that is, its decisions must be made in the right sequence and with the right timing and right intensity. In the long run, a well managed organisation must adapt to its external environment. The entrepreneurial role focuses on the adaptive changes, which requires creativity and risk taking. And to ensure that the organisation can have a life span longer than that of any of its key managers, the fourth role – integration – is necessary to build a team effort. Effective and efficient management over the short and long term requires the use of all four roles.

☐ Ichak Adizes, author, 1978

Leadership on the other hand is concerned with setting direction, communicating and motivating. It is about broad principles and emotion and less detail. It is particularly concerned with change. It is, therefore, quite possible for an organisation to be over-managed but under-led, or vice versa. In a start-up good leadership is essential – but easily delivered to a small workforce – while effective management quickly becomes increasingly important to get things done. A larger organisation, therefore, needs to be both effectively led and managed.

The consensus of opinion now is that leaders, unlike entrepreneurs, are not born. The idea that they may have traits or characteristics which typify them has largely been discredited. However, like entrepreneurs, they are shaped by their history and experience. The one characteristic that separates them from others is the obvious one that they have willing followers. Their characteristics and personality traits tell us very little. Leadership is about what you do with who you are – your relationships with followers – rather than just who you are. And as we have seen entrepreneurs are rather good at relationships.

Blank (1995) argues that leadership is an 'event' – a 'discrete interaction each time a leader and a follower join … Leadership can appear continuous if a leader manifests multiple leadership events.' One consequence of this is that, like entrepreneurs, leaders can have roller coaster careers as they exhibit leadership characteristics at certain discrete times and with different people, but not at others. Winston Churchill was widely acknowledged as a great war-time leader but a poor peace-time leader. Therefore entrepreneurs can be good leaders for the business at start-up but no good for either the growth or the maturity phase unless they adapt and change their style.

Our traditional view of leaders is that they are special people – often charismatic heroes like Churchill – who set direction, make key decisions and motivate staff, often prevailing against the odds at times of crisis. They have vision – something entrepreneurs certainly have. They are strategic thinkers and are effective communicators whilst still being able to monitor and control performance. Above all, they create the appropriate culture within the organisation to reflect their priorities.

Our image of a leader tends to propagate the myth of the individual focusing on short-term results, often overcoming some sort of crisis, rather than the systematic pursuit of long-term excellence. The image is often based on implicit assumptions of the general powerlessness, lack of personal vision and inability or other people's unwillingness to change. But in reality successful entrepreneurial leaders are different. As already mentioned, Timmons (1999) described successful entrepreneurs as 'patient leaders, capable of instilling tangible visions and managing for the long haul. The entrepreneur is at once a learner and a teacher, a doer and a visionary.' This is all very different from the charismatic hero much loved by folklore. Timmons talks about six dominant themes for successful entrepreneurs:

> *Management is about communication and listening to people. I believe the people on the ground have the answer. If you can find what the answer is you'll get a much better solution for the business ... Leadership to me is picking good teams and putting them together. And also putting yourself out for those people in terms of helping them when they're stuck, finding out what their concerns are, navigating them through problems. That, to me, is what leadership is about – not doing it yourself, but putting in place people who can do it for you.*
> ☐ David Arculus, former MD, Emap group, Chief Operating Officer, United News and Media and chairman, IPC, *The Times*, 3 May 2004

1 Leadership;
2 Commitment and determination;
3 Opportunity obsession;
4 Tolerance of risk, ambiguity and uncertainty;
5 Creativity, self-reliance and ability to adapt;
6 Motivation to excel.

If ever the job definition for a leader were written it would probably include five elements:

1 *Having vision and ideas* It is this that gives people a clear focus on the key issues and concerns facing the firm, the values it stands for, where it is going and how it will get there. Entrepreneurs, typically, find this part of the job definition easiest. They have vision and ideas in abundance, indeed often too many ideas and the problem is persuading them to focus on any one at a time.

2 *Being able to undertake long-term, strategic planning* It is one thing to know where you want to go, it is quite another to know how to get there. The heart of leadership is about being able to chart a course for future development that steers the firm towards the leader's business aims. Most textbooks talk about strategies being deliberate, consciously intended courses of action. Entrepreneurs often believe they are bad at this. However, strategies can also emerge as consistent patterns that lead to success over a period of time or course of events. They 'emerge' without advance deliberation. The trick for entrepreneurs is to spot the successful patterns, capitalise upon them and use them as part of future strategy. Body Shop's characteristic green-painted pine decor was as much born out of lack of cash as anything else, yet it came to symbolise its 'no-frills' approach to retailing. Any start-up needs some luck to survive, but the skill for the entrepreneur is to recognise what works and what is needed to build upon that success.

3 *Being able to communicate effectively* Even if entrepreneurs have a vision and a strategy, they still have to communicate it to the stakeholders in the business.

> *If there is a spark of genius in the leadership function at all, it must lie in the transcending ability, a kind of magic, to assemble ... out of a variety of images, signals, forecasts and alternatives ... a clearly articulated vision of the future that is at once simple, easily understood, clearly desirable, and energising.*
>
> ☐ Warren Bennis and Burt Nanus, authors, 1985

This is about inspiring and motivating staff, customers and financiers so that they understand where the business is going, how it is going to get there and motivating them to make it happen. It is about persuading them that the firm can deal with an uncertain environment and manage that most difficult thing of all, rapid change.

4 *Creating an appropriate culture within the firm* We defined culture in Chapter 2 as 'the collective programming of the mind which distinguishes one group of people from another.' At a firm level we might simply call it 'how it is around here' – that pattern of taken-for-granted assumptions. Creating an appropriate culture in the firm is the single most important thing a leader has to do.

5 *Monitoring and controlling performance* This is the routine task that entrepreneurs like least and are probably worst at doing. Typically, entrepreneurs prefer informal systems which involve direct, personal supervision and control, rather than formal systems which involve checking information and dealing with paperwork. However, as the firm grows the informal systems start to break down and need to be replaced by regular, routine procedures and some elements of a hierarchical organisation structure are bound to appear.

⚲ The evolving vision

Entrepreneurs have a vision for their business at start-up – and ideas aplenty. However, having your own individual vision is relatively easy. Building a shared vision with staff as the business grows is no easy task – it is not simply about going off and writing that vision statement, as we did in Chapter 11. Visions are living things that evolve over time. Developing the vision is a continuous process. It involves continually checking with staff to ensure that the vision has a resonance with them – modifying it little by little, if appropriate. Entrepreneurs can find this difficult and frustrating as they are more used to setting goals and seeking compliance. But to survive in a larger organisation they need to develop their political skills.

Good visions motivate. Two strong motivations for people are fear and aspiration. Fear is probably the strongest motivation that helps galvanise action and force people to change, but probably lasts only a short time. This motivation worked well for Winston Churchill in the Second World War. However, aspiration – what we might become – has greater longevity and is altogether a more positive motivator. It is the one that underpins most entrepreneurial organisations. It emphasises striving – a continuous journey of improvement.

It is not sufficient simply to have a vision; that vision must also be communicated. In this respect the leader is often held out as being a storyteller. Gardner (1995) maintains this is the key leadership skill. This storytelling skill can be either verbal or written, however, leaders must 'walk the talk' – practise what they preach – otherwise they have no credibility and are not believed. Gardner maintains that the most successful stories are simple ones that hit an emotional resonance with the audience, addressing questions of identity and providing answers to questions concerning personal, social

Are you a visionary leader?

In *Becoming a Visionary Leader* (HRD Press, Amherst, MA, 1996) Marshall Sashkin defines a visionary leader as one who:

▷ Provides *clear* leadership which focuses people on goals that are part of a vision and on key issues and concerns;
▷ Has good *interpersonal communication skills* that get everyone to understand the focus and to work together towards common goals;
▷ Acts *consistently* over time to develop trust;
▷ *Cares and respects* others, making them self-confident, whilst having an inner self-confidence themselves;
▷ Provides *creative* opportunities that others can buy into and 'own' – empowering opportunities that involve people in making the right things their own priorities.

The booklet contains a series of questions designed to see whether you might be a visionary leader. These start with an 'Impact Focus Scale' which looks at your motivations for wanting to be a leader. These are measured in three dimensions or scores. Effective leaders score high in each area:

▷ *Impact belief score* – This measures your belief that you can make a difference within the organisation.
▷ *Social power need* – This measures the value you place on power and influence for the good that you can do with it within the organisation.
▷ *Dominance avoidance* – This measures your need for dominance or vice versa. Effective leaders do not need to dominate.

The second part involves a 'Cultural Functions Inventory' which is designed to help decide whether an organisation's culture is effective at facilitating certain crucial functions. The resulting scores measure the ability to adapt to change, attain goals, coordinate teamwork, and systems stability.

Finally, Sashkin has produced the *Leader Behaviour Questionnaire* (available on www.hrdpress.com/visionary-leader-questionnaire-set-5-pack-VLQS), which is a 360-degree assessment instrument that measures visionary leadership behaviours, characteristics and contextual effects (filled out by 3–6 colleagues). The behaviours measured are:

▷ How well you manage to focus people's attention on key issues;
▷ How effective you are at communication, including 'active listening';
▷ How consistent your views and actions are and how you develop trust;
▷ Whether you demonstrate respect and regard for others;
▷ Whether you come up with ideas and opportunities that others find attractive and wish to take part in.

and moral choices. Is it any wonder that entrepreneurs skilled at developing personal relationships can also become powerful leaders?

Senge (1992) highlights the creative tension this storytelling must create:

> The leader's story, sense of purpose, values and vision establish the direction and target. His relentless commitment to the truth and to inquiry into the forces underlying current reality continually highlight the gaps between reality and the vision. Leaders generate and manage this creative tension – not just themselves but in an entire organisation. This is how they energise an organisation. That is their basic job. That is why they exist.

> ## Kotter's Seven Principles for successfully communicating a vision
>
> ▷ *Keep it simple*: Focused and jargon-free.
> ▷ *Use metaphors, analogies and examples*: Engage the imagination.
> ▷ *Use many different forums*: The same message should come from as many different directions as possible.
> ▷ *Repeat the message*: The same message should be repeated again, and again, and again.
> ▷ *Lead by example*: Walk the talk.
> ▷ *Address small inconsistencies*: Small changes can have big effects if their symbolism is important to staff.
> ▷ *Listen and be listened to*: Work hard to listen, it pays dividends.
>
> Adapted from Kotter (1996).

He goes on to underline how this can create within an entire organisation the sense of internal locus of control – emphasising the belief in control over destiny – that is an essential part of the entrepreneurial character: 'Mastering creative tension throughout an organisation leads to a profoundly different view of reality. People literally start to see more and more aspects of reality as something that they, collectively, can influence.' And this is one important psychological way that individuals within the entrepreneurial organisation deal with the uncertainty they face. You might recognise it as one aspect of 'empowerment'.

Bennis and Nanus (1985) talk about a 'spark of genius' in the act of leadership which 'operates on the emotional and spiritual resources of the organisation.' For them the genius of the leader lies in 'this transcending ability, a kind of magic, to assemble – out of a variety of images, signals, forecasts and alternatives – a clearly articulated vision of the future that is at once simple, easily understood, clearly desirable, and energising'. But entrepreneurial leadership that is to perpetuate itself is more than just charismatic leadership. Charismatic leaders deal in visions and crises, but little in between. Entrepreneurial leadership is about systematic and purposeful development of leadership skills and techniques – which can take a long time. It is about developing relationships. It is about creating long-term sustainable competitive advantage. And most of all it is about making the organisation systematically entrepreneurial – a topic we shall return to in the next chapter.

♀ Leadership style

The role of leader is normally based on some sort of authority. Authority can derive from role or status, tradition, legal position, expert skills or their charismatic personality. Timmons (op. cit.) believes that in successful entrepreneurial ventures leadership is based on expertise rather than authority and this then means there is no competition for leadership. Many of the best known, successful entrepreneurs clearly also have charisma.

It is a myth to think that leaders are born, not made. Leadership is a skill that can be developed. However, it is a complex thing. As represented in Figure 17.5, the appropriate leadership style depends upon the interactions

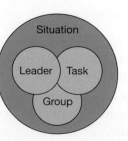

and interconnections between the leader, the task, the group being led and the situation or context. A leader may prefer an informal, non-directional style, but faced with a young apprentice working a dangerous lathe he might be forgiven for reverting to a fairly formal, directive style with heavy supervision. In that situation the change in style is appropriate. Try the same style with a group of senior creative marketing consultants and there would be a problem. Many different styles may be effective, with different tasks, different groups and in different contexts. What is more, there is no evidence of any single leadership style characterising successful businesses. Nevertheless, by picking off the individual elements of these four factors we can understand what style is best suited to different circumstances. The question is, can leaders adapt their style to suit different circumstances?

Leader and task

The leadership grid shown in Figure 17.6 was developed by Blake and Mouton (1978). It shows style as dependent upon the leader's concern for task compared to their concern for people. Entrepreneurs are usually more concerned with completing the task but, as the firm grows, must become more concerned with people if the tasks are to be accomplished. Task leadership may be appropriate in certain situations, for example emergencies, but concern for people must surface at some point if effective, trusting relationships are to develop. Low concern for both people and task is hardly leadership at all. High concern for people – the country-club style – is rare in business but can be appropriate in community groups, small charities or social clubs where good relationships and high morale might be the dominant objectives. You can find your preferred style on this grid by undertaking the interactive leadership test on the website accompanying this book.

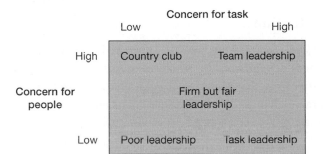

F17.6 Leader and task

Timmons (op. cit.) believes that the emphasis in successful entrepreneurial ventures is more on performing task-orientated roles although 'someone inevitably provides for maintenance and group cohesion by good humour and wit'. If this is the case then it is even more important to ensure that there is an appropriate and effective management team in place.

Leader and group

Leadership style also depends on the relationship of the leader with the group they are leading. Figure 17.7 shows this in relation to the leader's degree of authority and the group's autonomy in decision-making. If a leader has high authority but the group has low autonomy, the leader will tend to adopt an autocratic style, simply instructing people what to do. If they have low authority, for whatever reason, they will tend to adopt a paternalistic style, cajoling the group into doing things, picking off

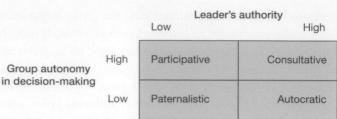

individuals and offering grace and favour in exchange for performance. If the leader has low authority and the group has high autonomy, then they will tend to adopt a participative style, involving all of the group in decision-making and moving forward with consensus. If the leader has high authority then they will seek opinions but make the decision themselves using a consultative style.

A survey of small business managers in Britain, France, Germany, Spain and Italy showed that most used a consultative style (Burns and Whitehouse, 1996). However, 20–30 per cent of managers in all countries other than Germany used an autocratic style. It has been said that growth-orientated companies are initially characterised by an autocratic or dictatorial style, but as the company grows, a more consultative style develops (Ray and Hutchinson, 1983). The survey confirmed this. Leadership styles also seem to be influenced by national culture. The survey revealed that a significant proportion (35 per cent) of German managers use a participative style, despite the fact that none of them thought their subordinates liked it. This probably reflects cultural differences at a national level, where consultative or participative decision-making is the norm, particularly when unions are involved. However, this mismatch between actual style, dictated by cultural norms, and desired style must create tension for German entrepreneurs.

Leader and situation

John Adair (1984) put forward the view that the weight the leader should put on these different influences depends on the situation or context they find themselves in. In an entrepreneurial firm that situation can be characterised as one of uncertainty, ambiguity and rapid change. What does that tell us about the context? Timmons (op. cit.) observed that:

> There is among successful entrepreneurs a well-developed capacity to exert influence without formal power. These people are adept at conflict resolution. They know when to use logic and when to persuade, when to make a concession, and when to exact one. To run a successful venture, an entrepreneur learns to get along with different constituencies, often with conflicting aims – the customer, the supplier, the financial backer, the creditor, as well as the partners and others on the inside. Success comes when the entrepreneur is a mediator, a negotiator, rather than a dictator.

How good entrepreneurial leaders approach any task, with any group, therefore depends on the situation they face. But entrepreneurial firms face an environment that is constantly changing, which can often lead to conflict as they try to get people to do different things or things differently. The Thomas-Kilmann Conflict Mode Instrument gives us an insight into how conflict might be handled. Whilst each style has its advantages in certain situations, generally compromise or, better still, collaboration is generally thought to be the best way for a team to work.

How do you behave in situations involving conflict?

Often in business you find yourself at odds with others who hold seemingly incompatible views. For leaders to be effective they need to understand how they handle these conflict situations and be able to modify their behaviour to obtain the best results from others. Based on research by Kenneth Thomas and Ralph Kilmann, the Thomas–Kilmann Conflict Mode Instrument (available on www.kilmann.com/conflict.html) shows how a person's behaviour can be classified under two dimensions:

▷ Assertiveness – the extent to which individuals attempt to satisfy their own needs;
▷ Cooperativeness – the extent to which they attempt to satisfy the needs of others.

These two dimensions lead the authors to identify five behavioural classifications which the questionnaire can identify in individuals:

High	Competing	Collaborating
Assertiveness	Compromising	
Low	Avoiding	Accommodating
	Low	High
	Cooperativeness	

1 *Competing* is assertive and uncooperative. Individuals are concerned for themselves and pursue their own agenda forcefully, using power, rank or ability to argue to win the conflict. This can be seen as bullying with less forceful individuals or, when others use the same mode, it can lead to heated, possibly unresolved, arguments.

2 *Accommodating* is unassertive and cooperative, the opposite of competing. Individuals want to see the concerns of others satisfied. They might do so as an act of 'selfless generosity' or just because they are 'obeying orders', either way they run the risk of not making their own views heard.

3 *Avoiding* is both unassertive and uncooperative. It may involve side-stepping an issue or withdrawing from the conflict altogether. In this mode any conflict may not even be addressed.

4 *Collaborating* is both assertive and cooperative, the opposite of avoiding. Issues get addressed but individuals are willing to work with others to resolve the conflict, perhaps finding alternatives that meet everybody's concerns. This is the most constructive approach to conflict for a group as a whole.

5 *Compromising* is the 'in between' route, the diplomatic, expedient solution to conflict which partially satisfies everyone. It may involve making concessions.

Each style of handling conflict has its advantages and disadvantages and can be effective in certain situations. However, management teams or boards of directors, if they are to get the most from each member over a longer period of time, work best when all members adopt the collaborating or compromising modes. A team made up of just competers would find it difficult to get on and, indeed, to survive. A team made up of just accommodaters would lack assertiveness and drive.

Entrepreneurial leaders face uncertainty and ambiguity, trying to manage people who often have unclear job definitions because they are having to cope with change. This can create conflict that has to be resolved on an everyday basis. The implications of the entrepreneurial situation are:

▷ Entrepreneurial leaders must move away from using an autocratic or dictatorial leadership style, especially with their senior management team, if they want staff to take more control over their actions and develop an entrepreneurial organisation.
▷ Entrepreneurial leaders must be adept at using informal influence. Their powers of persuasion and motivation are important. They should meet and influence people. Relationships and organisational culture are important.
▷ Entrepreneurial leaders must be adept at conflict resolution. In these situations Timmons (op. cit.) observes: 'Successful entrepreneurs are interpersonally supporting and nurturing – not interpersonally competitive.' In terms of the Thomas–Kilmann Conflict Modes this is the 'collaborating' or 'compromising' mode.

This means that entrepreneurial leaders have to be flexible and adapt their leadership style to suit different and changing circumstances. These changes are a lot to ask of anybody and many entrepreneurs cannot make the transition. Some learn that they are best at start-ups and sell the business at the point where proper controls and procedures need to be put in place and management teams developed, recognising their strengths but equally their weaknesses.

💡 Building the management team

Entrepreneurs will only succeed in growing their company if they get a good management team to work with. Attracting good staff is always difficult for small firms because of perceived lack of job security, uncertainty about promotion prospects and the fact that it is often difficult for new people to fit into an existing team. Hence the need, often, to offer shares in the company.

Selecting a team will depend upon the mix of functional skills and market or industry experience required in the firm, as well as the personal chemistry between its members. For a team to be effective individuals also need to have the right mix of a certain set of personal characteristics. Meredith Belbin (1981) identified nine clusters of personal characteristics or attributes which translate into the 'team roles', outlined opposite. Individuals are unlikely to have more than two or three of them, yet all nine clusters of characteristics need to be present in a team for it to work effectively.

It has been suggested that the 'prototypical entrepreneur' might be a plant (creative, ideas person), shaper (dynamism, full of drive and energy) and a resource investigator (enthusiastically explores opportunities) (Chell, 2001). In this case the first team member should not be strong in any of these categories, but ideally should be an implementer (reliable, efficient and able to turn ideas into practical action). The implementer will want a completer-finisher (conscientious, delivers on time), a teamworker (cooperative and unchallenging) and possibly a specialist (with particular knowledge or skills) working under him or her.

The leader's role is to select the team and then to build cohesion and motivation. In most cases this involves building consensus towards the goals of the firm, balancing multiple viewpoints and demands. However, too great a reliance on achieving consensus can lead to slow decision-making, so a balance is needed that will strain the interpersonal skills of the leader. However, in the best entrepreneurial firms leadership seems to work almost by infection. The management team seem to be infected by the philosophies and attitudes of the entrepreneur and readily buy into the goals set for the firm, something that is helped if they share in its success.

All personal relationships are based upon trust and this is the cornerstone of a good team. It is imperative that the management team trust the entrepreneurial leader. For the leader this involves being firm but fair, flexible but consistent in values and in dealings with individuals and always placing the interests of the firm first, also being supportive for individuals and having their interests at heart. Trust also has to be built up between other members of the management team. It takes time to build and needs to be demonstrated with real outcomes.

Once you have a business up and running the best way to keep in touch is to employ great people and empower them. This brings with it trust, communication and team spirit. When you work as a team you are in touch. My business style is non-aggressive, non-confrontational – it's who I am. It's important to be yourself. It comes from a background where you have to get on with people to get on. I believe that if you treat people like dirt on the way up it will come to haunt you as you find yourself on the way down.

☐ Jonathan Elvidge, founder of Gadget Shop, *The Times* 6 August 2002

I can't remember a single day when I didn't want to go to work. I had such a good team. There was an incredible feeling of trust. None of the boys would let me down.

☐ Tom Farmer, founder of Kwik-Fit, *Daily Mail* 11 May 1999

Effective teams, therefore, do not just happen, they have to be developed, and that can take time. It is said that teams go through a four-stage development process:

1 The group tests relationships. Individuals are polite, impersonal, watchful and guarded.
2 Infighting starts in the group and controlling the conflict is important. However, whilst some individuals might be confrontational, others might opt out and avoid the conflict altogether. Neither approach is good. Collaboration is best. This is a dangerous phase from which some groups never emerge.
3 The group starts to get organised, developing skills, establishing procedures, giving feedback, confronting issues.
4 The group becomes mature and effective, working flexibly and closely, making the most of resources and being close-knit and supportive.

The whole process of team formation and development has been likened to courtship and marriage, involving decisions based partly on emotion rather than logic. For

What sort of team player are you?

Developing a successful team depends not just on the range of professional skills it has, but also on the range of personal characteristics – the chemistry of the team. Based upon research into how teams work, Dr Meredith Belbin (1981) identified nine clusters of personal characteristics or attributes which translate into 'team roles'. The roles are:

The Shaper: This is usually the self-elected task leader with lots of nervous energy. They are extrovert, dynamic, outgoing, highly strung, argumentative, a pressuriser seeking ways around obstacles. They do have a tendency to bully and are not always liked. However, they generate action and thrive under pressure.

The Plant: This the team's vital spark and chief source of new ideas. They are creative, imaginative and often unorthodox. However, they can be distant and uncommunicative and sometimes their ideas can seem a little impractical.

The Coordinator: This is the team's natural chairman. They are mature, confident and trusting. They clarify goals and promote decision-making. They are calm with strong interpersonal skills. However, they can be perceived as a little manipulative.

The Resource Investigator: This is 'the fixer' – extrovert, amiable, six phones on the go, with a wealth of contacts. They pick other people's brains and explore opportunities. However, they can be a bit undisciplined and can lose interest quickly once initial enthusiasm has passed.

The Monitor-Evaluator: This is the team's rock. They are introvert, sober, strategic, discerning. They explore all options and are capable of deep analysis of huge amounts of data. They are rarely wrong. However, they can lack drive and are unlikely to inspire or excite others.

The Team-Worker: This is the team's counsellor or conciliator. They are mild mannered and social, perceptive and aware of problems or undercurrents, accommodating and good listeners. They promote harmony and are particularly valuable at times of crisis. However, they can be indecisive.

The Implementer: This is the team's workhorse. They turn ideas into practical actions and get on with the job logically and loyally. They are disciplined, reliable and conservative. However, they can be inflexible and slow to change.

The Completer-Finisher: This is the team's worry-guts, making sure things get finished. They are sticklers for detail, deadlines and schedules and have relentless follow-through, picking up any errors or omissions as they go. However, they sometimes just cannot let go and are reluctant to delegate.

The Specialist: This is the team's chief source of technical knowledge or skill. They are single-minded, self-starting and dedicated. However, they tend to contribute on a narrow front.

Most individuals are naturally suited to two or three roles. However, to work effectively a team must comprise elements of all nine roles. If a team lacks certain 'team roles' it tends to exhibit weaknesses in these areas.

that reason it is important that the team shares the same values and is committed to the same goals. They may disagree on tactics but they all agree on the destination and how they are going to get there. It is also important that team roles are clearly defined, although given the uncertainty involved with rapid growth, it is also important that flexibility is maintained – which brings us back to the way conflict is handled. An effective team will generate team norms of behaviour and that can be a powerful force for conformity and suggests skilful handling.

> *My philosophy is to get the best people and let them get on with it and trust them implicitly. Remember that it's a team effort that's going to make your business successful.*
>
> ☐ Martyn Dawes, founder of Coffee Nation, Startups: www.startupsco.uk

♀ The board of directors

In many firms the management team will also function as the legal board of directors of the company. The legal duties and responsibilities of directors arise out of common law and statute. Directors have a fiduciary duty to act honestly and in good faith, exercise skill and care and undertake their statutory duty. The broad functions of the board are summarised in Figure 17.8 along the dimensions of inward/outward looking and past/future orientation. The prime function of the board is to establish corporate strategy and policy:

▷ Overall strategic planning;
▷ Approval of strategies in key areas;
▷ Changes in the scope or nature of operations;
▷ Changes in organisational structure;
▷ Major company decisions.

The other responsibilities include:

▷ Monitoring and supervising management performance;
▷ Planning for management succession;
▷ Setting remuneration levels;
▷ Providing proper accountability to other stakeholders in the firm, for example, by appointing auditors and approving the annual financial statements, as well as ensuring that the company complies with all aspects of the law.

Whilst establishing corporate strategy and policy is the most important job for the board, it is unlikely that it will be given the appropriate weighting in terms of time allocation. Most boards spend too much time on the other functions, particularly monitoring management performance.

Whilst corporate governance and business ethics are high on the agenda of many high-profile public companies, that is not necessarily the case for smaller firms. Research shows that business ethics for smaller firms tends to take the form of informal codes of practice and an understanding of acceptable and unacceptable behaviour

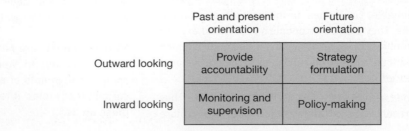

F17.8 The role of the board of directors

Strategy: Guiding strategic direction	People: Practising 'human' skills
Strategic thinking Systems thinking Awareness of external environment Entrepreneurial thinking Developing the vision Initiating change Championing causes	Communicating Creating a personal impact Giving leadership Promoting development of others Networking
Culture: Developing organisation culture	Operations: Exercising executive control
Customer focus Quality focus Teamwork focus People resource focus Organisational learning focus	Governance Decision-making Contributing specialist knowledge Managing performance Analysing situations Awareness of organisational structure

F17.9 The Institute of Management model of board-level competencies

rather than standardised, formal procedures, which are a feature of the larger firm (Spence, 2000). There are, of course, exceptions and the situation does seem to be changing rapidly.

A strong management team and board of directors is invaluable and their worth is no more evident than in the criteria venture capitalists use for investment: management, management and management. To help boards develop and operate more effectively, the Institute of Management has published a useful set of best practice checklists based upon a model of board-level competencies (Allday, 1997). Twenty-three board-level skills were identified grouped together under the four key headings shown in Figure 17.9. These generic competencies need to be balanced and tailored to particular circumstances and specific functional board roles.

More than 90 per cent of the *Financial Times* Stock Exchange (FTSE) companies comply with the recommendation that they have non-executive directors. However, in small unquoted companies the proportion is much, much smaller. Often non-executive directors are imposed by financial backers to oversee their investment. However, non-executive directors have a valuable role in bringing different skills, an independent and objective perspective and a new network of contacts. They should act as an early warning system for potential future difficulties, and as we saw in Chapter 16, their role can be particularly valuable in family firms.

Entrepreneurial structures

Entrepreneurial organisation structures, seen most clearly at the start-up phase, have been likened to the spider's web shown in Figure 17.10. The entrepreneur sits at the centre of the web with each new member of staff reporting to them. The management style tends to be informal, one of direct supervision. Just as entrepreneurs prefer informal marketing techniques, building on relationships, they prefer informal organisation structures and influences rather than rigid rules and job definitions.

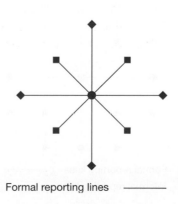

Formal reporting lines ———

F17.10 The entrepreneurial spider's web

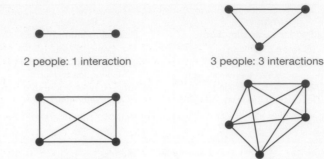

2 people: 1 interaction

3 people: 3 interactions

4 people: 6 interactions

5 people: 10 interactions

They persuade and cajole employees, showing them how to do things on a one-to-one basis, rather than having prescribed tasks. They rely on building personal relationships. After all, the business is growing rapidly and there are no precedents to go by. The future is uncertain, so flexibility is the key. The pace of change probably means that rigid structures would be out of date quickly. What is more, in a small firm everybody has to be prepared to do other people's jobs because there is no cover, no slack in the system if, for example, someone goes off sick. It is also perfectly flat and therefore efficient – overheads are reduced – and it is responsive – communication times are minimised. This is the typical small, entrepreneurial structure with the entrepreneur leading by example and communicating directly.

The entrepreneurial structure works quite well up to a couple of dozen employees. There are two reasons why it is less effective in bigger organisations. Firstly, communication becomes more complicated, with greater opportunity for misunderstanding and conflict as the number of people interacting increases. Figure 17.11 shows the number of interactions possible with groups of two, three, four and five people. The number of interactions is represented by the mathematical formula:

$$n \times \frac{n-1}{2}$$ where n represents the number of people.

Thus, five people generate ten interactions, ten people generate 45 and 15 people generate 105. Postulated by Northcote Parkinson, 'Parkinson's Coefficient of Inefficiency', proposes that the optimum *inefficient* number for a group is 21, at which point group interaction becomes impossible. Entrepreneurs beware!

The second reason relates to the character of the entrepreneur themselves. Their internal locus of control means that they tend to want to get invoved and do things themselves. Even when they try to delegate and introduce new staff who report to existing members of staff, entrepreneurs tend to meddle and the new employees soon find an informal reporting line to the entrepreneur, short circuiting the manager or supervisor they are supposed to report to, as in Figure 17.12. It is no wonder that this creates frustration, resentment and an unwillingness to accept responsibility in the manager. Why should they take responsibility when their decisions are likely to be questioned or reversed, or when staff supposedly reporting to them are constantly being checked up on by the entrepreneur?

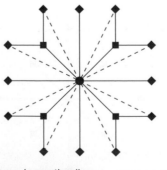

Formal reporting lines ———
Informal reporting lines - - - - -

The root cause of this problem lies in the entrepreneurial character and, in particular, the strong need for control that can exhibit itself in some entrepreneurs. Derek du Toit (1980), an entrepreneur himself, said that 'an entrepreneur who starts his own business generally does so because he is a difficult employee'. He probably finds it difficult to be in the alternating dominant and then submissive role so often asked of middle management. He hates being told what to do and wants to tell everybody what to do. He also believes he can do the job better than others, which may be true, but he must find a way of working through others if the business is to grow successfully.

Kets de Vries (1985) was probably the first to argue that these traits can lead to entrepreneurs wanting to over-control their business – becoming 'control freaks'. This is not such a problem in a micro business, where the owner-manager does everything themselves anyway because their business is their life and their life is the business. Indeed it can be a virtue – making certain everything gets done properly. However, as the business grows this characteristic starts to be a problem. For example, in a fruit juice bottling plant with about 200 employees the owner-manager could not bear to relinquish any control to senior managers and insisted that copies of all external correspondence came to him. In this way he believed he still had some control. Kets de Vries says employees in these situations become 'infantilised', expected to behave as incompetent idiots, taking few decisions and circulating little information. The better ones just do not stay.

💡 Traditional large firm structures

Structures create order in an organisation. Although there is no one 'best' structure, different types of structure are good for particular types of task. The most appropriate structure depends on a number of factors: the nature of the organisation, the strategies it is employing, the tasks to be undertaken, the environmental conditions under which the firm operates and the size of the firm. And size does seem to matter. Large organisations are more complex than small and complexity impedes information flows, lengthens decision-making and can kill initiative.

Despite the fact that there is no single 'correct' organisation structure, the entrepreneurial structure must evolve to become more formal, although not bureaucratic. Whilst keeping levels of management to a minimum, there needs to be a hierarchy of some sort that gives managers confidence that they have the authority to manage. The bureaucratic form of hierarchical structure (Figure 17.13), with its universal organisation structure, marks the earliest influential theory of organisational design. Based on the work of Weber (1947), it stresses rationality and functional efficiency. The literature was broadened by Chandler (1962), as technical and organisational complexity increased, by the inclusion of divisions – a development that was seen as

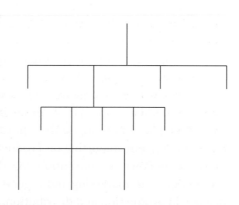

F17.13 The hierarchical structure

a rational solution to increasing scale and complexity. However, much of the later literature focuses on the dysfunctional consequences of this structure, where people got in the way of rational efficiency (Pugh and Hickson, 1976).

It was the contingency theorists of the late 1950s and 1960s that concluded there was no single best way of organising a business. The choice depends on the extent to which a structure furthers the objectives of the firm, but in particular it depends on:

▷ The environment it faces (Stinchcombe, 1959; Burns and Stalker, 1961; Emery and Trist, 1965; Haige and Aiken, 1967; Lawrence and Lorsch, 1967);
▷ The technology it uses (Woodward, 1965; Perrow, 1967);
▷ Its scale of operation (Pugh et al., 1969; Blau, 1970).

In all cases, variations in structure can be rationalised in terms of task predictability and diversity. However, these approaches tend not to explain the underlying processes – how things actually happen.

The matrix or task structure (Figure 17.14) came out of the contingency school. First posited by Galbraith (1973), it is based on the work of Lawrence and Lorsch (1967) and is essentially an overlay on what is still a bureaucratic structure with hierarchical distributed power and decision-making. It spawned the development of teams and task forces. Galbraith also observed how task complexity increased with task uncertainty and the amount of information that needed to be processed by the decision-maker.

The matrix or task structure is often seen in organisations undertaking project work, for example consultancies. But it can also be combined very effectively with the hierarchical structure so that individuals in different branches of the hierarchical structure come together as a team to undertake projects or tasks within the matrix structure. So, for example, the hierarchical structure might reflect functional areas such as design, production, marketing, sales and finance. Individuals from these areas, at appropriate levels in the hierarchy, might come together to form a matrix team to tackle a project such as new product development.

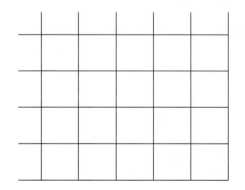

F17.14 The matrix structure

💡 Structure, change and task complexity

On its own, the traditional hierarchical structure shown in Figure 17.13 is mechanistic, bureaucratic and rigid. It has been called a 'machine bureaucracy' because it is most appropriate where the organisation (or sub-organisation) is tackling simple tasks with extensive standardisation, in stable environments, and/or where security is important and where plans and programmes need to be followed carefully. Well developed information systems reporting on production/processing activity need to exist for it to be effective. Power is concentrated in the top executives. It is more concerned with production than marketing and is good at producing high volumes and achieving efficiency in production and distribution. As such, it is particularly appropriate when a product is at the mature phase of its life cycle and is being 'milked' as a 'cash cow'. It is, in short, designed to stifle individual initiative.

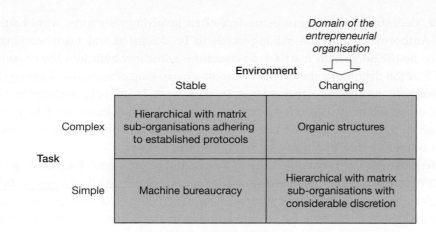

As the environment becomes more liable to change, standardisation becomes less viable and responsibility for coping with unexpected changes needs to be pushed down the hierarchy. Complex tasks in stable environments mean that it becomes worthwhile to develop standard skills to tackle the complexities. In both these cases the matrix organisation can be an effective sub-structure within a more hierarchical organisation. In a stable environment the matrix team can work on their complex tasks within set protocols – as they do, for example, in a surgical operation. In a changing environment the matrix team must have a high degree of discretion because established protocols may be inappropriate to the changing circumstances, even for the simple tasks they face. The implications for organisation structure of differences in task complexity and environmental stability are summarised in Figure 17.15.

The main characteristic of the entrepreneurial environment is that it is one of change. In a changing environment where there is high task complexity an innovative,

🗂 Case insight David Poole and DP&A

David Poole is CEO of DP&A, a direct marketing agency. In 2000 he owned 60 per cent and fellow directors Tony Appi and Dan Douglas each owned 20 per cent. He wanted to expand but a newspaper article on him and his firm highlighted some of the dilemmas he believed he faced.

'I have got to do things my way and prove I've got what it takes ... I love my business and find it massively stimulating, but I guess it all boils down to ego.

I haven't spent a lot of time on strategic planning ... I have an open and honest relationship with my fellow directors, but they haven't yet been involved in strategic planning. I don't want to distract them from their core work. I'm capable of taking the decisions myself ... A venture capitalist will have a strategy that is not necessarily in line with the best interests of the company and will always be looking towards a profitable exit, so effectively I would not be in charge.

[Going to the stock market] would give access to funding for development and provided I continued to perform well then I would keep control [but] quite simply we are too small.'

Sunday Times 20 February 2000

☐   Up-to-date information on DP&A can be found on their website: www.dpa.co.uk

flexible, decentralised structure is needed, often involving structures within structures. Authority for decision-making needs to be delegated and team working is likely to be the norm with matrix-type structures somehow built into the organisation. Clear job definitions should never lead to a narrowing of responsibilities so that people ignore the new tasks that emerge. In many ways, far more important than the formal organisation structure for a firm of this sort is the culture that tells people what needs to be done and motivates them to do it. This is often called an 'organic structure' and we shall examine it further in the next chapter.

Where there is low task complexity in a changing environment there is scope for greater centralisation but the structure still needs to be responsive to change, probably through a degree of central direction and supervision. The structure, although hierarchical, should be relatively flat with few middle-management positions. However, culture is still important because the workforce still need to be motivated to make these frequent changes to their work practices. A business is a little like a house. If the organization structure is the plan and people are the bricks then culture is the cement that holds the whole thing together. Ignore any one element at your peril.

♀ Creating culture

Edgar Schein (1990) says that the only important thing that leaders do may well be constructing culture. He says that an organisation's culture is grounded in the founder's basic beliefs, values and assumptions. So, how do you go about creating culture in an organisation? We have identified and explored the crucial role of values – what is worth having or doing – and vision – where we are going and how we will get there – and how it is communicated in creating culture. Having entrepreneurship at the core of these values is fundamental and essential for the success of the entrepreneurial organisation. Values related to entrepreneurship include creativity, achievement, ownership, change and perseverance.

This is the first step, a necessary but not a sufficient condition. It underpins everything else. Beyond this, Bowman and Faulkner (1997) talk about organisational culture being formed or embedded in an organisation from three influences; organisational processes, cognitive processes and behaviours. All these influences are represented in Figure 17.16.

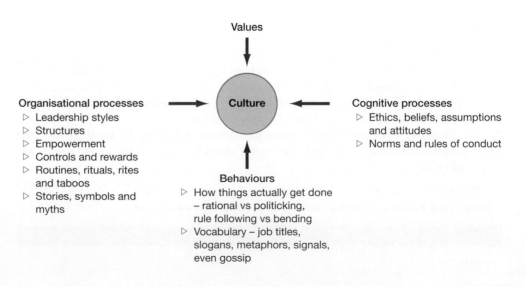

F17.16 Constructing culture

Organisational processes

These can be deliberate or emergent, evolving organically from within the organisation and may not be intended. There are many influences on this:

▷ The organisational structure can influence culture. Hierarchical organisations can discourage initiative. Functional specialisation can create parochial attitudes and sends signals about which skills might be valued.

▷ The power to make decisions is an important dimension for entrepreneurial organisations. Flat, decentralised structures send signals about encouraging decision-making, although sometimes informal power can lie outside formal hierarchies.

▷ Controls and rewards send important signals about what the firm values. People take notice of what behaviour gets rewarded – as well as what gets punished – and behave accordingly. Status, praise and public recognition are powerful motivators.

▷ Management and leadership styles, as we shall see later in the chapter, are an important influence. They send signals about appropriate behaviour. How managers allocate time sends signals about priorities.

▷ Routines and rituals can have a strong subconscious influence. They form the unquestioned fabric of everyday life, but they say a lot about the organisation.

▷ Stories and symbols have a part to play in preserving and perpetuating culture. Who are the heroes, villains and mavericks in the firm? What do staff talk about at lunch? Are there symbols of status that are important such as car or office size? How do staff talk about customers? How do staff talk about the entrepreneur and other senior managers?

Cognitive processes

These are the beliefs, assumptions and attitudes that staff hold in common and take for granted. They are embedded and emanate from the organisation's philosophy, values, morality and creed. As we have seen, CSR issues can resonate strongly with staff. These beliefs are likely to be strongest in firms that have a long history and where staff join young and stay in the firm for most of their careers.

Norms – rules or authoritative standards – in an organisation exist to enforce values and ensure conformity with the culture. An entrepreneurial firm may struggle with norms because one natural norm might well be to always ask the question 'why?', and to question the norms themselves. Because norms are questioned it is all the more important to have some deep values and beliefs underpinning the business. Morris and Kuratko (2002) talk about entrepreneurial organisations having a culture of 'healthy discontent' – one where there is a constant questioning, critiquing and changing of the way things are done. However, they do point out that this requires a balancing act, since too much discontent can easily become negative and destructive, and lead to political gamesmanship.

In a new, entrepreneurial firm these beliefs can be moulded and developed by the enthusiasm and personality of the entrepreneur. In larger firms this can be developed through more formal training and communication processes. They are strongly influenced by what the leaders in the organisation really pay attention to – not just what they say. But the important point is that they take time to frame. They do not happen overnight.

Behaviour

This is what actually happens in an organisation. It decides whether outcomes are rational, transparent or the result of politicking. It influences whether the organisation does actually follow rules, or is about bending them in the appropriate circumstances. Behaviour is about vocabulary – job titles, slogans, metaphors, signals, even gossip. Language is laden with value judgements that we do not realise most of the time – but they subconsciously influence the culture of the organisation. Take an extreme example – a 'private' in the army 'salutes' an 'officer'. What messages do the words and actions convey and what culture do they reinforce? So, what are the behaviours that reinforce the message that this is an entrepreneurial, in contrast to a bureaucratic, organisation?

Behaviour in organisations normally reflects and reinforces culture. However behaviour can also be influenced by a wide variety of external influences, within society as a whole, within a profession or within a sector or industry. Schneider and Barsoux (1997) observe that the culture in Nordic and Anglo-Saxon countries dictates that they frequently adopt 'controlling' strategies – rational-analytic with a desire to control the external environment – whereas the Latin Europeans and Asians tend to adopt 'adapting' strategies – with a belief in a less certain and less controllable environment. Behaviour that becomes routine can be difficult to change. However, attitudes can be influenced over time by getting people to behave in certain ways. Change behaviour first and attitudes will, eventually, follow.

Hofstede et al. (1990) looked at the different dimensions of organisational culture in an attempt to discriminate between entrepreneurial and what they called 'administrative' (or bureaucratic) organisations. These were not so much dimensions as descriptors of what an entrepreneurial culture might look like compared to an administrative or bureaucratic one. These descriptors are shown in Table 17.4. Most small firms start life with a 'task culture' – getting the job done and results achieved. If the entrepreneur finds it difficult to delegate that may turn into a 'power culture' – where people vie to have power and influence over the entrepreneur. As this sort of firm grows, especially if the delegated authority is not genuine, there is a danger of developing a 'role culture' whereby job titles become too important. These cultures are not conducive to success and are to be avoided.

Entrepreneurial	Administrative
▷ Results orientation	▷ Process orientation
▷ Job orientation	▷ Employee orientation
▷ Parochial interest	▷ Professional interest
▷ Open system	▷ Closed system
▷ Loose control	▷ Tight control
▷ Pragmatic orientation	▷ Normative orientation

Source: Hofstede et al. (1990).

T17.4 Entrepreneurial vs administrative cultures

Timmons (op. cit.) says that a successful entrepreneurial culture can be described along six dimensions:

▷ The degree of organisational clarity in terms of goals, tasks, procedures and so on;
▷ The degree to which high standards are expected;
▷ The extent to which employees are committed to the firm's goals;
▷ The extent to which they feel responsible for these goals without being constantly monitored;
▷ The extent to which they feel they are recognised and rewarded for high performance;
▷ The extent to which there is a sense of cohesion and team working within the firm.

An entrepreneurial culture needs to motivate people to do the right things, in the right way, for the organisation as well as for themselves. Entrepreneurs are good at doing this by example – 'walking the talk' – but as the firm grows they need to find different ways of communicating with more people. Equally simple things can tell you a lot about the culture of the firm. What impression does a firm with reserved parking spaces and managers in offices 'guarded' by secretaries give you? If salaries are based mainly on sales bonuses and there is a monthly league table of the best sales people, what does this tell you about the firm, its values and its goals? The culture of a firm comes from the entrepreneur, it reflects their personal values, but it is made up of a lot of small items of detail. Cultures can come about by chance, but if entrepreneurs want to plan for success, they need to plan to achieve the culture they want. And it is a vital element in maintaining the entrepreneurial focus in a larger organisation.

💡 Entrepreneurial leadership skills

Kirby (2003) likens entrepreneurial leaders to the leaders of jazz bands. They decide on the musicians to play in the band and the music to be played but then allow the band to improvise and use their creativity to create the required sounds. In the process they have fun as the leader brings out the best in them. The leader's authority comes from their expertise and values rather than their position. They lead by example – playing themselves. They empower their teams and nurture leaders at all levels – encouraging solo performances.

An entrepreneurial leader must combine many of the traditional skills of management with those of the entrepreneur. They must also reconcile the conflict between the impatience of the entrepreneur with the constraints imposed by an organisation in its desire to control events. That is where different structures can be important as well as the role of change agents such as intrapreneurs. The leader's role, however, is more than that of the change agent, championing individual initiatives. Pursuing innovative ideas may be exciting but the leader needs to give the firm a sense of direction and purpose by aligning these developments to the vision and direction of the organisation. That means standing back from the developments and providing a measure of impartial and objective evaluation. The leader must take an overview; reconciling differing perspectives – which may involve conflict resolution, creating

the focus on a low-cost/low-price marketing strategy has been maintained. The business model has been consistent and followed relentlessly:

▷ Sell directly to consumers;
▷ Keep prices low and quality high;
▷ Offer solid technological support to customers.

> 'We built the company around a systematic process: give customers the high-quality computers they want at a competitive price as quickly as possible, backed by great service.'

A custom-built Dell computer is shipped within 36 hours of being ordered through the company's website or by phone. The company maintains an extremely low inventory of computer parts, sufficient at any time to meet only a few days of orders. This strategy not only reduces costs but also the need for warehouse space as well as ensuring only the most up-to-date parts are in stock. The company's steady growth rate has been achieved by expanding its customer base in the USA and overseas – selling not just to individual consumers but also to large and small companies, educational institutions, and government agencies. The company has also expanded its product portfolio to include network servers, storage systems, handheld computers, HDTVs, cameras, printers, MP3 players and printers all built by other manufacturers.

> 'We were moving in the right direction with our emphasis on liquidity, profitability and growth. But we were also challenged by a cultural issue. We had created an atmosphere in which we focused on growth ... We had to shift to focus away from an external orientation to one that strengthened our company internally.
>
> For us growing up meant figuring out a way to combine our signature informal, entrepreneurial style and want-to attitude with the can-do capabilities that would allow us to develop as a company. It meant incorporating into our everyday structures the valuable lessons we'd begun to learn using P&Ls [profit and loss accounts]. It meant focusing our employees to think in terms of shareholder value. It meant respecting the three golden rules at Dell:
>
> 1. Disdain inventory.
> 2. Always listen to the customer.
> 3. Never sell indirect.'

Dell's mission is to be the most successful computer company in the world at delivering the best computer experience in markets we serve. In doing so, Dell sets out to meet customer expectations of:

▷ Highest quality;
▷ Leading technology;
▷ Competitive pricing;
▷ Individual and company accountability;
▷ Best-in-class service and support;
▷ Flexible customization capability;
▷ Superior corporate citizenship;
▷ Financial stability.

Dell calls its corporate philosophy the 'Soul of Dell'. It sees its core elements as:

▷ *Customers* – We believe in creating loyal customers by providing a superior experience at a greater value. We are committed to direct relationships, providing the best products and services based on standards-based technology, and outperforming the competition with value and a superior customer experience.

▷ *The Dell team* – We believe our continued success lies in teamwork and the opportunity each team member has to learn, develop and grow. We are committed to being a meritocracy, and to developing, retaining and attracting the best people, reflective of our worldwide market place.

▷ *Direct relationships* – We believe in being direct in all we do. We are committed to behaving ethically: responding to customer needs in a timely and reasonable manner; fostering open communications and building effective relationships with customers, partners, suppliers and each other; and operating without inefficient hierarchy and bureaucracy.

▷ *Global citizenship* – We believe in participating responsibly in the global market place. We are committed to understanding and respecting laws, values and cultures wherever we do business; profitably growing in all markets; promoting a healthy business climate globally; and contributing positively in every community we call home, both personally and organizationally.

▷ *Winning* – We have a passion for winning in everything we do. We are committed to operational excellence, superior customer experience, leading in the global markets we serve, being known as a great place to work, and providing superior shareholder value over time.

Michael Dell has always been keen on developing relationships – with customers, employees and suppliers. This underpins his direct selling strategy and his integrated supply chain network. Dell has been a pioneer of e-business. What makes Dell special today is its 'fully integrated value chain' – B2B2C. Suppliers, including many small firms, have real-time access to information about customer orders and deliveries via the company's extranet. They organise supplies of hard drives, motherboards, modems and so on, on a 'just-in-time' basis so as to keep the production line moving smoothly. From the parts being delivered to the orders being shipped out takes just a few hours. Inventories are minimised and, what is more, the cash is received from the customer before Dell pays its suppliers. Dell have created a three-way 'information partnership' between itself and its customers and suppliers by treating them as collaborators who together find ways of improving efficiency.

Courtesy of Dell Inc.

> 'The best way I know to establish and maintain a healthy, competitive culture is to partner with your people – through shared objectives and common strategies ... Dell is very much a relationship orientated company ... how we communicate and partner with our employees and customers. But our commitment doesn't stop there. Our willingness and ability to partner to achieve our common goals is perhaps seen in its purest form in how we forge strong alliances with our suppliers.'

Michael Dell has moved from being an entrepreneur, wheeling and dealing in cheap components, then innovating in direct marketing techniques, to being a visionary leader, understanding where his competitive advantage lies and then putting into place the systems and processes to keep his company two steps ahead of the competition. However, it has not always been like this. Michael's managerial experience was extremely limited. In the early days he was said to be most comfortable with the company's engineers. Although those who worked with him closely described him as likable, he was so shy that some employees thought he was aloof because he never talked to them. It was probably Lee Walker, a mature venture capitalist brought in during the company's organisation-building years, who gave Michael the insight into management and leadership that he needed and

➡

skills and exercise effective executive control. Non-executive directors are valuable in providing different skills, objectivity and a new network of contacts. They can be particularly valuable for family firms.

▷ An entrepreneurial organisation structure at start-up is a spider's web, with the entrepreneur at the centre. Whilst this may be flat and efficient, it only works up to a certain size. Entrepreneurs prefer informal structures and management styles relying on building personal relationships and influence. They lead by example. However, these elements combine to give the impression that they want to control everything and managers can find that this undermines their authority, and that can lead to frustration, even 'infantilisation'. Whilst avoiding bureaucracy, more formal structures need to be introduced as a business grows. The entrepreneur needs to recruit managers from outside and learn to delegate.

▷ Creating an appropriate culture in the firm is the most important, and probably the most difficult,

task. Culture is influenced by organisational and cognitive processes and behaviour. It can be based upon the entrepreneur's strongly held beliefs and values. It can be deliberate or emerge organically. Entrepreneurs 'infect' staff with a culture that motivates them to do the right things, in the right way. They create culture by example. However, as the firm grows culture can be influenced through training. Most firms start with a 'task culture' which can easily evolve into a 'power' or 'role' culture if care is not taken. An effective entrepreneurial culture involves:

▷ Clear goals;
▷ High standards;
▷ Commitment;
▷ Recognition;
▷ Team cohesion.

▷ As **Gary Redman** of **Now Recruitment** found, leaders of entrepreneurial organisations need the range of skills listed in Table 17.5. They need to use all the levers available to them to shape the organisation. Above all, however, they need good interpersonal skills.

⏻ **Further resources are available at www.palgrave.com/business/burns**

🗎 Essays and discussion topics

1 How do the role of and skills required by the founder change as the business grows?
2 Is the Greiner growth model an accurate predictor of the growth process?
3 How are the antecedent influences on an entrepreneur likely to improve their chances of successfully growing the firm?
4 What are the advantages and disadvantages of an entrepreneurial organisation?
5 What are the possible negative consequences of the internal locus of control that is characteristic of so many entrepreneurs.
6 Discuss how the typical entrepreneur's preference for physical intervention and informal, personal controls shows itself. Is this a good thing?
7 Critically evaluate the three growth models by Churchill and Lewis, Scott and Bruce, and Burns.

8 Is operational capability more important than strategic capability at start-up?
9 How is the marketing function likely to change as the firm grows?
10 As long as small firms are not homogeneous, growth models will not work. Discuss.
11 How are the recurrent crises facing the growing firm likely to affect the entrepreneur and how do they react to them?
12 How does the role of leader differ from that of entrepreneur?
13 What is culture and how can it be developed?
14 What is an entrepreneurial culture? Do Timmons' six dimensions adequately describe it?
15 What is the relationship between an entrepreneurial culture within a firm and an entrepreneurial national culture? Can one exist without the other?

▷ *The Dell team* – We believe our continued success lies in teamwork and the opportunity each team member has to learn, develop and grow. We are committed to being a meritocracy, and to developing, retaining and attracting the best people, reflective of our worldwide market place.

▷ *Direct relationships* – We believe in being direct in all we do. We are committed to behaving ethically: responding to customer needs in a timely and reasonable manner; fostering open communications and building effective relationships with customers, partners, suppliers and each other; and operating without inefficient hierarchy and bureaucracy.

▷ *Global citizenship* – We believe in participating responsibly in the global market place. We are committed to understanding and respecting laws, values and cultures wherever we do business; profitably growing in all markets; promoting a healthy business climate globally; and contributing positively in every community we call home, both personally and organizationally.

▷ *Winning* – We have a passion for winning in everything we do. We are committed to operational excellence, superior customer experience, leading in the global markets we serve, being known as a great place to work, and providing superior shareholder value over time.

Courtesy of Dell Inc.

Michael Dell has always been keen on developing relationships – with customers, employees and suppliers. This underpins his direct selling strategy and his integrated supply chain network. Dell has been a pioneer of e-business. What makes Dell special today is its 'fully integrated value chain' – D2B2C. Suppliers, including many small firms, have real-time access to information about customer orders and deliveries via the company's extranet. They organise supplies of hard drives, motherboards, modems and so on, on a 'just-in-time' basis so as to keep the production line moving smoothly. From the parts being delivered to the orders being shipped out takes just a few hours. Inventories are minimised and, what is more, the cash is received from the customer before Dell pays its suppliers. Dell have created a three-way 'information partnership' between itself and its customers and suppliers by treating them as collaborators who together find ways of improving efficiency.

> 'The best way I know to establish and maintain a healthy, competitive culture is to partner with your people – through shared objectives and common strategies ... Dell is very much a relationship orientated company ... how we communicate and partner with our employees and customers. But our commitment doesn't stop there. Our willingness and ability to partner to achieve our common goals is perhaps seen in its purest form in how we forge strong alliances with our suppliers.'

Michael Dell has moved from being an entrepreneur, wheeling and dealing in cheap components, then innovating in direct marketing techniques, to being a visionary leader, understanding where his competitive advantage lies and then putting into place the systems and processes to keep his company two steps ahead of the competition. However, it has not always been like this. Michael's managerial experience was extremely limited. In the early days he was said to be most comfortable with the company's engineers. Although those who worked with him closely described him as likable, he was so shy that some employees thought he was aloof because he never talked to them. It was probably Lee Walker, a mature venture capitalist brought in during the company's organisation-building years, who gave Michael the insight into management and leadership that he needed and

→

gave him the instinct for motivating people and winning their loyalty and respect. He can delegate effectively and believes in team working.

> 'The right people in the right jobs are instrumental to a company's success ... If you assume that people can grow at the same rate as your company – and still maintain the sharp focus that is critical to success – you will be sadly disappointed. When a business is growing quickly, many jobs grow laterally in responsibility, becoming too big and complex for even the most ambitious, hard-working person to handle without sacrificing personal career development or becoming burned out ... The ability to find and hire the right people can make or break your business. It is as plain as that. No matter where you are in the life cycle of your business, bringing in great talent should always be a top priority.'

He is an accomplished speaker and his quiet, reflective manner now gives him an air of maturity. However, this probably disguises the competitive personality who has taken risks to make his business grow.

> 'Communicating is one of the most important tools in recovering from mistakes. When you tell someone, be it a designer, a customer, or the CEO of the company, 'Look, we've got a problem. Here's how we're going to fix it,' you diffuse the fear of the unknown and focus on the solution.'

In 2004 Michael Dell stepped aside as CEO of Dell while retaining his position as Chairman of the Board, Kevin Rollins became the new CEO. But under Kevin Rollins the company struggled – revenue targets were missed, the share price suffered and Dell lost its coveted number one position in the PC market to Hewlett-Packard. In 2007 the board decided it wanted Michael Dell back as CEO.

According to *Director* magazine (April 2009) Kevin Rollins had kept 'an emotional distance' from staff and Michael Dell's team building track record made him ideal to 'glue the company back together again'. However, it reported that John Enck, managing vice-president of research analysts Gartner, thought Michael Dell had changed his management style to become more inclusive: 'I've seen a big difference in the two reigns ... The leadership of Dell isn't as autocratic as it used to be. When Michael was originally CEO he was the decision-maker. Coming back, he created a leadership board and did a very good job of delegating decisions and responsibility to his executive team. That will theoretically allow Dell to be more nimble.' *Director* magazine also reported that Michael Dell did not agree: 'That question assumes that during the entire 20-year period I only used one approach, which would be wrong. I constantly adjust my approach and way of doing things based on all the inputs and opportunities that I see.'

Michael has reverted to his tried and tested strategies: cutting costs, improving customer service (which had slipped very noticeably), introducing new products and investing in innovation. By 2009 he had made ten acquisitions, cut more than 10 000 jobs, outsourced 40 per cent of production and entered the smart phone market in China. Product inspiration now also comes from a Dell community website – www.ideastorm.com – that allows customers to identify and vote on new lines, while also rating current ones. The goal is to diversify beyond the mature PC market, which still accounts for more than half of revenues, into new markets such as computer storage and services. At the same time Dell is trying to enter new market sectors – for example by the purchase of Perot Systems in 2009 which enabled it to enter the health care sector.

Will Michael Dell pull his company around? Time will tell.

Courtesy of Dell Inc.

☐ Up-to-date information on Dell can be found on their website: www.dell.com

QUESTIONS

1 What characteristics of an entrepreneur and a leader does Michael Dell exhibit?

2 Why has Dell been successful, at least until Michael Dell stepped down as CEO?

3 What do you think about Michael Dell's final comments about varying his management style?

▷ Summary

▷ As they develop, firms typically go through a period of growth, followed by crisis and then a period of consolidation. In going through each crisis the entrepreneur faces a roller coaster of human emotion that they may not be able to handle. The classic change/denial curve seeks to describe their emotions at each stage. This range of feelings was expressed by **David Poole** of **DP&A**.

▷ Greiner's growth model predicts the causes of growth and the associated crises a firm will face as it grows. These are:

1 Growth through creativity leading to crisis of leadership.
2 Growth through direction leading to crisis of autonomy.
3 Growth through delegation leading to crisis of control.
4 Growth through coordination leading to crisis of red tape.

▷ The Churchill and Lewis growth model summarises management style, organisational characteristics, formality of systems and major strategies at different stages of the firm's life. It distinguishes between lifestyle and growth firms at the 'success' stage and highlights the changes that take place at this point for the different types of firm. It emphasises the importance of the entrepreneur's strategic abilities, compared to their operating abilities, as the firm grows.

▷ As firms grow the role of the founder needs to change. Like **Michael Dell**, the founder needs to metamorphosise into a leader. This change is not easy. Some choose to only do what they enjoy and are good at – start-ups – and become serial entrepreneurs.

▷ A job definition for a leader would include five elements:

1 Vision and ideas;
2 Strategic planning;
3 Effective communication;
4 Creation of culture;
5 Monitoring and controlling performance.

▷ Entrepreneurs are defined by Timmons (1999) as 'patient leaders, capable of instilling tangible visions and managing for the long haul … a learner and a teacher, a doer and a visionary.' Having and communicating a vision is a key skill of both entrepreneurship and leadership. Developing the vision is a continuous process, checking with staff that it resonates with them, modifying it to suit changing circumstances.

▷ Leadership stems from authority. Entrepreneurial authority, in the main, comes from expertise. There is no single best leadership style. The appropriate style depends upon the leader, the group, the task and the situation or context they are in. An autocratic or dictatorial style is unlikely to be appropriate in the context of a growing firm. Entrepreneurial leaders must be adept at using informal influence to get their way. Entrepreneurs must also be adept at resolving conflict, through a collaborative or compromising approach.

▷ Picking a good team is not just about selecting people with appropriate functional skills. It is also about assembling a mix of different personalities. Belbin identified nine characteristics that need to be present to form an effective team: shaper, plant, coordinator, resource investigator, monitor-evaluator, team-worker, implementer, completer-finisher and specialist. Building a team takes time and the team is likely to go through a four-stage process in its development:

1 Testing;
2 Infighting;
3 Getting organised;
4 Mature effectiveness.

▷ The board of directors becomes an increasingly important team as a company grows. Its most important functions are strategy and policy formulation. It also has to monitor the performance of management and provide accountability to stakeholders. Members therefore need to be able to give that strategic direction, develop organisational culture, practise 'human' skills and exercise effective executive control. Non-executive directors are valuable in providing different skills, objectivity and a new network of contacts. They can be particularly valuable for family firms.

▷ An entrepreneurial organisation structure at start-up is a spider's web, with the entrepreneur at the centre. Whilst this may be flat and efficient, it only works up to a certain size. Entrepreneurs prefer informal structures and management styles relying on building personal relationships and influence. They lead by example. However, these elements combine to give the impression that they want to control everything and managers can find that this undermines their authority, and that can lead to frustration, even 'infantilisation'. Whilst avoiding bureaucracy, more formal structures need to be introduced as a business grows. The entrepreneur needs to recruit managers from outside and learn to delegate.

▷ Creating an appropriate culture in the firm is the most important, and probably the most difficult,

task. Culture is influenced by organisational and cognitive processes and behaviour. It can be based upon the entrepreneur's strongly held beliefs and values. It can be deliberate or emerge organically. Entrepreneurs 'infect' staff with a culture that motivates them to do the right things, in the right way. They create culture by example. However, as the firm grows culture can be influenced through training. Most firms start with a 'task culture' which can easily evolve into a 'power' or 'role' culture if care is not taken. An effective entrepreneurial culture involves:

▷ Clear goals;
▷ High standards;
▷ Commitment;
▷ Recognition;
▷ Team cohesion.

▷ As **Gary Redman** of **Now Recruitment** found, leaders of entrepreneurial organisations need the range of skills listed in Table 17.5. They need to use all the levers available to them to shape the organisation. Above all, however, they need good interpersonal skills.

⏻ **Further resources are available at www.palgrave.com/business/burns**

🗎 Essays and discussion topics

1 How do the role of and skills required by the founder change as the business grows?
2 Is the Greiner growth model an accurate predictor of the growth process?
3 How are the antecedent influences on an entrepreneur likely to improve their chances of successfully growing the firm?
4 What are the advantages and disadvantages of an entrepreneurial organisation?
5 What are the possible negative consequences of the internal locus of control that is characteristic of so many entrepreneurs.
6 Discuss how the typical entrepreneur's preference for physical intervention and informal, personal controls shows itself. Is this a good thing?
7 Critically evaluate the three growth models by Churchill and Lewis, Scott and Bruce, and Burns.

8 Is operational capability more important than strategic capability at start-up?
9 How is the marketing function likely to change as the firm grows?
10 As long as small firms are not homogeneous, growth models will not work. Discuss.
11 How are the recurrent crises facing the growing firm likely to affect the entrepreneur and how do they react to them?
12 How does the role of leader differ from that of entrepreneur?
13 What is culture and how can it be developed?
14 What is an entrepreneurial culture? Do Timmons' six dimensions adequately describe it?
15 What is the relationship between an entrepreneurial culture within a firm and an entrepreneurial national culture? Can one exist without the other?

16 Is there such a thing as an effective leadership style for a growing business?

17 Why is an ability to handle conflict important in the growing firm?

18 How do you build an effective team?

19 How do you generate trust?

20 What is the role of the non-executive director? How important are they for the growing firm?

21 Leaders are born not made. Discuss.

22 In what contexts might Lessem's five entrepreneurial archetypes succeed?

☝ Exercises and assignments

1 List the questions you would ask an entrepreneur who has successfully grown their business to try to assess how they and the skills they have needed have changed as the firm grew.

2 Based upon these questions, interview a successful entrepreneur and write an essay describing the changes they have faced and how they coped.

3 Based upon a small firm with about a dozen employees, draw the formal organisation chart and then, based upon interviews with employees, draw the informal organisation.

4 Answer the Leadership Styles Questionnaire on the website and plot your score on the Leadership Grid at the end of this chapter.

5 Obtain the Thomas–Kilmann Conflict Mode Instrument and evaluate how you handle conflict.

6 Obtain the Belbin Instrument and evaluate your preferred team roles.

📖 References

Adair, J. (1984) *The Skills of Leadership*, London: Gower.

Adizes, I. (1978) 'Organizational Passages: Diagnosing and Treating Life Cycle Problems of Organizations', Organizational Dynamics, Summer.

Allday, D. (1997) *Check-a-Board: Helping Boards and Directors become More Effective*, London: Institute of Management.

Bennis, W. and Nanus, B. (1985) *Leaders: The Strategies for Taking Charge*, New York: Harper & Row.

Belbin, R.M. (1981) *Management Teams – Why They Succeed and Fail*, London: Heinemann Professional Publishing.

Blake, R. and Mouton, J. (1978) *The New Managerial Grid*, London: Gulf.

Blank, W. (1995) *The Nine Laws of Leadership*, New York: AMACOM.

Blau, P.M. (1970) 'A Formal Theory of Differentiation in Organisations', *American Sociological Review*, 35(2).

Bowman, C. and Faulkner, D.O. (1997) *Competitive and Corporate Strategy*, London: Irwin.

Burns, P. (1996) 'Growth', in P. Burns and J. Dewhurst (eds), *Small Business and Entrepreneurship*, London: Macmillan – now Basingstoke: Palgrave Macmillan.

Burns, P. and Whitehouse, O. (1996) 'Managers in Europe', European Venture Capital Journal, 45, April/May.

Burns, T. and Stalker, G.M. (1961) *The Management of Innovation*, London: Tavistock.

Chandler, A.D. (1962) *Strategy and Structure: Chapters in the History of the American Industrial Enterprise*, Cambridge, MA: MIT Press.

Chell, E. (2001) *Entrepreneurship: Globalization, Innovation and Development*, London: Thomson Learning.

Churchill, N.C. and Lewis, V.L. (1983) 'The Five Stages of Small Business Growth', *Harvard Business Review*, May/June.

du Toit, D.E. (1980) 'Confessions of a Successful Entrepreneur', *Harvard Business Review*, November/December.

Emery, F.E. and Trist, E.L. (1965) 'The Causal Texture of Organisational Environments', *Human Relations*, 18.

Galbraith, J.R. (1973) *Designing Complex Organisations*, Reading, Mass: Addison-Wesley.

Gardner, H. (1995) *Leading Minds: An Anatomy of Leadership*, New York: John Wiley.

Greiner, L.E. (1972) 'Evolution and Revolution as Organisations Grow', *Harvard Business Review*, July/August.

Haige, J. and Aiken, M. (1967) 'Relationship of Centralisation to other Structural Properties', *Administrative Science Quarterly*, 12.

Hofstede, G., Neuijen B., Ohayv, D. D. and Sanders, G. (1990) 'Measuring Organizational Cultures: A Qualitative and Quantitative Study across Twenty Cases', *Administrative Sciences Quarterly*, 35.

Kakabadse, A. (1983) *The Politics of Management*, London: Gower.

Kets de Vries, M.F.R. (1985) 'The Dark Side of Entrepreneurship', *Harvard Business Review*, November/December.

Kirby, D. (2003) *Entrepreneurship*, London: McGraw Hill.

Kotter, P. (1996) *Leading Change*, Boston: Harvard Business School Press.

Lawrence, P.R. and Lorsch, J.W. (1967) *Organisation and Environment: Managing Differentiation and Integration*, Boston MA: Division of Research, Graduate School of Business, Harvard University.

Lessem, R. (1987) *Intrapreneurship*, Aldershot: Gower.

Morris, M.H. and Kuratko, D.F. (2002) *Corporate Entrepreneurship*, Orlando: Harcourt College Publishers.

Perrow, C. (1967) 'A Framework for the Comparative Analysis of Organisations', *American Sociological Review*, 32.

Pugh, D.S. and Hickson, D.J. (1976) *Organisational Structure in its Context: The Aston Programme 1*, Farnborough, Hants: Saxon House.

Pugh, D.S. Hickson, D.J. and Hinings, C.R. (1969) 'The Context of Organisation Structures', *Administrative Science Quarterly*, 13.

Ray, G.H. and Hutchinson, P.J. (1983) *The Financing and Financial Control of Small Enterprise Development*, London: Gower.

Schein, E.H. (1990) 'Organisational Culture', *American Psychologist*, February.

Schneider, S. C. and Barsoux, J.-L. (1997) *Managing across Cultures*, London: Prentice Hall.

Scott, M. and Bruce, R. (1987) 'Five Stages of Growth in Small Businesses', *Long Range Planning*, 20(3).

Senge, P. M. (1992) *The Fifth Discipline*, London: Century Business.

Spence, L.J. (2000) *Priorities, Practice and Ethics in Small Firms*, London: The Institute of Business Ethics.

Stinchcombe, A.L. (1959) 'Social Structure and Organisation', in J.G. March (ed.), *Handbook of Organisations*, Chicago: Rand McNally.

Timmons, J.A. (1999) *New Venture Creation: Entrepreneurship for the 21st Century*, Singapore: Irwin/McGraw Hill.

Weber, M. (1947) *The Theory of Social and Economic Organisation*, Glencoe, IL: The Free Press.

Woodward, J. (1965) *Industrial Organisation: Behaviour and Control*, Oxford: Oxford University Press.

18 Corporate entrepreneurship

▷ **Defining corporate entrepreneurship**
▷ **Entrepreneurial architecture**
▷ **Learning organisations**
▷ **Building the architecture for entrepreneurial transformation**
▷ **The role of culture**
▷ **The role of structure**
▷ **Management, structure and control**
▷ **Intrapreneurship**
▷ **Organising new venture ideas**
▷ **Corporate venturing**
▷ **Summary**

Case insights
▷ Julian Metcalf, Sinclair Beecham and Pret a Manger
▷ Richard Branson's Virgin Group

Cases with questions
▷ David Hall and HFL
▷ Nokia
▷ 3M

Learning outcomes

By the end of this chapter you should be able to:

▷ Explain what is meant by the term 'corporate entrepreneurship' and the basic schools of thought that have contributed to its development;

▷ Explain what is meant by the term 'entrepreneurial architecture', how it might be shaped and how it might lead to sustainable competitive advantage in the appropriate environment;

▷ Explain what is meant by the term 'learning organisation' and how it underpins the entrepreneurial architecture in a larger firm;

▷ Explain what is meant by the term 'entrepreneurial management' and the differences between it and traditional management;

▷ Explain what an entrepreneurial culture means in an organisation and how it can be measured;

▷ Explain how structure and size can encourage and contribute to the development of corporate entrepreneurship;

▷ Describe the balance between freedom and control needed in an entrepreneurial organisation and explain the dimensions on which it can be measured;

▷ Describe the role of the intrapreneur in larger entrepreneurial firms;

▷ Explain how organisations might encourage and facilitate the work of the intrapreneur;

▷ Describe the options for dealing with new venture developments and explain which are best in different circumstances;

▷ Explain why large organisations undertake corporate venturing and what is needed to make such a strategy successful.

♀ Defining corporate entrepreneurship

Greiner (1972) predicts that the final crisis facing a business is one of 'red tape' or bureaucracy – the loss of its entrepreneurial nature (see previous chapter). And with the loss of entrepreneurship there is the danger that the firm will cease to change and innovate. But is this inevitable? Can it be delayed or even prevented? In fact, many truly successful innovations, particularly product innovations but certainly the ones involving large amounts of capital, originate from large not small companies. There are few Dysons in this world who successfully struggle to bring a genuinely new product to the market themselves, against all the odds. (James Dyson invented a completely new 'cyclone' vacuum cleaner and then successfully claimed against Hoover for infringing his patents with their 'vortex' cleaner.) There are just too many problems to sort out – not least of which is finding the finance. Moreover it is easier for a middle or large company to sort out these problems because it has more resources, more experience – more of everything to throw at a problem.

There is a real need for corporate entrepreneurs at the moment. For too long the prevailing consensus has been if it ain't broke, don't fix it but entrepreneurs recognise that action and change are crucial for maximising potential and taking advantage of opportunities. You have to be tough and outgoing and not afraid of leaving calm waters to ride the waves of a storm. I consider myself to be a corporate entrepreneur. I have not created the company I am in charge of, but I have changed the way it is run and have made a real difference. I think times have changed and entrepreneurs don't have to be totally out on a limb. There are plenty of opportunities for entrepreneurialism in large companies too.

☐ Diane Thompson, Chief Executive, Camelot (also founder of an advertising agency), *Sunday Times* 17 March 2002

Incremental improvements to products and services are one thing. They can be addressed systematically. But these changes, important as they are, do not conquer new markets. Often what is needed is the mould-breaking innovation and big companies can put bureaucratic barriers in the way of this. When the personal computer was first introduced it was considered simply a toy and the market leader in computers, IBM, ignored it for many years. However, the personal computer turned the whole computer industry on its head and nearly caused the demise of IBM. Not only did IBM not lead in this major innovation, it also tried to ignore it – and paid the price.

'Corporate entrepreneurship' is the term used to describe entrepreneurial behaviour in an established, larger organisation. The objective of this is simple – to gain competitive advantage by encouraging innovation at all levels in the organisation – corporation, division, business unit, functional or project team levels. Even as late as the 1980s some academics still believed it was difficult, if not impossible, for entrepreneurial activity to take place in larger, bureaucratic organisations (Morse, 1986). Nevertheless there is a large literature on the general phenomenon stretching back over 30 years. Despite this there is no real consensus on what the term means. Vesper (1984) suggested it was characterised by three activities:

▷ The creation of new business units by an established firm;
▷ The development and implementation of entrepreneurial strategic thrusts;
▷ The emergence of new ideas from various levels in the organisation.

In the years ahead all big companies will find it increasingly difficult to compete with – and in general will perform more poorly than – smaller, speedier, more innovative companies. The mindset that in a huge global economy the multinationals dominate world business couldn't have been more wrong. The bigger and more open the world economy becomes, the more small and middle-sized companies will dominate. In one of the major turnarounds of my lifetime, we have moved from economies of scale to 'diseconomies of scale'; from bigger is better to bigger is inefficient, costly, wastefully bureaucratic, inflexible, and, now, disastrous. And the paradox is that that has occurred as we move to a global context: The smaller and speedier players will prevail on a much expanded field … Corporations have to dismantle bureaucracies to survive. Economies of scale are giving way to economies of scope, finding the right size for synergy, market flexibility and, above all, speed.

☐ John Naisbitt, entrepreneur and author, 1994

Notwithstanding this, Zahra (1991) still defined corporate entrepreneurship as 'activities aimed at creating new businesses in established companies'. Guth and Ginsberg (1990) expanded this to include 'transformation of organisations through strategic renewal' and Zahra et al. (1999) have since suggested that there are many facets to entrepreneurship at firm level which reflect different combinations of:

▷ The content of entrepreneurship – corporate venturing, innovation, proactivity;
▷ The sources of entrepreneurship – both internal and external;
▷ The focus of entrepreneurship – formal or informal.

These views cover a wide range. Trying to pull together the different strands, Birkinshaw (2003) identified four strands of the literature that he calls 'basic schools of thought':

1 Corporate venturing;
2 Intrapreneurship;
3 Bringing the market inside';
4 Entrepreneurial transformation.

Corporate venturing

This is concerned with larger businesses needing to manage new, entrepreneurial businesses separately from the mainstream activity. It is concerned with investment by larger firms in strategically important smaller firms and different forms of corporate venturing units (Chesbrough, 2002). The reasons for doing so rarely involve short-term financial gain but more normally relate to issues of innovation and strategic foresight. Small firms are often good at innovation and larger firms therefore have to buy them out to capitalise on their 'first-mover advantage' in a critical area of new technology development. This happens frequently in the pharmaceutical industry. It

---

📋 Case insight Julian Metcalfe, Sinclair Beecham and Pret a Manger

Julian Metcalfe and Sinclair Beecham opened their first Pret A Manger sandwich bar in Victoria Street, central London, in 1986. They made sandwiches in the basement from fresh ingredients bought every morning at Covent Garden market. They built Pret on the simple concept of providing gourmet, fresh and organic fast food in modern, clean surroundings. Pret now sells sandwiches, baguettes, soups, salads, coffees and desserts. It still emphasises its use of fresh, natural ingredients only. Sandwiches are made on the day of purchase in kitchens at the location. Those not sold on the day they are made are given to charity. The formula has proved successful.

By 2001 Pret had 103 stores in the UK and one in New York, producing a turnover of £100 million and profits of £3.6 million. But Pret does not franchise and finding the funding for expansion was proving challenging. However it came as quite a surprise when McDonald's bought a non-controlling 33 per cent interest in the company for an estimated £26 million. The motives were simple enough. McDonald's could provide not only cash but also the support for Pret's

global expansion plans and they were happy not to change the Pret formula in any way. McDonald's, who also owned the Aroma coffee bar chain, saw this as a strategic purchase that would advance their long-term strategy of gaining a greater share of the diverse informal eating-out market and spreading their product portfolio into newer, higher-growth market segments.

In February 2008 Julian and Sinclair sold Pret for £345 million to private equity firm Bridgepoint and US investment bank, Goldman Sachs, retaining 25 per cent of the company for management. McDonald's sold its share in the company as part of the deal. The buy-out firm said it intended to change Pret 'from a domestic to an international business through controlled expansion of its already profitable but small US presence'. There are now some 225 shops worldwide but more than three-quarters of them are in the UK and less than 30 are in the USA.

☐ Up-to-date information on Prét a Manger can be found on their website: www.pret.com

also happens far more in the USA than in the UK with firms like General Electric, Monsanto, Xerox, Apple, IBM and Kyocera being particularly active.

Corporate venturing is also concerned with the organisational structures needed to encourage new businesses whilst aligning them to the company's existing activities (Galbraith, 1982; Burgelman, 1983; Drucker, 1985). It also deals with how companies can manage disruptive technologies (Christensen, 1997). We shall return to corporate venturing later in this chapter.

Intrapreneurship

This is concerned with individual employees and how they might be encouraged to act in an entrepreneurial way within a larger organisation. They are entrepreneurs in larger organisations. Rarely the inventor of the product, they work with teams to cut through the bureaucracy of the organisation to develop the product for the market place as quickly as possible. They share many of the characteristics of the entrepreneur, and may ultimately become the managing director of a company set up by its larger parent to exploit the idea. However, essentially, like Art Frye with his Post-It Notes at 3M (see Case at the end of this chapter), intrapreneurs work within the larger organisation and will have come from within it. They are therefore likely to be hybrids, having to work hard to create entrepreneurial structures and cultures around them, but always having to communicate with the more bureaucratic organisation that employs them.

The literature looks at the systems, structures and cultures that inhibit this activity and how they might be circumvented or even challenged. It is concerned with the character and personality of this strange hybrid of entrepreneur and 'company-man'. The term was introduced and popularised by Gifford Pinchot (1985) building on the earlier work of Ross Kanter (1982, 2004). In many ways it was this school that launched the idea that large organisations could change and be something different to what, all too often, they had become. We shall return to it later in this chapter.

Bringing the market inside

This focuses mainly on the structural changes needed to encourage entrepreneurial behaviour and argues for a market approach to resource allocation and people management systems using market-based techniques such as spin-offs and venture capital operations (Hamel, 1999; Foster and Kaplan, 2001). For example, Monsanto, Apple, 3M and Xerox use independent venture capital conduits to finance their spin-outs from in-house research. We shall look at how new venture ideas coming out of larger organisations might be organised later in this chapter.

Entrepreneurial transformation

The premise behind this strand of literature is that large firms need to adapt to an ever-changing environment if they are to survive, and to do so they need to adapt their structures and cultures so as to encourage entrepreneurial activity in individual employees (Peters and Waterman, 1982; Kanter, 1989; Tushman and O'Reilly, 1996; Ghoshal and Bartlett, 1997). According to this school individual behaviour is fashioned by the leadership, strategy, systems, structures and culture in the organisation – called by Burns (2005) 'the entrepreneurial architecture'. To the writers in this school the previous three 'schools' are simply techniques that can help bring about the entrepreneurial transformation. To understand how an entrepreneurial architecture can be created, we need to first understand the term architecture.

♀ Entrepreneurial architecture

Architecture is the term originally used by John Kay (1993) to describe the relational contracts within and around the organisation – with customers, suppliers and staff. These are long-term relationships, although not necessarily just legal contracts, which are only partly specified and only really enforced by the need of the parties to work together. Like all relationships, architecture is based upon mutual trust, although underpinned by mutual self-interest. This self-interest discourages one party from acting in some way at the expense of another because it is important that they continue to work together. We have already stressed the importance of relationships in the way the entrepreneur does business.

Just as entrepreneurs use networks of relationships to help them operate in a way that allows them to seize opportunities quickly, architecture allows the entrepreneurial firm to respond quickly and effectively to change and opportunity. Developing organisational architecture is a systematic exploitation of one of the main distinctive capabilities of entrepreneurs. It builds in dynamic capabilities that are difficult to copy. It does this by creating within the organisation the knowledge and routines that enable this to happen smoothly and unhindered. Staff are somehow motivated in themselves to make this happen, knowing it is good for the organisation – what has been called empowerment. Architecture can create barriers to entry and competitive advantage by institutionalising these relationships. It is difficult to copy because it is not a legal contract and not written down anywhere, relying instead on the complex network of personal relationships throughout the organisation. Architecture is created partly through appropriate strategies, partly through appropriate structures, but mainly through developing the appropriate culture in the organisation.

Using examples of small and large organisations, Kay emphasises that architecture comprises patterns of long-term relationships which are 'complex, subtle and hard to define precisely or to replicate' and he observes that it is easier to sustain than to create and even more difficult to create in an organisation that does not have it in the first place. Individuals participate in these relationships voluntarily because of a strong personal feeling that it is in their interests because they are participating in a 'repeated game' in which they share the rewards of collective achievement. The relationships solve problems of cooperation, coordination and commitment. They set the rules of the game and if you cheat you would find it difficult to play the game again with the same players. These relationships are characterised as having a high but structured degree of informality, something that can be mistaken as haphazard, chaotic or just lucky. But, as Kay points out, 'truly chaotic organisations rarely perform well' and, as we have seen, entrepreneurs create their own luck. In this way the architecture is distinctive and difficult to copy because individuals only know or understand a small part of the overall structure.

With this description we start to glimpse reflections of the start-up entrepreneur in the middle of a spider's web of informal, personal relationships, recognising opportunity everywhere, trying to innovate and trying to replicate success, using networks, relying on personal relationships with customers, staff and suppliers. They prefer influence and informal relationships to formal contracts. They use these to secure repeat sales at the expense of competitors and to secure resources or competitive advantage that they might not otherwise have. Close partnerships with suppliers where information and knowledge are shared can lead to significant advantages in lowering costs, lead times and inventories. All these relationships are based on trust – 'my word is my bond' – and most involve a degree of self-interest. The challenge is to replicate these relationships across the organisation and develop that entrepreneurial architecture.

Kay (op. cit.) sees no conflict in the need for stability and continuity in relationships and the equal need for change and flexibility in an entrepreneurial firm:

> It is within the context of long-term relationships, and often only within that context that the development of organisational knowledge, the free exchange of information, and a readiness to respond quickly and flexibly can be sustained.

And here lies an important by-product of this architecture – it creates organisational learning and knowledge that can be used to create competitive advantage. Entrepreneurs learn by doing, and they learn quickly not to repeat mistakes but to capitalise on success. Because they are one person, knowledge and learning is transferred continuously, quickly and without barriers. As the organisation grows the challenge is for knowledge and learning to continue to be transferred in this way. But how do you translate what happens in the brain of one person into the operations of an entire organisation? And what does learning really mean? The answer to this lies in the concept of the 'learning organisation'.

♀ Learning organisations

The person most associated with the concept of learning organisations is Peter Senge. His book, *The Fifth Discipline: The Art and Science of the Learning Organisation* (1990), was a loose collection of ideas about change, learning and communication drawn from an eclectic variety of sources. However the central concept was inherently attractive:

> As the world becomes more interconnected and business becomes more complex and dynamic, work must become more 'learningful' … It is no longer sufficient to have one person learning for the organisation … It's just not possible any longer to 'figure it out' from the top, and have everyone else following the orders of the 'grand strategist'. The organisations that will truly excel in the future will be the organisations that discover how to tap people's commitment and capacity to learn at all levels in the organisation.

If the grand strategist is the entrepreneur, then you can see that the challenge is one of making the whole organisation entrepreneurial. A learning organisation has been defined as one that 'facilitates the learning of all its members and continuously transforms itself … adapting, changing, developing and transforming themselves in response to the needs, wishes and aspirations of people, inside and outside' (Pedler et al., 1991). Writings on the learning organisation stress how it is flexible, adaptable and better equipped to thrive in a turbulent environment – the very environment that entrepreneurs and

There are countless successful companies that are thriving now despite the fact that they started with little more than passion and a good idea. There are also many that have failed, for the very same reason. The difference is that the thriving companies gathered the knowledge that gave them the substantial edge over their competition, which they then used to improve their execution, whatever their product or service … The key is not so much one great idea or patent as it is the execution and implementation of a great strategy.

☐ Michael Dell (1999)

entrepreneurial firms inhabit. A learning organisation facilitates learning for all its members and continually transforms itself:

▷ Encouraging systematic problem-solving;
▷ Encouraging experimentation and new approaches;
▷ Learning from past experience and history;
▷ Learning from best practice and outside experience;
▷ Being skilled at transferring knowledge in the organisation.

Peter Senge (1992) even observes that learning organisations can only be built by leaders with fire and passion: 'Learning organisations can be built only by individuals who put their life spirit into the task.' The similarity to the entrepreneur is striking. Indeed the similarities can also be seen from the literature about entrepreneurs. Timmons (1999) says successful entrepreneurs are: 'patient leaders, capable of instilling tangible visions and managing for the long haul. The entrepreneur is at once a learner and a teacher, a doer and a visionary.' Being a learner and a teacher are two of the prime tasks for a leader in a learning organisation. Truly entrepreneurial organisations, therefore, are in fact learning organisations. This goes to the heart of their architecture.

A learning organisation thrives in turbulent and changing environments. It is fast and responsive. It requires unitarism – a belief that the interests of the organisation and the individual are the same. Shared values are at the core of this, as is being part of a team or an 'ingroup' (terminology used by Hofstede in his analysis of culture and explained later in this chapter). This results in staff feeling empowered to influence the direction of the organisation and believing that continually developing, learning and acquiring new knowledge is the way to do this.

Continually developing, learning and acquiring new knowledge is therefore at the heart of a learning organisation. But knowledge is about more than just information sharing. It is about learning from each other and from outside the organisation. It is about a better understanding of inter-relationships, complexities and causalities. Daniel Kim (1993) suggests that effective learning can be considered to be a revolving wheel – the wheel of learning (Figure 18.1). During half the cycle, you test existing concepts and observe what happens through experience – learning 'know-how'. In the second half of the cycle, you are reflecting on the observations and forming new

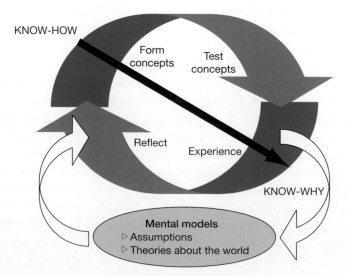

F18.1 The wheel of learning and our mental models

concepts – learning 'know-why'. This is often called 'double-loop learning'. It is this second sort of learning that is of particular value to the organisation because it is at this point that root causes of problems are diagnosed and systematic solutions put in place.

So real learning is about application, continuous problem-solving, and understanding the root cause of problems rather than being distracted by the symptoms. It is about continually challenging the mental models we hold – deeply-held beliefs about how the world works that are shaped by our experiences and shape our experiences. It occurs when people within organisations share, explore and challenge their mental models. When this happens the wheel of learning both affects and is affected by our mental models, shown in Figure 18.1. Once we start to share our knowledge of know-how and/or know-why with others, organisational learning takes place. The difficulties in doing this increase with the size of the organisation. However, the constantly increasing amount of know-how and know-why, accumulated through years of turning the wheel of learning and sharing of mental models, becomes part of the collective memory of the organisation. Although this accumulated knowledge is tacit, shadowy and fragile it is unique and can be part of the organisational architecture that underpins its competitive advantage.

Again, there are pronounced similarities with how entrepreneurs operate. The learning organisation literature stresses incrementalism and learning by doing on the job, rather than in the classroom. It stresses questioning of the status quo. What is more it explains why entrepreneurs are more comfortable continuously strategising and why strategy tends frequently to emerge, based on the learning that is continuously taking place.

The ability to adapt is what makes the difference between survival and growth in an uncertain, turbulent environment and an organisation's ability to adapt is the direct result of its ability to learn collectively about the factors that influence it. Constant learning by organisations requires the acquisition of new knowledge and skill and the willingness to apply it to decision-making (Miller, 1996). It includes the unlearning of old routines (Markoczy, 1994) so that the range of potential behaviour is altered (Wilpert, 1995).

Our mental models, those deeply-held images of how the world works, are both shaped by our experiences and help shape our experiences. And from school onwards, all too often, conformity is rewarded, mistakes punished and too much questioning discouraged. How can we possibly make the leap of faith required to convince us things could be different? And how robust are our learning processes? Do we have the skill, let alone the time, to reflect in this modern world? Can these learning processes ever be sufficiently robust to get us to see how information, action and results form a chain of causality – the key to understanding the root cause of a problem? And how can an organisation encourage all this to take place? These questions bring us back to the challenge of building an entrepreneurial architecture that encourages these qualities.

♀ Building the architecture for entrepreneurial transformation

Burns (op. cit.) claims that an entrepreneurial architecture must reflect the very DNA of the entrepreneur – their personality and how they do business. This is replicated through the structures (including systems and processes) and culture in the

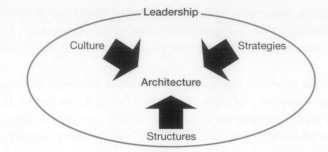

F18.2 Building entrepreneurial architecture

organisation and reinforced through the strategies that it follows. Effective entrepreneurial leadership is the key to putting the architecture in place since it is the leader that puts in place the structures, builds the culture and helps develop and implement the strategy. All this is shown in Figure 18.2. The leader's role is vital.

We know that the key characteristic of entrepreneurs is their search for opportunity and their ability to innovate and this book has built up that profile of the entrepreneur and how they manage – their DNA. In the context of a larger organisation, what we might call 'entrepreneurial management' is about encouraging opportunity seeking and innovation in a systematic manner throughout the organisation, always questioning the established order, seeking ways to improve and create competitive advantage. It is about encouraging the qualities enjoyed by successful entrepreneurs such as vision and drive. It is about learning new ways to manage organisations involving relationships and culture rather than discipline and control. It is about new ways of dealing with risk, uncertainty and ambiguity so as to maintain flexibility – and allowing failure. It is about institutionalising a process of continuous strategising, learning from customers, competitors and the environment. It is about encouraging change and managing rapid growth. And it is about doing these things throughout an organisation so that it reflects the entrepreneurial characteristics of its managers – responding quickly and effectively to opportunities or changes in the market place. Entrepreneurial management is therefore about a different set of imperatives to traditional management. These are summarised in Table 18.1.

Entrepreneurial architecture, therefore, should seek to encourage entrepreneurial management at all levels within the organisation. This entrepreneurial architecture creates within the organisation the knowledge and routines that allow it to respond flexibly to change and opportunity in the way the entrepreneur does. These organisations will thrive in changing, unstable or disruptive environments – even chaos. They will thrive in environments where change is the norm and opportunities are constantly presenting themselves. These environments are characterised by a high degree of uncertainty – even contradiction – and larger firms traditionally find them difficult to operate in. An entrepreneurial architecture is therefore a very real and valuable asset. It creates competitive advantage and can be sustained.

Internal architecture focuses on employees, generating a strong sense of collectivism rather than individuality and implying strong job security. This collectivism comes from shared objectives and commonly accepted strategies. And this brings with it potential weaknesses: 'Firms with strong internal architecture tend to restrict individuality and recruit employees of characteristic, and familiar type, inflexibility is a potential weakness' (Kay, op. cit.). These we also recognise as familiar potential weaknesses for entrepreneurs in growing firms. However, whilst adopting certain administrative traits is critical for successful growth (Cooper, 1993), both the

Traditional management	Entrepreneurial management
▷ Encouraging control	▷ Encouraging opportunity seeking
▷ Encouraging discipline	▷ Encouraging innovation
▷ Encouraging uniformity	▷ Encouraging questioning of the status quo
▷ Encouraging conformity	▷ Encouraging vision
▷ Encouraging efficiency	▷ Encouraging drive
▷ Encouraging effectiveness	▷ Encouraging relationships within and
▷ Encouraging contractual relationships	outside the organisation
only	▷ Encouraging strategising at all levels in
▷ Encouraging long-term planning	the organisation
▷ Encouraging 'training'	▷ Encouraging learning
▷ Encouraging functional management	▷ Encouraging the rapid transfer of
▷ Compartmentalising knowledge and	knowledge and information
information	▷ Encouraging cooperation
▷ Trying to create certainty and clarify	▷ Tolerating uncertainty and ambiguity
ambiguity	▷ Taking risks
▷ Avoiding risk	▷ Allowing failure
▷ Discouraging failure	▷ Accepting and embracing change
▷ Seeing change as a threat	▷ Not controlling too strongly

T18.1 Traditional vs entrepreneurial management

entrepreneur and the organisation must also remain essentially entrepreneurial. Retaining a balance is crucial, building on the distinctive traits, skills, capabilities and approach to business of the entrepreneur and institutionalising elements of their approach – replicating their DNA within the organisation's culture.

External architecture focuses on external relationships. It is found where firms share knowledge with outsiders, which encourages flexibility and fast response times. It is based on deep relationships and is often found in networks or clusters of small firms in particular geographic areas where they depend on each other for various aspects of their commercial activity. For example, in the UK there is a cluster of small firms in South Wales which manufacture sofas. Around them is a skilled workforce and the infrastructure needed to support them. Italy has developed these clusters in numerous industries from knitwear and ties to tiles, all based in different geographic clusters. Some larger firms, such as Dell, have developed competitive advantage based upon the development of distinctive global supply networks – which are also based on effective external architecture. The strongest architectures develop both strong internal and external relationships.

Whether internal or external, architecture is based upon mutually supportive, long-term relationships. Any relationship is based upon trust, and trust can take a long time to build but can be lost very quickly. It is also based on mutual self interest – there must be something in it for both parties. It is based on knowledge and information and is essentially informal rather than formal. It can be planned and it can be engineered, but is not easy to achieve. It needs cultivating and managing and its roots lie deep in the interpersonal relationships in the organisation.

The primary role of the good entrepreneurial leader is to build an entrepreneurial architecture. As Collins and Porras (1994) eloquently explain:

> Imagine you met a remarkable person who could look at the sun or stars at any time of day or night and state the exact time and date: 'It's April 23, 1401, 2:36 am, and 12 seconds.' This person would be an amazing time teller, and

we'd probably revere that person for the ability to tell the time. But wouldn't that person be even more amazing if, instead of telling the time, he or she built a clock that could tell time forever, even after he or she was dead and gone.

Having a great idea or being a charismatic, visionary leader is 'time telling'; building a company that can prosper far beyond the presence of any single leader and through multiple product life cycles is 'clock building'. The builders of visionary companies tend to be clock builders, not time tellers ... And instead of concentrating on acquiring the individual personality traits of visionary leadership, they take an architectural approach and concentrate on building the organisational traits of visionary companies.

♀ The role of culture

Culture is an important part of architecture. So what are the features of a culture that underpins an entrepreneurial architecture? Entrepreneurial culture is far harder to describe than it is to recognise – not unexpected given the lack of scientific measures available. Burns (op. cit.) talks about five 'high level' elements that really set the culture of the organisation apart as being entrepreneurial:

▷ Creativity and innovation;
▷ Empowerment;
▷ Strong relationships;
▷ Continual learning;
▷ Measured risk-taking.

They represent the very DNA of the entrepreneur and are supported by the 25 detailed elements, all shown in Figure 18.3. Many of these detailed elements aid recognition and are important in contributing to the overall culture. However many elements are just detail and can get in the way of the big picture.

The constant theme coming through both the entrepreneurship literature and the learning organisation literature is the need to empower and motivate employees to do 'the right thing', without having to be ordered to do so. This implies more of a consensus form of decision-making that can militate against speed of action. In some circumstances this might just not be possible if an opportunity is to be seized. This is when the organisation moves back from collectivism to individualism as entrepreneurs assert themselves. Often the different scenarios will already have been considered as the organisation continuously strategises and evaluates the options open to it. However, ultimately there may be a problem here that only considerations of size and structure can address. If the decision-making group is too large, the organisation may well not be able to react with sufficient speed to changing circumstances.

Creating a culture in which every person in your organisation, at every level, thinks and acts like an owner means that you need to aim to connect individual performance with your company's most important objectives ... A company composed of individual owners is less focused on hierarchy and who has a nice office, and more intent on achieving their goals.

☐ Michael Dell (1999)

An entrepreneurial culture needs to motivate people to do the 'right things', in the right way, for the organisation as well as for themselves. It needs to help them cope with an uncertain future by giving them a vision and a belief that they can achieve it. Entrepreneurs are naturally good at motivating staff by the example they set – 'walking the talk' – but as the firm grows the leader needs to find different ways of communicating with more people, infecting them with the entrepreneurial virus. The culture

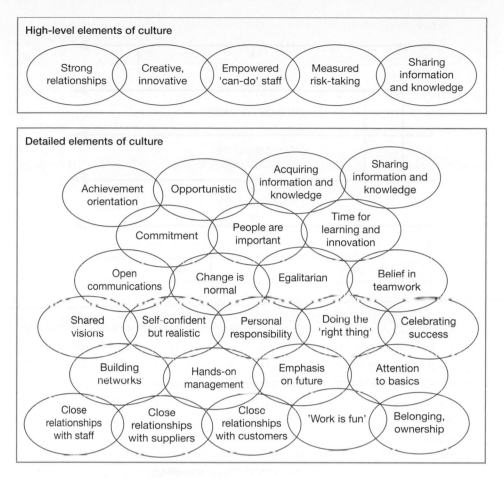

High-level elements of culture

Strong relationships — Creative, innovative — Empowered 'can-do' staff — Measured risk-taking — Sharing information and knowledge

Detailed elements of culture

Achievement orientation — Opportunistic — Acquiring information and knowledge — Sharing information and knowledge

Commitment — People are important — Time for learning and innovation

Open communications — Change is normal — Egalitarian — Belief in teamwork

Shared visions — Self-confident but realistic — Personal responsibility — Doing the 'right thing' — Celebrating success

Building networks — Hands-on management — Emphasis on future — Attention to basics

Close relationships with staff — Close relationships with suppliers — Close relationships with customers — 'Work is fun' — Belonging, ownership

F18.3 The cultural web hierarchy in an entrepreneurial organisation

Source: Burns (2005).

of a firm comes from the leader, it reflects their personal values and their vision, but it is made up of a lot of small items of detail. Cultures can come about by chance, but if leaders want to plan for success, they need to plan to achieve the culture they want.

Burns (op. cit.) maps the elements of culture in Figure 18.3 onto Hofstede's four dimensions. This is summarised in Figure 18.4. It allows us to describe an entrepreneurial organisation culture in a more structured way. It also allows us to contrast it with the national culture that encourages individual entrepreneurship that we discussed in Chapter 2. In terms of Hofstede's fifth dimension, an entrepreneurial organisation clearly has a long-term orientation as it has a long-term vision (strategic intent), is egalitarian with open communication and a lack of hierarchy.

The move from an individual entrepreneurial culture to an organisation entrepreneurial culture involves:

▷ *A move from individualism to collectivism* as the organisation grows and the entrepreneur must depend more upon a team. This implies cooperation and the development of relationships and networks with a strong sense of 'ingroup', with a clear identity and a feeling of competition against 'outgroups'. However, there is a careful balance to be achieved between the need for individual initiative and cooperation and group working. A cross-cultural, empirical investigation (Morris et al., 1994) supports this, observing that entrepreneurship appears to decline the more collectivism is emphasised, but, equally, dysfunctionally high levels of individualism can have the same effect.

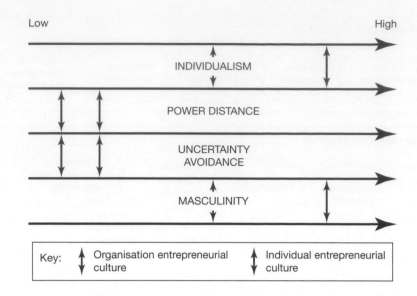

F18.4 Entrepreneurial culture summarised in Hofstede's dimensions

▷ *Low power distance*. This implies an egalitarian organisation with flat structures and open and informal relationships and unrestricted information flows. To reinforce this point Hall (2005) found in his study of organisational culture that innovation cannot occur in a high power distance culture.

▷ *Low uncertainty avoidance*. This implies a tolerance of risk and ambiguity, a preference for flexibility and an empowered culture that rewards personal initiative. It implies that failure may occasionally occur.

▷ *A balance between 'masculine' and 'feminine' dimensions* to build a culture of achievement against 'outgroups' through co-operation, networks and relationships with the 'ingroup'.

♀ The role of structure

Structures create order in an organisation but there is no single 'best' structure. As we saw in the last chapter, the most appropriate structure depends on the nature of the organisation, the strategies it employs, the tasks it undertakes, the environment it operates in and its size.

Structure also is integral to creating the entrepreneurial architecture in a larger organisation. And size does seem to matter. Large organisations are more complex than small and complexity impedes information flows, lengthens decision-making and can kill initiative. To be entrepreneurial, a large organisation needs to find ways of breaking itself down into a number of sub-organisations with varying degrees of autonomy. The span of control for management does seem to matter – 'walking the talk' only seems possible up to a certain size. But large organisations can structure themselves so that they comprise smaller 'units'. Again there are no prescriptive 'correct' approaches. However, large companies have been seeking to replicate the flexibility of the small firm and encourage entrepreneurial management by 'deconstructing' themselves – that is, breaking themselves down into smaller units – for some time. Peter Chemin, CEO of the Fox TV empire believes that 'in the management of creativity, size is your enemy' (*Economist*, 4 December 1999). He has tried to break down the studio into small units, even at the risk of incurring higher costs.

Small organisational units are more responsive to the environment and large firms have responded to the entrepreneurial challenge by experimenting with different organisational forms. There is an accelerating trend to downsize and deconstruct large firms – breaking them down to smaller components so that even the core is better able to act entrepreneurially. More firms are outsourcing non-core activities, downscoping and using project forms of organisation. They are developing strategic alliances with smaller firms and using them to 'outsource innovation'. They are flattening organisational structures, investing in information technology and new HRM techniques to make this happen.

Structures evolve as organisations grow and survival depends on swift adaptation. For larger firms, both hierarchical and matrix structures, or a combination, can be appropriate in different circumstances. However the traditional hierarchical structure tends to be mechanistic, bureaucratic and rigid. As shown in Figure 17.4, it is most appropriate for simple tasks in stable environments. Entrepreneurial organisations typically face a high degree of environmental turbulence. If the tasks they need to undertake are complex, they are best served by an organic organisation structure – one that changes and adapts to suit circumstances. Miller (1986) defines an organic structure as having 'limited hierarchy and highly flexible structure. Groups of trained specialists from different work areas collaborate to design and produce complex and rapidly changing products. The emphasis is on extensive personal interaction and face-to-face communication, frequent meetings, use of committees and other liaison devices to ensure collaboration. Power is decentralised and authority is linked to expertise. Few bureaucratic rules or standard procedures exist. Sensitive information-gathering systems are in place for anticipating and monitoring the external environment.'

So what will an organic structure look like? Unfortunately that is difficult to answer because, by its very definition, it is constantly forming and reforming to meet the changes it faces as it undertakes those complex tasks. Figure 18.5 is an example of one highly organic structure which comprises a series of spider's-web organisations within one large spider's web. There is no hierarchy. The organisation is flat. In this organisation the reporting lines between the smaller spider's webs are informal. Each operates

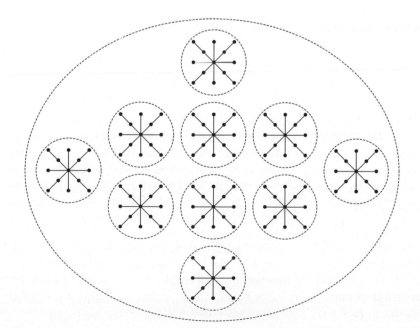

F18.5 An organic structure

almost autonomously and, in that sense, this may be seen more as a loose coalition of entrepreneurial teams, perhaps forming and reforming as opportunities appear. The danger is that each might operate with too much autonomy and too little direction, resulting in anarchy. In many organisations, particularly larger ones, more structure and hierarchy may therefore be needed.

Remember that it is unlikely that one organisational structure – even an organic one – will suit all situations. Greiner (op. cit.) emphasised how organisations naturally change and adapt and Galbraith (1995) underlines the importance of change and variety rather than rigidity and conformity: 'Organisational designs that facilitate variety, change, and speed are sources of competitive advantage. These designs are difficult to execute and copy because they are intricate blends of many different policies.' So flexibility and ability to change quickly are the keys. Like the chameleon, the entrepreneurial organisational structure will adapt to best suit the environment it finds itself in.

Like the chameleon, entrepreneurial organisational structure adapts to its environment

The common themes are that the organic structure will be flexible, decentralised with a minimum of levels within the structures. It will be more horizontal than vertical. Authority will be based on expertise not on role and authority for decision-making will be delegated and individuals empowered to make decisions. It will be informal rather than formal, with loose control but an emphasis on getting things done. Spans of control are likely to be broader. Team working is likely to be the norm. There will be structures within structures that encourage smaller units to develop, each with considerable autonomy, but there will be structures in place that encourage rapid, open, effective communication between and across these units and through any hierarchy. The success of these units will depend on the degree of fit with the

📖 Case insight Richard Branson's Virgin Group

The Virgin Group is characterised as being informal and information-driven – one that is bottom-heavy rather than strangled by top-heavy management.

Richard Branson describes Virgin as a 'branded venture capital company'. He comments: 'Despite employing over 20 000 people, Virgin is not a big company – it's a big brand made up of lots of small companies.' In fact it is made up of some 270 separate, semi-independent companies and Richard has been adept at setting up in partnership with other firms or even selling off part of his companies' shares to finance Virgin's global expansion. The Virgin brand can now be found on aircraft, trains, cola, vodka, mobile phones, cinemas, a radio station, financial services and most recently the internet.

Richard runs the Virgin empire from a large house in London's Holland Park. Although there does not appear to be a traditional head office structure, Virgin employs a large number of professional managers. It has a devolved structure and an informal culture. Employees are encouraged to come up with new ideas and development capital is available. Once a new venture reaches a certain size it is launched as an independent company within the Virgin Group and the intrapreneur takes an equity stake. Will Whitehorn, Branson's right hand man for the last 16 years, says of Richard: 'He doesn't believe that huge companies are the right way to go. He thinks small is beautiful ... He's a one-person venture capital company, raising money from selling businesses and investing in new ones, and that's the way it will be in the future' (*The Guardian*, 30 April 2002).

☐ Up-to-date information on the Virgin Group can be found on their website: www.virgin.com

mainstream organisation requiring a high degree of awareness, commitment and connection between the two (Thornhill and Amit, 2001).What is more, with such a loose structure, strong entrepreneurial leadership and culture will be needed to keep the organisation together and moving in the right direction.

♀ Management, structure and control

Management is an art not least because the structures of the organisation affect how you undertake it – and vice versa. As an entrepreneurial firm moves away from centralised, formal hierarchies to flatter structures with more horizontal communication the need for managers and tight management control lessens. The 'style' of leadership and management influences, and is influenced by, the organisational architecture just as much as structure and culture. If you are looking for 'dazzling breakthroughs' then autonomy and flexibility are crucial. But if the degree and frequency of entrepreneurship is less, the need for controls will increase. Again, it is all a question of balance.

In this context, Covin and Slevin (1990) argue that entrepreneurial behaviour within an organisation is positively correlated with performance when structures are more organic, as shown in Figure 18.6. In reality the dimension of structure from organic to mechanistic is a continuum and ought to correspond to the managerial dimension from entrepreneurial to administrative. A mechanistic structure is appropriate for a bureaucratic or administrative style of management because it will result in an efficient albeit bureaucratic organisation. However, it will stifle, if not kill, an entrepreneurial style. On the other hand an organic structure facilitates an effective entrepreneurial management style. The management style should be appropriate for the structure of the organisation and the structure of the organisation should be appropriate for the management style. Organisations are much more problematic, to the point where they can become dysfunctional, when there is an incongruity between structure and style.

STRUCTURE

	Organic structure	Mechanistic structure
Channels of communication	Open, free flow throughout the organisation	Highly structured and restricted
Operating styles	Allowed to vary freely	Uniform and restricted
Authority for decisions	Based upon expertise of individual	Based on formal line-management position
Ability to adapt	Free to adapt to changing circumstances	Reluctant to change from tried and tested principles
Emphasis	On getting things done, unconstrained by procedures	Reliant on procedures and tried and tested principles
Control	Loose and informal with emphasis on cooperation	Tight control through sophisticated systems
On-the-job behaviour	Shaped by the situation and the personality of the individual	Constrained to conform to job descriptions
Decision-making	Participation and consensus frequently used	Superiors make decisions with minimum consultation
Entrepreneurial		Bureaucratic

MANAGEMENT STYLE

F18.6 Organisational structure and management style

Source: Adapted from Covin and Slevin (1990)

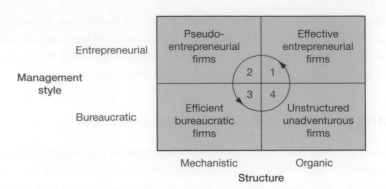

F18.7 Organisational structure, management style and the concept of cycling

Source: Covin and Slevin (1990)

This incongruity is shown in Figure 18.7. It demonstrates what Covin and Slevin call 'cycling', where a successful firm can move backwards and forwards between quadrants 1 and 3 as it moves from periods of opportunity, innovation and change to periods of consolidation and stability – when greater bureaucratic control is needed. This mirrors quite closely the strategy formulation cycle described in Figure 11.8 and may give one more reason why the transition from growth to consolidation is so often interspersed with a crisis – management style and organisational structures are out of sync and firms get stuck in quadrants 2 and 4. Change, if it is to be successfully managed must be along both dimensions simultaneously.

It must be remembered, however, that it is quite possible to have different units, departments or divisions within an umbrella organisation that have different, but in their own way, appropriate organisational structures and management styles – particularly as a product or service moves through its life cycle. The only issue is that the interface between them needs to be managed carefully. One example of this is the Virgin Group with its 'branded venture capital' organisation structure spanning many different industry sectors.

Most organisational control systems are aimed at eliminating risk and uncertainty – something the entrepreneurial firm must tolerate – and promoting efficiency and effectiveness – which can be at the expense of innovation. Innovation requires organisational 'slack' or 'space' – a looseness in resource availability which allows employees to 'borrow' expertise, research, materials, equipment and other resources as they develop new concepts. 3M have built slack into the organisation by allowing researchers to spend 15 per cent of their time on their own projects. Garud and Van de Ven (1992) confirm that entrepreneurial activity in a large organisation is more likely to continue, despite negative outcomes, when there is slack in resource availability and a high degree of ambiguity about the outcomes. A highly efficient organisation has no slack. Everything is tightly controlled, every penny accounted for, all jobs are defined and individuals made to conform. This environment might lead to high degrees of efficiency but it does not encourage entrepreneurship and innovation.

The leader in an entrepreneurial firm, therefore, faces a crucial dilemma – the amount of freedom given to the management team. Too much and anarchy or worse might result. Too little and creativity, initiative and entrepreneurship will be stifled. It is all well and good talking about empowerment, but at what stage does it become licence?

The answer is a question of 'balance'. Birkinshaw (op. cit.) explains the model used by BP to help guide and control entrepreneurial action. BP's philosophy is that 'successful business performance comes from a dispersed and high level of ownership of, and a commitment to, an agreed-upon objective'. Within BP there are a number of business units. Heads of units have a 'contract' agreed between them and the top executives in the organisation. Once agreed they have 'free rein to deliver on their contract in whatever way they see fit, within a set of identified constraints'. BP's model uses four components to help guide and control entrepreneurial action:

▷ *Direction* – the company's broad strategy and goals;
▷ *Space or slack* – the degree of looseness in resource availability (monetary budgets, physical space and supervision of time);
▷ *Boundaries* – the legal, regulatory and moral limits within which the company operates;
▷ *Support* – the information and knowledge transfer systems and training and development programmes provided by the company to help business unit managers do their job.

All four need to be in balance. If they are too tight they constrain the business unit, but if too slack they might result in chaos. This is shown in Figure 18.8. These elements need to be looked at as a whole rather than individually. And balance is the key. Birkinshaw observes that most companies operate in the 'constrained' area in Figure 18.8 – direction defined too tightly, too little space, overtight boundaries and overly complex support structures – rather than the 'chaos' area, so most central management probably needs to 'let go' a little. This BP approach to management perhaps gives us some insight into how the Gulf oil spill in 2010 could happen, which in turn underlines the inherent risks of entrepreneurial management – mistakes will happen. The point is that management is an art, not a science, and it involves some fine judgements about the individuals you work with – their strengths and weaknesses – as well as their personal characteristics.

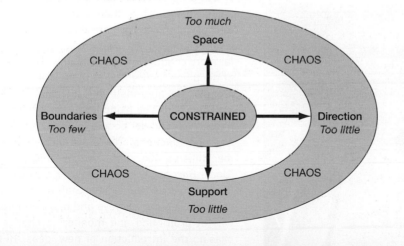

F18.8 Freedom vs control

Source: Birkinshaw (2003)

🗀 Case with questions David Hall and HFL

Based in Newmarket at the heart of the UK's best-known horse racing and breeding area, HFL started life in 1963 owned by the UK Horserace Betting Levy Board (HBLB – a quasi-governmental body, or quango). It enjoyed a steady stream of guaranteed income from the monitoring of racehorses and greyhounds to ensure that their performance was not artificially influenced by illegal substances. As a public sector organisation, it had a bureaucratic, government-style organisation structure and was not driven by profitability.

→

This, therefore, seems an unlikely organisation to look to as an exercise in change management and corporate entrepreneurship. But change it did, and by 2007 it had diversified into drug testing on humans and had been sold for £20.25 million to Quotient Bioresearch Ltd which is owned by a consortium of investors, including a minority holding by HFL's Chief Executive David Hall and other senior managers. HFL is now the UK's pre-eminent drug surveillance company, and a major competitor within the contract research market (testing for pharmaceuticals and biotechnology companies). It is the only laboratory in the world engaged in both sport drug surveillance and contract research. It has undertaken funded research for the World Anti-doping Agency as well as extensively for British Horseracing. HFL has pioneered sports doping control research and surveillance in the UK, testing athletes and racing animals as part of forensic doping control processes and providing research and bio-analysis testing services to pharmaceutical, food, consumer products and health care clients. Quotient Bioresearch at the Newmarket site now has a turnover approaching £20 million, employs some 200 people and enjoys a far more entrepreneurial culture.

The change catalyst was the appointment of David Hall as Chief Executive in 2001. His brief was to broaden the business base away from racehorses and greyhounds, and he effectively paved the way for the 'privatisation' of the company. David is a scientist – Chartered Engineer with a PhD – but he also has an MBA, which is the source of his theoretical knowledge of how to change the culture of an organisation. The challenge was to put it into practice at HFL. David would say that his passion for creativity and innovation and the pursuit of a perfect culture provided a common thread throughout his career before joining HFL. For example, he set up a technology transfer organisation in London – Thames Gateway Technology. The challenge, as David sees it, is to get the very best from your staff and to truly differentiate your company on the basis of its people. The HFL culture demands involvement across all levels and functions. It is a culture where knowledge is shared and communication is a vital element in this process. David wants it to run downwards, upwards and sideways through all feasible routes, so there is no excuse for 'not knowing'.

David's preferred leadership style is to 'animate and facilitate' rather than 'command and control'. Because of this his preferred communication style involves limiting group size to 20, which he sees as far more conducive to participation. He gives 'state of the union' addresses to these groups every six months. He also instituted informal 'coffee and cakes' sessions on Monday mornings to help communication and get people to mix across boundaries and functions. There are also more formal mechanisms like team briefs and a mythical 'Uncle Bernard' who will answer e-mailed questions from staff. The elected Staff Association also conducts regular surveys and plays an important part in promoting and monitoring change, even chasing the introduction of new ideas. HFL also uses cross-functional teams for project work and senior managers have had spells of doing other people's jobs. Staff work closely together in a culture that encourages team working.

HFL's scientific work depends critically on new ideas, which is why David is keen to encourage creativity. To do this he set up a Creativity Club and an Innovation Club. Each provides an environment for the free exchange of ideas, to push boundaries, and to harness the creative energies of staff. David drives the Creativity Club, which initially met monthly but now more simply as key problems are identified and creative ideas then generated. Creativity Club meetings are limited to one hour and operate under the terms of the 'Creativity Charter'. The ideas or problems brought to the Club use a wide range of creativity

→

techniques (see Chapter 5) to take the ideas forward or seek solutions to the problems. Every idea is posted on the company's intranet and staff are invited to comment. The best ideas might be taken forward by project teams. The senior managers also use the Club as a forum to take forward strategic issues that require a 'different way of thinking'. The Innovation Club focuses more on issues of strategic importance and on implementation – corporate innovation. All staff are automatically members and the Club meets quarterly at lunch time.

The company also has a book club that encourages the reading of business books, which also can lead to the introduction of new ideas. There is also the Business Intelligence Group, established to trawl the outside world for new ideas and to establish benchmarks for its activities. Everyone who sees or hears things outside the company is debriefed and the ideas are passed on or project teams are set up to take the idea further.

David is a great believer in the power of positive thinking – another attitude he likes to encourage in staff. He believes it can raise the proportion of time people spend working at maximum output. He has arranged in-house training sessions on the topic which resulted in individuals producing 'affirmations' to complete challenging personal tasks. David participated in the training and his 'affirmation' led to him cycling coast-to-coast and back to raise money for charity. HFL has performance reviews and a bonus scheme based upon four performance classifications: outstanding, achieving, aspiring and unacceptable. Staff are not paid bonuses if their performance in unacceptable. HFL has 'Investors in People' status and in 2005 was voted by its staff into the list of The Times '100 Best Companies to Work For'. But David will also admit that there have been casualties along the way, with less willing staff being replaced. And new managers have had a crucial part to play in changing the culture. David recruited Anne Stringer from a Cambridge wine business, nominally as finance director, but also with responsibility for HR and IT, to head up 'Central Services'.

HFL uses what it calls a 'strategy map' divided into four interconnecting areas: customer, reputation, people and finance. The aim in the 'customer' area is to become, or remain, 'first choice for analytical chemistry by improving loyalty, building relationships and innovating'. HFL aims to be the best customer choice, but not necessarily the cheapest. To achieve this it has to remain at the leading edge of its science and at the forefront of innovation. But innovation need not always be scientific. Staff involvement and enthusiasm at HFL is no accident. It is carefully nurtured with formal and informal techniques.

☐ Up-to-date information on HFL Ltd can be found on their website: www.hfl.co.uk

QUESTIONS

1 Describe the culture in HFL. How is this further encouraged?
2 Why is effective communication so important in changing culture?
3 What are the techniques HFL uses to promote internal and external communication? How do the 'informal' reinforce the 'formal' techniques?
4 Why is creativity and innovation important at HFL? How is it promoted and what benefits has it brought?
5 Give examples of how HFL has used technology to achieve its aims.
6 How important was David Hall to the process of change experienced at HFL? Give examples.
7 Why is it important to replace senior managers who block change?

♀ Intrapreneurship

Intrapreneurs can play an important role in entrepreneurial transformation. It may be an isolated activity, designed to see a new project into the market place, either as part of the existing organisation or as a spin-off from it. On the other hand, it may be part of a broader strategy to reposition or reinvigorate the whole organisation or even reinvent an entire industry. It can be undertaken at the corporate, divisional, functional or project level. It may be happening at a number of different levels, based on different individuals, at the same time. It is an attempt to compartmentalise the change agent(s) and reduce risk, whilst still pursuing fleeting opportunities.

Ross and Unwalla (1986) characterise the best intrapreneurs as result-orientated, ambitious, rational, competitive and questioning. They dislike bureaucracy and are challenged by innovation, but have an understanding of their organisation and a belief in their colleagues. They are adept at politics and good at resolving conflict – and need to be because they will face a lot of it as they smooth the connections with 'conventional' management. Kanter (op. cit.) found that intrapreneurs were comfortable with change, had clarity of direction, thoroughness, a participative management style and an understanding that they needed to work with others to achieve their goals.

Pinchot (op. cit.) also characterises them as goal-orientated and self-motivated but, unlike entrepreneurs, he says they are also motivated by corporate reward and recognition. They are able to delegate but not afraid to roll their sleeves up and do what needs to be done themselves. Like entrepreneurs, they need to be self-confident and optimistic. They may well be cynical about the bureaucratic systems within which they operate, although they do believe they can circumvent or manipulate them. In that sense they are good at working out problems within the 'system' – or even bypassing the system – rather than leaving the organisation. They are often good at sales and marketing and can bring those skills to bear both internally and externally. Like entrepreneurs they are strongly intuitive, but unlike entrepreneurs their corporate background means they are willing to undertake market research. They are risk-takers and believe that, if they lose their jobs, they will quickly find new ones. However, they are sensitive to the need to disguise risks within the organisation so as to minimise the political cost of failure. They are adept communicators with strong interpersonal skills that make them good at persuading others to do what they want. In this respect they are somewhat more patient than entrepreneurs. This process of influencing without authority, based upon reciprocity, is at the heart of the skill of intrapreneurs (Cohen and Bradford, 1991). They need to identify potential allies, diagnose their world – its language and what they value (and which things of value the intrapreneur controls) – and then establish a working relationship in which exchanges of value might take place.

To work effectively, intrapreneurs need a certain amount of 'space' since they will end up 'breaking the rules', but equally they need to be kept under control. A balance is required. They also need a high-level sponsor to protect them when times are difficult or vested interests are upset, and to help them unblock the blockages to change as they occur. The sponsor will help secure resources, provide advice and contacts. He or she will need to nurture and encourage the intrapreneur, particularly early on in the life of the project or when things go wrong, and will need to endorse and create visibility for the project at the appropriate time. Underpinning this must be a good relationship between the sponsor and the intrapreneur, based on mutual trust and respect.

Often intrapreneurs need to build a team around them. To do this they need to be able to identify key players that complement their own competencies (Stopford and Baden-Fuller, 1994). Often the intrapreneurial team works outside traditional lines of authority – in the USA it is called 'skunk working'. This eliminates bureaucracy, permits rapid progress and promotes a strong sense of team identity and cohesion – Hofstede's 'ingroup'. Intrapreneurs subvert the prevailing corporate culture in an attempt to counter the stagnation or inertia often encountered as organisations get larger or older. Often they will 'bootleg' resources – time, materials and so on – because none are formally made available to them.

The level of intrapreneurship varies and can be adapted to suit different organisations but, whilst not dependent upon the size of the organisation (Antoncic and Hisrich, 2003), the practice of intrapreneurship does become more difficult as the firm grows (Ross, 1987). Some intrapreneurs just emerge in organisations. Others will have to be identified. Pinchot (op. cit.) observes that if there are too few intrapreneurs within an organisation there are two solutions: attracting successful intrapreneurs from other companies or recruiting managers with an intrapreneurial character and growing them. Galloway (2006) stresses the importance of transferring and disseminating intrapreneurial knowledge through appropriate structures and cultures, observing that it is not enough to simply recruit intrapreneurs from outside. Without the appropriate structure and culture they will not flourish.

⚲ Organising new venture ideas

Once the flow of new venture ideas has started to come from an entrepreneurial organisation the question will arise as to what to do with them? This is where some of the ideas from 'bringing the market inside' are useful. Burgelman (1984a, b) uses the typology shown in Figure 18.9 to answer this. He suggests that the answer depends on how strategically important the development is for the business and how operationally related it is – and a spin-off is not always the answer. Generally, the more important the development and the more operationally related it is, the more it is likely to be kept 'in-house'. If there is little or no operational relatedness and the development has little or no strategic importance to the existing business then it should be completely spun-off, with no ownership retained. The most important condition for a spin-off, according to Garvin (1983), is that the core competencies are embodied in skilled labour rather than physical assets because the individuals transfer the knowledge to new firms. He argues that when new market segments develop opportunities for industries in the mature stage of their life cycle these industries are most likely to generate spin-offs because of the information advantage of insiders:

> An industry whose technology is embodied in skilled human capital is a prime candidate for spin-offs, for techniques, designs, and ideas are readily appropriable by individuals and transferable to new firms. Spin-offs in particular are encouraged by the existence of multiple market segments, information and start-up advantage accruing to members of established firms, readily transferable technologies, and environments in which skilled human capital is the critical factor of production.

Looking at Burgelman's other typologies:

▷ *Direct integration* – this is recommended where the development is both strategically important and operationally related, for example, when a new product development is integrated into a product range.

Operational relatedness		Very important	Uncertain	Not important
	Unrelated	Special business units	Independent business units	Complete spin-off
	Partly related	New product business departments	New venture division	Contracting
	Strongly related	Direct integration	Micro new business departments	Nurturing and contracting

Strategic importance

F18.9 Dealing with new venture developments

Source: Adapted from Burgelman (1984)

▷ *New product business departments* – these remain in-house because of their importance but for some operational reason a new department needs to be established to get the product to market. This might be the case with product extension.

▷ *Special business unit* – where operational relatedness is minimal, new staff with different skills may have to be recruited and the unit given greater independence and operational freedom, whilst still retaining ownership.

▷ *Micro new business departments* – where the strategic importance is uncertain the situation needs to be clarified before a final decision is made. This option keeps the development 'in-house' within a department because of the strong operational relatedness, pending that final decision.

▷ *New venture division* – such a division should be used to deal with developments that require further investment before their final fate is decided. They could ultimately be spun out or integrated into the mainstream, depending on the final assessment.

▷ *Independent business units* – these have greater independence than other formats. Often they are joint ventures with other strategic partners and may ultimately be spun off completely.

▷ *Nurturing and contracting* – these are appropriate where the core competencies are embodied in some physical assets or processes that are owned by the company but they are of little strategic importance. These can then be offered for use by other firms on a contracting basis.

♀ Corporate venturing

As well as spinning out businesses, larger organisations may need to invest in smaller businesses as part of their entrepreneurial transformation. The key to successful corporate venturing is 'strategic fit' – either finding investment where there is a strong relationship with the core competencies of the venturing company or acquiring skills, technologies or customers and market segments that complement the strategic direction of the venturing company. Ideally there should be strong synergy between the venture company and its smaller 'partner'. For the smaller company there can be advantages in gaining resources (money and advice) or access to markets that it might not otherwise have.

The advantages of corporate venturing to the larger organisation are that:

▷ It brings innovation and knowledge into the organisation from external sources;
▷ External sources of finance may be more easy to access;
▷ It facilitates the creation of semi-autonomous operating units with their own cultures, incentives and business models;
▷ It is often highly motivating to the staff involved.

The disadvantages are that:

▷ It requires investment, normally in the form of equity, which can be risky;
▷ It requires the investing company to invest in mechanisms that set up venture management and networks that search out, evaluate and generate deal flows;
▷ The investing company will not be in complete control of the innovation.

🖾 Corporate Entrepreneurship Audit Tool

The Corporate Entrepreneurship Audit Tool provides a check on the potential for the organisation to be entrepreneurial, as well as the appropriateness of this orientation in terms of its environment. It looks at entrepreneurial characteristics in the four dimensions of architecture outlined in this chapter: Leadership, Culture, Structure, Strategy.

These must be placed in the context of the environment within which the organisation operates. Only if the environment is suitable will an entrepreneurial response be appropriate.

This interactive tool assesses the environment and each of the four dimensions of architecture by answering 15 questions on a scale of 0–4 (low–high). The results are mapped onto an Audit Grid that measure entrepreneurial potential in four dimensions – shown as a red diamond – and the appropriateness of entrepreneurship for the competitive environment facing the organisation – shown as a blue circle. The further from the centre (measured on a 60-point scale), the more entrepreneurial is the architecture and the environment. The environmental footprint, ideally, should map onto the entrepreneurial potential, otherwise there is a mismatch.

The illustrated example shows an organisation with strong entrepreneurial leadership (score: 52) and strategies (50) but some work still to be done to bring about an entrepreneurial culture (18) with an adequate organisational structure (28). This would be a consistent pattern for an organisation in the process of becoming entrepreneurial, as culture takes time to change. The environment is shown by the circle with a diameter of 50 – indicating that the competitive environment is entrepreneurial. If the context for this organisation is that new entrepreneurial leadership has introduced new strategies and structures but cultures are taking longer to change, then the organisation is indeed moving in the right direction.

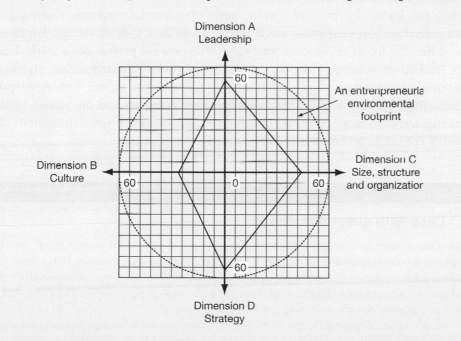

This diagnostic tool can be applied to any level of organisation – the organisation overall, division, department and so on. It provides a means of analysing potential areas for improvement, rather than a crude pass/fail test. This involves making informed judgements about certain criteria and, as such, is subjective rather than objective. Where benchmark comparisons are required, they should be made against competitor organisations.

Go to the website www.palgrave.com/business/burns to try out the tool.

For corporate venturing to work a number of things need to be in place. Firstly, as with most initiatives, it needs the commitment of senior management. Secondly, it needs to be consistent with corporate strategy, in such a way that an investment 'road map' can be produced, listing the areas to be investigated and invested in, the rationale for this and the mechanisms for searching out investments. However, the search mechanism needs to be sufficiently flexible to react to unexpected opportunities. It is important that the strategy is integrated into the overall corporate strategy for growth and innovation. A company can only beat venture capitalists at their own game if it adds value to the process in some way and the venture portfolio is aligned to its overall corporate strategy. It is this ability to share and leverage industry knowledge between portfolio companies and the business units of the investing company that creates added value. Thirdly, there need to be effective HR policies in place to encourage the retention of talented staff and encourage continuity. There is not much point in acquiring a company only to find that key staff leave shortly after acquisition which, as we have seen, is what happens all too often. Finally, the investing firm needs to have access to sufficient capital to use corporate venturing in this strategic way.

Corporate venturing is also used to spin out non-core, but still very profitable, opportunities coming from in-house research, whilst maintaining an equity stake in the new technologies. Monsanto, Apple, 3M and Xerox have used independent venture capital conduits for this purpose. Finally, large companies also sometimes run funds with other investment criteria, such as creating jobs in areas where the company has made redundancies. Many of these funds have 'non-profit' objectives and are part of a larger CSR agenda for the company.

Effective knowledge transfer is at the heart of successful corporate venturing for commercial purposes and many mechanisms can be used to facilitate this. For example, within the Intel Corporation, Intel Capital investment professionals work alongside Intel business units to identify venture investments. Similarly within Motorola, Motorola Ventures has a knowledge transfer team that is tasked with developing relationships between each start-up or investment company and the parent. In this way engineers can monitor whether the technology acquired meets expectations and identify opportunities between it and existing business units.

🗐 Case with questions Nokia

Nokia has a number of integrated mechanisms and organisations for encouraging, searching for and commercialising innovation. It has a traditional research centre, *Nokia Research Centre*. It has its own venturing organisation called *Nokia Ventures Organization* which seeks out internal and external opportunities. Finally it has three corporate venturing arms; *Nokia Venture Partners*, *Nokia Innovent*, and *Nokia Growth Partners.*

Nokia Ventures Organization has as its mission 'the renewal of Nokia'. Nokia's venturing activities have created independent businesses, contributed to the growth and profitability of core business, provided financial returns in their own right and provided intangible assets and insights. It approaches its mission from two directions. Firstly it tries to identify broad opportunities based upon industry analysis and developing new ventures from Nokia employees' ideas as well as those from external sources. Nokia has an annual Venture Challenge ideas campaign for employees. But it also collects ideas from a broad network that extends beyond Nokia and includes external research centres, academics, business

➡

partners and entrepreneurs. In collaboration with other Nokia units it systematically scans emerging trends and disruptions from the perspectives of technology, business and users to spot opportunities.

The *Nokia Research Centre* explores new concepts, applications and technologies. On the one hand the Centre develops disruptive technologies that go beyond the current state of the art and on the other hand it supports the locally-based product development units with technological expertise. The business units fund the majority of the research undertaken by the Centre. In both cases the Centre helps develop new business/venture ideas. Ideas are collected and evaluated by New Business Development teams across Nokia. New business cases are developed for the most promising ideas and, where appropriate, these are developed further in incubation units of the business unit where the objectives and competencies best match the scope of the idea and the resources needed to develop it. Projects where the business case is not yet clear or where there are many opportunities to be explored continue to be incubated in the Research Centre's incubator unit. Later, when the business case is clear, they are transferred to *Nokia Ventures Organization*.

If the technology to support the business idea has not yet been developed, *Nokia Ventures Organization* will commission technology research and development from the Research Centre or outside partners. Nokia uses the same venturing process throughout the organisation. The process ensures essential services and tools are available, facilitating the whole venturing process. Support includes personal guidance, dedicated resources, business planning and technology validation. A series of milestone reviews ensure projects move along.

Details of the three corporate venturing arms are:

▷ *Nokia Venture Partners*, which offers seed finance for early-stage business ideas to both internal and external ventures. It also offers support on legal, communications and human resources issues. Technology experts from the Research Centre also support Venture Partners in evaluating technologies that may be invested in.
▷ *Nokia Innovent*, which is its early-stage development team focusing only on external opportunities.
▷ *Nokia Growth Partners*, which invests in mid- to late-stage mobile technology companies. It also provides external funding only and focuses on Nokia's broad vision of 'Life Goes Mobile'.

Examples of Nokia's innovations coming through this integrated network include:

▷ *Nokia One Mobile Connectivity Service* – This offers corporate employees easy and secure access to mobile email, calendar, directory, contacts and mission-critical corporate applications from a mobile phone.
▷ *Nokia Mobile RFID Kit* – This Radio Frequency Identification (RFID) Kit integrates reader technology with the phone and allows mobile phones to be used to access data and initiate familiar mobile phone functions simply by touching a smart object with the phone. It is designed for use by security and maintenance service personnel.
▷ *Nokia Lifeblog* – This is a PC and mobile phone software combination that allows you to keep a real-time multimedia diary – text, photos, videos, text messages – with clear chronology.

☐ Up-to-date information on Nokia can be found on their website: www.nokia.com

QUESTIONS

1 What do you think of this integrated approach to encouraging, searching for and commercialising innovation? What are the advantages and disadvantages of this approach?

2 What category of corporate entrepreneurship does this fall into?

3 Compare and contrast this approach to that of 3M.

📋 Case with questions 3M

3M has been known for decades as an entrepreneurial company that pursues growth through innovation. It generates a quarter of its annual revenues from products less than five years old. 3M started life as the Minnesota Mining and Manufacturing Company back in 1902. Its most successful product – flexible sandpaper – still forms an important part of its product line but this now comprises over 60 000 products that range from adhesive tapes to office supplies, medical supplies and equipment to traffic and safety signs, magnetic tapes and CDs to electrical equipment. Originally innovation was encouraged informally by the founders, but over more than a century some of these rules have been formalised. But most important of all, there has built up a culture which encourages innovation. And because this culture has created a history of success, it perpetuates itself.

3M started life selling a somewhat inferior quality of sandpaper. The only way they could do this was by getting close to the customer – demonstrating it to the workmen who used it and persuading them to specify the product – an early form of relationship selling. This was the first strategic thrust of the fledgling business – get close to customers and understand their needs.

However, the company was desperate to move away from selling a commodity product and competing primarily on price and its closeness to the customer led it to discover market opportunities that it had the expertise to capitalise on. The first such product was Three-M-Ite™ Abrasive – an abrasive cloth using aluminium oxide for durability in place of a natural abrasive. This was followed by waterproof sandpaper – an idea bought from an inventor who subsequently came to work for 3M. This was followed shortly by Wetordry™ – a product designed for use by the car industry in finishing bodywork. And with this the second strategic thrust of the company was developed – to seek out niche markets, no matter how small, which would allow it to charge a premium price for its products. The company began to realise that many small niche markets could prove to be more profitable than a few large ones.

In the 1990s this began to change somewhat, to the extent that some technologies became more sophisticated and the investment needed to develop new products increased. Therefore the return required became larger and markets needed to be correspondingly bigger. Luckily the world was increasingly becoming a global market place. At the same time, competition was becoming tougher and the rapidity of technological change and shortening of product life cycles made 3M recognise the need to dominate any market niche quickly. Speed of response was vital. By the 1990s, many of the market niches 3M was pioneering were turning out to be not that small at all, particularly in the global market place. So, the approach remained the same, but the speed of response and size of market niche, worldwide, increased.

The company really started to diversify when it entered the tape market in the 1920s, but even this built on its expertise in coatings, backings and adhesives. What is more the way the first product evolved demonstrates perfectly how an entrepreneurial architecture works. By being close to its customers 3M saw a problem that it was able to solve for them through its technical expertise. In selling Wetordry™ to car-body finishers, an employee realised how difficult it was for the painters to produce the latest fad in car painting – two tone paintwork. The result was the development of masking tape – imperfect at first, but developed over the years 'out-of-hours' by an employee to what we know it to be today and from that technology developed the Scotch™ range of branded tapes. So, the third strategic thrust was developed – having identified a market opportunity through closeness to the customer, diversify into these related areas. Once 3M found a niche product to offer in a new market, it soon developed other related products and achieved a dominant position in the new market. In the 1990s 3M came to recognise that it did best when it introduced radically innovative products into a niche market in which it already had a toe hold.

→

This experience also taught 3M the value of research but in particular to value maverick inventors who were so attached to their ideas that they would push them through despite the bureaucracy of the company. It was in the late 1920s that it developed the policy of allowing researchers to spend up to 15 per cent of their time working on their own projects. To this day, it tries to make innovation part of the corporate culture by encouraging staff to spend 15 per cent of their time working on pet ideas that they hope one day will become new products for the company. They can also get money to buy equipment and hire extra help. To get an idea accepted, they must first win the personal backing of a member of the main board. Then an inter-disciplinary team of engineers, marketing specialists and accountants is set up to take the idea further. Failure is not punished, but success is well rewarded.

Perhaps the best known contemporary example of the success of this policy is the development of the Post-It Note by Art Frye in the 1980s. He was looking for a way to mark places in a hymn book – a paper marker that would stick, but not permanently. At the same time the company had developed a new glue which, unfortunately as it seemed at the time, would not dry. Art spotted a use for the product but what was different was the way he went about persuading his bosses to back the project. He produced the product, complete with its distinctive yellow colour, and distributed it to secretaries who started using it throughout 3M. Art then cut their supplies, insisting that there would be no more unless the company officially backed the product. The rest is history.

So the fourth strategic thrust of the company was developed – to pursue product development and innovation at every level in the organisation through research. This was formalised when the Central Research Laboratory was set up in 1937, but maverick research continued to be encouraged. In 1940, a New Product Department was developed to explore the viability of new products or technologies unrelated to existing ones. In 1943, a Product Fabrications Laboratory was set up to develop manufacturing processes. In the 1980s four Sector Labs were created with a view to being more responsive to the market place and undertaking medium-term research (5–10 years); Industrial and Consumer, Life Sciences, Electronic and Information Technologies and Graphic Technologies. The Central Lab, renamed the Corporate Lab, was maintained to undertake more long-term research (over 10 years). In addition most of the Divisions had their own Labs undertaking short-term, developmental research (1–5 years).

3M has always been admired for its ability to share knowledge across the organisation and link technologies to produce numerous products that could be sold in different markets. One example of this is Scotchlite™ Reflective Sheeting used for road signs, developed in the 1940s – in fact as a result of failed research to develop reflective road markings. This combined research from three different laboratories to produce signs with a waterproof base onto which a covering of an opaque, light-reflecting pigment was added followed by microscopic beads. This was all sealed with a thin coat of plastic to ensure weather durability. Strategy five had emerged – get different parts of the organisation to communicate and work together and, most important of all, share knowledge.

This became formalised in the 1950s with the establishment of the Technical Forum, established with the aim of sharing knowledge across the company. It held annual shows. Out of this came the Technical Council, made up of technical directors and technical personnel, which met several times a year to review research and address common problems. Alongside this the Manufacturing Council and then the Marketing Council were established. At the same time technical directors and researchers regularly moved around the different divisions. The fifth strategy was in place – share knowledge.

The culture in 3M evolved out of its place of origin and has been called 'Minnesota nice'. It has been described as non-political, low ego, egalitarian and non-hierarchical as well as hardworking and self-critical. It has also, at least in its earlier days, been described as paternalistic in its approach to employees. Above all, 3M has always been achievement-orientated and achievement, particularly in research, was rewarded,

→

often through promotion. For example successful new product teams were spun off to form new divisions. The leader of the team often became general manager of the new division and this was seen as a great motivator. Lesser achievements were also acknowledged. Researchers who consistently achieved 'high standards of originality, dedication and integrity in the technical field' – as judged by their peers, not management – were invited to join the exclusive 'Calton Society'. The 'Golden Step' and 'Pathfinder' awards were also given to those helping develop successful new products. Achievement was lauded at all levels. Strategy six was emerging – encourage achievement through reward.

Today 3M faces many challenges to maintaining its reputation for innovation. As it becomes larger and more complex, involved in different markets with different products and technologies, at different stages of their life cycle, it recognises that different managerial approaches may be necessary. The 'maverick', high-risk approach to research and development may not be appropriate in certain sectors. The 25 per cent rule – the proportion of new product sales – may not be achievable by all divisions. 3M also faces stiffer competition which means that cost economies have had to be made to maintain profitability. As a result the 15 per cent rule – slack time to research new products – is under severe pressure, to the point where it is described as more of an attitude than a reality. Nevertheless, 3M has for over a century successfully practised corporate entrepreneurship.

☐ Up-to-date information on 3M can be found on their website: www.3M.com

A series of case studies on 3M, tracking its history and development since its inception in 1902, have been written by Research Associate Mary Ackenhusen, Professor Neil Churchill and Associate Professor Daniel Muzyka from INSEAD. They can be obtained from the Case Clearing House, England and USA.

QUESTIONS

1 Describe the organisational structures and devices 3M uses to encourage entrepreneurial activity. Why do they work?
2 How does 3M distinguish between incremental and fundamental innovations?
3 Describe, as best you can from the case, the culture of the organisation. What does this depend upon?
4 Why has 3M been such a successful innovator for so long?
5 Can other companies just copy 3M's structures and culture and become successful innovators also?

▷ Summary

▷ Corporate entrepreneurship is the term used to describe entrepreneurial behaviour in an established, larger organisation. It is an emerging discipline. A more precise definition is difficult but there are four identifiable strands of literature:

1 Corporate venturing – e.g. the purchase of **Pret A Manger** by **McDonald's**.
2 Intrapreneurship – e.g. **Art Frye** at **3M**.
3 Bring the market inside – e.g. as at **Nokia**.
4 Entrepreneurial transformation – e.g. as at **HFL** and **3M**.

▷ Entrepreneurial transformation is about adapting large firms through their leadership, strategies, systems, structures and cultures so that they are better able to cope with change and innovation. This is called creating entrepreneurial architecture.

▷ Entrepreneurial architecture is the network of relational contracts within or around an organisation – its employees, suppliers, customers and networks. It creates within the organisation the knowledge and routines that allow it to respond flexibly to change and opportunity in the very way the entrepreneur does. It is not necessarily based on legal contracts and often only partly specified, therefore it is not easy to copy. It is based upon trust and mutual self-interest. Because it is complex, architecture can be a major source of sustainable competitive advantage. Strong architecture is based on deep personal relationships, either internal or external. **Dell** gains some of its competitive advantage from partnering with suppliers (external architecture).

▷ Entrepreneurial management is about the ability to lead and manage this larger entrepreneurial organisation – a need endorsed by **Diane Thompson** of **Camelot**. It involves the development of an entrepreneurial architecture.

▷ Learning organisations thrive in turbulence. Real knowledge means using the wheel of learning (Figure 18.1) to understand the root cause of problems so as to put in place systematic solutions to problems – 'knowing-how', 'knowing-why' and doing something about it. It means linking this to our mental models so as to challenge how things are. The most important learning occurs on the job. It is social and active. It is about learning tacit knowledge – intuition, judgement and expertise.

▷ Entrepreneurial firms thrive in environments of change, chaos, complexity, competition, uncertainty even contradiction. The exact nature of effective entrepreneurial architecture depends on the environment. It can be sectorally and geographically dependent. It can also vary with the nature of the entrepreneurial intensity. The point is that there can be no prescriptive blueprint for entrepreneurial architecture.

▷ Figure 18.3 shows the cultural web of an entrepreneurial organisation, but it distinguishes between 'high-level' elements of culture – strong relationships, creativity and innovation, empowerment, measured risk-taking and continual learning – and the detailed elements of culture.

▷ Structures create order in an organisation but there is no single 'best' solution. The most appropriate structure depends on the nature of the organisation, the strategies it employs, the tasks it undertakes, the environment it operates in and its size.

▷ Small organisational units are more responsive to the environment and large firms have responded to the entrepreneurial challenge by experimenting with different organisational forms.

▷ An organic structure has limited hierarchy and is highly flexible, decentralised with a minimum of levels within the structures. It is more horizontal than vertical. Authority is based on expertise not on role, and authority for decision-making is delegated and individuals empowered to make decisions. It is informal rather than formal, with loose control but an emphasis on getting things done. Spans of control are likely to be broader. Team working is likely to be the norm.

▷ There are structures within structures that encourage smaller units to develop, each with considerable autonomy, but there are also structures in place that encourage rapid, open, effective communication between and across these units and through any hierarchy.

▷ **Richard Branson** understands this, and his **Virgin** empire comprises some 270 separate, semi-independent companies, often set up in partnership with other individuals and organisations.

▷ Managers must give up control to gain control. Entrepreneurial firms need loose control but tight accountability. Too much control stifles creativity, innovation and entrepreneurship. However, too little control can lead to chaos. Most firms place too many constraints and controls on managers. What is needed is 'balance', as in **BP**'s model which involves:

  ▷ Space or slack – a looseness in resource availability;
  ▷ Direction – the broad strategy and goals;
  ▷ Support – like knowledge transfer and training systems;
  ▷ Boundaries – not just rules but underlying morals and ethics.

▷ For an organisation to work effectively, the organisation structure and the style of management need to be in sync. As an entrepreneurial firm moves away from centralised, formal hierarchies to flatter structures with more horizontal communication the need for managers and tight management control lessens. If you are looking for 'dazzling breakthroughs' then autonomy and flexibility are crucial. But if the degree and frequency of entrepreneurship is less, the need for controls will increase. Again, it is all a question of balance. Many successful firms cycle between organic/entrepreneurial structure and styles and mechanistic/bureaucratic as they grow – mirroring the growth/crisis/consolidation process noted in strategy development.

▷ An intrapreneur pushes through innovations within a larger organisation in an entrepreneurial fashion. Intrapreneurship can be an isolated activity, designed to see a new project into the market place, either as part of the existing organisation or as a spin-off from it, or it can be part of a broader strategy to reposition or reinvigorate the whole organisation – or even reinvent an industry.

▷ Intrapreneurs are results-orientated, ambitious, rational, competitive and questioning and must be adept at handling conflict and the politics of the larger organisation in which they operate. Their work needs to be facilitated by a high-level sponsor in senior management and an organisational structure that encourages them.

▷ What to do with a new development depends on how strategically important and how operationally related it is to the business. Generally, the more important the development and the more operationally related it is, the more likely it is to be kept in-house. If there is little or no operational relatedness and the development has little or no strategic importance to the existing business then it should be completely spun off, with no ownership retained.

▷ Some firms prefer corporate venturing – investing in smaller businesses in order to capitalise on their innovations. This is one of the reasons why **McDonald's** bought **Pret A Manger**. For corporate venturing to work it needs the commitment of senior management; consistency and integration with corporate strategy; to add value through effective knowledge transfer, leveraging knowledge from itself and the firm it acquires; effective HR policies to encourage the retention of talented staff and encourage continuity; and finally to have access to sufficient capital.

⏻ **Further resources are available at www.palgrave.com/business/burns**

🗋 Essays and discussion topics

1 Can large firms also be entrepreneurial? Is it in their interests to be so? What pressures are there for them not to be entrepreneurial?

2 What is corporate entrepreneurship?

3 What do you think of the four 'schools' of literature identified by Birkinshaw?

4 What do you understand by the term 'entrepreneurial architecture'? Why are relationships rather than legal contracts important?

5 What is needed to build long-term relationships?

6 How can entrepreneurial architecture be shaped?

7 Why can the architecture of a firm give it sustainable competitive advantage?

8 Is the learning organisation a romantic dream?

9 Is the entrepreneurial organisation really a learning organisation?

10 How do you spread learning and knowledge in an organisation?

11 Should an entrepreneur find building this architecture easier than other people?

12 What is entrepreneurial management? How does it differ from traditional management? How is it different from being an entrepreneur or intrapreneur?

13 Can a traditional manager become an entrepreneurial manager?

14 Why is the leader's role crucial in developing an entrepreneurial organisation?

15 Will an entrepreneurial organisation succeed in all environments?

16 In what circumstances might a bureaucratic organisation be more successful than an entrepreneurial organisation?

17 How might the geographic environment affect an entrepreneurial architecture?

18 What are the five 'high level' elements of entrepreneurial culture? Explain 'high level'.

19 Do you agree that the most important elements of an entrepreneurial culture are creativity and innovation, empowerment, strong relationships, continual learning and measured risk-taking?

20 What do you understand by an organic structure? Try drawing one.

21 Why does tight control stifle creativity, innovation and entrepreneurship?

22 Why is slack or space so important for creativity, innovation and entrepreneurship within a larger organisation? Why is it not mentioned in the literature on entrepreneurship?

23 How do you achieve 'balance' between freedom and control? Who makes the judgement?

24 How can you have loose control but tight accountability? Give examples.

25 With freedom comes accountability. Discuss.

26 What is corporate venturing?

27 What is intrapreneurship? How is it different to entrepreneurship?

28 How is an intrepreneur different to an entrepreneur? Is it easier to be an intrapreneur or an entrepreneur?

29 Under what conditions might intrapreneurship thrive?

30 How important is the intrapreneur as a tool of entrepreneurial management?

31 How much 'space' does an intrapreneur need? Why is this not important for an entrepreneur?

32 Real entrepreneurs leave an organisation to set up their own new venture rather than run one belonging to a big company. Discuss.

33 Why are operational relatedness and strategic importance important determinants of what to do with new ventures?

34 Is there any relationship between Burgelman's typology (Figure 18.1) and the Ansoff matrix (Figure 12.1)?

35 Is corporate venturing any more than an excuse for buying up successful small firms?

36 What needs to be in place for corporate venturing to work?

37 Explain the importance of effective knowledge transfer for corporate venturing to work best.

38 Why should a large company want to spin out a new venture with good opportunities?

⎌ Activities

1 Apply the Corporate Entrepreneurship Audit Tool to a growing company or a division/department of a larger organisation. Assess its entrepreneurial architecture and the commercial environment in which it operates. Be sure to justify your evaluations with evidence and examples.

2 List the types of organisations and market sectors or environments that face high degrees of turbulence. Select a particularly turbulent sector and research how the organisations within it are organised and the success, or otherwise, they have in dealing with it.

3 Select two organisations, one that you would describe as entrepreneurial, the other that you would describe as administrative or bureaucratic. Referring back to Hofstede's work and the five high-level elements of culture in Figure 18.3, describe their cultures in a brief report.

4 Give some specific examples of an industry where a hierarchical, bureaucratic structure should be the best way to organise. Select a company in this industry and investigate their organisational structure. Explain why their structure conforms or does not conform to your expectations, taking into account the success of the business in that industry.

5 Select a large company spin-out. Research and write up its history and describe its success or failure. What lessons are to be learnt from this?

6 Find an example of corporate venturing that has proved unsuccessful and analyse why. What lessons can be learned from this?

📖 References

Antoncic, B. and Hisrich R. (2003), 'Clarifying the Intrapreneurship Concept', *Journal of Small Business and Enterprise Development*, 10(1).

Birkinshaw, J.M. (2003) 'The Paradox of Corporate Entrepreneurship', *Strategy and Business*, 30, Spring.

Burgelman, R.A. (1983) 'A Process Model of Internal Corporate Venturing in the Diversified Major Firm', *Administrative Science Quarterly*, 28.

Burgelman, R.A. (1984a) 'Designs for Corporate Entrepreneurship in Established Firms', *California Management Review*, 16(3).

Burgelman, R.A. (1984b) 'Managing the Internal Corporate Venturing Process', *Sloan Management Review*, Winter.

Burns, P. (2005) *Corporate Entrepreneurship: Building an Entrepreneurial Organisation*, Basingstoke: Palgrave Macmillan.

Chesbrough, H.W. (2002) 'Making Sense of Corporate Venture Capital', *Harvard Business Review*, March.

Christensen, C.M. (1997) *The Innovator's Dilemma: When New Technologies Cause Great Firms to Fail*, Boston: Harvard Business School Press.

Cohen, A.R. and Bradford, D. (1991) *Influence without Authority*, New York: Wiley.

Collins, J.C. and Porras, J.I. (1994) *Built to Last: Successful Habits of Visionary Companies*, New York: Harper Business.

Cooper, A.C. (1993) 'Challenges in Predicting New Firm Performance', *Journal of Business Venturing*, May.

Covin, D. and Slevin, J. (1990) 'Judging Entrepreneurial Style and Organisational Structure: How to Get Your Act Together', *Sloan Management Review*, 31 (Winter).

Dell, M. (1999) Direct from Dell: Strategies that Revolutionised an Industry, New York: Harper Business.

Drucker, P.F. (1985) *Innovation and Entrepreneurship: Practice and Principles*, London: Heinemann.

Foster, R.N. and Kaplan, S. (2001) *Creative Destruction: Why Companies that are Built to Last Underperform the Market – and How to Successfully Transform Them*, New York: Currency Doubleday.

Galbraith, J. (1982) 'Designing the Innovating Organisation', *Organisational Dynamics*, Winter.

Galbraith, J. (1995) *Designing Organisations*, San Francisco: Jossey-Bass.

Galloway, L. (2006) 'Identifying Intrapreneurship in Organizations: A Human Resources Study', presented at Institute for Small Business and Entrepreneurship conference, Cardiff.

Garud, R. and Van de Ven, A. (1992) 'An Empirical Evaluation of the Internal Corporate Venturing Process', *Strategic Management Journal*, 13 (Special Issue).

Garvin, D.A. (1983) 'Spin-offs and New Firm Formation Process', *California Management Review*, 25(2).

Ghoshal, S. and Bartlett, C.A. (1997) *The Individualised Corporation: A Fundamentally New Approach to Management*, New York: Harper Business.

Greiner, L. (1972) 'Revolution and Evolution as Organisations Grow', *Harvard Business Review*, 50, July/August.

Guth, W.D. and Ginsberg, A. (1990) 'Corporate Entrepreneurship', *Strategic Management Journal*, 11 (Special Issue).

Hall, D. (2005) 'Insight from Facilitating Entrepreneurial Business Development within Established Organisations', presented at the Institute for Small Business and Entrepreneurship, Blackpool, UK.

Hamel, G. (1999) 'Bringing Silicon Valley Inside', *Harvard Business Review*, September.

Hofstede, G., Neuijen, B., Daval Ohayv, D. and Sanders, G. (1990) 'Measuring Organizational Cultures: A Qualitative and Quantative Study across Twenty Cases', *Administrative Sciences Quarterly*, 35.

Kanter, R.M. (1982) 'The Middle Manager as Innovator', *Harvard Business Review*, July.

Kanter, R.M. (1989) *When Giants Learn to Dance: Mastering the Challenge of Strategy, Management and Careers in the 1990s*, New York: Simon & Schuster.

Kanter, R.M. (2004) 'The Middle Manager as Innovator', *Harvard Business Review*, 82 (7/8) (Special edition).

Kay, J. (1993) *Foundations of Corporate Success*, Oxford: Oxford University Press.

Kim, D.H. (1993) 'The Link between Individual and Organizational Learning', *Sloan Management Review*, Fall.

Markoczy, L. (1994) 'Modes of Organisational Learning: Institutional Change and Hungarian Joint Ventures', *International Studies of Management and Organisations*, 24, December.

Miller, A. (1996) *Strategic Management*, Maidenhead: Irwin/McGraw-Hill.

Miller, D. (1986) 'Configurations of Strategy and Structure: Towards a Synthesis', *Strategic Management Journal*, 7.

Morris, M.H., Davies, D.L. and Allen, J.W. (1994) 'Fostering Corporate Entrepreneurship: Cross Cultural Comparisons of the Importance of Individualism versus Collectivism', *Journal of International Business Studies*, 25(1).

Morse, C.W. (1986) 'The Delusion of Intrapreneurship', *Long Range Planning*, 19(2).

Naisbitt, J. (1994) *Global Paradox: The Bigger the World Economy, the more Powerful its Smaller Players*, London: BCA.

Pedler, M., Burgoyne, J.G. and Boydell, T. (1991) *The Learning Company: A Strategy for Sustainable Development*, London: McGraw-Hill.

Peters, T. and Waterman, R. (1982) *In Search of Excellence: Lessons from America's Best-Run Companies*, New York: Harper Row.

Pinchot, G. (1985) *Intrapreneuring: Why You Don't Have to Leave the Company to Become an Entrepreneur*, New York: Harper Row.

Ross J. (1987) 'Intrapreneurship and Corporate Culture', *Industrial Management*, 29(1).

Ross, J. E. and Unwalla, D. (1986) 'Who is an Intrapreneur?', *Personnel*, 63(12).

Senge, P. (1990) *The Fifth Discipline: The Art and Science of the Learning Organisation*, New York: Currency Doubleday.

Senge, P. (1992) 'Mental Models', *Planning Review*, March–April.

Stopford, J.M. and Baden-Fuller, C.W.F. (1994), 'Creating Corporate Entrepreneurship', *Strategic Management Journal*, 15(7).

Thornhill, S. and Amit, R. (2001) 'A Dynamic Perspective of Internal Fit in Corporate Venturing', *Journal of Business Venturing*, 16(1).

Timmons, J.A. (1999) *New Venture Creation: Entrepreneurship for the 21st Century*, Singapore: Irwin/McGraw Hill.

Tushman, M.L. and O'Reilly, C.A. (1996) 'Ambidextrous Organisations: Managing Evolutionary and Revolutionary Change', *California Management Review*, 38(4).

Vesper, K.H. (1984) 'The Three Faces of Corporate Entrepreneurship: A Pilot Study', in J.A. Hornaday et al. (eds), *Frontiers of Entrepreneurial Research*, Wellesley, MA: Babson College.

Wilpert, B. (1995) 'Organisational Behaviour', *Annual Review of Psychology*, 46, January.

Zahra, S.A. (1991) 'Predictors and Financial Outcomes of Corporate Entrepreneurship: An Exploratory Study', *Journal of Business Venturing*, 6(4) (July).

Zahra, S.A., Jennings, D.F. and Kuratko, D.F. (1999) 'The Antecedents and Consequences of Firm Level Entrepreneurship: The State of the Field', *Entrepreneurship: Theory and Practice*, 24.

Further reading and journals

Selected further reading

Entrepreneurship and small business

Blundel, R. and Lockett, N. (2010) *Exploring Entrepreneurship: Practice and Perspectives*, Oxford: Oxford University Press.

Bolton, B. and Thompson, J. (2004) *Entrepreneurs: Talent, Temperament, Techniques*, 2nd edn, Oxford: Butterworth-Heinemann.

Burke, G., Clarke, L. Molian, D. and Barrow, P. (2008) *Growing Your Business: A Handbook for Ambitious Owner-Managers*, Abingdon: Routledge.

Bygrave, W.D. and Zacharakis, A. (eds) (2004) *The Portable MBA in Entrepreneurship*, 3rd edn, New York: John Wiley & Sons.

Deakins, D. and Freel, M. (2009) *Entrepreneurship and Small Firms*, 5th edn, Maidenhead: McGraw Hill.

Hisrich, R. D., Peters, M. P. And Shepherd, D. A. (2005) *Entrepreneurship*, 6th edn, Maidenhead: McGraw Hill.

Kuratko, D.F. (2009) *Entrepreneurship: Theory, Process, Practise*, 8th edn, Mason: South-Western Cengage Learning.

Selected topics in alphabetic order

Corporate entrepreneurship

Burns, P. (2008) *Corporate Entrepreneurship: Building an Entrepreneurial Organisation*, 2nd edn, Basingstoke: Palgrave Macmillan.

Morris, M.H. and Kuratko, D.F. (2007) *Corporate Entrepreneurship and Innovation*, Fort Worth: Harcourt College Publishers.

Sathe, V. (2003) *Corporate Entrepreneurship: Top Managers and New Business Creation*, Cambridge: Cambridge University Press.

Culture

Guirdham, M. (2005) *Communicating across Cultures at Work*, Basingstoke: Palgrave Macmillan.

Hofstede, G. and Hofstede, G. J. (2005) *Culture and Organizations: Software of the Mind*, 2nd edn, Maidenhead: McGraw Hill.

Samovar, L. A. Porter, R. E. and McDaniel, E. R. (2009) *Communicating between Cultures*, Boston: Wadsworth Cengage Learning.

Economists' perspective and policy on small business

Bridge, S., O'Neill, K. and Martin, F. (2009) *Understanding Enterprise, Entrepreneurship and Small Business*, Basingstoke: Palgrave Macmillan.

Casson, M. (2003) *The Entrepreneur: An Economic Theory*, 2nd edn, Cheltenham: Edward Elgar Publishing.

Parker, S.C. (2005) *The Economics of Entrepreneurship: What We Know and What We Don't*, Hanover: Now Publishers.

Schumacher, E.F. (1974) *Small is Beautiful: A Study of Economics as if People Mattered*, London: Abacus.

Storey, D.J. and Greene, F.J. (2010) *Small Business and Entrepreneurship*, Harlow: Pearson Education.

Family firms

Kenyon-Rouvinez, D. and Ward, J.L. (eds) (2005) *Family Business: Key Issues*, Basingstoke: Palgrave Macmillan.

Leach, P. (1996) *The BDO Stoy Hayward Guide to the Family Business*, London: Kogan Page.

Poutziouris, P.Z. and Smyrnios, K.X. (eds) (2008) *Handbook of Research on family Business*, Cheltenham: Edward Elgar Publishing.

Innovation

Drucker, P.F. (1985) *Innovation and Entrepreneurship: Practice and Principles*, London: Heinemann.

Tidd, J. and Bassant, J. (2009) *Managing Innovation: Integrating Technological, Market and Organisational Change*, 4th edn, New York: Wiley.

International entrepreneurship

Dicken, P. (1998) *Global Shift: Transforming the World Economy*, London: Paul Chapman Publishing.

Giddens, A. (2000) *Runaway World: How Globalisation is Reshaping our Lives*, Andover: Routledge.

Social entrepreneurship

Brinckerhoff, P. (2000) *Social Entrepreneurship: The Art of Mission-Based Venture Development*, Hoboken, NJ: Wiley.

Dees, J.G., Emerson, J. and Economy, P. (2001) *Enterprising Nonprofits: A Toolkit for Social Entrepreneurs*, Hoboken, NJ: Wiley.

Ebrhim, A. (2004) *NGOs and Organisational Change*, Cambridge: Cambridge University Press.

Mair, J. Robinson, J. and Hockerts, K. (eds) (2006) *Social Entrepreneurship*, Basingstoke: Palgrave Macmillan.

Strategy

Johnson, G., Scholes, K. and Whittington, R. (2008) *Exploring Corporate Strategy*, 8th edn, Harlow: Pearson Education.

Kay, J. (1998) *Foundations of Corporate Success*, Oxford: Oxford University Press.

Mintzberg, H. (1994) *The Rise and Fall of Strategic Planning*, New York: Free Press.

Mintzberg, H., Ahlstrand, B. and Lampel, J. (1998) *Strategy Safari*, New York: Free Press.

Wickham, P.A. (2006) *Strategic Entrepreneurship*, 4th edn, Harlow: Pearson Education.

Selected journals

There are a number of journals that are specifically concerned with entrepreneurship and small business. The list below also shows the 2009 Association of Business Schools' quality ranking (4 = high to 1 = low):

4   *Entrepreneurship, Theory and Practice*
    Journal of Business Venturing
3   *Entrepreneurship and Regional Development*
    International Small Business Journal
    Journal of Small Business Management
    Small Business Economics
    Strategic Entrepreneurship Journal
2   *Family Business Review*
    International Journal of Entrepreneurial Behaviour and Research
    International Journal of Entrepreneurship and Innovation
    Journal of Small Business and Enterprise Development
    Venture Capital: An International Journal of Entrepreneurial Finance
1   *International Entrepreneurship and Management Journal*
    Journal of Enterprising Culture
    Journal of Entrepreneurship
    Journal of International Entrepreneurship
    Social Enterprise Journal

Not classified
    Enterprise and Innovation Management studies
    Entrepreneurship, Innovation and Change
    International Journal of Entrepreneurship and Innovation Management
    International Journal of Entrepreneurship Education
    Journal of Developmental Entrepreneurship
    Journal of Entrepreneurship Education
    Journal of Family Business Strategy
    Journal of Small Business and Entrepreneurship
    Journal of Small Business Strategies
    Small Enterprise Research
    World Review of Entrepreneurship, Management and Sustainable Development

Articles on entrepreneurship in general also appear in most business and management journals, particularly in the subject areas of strategy and human resources. The easiest way to find academic articles on a topic related to small firms is to use a web-based search engine. Your library will advise you on the most appropriate one to use.

Subject index

Note: '*see website*' and '*see also website*' are references to the book website – **www.palgrave.com/business/burns**

3M   127, 473, 486, 494

A
ABC analysis   338–9
Abel and Cole   302
accounting records/systems   *see*
   financial records/systems
ACORN   178
acquisition   355–7
advertising   170–1, 379
advice/help   *see website*
aged listing of debtors   235
agency dilemma   213–14
Alternative Investment Market
   (AIM)   273–5
Amazon   131
America On-Line (AOL)   128, 355, 356
analogy   119
Andreesen, Marc   128
Ansoff matrix   *see* product/market
   matrix
antecedent influences   10, 42–4, 433
Apple   150, 473, 494
asset efficiency   306, 307
AT&T   355, 356
attribute analysis   119
average cost   173, 176

B
bad debts   210
balance sheet   227, 229–31, 266
Bang & Olufsen   177
bankruptcy   396
   see also failure
banks/bankers   265, 267–70, 374–5
   see also website
Barclays   178
barriers to entry/exit   10, 147, 203,
   212, 310, 347–8
   see also Porter's Five Forces

barriers to growth   *see* growth
Bell Laboratories   125
benchmark/benchmarking   235, 238,
   303, 304, 306, 310
benefits of a product/service   169–70,
   186, 299
BMW   177
board of directors   422–3, 450–1
body language   186, 187
Body Shop, The   85, 181, 299
Boo.com   128
Boots   205
bootstrapping   124, 155
Boston matrix   *see* portfolio of
   products
BP   70, 294, 484
brainstorming   116–18, 309
brainwriting   118
brand/branding   95, 154, 177–8, 188,
   190, 192, 210, 311, 328, 332, 336,
   348–9, 351, 353, 413
   familial   413
Branson, Richard   9, 12, 177, 291,
   347
break-even   174–5, 234–5, 236–42,
   268, 301, 368–9, 375, 379–80, 402
British Business Angel
   Association   271, 283
British Franchise Association   193
British Venture Capital Association
   (BVCA)   271, 283
BT   178
budgets   232–3, 246–52, 306, 367–9
business angels   260, 261, 270–3,
   375–7
Business Link   91, 157, 261, 271
   see also website
business plan   159–60, 181, 232–3, 268,
   292, 365–81
buying signals   187

C
Cadbury   85, 296, 346, 348, 349, 355,
   356, 413, 414
CAMPARI   268
capital   94, 155–6, 223, 224–8, 229–30,
   252–6
cash   223, 224, 226, 230, 233
cash book   252–3
cash cow   *see* portfolio of products
cash flow   223–5, 228, 301, 332, 338,
   389, 392, 395, 435, 436
cash flow forecast   223–4, 246–52,
   368–74, 381
Centre for Interfirm Comparison   303,
   306
Chamber of Commerce   157, 211, 217
   see also website
change agents   78
change/denial curve   439
channels of distribution   170–2, 196,
   213, 328, 335
character traits (entrepreneurial)   10,
   36–42, 143–4, 291, 390–1
charitable social enterprise   90
charitable incorporated organisation
   (CIO)   90–1
Churchill, Winston   442
churn/churning   24, 25
CISCO   291
civic enterprise/
   entrepreneurship   85–102
Clark, Jim   128
clusters   77, 205, 479
cognitive processes   456–7
cognitive theory   42–4
collateral   266–7
commodity supplier   *see* generic
   marketing strategies
community benefit society
   (BenCom)   90

community interest company (CIC) 90
Companies Act 191, 252
company valuation *see* valuation
competitive advantage 65–9, 293, 298, 299–300, 308, 310, 311–14, 379, 437–8, 444, 449, 471, 474–5, 477–9, 484
competitors 145, 146–8, 169, 170, 179–80, 182–4, 378, 366, 370
conflict 414–16, 419–23, 446–7
conglomerate 352, 356–7
Connectair 144
contribution *see* break-even
control, organisational 223–256, 421, 434, 442, 485–7
   see also locus of control
Co-op Bank 178, 295, 296
cooperatives 90, 503
copyright 135–6
corporate entrepreneurship 338, 471–97
   definition 471–2
Corporate Entrepreneurship Audit Tool 493
corporate social responsibility (CSR) 70, 293–7, 494
corporate venturing 472–3, 492–4
cost plus pricing 173–6
cost–profit–volume *see* break-even
Coutts 178
creative destruction 10, 72
creativity 65, 74–5, 92, 111–36, 433, 434, 480, 482
   barriers 113
   definition 111
   laboratory 116
   resources 121
creditors 227–8, 252, 254, 387, 396, 398, 399
crises 433–5, 439–43
critical success factors 366
cross elasticity of demand 66, 176
culture
   definition 49
   enterprise/entrepreneurial 9, 22, 24, 25
   family 411, 414–16
   firm/organisation 449–52, 476, 480–2
   national 49–53
current ratio 306, 307
customer loyalty ladder 178
customers 114, 119, 120–1, 124, 128, 145–6, 169, 178–80, 203, 291, 294–5, 299, 301, 302, 308, 311–12, 327, 335–6, 346, 348, 349, 353–4, 366
cycling 486

D
Dangdang.com 131
Death Valley Curve 223–5, 338, 374, 392
debtors 227–8, 235, 252, 254, 260, 265, 266, 305, 307
decision-making 17–9, 238–42, 315, 381–92
decision-making unit (DMU) 185
deconstruction (of large companies) 9, 483
Dell 6, 9, 131, 150, 157, 203, 291, 298, 355, 479
de Mestral, Georges 119
depreciation 227
differentiation 177–8, 314
   see also generic marketing strategies
Direct Line 66, 70
directors *see* board of directors
Disney Corporation 413
distribution channels *see* channels of distribution
distributor *see* sales agent
diversification 152, 350–2
dot.com *see* internet
Duckworth, Cecil 126
due diligence 356, 377
Dyson 75, 112, 127, 471

E
easyJet 298
eBay 70
early adopters 328
e-business/commerce *see* internet
economic growth 10–11, 25, 71–3, 76
economics of entrepreneurship 9–11, 33
economies of scale 11, 147, 149–51, 159, 174, 177, 182, 192, 205, 206, 303, 311, 349
economies of small scale 150–1, 303
Edison 65
elasticity of demand *see* cross elasticity of demand
emergent strategy *see* strategy development and strategising
employee rights *see* website
empowerment 444, 449, 456, 474, 480, 486
Enterprise Finance Guarantee 260, 263
Enron 293
entrepreneur, definition 11–15
entrepreneurial
   architecture 473–5, 477–80
   character/personality *see* character traits

management/leadership 478–9; *see also* leadership
   marketing 180–2
   transformation 473, 477–80
equity investor 259, 260, 262, 270–6, 367, 370, 371, 374, 375–7
ethnicity 25, 44–6, 49, 92, 278–81
European Commission/Union 6, 7, 16, 21–2, 413
European Franchise Association 193
exporting 210–13, 207, 349

F
factoring 259, 261, 262, 263
failure 387–404
   company 397–400
   prediction 394–5
   sole trader 396–70
family firms 411–28
   definition 413–14
   constitution 422–3
   culture *see* culture
   life cycle 418
   strategic plan 422–3
   succession 417–18, 425–8
features of a product/service *see* benefits
Fifteen 87
financial control *see* financial records/systems and financial drivers
financial drivers 233–5
financial gearing/leverage *see* gearing
financial ratios/performance analysis 303, 304–7, 374
financial records/systems 252–6, 263
financing gap 259, 275–6
first mover advantage 205–6, 208
fixed asset turnover 305
fixed costs 9, 19
focus 178–80
Ford 69, 351, 353, 413
franchise 192–3, 214
futures thinking 309

G
gap analysis 119–20
Gates, Bill 6, 9, 77, 291
gearing
   financial 236–7, 306, 375
   operating 236–7, 375
gender 25, 46–7, 49, 278–81
General Enterprise Tendency (GET) test 54
generic marketing strategies 148–54, 172, 179, 180, 293, 303, 311, 332, 345, 367

Global Entrepreneurship Monitor
    (GEM)   24–5, 43, 46, 85, 92
goodwill   403
grants   261, 263
Greiner's growth model   433–6
gross profit margin   305, 307
growth   345–9
    economic   *see* economic growth
    firms   19–20, 48–9
    influences   72–3
    models   94–5, 316, 433–8

H
Hallmark   114
Harvard   5
Health & Safety   *see website*
help and advice   *see website*
hire purchase (HP)   259, 260
H.J. Heinz   413
Hoover   65
horizontal integration   351
human capital   155–6

I
IBM   6, 50, 52, 150, 296, 353, 471,
    473
ICC Business Ratios   303
ideas for businesses   125–36
immigration   *see* ethnicity
industrial economics   10
industrial evolution theory   11, 74
information asymmetry   11, 211, 266,
    269, 395
innovation   10–11, 65–78, 97, 121, 124,
    471, 483
    and location   77
    and size   75–6
    definition   65–9
    discontinuous   69–71
    open   157
innovative milieu theory   77
Innovative Potential Indicator
    (IPI)   78
innovators   67
insolvency   *see* failure
intellectual property (IP)   131–6, 178
    see also website
Intel   494
interest cover   307
internationalisation   203–15, 349
internet   9, 70, 73, 77, 128–31, 180,
    188–90, 309, 349
interstices (of the economy)   151
intrapreneur/intrapreneurship   96,
    473, 489–91
introvert firm   421–2
invent/inventor/invention   65, 125
invoice discounting   *see* factoring

J
Jaguar   177
J. Barbour & Sons   171, 413
John Lewis Partnership   14, 296
joint venture   203, 209, 214, 354

K
Kestenbaum, Jonathan   87
knowledge   77, 122, 156
    filters/spill-over/transfer etc.   11, 74,
        77, 157–9
    network   77, 157–8
    see also learning organisation
Kondratieff   72

L
labour market economics   10
laggards   328
Land, Edwin   127
Lastminute   70, 128, 131
launch strategy   148–54, 169–82, 328
leadership
    role   440–2
    skills   459–61
    style   416, 437–8, 444–8, 485–7
learning
    organisation   475–7
    theory   210
lease/leasing   259, 260, 261, 263
legal forms of business   190–3, 503
Lego   114, 413
leverage   *see* gearing
Levi Strauss   413
LG   114
licences   *see website*
life cycle of product   68, 207, 303,
    327–30, 345, 367
lifestyle firms   19–20, 211, 347, 436,
    437
limited companies   13, 191–2, 503
limiting resources   241–2
liquidation   *see* failure
loans   259–69
Local Investment Network Company
    (LINC)   271
location   *see* clusters
logistics   *see* supply chain
London Stock Exchange   274
luck   291, 315
Lush   85, 171, 177, 181, 302, 376

M
M&S   70, 205, 295, 296, 297
management buy-ins/buy-outs   270,
    401, 403, 425
management team   *see* teams
Mansfield Motors   207
marginal cost   273, 276
marginal revenue   273

margin of safety   234–5, 268, 273
market
    development   236, 249–50
    niche   9, 151–3, 158, 205, 210, 330,
        366; *see also* generic marketing
        strategies
    penetration   177, 332, 346–7
    research   182–5, 303, 378
    segment/segmentation   178–80,
        301, 327–8, 330, 332, 389
    traders   *see* generic marketing
        strategies
marketing
    mix   151–2, 170–1, 301, 328, 367–9,
        379
    strategy   148–54, 169–90, 301,
        327–8, 330, 332, 389; *see also*
        generic marketing strategies
Mars   413
Marxism   9
matrix structure   454, 455
McDonald's   177, 205, 329, 330, 349
Mercedes Benz   177, 349, 351, 354
mergers   *see* acquisitions
Microsoft   6, 52, 55, 128, 150
mission/mission statement   297–9,
    301, 366, 367, 368, 434
Monsanto   473, 494
Morgan Motor Company   413
Motorola   494
mutual guarantee schemes   267

N
nascent entrepreneurship   22, 24, 25
National Insurance   503
NCR   355, 356
NC Soft   131
net profit   224, 226, 307
Netscape   128
networks/networking   77, 155–6,
    157–9, 205, 209, 278–9
new products   *see* products
niche markets/marketing   *see* market
    niche
non-executive directors   273, 376
non-government development
    organisations (NGOs)   99
non-metric mapping   120
norms   457
not-for-profit organisation   99
    see also social enterprise

O
objectives   301, 366–8, 370, 371, 378
OFEX   273–5
operating
    gearing/leverage   *see* gearing
    risk   *see* margin of safety

opportunity recognition   121–5
organic structures   455, 483
organisation structure   92, 232, 434, 451–6, 482–7
    organisation slack   486–7
outstanding success   see generic marketing strategies
overdraft   259–63, 265, 269
overhead costs   see fixed costs
overtrading   389
    see also Death Valley Curve
owner-manager definition   13, 15

P
partnerships   191, 192, 252, 503
patents   133
penetration
    market   see market penetration
    price   see price
perceptual mapping   120
personal construct theory   120
personal guarantees   see collateral
personality traits   see character traits
planning   see business plan
Polaroid   127
policy   see small firms
Porter, Michael   74
Porter's Five Forces   146–8, 169, 303, 356, 366, 393
portfolio
    of lending/investments   266, 268, 273
    of products   303, 330–40, 345, 367
preference shares   270
premises   307
    see also website
price/pricing   172–7, 210, 328, 322, 366
price–earnings ratio   403
price elasticity   see cross elasticity of demand
Prince's Youth Business Trust   261
Procter and Gamble   157
product
    development   346, 348–9, 491–2
    extension   336
    life cycle   see life cycle
    modification   335–6
    new   158, 295, 327–40
    portfolio   see portfolio of products
product/market matrix   345–52
profit   224–9, 338–9, 403
    forecast/statement   228–9, 246–52, 301, 368–70, 379
    margin   233, 305, 307
profit–volume chart   236
promotion   170–1, 188, 301, 368, 379

PROWESS   278
push/pull factors   53–4, 279

Q
Quad Electroacoustics   302, 413
quality of earnings   403
quick ratio   306, 307

R
R&D   76, 77, 150, 205, 308, 355, 356, 375
ratio analysis   see financial ratios
registered design   134–5
relationship marketing   170–1, 180, 346, 348, 438
relationships   15, 18, 50, 92, 94, 156, 269–70, 348, 439–40, 443–5, 447–9, 451–2, 461, 474–5, 476, 479, 480–2, 490
repertory grid   120–1
resources   86, 92, 94, 97, 143–4
retail/retailing   188–90
return on investment   270, 272
return on total assets   305, 307, 403
return to shareholders   304, 307
R. Griggs Group   413
risk   9, 12, 19, 350–1, 352–5, 421, 447
    see also break-even margin of safety and gearing/leverage
Roddick, Anita   411
routes to market   see channels of distribution

S
Saga   349
Sainsbury   205
sales
    agent   207, 213–15
    commission   355
    mix   240–2, 247
scenario planning   310
School for Social Entrepreneurs   93
search engine optimisation   189
segment/segmentation   see market segment/segmentation
selling potential matrix   185
selling skills   185–8
share capital   224, 229, 259, 270
Shell   178
Shockley, William   125
skimming   see price premium
skunk working   490
slack   see organisation slack
SLEPT analysis   303, 309–10
small firm(s)
    characteristics   18–19
    definition   16–19
    economic contribution (GDP, employment etc.)   21–4

failure   see failure
policy   22, 55
starts, stops and stocks   21–4
SMEs   see small firm(s)
Smith, Adam   73
social capital   94, 155–6, 276
social economy   87–8
social enterprise/entrepreneurship   85–102
    definition   86
    legal forms   88–91
    life cycle   94–5
social entrepreneur   92–4
social media   70
sole traders   190, 192, 224, 226, 252
    see also website
spider's web   435, 451–3, 474
spin-offs   491–2, 494
stage models
    of growth   see growth models
    of internationalisation   207–9
standard industrial classification (SIC)   179
start-up(s)
    influences on   33–55
    international   205–7
stock exchange/market   273–5, 297, 402
stock turnover   235, 305, 307
strategic
    alliance   157–9, 205, 209, 354, 483
    fit   492
    intent   310, 315
    structure   see organisation structure
strategising   301, 314–15, 477–9
strategy   291, 300, 345–6, 367, 370
    development/formulation   292–3, 314–16, 477–9; see also strategising
    for growth   see growth strategies
succession   see family firms
supply chain   295, 308–9
    see also value chain
sustainable competitive advantage   see competitive advantage
sustainability   see corporate social responsibility
Swatch   354
switch costs   146–7, 309
SWOT analysis   291, 292, 300–3, 310, 311, 366–9, 392
synergy   159, 352, 356–7, 492

T
tax/taxation   211, 212, 224, 226, 246, 309, 376, 399, 402, 404, 426
    see also VAT and website
teams   340

team building/working   448–50
    see also management team
technology   9, 205
Thatcher, Margaret   55, 70
Third Way   85, 99
Thomas–Kilmann conflict
    modes   422–3, 446–7
Timberland   85, 297, 336, 351
Time Warner   128, 355, 356
total entrepreneurial activity
    (TEA)   24–5
trade associations   506
trade mark   134
trait theory   *see* character traits
triggers for self employment   53
trusts   89

U
uncertainty   *see* risk
unique selling proposition (USP)   151,
    153, 366, 371, 437–8

unincorporated associations   88
unitarism   476
UK   7, 19–24, 43, 46, 49, 51, 52, 85,
    88–91, 92, 133, 191–2, 204, 260, 261,
    271, 276, 279, 291, 396–9, 413
USA   7, 21–2, 24, 42, 43, 46, 47, 50, 51,
    52, 85, 99, 132, 157, 291, 295, 297,
    413

V
valuation (company)   357, 400–4
value chain   303, 308–9
values   178, 299–300, 413, 415, 441,
    443, 448, 450, 456–9
variable cost   173–6, 233–4, 237, 238,
    240–2
VAT   246–52, 399
    see also website
venture capital/capitalists   260,
    262–3, 270–3, 371, 374, 375–7

viral marketing   189
vision   206, 292, 297–300, 301, 315,
    366–8, 436–7, 441–4
    see also mission
voluntary liquidation/
    arrangements   387, 396, 398
Virgin   55, 177, 347, 349, 351, 486

W
website (company)   188–9
what if? questions   238, 239–40
why? why? diagrams   123–4
Wilkin & Sons   296, 413, 414
Wilkinsons   85
Worcester Engineering   126
Wright, Robert   144

Z
Z score   395

Author index

3i   153, 313, 314

A

Abdesselam   55
Abell   345
Acce   69
Acemoglo   73
Acs   10, 33, 73, 76
Adair   446
Aggarwal   203, 206
Aghion   10, 73
Ahl   279
Aiken   454
Aldrich   157, 209, 279, 280
Alexander   99
Allday   451
Allen   279
Altman   394
Amit   485
Anderson   158
Andersson   36
Annual Population Survey   45, 46
Ansoff   345, 352
Antoncic   490
Aston Business School   276
Atkinson   18
Audretsch   10, 11, 33, 68, 73, 76
Autio   210

B

Baden-Fuller   490
Bank of England   260, 265, 281
Bannock   270, 387
Barney   40
Barrett   24
Barsoux   458
Bartlett   298, 473
Bassant   132
Baty   36
Bauerschmidt   208
Bayus   171

Beaver   5, 391, 394
Belbin   448, 9
Bell   36
Bennis   444
Berkhout   70, 295
Berryman   389
Bessant   68
Bhidé   155
Bill   22
Binks   267, 270
Birch   6
Birkinshaw   472, 486
Birley   151, 313
Blackburn   391
Blake   445
Blanchflower   361
Blank   440
Blau   454
Bodden   278
Boldrin   132
Bolton   16, 21, 43, 74, 127
Bond   52
Boschee   85
Boston Consulting Group   313
Bowman   352, 456
Box   99
Bradford   490
Brady   190
Brassington   179
Bridge   22
Brinckerhoff   85
Brockhaus   36
Bruce   437
Brush   36, 278, 279
Burgelman   473, 491
Burke   294, 297
Burns   5, 152, 210, 260, 261, 265, 313,
       352, 402, 418, 428, 437–8, 446, 545,
       473, 477, 480, 481
Busenitz   40
Buttner   36
Buzell   313

C

Cachon   42
Caird   36
Camagni   77
Cannon   5, 353
Cantillon   13, 14
Capello   77
Carr   5, 52
Carson   182, 204
Carter   42, 46, 278, 279
Casson   19
Center for Women's Research   47
Chandler   453
Chaston   180, 369
Chell   35, 36, 448
Chen   44
Chesbrough   157, 472
Chittenden   233, 413, 417
Choudhry   212
Christensen   69, 473
Churchill   418, 435–6
Cliff   46, 279, 280
Clute   389, 392
Cohen   490
Coleman   279
Collins   479
Cook   99
Cooper   478
Cosh   146, 160, 276, 369, 392
Coviello   206, 209
Covin   485, 486
Crainer   5
Crick   212
Cuba   36

D

Daley   387
Dalgic   179
Davidson   22
Deakins   76
Dearlove   5
de Bono   36, 111, 113

de Cole   297
de Geus   6
de Leon   99
Denhardt   99
Dewhurst   5
Dex   24
Dicken   207
Dixon   270
Dosi   132
Drucker   14, 121, 124, 473
D'Silva   395
Dubini   157, 209
Dunkelberg   314
du Toit   453

E
Edwards   24
Eikenberry   99
Ely   14
Emery   454
Ennew   270
Environomics International   294
Epstein   297
Ericson   11
ESRC   146
Etemad   14
European Commission   22
Eurostat   7, 21, 23, 24
Evans   42, 388
Everett   393

F
Faulkner   352, 456
Firkin   278
Fisher   209
Foster   473
Fowler   86, 99
Fraser   267, 279, 281
Freel   76

G
Galbraith   454, 473, 484
Gale   313
Galloway   491
Gardner   442
Garud   486
Garvin   491
Gaskill   391
GEM   25, 85, 92
Ghoshal   158, 298, 473
Gilligan   212
Ginsberg   472
Goldhar   157
Gonella   297
Goss   96, 97
Green   22, 70, 279, 295
Greiner   433–4, 471, 484
Guiltinan   338
Gumperter   345

Gundry   280
Guth   472

H
Haige   454
Halbauer   214
Hall   482
Hamel   301, 473
Handy   157
Harper   46
Harrison   7, 291, 313
Haswell   392
Hatten   418
Hayek   14
Hess   14
Hibbert   89
Hickson   453
Hirsch   36
Hisrich   279, 490
HLB Kidson   274
Hofstede   49, 50, 52, 458
Holliday   416
Holmes   392
Hölzl   22
Hoon-Halbauer   214
Hopenhayn   11
Horwitz   36
Howitt   10, 73
Hughes   146, 160, 267, 270, 276, 369, 392
Hurmelinna-Laukkaneu   132
Hutchinson   313, 446

I
Institute for Small Business Affairs/Entrepreneurship (ISBA/E)   279, 413

J
Jankovicz   11
Jennings   391
Johanson   203, 207, 210
Johnsen   278
Johnson   157, 206, 209, 352
Jovanovic   266, 291
Joyce   314

K
Kakabadse   439
Kalleberg   46
Kanter   36, 85, 473, 489
Kaplan   473
Karagozoglu   212
Katsikeas   208
Kay   314, 473, 478
Keasey   394
Keeble   77
Kets de Vries   453
Kiggundu   391

Kim   476
King   99
Kinsella   365
Kirby   96, 111, 459
Kirton   67
Kirzner   14, 36
Klepper   11
Kluver   99
Knight   14
Knotts   392
Kotter   444
Kuratko   67

L
Lambson   11
Larson   157, 209, 391, 392
Lawrence   454
Leadbeater   85, 86, 92, 94, 95, 96, 97
Leach   411, 413, 420, 426
Leavy   315
Leeuw   179
Lei   157
Leicht   46
Leighton   42
Leonidou   208
Leppard   123
Lessem   460
Levenson   279
Levine   132
Levingson   420
Lewis   158, 435–6
Lindbolm   315
Lindell   212
Litvak   206
Logsdon   294, 297
Lorange   158
Lord   210
Lorenz   77
Lorsch   454
Lott   270
Loustarinen   208
Love   395

M
Macmillan   259
MacPherson   77
Macrae   313
Majaro   112
Markoczy   477
Marlow   278, 279
Martinez   36
Mathewson   315
Matlay   24
McCarthy   315
McClelland   36
McDougall   157, 206, 209
McGovern   24
McMahon   278

Meager 18
Menger 14
Meyer 36
Michelacci 73
Miller 477, 483
Mintzberg 66, 113, 315
Mitra 77
Montgomery 352
More 36
Morris 52, 67, 279
Morse 471
Mort 86, 93
Mouton 445
Munroe 206, 209
Murray 270

N
Nahapict 158
Namiki 210
Nanus 297, 444
Nelton 411, 414
Nohria 314
Nonaka 300
Norburn 151
Nucci 278

O
Oakley 206
O'Connor 52
OECD 7
Ohmae 158
O'Reilly 473
Oviatt 157, 205, 206, 209

P
Page 111
Pakes 11
Parkhurst 111
Patton 279
Paul 338
Pavitt 76
Pearce 87, 88
Pedler 475
Perrow 454
Peters 345, 473
Pettitt 179
Pham 131
Pinchot 36, 96, 473, 490
Porras 479
Porter 65, 66, 77, 146, 148, 352, 356
Post 92
Poutziouris 413, 414, 417
Prahalad 301
Pugh 453, 454
Puumalainen 132

R
Rainnie 24
Ram 24, 281, 416

Ranft 210
Ray 313, 446
Reid 392
Reuber 209
Rogers 327
Roos 158
Rosa 36, 46, 279
Rosenblatt 414
Ross 96, 489, 490
Rothwell 76
Roy 297
Rumelt 352

S
Sapienza 273
Sashkin 443
Say 14
Schein 36, 456
Schmidt 69
Schneider 458
Scholes 352
Schumacher 5, 10
Schumpeter 10, 14, 36, 66, 71
Schwartz 36
Scott 36, 279, 437
Selassie 210
Senge 443, 475, 476
Shapero 14, 36, 131
Shaver 36
Shaw 46, 280
Siegel 313
Slevin 485, 486
Smith 24, 397
Solem 313, 314
Sonnenfield 426
Spence 451
Stalker 454
Stanworth 44
Steiner 313, 314
Stevenson 155, 345
Stiglitz 266
Stinchcombe 454
Stokes 171, 391
Stopford 490
Storey 7, 19, 22, 36, 42, 44, 54, 76, 146, 151, 276, 291, 313, 314, 388
Strivers 99
Sullivan 208
Sykes 19, 36

T
Taffler 394
Taylor 7, 291, 313
Teece 159
Tellis 329
Terry 99
Thompson 43, 74, 86, 92, 127
Thornhill 485

Tidd 69, 132, 158
Timmons 50, 273, 365, 473, 441, 444, 445, 447, 459
Treacy 302
Treichel 279
Trist 454
Tushman 473

U
Unwalla 96, 489
Utterback 69

V
Vahlne 203, 207, 210
Valery 121
Van de Ven 486
Van Grundy 85
Vernon 207
Verschoor 295
Vesper 471
Von Oech 113, 115
Vossen 76
Vyakarnham 123

W
Waddock 92, 93
Walters 24
Waterman 345, 473
Watkins 391
Watson 278, 279, 393, 394
Weber 453
Webster 180
Weiss 266
Weitz 158
Welch 208
Welsch 50, 280
Wernerfelt 352
Westhead 313
Whitehouse 151, 260, 261, 402, 428, 446
Wichmann 392
Wickham 299
Wiedershheim-Paul 203
Wiersema 302
Wilkinson 77
Willard 279
Wilpert 477
Wilson 212
Woo 314, 365
Wood 294
Woodward 454
Wynarczyk 19, 314

Y
Yelle 313

Z
Zahra 472

Quotes index

A

Adizes, Ichak (author) 440
Arculus, David (Emap Group) 441

B

Bannatyne, Duncan (Dragon) 144, 278,
 300, 371
Baxter, Audrey (Baxter's Soups) 413
Bennis, Warren (author) 442
Blackmore, Adele (Community Action
 Network) 87
Branson, Richard (Virgin) 38, 41

C

Cadbury, Adrian (Cadbury) 312, 411
Castle, Nin (Goodone) 154
Coe, Ruth (Bespoke Beauty) 279, 369
Collin, Derrick (Brulines) 298
Constantine, Mark (Lush) 53, 156, 391

D

Dowes, Martyn (Coffee Nation) 36, 41,
 144, 145, 152, 377, 476, 480
Dell, Michael (Dell Corporation) 11, 113,
 121, 302, 314, 367, 475
Deshpande, Gururaj (Sycamore
 Networks) 298

E

Elvidge, Jonathan (Gadget Shop) 37, 38,
 121, 448

F

Farmer, Tom (Kwik-Fit) 40, 448
Frank, Gary (Fabulous Bakin Boys) 143

G

Garland, Chey (Garland Call
 Centres) 36

H

Haji-Ioannou, Stelios (easyJet) 433
Hamel, Gary (author) 9
Hoberman, Brent (Lastminute.com) 37

I

Ingram, Chris (Tempus) 40

K

Kelly, Neil (PAV) 39
King, Will (King of Shaves) 111, 374, 389

L

Lane Fox, Martha (Lastminute.com) 40

M

Muirhead, Charles (Orchestream) 37
Murray, Sara (Confused.com) 156

N

Naisbitt, Joghn (author) 471
Nanus, Burt (author) 446
Notley, Ann (The Iron Bed
 Company) 42

P

Peters, Mike (Universal
 Laboratories) 41

R

Redman, Gary (Now Recruitment) 33
Roddick, Anita (The Body Shop) 126

S

Shah, Bharat (Sigma
 Pharmaceuticals) 45, 418
Shah, Eddy (Messenger Group) 36
Spurgeon, Julie (Material Pleasures) 365

T

Thompson, Diane (Camelot) 471
Thompson, Richard (EMS) 38
Timmons, Jeffrey (author) 9

V

Valentine, Andrew (Streetcar) 156

W

Waring, Stephen (Green Thumb) 36
Worcester, Bob (MORI) 40

Y

Yip, Wing (W. Wing Yip & Brothers) 41
Young, Jean 38